WATER RESOURCES
ATLAS OF FLORIDA

EDITORS

EDWARD A. FERNALD
STATE GEOGRAPHER

ELIZABETH D. PURDUM

PROJECT DIRECTOR
JAMES R. ANDERSON, JR.

ASSOCIATE EDITOR
CAVELL KYSER

CARTOGRAPHER
PETER A. KRAFFT

ASSOCIATE CARTOGRAPHER
LOUIS CROSS III

INSTITUTE OF SCIENCE AND
PUBLIC AFFAIRS   FLORIDA STATE UNIVERSITY

Marsh grasses move in concert with the clouds and wind, Observation Shoal, Lake Okeechobee

Early morning fog envelopes a cypress along the Santa Fe River, Gainesville

The Myakka River expands into the Wilderness Preserve creating Lower Myakka Lake, Myakka River State Park, Sarasota

Alum Bluff is the highest bluff in Florida forming The Nature Conservancy's Apalachicola Bluffs and Ravines Preserve, Liberty County

ii

Pond cypress create the beginnings of a cypress dome, Corkscrew Regional Ecosystem Watershed, Collier and Lee counties

Swamp lilies adorn marl prairie cypress savannahs, Big Cypress National Preserve

Special Recognition
The Elizabeth Ordway Dunn Foundation
Quest Foundation

LIBRARY OF CONGRESS CATALOG NUMBER 98-072985
ISBN 0-9606708-2-3

Greetings:

Water resources are among Florida's most important natural assets. Freshwater supplies are vital for our daily lives, future residents and visitors, natural systems, recreation and agriculture.

Florida's freshwater supplies are finite and the demands of a growing population and the need to sustain our rivers, lakes, wetlands and estuaries requires the utmost care and thoughtfulness in planning and using our freshwater supplies.

The *Water Resources Atlas of Florida* contains a wealth of scientific information not previously compiled into a single document. It has been invaluable in planning for wise use and protection of our natural resources.

I am extremely pleased that the *Water Resources Atlas of Florida* has been updated with this new edition. Today, more than any other time in our State's history, the availability of objective information on Florida's water resources for research, teaching, planning and management, and for the public's use is of paramount importance.

Governor

Staff

Melissa Hall

Michelle Hane

Kristine Hernandez

Iris Kahrmann

Shell Kimble

Chris Wilkes

Contributors

Chapter/authors/affiliation

1. Donald J. Patton, Florida State University (retired)
   Rodney S. DeHan, Florida Department of Environmental Protection

2. James A. Henry, East Tennessee State University

3. Marian P. Berndt, Edward T. Oaksford, Gary Mahon, U.S. Geological Survey
   Walter Schmidt, Florida Department of Environmental Protection

4. Joann Mossa, University of Florida

5. Randy S. Kautz, Theodore S. Hoehn, Florida Game and Fresh Water Fish Commission
   Kenneth Haddad, Thomas Rogers, Tom Atkeson, Florida Department of Environmental Protection
   Ernest D. Estevez, Mote Marine Laboratory

6. Richard L. Marella, U.S. Geological Survey
   David W. York, Florida Department of Environmental Protection

7. Eric Livingston, Joe Hand, Mary Paulic, Tom Seal, Thomas M. Swihart, Gary Maddox, Jay Silvanima, Charles Coultas, Kenna Study, Michael Scheinkman, Tricia McClenahan, Bob Fisher, Donnie McClaugherty, Steve Partney, Rich Deuerling

8. Elizabeth D. Purdum, Florida State University
   Louis C. Burney, Thomas M. Swihart, Florida Department of Environmental Protection

9. Elizabeth D. Purdum, Florida State University
   Georgann Penson, Northwest Florida Water Management District
   with assistance from Ron Bartel, Duncan Cairns, William Cleckley, George Fisher, Guy Gowens, Tyler Macmillan, Tom Pratt, Nick Wooten

10. Marvin Raulston, Cindy Johnson, Kirk Webster, Carolyn Purdy, Ron Ceryak, Suwannee River Water Management District

11. Linda McGrail, Kenneth Berk, Donald Brandes, Douglas Munch, Clifford Neubauer, William Osburn, Donthamsetti Rao, John Thomson, David Toth with assistance from Don Boniol, Dean Campbell, Wesley Curtis, Stewart Dary, Bruce Florence, Walter Godwin, Paul Haydt, John Hendrickson, Lawrence Keenan, Margaret Lasi, Cynthia Moore, Lisa Northrup, Gilbert Sigua, Joel Steward, Karen Warr

12. Wes Wheeler, Richard Owen, Terry Johnson, Southwest Florida Water Management District with assistance from Sandra Haley, John Walkinshaw, Dean Rusk, Margit Crowell, Mary Ann Wolf

13. Joel VanArman, Winnie Park, Patti Nicholas, Patricia Strayer, Agnes McLean, Barry Rosen, Jim Gross
    with assistance from Jennifer Barnes, Lynn Gulick, Barbara Brown, Jeff Herr, Matt Hinton, Jimmy Kramp, Jerry Krenz, Tim Lieberman, Maryam Mayashenkhi, Chris McVoy, Tracey Needle, Moysey Ostrovsky, Ahmad Poudratchi, Mike Rose, Kurt Saari, Cindy Whelan, Chris Burns, Jane Walters

14. Jay W. Yingling, C. Donald Rome, Jr., Southwest Florida Water Management District
    Grace M. Johns, Hazen and Sawyer, P.C.
    William Hutchinson, Planning and Economics Group
    Richard A. March, South Florida Water Management District
    with assistance from David W. Carter

15. Richard Hamann, University of Florida

ACKNOWLEDGMENTS

Over three years and the efforts of many people throughout the state have gone into the production of the *Water Resources Atlas of Florida*. The atlas would not have been possible without fiscal and other support from the state's five water management districts and the Florida Department of Environmental Protection. Support from FSU President Sandy D'Alemberte and Vice President for Research Susan Allen for the atlas project is also gratefully acknowledged.

The members of the water atlas revision committee listed below generously gave of their time in reviewing the original atlas and planning the new atlas: Patti Nicholas and Joel VanArman, South Florida Water Management District; Stewart Dary and John Hall, St. Johns River Water Management District; Cindy Johnson and Marvin Raulston, Suwannee River Water Management District; Georgann Penson and Ron Bartel, Northwest Florida Water Management District; Richard Owen and John Walkinshaw, Southwest Florida Water Management District; Rodney DeHan and Tom Swihart, Florida Department of Environmental Protection; and Edward Oaksford and Gary Mahon, U.S. Geological Survey.

Marian Berndt, Rodney DeHan, Randy Kautz, Richard Marella, Georgann Penson, Marvin Raulston, Walt Schmidt, and Joel VanArman deserve special acknowledgment for their support, assistance, and enthusiasm far beyond their recognition as contributions on individual chapters. We also thank Rick Copeland, Linda McGrail, Winnie Park, Tom Scott, Eric Livingston, and Jay Yingling for their dedication in the final weeks of atlas preparation.

Special assistance was provided by Niki Gandy and Tom Smith of Gandy Printing in color correction of the photographs. We also would like to thank Pat Boling, Chris Casey, Kris Felss, Barbara Hagen, Ric Hastings, and Rob Krehbiel of the C.J. Krehbiel Company for their invaluable assistance in preparing the book for printing and the printing of the atlas.

Stephen Hodge and Georgianna Strode of the Florida Resources and Environmental Analysis Center at Florida State University assisted in converting GIS map files to atlas requirements and provided computer support. Chengxia You of the Florida Natural Areas Inventory provided up-to-date computer files of conservation lands. Phyllis Sullivan was very helpful in developing printing specifications. Morton D. Winsberg, retired professor of geography at FSU, generously reviewed material contained in the atlas.

for

Donald J. Patton, scholar, teacher, environmentalist, friend

PREFACE

Fourteen years have passed since we completed the first *Water Resources Atlas of Florida*. Our goal has remained the same: to compile in maps and graphs, text, and photographs all aspects of our state's most precious resource. This book is not simply a revised edition, but a new book. Although many of the chapter titles remain the same, the content is new. We have expanded the ecosystems of surface water chapter to include all natural systems since they are all linked together and all depend on water. We have expanded the groundwater and surface water chapters to include watersheds in neighboring Georgia and Alabama, and have included discussions of El Niño and global warming in the weather and climate chapter. The chapters by each of the state's five water management districts are more consistent in content than they were in the first atlas. In these chapters you will also find descriptions of the numerous restoration projects occurring around the state. The economics chapter presents a wealth of data on the costs of water and responses to costs as well as a discussion of the controversial subject of water markets. The legal chapter introduces legal and policy issue that will continue to be of concern into the next millennium.

Although preparation of this book was funded in part by generous support from each of the water management districts and the Department of Environmental Protection, it is not intended as an official publication of the positions or views of these organizations. We have encouraged authors, many of whom are from the districts and the Department of Environmental Protection, to express their own views.

Much has happened since 1984: new laws and regulations; major land acquisition programs; development of new sources of supply (reuse, desalination, aquifer storage, conservation); progress in establishing minimum levels and flows to assure the freshwater needs of natural systems; ongoing efforts to restore many parts of the state degraded by human activities, including the Everglades, the Kissimmee River, Lake Apopka, the St. Johns River, and the Indian River Lagoon; signing of an interstate compact between Florida, Alabama, and Georgia to manage the Apalachicola River. In spite of these very positive steps, a 1998 survey of Florida educators, scientists, natural resource administrators, citizens, and tourists by Mark Damian Duda and Associates concluded that water resource issues remain "the most important and salient environmental concern to Floridians." We hope that this book will help all Floridians make more informed decisions about water and the environment.

CONTENTS

I

INTRODUCTION

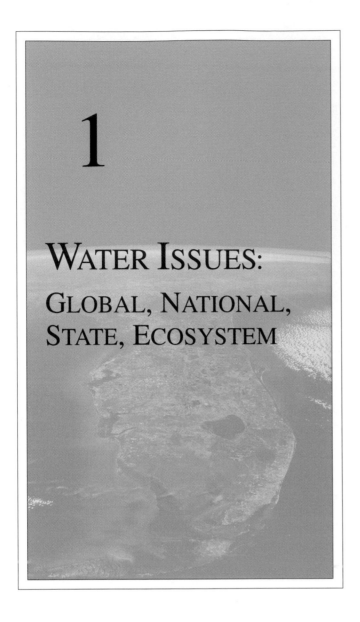

1

WATER ISSUES:
GLOBAL, NATIONAL, STATE, ECOSYSTEM

(Postel 1996). Because water resources are often scarce, even in humid Florida, problems relating to the allocation and use of a scarce resource arise. Other water problems are caused by the mobility of the resource, not only in its passage from place to place on and beneath the surface of the earth but also in its transformation from its liquid form as it vaporizes in evaporation and transpiration. Some of the problems associated with water, such as the manifold ways in which it can be polluted, arise from its very special physical and chemical attributes. For these and other reasons, water, despite its incalculable ultimate value to society, concurrently confronts society with problems as it is brought into use.

This chapter introduces the subject of water resources and water problems, first at the extremely broad scale of the entire globe, then at the intermediate scale of the United States, and finally at the still more detailed scale of Florida and even of regions within Florida. Although world and national water problems are not a principal concern of this atlas, they are addressed

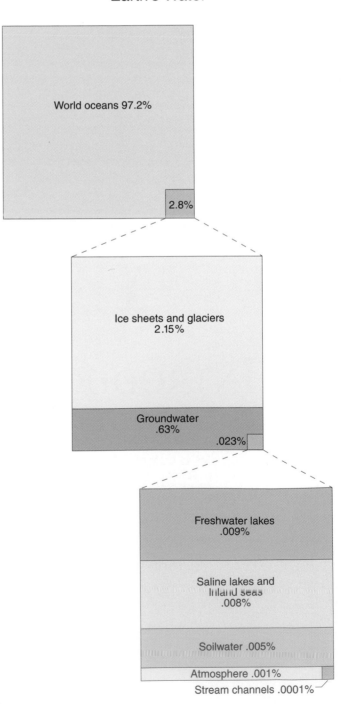

Earth's Water

2   A cardinal purpose of the *Water Resources Atlas of Florida* is to display Florida's water resources in maps and graphs, in photographs and drawings, and in tables and text. The information contained in this atlas is designed not only for those who must make decisions that in some way relate to water resources but also for those who have an interest in the state's water resources and the ways in which those resources are used. This atlas has an interrelated second purpose, however: to focus on Florida's water issues and problems. The people of Florida face serious but not insolvable difficulties with respect to the state's waters, and promising beginnings have been made toward their eventual resolution. Floridians, nevertheless, need to be keenly aware of their state's water problems and of the need to address these problems in the broader context of ecosystem protection and growth management.

Water problems arise for many reasons. The most fundamental is the limited amount of freshwater on earth, most of which is frozen or underground. In spite of the finite nature of water worldwide, water use has more than tripled since 1950

Donald J. Patton and Rodney S. DeHan

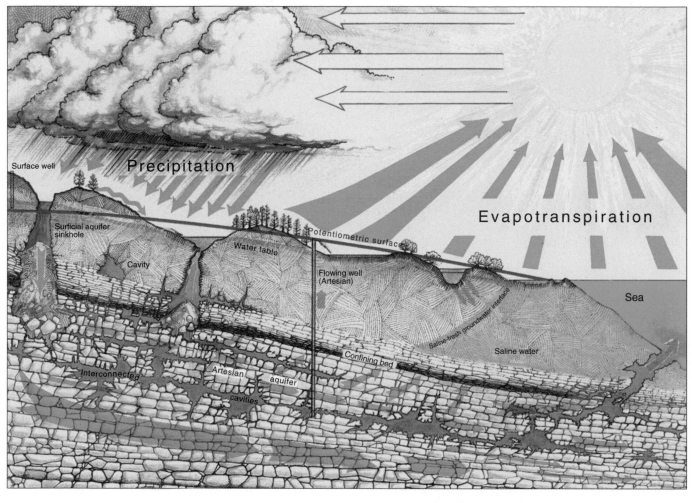

in this first chapter in order to give some perspective on water resources problems in Florida. As the focus shifts from the globe to the nation and then to the state, differences emerge in the nature of water-related problems and how those problems are stated and addressed, but common themes also become apparent.

The Global Hydrologic Cycle

The hydrologic cycle is essentially a closed system with regard to water. The same water circles endlessly through its different phases, moving from sea to atmosphere to the land and back to the sea. Approximately 80,000 cubic miles of water evaporate annually from the world's oceans. The power source for the hydrologic cycle is solar energy, which induces evaporation. Although annual incoming radiant energy from the sun is greatest in the equatorial zone, the solar radiation reaching the earth's surface is reduced by the high cloudiness of that zone, and this reduced solar radiation, in addition to the high humidity, reduces evaporation. Highest evaporation occurs in the zones of highest solar radiation intensity at the earth's surface which are located to the north and south of the equator in the subtropical high pressure and trade-winds belts. King (1962) identified 20°N and 10°S as the latitudes with the highest levels of evaporation.

Once evaporated, water is carried through the atmosphere as clouds and vapor, forming an integral part of the earth's weather. When atmospheric conditions are right, water vapor condenses and falls as precipitation, such as rain, snow, sleet, or hail. Some precipitation bypasses part of the cycle and either evaporates while in the air or falls into the ocean. Other precipitation falls on the land.

Precipitation that falls on the land flows through many different pathways. Some precipitation will flow on the surface as runoff or overland flow. This water eventually makes its way to bodies of surface water, such as lakes, wetlands or rivers, where it will reside temporarily. Eventually, the surface water evaporates back into the atmosphere, makes its way to the ocean by way of a river system, or seeps through the lake, wetlands, or stream bottom into the underlying rocks or sediments.

Some precipitation seeps into the ground on which it falls, a process known as infiltration. As the water percolates downward through the soil, some may be removed by growing plants and recycled back into the atmosphere by transpiration from leaf surfaces. Some soil moisture will remain, clinging to the soil particles. Excess moisture is pulled downward by gravity until it reaches the zone of saturation or water table. Water below the water table is called groundwater. Much, but not all, groundwater flows beneath the land surface through layers of soil and rock until it reaches points of discharge, such as springs, wells, or seeps. Most groundwater discharges to streams and ultimately flows to the ocean, however long or deep the journey. Some of the very old groundwater, however, known as connate water, may stay beneath the land surface for millions of years. Connate water, which is highly mineralized because of its long contact with rock materials, is water that became trapped in sediments when they were deposited and subsequently was buried by younger sediments. Typically, however, the age of groundwater ranges from a few tens of years to tens of thousands of years (Bouwer 1978).

Water is added to the hydrologic cycle in minute amounts each year from deep within the earth by volcanic eruptions. This water is called juvenile water or primary water and is a

3

Morocco 1984 during the third consecutive year of drought. Single wells such as this one are the only source of water for large areas. Clustering of people and animals around the well causes further problems such as overgrazing and desertification.

component of deep rock and magma. This added water is balanced by water removed from the hydrologic cycle each year by combination with newly deposited hydrated minerals, such as gypsum, a mineral whose chemical formula contains water molecules.

Global Water Problems

The paramount world water problem is the sheer unavailability of water supplies in many regions. The accompanying map shows that a third of the earth's land surface is arid and much of its remaining land area is semiarid. Even in these dry lands, however, concentrated water supplies do exist, both as lenses of groundwater and as exotic rivers such as the Nile that arise in humid mountain lands and have sufficient flow to be able to make their way far out into and even across vast deserts. But such waters are elusive. Groundwater and stream flow are often really potential, not actual, supplies for the populations of the dry lands because the works that could deliver them for human use are inadequate or entirely lacking. Those supplies that are tapped by methods both ancient and modern are often cruelly deficient for the water-dependent populations as many of these dry regions are in the Third World where most families continue to depend directly on agriculture or on livestock rearing for their slender support.

The problem of water scarcity in the arid and semiarid realms of the earth is compounded by rainfall variability. An accompanying map shows that as total mean annual rainfall declines, relative rainfall variability from year to year tends to increase. Dry years, moreover, may cluster as they did during the dust-bowl years on the American Great Plains. Although the most directly affected in the drier years would likely be those who grow crops or graze livestock without benefit of irrigation, such as the refugees who streamed southward out of the Sahel in Africa during the 1970s, the effects also reach out to those who tap concentrated water supplies derived from the erratic rainfall. Even minor differences of a few inches in total rainfall from year to year result in relatively much larger fluctuations in surface flows, in amounts of water collected in cisterns and ponds, and in depths to groundwater reached by wells. Dry wells and cracked, desiccated mud at the bottom of ponds are inevitable signs of recurring stress. Yet rural population densities in these regions of very uncertain rainfall may be relatively high; the Brazilian northeast and the African nations from Senegal east to Niger are cases in point. Food is often in very short supply, especially in the developing countries of Africa and South Asia as well as Latin America, and it is water rather than land that is usually the limiting factor in food production.

Global warming will further complicate water resources management. In 1995 the United Nations Panel on Climate Change predicted that if emissions from fossil fuels continue at current levels, the earth's temperature will increase by as much as 6 degrees F in the next 100 years. Sea level may rise by as much as 14 inches in some places. Warming will also increase the possibility of stronger and more frequent hurricanes. In semiarid midlatitude climates currently dependent on snowmelt, water supply is likely to decrease (Loaiciga et al. 1996).

Throughout much of the globe, agricultural output per unit area is much higher in irrigated than in unirrigated areas. Seemingly, therefore, water-related problems should be less severe in irrigated districts, particularly in the Third World. The evidence, however, is otherwise. Irrigation exists in humid as well

4

Annual Precipitation

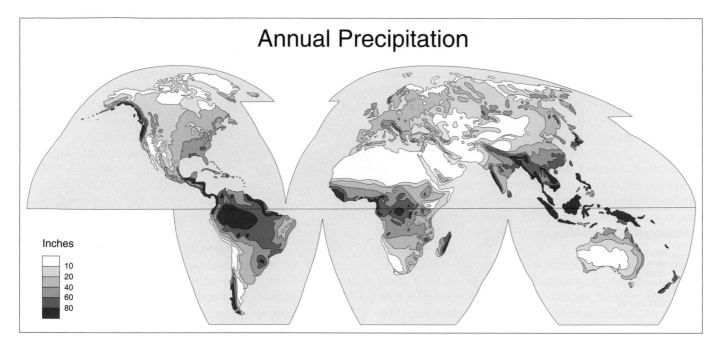

Inches
10
20
40
60
80

as arid and semiarid lands, but it is primarily on the irrigated tracts in arid and semiarid regions of developing countries that water problems are particularly grave.

Irrigation is clearly the largest consumer of freshwater in the world. It accounts for two-thirds of the freshwater withdrawn around the world from lakes, rivers, and aquifers (Gardner 1996). In the face of possible food shortfalls, and prompted by the expectation of higher food yields under irrigation, it is easy to see why new irrigation projects tend to gain political support in lesser-developed countries in particular. But the high value put on water by peoples living in the dry lands of the earth—including the American West—leads paradoxically to its being persistently oversupplied to crops under irrigation. Moreover, in the developing countries especially a broad gap exists between technical knowledge of how to irrigate, possessed by the few, and actual field practice of the many. Heavy government subsidies of irrigation have encouraged waste in many parts of the world including the United States. Many nations, including China, India, Iran, Libya, Pakistan, Saudi Arabia, and the U.S., are withdrawing groundwater faster than it can be replenished by rain. On the Arabian Peninsula, 75 percent of the groundwater was trapped below the surface thousands of years ago and will never be replenished. In other places, overextraction of groundwater can cause subsidence (sinkhole formation) and compaction in the aquifer eliminating the spaces that once held water.

The consequences of overuse and misuse of water in irrigation are waterlogging and enhanced salinity. Harvests decline and field abandonment eventually ensues. Half the irrigated area of the earth is affected. It is estimated that each year farmers give up from 500,000 to 1,000,000 acres (Holdgate and White 1977). In the U.S., water shortages forced farmers drawing water from the Ogallala Aquifer to decrease irrigated acreage by 10 percent (Gardner 1996). As much as 40,000 acres of irrigated land have gone out of production each year in Pakistan alone as a result of salinity and waterlogging. Some 60 percent of the soils in the Tigris-Euphrates floodplain suffer from excess salt content, as do one-half the irrigated soils in Syria. Diversion of river water for irrigation of cotton fields has had dramatic consequences for the Aral Sea and surrounding land in Kazakhstan and Uzbekistan. Once the earth's fourth-largest lake, the Aral Sea has lost half its area and three-fourths

its volume. Concentrated salts and toxic chemicals have killed fish. Salt blown from the dry sea bed has harmed or killed crops on surrounding land. Crop output in a quarter of the Nile delta is reduced as a consequence of excessively high water tables (White 1960).

Replacement of declining crop harvests and abandoned fields with new irrigation projects has always been at the cost of socioeconomic disruption and stress within the affected countries. Insofar as the new projects are capital-intensive, depending in part on new engineering works, a further problem arises from the costs that are now inflated by high interest rates of hard-currency, technology-exporting countries to which the developing countries often must turn.

Water resources development in the twentieth century has commonly employed structural approaches, the central feature of which has been a dam to impound streamflow for a reservoir. The United States in particular pioneered large-scale, multiple-purpose water resources development earlier in the twentieth century as technological innovations in earth-moving machinery, use of concrete, and dam design opened a new era in water manipulation. At present, however, dams and reservoirs are widespread around the earth and plans for their construction are increasing. According to Dan Beard, former Commissioner of the U.S. Bureau of Reclamation, "it is a serious mistake for any region in the world to use what we did on the Colorado and Columbia rivers as examples to be duplicated," but this is precisely what is occurring (quoted in Abramovitz 1996:66). Laos, for example, plans to build 23 dams by 2010, and in 1996 work was underway on the Three Gorges Dam across the Yangtze River in China. The dam, expected to take over a decade to construct, will be 1.5 miles across and 600 feet high. The resulting 396-mile-long reservoir will displace over a million people who for centuries have farmed the fertile upper Yangtze River valley.

Some of the globe's largest dams and reservoirs are now in the lesser-developed countries. The waters of the powerful Zambezi River in southern Africa emerge from the deep gorge below Victoria Falls and spread out in the 175-mile-long Kariba Lake before plunging downward again at Kariba Dam. Although dams and reservoirs may be hailed as proof of national modernity in water development, especially in the developing countries, the sudden implantation of such works into rivers

5

lion pounds of severely restricted pesticides including carbofuran, chlordane, and heptachlor were exported during this same period (Foundation for Advancements in Science and Education 1996).

National Water Problems

In the 1970s the National Water Commission, in an exhaustive review of American water problems, concluded that the United States required new water resources policies to reflect and provide for present and future national water needs (National Water Commission 1973). Concerns of the nation had changed. The country no longer needed toll-free improved inland waterways as it did in the 19th century. Likewise earlier policies to dispose of federal land, to expand settlement into new regions, and to increase agricultural production were no longer applicable. A policy of construction of engineering works to contain flood waters initiated earlier in the twentieth century and prompted by a felt need to protect population already domiciled in floodprone areas was now inappropriate for stemming further encroachments onto floodplains. By the 1970s the nation had new conditions, desires, and expectations. The population was predominantly urban. People were concerned with environmental and aesthetic values as well as with the recreational possibilities of water resources. Water pollution had befouled the nation's surface waters and increasingly threatened groundwaters as well.

Complicating development of new national water policies are differences between much of the eastern and much of the western halves of the forty-eight coterminous states in their overall water supplies, shown here in terms of deficiency or surplus measured by a moisture index. This difference between East and West in water supply is so deep-seated that historically it has shaped two different systems of water law.

The debate on the nature, causes, and resolution of U.S. water problems raging in the 1970s continues, although in the last two decades new legislation has led to some improvements in conservation and environmental protection in the United States. The Clean Water Act, the Safe Drinking Water Act, Superfund, the Resource Conservation and Recovery Act, and the Toxic Substances Control Act (TOSCA) were all adopted and implemented during this period. The majority of these improvements, however, have been made in reaction to a crisis or to the discovery of a problem rather than on the basis of systematic and comprehensive policies designed to prevent environmental degradation. Water Quality 2000 concluded that "progress has been made in improving the conditions of the nation's water over the last 20 years, but the national goal of fishable and swimmable waters [set by the Clean Water Act] has not been attained in many areas" and "much work remains (to be done) to restore and maintain the chemical, physical, and biological integrity of the nation's waters" (Water Environment Federation 1993). Thirty-seven percent of the nation's lakes and estuaries and 36 percent of its rivers have levels of pollution that are too high to allow them to meet basic uses such as fishing and swimming (U.S. Geological Survey 1995).

The quality of many of the nation's water bodies still remains unknown. Only small portions of the nation's surface waters are being assessed by the states, the U.S. Geological Survey (USGS), or the U.S. Environmental Production Agency (EPA), and these assessments, which only employ a fraction of possible monitoring parameters, are not encouraging. Current monitoring programs have shown U.S. surface waters to be degraded by siltation, pathogens, nutrients, toxic organics, pesticides, metals, and other toxins.

Although until 1992 EPA did not ask states to report on groundwater quality, a 1994 EPA report entitled "The Quality of Our Nation's Water" did find enough data to show contamination in many aquifers with fertilizers, pesticides, and pathogens from feedlot operations, septic systems, and agricultural activities. Groundwater has also been polluted with petroleum products, manufacturing operations products, metals,

8

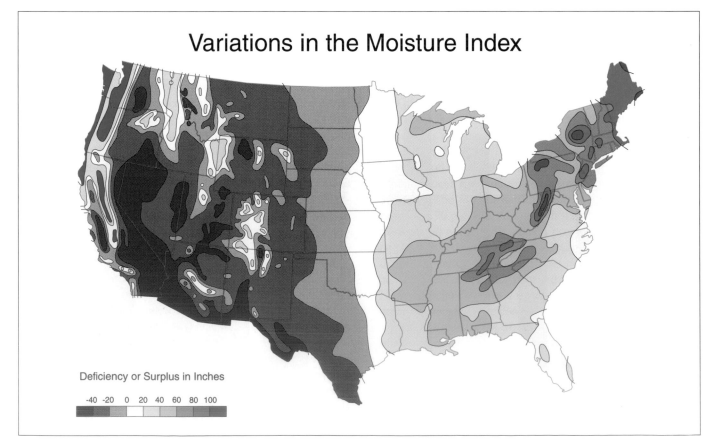

Variations in the Moisture Index

Deficiency or Surplus in Inches

-40 -20 0 20 40 60 80 100

inorganics, toxic organics and other industrial and hazardous material from spills, dumps, or leaking underground storage tanks. In Florida and other coastal states, saltwater intrusion into coastal aquifers due to overpumping is an additional problem addressed in more detail elsewhere in the atlas. Monitoring the impact of these pollutants on the ambient groundwater quality is obviously more difficult and expensive than monitoring surface water. Chapter 3 illustrates the complexity of hydrogeologic systems in Florida. For these reasons very few states (Florida among them) have any programs to monitor the ambient quality of groundwater.

Monitoring the receiving waters for regulatory purposes is a more common and well-funded effort since it is mandated by federal and state legislation. As such, it has generated huge amounts of analytical data on groundwater and surface-water quality in the last two decades. Unfortunately, this information is of a limited value in determining the overall health of watersheds. This is primarily because such monitoring is traditionally designed to measure the effects of discharge of contaminants in terms of Maximum Contaminant Levels (MCLs) from specific facilities to certain segments of the receiving water, rather than the aquatic system as a whole. Useful as the MCLs may be in estimating the effects of pollutants on human health, they are of little value, if not actually misleading, as indicators of the health of ecosystems. This is largely because biological communities living in these systems are more sensitive, and react in different ways than humans, to the same concentration of pollutants.

The Great Midwest Flood of 1993 during which the Mississippi in essence reclaimed its floodplain brought into relief the continuing failure of past water policies even to protect human lives and property. The Interagency Floodplain Management Task Force, established after the flood, recommended floodplain restoration—instead of the historic response of more engineering works—and managing the river as a whole ecosystem. The conclusion of the task force is consistent with a new paradigm for managing and protecting the environment that emerged in the late 1980s and early 1990s: ecosystem management. The federal government and many state governments have embraced this concept. A 1994 memorandum of understanding among 14 federal agencies and departments called for the adoption of ecosystem management in the operation of their programs. By contrast, traditional "command and control" policies for environmental management and protection have focused primarily on human health and safety and have applied rigid regulatory remedies to artificially compartmentalized components of the ecosystem, such as groundwater, surface water, soil, sediments, and atmospheric deposition. Ecosystem management demands evaluating and understanding the condition of, and relationship between water, air, soil, plants and animals and how humans, as integral parts of the system, are responsible for short- and long-term changes to these resources. Restoring or sustaining the health of ecosystems depends on adequate scientific information obtained through well-thought-out monitoring programs.

Although a philosophical shift has occurred in the United States in the way water and other aspects of the environment are discussed, problems remain. Answers to basic questions of ecosystem health remain elusive despite tens of billions of dollars spent on monitoring. Federal and state monitoring programs continue to focus on specific water media (or water bodies) in response to statutory or regulatory mandates. More than 30 major federal monitoring programs for assessing natural resources and associated problems are in place at a cost of about $500 million annually. Although many of these programs are effective in providing information about specific resources, such as forests, fisheries, rangeland, and water, they were created in response to narrowly focused legislation designed to manage each of the components of the ecosystem indi-

National Water Assessment
1992

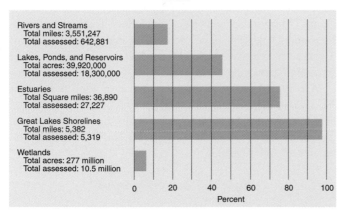

Rivers and Streams
Total miles: 3,551,247
Total assessed: 642,881

Lakes, Ponds, and Reservoirs
Total acres: 39,920,000
Total assessed: 18,300,000

Estuaries
Total Square miles: 36,890
Total assessed: 27,227

Great Lakes Shorelines
Total miles: 5,382
Total assessed: 5,319

Wetlands
Total acres: 277 million
Total assessed: 10.5 million

Percent

Contamination of Assessed Surface Water in the U.S.
1992

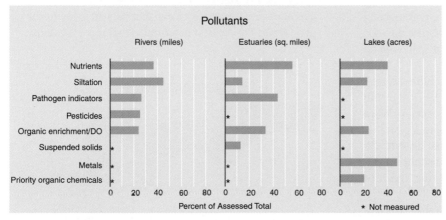

Pollutants

Rivers (miles)   Estuaries (sq. miles)   Lakes (acres)

Nutrients
Siltation
Pathogen indicators
Pesticides
Organic enrichment/DO
Suspended solids
Metals
Priority organic chemicals

Percent of Assessed Total   ★ Not measured

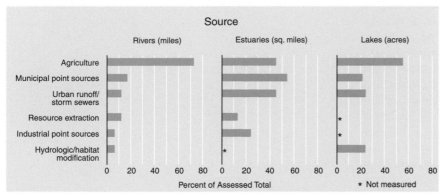

Source

Rivers (miles)   Estuaries (sq. miles)   Lakes (acres)

Agriculture
Municipal point sources
Urban runoff/storm sewers
Resource extraction
Industrial point sources
Hydrologic/habitat modification

Percent of Assessed Total   ★ Not measured

9

vidually with little attention to how these components react with and influence each other and the system as a whole. Even less effort is expanded correlating these data with land use and other activities such as alteration of habitat, overwithdrawal of water, lowering of water tables, reducing stream flow, or introduction of exotic species. This lack of adequate data and area coverage can lead to conflicting assessments of the progress the United States has made in preserving, managing, or restoring its ecosystems, and makes practical decisions of allocation and use of water resources, on the basis of watershed sustainability, extremely difficult.

Monitoring is also conducted by thousands of other public agencies and private organizations using different parameters, methods, and quality control and assurance measures that render integration of data extremely difficult if not impossible. In 1995 the Intergovernmental Task Force on Monitoring Water Quality concluded, "In the last decade it has become clear that monitoring activities need to be improved and integrated better to meet the full range of needs more effectively and economically." At an even more fundamental level, disagreement continues among scientists and managers in different disciplines as to what constitutes an ecosystem, what are its components, and how to measure its health.

The 1990s have seen efforts by some members of Congress through the Republican majority's so-called "Contract with America" and other measures to decrease government's role in environmental regulation by such actions as drastically reducing EPA's enforcement budget and authority, weakening the Clean Water and Safe Drinking Water acts, requiring the federal government to compensate property owners if the value of their property is reduced by regulatory actions, moratorium on the listing of new endangered species, limiting EPA's authority to regulate activities in wetlands by changing the definition of wetland, and accelerating logging in Alaska's Tongas National Forest. The general public (as well as the Clinton administration) reacted strongly by opposing these measures in surveys and polls (Groundwater Protection Council 1996). Vice President Gore in a 1995 speech before the National Academy of Sciences addressing global warming and other environmental problems urged that "more attention, not less, should be devoted to understand the huge impact human civilization is having on the earth" (Clarke 1995:8).

The Vice President reiterated that admonition more recently, by directing the federal agencies on October 18, 1997 (the 25th anniversary of the adoption of the Clean Water Act), to work with each other and with the public in developing a plan that charts the course toward fulfilling the goals of that historic act. In February 1998 the agencies responded by publishing a document entitled "Clean Water Action Plan: Restoring and Protecting America's Waters."

The plan recounts the significant progress in restoring and protecting our waters achieved since the adoption of the act in 1973. However, it also cautions that the job is far from complete, as judged by these facts: 36 percent of the rivers and streams surveyed are either partially or fully impaired, and 8 percent are threatened; 39 percent of the lakes surveyed are either partially or fully impaired and 10 percent are threatened; 38 percent of the coastal estuaries surveyed are either partially or fully impaired and 4 percent are threatened; 97 percent of Great Lakes shoreline surveyed are either partially or fully impaired and 1 percent is threatened.

The plan reaffirms the need for managing and protecting water resources on the basis of the overall health of *water-*

Threats to Groundwater in the United States
400,000 leaky underground tanks, many containing gasoline or other hazardous or toxic materials
23 million domestic septic systems in operation and 500,000 new systems installed annually
250,000 solid waste landfills. Only 25 percent of the 6,000 municipal landfills monitor groundwater. The majority of these landfills have no barrier between the waste and groundwater. In Florida virtually all landfills are located over potable water aquifers.
Of the 1.1 billion pounds of pesticides produced annually in the U.S., 77 percent are applied on land underlain by potable drinking water aquifers.
Groundwater has been contaminated at 42 percent of the 33,000 abandoned hazardous waste sites identified nationally.

sheds, and reports the water quality of 16 percent of the more than 2,000 watersheds in the continental United States is "good." Thirty-six percent have "moderate" water quality problems and 21 percent have "serious" water quality problems. Twenty-seven percent lack sufficient data upon which to make on overall assessment.

The President has proposed a budget of $568 million for FY 1999 to help implement the plan's numerous and detailed action steps that should lead to the realization of the original goal of the Clean Water Act—*"fishable and swimmable"* waters for all Americans.

State and Ecosystem Issues

People, especially from the parched western states, often wonder why Florida, with an average rainfall of 53 inches annually, still has water problems. Florida's water problems can be traced to a few facts (Betz 1984):

1) Florida's abundant rainfall is unevenly distributed in time and space. The southern 50 percent of the state gets all its freshwater from rain that falls on it. Hydrologist Garald Parker first determined that there is almost

Hydrologic Divide

10

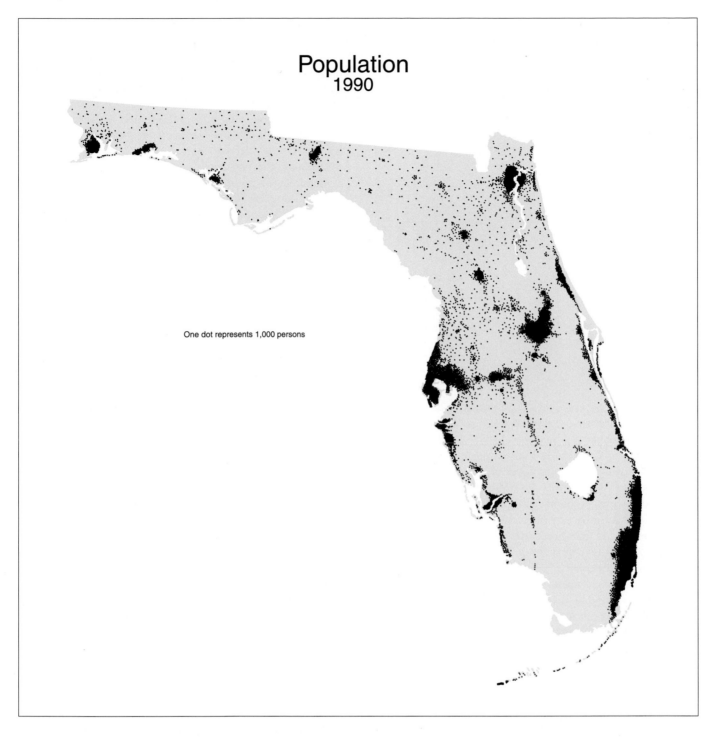

Population
1990

One dot represents 1,000 persons

Florida Department of Commerce

Urban coastal development

no net movement of either surface water or groundwater across a line snaking from Cedar Key on the Gulf to New Smyrna Beach on the Atlantic.

2) Between 1940 and 1990, Florida's population grew from 1.8 million to 14 million.

3) Large areas of the state are generally unsuitable for dense human habitation and had to be altered both ecologically and hydrogeologically, to accommodate people and the needs of agriculture and industry.

4) Forty million additional people visit Florida annually.

5) The state's main attraction (its aquatic environments) is one of the most ecologically sensitive areas in North America, if not the world. Nine out of the twenty-one most threatened ecosystems in the country are located in Florida (U.S. EPA 1994).

Almost every facet of life in Florida has a close association with water. Florida has 1,197 miles of coastline, 7,700 lakes

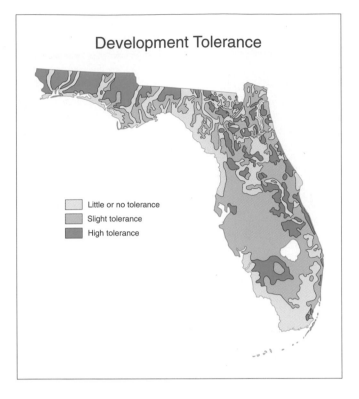

Development Tolerance

Little or no tolerance

Slight tolerance

High tolerance

greater than 10 acres, more than 1,700 streams, 3 million acres of wetlands, and 27 first-magnitude springs (those with flows exceeding 100 cubic feet per second). These water resources are intricately and delicately interwoven into an interactive system. Rain water recharges aquifers that discharge to wetlands and rivers. The majority of surface-water bodies are supplied by discharged groundwater that underlies most of the peninsula and forms over 90 percent of the base flow of surface waters. Rivers flow to estuaries and maintain the salinity regimes necessary for the growth and survival of aquatic organisms and vegetation.

These relationships contribute to the system's extreme vulnerability to degradation. Anthropogenic, and occasionally natural, pollutants introduced into one component of the system can, and do, move freely to other components making detection, assessment, and restoration both difficult and costly. Withdrawals of groundwater and surface water may also have far-reaching effects.

Since the 1800s massive alterations to Florida's natural systems have been made particularly in South and Southwest Florida to facilitate navigation and to drain land for agriculture and residential development. The Kissimmee River was straightened, the Cross-Florida Barge Canal begun, and thousands of miles of canals and dikes constructed. In the Kissimmee River-Lake Okeechobee watershed, nutrient-laden runoff from massive sugarcane farms and other agricultural activities has degraded both groundwater and surface-water quality and has harmed the flora and fauna of Everglades National Park and Florida Bay. Farther south, in the Florida Keys, septic tanks and drainage wells have contaminated shallow groundwater and jeopardized the health of the only remaining coral reef off the continental United States (Paul et al. 1995a, 1995b).

The state is now attempting to recover from the environmental and ecological effects of these alterations. In 1995 the Florida legislature passed the Everglades Forever Act, a detailed strategy for saving the River of Grass from catastrophic loss. In 1992 Congress authorized the dechannelization of the Kissimmee River. Attempts have also been made to levy a tax

on sugar to force the industry to pay its share of the cleanup costs.

To help offset the cost of saving the Everglades and cleaning up the Florida Bay, an amendment to the state constitution, authorizing the state to levy a sales tax on sugar, was successfully placed on the ballot in 1996. However, the amendment was narrowly defeated by a concentrated, well-financed and orchestrated political and media campaign by the sugar industry. The effort did serve to focus national attention on the plight of the South Florida ecosystem and resulted in the allocation of hundreds of millions of federal dollars to the so-called "Florida Initiative"—a collaborative local, state, and federal effort to restore what the Clean Water Action Plan calls a "nationally significant watershed."

Nowhere are political disputes over water more intense than in the southwestern counties of Hillsborough, Pinellas, Pasco, and Hernando. Water wars in this area have cost local governments and regional agencies over $3 million in attorneys' fees alone. In some areas of the Southwest Florida Water Management District, the demand for water already exceeds supply, forcing the water management district and the regional water supply authority to impose restrictions on water withdrawal, to increase the use of reclaimed water, and to consider the increased use of water from rivers and springs.

The impacts of water shortages are never limited to human communities. Natural systems also depend on the right amount of good quality water at the proper time. Water withdrawals for human use have adversely affected natural systems in southwest Florida by lowering lake levels, drying up wetlands, and reducing base flow to streams. Overwithdrawal has resulted in earth subsidence (sinkhole development), drying up of private wells, and increased saltwater intrusion.

This area of the state has been affected by phosphate mining and associated phosphoric acid production. Gypsum stacks from phosphate mining have contaminated groundwater and wetlands with radioactive and other pollutants. In 1994 a portion of a gypsum stack collapsed through a sinkhole into the underlying aquifer, and in 1997 a phosphogypsum impoundment was breached spilling millions of gallons of acidic wastewater into a tributary of the Alafia River and resulting in one of the largest fish kills ever documented in a Florida river. In 1995 Florida adopted a phosphogypsum rule to govern construction and operation of gypsum stacks. In 1998 the Florida legislature directed the Florida Department of Environmental Protection to write regulations governing the construction of phosphogypsum impoundments.

The Atlantic coast and the Jacksonville and Orlando regions are not immune to water woes (albeit less serious than those in south and southwest Florida). In these regions of exploding population, localized water shortages may be expected. The area's groundwater quality is also threatened by a large number of drainage wells that discharge stormwater runoff directly into the public water supply: the Floridan aquifer. The St. Johns River has historically been used for disposal of domestic and industrial effluents. Despite years of regulatory measures to reduce pollution, the Lower St. Johns is still not meeting the "fishable and swimmable" designation of the Clean Water Act.

The northern and northwestern parts of the state are generally water-rich and are more likely to suffer from floods than from water shortages. Projections for future availability of water in these regions are encouraging. In the Suwannee River watershed, a coalition of local, regional and federal agencies and stakeholders from Florida and Georgia have been collaborating on the development of plans to manage and protect the relatively pristine quality of this basin that straddles both states. The Suwannee coalition will have to address legislative bills proposing to divert some of the river's water to the water-starved Tampa Bay area to satisfy the demand of the ever-increasing population of that region. Levels of nitrates are also increasing in both the river and some of the underlying aquifers. These are indicative of pollution from concentrated feed lot operations and the proliferation of septic systems.

In northwest Florida water quality and availability projections are generally reassuring, with the exception of the Apalachicola River watershed and rapidly developing coastal areas. The Apalachicola River, a critical component of one of the most biologically productive estuaries in the country, has been plagued with water quality problems largely owing to point and nonpoint source discharges from Georgia and Alabama.

Florida has been in the forefront among states in the nation in the development of water resources legislation, although much remains to be done. The National Water Commission recognized the Water Resources Act of 1972 (Chapter 373 of the Florida Statutes) as a model water statute. The act was particularly innovative for establishing regional administration and calling for development of a comprehensive state water plan. Water management districts, established primarily in accord with surface water features, were to regulate water through a consumptive use permitting system. They were also to adopt minimum flows and levels for all surface waters and aquifers below which withdrawals were to be prohibited as harmful to natural systems. Twenty-five years later minimum flows and levels have not been established for most of Florida's waters, and those that have been or are being set are subject to controversy as the amount of water required to maintain various types

of natural systems is debated in the scientific community.

In the 1980s and 1990s Florida turned to land acquisition as a means of preserving and protecting water and other natural resources. The Florida legislature adopted Preservation 2000 in 1990 which authorized $300 million annually for 10 years to purchase ecologically valuable lands. Many believe land acquisition programs alone will not be adequate to preserve the minimum necessary for healthy ecosystems. In 1994, the Florida Game and Fresh Water Fish Commission estimated that the state would have to increase its conservation lands from the current 7 million acres to 11.7 million acres in order to protect the state's wildlife and its habitat (Cox et al. 1994).

In 1995 the Florida Department of Environmental Protection completed the Florida Water Plan. The plan identified four major issues still facing Florida:

Issue 1: Inadequate links between land and water planning, and between planning and program implementation, causing program conflicts and inefficiencies.

Issue 2: Government, the private sector, and the general public frequently do not take shared responsibility for sustaining Florida's water resources, thereby hindering the effectiveness of water management efforts.

Issue 3: Water management usually has not been approached on a comprehensive watershed basis, which has impaired our ability to protect water resources and related natural systems.

Issue 4: Information and research to support water resource protection, restoration and management actions is inadequate.

The Florida Water Plan identifies many ways to address these issues. Most of these, however, are not legislatively mandated and are thus not adequately funded. Following the national trend the Florida Water Plan calls for ecosystem management through which watershed-specific plans are developed

13

Gary Knight

Freshwater lake behind dunes, Topsail Hill, Walton County, land purchased through P2000

and implemented in cooperative partnerships between governments at all levels, the regulated community, and affected citizens.

Florida's efforts at ecosystem management as the best way to protect water and other resources have been subject to some of the same criticisms as national efforts. Implementation of this new philosophy will require restructuring of organizations as well as shifting of funding priorities. Changes at the federal level are considered necessary for propelling Florida (and other states) toward ecosystem management. Federal and state agencies still need to redesign or redirect monitoring programs to generate the information necessary for assessment of watersheds and ecosystems. Watersheds have traditionally been considered synonymous with river basins and rarely, if ever, have groundwater (which contributes over 90 percent of Florida's surface water base flow), sediments, soil, or atmospheric deposition been evaluated as essential components of ecosystems.

Issues of scale and boundaries of watersheds have not received adequate attention. Determining scale and boundaries is essential, not only for data analysis and management, but also for construction of GIS-based decision-making models to allow managers and policy makers to base their decisions on solid foundations.

The quality of our water depends on the health of the ecosystem of which it is a part. By the time we notice that the quality or quantity of water has declined it may be too late. To protect our water resources we need to look at other indicators of system stress, such as loss of habitat, alteration of vegetative cover, increased sedimentation, reduction of surface water flow, lowering of water table elevation, or introduction of exotic species. In July 1996 EPA administrator Carol Browner stated: "In Florida we have 200 beach closures a year. Across the country you cannot eat the fish in thousands of rivers and lakes." All these are indications that the job is not done.

REFERENCES

A source for a map or figure has a number in parentheses following the entry. This number refers to the page in this atlas for which the source was used.

Abramovitz, J.N. 1996. "Sustaining Freshwater Ecosystems." In *State of the World*. L.R. Brown, ed. New York, N.Y.: W.W. Norton.

Ackermann, W.C., G.F. White, and E.B. Worthington, eds. 1973. *Man-Made Lakes: Their Problems and Environmental Effects*. American Geophysical Union. Geophysical Monograph 17. Washington, D.C.

Betz, J. 1984. "Water Use" In *Water Resources Atlas of Florida*. E.A. Fernald and D.J. Patton, eds. pp 108–115. Tallahassee, FL: Institute of Science and Public Affairs.

Bouwer, H. 1978. *Groundwater Hydrology*. New York, N.Y.: McGraw Hill.

Carter, L.J. 1974. *The Florida Experience: Land and Water Policies in a Growth State*. Baltimore and London: Johns Hopkins University Press. (map, 12)

Clarke, D.C., ed. 1995. *Risk Policy Report*. September 22. Washington, D.C.: Inside Washington Publishers.

Clarke, R. 1993. *Water: The International Crisis*. Cambridge, MA: M.I.T. Press.

Cox, J., R. Kautz, M. MacLaughlin, and T. Gilbert. 1994. *Closing the Gaps in Florida's Wildlife Habitat Conservation System*. Florida Game and Fresh Water Fish Commission, Tallahassee.

Crosson, P.R., and K.D. Frederick. 1983. *The World Food Situation*. Washington, D.C.: Resources for the Future, Inc.

Crosson, P.R., R.R. Cummings, and K.D. Frederick, eds. 1978. *Selected Water Management Issues in Latin American Agriculture*. Baltimore, MD: Johns Hopkins University Press.

Espenshade, E.B., ed. 1978. *Goode's World Atlas*. Chicago, IL: Rand McNally. (maps, 5, 6)

Foundation for Advancements in Science and Education. 1996. *Exporting Risk: Pesticide Exports for U.S. Ports, 1992–1994*. Foundation for Advancements in Science and Education Research Report, Spring 1996.

Frederick, K.D. 1996. "Water as a Source of International Conflict." *Resources* 123 (Spring):9–12.

Gardner, G. 1996. "Preserving Agricultural Resources." In *State of the World*. L.R. Brown, ed. New York, N.Y.: W.W. Norton.

Ground Water Protection Council. 1996 (May–June). *The Ground Water Communique*. Oklahoma City, OK.

Holdgate, M.W., and G.F. White, eds. 1977. *Environmental Issues. Scientific Committee on Problems of the Environment*. Report No. 10. London: John Wiley and Sons.

Kolais, J.F., and J.D. Nystuen. 1975. *Physical Geography: Environment and Man*. New York, N.Y.: McGraw-Hill. (map, 8)

King., C.A. 1962. *An Introduction to Oceanography*. New York, N.Y.: McGraw-Hill.

Loaiciga, H.A., J.B. Valdes, R. Vogel, and J. Garvey. 1996. "Global Warming and the Hydrologic Cycle." *Journal of Hydrology* 174: 83–127.

National Water Commission. 1973. *National Water Commission Report*. Washington, D.C.

Odingo, R.S. 1977. "African Experience: Some Observations from Kenya." In *Environmental Effects of Complex River Development*. G.F. White, ed. Boulder, Colorado: Westview Press.

Paul, J., J. Rose, S. Jiang, C. Kellogg, and E. Shinn. 1995a. "Occurrence of Fecal Indicator Bacteria in Surface Waters and the Subsurface Aquifer in Key Largo, Florida." *Applied and Environmental Microbiology* 6:2235–2241.

Paul, J., J. Rose, S. Jiang, C. Kellogg, and E. Shinn. 1995b. "Viral Tracer Studies Indicate Contamination of Marine Waters by Sewage Disposal Practices in Key Largo, Florida." *Applied and Environmental Microbiology* 61: 2230–2234.

Pearce, F. 1992. *The Dammed Rivers, Dams, and the Coming World Water Crisis*. London: Bodley Head.

Platt, A.E. 1996. "Confronting Infectious Disease." In *State of the World*. L.R. Brown, ed. New York, N.Y.: W.W. Norton.

Postel, S. 1996. "Forging a Sustainable Water Strategy." In *State of the World*. L.R. Brown, ed. New York, N.Y.: W.W. Norton.

Strahler, A., and A. Strahler. 1994. *Introducing Physical Geography*. New York: John Wiley and Sons. (figure, 2)

U.S. Department of Commerce. Bureau of the Census. (map, 11)

U.S. Environmental Protection Agency. 1994. *The Quality of Our Nation's Water*. EPA 841-5-94-002. (graphs, 9)

U.S. Geological Survey. 1995. *Final Report of the Intergovernmental Task Force on Monitoring Water Quality*.

Water Environment Federation. 1993. *Water Quality 2000*. Washington, D.C.

Water Environment Federation. 1993. *A National Water Agenda for the 21st Century*. Washington, D.C. (table, 10)

White, G.F. 1960. *The Changing Role of Water in Arid Lands*. University of Arizona Bulletin Series. 32.

Worldwatch Institute. 1990. Worldwatch Database Disk. (graphs, 7)

II

FLORIDA'S WATER RESOURCES

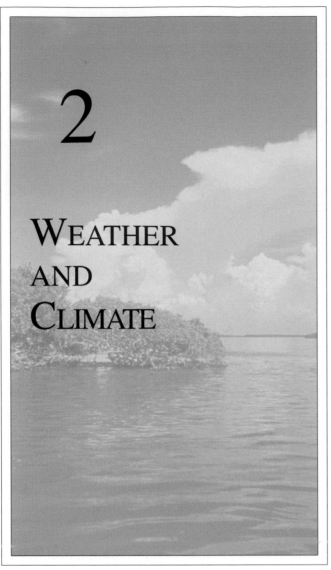

2
WEATHER
AND
CLIMATE

James A. Henry

Köppen, divides the state into two major climate types. A tropical savanna, also called a tropical wet-and-dry climate, occurs in the southern portion of the peninsula and the Keys. Here all months average above 64°F and pronounced wet and dry seasons occur. The rainy season, typically June through September, has frequent afternoon thunderstorms and some months exceed 10 inches of rainfall. The dry season, winter, may have very little or no rainfall for weeks, occasionally for months. Extending along the coast from about Ft. Pierce to Miami is a transitional tropical climate, which has a relatively short dry season. The northern three-quarters of the state has a humid subtropical climate; this type covers much of the southeastern portion of the country. This climate is subtropical rather than tropical because some months have an average temperature of less than 64°F. Also, this part of Florida does not experience such a pronounced dry season as the tropical southern section.

Another climate classification, called the Thornthwaite system, is used frequently by water resource scientists and divides Florida into three types, rather than two. This system includes an indicator of precipitation effectiveness, which considers evapotranspiration as well as rainfall, and it is this indicator (not the humidity of the air) that determines the boundary between humid and subhumid climate types. As can be seen in the figure, the humid tropical class of the Thornthwaite system corresponds approximately with the tropical savanna of the Köppen system.

A third way of denoting regional climate distinctions is the climatological division scheme. Each division is, as nearly as possible, a region of relatively uniform climate within a state. The divisions, of which there are 344 in the conterminous states, are primarily modifications of the old U.S. Department of Agriculture crop reporting districts. Florida has seven climatological divisions, the names of which relate to their geographical location in the state. This approach yields boundaries that are very different from the Köppen and Thornthwaite classifications.

Although some rainfall data are reported on a climatological division basis, such as certain drought indices, nearly all data are for individual stations. Values for 95 stations in Florida are used to describe the climate of the state, emphasizing rain-

Climate is often stated to be one of Florida's most important resources. Although the state is located at the same latitude as some of the world's major deserts, Florida is one of the wettest states in the country. Its average rainfall per year is 53 inches; only Alabama has this same amount, and both are exceeded only by the 55-inch average of Louisiana. Florida has many unique rainfall characteristics in addition to being one of the wettest states. For example, it is first or tied for first in the nation in the following categories: proportion of summer versus winter rainfall; percentage of the months of June through September in which rainfall exceeds four inches; rainfall in the average wettest month; difference in rainfall between the average wettest and driest months; and maximum expected 30-minute rainfall.

Despite the fact that Florida is a low peninsula with a relatively homogeneous topographic nature, extending over just six and one-half degrees of latitude, it is not uniform in rainfall characteristics, or even in general climate types. The most commonly used climate classification, developed by Wladimir

Köppen Climate Types

Humid subtropical

Vero Beach

Punta Gorda

Tropical savanna

fall characteristics. To facilitate comparison of general climatic maps, international agreement has led to the use of what is called a climatic normal, which is an average of a climatic element, such as rainfall, over a 30-year period, ending with a decade. The averages are computed from the data for the preceding three decades. For some aspects, such as extremes and long-term trends, it is preferable to use all data available for the entire period of collection for each station. Most stations in Florida have nearly complete records since 1948.

Annual Rainfall

Average Annual Rainfall

The map of average annual rainfall for Florida exhibits substantial variation; values range from 69 inches at Wewahitchka in the panhandle to 40 inches in Key West.

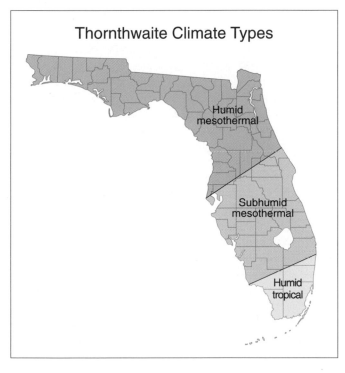

Twenty-five stations receive between 40 and 49 inches yearly, 58 average between 50 and 59 inches, and 12 receive between 60 and 69 inches. Eight of the stations that average 60 or more inches yearly are in the panhandle, including the seven wettest cities in the state. Tallahassee's 66 inches ranks third in the state, exceeded only by 69 inches at Wewahitchka and 68 inches at Milton. The other region of highest rainfall is in the southeastern part of the state, including Hialeah (63 inches), Ft. Lauderdale (61 inches), and West Palm Beach (61 inches).

The high rainfall values in the panhandle are primarily due to the relatively abundant rainfall received throughout the year. In summer this region receives substantial convective rainfall (a typically sudden-onset, localized showery type), as do generally all parts of the state, but in addition receives more winter rainfall from large-scale frontal systems than any other portion of the state. This area also has more days with intense rainfall; Tallahassee averages 40 days annually that receive rainfall of 0.5 inch or more. This section of the state, along with the southeastern portion, experiences the most days in a year with at least 0.1 inch of rainfall, averaging more than 80 days.

Several interacting factors account for the relatively high rainfall in the southeastern portion of the state. Here the Gulf Stream approaches the land closer than any other point in the state, which contributes moisture to the air and aids in producing instability, both of which enhance the likelihood of rainfall. Intense, convective rainfall is very frequent for six months, and unlike anywhere else in the state, nighttime convective rainfall is often significant, particularly just inland from the coast. Also enhancing rainfall are wind direction, upper-atmospheric pressure systems, and the sea breeze, a significant producer of locally heavy rainfall. This is also one of the sectors of the state most frequently affected by tropical storms and hurricanes.

Lowest average annual rainfall occurs in the Keys and the central portion of the peninsula. Key West's 40 inches is the lowest, followed by Tampa (44 inches). Six stations receive 45 inches, including Tavernier, also in the Keys, and Miami Beach. The islands of the Keys are not of sufficient size to produce convection and the resulting rainfall in summer that occurs

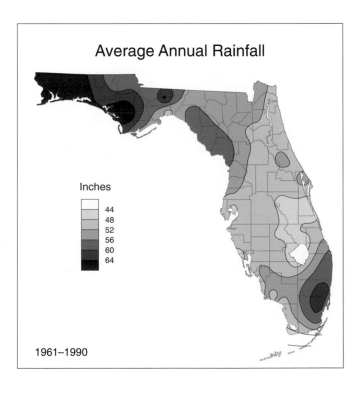

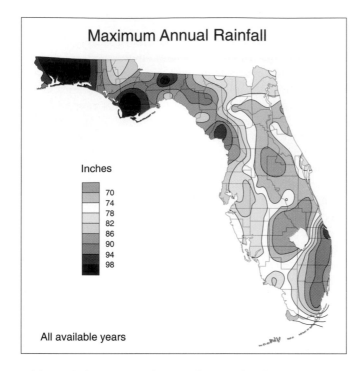

Maximum Annual Rainfall

Inches

70
74
78
82
86
90
94
98

All available years

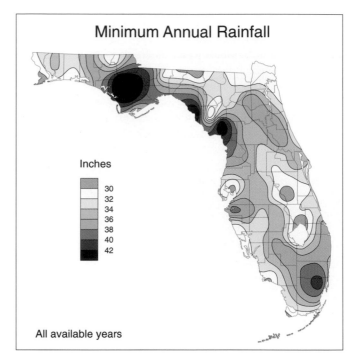

Minimum Annual Rainfall

Inches

30
32
34
36
38
40
42

All available years

with regularity on the main part of the peninsula. Here only 24 days per year have rain of 0.5 inch or more, and fewer fronts and the rain they produce penetrate these southern regions compared with the northern sections of the state.

Although not distinctly apparent on the map, rainfall definitely increases a few miles inland from the coast in most sections of the state. This effect is very strongly revealed in a comparison of Miami Beach and the Miami airport. The former averages 45 inches annually, and just eight miles inland the airport receives 56 inches. Also not revealed on the map is the influence of Lake Okeechobee. Rainfall is reduced by about 15 percent annually directly over the lake because of reduction of convection over its waters. This also results in a slight reduction of rainfall downwind of its surface.

Extreme Annual Rainfall

Year-to-year rainfall variability is significant at nearly all cities in Florida. This is true on a calendar-year basis, as well as a 12-month basis (not necessarily coinciding with a calendar year). The maps included here show the maximum and minimum rainfall that has occurred in any calendar year at each station; all years of data available (not restricted to 1961 through 1990) were used. Five Florida stations have received 100 inches or more rainfall in a calendar year, led by Milton's 105 inches received in 1975, and the 104 inches that fell on Wewahitchka in 1965 and on Tallahassee in 1964. The other cities that have received 100 inches or more are Niceville (101 inches), also in the panhandle, and Stuart (100 inches) on the southeastern coast. Sixteen cities have received 90 inches or more in a calendar year, and all but two are in the panhandle or on the southeastern coast. Of these 16 stations, three had their rainiest year in 1964, three in 1975, and three in 1994. However, even stations in very close proximity recorded maximum values in different years. This is also true of four of the five cities with the least extreme high values of one-year rainfall: they are closely clustered north of Lake Okeechobee but achieved their maximum rainfall in four different years. Key West's greatest annual rainfall occurred in 1969, and at just 63 inches it is the lowest value in the state.

When any 12-consecutive-month period is considered, maximum rainfall values and patterns are somewhat different from that of calendar-year data. Six stations, compared with five when calendar-year data are used, have exceeded 100 inches over a 12-month period, and nearly all stations in the panhandle and along the southeastern coast have received 90 inches or more. The maximum of 112 inches occurred in Wewahitchka (1965–1966). Many stations statewide have accumulated more than 75 inches, and a large majority of cities have reported values of at least 70 inches. Most of the high-rainfall years have been produced by very wet warm seasons, including contributions from hurricanes, rather than winter storms, although exceptions have occurred.

The map of minimum rainfall on a calendar-year basis reveals relatively little variation in values: most stations are between 29 and 37 inches. However, 12 cities have had at least one year with less than 30 inches. The lowest amount, 20 inches, occurred at Key West in 1974. Tied for second lowest is also a city in the Keys—Tavernier with 25 inches in 1951. Other minimum values are scattered over the entire length of the peninsula. Cross City, also with a value of 25 inches (1972), is in the northern part of the peninsula, while the next three driest cities (all standing at 27 inches) are Tampa, on the central west coast; Miami Beach, on the lower east coast; and Okeechobee, between these two cities in a central non-coastal location. Only two of these six stations, Miami Beach and Tampa, recorded their minimum rainfalls in the same year (1956). Wewahitchka has the highest minimum amount of rainfall, receiving 49 inches in its driest year on record.

Minimum rainfall amounts on a 12-month, non-calendar basis also present a complex pattern. Between Lake Okeechobee and Jacksonville are several east-west trending bands of varying minimum rainfall amounts extending across the entire peninsula. Several of the included stations have values less than 32 inches, which is also the case around the Apalachicola and Tampa Bay regions. Key West has received less than 20 inches, the lowest rainfall amount in the state over a 12-month period. This minimum value, coupled with the yearly rainfall amounts exceeding 100 inches received in the wettest years in some locations, gives Florida a ranking of sixteenth among the 48 contiguous states for rainfall variability.

Monthly and Seasonal Rainfall

Average Monthly Rainfall

The graph of average monthly rainfall for the entire state reveals that July is the wettest month, and November, with less than one-third the rainfall of July, the driest. Rainfall markedly increases from May to June, and at many individual stations a more than twofold increase exists between these months. An even more abrupt change occurs from September to October. Rainfall decreases significantly statewide in April: more than one-half of the cities experience less rainfall in this month than the prior month.

The six months shown in the maps represent various phases of the yearly rainfall regime. January is the average coldest month; April shows a statewide decrease of rainfall compared with the preceding and following months; June is most frequently the first month of Florida's rainy season in most sections of the state; July is the wettest month and generally the warmest; September is the last month of the rainy season in most sections; and November receives the least rainfall statewide. The rainfall patterns are much more complex in June and July than in the drier months. There is a difference of 6.5 inches of rainfall between the wettest (9.8 inches) and driest (3.3 inches) cities in the state in July, and just 3.2 inches between the maximum and minimum values in November (4.7 and 1.5 inches, respectively).

Although July is the wettest month and November is the driest month for the state as a whole, other months have the distinction of receiving the most and least rainfall. The map showing the distribution of the wettest average month reveals that July is the wettest only in the panhandle and in relatively small sections near the center of the peninsula. June is the wettest month in most of the southern half of the peninsula, August for most of the other half, and September in Key West, Apalachicola, and most stations on the east coast of the state. Only in Pompano Beach, with an October maximum, does the wettest month not occur in June through September.

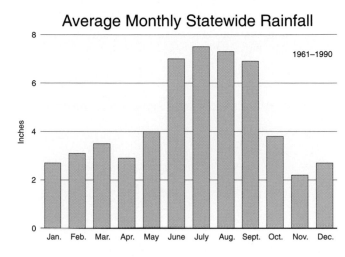

19

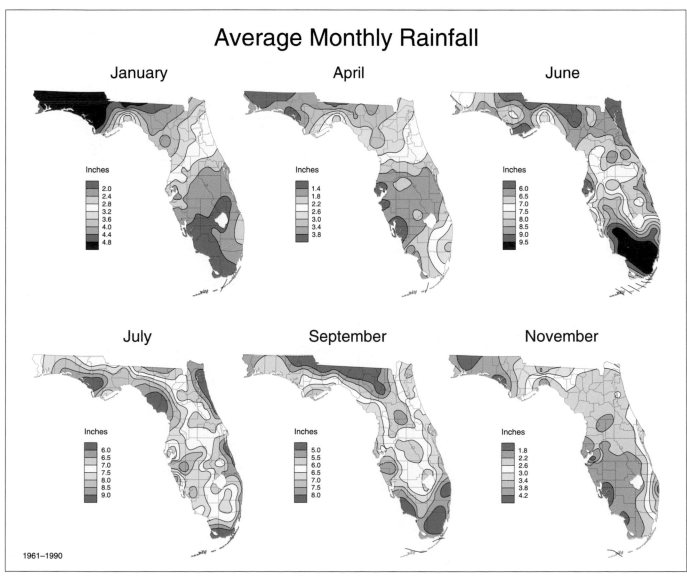

The pattern of the driest average month reveals that November, despite being the driest month when rainfall is averaged for the entire state, is the driest month at only 5 of the 95 individual Florida stations, all of which are located in the northeastern section. April, October, and December are the driest average months in most sections of the state. March is the driest month in the Keys, and only in Apalachicola is May the month of least average rainfall.

The maps showing the average rainfall of the month with the greatest and least average rainfall reveal that a complex pattern emerges in the wet season, with highest values in the southeastern portion of the state and along the western portion of the peninsula. Very little variation occurs throughout the state in rainfall during the average driest month at each city; values vary by only a few inches.

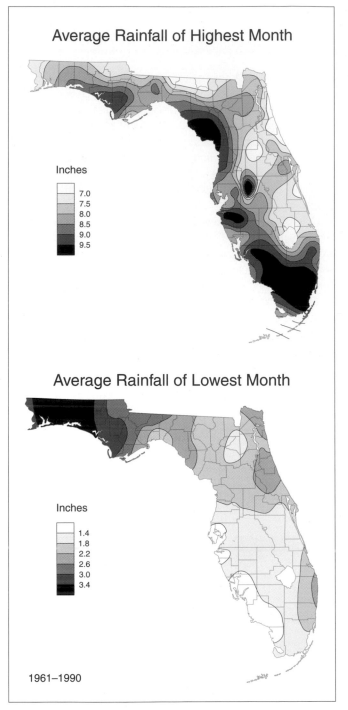

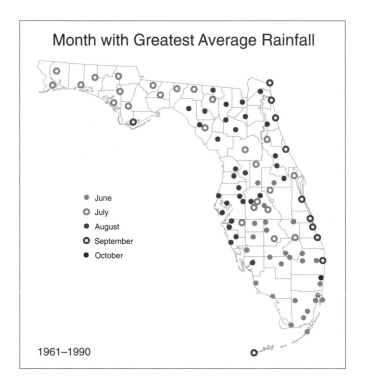

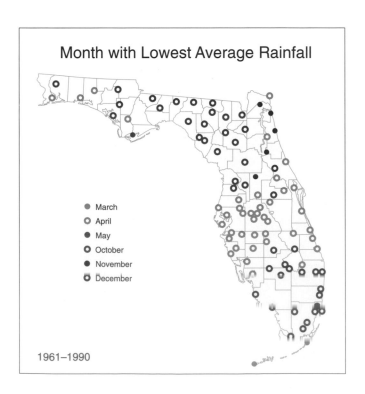

Extreme Monthly Rainfall

The maximum rainfall ever recorded during any month at each station, using all available years, was used to produce the maximum monthly rainfall map. The highest ever reported was just over 42 inches during October 1965 at a station located in the yacht basin in Ft. Lauderdale. This stands as the sixth highest monthly total in the country. (Although this value was recorded at a regular climatological station, it is not the same Ft. Lauderdale station that the National Climatic Data Center includes in its general Florida climatic database.) This prodigious amount resulted from two stationary localized storms that yielded 26 inches during three days in the middle of the month and nearly 14 inches on the last two days of the month. Pompano Beach, eight miles to the north, in the same month received its record monthly rainfall, a total of 34.4 inches, nearly all received from the same two storms that inundated the Ft. Lauderdale yacht basin. However, two stations less than 10

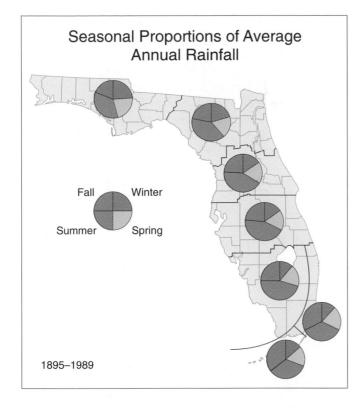

Seasonal Proportions of Average Annual Rainfall

Fall　Winter

Summer　Spring

1895–1989

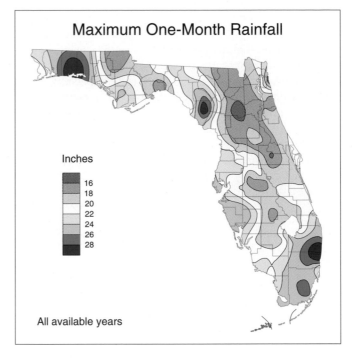

Maximum One-Month Rainfall

Inches

16
18
20
22
24
26
28

All available years

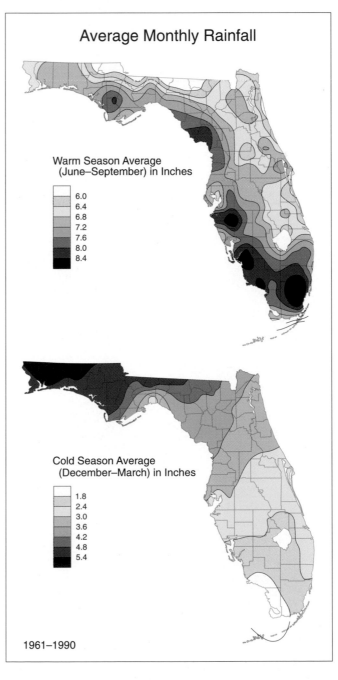

Average Monthly Rainfall

Warm Season Average
(June–September) in Inches

6.0
6.4
6.8
7.2
7.6
8.0
8.4

Cold Season Average
(December–March) in Inches

1.8
2.4
3.0
3.6
4.2
4.8
5.4

1961–1990

miles from the yacht basin recorded entire monthly totals of only 10 to 14 inches.

Other high monthly totals include 32.0 inches during July 1985 at Cross City, 31.4 inches at Niceville during July 1994, and 30.8 inches in August 1995 at Jacksonville Beach. Nearly all of the maximum monthly values for each station were recorded in June through September, primarily June and September in the southern half of the state, July and August in most of the rest of the state, with September dominant in the northeastern section and the region around Tallahassee. Several high monthly values are associated with hurricanes, and will be discussed in the section on hurricanes and tropical storms.

A map of minimum monthly rainfall was not prepared because all stations had several months with no or very nearly no rainfall. These minimum values occur mainly in midwinter in the southern portion of the state, but during the fall or spring in the remainder of the state.

Seasonal Rainfall

The map of seasonal variation of rainfall for 18 selected Florida cities and a map showing seasonal proportional rainfall for the seven climatological divisions, coupled with maps of warm season (June–September) and cold season (December–March) rainfall and the previous maps of six significant rainfall months, reveal three general seasonal rainfall regimes in the state. These regimes have been described by Henry et al. (1994) and are summarized here. The first regime, covering the panhandle and most of the northern and central peninsula to approximately the Tampa Bay region, has two peaks in the rainfall cycle: summer and late winter/early spring. The summer maximum, which is almost always greater than the winter/spring maximum, is the result of the sea breeze and convection caused by heating of the land. There is also at this time a pronounced near-coastal maximum compared with inland locations. The cold season maximum, which may include snow, generally peaks in March at most central and northern cities.

21

There is no significant coastal-inland difference in rainfall amounts in these cooler months. Rainfall at this time is mostly the result of mid-latitude cyclonic storms, cold fronts, and low-pressure systems that move from the Gulf of Mexico northeastward over the northern half of the state, especially affecting the panhandle. The graph of the average number of fronts affecting various parts of the state does not include those associated with major, fully developed mid-latitude cyclones; only about ten such storms affect north Florida per year, and this reduces to an average of five near the latitude of Daytona Beach. As much as slightly more than 90 percent of the rainfall from

November through March results from fronts of all types. This activity keeps late winter/early spring from being the driest time of year in the panhandle. Rainfall in the northern section of the state averages around five inches monthly at this time of year. In this northern rainfall regime October or November is generally the month of least rainfall. A secondary minimum often occurs in April and sometimes May.

A second general seasonal rainfall regime exists in the southeastern portion of the state, especially along the coast. Convection is active for six months here, with peaks in rainfall in June and September through October. In the Miami region

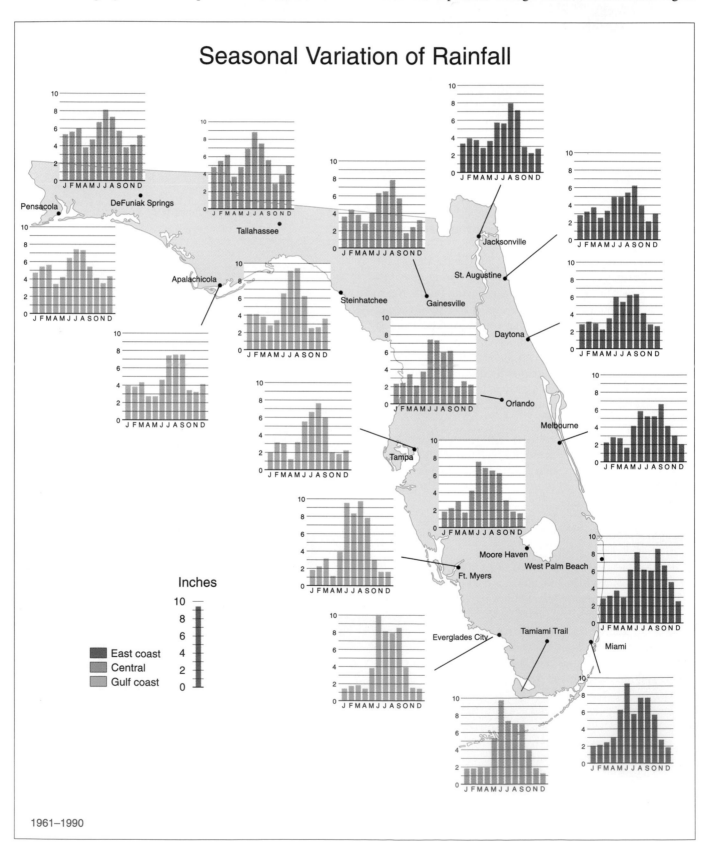

Seasonal Variation of Rainfall

Inches

East coast
Central
Gulf coast

1961–1990

22

the former peak is the larger, but north of Miami, including West Palm Beach, September is the peak month. A definite coastal to inland rainfall gradient occurs here, with the maximum rainfall recorded very near the coast. A significant decrease in July and August is primarily due to the westward migration, away from Florida, of an elongated region of low pressure in the upper atmosphere, which induces rainfall while it is over a region, but decreases amounts when it migrates from the region. It moves back over the southern peninsula in September and October, producing a second rainfall peak. Also influencing rainfall in the southeastern part of Florida, and other sections of this part of the country, is the anticyclone, or high-pressure system, situated in the Atlantic Ocean. Often called the Azores-Bermuda high because of its location relative to these areas, the maps of its seasonal migration show that a western extension, or ridge, occasionally extends over Florida, reaching a maximum in summer. The accompanying subsidence and rain-inhibiting effects reduce rainfall at this time, although the reduction is not as much as would occur if it were not for the strong convection over the peninsula induced by high summer land temperatures and an active, strong sea breeze, both inducing rising air, which enhances rainfall. Despite reduced rainfall amounts in July through August, the main dry season in the southeastern part of the state is December through February, when the only significant source of moisture is the few fronts passing over the area. Because fronts produce large-scale rather than localized rainfall, there is no coastal-inland rainfall gradient at this time of year.

The third major seasonal rainfall regime exists in the Keys, the overall driest portion of the state. Here the timing of the wet and dry seasons is quite similar to that of the southeastern coastal regime, but the difference between the wet and dry season is less distinct. In the Keys rainfall is more consistently distributed in all seasons compared with the coastal area between Miami and West Palm Beach.

Other seasonal aspects of rainfall in Florida exist. In the southern portion, except the Keys, the dry season is usually drier and the wet season is often wetter than in the north. October is normally the driest month in the northwest, but is typically one of the wettest months along the southeastern coast.

The wet season begins on the southern portion of the peninsula in June on both coasts, but extends only through September on the west coast while lasting through October on the east coast. The most consistent rainfall throughout the year occurs in the Keys, the driest section of the state, and in the relatively wet panhandle. Averaged over a year, most of the east coast of the peninsula receives more rainfall than the west coast, but summer amounts are about the same on both coasts. The winter pattern is complex with few consistencies.

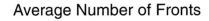

Average Number of Fronts

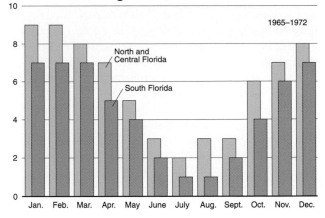

1965–1972

North and Central Florida

South Florida

Azores-Bermuda High Pressure System
Average Strength (in millibars) and Position

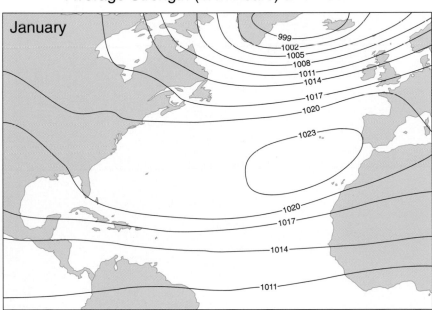

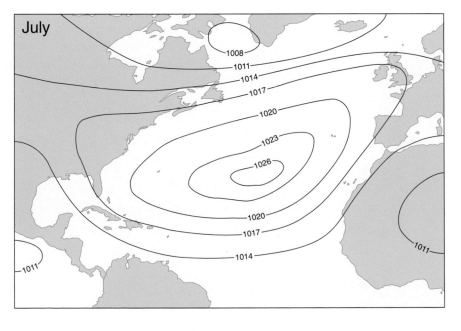

23

As revealed on the maps of warm season and cold season rainfall, the amount in the former is greater than that of the cold season by approximately 40 percent in the panhandle, but by as much as 400 percent in the southern peninsula. For the entire state, the average rainfall for June through September (the warm season) is approximately 29 inches, or 55 percent of the annual total. Patterns of maximum and minimum warm season and cold season rainfall (not mapped) are complex, especially for minimum warm-season rainfall.

Daily Rainfall

The pattern of greatest daily rainfall in Florida is very irregular. Two cities have reported 30 or more inches in a 24-hour period, two have experienced between 20 and 30 inches in a day, and 43 stations have received 10 to 19 inches in a day. These extreme rainfall values are spread throughout the state. The two greatest 24-hour amounts occurred during storms of tropical origin. A state-record 38.7 inches fell in Yankeetown

in a 24-hour period extending over September 5–6, 1950, during Hurricane Easy. This remained the North American record until it was eclipsed by a 43-inch amount produced near Houston, Texas, by a tropical storm. The second greatest daily amount in Florida occurred in Trenton, north of Yankeetown, where 31 inches of rain fell during the passage of a weak tropical disturbance in October 1941. Key West, the driest city in the state in terms of average annual rainfall, received 23.3 inches (some accounts say 22.8 inches) in 24 hours in November 1980, and Fernandina Beach reported 22 inches in one day in November 1969. Heavy rainfall events, with three or more inches of rainfall over two consecutive days, occur in the panhandle (as represented by Apalachicola) an average of 3.2 times per year, which is among the highest values in the southeastern United States. Peninsular Florida (represented by St. Leo and Belle Glade) experiences an average of 2.5 such events annually, also greater than nearly all other sections of the southeastern region of the country. Additionally, individual storm events last an average of seven to eight hours over nearly all

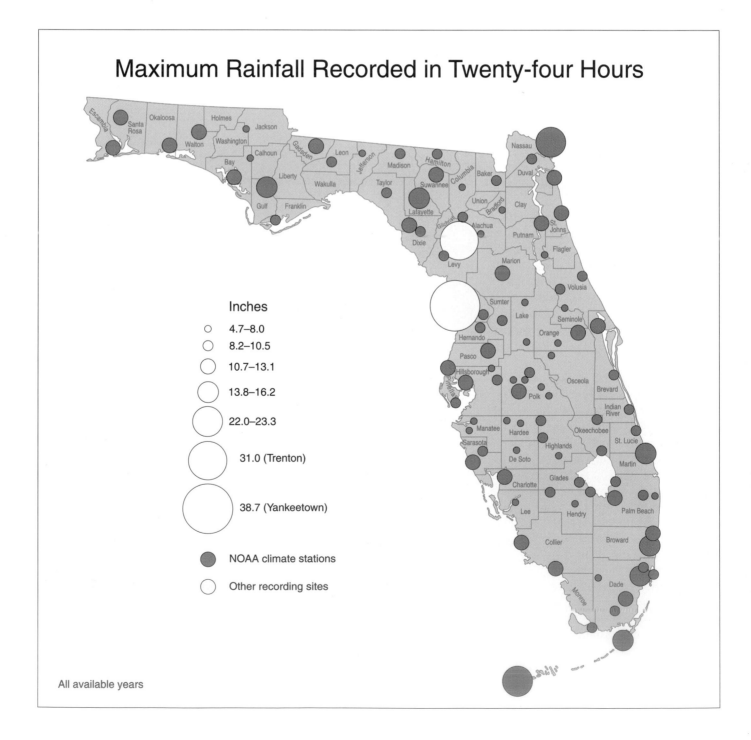

Maximum Rainfall Recorded in Twenty-four Hours

Inches

○ 4.7–8.0

○ 8.2–10.5

○ 10.7–13.1

○ 13.8–16.2

○ 22.0–23.3

○ 31.0 (Trenton)

○ 38.7 (Yankeetown)

● NOAA climate stations

○ Other recording sites

All available years

the state; although this is the lowest average for a major region in the eastern half of the country, the amount of rainfall per storm event exceeds 0.65 inches throughout the panhandle, and is between 0.60 and 0.65 inches for the peninsula—values that are among the highest in the southeastern United States. Also, it has been estimated that individual storms that produce more than 15 inches of rainfall probably occur in the state at least once a year.

Considering all stations in the state, maximum daily values have occurred in all months except February. September has had the most such occurrences, with 28 percent, followed by June (16 percent) and October (12 percent). In September and October convective rainfall and hurricane occurrence are still significant. During June, the second most common month in which extreme daily rainfalls have occurred, the sea breeze and its accompanying convective rainfall are very intense and occur on a daily basis. A rain shower occurs somewhere within the state on almost every day during summer, and the chance of no place in the state south of Orlando experiencing a summer day with no rainfall is considerably less than 1 in 500.

Hourly Rainfall

Rainfall varies considerably relative to time of day. The hourly variation is shown for three selected cities, representative of the northern, central, and southern portions of the state. The graphs indicate the percentage of the total daily rainfall that occurs during each hour, for the cold and warm seasons. A pronounced afternoon maximum, reaching a peak around 4 P.M., occurs during the warm season for all three stations. This effect is especially strong at Orlando, where nearly 60 percent of the rain in summer occurs from 2:00 to 7:00 P.M. Considering just July in Orlando, more than two-thirds occurs in the same hours, while less than five percent falls in the 14 hours between 8:00 P.M. and 10:00 A.M. The afternoon peak also exists at most coastal cities, but is not as evident as at those farther inland. This diurnal variation and coastal-versus-inland effect is primarily the result of the movement of the sea breeze, which moves inland from both coasts and often produces a convergence near the central portions of the state, generally yielding considerable inland rainfall around 4 P.M. Only in the extreme eastern portion of the panhandle and the Keys is there no significant afternoon concentration of rainfall. In these two locations the sea breeze convergence is weaker or nearly absent.

A more uniform distribution of rainfall occurs throughout the day in December through March, especially in the panhandle, where only a very slight tendency exists for more morning than afternoon or evening rainfall. A small late afternoon/early evening maximum occurs for cities located on the peninsula, particularly in the southern section, indicating that convective activity is still evident at this time of year. However, most of the cold season rainfall in all sections is produced by mid-latitude cyclones and fronts, which move across the state at all hours of the day with no apparent hourly maximum.

The hourly distribution of rainfall in the spring and fall varies considerably from month to month as well as from year to year. At these times convection and traveling frontal storms may be individually or simultaneously producing rainfall. An hourly maximum may be evident when convection is the dominant control, but no such peak in rainfall generally occurs when frontal or both types of rainfall occur. Hourly patterns are especially complex at coastal locations, where the sea breeze as well as an occasional land breeze may interact.

Hourly rainfall data also reveal that intense rainfall is common in the state. Miami experiences 68 hours per year with a rainfall rate of at least 0.25 inch per hour—this places the city first in this category of 100 major cities in the country. Miami also ranks first with 27 hours per year with at least 0.50 inch of rain. Also indicative of the rainfall intensity in the southern portion of the peninsula is the fact that although it rains an average of 122 days per year in Miami, the rain falls during only five percent (434) of the possible hours in a year.

Several Florida cities have experienced extreme hourly rainfall. The previously mentioned Yankeetown 24-hour rainfall record in the state yields an average rate of more than an inch and a half per hour. Detailed records of the Trenton extreme rainfall in October 1941 indicate a rate of 13 inches in six hours, 28 inches in 15 hours, and 31 inches in 24 hours. In Key West the following values were recorded during a nontropical storm that occurred in November 1980: 4.5 inches in one hour, 8.3 inches in two hours, nearly 15 inches in six hours, and 23.3 inches in 24 hours.

Other extreme short-term rainfall values have been recorded. In five hours 16 inches of rainfall fell at West Palm Beach in January 1957, and just over 8 inches fell in a two-

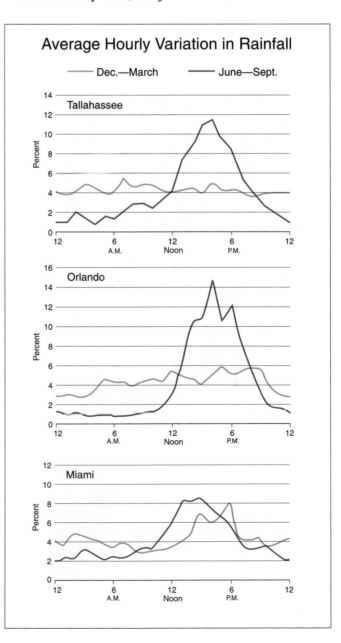

25

hour period in April 1942. Approximately 6 inches fell in about one hour from a 1947 hurricane over Ft. Lauderdale. Boca Raton experienced 5.9 inches in one hour during January 1942. More than 5.5 inches of rain fell in an hour from an October hurricane in 1947 at Hialeah, with another 1.3 inches at Miami, during the same storm.

Thunderstorms

Florida experiences more thunderstorms than any other state or region in North America, and the rainfall from these storms is a major portion of the total precipitation in the state. Florida is perfectly designed as a thunderstorm spawning ground, primarily because of its peninsular shape, converging sea breezes, position relative to the Atlantic high pressure system, and tropical/subtropical location.

The pattern of the average annual number of days with thunderstorms shows a distinct maximum in the south central and southwestern portions of the peninsula, where more than 90 days per year in some cities experience thunder. Minimum values of fewer than 70 days occur primarily in the panhandle, in the northern section of the peninsula, and in the Keys. Coastal regions have fewer days with thunderstorms than locations slightly inland, although the central portion of the peninsula does not experience maximum values. Most days with thunderstorms occur in the warm season, especially in July and August. Some southwestern cities experience up to 80 percent of the annual total in June through September, and in Ft. Myers thunder occurs on two out of three days throughout this four-month period; this city also experiences more days with thunderstorms in a month than any other, averaging 23 days in July. Minimum state values during July and August are reported at Key West, Jacksonville, and Apalachicola, each averaging 13 to 15 days per month with thunderstorms.

The number of days with thunderstorms declines noticeably after August and drops off even more in October. For the entire cold season the percentage of thunderstorm days varies from about 5 percent in south Florida to about 15 percent in the western section. Thunderstorm activity again begins to be significant in May, and that month's number of days with thunderstorms doubles in June.

The pattern of average annual hours of thunderstorms is somewhat similar to that of the annual number of days with thunderstorms. Much of the southwestern section experiences over 200 hours annually, with some cities enduring more than 230 hours. However, there is a great deal of year-to-year variability. In Miami thunderstorm hours per year have ranged between 47 and 229, and Melbourne has recorded as few as 27 and as many as 209 in a year. Tallahassee has one of the smallest ranges in thunderstorm hours in a year, varying from 119 to approximately 230 hours. The duration of individual thunderstorms is typically greatest in the northern one-third of the state, averaging about one and three-quarters hours. The central portion of the state has thunderstorms usually lasting about one and one-half hours, with the shortest times of less than

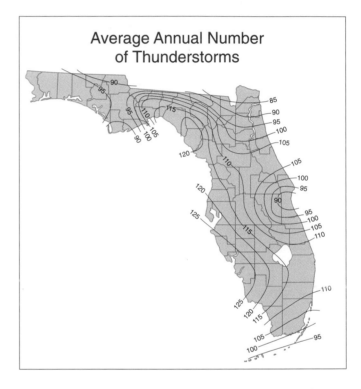

Average Annual Number of Thunderstorms

26

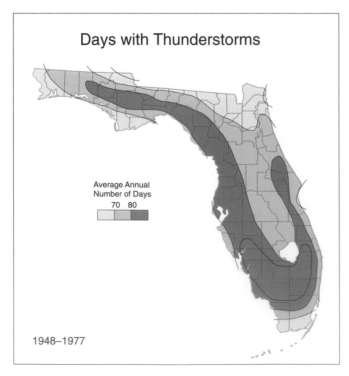

Days with Thunderstorms

Average Annual
Number of Days
70 80

1948–1977

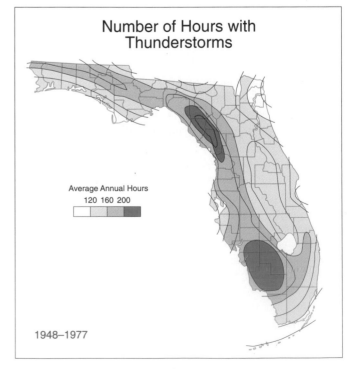

Number of Hours with Thunderstorms

Average Annual Hours
120 160 200

1948–1977

one and one-third hours occurring in the Keys. However, several cities have experienced single storms lasting well in excess of two hours.

The determination of the actual number of thunderstorms is more complex than the determination of days and hours with thunderstorms. A thunderstorm is determined to begin when thunder is first heard, but does not officially terminate until 15 minutes have elapsed after the last thunder is heard. The map of average annual number of thunderstorms for the state shows, in like fashion as the other thunderstorm maps, highest values in the southwestern part of the state. July has more than other months, averaging about 20 thunderstorms over most of the state; August is the main month in the southernmost section. Often two or more thunderstorms occur per day at many locations, with some cities citing six in a day in the summer. Most thunderstorms occur during the daylight, but actual time of the maximum varies. In the southwestern section, where thunderstorms are most prevalent, activity typically peaks in the late afternoon.

Hurricanes

Hurricanes often yield 5 to 12 inches of rain over much of the affected area. This prodigious amount of rain, coupled with the fact that nearly 40 percent of all hurricanes that have impacted the country have struck Florida, indicates that hurricanes often contribute significant rainfall in the state during the six-month hurricane season of June through November. Although the number of hurricanes (and tropical storms, which have wind speeds of 39 to 73 miles per hour) and associated rainfall amounts vary widely, the long-term average contribution of these tropical systems to statewide summer/fall rainfall is 10 to 15 percent. The percentage is about 30 percent for central Florida during October, and nearly one-third of the rainfall for much of the northern part of the state in September. As previously mentioned, several of the greatest one-day and one-hour rainfall rates in the state have been produced by hurricanes or other forms of tropical systems. Ironically, rainfall amounts are not closely related to strength of the storm; prodi-

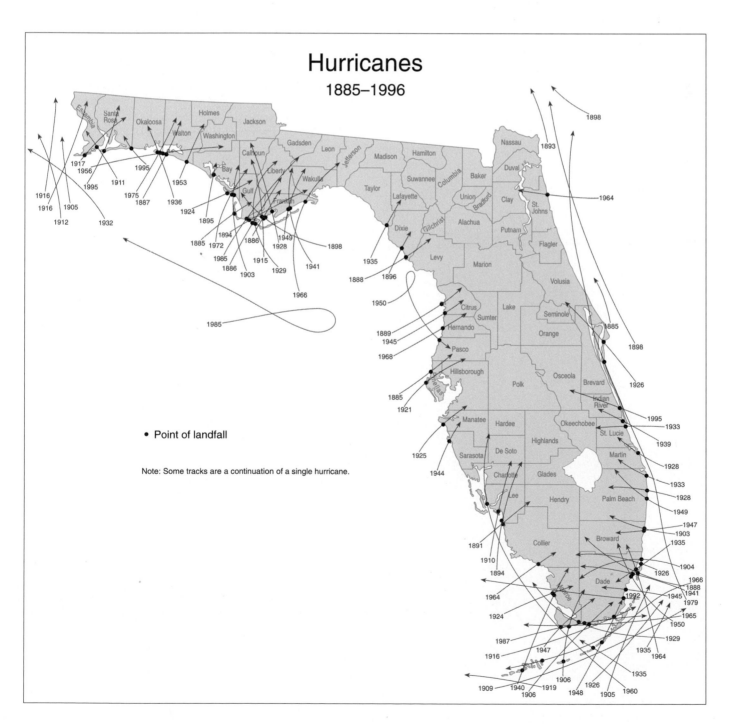

Hurricanes
1885–1996

• Point of landfall

Note: Some tracks are a continuation of a single hurricane.

27

Florida Hurricanes

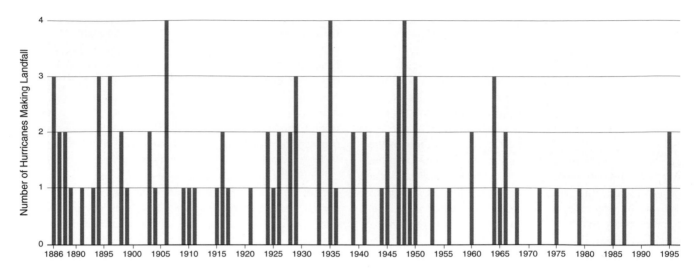

gious amounts have been produced by very weak hurricanes and storms that never reached hurricane strength, as noted in the sections on daily and hourly rainfall.

The map of hurricanes (tropical storms are not included) that struck or approached very near the state between 1885 and 1996 indicates that the panhandle and the southern portion of the peninsula have been most affected. Eighty-eight hurricanes impacted Florida in this period. Twenty-three struck the panhandle between Apalachicola and Alabama; the second most frequently hit sector of the state is the Key Largo to Jupiter area, followed closely by the Ft. Myers to Key Largo region and the Keys south of Key Largo. The graph of the years in which Florida was hit reveals that in three different years, four hurricanes struck the state. More than 30 of the 88 strikes occurred during September, with slightly more than 20 during October.

Rainfall amounts vary significantly among hurricanes. Although amounts are typically 5 to 12 inches, extremes range from the 38.7 inches in 24 hours at Yankeetown to less than 0.5 inch by a 1941 hurricane that had winds of 123 miles per hour. Rainfall is normally greatest in the right front quadrant, and rates of rainfall are greatest ahead of the center of the storm, compared with the rear half. Coastal areas usually receive more hurricane rainfall than inland areas, because the storms almost

28

South Florida Water Management District

Hurricane Andrew aftermath, 1992

always start to decay rapidly after landfall. However, there have been notable exceptions, including Hurricane Agnes in 1972, which was only minimal strength when it went ashore near Apalachicola and caused only limited damage in Florida, but created massive flooding from very heavy rainfall far inland, long after it had been downgraded from a hurricane.

Drought

Florida is occasionally afflicted with droughts, despite being one of the wettest states. A concise, simple definition and determination of what constitutes a drought have been very problematic for atmospheric scientists. A mere lack of rainfall over a specified period is not an ideal way of specifying a drought, because this technique does not address moisture supply versus demand. When this technique is applied to Florida, for example, the southern portion of the state would essentially experience a drought nearly every winter; all major cities in every section of the state have experienced at least 49 consecutive dry days (0.1 inch or less), and runs exceeding 15 dry days have occurred very frequently. Not all of these situa-

tions, however, involved a water deficiency in terms of water supply and demand, and thus could not be specified as actual droughts.

Two drought indices have been widely adopted: the Palmer Drought Severity Index (PDSI) and Palmer Hydrological Drought Index (PHDI). The former is a meteorological drought index that classifies spells of weather and responds relatively quickly to changes in atmospheric conditions. The PHDI is a hydrological drought index which more closely reflects soil moisture, streamflow, and lake levels, and measures long-term moisture supply and abnormalities. This index was designed to be insensitive to so-called man-made droughts created by large-scale changes in local water usage, such as new reservoirs and increased demand for irrigation or industrial water. The PHDI is often the more useful of the two indices to water managers and is used in the graphs presented here. Moisture abnormality is designated by the PHDI with the use of a numerical scale, negative values denoting dry conditions and positive values indicating wet conditions. Nearly all values are between +6 and -6; values of 0 to -0.49 represent near-normal conditions, -0.5 to -0.99 incipient drought, -1 to -1.99 mild drought, -2 to -2.99 moderate drought, -3 to -3.99 severe drought, and values of -4 and below indicate extreme drought. Similar adjectives are used for corresponding categories of excess moisture (positive values).

Statewide PHDI values (not graphed) indicate that Florida has experienced many moderate droughts since 1891; severe droughts have not been rare, but only a very few extreme droughts have occurred. Because droughts rarely occur in all parts of the state simultaneously, graphs of PHDI data are shown for three climatological divisions (see map of the seven state divisions in the introduction). The Northwest division covers the panhandle, the North Central division is representative of the central portion of the peninsula, and the Lower East Coast division includes the southeastern coastal section. The midsection of the state has experienced more severe droughts (-3 to -3.99) than the panhandle or the southeastern section, al-

Palmer Hydrological Drought Index
Northwest Division

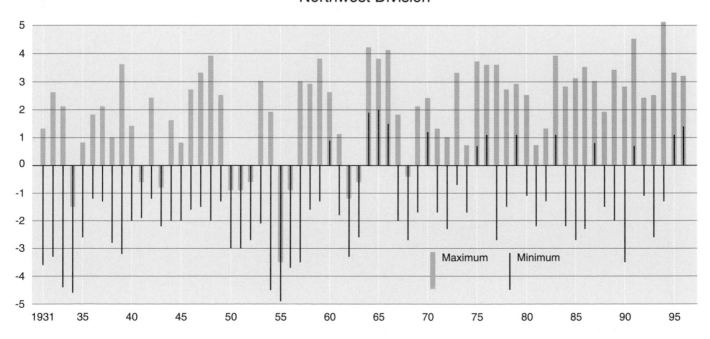

though the latter section of the state has endured more extreme droughts, and experienced the state-record minimum of -6.0 in 1990. February 23 of that year was designated "Drought Awareness Day" in Florida by the National Weather Service.

The time series of PHDI values shows that droughts seldom occur throughout the entire state at the same time. One section may experience drought conditions while others are receiving above-normal rainfall. This is also true of the state in general, relative to the rest of the southeastern United States. Florida was out of phase in moisture conditions relative to nearby states for approximately one-third of all months from 1931 to 1984. One example includes most of the 1930s, when much of the southeastern section of the country was experiencing significantly dry conditions, but south Florida was not; it was occasionally having only moderately dry conditions and was receiving sufficient rainfall in many months. Also, in 1986 most sections of the state did not experience the often devastating drought conditions that occurred throughout much of the rest of the Southeast.

The complex behavior of drought within Florida and the southeastern portion of the country can be explained by the several causes of drought. A change in the tracks of mid-latitude cyclonic storms is caused by movement of upper-level winds, particularly the jet streams. A northward displacement of these systems brings fewer rain-bearing storms to Florida. There are also fewer low-pressure systems when a well-defined subtropical jet stream fails to form; this upper-level wind is a main triggering mechanism for storm development in Florida.

Another main cause of drought is air subsiding from high to lower levels in the atmosphere. This happens over Florida when the Azores-Bermuda high pressure cell in the Atlantic has an extension that reaches westward to the state. Subsidence is also induced from migrating high-pressure systems advancing from the west and stagnating over the Southeast, often for many weeks. A third cause of subsidence is the formation of a ridge in upper-atmospheric pressure and wind systems over the central portion of the country, resulting in winds at about three miles in altitude flowing southward over Florida, inducing subsidence and dry conditions.

One suggested cause of drought in the southern portion of the state relates to the large-scale drainage of wetlands. Sixty percent of the wetlands in the southern part of the peninsula have been drained, according to one estimate. This reduces the moisture evaporated into the atmosphere, which may in turn reduce the amount of rainfall. One computer simulation showed that rainstorms form more slowly over non-water areas of south Florida compared with wetland regions. However, studies reveal that the majority of the moisture in the atmosphere over this part of the state comes from the Gulf of Mexico and Atlantic Ocean, and that any droughts in the southern peninsula more than likely are the result of much larger-scale processes affecting these much greater water sources.

Rainfall in the state is also strongly influenced by the temperature of ocean surface waters, in the Pacific as well as the Atlantic. When the temperature of the Atlantic water near the equator is higher than normal, wind patterns cause a reduction in the amount of moisture that is brought from the Gulf of Mexico over Florida. Even more influential is a phenomenon that occurs in the Pacific Ocean—El Niño. This term originally was applied only to the extreme southward displacement of the warm ocean current along the coast of Peru, Ecuador, and northern Chile. In the late 1960s it became recognized that El Niño events are closely linked to the Southern Oscillation (SO), a climatic fluctuation primarily apparent in atmospheric pressures over the southeastern Pacific. Later studies revealed that El Niño and the SO are essentially part of a single phenomenon, referred to as ENSO.

ENSO involves the entire ocean-atmosphere system in the tropical Pacific, including ocean currents, sea surface temperatures, wind patterns, and atmospheric pressure oscillations. ENSO has two main phases: El Niño, also referred to as a warm episode or phase, and La Niña (also El Viejo and formerly anti-El Niño), which is the cold episode or phase of ENSO. An

Palmer Hydrological Drought Index
North Central Division

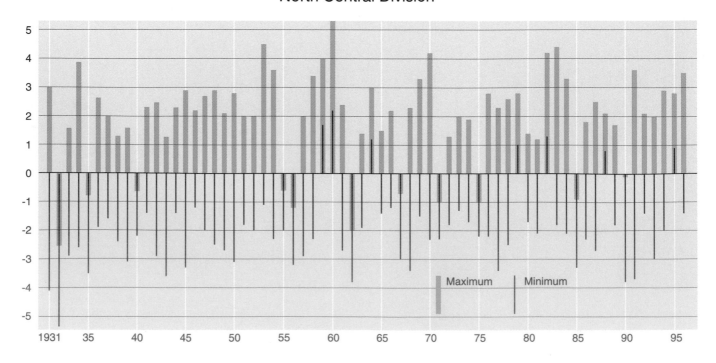

El Niño generally occurs about every three to seven years, beginning around Christmas, and lasts an average of about a year to 15 months, although the time between recurrence has exceeded 10 years, and many have persisted for several years, including one that began in the early 1990s. La Niñas form between occurrences of El Niño.

The El Niño or warm phase has especially noticeable effects and has been stated to be second only to the march of the seasons in its impact on world climate. During this phase of ENSO a massive area of warm surface water exists in the eastern equatorial Pacific, which shifts the jet streams into patterns that generally bring more rainfall to Florida. October through March rainfall was above normal in Florida during more than 80 percent of the El Niño events since 1875. The El Niño of 1982–1983 was one of the strongest ever recorded, and rainfall in that winter-spring in south Florida was three times the normal amount, and the storms that moved into the state from the Gulf of Mexico at that time were more frequent and more intense than usual. Especially noticeable effects on Florida rainfall occur when an El Niño is moderate or strong and lasts at least two years. In the first year rainfall exceeds normal amounts during summer in the central part of the state, and above normal in the south during spring. An even stronger effect occurs in the second year, when throughout the state spring and winter rainfall are often well above normal, and south Florida has experienced increases of 66 percent above normal amounts in winter.

ENSO events can also contribute to below-normal rainfall and droughts in diverse regions of the world, including Florida. Although the El Niño phase of ENSO produces conditions conducive to rainfall in some seasons and some sections of Florida, often in the first year of a two-year event the rainfall for September through November may be less than normal, except in the northernmost part of the state. Also, El Niños are inimical to hurricane formation. Since 1900 none of the 22

South Florida Water Management District

Drought, Everglades National Park

Palmer Hydrological Drought Index
Lower East Coast Division

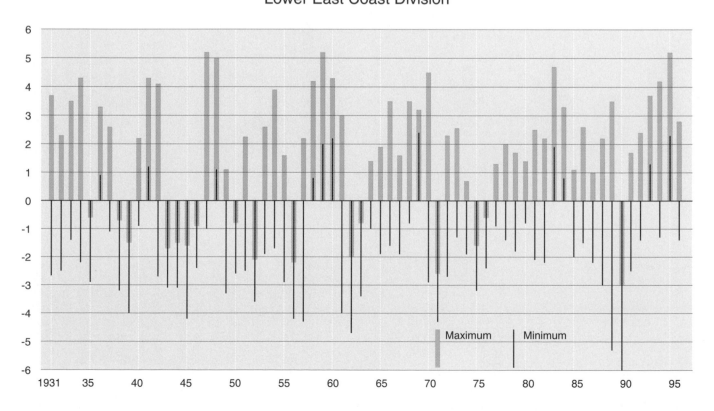

years with the greatest number of days on which hurricanes occurred were years in which an El Niño formed, and 1983, the second year of the particularly strong El Niño, experienced only extremely light tropical activity. However, the primary way that ENSO contributes to drought conditions in the state is through a reversal of the conditions that produce an El Niño. Winds in the tropical Pacific move warm water westward, eventually leading to opposite conditions of an El Niño. These occurrences, La Niñas, are often related to droughts in all parts of the state, because they shift jet streams and the related storm tracks in a manner that steers them away from Florida, aiding drought conditions.

Atmospheric Moisture

Relative Humidity

The most common way of expressing atmospheric moisture is relative humidity, which is the amount of moisture in the air compared to the amount that would exist in the air at its saturation point. Because relative humidity varies with temperature as well as with actual changes in the amount of moisture in the air, there is a definite hourly as well as seasonal pattern of relative humidities. Measurements are made four times daily: every six hours beginning at 1:00 A.M. The maps of cool and warm season average maximum and average minimum values are from data acquired at 7:00 A.M., nearly always the time of the maximum recorded value, and 1:00 P.M., usually the hour of the lowest recorded value. Relative humidities vary little from city to city throughout the northern three-quar-

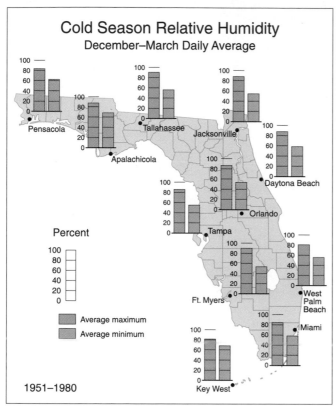

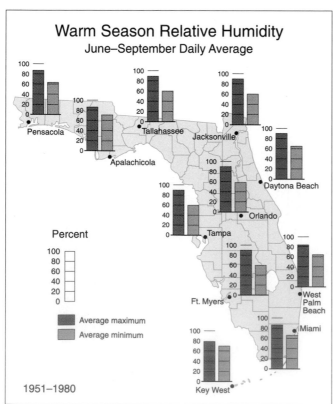

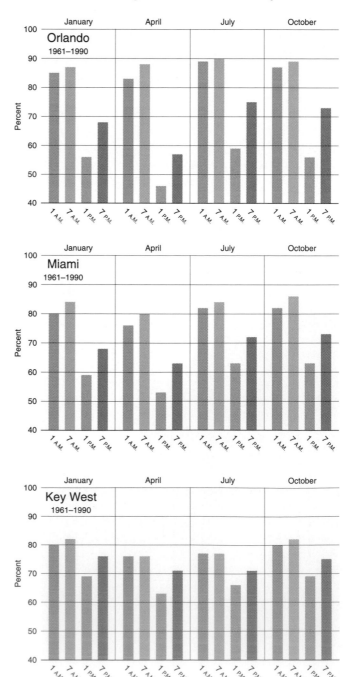

32

ters of the state. In the graph of average relative humidity percentages, Orlando values are very representative of nearly the entire state north of Miami. In the morning Key West has consistently lower readings compared with Orlando, but almost always has comparatively higher values in afternoons and evenings. This pattern is due primarily to Key West's very different temperatures compared with most of the rest of the state, rather than to significant differences in actual amount of atmospheric moisture.

Precipitable Water

Another measure of moisture in the air is precipitable water, which is the amount of water vapor in a vertical column of air expressed in terms of the depth in inches that would result if all that vapor were condensed into liquid water (i.e., the liquid water equivalent of the water vapor in the column of air). If the column of air used in the determination extends from the earth's surface to the upper limit of the atmosphere, then a

value termed total precipitable water is given. Such data are available for relatively few stations. Although the values in the graph may seem rather small, with a maximum of 1.7 inches, this is a great deal of total moisture, and there is a definite correlation between rainfall amounts in individual storms and the total precipitable water. This vapor is converted to rainfall by several rain-forming processes, the predominant one in Florida being convection.

Evaporation and Water Budgets

The map of evaporation was determined from pan evaporation data, the values determined by water evaporating from a metal pan 10 inches deep and about 4 feet in diameter. Only very general maps for the state are possible, as few stations have long-term evaporation measurements. Most all station values are in the range of 60 to 70 inches annually. May is generally the month with the most maximums, and December has the lowest evaporation. Evaporation from lakes is usually less than pan evaporation. Lake evaporation values are generally about 50 to 54 inches per year in the southern peninsula, 46 to 50 inches in the central part of the state and much of the panhandle, and approximately 45 to 46 inches in the northern portion of the peninsula.

Another way that water is transferred to the atmosphere is through evapotranspiration, the combined processes of evaporation from water surfaces and the land and transpiration by plants. The term potential evapotranspiration refers to the amount of water that would be evapotranspired if there was always enough water available for plants to transpire at the maximum rate possible (i.e., no soil water deficiency). This map reveals annual values of 39 inches in the northern panhandle up to 53 inches at Key West.

Actual and potential evapotranspiration data, when coupled with rainfall, allow the determination of a climatic water budget, also called climatic water balance, which is an accounting of the precipitation input and the total water outflow and soil

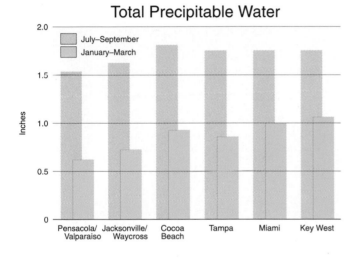

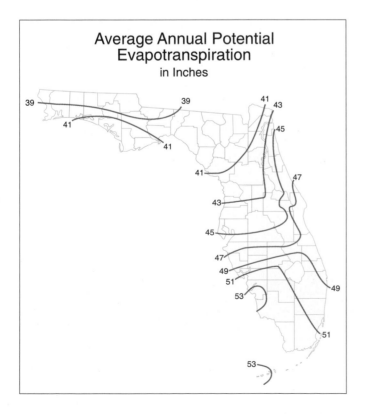

33

moisture storage at a location. The climatic water budget can be represented by the equation:

$$PRECIP = (POTET - DEFICIT) + SURPLUS \pm \Delta STORAGE$$

where:

  PRECIP is precipitation, indicating the atmospheric moisture supply

  POTET is potential evapotranspiration, representing moisture demand

  DEFICIT is the moisture shortage; (POTET - DEFICIT) indicates the actual evapotranspiration

  SURPLUS is the moisture surplus

  ΔSTORAGE is soil moisture storage change.

Soil moisture is recharged when rainfall is greater than actual evapotranspiration, but soil moisture is utilized when rainfall is less than evapotranspiration. A water deficiency is said to exist when potential evapotranspiration exceeds actual evapotranspiration.

This form of the water budget, which can also be determined on a weekly and even daily basis, has a wide range of applications. A deficit (moisture shortage), which indicates there is not sufficient water for naturally replenishing soil moisture or for providing runoff, can be used as an index of irrigation requirements for an area. A surplus of moisture indicates the availability of the amount of water for recharging groundwater supplies, and if any runoff is sufficient to be potentially useful for water-resource projects, sewage disposal, or industrial uses. The water budget concept is also used in the calculation of the Palmer Drought Severity Index, previously discussed in the drought section of this chapter.

Climatic water budget graphs for 11 Florida cities show that a water deficiency exists throughout the year in Key West.

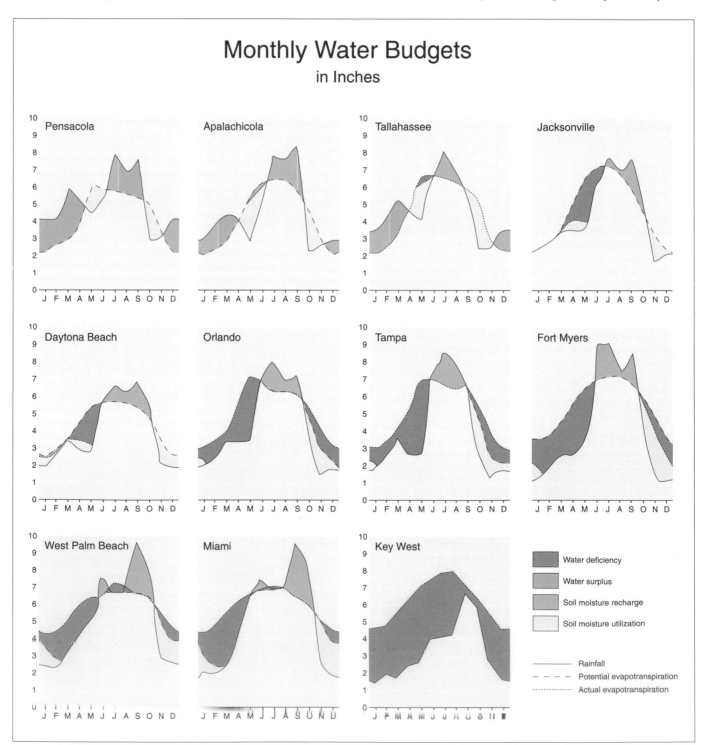

Monthly Water Budgets
in Inches

In the peninsula, deficiencies are common in winter and spring. Moisture shortages are relatively rare in the panhandle.

Rainfall Trends and Cycles

The graph of annual rainfall for 1895 through 1991 averaged over the entire state, which has been mathematically smoothed to emphasize any long-term trend, reveals no generally increasing or decreasing trend, although the 96-year period was punctuated with several significant wet and dry years, and yearly variation of rainfall above the average has been much greater since the late 1940s. This is also true when the data are analyzed on a seasonal basis. A noticeable change, however, has occurred in September rainfall, which has decreased significantly, and is especially apparent when the average rainfall of this month from 1961 to 1990 is compared with 1941 to 1970, throughout the entire state. The lack of an overall statewide significant change in rainfall contrasts with the trend for the southeastern section of the country, which showed an increase during 1895 to 1990 of more than two inches in the annual average.

Although the state as a whole shows no rainfall trend, and the general spatial pattern of rainfall throughout the state has remained the same for the past several decades, some regional changes in the amount of rain have occurred in certain sections of the state. Many stations in the panhandle have displayed an increase of several inches when the 1931 to 1960 averages are compared with those of the 1961 to 1990 values. Tallahassee has witnessed an increase of approximately 10 inches in its annual average rainfall, although much of this increase has been attributed to two station location changes, resulting in a position closer to the coast, where rainfall is greater than farther inland. Increases have also occurred on the peninsula, most notably in the northwestern portion, including Perry, Steinhatchee, Cross City, and Usher Tower, and in the southeastern section near the coast. The most significant decrease between 1931 to 1960 and 1961 to 1990 occurred just inland from the southeastern coastal area, where differences of more than five inches in average annual amounts occurred.

Localized summer storm   Suwannee River Water Management District

The search for cycles in rainfall has revealed the existence of a somewhat regular, albeit weak, 5- to 6-year cycle in some sections of the state. This cycle is most common in the southern portion, but even there only approximately two-thirds of the stations exhibit such a tendency. The Keys display a slight tendency toward a repeating pattern of rainfall approximately every five years. The data from six of eight stations distributed throughout the state have cycles of 5.5 to 7.5 years, but the consistency is not strong, although the length of the cycles closely coincides with the return period of El Niño. Also, as previously noted, winter-spring rainfall in Florida is most strongly related with occurrences of El Niños, and it is these same two seasons that exhibit the strongest tendencies toward cyclical patterns in rainfall.

Global Warming and Potential Effects

A general increase in average global temperature is often cited as the one aspect of climate change with the greatest potential for affecting Florida's future water supply. Several hydrological studies suggest that one of the most significant consequences of any future global warming would be an alter-

35

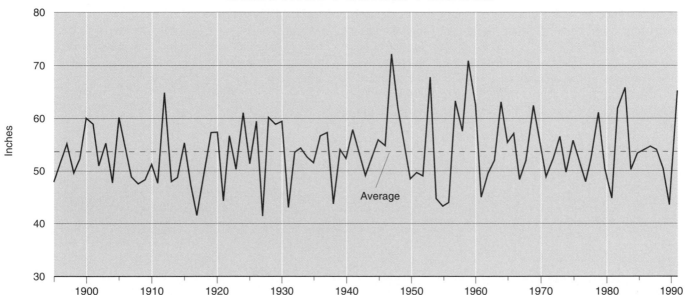

Statewide Annual Rainfall

ation of the global and regional hydrologic cycles, which would have a major impact on the availability of water. Intensive study has been applied to potential changes in rainfall intensity, frequency, regional distribution and trends, and changes in hurricane frequency and intensity that might accompany rising global temperatures.

Global warming, which has been predicted by many to continue, has most often been attributed to the human addition of various gases to the atmosphere. These include primarily carbon dioxide, water vapor, methane, nitrous oxide, and several types of chlorofluorocarbons. Collectively these gases are referred to as greenhouse gases, and they allow some of the solar radiation in but trap nearly all of the energy reradiated by the surface and atmosphere. Carbon dioxide has produced the most change—an estimated 60 percent of observed warming. More than 5 billion tons of this gas were produced worldwide in 1990, primarily by power plants and automobiles. Florida added about 186 million tons in that year, an amount exceeded by only nine other states.

Global temperature increased about 1°F between 1860 and 1996, although this is reduced to a 0.5 to 0.7°F rise when warming attributed to expansion of cities is subtracted from the measured increase. (Several Florida cities, including Jacksonville, Lake City, Gainesville, Tampa, and West Palm Beach have been shown to be warmer than surrounding rural areas, and cities exceeding 200,000 in population are predicted to warm at rates of up to 0.3°F per decade.) The four warmest years from 1860 to 1996, were, in descending order, 1995, 1990, 1991, and 1994. The year 1996 was the eighth warmest in that period, and was the eighteenth consecutive year with a positive global temperature anomaly. However, this warming has not been consistent throughout the period, but can best be characterized as an average of regional above-and-below-normal temperatures, with the warm anomalies predominating, especially from about 1920 to 1940 and 1976 through 1996, the last year of this measurement period.

In contrast to global temperatures, the southeastern section of the United States did not experience an overall warming trend, and indeed the result of various cooling and warming periods was a decrease in this area of about 0.5°F, while the average global temperature was increasing by approximately this amount in the same time period. Florida temperatures have closely followed those of the southeastern United States: a warming trend until 1950 was followed by more than 30 years of general cooling of almost 3°F throughout the state, except Key West, where a further warming of about one-half degree occurred after 1950. Winter temperatures in the state followed a different pattern than that observed for annual average temperatures: a decrease of about 3°F in the southern and central peninsula occurred from 1920 into the 1990s, with a decrease of approximately 4°F in the northern portion of the state.

Despite the lack of any consistent long-term warming in Florida, several aspects of the state's climate are predicted to be impacted by any future global warming that may occur, although the changes will likely be less here than for many other regions of the country because of Florida's relatively low latitude and peninsular configuration. The most probable change in predicted rainfall for the state is a slight decrease as temperatures rise, in contrast to an increase predicted for the globe. Reduced rainfall would be a consequence of a probable northward shift of jet stream and storm tracks, resulting in fewer mid-latitude storms penetrating far enough south to impact Florida; this would especially yield less winter rainfall. Summer thunderstorms and attendant rainfall may be reduced due to a westward shift, coupled with an intensification and expansion of the Azores-Bermuda high pressure cell in the Atlantic. However, one study indicated a positive correlation between annual frequency of heavy-rainfall storms and temperature in the panhandle, suggesting that rising temperatures may produce conditions conducive to greater summer rainfall. This finding has been corroborated by other studies indicating that heavy-rainfall events are likely to increase in a warmer world. Paradoxically, droughts may also be more severe if temperatures rise, because rainfall would likely be more variable.

Research suggests that the distribution of relative humidity will remain mostly unchanged in warmer conditions. However, evaporation and transpiration will likely increase. More evaporation from reservoirs would not only reduce water supplies, but could lead to increased nutrient loading and faster eutrophication in these water bodies.

Of particular significance to Florida is whether the frequency and characteristics of hurricanes will change during significant global warming. Most of the analysis in this field has been computer simulation of potential future climate change and possible related consequences. Many early simulations indicated more frequent and intense hurricanes in a warmer world. For example, one suggested that it would be reasonable to expect a 60 percent increase in the maximum destructive potential of the most powerful hurricanes if the atmospheric carbon dioxide level reached twice that of 1987. Another indicated that if the ocean surface increased by just over 2°F, the number of hurricanes could increase by 40 percent and the maximum wind speed could go up 8 percent; an ocean warming of just 1°F would likely lengthen the hurricane season by approximately 20 days. Later studies indicated the earlier ones were probably too simplistic. These later results, coupled with a lack of a consistent relationship between rising ocean warmth and hurricane frequency or intensity, indicate that the threat from hurricanes will not likely increase significantly in the near future.

REFERENCES

A source for a map or figure has a number in parentheses following the entry. This number refers to the page in the atlas for which the source was used. Unless otherwise indicated the source of data to construct the graphics was EarthInfo (1996).

Artusa, A.M. 1988. "Tropical Cyclone Statistics for the State of Florida, 1886–1986." Master's thesis, Department of Meteorology, Florida State University, Tallahassee.

Baldwin, J.L. 1974. *Climates of the United States.* Washington, D.C.: U.S. Department of Commerce, National Oceanic and Atmospheric Administration, Environmental Service. (average annual pan evaporation map, 33)

Barada, W.R. 1983. Human Impact on Florida's weather. *ENFO* 1–10.

Blanchard, D.O., and R.E. Lopez. 1985. "Spatial Patterns of Convection in South Florida." *Monthly Weather Review* 113:1282–1299.

Boyle, R.H., and R.M. Mechem. 1982. "Anatomy of a Man-Made Drought." *Sports Illustrated* 56:46–54.

Brandes, D. 1981. "The Significance of Tropical Cyclone Rainfall in the Water Supply of South Florida." Ph.D. dissertation, Department of Geography, University of Florida, Gainesville.

Brandes, D. 1982. "Hurricane Rainfall in South Florida." *Florida Geographer* 16:17–24.

Burpee, R.W., and L.N. Lahiff. 1984. "Area-Average Rainfall Variations on Sea Breeze Days in South Florida." *Monthly Weather Review* 112:520–534.

Carlson, T.N. 1967. "Isentropic Upslope Motion and an Instance of Heavy Rain over Southern Florida." *Monthly Weather Review* 95:213–220.

Chen, E. 1990. "Climate." In *Ecosystems of Florida*, R. L. Myers and J. J. Ewel, eds. Orlando: University of Central Florida Press.

Coleman, J.M. 1982. "Recent Seasonal Rainfall and Temperature Relationships in Peninsular Florida." *Quaternary Research* 18:144–151.

Coleman, J.M. 1988. "Climatic Warming and Increased Summer Aridity in Florida, U.S.A." *Climatic Change* 12:165–178.

Dohrenwend, R.E. 1976. The Climate of Florida. Unpublished paper, Department of Botany, School of Forest Resources and Conservation, University of Florida, Gainesville. (average annual potential evapotranspiration map, 33)

Dohrenwend, R.E. 1977. "Evapotranspiration Patterns in Florida." *Florida Scientist* 40:184–192.

Eagleman, J.R. 1973. *Visualization of Climate.* Lawrence, Kansas: Environmental Publications. (graphs, 34)

EarthInfo. 1996. NCDC. Summary of the Day. Boulder, Colorado.

Emanuel, K.A. 1987. "The Dependence of Hurricane Intensity on Climate." *Nature* 326:483–485.

Fernald, E.A., and E.D. Purdum, eds. 1996. *Atlas of Florida.* Gainesville: University Press of Florida.

Gerber, J. 1985. "Is the Climate Changing in Florida?" *The Citrus Industry* 66:42–49, 70.

Gray, W.M. 1984. "Atlantic Seasonal Hurricane Frequency. Part I: El Niño and 30 mb Quasi-Biennial Oscillation Influences." *Monthly Weather Review* 112:1649–1668.

Hanson, K., and G.A. Maul. 1991. "Florida Precipitation and Pacific El Niño." *Florida Scientist* 54:160–168. (seasonal proportions of average annual rainfall map, 21).

Head, C.M, and R.B. Marcus. 1987. *The Face of Florida.* Dubuque, Iowa: Kendal/Hunt.

Henry, J.A., and S.E. Dicks. 1984. "Drought in Southeastern United States." *Florida Scientist* 47:114–129.

Henry, J.A., and D.W. LeBoutillier. 1990. "Comparison of Moisture Conditions in Peninsular Florida with Other Sections of the Southeastern United States." *Southeastern Geographer* 30:94–106.

Henry, J.A., K.M. Portier, and J. Coyne. 1994. *The Climate and Weather of Florida.* Sarasota, Florida: Pineapple Press. (seasonal proportion of average annual rainfall map, 21; average number of fronts graph, 23; maps, 23; average annual number of thunderstorms, 26; average annual pan evaporation, 33; graphs, 34)

Isaacs, J.A. 1980. "Precipitation Regimes of Florida: Spatial Analysis and Time Series." Master's thesis, Department of Geography, University of Florida, Gainesville.

Jordan, C.A. 1984. "Florida's Weather and Climate: Implications for Water." In *Water Resources Atlas of Florida*, E.A. Fernald and D.J. Patton, eds. Tallahassee, Florida: Institute of Science and Public Affairs. (map, 27; days with thunderstorms and hours with thunderstorms maps, 26; total precipitable water graph, 33; average hourly rainfall, 25; warm and cold season relative humidity, 32)

Keim, B.D. 1997. "Preliminary Analysis of the Temporal Patterns of Heavy Rainfall Across the Southeastern United States." *Professional Geographer* 49:94–104.

Lin, S., and J. Lane. 1982. "Preliminary Report on the Rainstorm of March 28–29, 1982." West Palm Beach: South Florida Water Management District.

Maier, M.W. Lightning Location and Protections, Inc. of Tucson, Arizona. (hours and days with thunderstorms maps, 26)

National Oceanic and Atmospheric Administration. Asheville, North Carolina: U.S. Department of Commerce, National Climatic Data Center. (drought graphs, 29, 30, and 31; average relative humidity, 32; statewide annual rainfall, 35)

Owenby, J.R., and D.S. Ezell. 1992. *Monthly Station Normals of Temperature, Precipitation, and Heating and Cooling Degree Days, 1961-90: Florida.* Climatography of the U.S. No. 81. Asheville, North Carolina: U.S. Department of Commerce, National Climatic Data Center.

Palmer, C.E. 1986. *Long Term Rainfall Deficits in Central Florida: Implications for Water Management.* Bartow, Florida: Water Resources Department, Environmental Services Division.

Rhoads, P.B., C.C. Shih, and R.L. Hamrick. 1987. "Water Resources Planning Concerns and Changing Climate: A South Florida Perspective." In *Proceedings of the Symposium on Climate Change in the Southern United States: Future Impacts and Present Policy Issues.* Washington, D.C.: U.S. Environmental Protection Agency, Office of Policy, Planning and Evaluation.

Ropelewski, C.F., and M.S. Halpert. 1986. "North American Precipitation and Temperature Patterns Associated with the El Niño/Southern Oscillation (ENSO)." *Monthly Weather Review* 114:2352–2362.

Schwartz, B.E., and L.F. Bosart. 1979. "The Diurnal Variability of Florida Rainfall." *Monthly Weather Review* 107:1535–1545.

Simpson, J., W.L. Woodley, and R.M. White. 1972. "Joint Federal-State Cumulus Seeding Program for Mitigation of 1971 South Florida Drought." *Bulletin of the American Meteorological Society* 53:334–344.

Sourbeer, R.H., and R.C. Gentry. 1961. "Rainstorm in Southern Florida, January 21, 1957." *Monthly Weather Review* 89:9–16.

Winsberg, M.D. 1990. *Florida Weather.* Orlando: University of Central Florida Press.

3

GROUNDWATER

ter in Florida is more than a quadrillion gallons—about one-fifth as much as in all of the five Great Lakes, 100 times that in Lake Mead on the Colorado River, and 30,000 times the daily flow to the sea of Florida's 13 major coastal rivers (Conover 1973).

Nearly all of Florida's groundwater originates from precipitation. Annual precipitation (1951–95) averages over 50 inches per year. Part of this precipitation percolates to the water table and recharges the groundwater reservoir. Annual recharge to groundwater ranges from near zero in some perennially wet, lowland areas to greater than 20 inches per year or more in well-drained upland areas. In much of the state, most of this recharge moves through the surficial sands and discharges downward to deeper aquifers (groundwater reservoirs) or laterally to nearby lakes and streams.

Florida is underlain virtually everywhere by aquifers capable of yielding at least small quantities of potable water to wells. Aquifers are defined on the basis of rock types, geologic confinement, and groundwater flow. An aquifer system consists of two or more hydraulically connected aquifers. A change in the condition of one aquifer affects the other aquifers in the system. In Florida three aquifer systems are used for water supply: the surficial aquifer system, the intermediate aquifer system, and the Floridan aquifer system. Two aquifers within the surficial aquifer system—the sand and gravel and the Biscayne aquifers—are important sources of supply where they occur.

Sequence of Aquifers

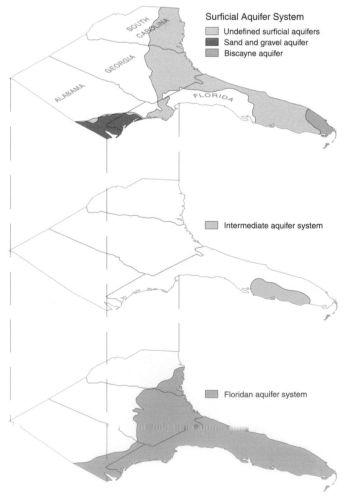

38 Groundwater is one of Florida's most valuable natural resources. Usable quantities of potable groundwater can be obtained throughout the state, with the exception of a few places, most of which are near the coasts. About 93 percent of Florida's population depends on groundwater for drinking water. Florida ranked fifth in the nation in the use of fresh groundwater in 1995. Because of its abundance and availability, groundwater is the principal source of freshwater for public supply and domestic (rural) and industrial uses. Of the total freshwater used in Florida in 1995, 60 percent was groundwater.

All of Florida is in the Coastal Plain physiographic province, a region of low relief underlain by unconsolidated to poorly consolidated sediments and hardened carbonate rocks. Florida is covered nearly everywhere by sands that overlie a thick sequence of limestone and dolomite. Together, the surficial sands and the limestone and dolomite form an enormous groundwater reservoir that provides more available groundwater than any other state (McGuinness 1963). Hydrologists have estimated that the total quantity of fresh groundwa-

Marian P. Berndt, Edward T. Oaksford, and Gary L. Mahon; Stratigraphy and hydrogeologic units, Walter Schmidt

Relationship of Regional Hydrogeologic Units to Major Stratigraphic Units

System	Series	Panhandle Florida		North Florida		South Florida	
		Stratigraphic Unit	Hydrogeologic Unit	Stratigraphic Unit	Hydrogeologic Unit	Stratigraphic Unit	Hydrogeologic Unit
Quaternary	Holocene	Undifferentiated terrace marine and fluvial deposits	Surficial aquifer system (Sand and Gravel aquifer)	Undifferentiated terrace marine and fluvial deposits	Surficial aquifer system	Terrace Deposits	Surficial aquifer system (Biscayne aquifer)
	Pleistocene					Miami Limestone Key Largo Limestone Anastasia Formation Fort Thompson Formation Caloosahatchee Marl	
Tertiary	Pliocene	Citronelle Formation		Miccosukee Formation Alachua Formation		Tamiami Formation	
		Undifferentiated coarse sand and gravel			Intermediate aquifer system or intermediate confining unit		Intermediate aquifer system or intermediate confining unit
	Miocene	Alum Bluff Group Pensacola Clay Intracoastal Formation Hawthorn Group Chipola Formation Bruce Creek Limestone St. Marks Formation Chattahoochee Formation	Intermediate confining unit	Hawthorn Group St. Marks Formation		Hawthorn Group	
			Floridan aquifer system				
	Oligocene	Chickasawhay Limestone Suwannee Limestone Marianna Limestone Bucatunna Clay		Suwannee Limestone	Floridan aquifer system	Suwannee Limestone	Floridan aquifer system
	Eocene	Ocala Limestone Lisbon Formation Tallahatta Formation Undifferentiated older Rocks	Sub-Floridan confining unit	Ocala Limestone Avon Park Formation Oldsmar Formation		Ocala Limestone Avon Park Formation Oldsmar Formation	
	Paleocene	Undifferentiated		Cedar Keys Formation	Sub-Floridan confining unit	Cedar Keys Formation	Sub-Floridan confining unit
Cretaceous and older		Undifferentiated		Undifferentiated			

39

Aquifers in Florida are composed of sedimentary rock units of varying composition and depositional history. These units are divided into geologic formations based on rock composition and physical characteristics. Many units are related by the similarities of the sediments while others may be defined on the sediment heterogeneity. An aquifer is defined as a body of rock that is sufficiently permeable to conduct groundwater and to yield economically significant quantities of water to wells and springs. They are identified independently from lithostratigraphic units and may include more than one formation or be limited to only a portion of a formation.

The stratigraphic and hydrogeologic framework of Florida has significant variability from north to south and west to east in the peninsula and the panhandle. The stratigraphic units that comprise the aquifer systems in Florida occur primarily as subsurface units with very limited surface exposures. As a result of the generally low relief of the state, most of the stratigraphic descriptions are from well cuttings and cores used to study the subsurface sediments and rocks.

The following description of the stratigraphy of the various units associated with the aquifer systems is brief and generalized. More complete information concerning these groups and formations can be obtained by referring to Florida Geological Survey and U. S. Geological Survey publications relating to specific areas and/or specific aquifers.

Paleocene Series

In general, most of the Paleocene sediments in the Florida peninsula form the sub-Floridan confining unit and only a limited portion of these rocks are part of the Floridan aquifer system.

Cedar Keys Formation

The Cedar Keys Formation consists primarily of dolostone and evaporites (gypsum and anhydrite) with a minor percentage of limestone (Chen 1965).

The Cedar Keys Formation forms the base of the Floridan aquifer system throughout the peninsula except in the northwestern-most peninsular area where the Oldsmar Formation forms the base (Miller 1986). The upper, porous dolostone comprises the lowest beds of the Floridan aquifer system. The lower Cedar Keys Formation is significantly less porous, contains evaporites, and forms the sub-Floridan confining unit.

W. Schmidt

Ocala Limestone, exposed at Haile Quarry, Alachua County

Eocene Series

The sediments of the Eocene Series that form portions of the Floridan aquifer system are carbonates. During the Early Eocene, deposition followed a distribution pattern similar to that of the Paleocene carbonate sediments. However, through the Eocene, carbonate-forming environments slowly encroached further north and west over what had been siliciclastic depositional environments during the Paleocene. The Eocene carbonate sediments comprise a large part of the Floridan aquifer system.

Claiborne Group

The Claiborne Group consists of the Tallahatta and Lisbon formations which are lithologically nearly identical and are not separated. The group is composed of glauconitic, often clayey sand grading into fine-grained limestone to the south (Allen 1987). The Claiborne Group ranges from 250 to 400 feet below NGVD and is up to 350 feet thick (Allen 1987).

Oldsmar Formation

The Oldsmar Formation is recognized throughout the Florida peninsula and consists predominantly of limestone interbedded with vuggy dolostone. Pore-filling gypsum and thin beds of anhydrite occur in some places, often forming the base of the Floridan aquifer system (Miller 1986; T. Scott, personal communication).

Avon Park Formation

The Avon Park Formation is primarily composed of fossiliferous limestone interbedded with vuggy dolostone. In a few, limited areas of west central Florida, evaporites are present as vug fillings in dolostone.

The Avon Park Formation occurs throughout the Florida peninsula and the eastern panhandle in a pattern very similar to the underlying Oldsmar Formation. The oldest rocks exposed on the surface in Florida are Avon Park Formation. These sediments are locally exposed on the crest of the Ocala Platform in west central peninsular Florida.

The carbonate sediments of the Avon Park Formation form part of the Floridan aquifer system and serve to subdivide it into an upper and lower Floridan in many areas. Miller (1986) recognized that portions of the Avon Park Formation are fine-grained and have low permeability, often acting as a confining bed in the middle of the Floridan aquifer system. In Brevard County, for example, these low permeability beds are relied upon to keep less desirable water injected into the lower Floridan from migrating into the potable water of the upper Floridan.

T. Scott

Avon Park Formation, Melbourne Area, Brevard County

Ocala Limestone

Dall and Harris (1892) referred to the limestones exposed in central peninsular Florida near the city of Ocala in Marion County as the Ocala Limestone. The sediments of the Ocala Limestone form one of the most permeable zones within the Floridan aquifer system. The Ocala Limestone comprises much of the Floridan aquifer system in the central and western panhandle. The extensive development of secondary porosity by dissolution has greatly enhanced the permeability, especially in those areas where the confining beds are breached or absent. The Ocala Limestone forms the lower portion of the Floridan in the western panhandle (Schmidt and Coe 1978, Wagner 1982). In much of the peninsular area, it comprises all or part of the upper Floridan. The surface and thickness of the Ocala Limestone are highly irregular due to dissolution of the limestone as karst topography developed.

W. Schmidt

Ocala Limestone, exposed near Steinhatchee

40

Oligocene Series

The carbonate sediments of the Oligocene Series form much of the upper portion of the Floridan aquifer system in Florida. The depositional pattern of the Oligocene sediments shows that carbonate sediments were deposited well updip to the north of the Florida Platform (Miller 1986). In the central panhandle and to the west, siliciclastic sediments began to be mixed with the carbonates.

F. Rupert

Suwannee Limestone, Wakulla County (note numerous fossil molds)

Suwannee Limestone

The Suwannee Limestone consists primarily of variably vuggy and muddy (carbonate) limestone (grainstone to packstone). It is absent throughout a large area of the northern and central peninsula probably due to erosion. Where Suwannee Limestone is present, it forms much of the upper portion of the Floridan aquifer system.

W. Schmidt

Sucrosic Suwannee Dolostone from Rocky Creek, Jackson County

Marianna Limestone

The Marianna Limestone is a fossiliferous, variably argillaceous limestone (packstone to wackestone) that occurs in the central panhandle (Schmidt and Coe 1978). The Marianna Limestone forms a portion of the uppermost Floridan aquifer system in the central panhandle region.

Bucatunna Clay Member of the Byram Formation

The Bucatunna Clay Member is silty to finely sandy clay. The sand content of the Bucatunna ranges from very minor percentages to as much as 40 percent (Marsh 1966). It occurs from the western end of the state eastward to approximately the Okaloosa-Walton County line where it pinches out (Marsh 1966, Clark and Schmidt 1982). The Bucatunna Clay Member provides an effective confining unit in the middle of the Floridan aquifer system in the western panhandle.

Chickasawhay Limestone

The Chickasawhay Limestone is composed of highly porous limestone and dolomitic limestone (Marsh 1966), often interbedded with porous to compact dolomitic limestone to dolostone. The Chickasawhay Limestone grades into the upper Suwannee Limestone eastward. The permeable sediments of the Chickasawhay Limestone form part of the upper Floridan in the western panhandle (Wagner 1982).

41

Miocene Series

The Miocene Epoch was a time of significant change in the depositional sequence on the Florida Platform and the adjacent Gulf and Atlantic Coastal Plains. During the early part of the Miocene, carbonate sediments continued to be deposited over most of the platform. Intermixed with the carbonates were increasing percentages of siliciclastic sediments. By the end of the Early Miocene, the deposition of carbonate sediments was occurring only in southern peninsular Florida. Siliciclastic deposition dominated the Middle Miocene statewide with this trend continuing into the Late Miocene.

The basal Miocene carbonate sediments often form the uppermost portion of the Floridan aquifer system. The remainder of the Miocene sediments form much of the intermediate aquifer system and intermediate confining system. In some instances, these sediments may also be included in the surficial aquifer system.

Unusual depositional conditions existed during the Miocene as is evident from the occurrence of abundant phosphate, palygorskite, opaline cherts and other uncommon minerals plus an abundance of dolomite within the Hawthorn Group (Scott 1988). The presence of these minerals may influence groundwater quality in areas where the Miocene sediments are being weathered. Groundwater quality may also be affected where these sediments form the upper portion of the Floridan aquifer system or portions of the intermediate aquifer system.

The Miocene sediments are absent from the Ocala Platform and the Sanford High. These sediments are as much as 800 feet thick in southwest Florida, 500 feet thick in the northeastern peninsula, and 900 to 1,000 feet thick in the westernmost panhandle (Miller 1986; Scott 1988).

Chattahoochee Formation

The Chattahoochee Formation is predominantly a fine-grained, often fossiliferous, silty to sandy dolostone which is variable to a limestone (Huddlestun 1988). Fine-grained sand and silt may also form beds with various admixtures of dolomite and clay minerals. Clay beds may also be common in some areas (Puri and Vernon 1964). The sediments of the Chattahoochee Formation comprise the upper zone of the Floridan aquifer system in the central panhandle.

St. Marks Formation

The St. Marks Formation is a fossiliferous limestone (packstone to wackestone). Sand grains occur scattered in an often very moldic limestone. This formation forms the upper part of the Floridan aquifer system in portions of the eastern and central panhandle.

Hawthorn Group

The Hawthorn Group is a complex series of the phosphate-bearing Miocene sediments in peninsular and eastern panhandle Florida. The carbonate sediments of the Hawthorn Group are primarily fine-grained and contain varying admixtures of clay, silt, sand, and phosphate. Dolostone is the dominant carbonate sediment type in the northern two-thirds of the peninsula while limestone predominates in the southern peninsula and in the eastern panhandle area.

The top of the Hawthorn Group is a highly irregular erosional and karstic surface. It can exhibit dramatic local relief especially in outcrop along the flanks of the Ocala Platform.

In the peninsula, the Hawthorn Group can be broken into a northern section and a southern section. In the northern section the sediments comprising the Hawthorn Group characteristically have low permeabilities and form an effective aquiclude, the intermediate confining unit. In a few areas, permeabilities within the Hawthorn sediments are locally high enough to allow the limited development of an intermediate aquifer system.

The southern section consists of a lower dominantly phosphatic carbonate section and an upper phosphatic siliciclastic section. Throughout much of south Florida, these sediments have limited or low permeabilities and form an effective intermediate confining unit. However, where the Tampa Member is present and permeable enough, it may form the upper portion of the Floridan aquifer system. In portions of southwestern Florida, the Hawthorn sediments are permeable enough to form several important producing zones in the intermediate aquifer system (Knapp et al. 1986, Smith and Adams 1988).

The Hawthorn Group, Torreya Formation sediments in the eastern panhandle are predominantly siliciclastics with limited amounts of carbonates (Scott 1988). The siliciclastic sediments are very clayey and form an effective intermediate confining unit. The carbonate sediments may locally be permeable enough to form the upper portion of the Floridan aquifer system.

T. Scott

Hawthorn Group sands and phosphatic clays, Devils Millhopper, Alachua County

Bruce Creek Limestone

Bruce Creek Limestone, a fossiliferous, variably sandy limestone (Schmidt 1984), occurs in the Apalachicola Embayment and coastal areas of the central and western panhandle. It forms part of the upper Floridan aquifer system in the central and western panhandle.

W. Schmidt

Intracoastal Formation and Bruce Creek Limestone Walton County

42

Alum Bluff Group

The Alum Bluff Group consists of clays, sands and shell beds which may vary from a fossiliferous, sandy clay to a pure sand or clay and occasional carbonate beds or lenses. Sediments comprising the Jackson Bluff Formation are very similar to those making up the Alum Bluff Group. The sediments comprising the Alum Bluff Group are generally impermeable due to the abundance of clay-sized particles. These sediments form an important part of the intermediate confining unit in the central panhandle.

Florida Geological Survey Archives
Outcrop showing gravels of Citronelle Formation overlying mottled sandy clays of Alum Bluff Group, Washington County

Pensacola Clay

The Pensacola Clay consists of three members: lower and upper clay members and a middle sand member. The Pensacola Clay forms the intermediate confining unit for the Floridan in the western panhandle.

Intracoastal Formation

The Intracoastal Formation is a "very sandy, highly microfossiliferous, poorly consolidated, argillaceous, calcarenitic limestone" (Schmidt 1984). Phosphate is generally present in amounts greater than one percent. The Intracoastal Formation forms part of the intermediate confining unit in the central to western panhandle (Wagner 1982).

Pliocene-Pleistocene Series

The sediments of the Pliocene-Pleistocene Series occur over most of the state. These sediments range from nonfossiliferous, clean sands to very fossiliferous, sandy clays and carbonates.

Coarse Clastics

The name *Coarse Clastics* has been applied to sequences of quartz sands and gravels in a number of areas around Florida. In the panhandle, the Coarse Clastics are variably clayey sands with gravel and some shell material (Clark and Schmidt 1982). These siliciclastics occur in Escambia, Santa Rosa, and western Okaloosa counties in the western panhandle. In southern peninsular Florida, the coarse siliciclastics are fine to very coarse quartz sands with quartz gravel and variable amounts of clay, carbonate, and phosphate.

These siliciclastic sediments form important aquifer systems in portions of southern and panhandle Florida. In the western panhandle, the Coarse Clastics form a portion of the sand and gravel aquifer, part of the surficial aquifer system. These sediments also comprise a portion of the surficial aquifer system in the peninsular area, especially in southern Florida.

Tamiami Formation

The various facies of the Tamiami occur over a wide area of southern Florida. The relationships of the facies are not well known due to: first, the complex set of depositional environments that were involved in the formation of the sediments and second, the Tamiami Formation most often occurs as a shallow subsurface unit. Many of the facies are important from a hydrogeologic perspective in an area of groundwater problems.

Sediments of the Tamiami Formation exhibit variable permeabilities and form the lower Tamiami aquifer and Tamiami confining beds of the surficial aquifer system (Knapp et al. 1986). Smith and Adams (1988) indicate that the upper Tamiami sediments form the basal portion of the "water table aquifer" overlying the Tamiami confining beds.

Citronelle Formation

The Citronelle Formation is composed of fine to very coarse siliciclastics. The unit is recognized from central Gadsden County on the east to the western boundary of the state. The Citronelle Formation is composed of very fine to very coarse, poorly sorted, angular to subangular quartz sand. The unit contains significant amounts of clay, silt, and gravel, which may occur as beds, lenses, or stringers and may vary rapidly over short distances. Limonite nodules and limonitic cemented zones are common.

The Citronelle Formation forms an important part of the sand and gravel aquifer in the western panhandle and locally produces up to 2,000 gallons of water per minute (Wagner 1982).

Miccosukee Formation

The Miccosukee Formation consists of interbedded and cross-bedded clay, silt, sand, and gravel of varying coarseness and admixtures (Hendry and Yon 1967). Limonite pebbles are common in the unit. The Miccosukee Formation occurs in the eastern panhandle from central Gadsden County on the west to eastern Madison County on the east. Due to its clayey nature, the Miccosukee Formation does not produce significant amounts of water. It is, however, generally considered to be part of the surficial aquifer system (Southeastern Geological Society 1986).

Cypresshead Formation

The Cypresshead Formation is composed entirely of siliciclastics; predominantly quartz and clay minerals. The unit is characteristically a mottled, fine- to coarse-grained, often gravelly, variably clayey quartz sand. As a result of weathering, the clay component of these sediments has characteristically been altered to kaolinite. Clay serves as a binding matrix for the sands and gravels. Clay content may vary from absent to more than 50 percent in sandy clay lithologies although the average clay content is 10 to 20 percent. The Cypresshead Formation appears to occur in the Central Highlands of the peninsula south to northern Highlands County, although the extent of the Cypresshead Formation has not been accurately mapped in this area. This unit may locally comprise the surficial aquifer system where clay content is low.

Nashua Formation

The Nashua is a fossiliferous, variably calcareous, sometimes clayey, quartz sand. The fossil content is variable from a shelly sand to a shell hash. The dominant fossils are mollusks. The extent of the Nashua in northern Florida is not currently known. It extends some distance into Georgia and appears to grade laterally into the Cypresshead Formation (Huddlestun 1988). The Nashua Formation may produce limited amounts of water in localized areas where it forms part of the surficial aquifer system.

Caloosahatchee Marl

The Caloosahatchee Marl consists of fossiliferous quartz sand with variable amounts of carbonate matrix interbedded with variably sandy, shelly limestones. Caloosahatchee Marl occurs from north of Tampa on the west coast south to Lee County, eastward to the east coast then northward into northern Florida (DuBar 1974).

In most hydrogeologic investigations of southern Florida, Caloosahatchee Marl is not differentiated from the Fort Thompson Formation due to the dominance of paleotological components. The undifferentiated sediments form much of the surficial aquifer system.

Fort Thompson Formation

The sandy limestones present in the Fort Thompson Formation were deposited under both freshwater and marine conditions. The sand present in these sediments is fine- to medium-grained. The sediments of Fort Thompson age in central Florida along the east coast, consist of fine to medium quartz sand with abundant mollusk shells and a minor but variable clay content.

The Fort Thompson Formation, as the Caloosahatchee Marl, is part of the undifferentiated sediments in southern Florida. It forms a portion of the surficial aquifer system.

Key Largo Limestone

The Key Largo Limestone is a coralline limestone composed of coral heads encased in a matrix of calcarenite (Stanley 1966). Key Largo Limestone occurs in the subsurface from as far north as Miami Beach to as far south as the Lower Keys (Hoffmeister and Multer 1968). The fossil reef tract represented by the Key Largo sediments may be as much as 8 miles wide (DuBar 1974). The Key Largo Limestone forms a part of the Biscayne aquifer of the surficial aquifer system. The Biscayne aquifer provides water for areas of Dade, Broward, and Monroe counties.

Miami Limestone

Miami Limestone is generally a variably sandy, recrystallized, fossiliferous limestone, including an oolitic and a bryozoan facies, covering Dade County, much of Monroe County and the southern part of Broward County (Hoffmeister et al. 1967). Miami Limestone forms a portion of the Biscayne aquifer of the surficial aquifer system. It is very porous and permeable due to the dissolution of carbonate by groundwater as it recharges the aquifer system.

Anastasia Formation

The Anastasia Formation consists of interbedded quartz sands and coquinoid limestones. The sand beds consist of fine to medium-grained, variably fossiliferous, calcareous, quartz sand. The contained fossils are primarily broken and abraded mollusk shells. The limestone beds, commonly called coquina, are composed of shell fragments, scattered whole shells and quartz sand enclosed in a calcareous matrix, usually sparry calcite cement.

The Anastasia Formation forms the core of the Atlantic Coastal Ridge through most of its length (White 1970). Natural exposures of this unit occur scattered along the east coast from St. Augustine south to southern Palm Beach County near Boca Raton. Cooke (1945) felt that the Anastasia Formation extended no more than three miles inland from the Intracoastal Waterway. Field work by the Florida Geological Survey suggests that the Anastasia may extend as much as 10 miles inland; although Schroeder (1954) suggested that this unit may occur more than 20 miles inland.

The Anastasia Formation forms a portion of the surficial aquifer system along the eastern coast of the state. Groundwater is withdrawn from the Anastasia Formation in many areas along the Atlantic Coastal Ridge where, locally, it may be the major source of groundwater. Near the southern extent of the Anastasia Formation, it forms a portion of the Biscayne aquifer (Hoffmeister 1974).

Florida Geological Survey Archives

Anastasia Formation, coast of Martin County

Undifferentiated Pleistocene-Holocene Sediments

The sediments referred to as the "undifferentiated Pleistocene-Holocene sediments" cover much of Florida effectively hiding most older sediments. Included in this category are marine "terrace" sediments, eolian sand dunes, fluvial deposits, freshwater carbonates, peats and a wide variety of sediment mixtures. These sediments often occur as thin layers overlying older formations and are not definable as formations. As such, these sediments have been referred to by many different names including Pliocene to Recent sands, Pleistocene sands, and Pleistocene Terrace Deposits.

The sediments included in this category are most often quartz sands. Gravel may be present in these sediments in the panhandle area. Other sediments included in this group include peat deposits, some clay beds, and freshwater carbonates. The freshwater carbonates occur in many freshwater springs and in large areas of the Everglades.

Locally, these sediments may form a portion of the surficial aquifer system. The greatest thicknesses of these sediments occurs infilling paleokarst features where more than 300 feet of undifferentiated Pleistocene-Holocene sediments have been recorded (Florida Geological Survey, unpublished well data).

Major Aquifers and Aquifer Systems

The surficial aquifer system consists mostly of unconsolidated sand and includes the sand and gravel and the Biscayne aquifers and all the undefined aquifers present at the land surface. In Florida the surficial aquifer system is used by a few small municipalities as well as by large numbers of individual households. The sand and gravel and Biscayne aquifers are separately recognized parts of the surficial aquifer system that consist of distinct rock types. The sand and gravel aquifer is the major source of water in northwest Florida and the Biscayne aquifer is the major source of water in southeast Florida. Between the surficial aquifers and the Floridan aquifer system in some parts of the state is the intermediate aquifer system. The intermediate aquifer system is an important source of supply in Sarasota, Charlotte, and Glades counties.

The Floridan aquifer system underlies the entire state of Florida and portions of Alabama, Georgia, and South Carolina and has been called "Florida's rain barrel" (Parker 1951). The Floridan provides water for many cities including Daytona Beach, Gainesville, Jacksonville, Lakeland, Ocala, Orlando, St. Petersburg, and Tallahassee as well as for hundreds of thousands of people in smaller communities and rural areas. The Floridan is also intensely pumped for industrial and agricultural supply. In several places where the Floridan contains saltwater, such as along the southeast coast, treated sewage and industrial wastes are injected into it. In the Orlando area large quantities of surface runoff are routinely diverted into the Floridan via drainage wells.

The different aquifers in the state have different capabilities of transmitting water. Transmissivity, expressed in feet squared per day, is a measure of the ease with which water moves through an aquifer. It is calculated by multiplying hydraulic conductivity (volume of water that moves in a unit of time under a unit gradient through a unit area) by the saturated thickness of the aquifer. Hydraulic conductivity is highest in aquifers with large conduits such as caves, sinkholes, and solution channels. However, a thick aquifer (hundreds of feet) will have a higher transmissivity than a thinner aquifer (tens of feet) that has the same hydraulic conductivity. In general, aquifers in Florida have high transmissivities. The highest transmissivities are found in the Floridan aquifer system (10,000 to greater than 1,000,000 feet squared per day) and Biscayne aquifer (100,000 to 1,000,000 feet squared per day), followed by the sand and gravel aquifer (10,000 feet squared per day), the surficial aquifer system (1,000 to 10,000 feet squared per day), and the intermediate aquifer system (200 to 13,000 feet squared per day).

Surficial Aquifer System

The surficial aquifer system in Florida includes aquifers present at the land surface. Even though the sand and gravel aquifer and the Biscayne aquifer are present at the land surface and are hydraulically connected to other surficial aquifers in the surficial aquifer system, they are discussed here as separate and distinct aquifers because of their importance as local water sources. Other parts of the surficial aquifer system occur throughout large portions of Florida and adjacent states and are important sources of water in some small municipalities and in rural areas. The surficial aquifer system is primarily used for individual household wells where the Floridan aquifer system is too deep or contains nonpotable water.

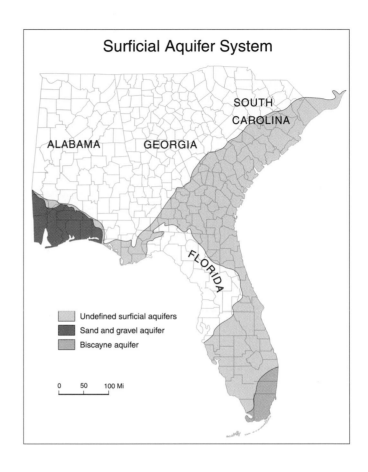

Surficial Aquifer System

SOUTH CAROLINA

ALABAMA GEORGIA

FLORIDA

- ☐ Undefined surficial aquifers
- ■ Sand and gravel aquifer
- ▨ Biscayne aquifer

0   50   100 Mi

Groundwater Flow

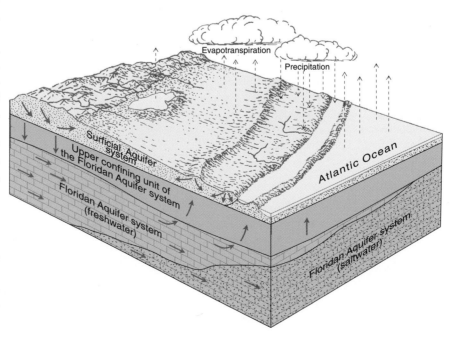

Evapotranspiration

Precipitation

Surficial Aquifer system

Upper confining unit of the Floridan Aquifer system

Floridan Aquifer system (freshwater)

Atlantic Ocean

Floridan Aquifer system (saltwater)

45

The surficial aquifer system consists mostly of sand, sandy clay, silt, clay, sandstone, limestone, and shell beds. Sandstone and limestone units occur primarily in southwestern Florida. In some places the clays are thick enough and continuous enough to divide the surficial aquifer into two or three separate layers, but generally the aquifer is undivided. Thicknesses of the surficial aquifer system vary across the state and range from tens of feet to several hundred feet in Indian River and St. Lucie counties. The surficial aquifer system is as much as 200 feet thick in Martin and Palm Beach counties and 150 feet thick in eastern St. Johns County. Elsewhere in Florida, the surficial aquifer system is generally less than 100 feet thick.

Groundwater in the surficial aquifer system is unconfined by overlying deposits. Water that enters the aquifer is from precipitation. A large amount of precipitation is returned directly to the atmosphere as evapotranspiration and does not enter the aquifer. Some of the water that enters the aquifer moves quickly along short flowpaths and discharges to lakes and streams. In some places, especially near the coast, water leaks upward from the underlying Floridan aquifer system through the clayey confining unit separating the surficial aquifer and the Floridan aquifer system. In other places, leakage occurs downward from the surficial aquifer to the Floridan aquifer system. The general movement of water in the surficial aquifer is illustrated in the idealized diagram representing the aquifers in south central and coastal Florida.

The altitude of the water table in the surficial aquifer system is generally a subdued replica of the land surface. Relatively steep gradients occur from ridges or hills to streams, and low gradients occur in the low, flat areas between streams and under large topographic highs. Arrows on the map show that the general direction of groundwater flow in the surficial aquifer is toward the Atlantic Ocean, the Gulf of Mexico, or toward major rivers. The directions of groundwater movement can change markedly within short distances.

Sand and Gravel Aquifer

The sand and gravel aquifer underlies more than 6,000 square miles of land surface in southwestern Alabama and the western Florida panhandle. It is the major source of groundwater in Escambia and Santa Rosa counties and is a secondary source in Okaloosa and Walton counties. As its name implies, it consists largely of interbedded layers of quartz-rich sand and gravel. Clay

46

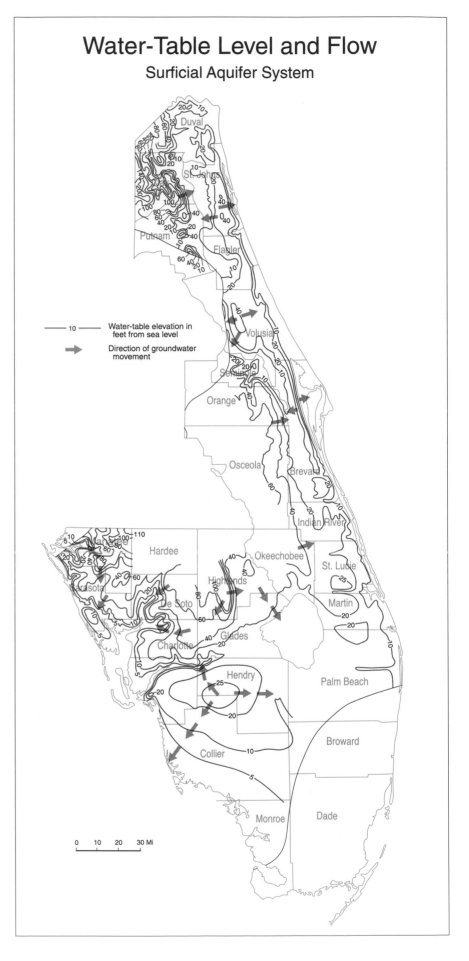

Water-Table Level and Flow
Surficial Aquifer System

beds and lenses are common throughout the aquifer and form local confining beds. The aquifer is wedge-shaped. It is thinnest at its northern and eastern limit and thickest (1,400 feet) in southwestern Alabama. The sand and gravel aquifer has been subdivided into three different hydrologic zones: the upper water-table zone, the intermediate zone, and the lower main producing zone. The upper zone consists mostly of unconsolidated sand of the Citronelle Formation, the intermediate zone

Hydrogeologic Cross Section

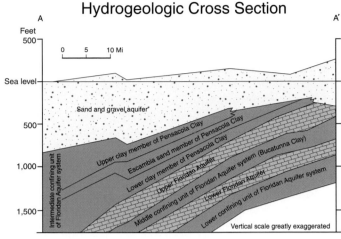

Sand and Gravel Aquifer

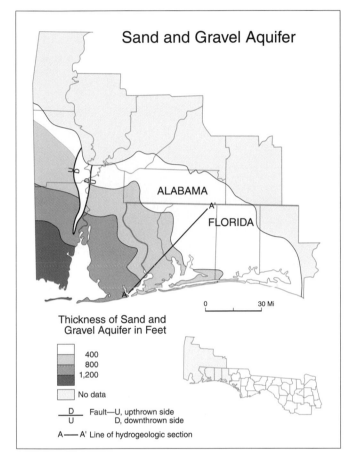

Thickness of Sand and
Gravel Aquifer in Feet

400
800
1,200

No data

$\frac{D}{U}$ Fault—U, upthrown side
D, downthrown side

A——A' Line of hydrogeologic section

consists of less permeable sand and clay deposits, and the main producing zone consists of Miocene age coarse sand and gravel beds. The main producing zone is recharged by downward leakage from the upper zone. The intermediate confining unit underlies the main producing zone inhibiting downward movement of groundwater. Wells in the main producing zone commonly yield more than 1,000 gallons per minute, and the transmissivity is as high as 20,000 feet squared per day.

Water in the aquifer is unconfined where overlying clay deposits are thin or absent and is under artesian conditions where clay deposits are thick and confine water movement. Water enters the sand and gravel aquifer as recharge from precipitation and moves generally downward and downgradient, either discharging to streams or moving toward the coast. The regional flow pattern is affected substantially by pumping. In some locations where heavy pumping from several well fields has occurred, water levels were reported to have dropped 20 to 25 feet from 1940 to 1973 (Trapp 1975). As is typical of other unconfined surficial aquifers, the sand and gravel aquifer is easily contaminated.

47

Potentiometric Surface and Flow
Sand and Gravel Aquifer

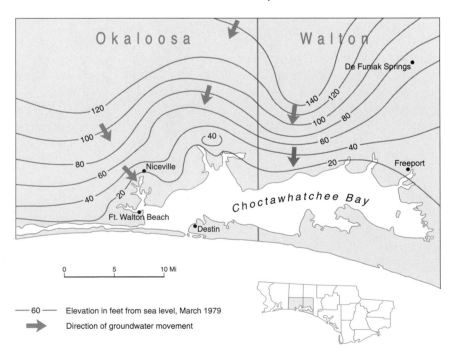

—— 60 —— Elevation in feet from sea level, March 1979

➡ Direction of groundwater movement

Biscayne Aquifer

The Biscayne aquifer underlies almost all of Dade and Broward counties and small parts of Palm Beach and Monroe counties. It also extends beneath Biscayne Bay and under the near shore of the Atlantic Ocean, where its highly permeable sediments contain saltwater. The Biscayne aquifer is the sole source of drinking water for over 3 million people in southern Florida. The Biscayne aquifer is wedge-shaped and ranges in thickness from 20 feet on its western edge, to more than 300 feet toward the coast in parts of coastal Broward and Palm Beach counties. The aquifer consists of highly permeable interbedded limestone and sandstone. These highly permeable rocks are covered in most places only by a thin veneer of porous soil. Accordingly, water levels in the aquifer rise rapidly in response to rainfall. The high permeability of the Biscayne aquifer is created largely by extensive dissolution of the carbonate minerals that comprise the limestone units. The thickest and most extensive geologic unit in the Biscayne aquifer is the Fort Thompson Formation. Other units that comprise the aquifer include the Anastasia Formation, Key Largo Limestone, Miami Limestone, and Pamlico Sand.

Before development in southern Florida, a large proportion of the abundant precipitation that fell on the flat, low-lying interior land during the wet season drained southward to the Gulf of Mexico and Florida Bay. Most of this drainage was in the form of wide, shallow sheets of water that moved sluggishly southward. This drainage was a major source of recharge to the Biscayne aquifer. Since the early 1900s, well fields, canals, control structures, levees, and conservation areas have substantially altered natural flow patterns of both surface water and groundwater.

Today, shallow, southward-moving surface water still provides some recharge to the Biscayne aquifer in addition to rain that falls directly on the aquifer. Where the Biscayne aquifer is exposed at the land surface or is covered by only a thin veneer of soil, the slowly moving surface water that passes over the aquifer is able to readily percolate downward into the aquifer. The general movement of water in the Biscayne aqui-

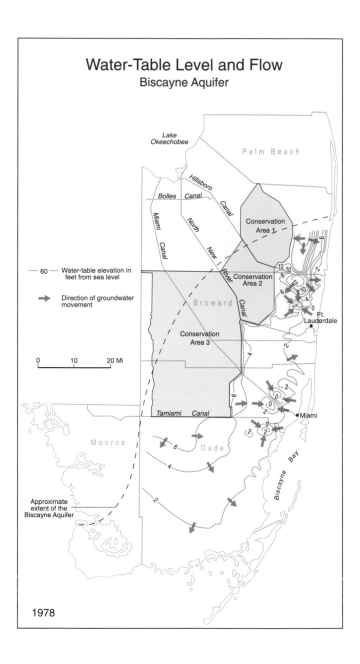

Water-Table Level and Flow
Biscayne Aquifer

— 60 — Water-table elevation in feet from sea level

→ Direction of groundwater movement

0   10   20 Mi

Approximate extent of the Biscayne Aquifer

1978

48

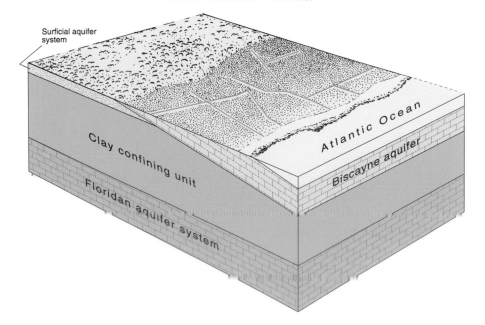

Sequence of Aquifers
Southeastern Florida

fer is seaward. Water levels are highest near water conservation areas and lowest near the coast. The closed depressions in the water table in eastern Broward and Dade counties are caused by pumpage from major well fields. Withdrawal of large volumes of groundwater has reversed the natural eastward flow pattern of groundwater to westward and has increased the possibility of saltwater intrusion from Biscayne Bay and the Atlantic Ocean.

Canals have been used extensively for drainage and flood control and have lowered groundwater levels and altered groundwater flow patterns in southeast Florida. Levees were also constructed, first to prevent flooding from Lake Okeechobee, and later to impound excess water in three large water conservation areas for later release. A system of canals, levees, control structures, pumping stations and water conservation (storage) areas are used to manage the water resources of southern Florida. The goals of this system are to conserve freshwater, provide flood control, and minimize saltwater encroachment. Saltwater encroachment has long been a concern in southeastern Florida. The installation of canal control structures combined with the impoundment of water in the conservation areas have stabilized the saltwater-freshwater interface near the coast and at the entrances to major canals.

Intermediate Aquifer System

The intermediate aquifer system consists of those water-bearing units located between the Floridan aquifer system and the overlying surficial aquifers, and consists of one or more water-bearing units separated by confining units. Because of the lower permeability and transmissivity of the intermediate aquifer system compared to the Floridan aquifer system, the intermediate aquifer system acts as a confining unit for the underlying Floridan aquifer system in some places. Because the intermediate aquifer system does not yield as much water as other aquifers, it is used only in places where water from surficial aquifers or the Floridan aquifer system is not adequate in amount or quality. In southwestern Florida, for example, the underlying Floridan aquifer system contains nonpotable water, thus the intermediate aquifer system is the main source of water supply for Charlotte, Lee, and Sarasota counties. The

intermediate aquifer system consists predominantly of sand beds and limestone of the Hawthorn Group; and sand, limestone, and shell beds of the Tamiami Formation. The aquifer also contains some sandy limestone, sandstone, and clay beds.

Water in the intermediate aquifer system is under confined conditions, except locally where an upper clay confining unit is absent. In most places, water moves downward through the upper confining unit of the intermediate aquifer system. Most of the water then follows short flowpaths and discharges to surface drainage. Some water percolates downward through the lower confining unit of the intermediate aquifer to recharge

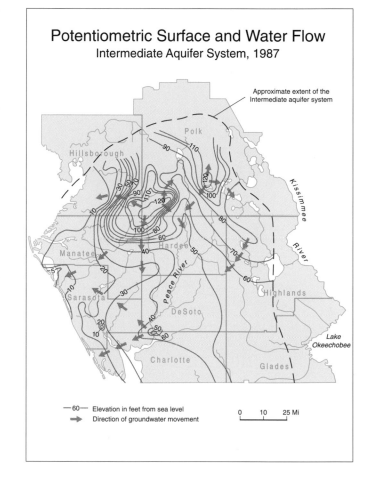

49

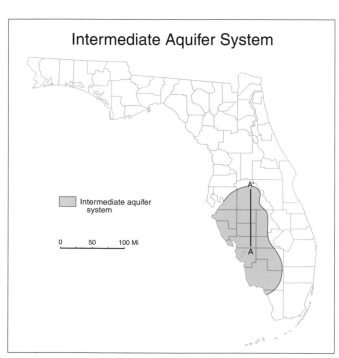

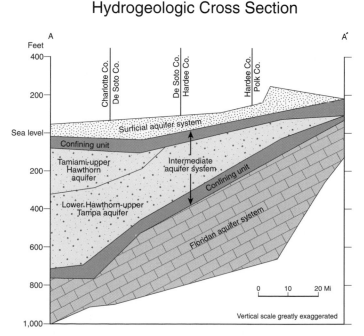

the underlying Floridan aquifer system. Locally, in Charlotte and Lee counties, some water leaks upward from the Floridan aquifer system to the intermediate aquifer system. In Polk County, where the potentiometric surface is more than 120 feet above sea level, the intermediate aquifer system water moves outward from two major recharge areas. From these areas, the lateral flow is toward major surface streams and the Gulf of Mexico. The two depressions in the potentiometric surface in western Sarasota County are caused by pumpage from local pumping stations.

Floridan Aquifer System

One of the most productive aquifers in the world, the Floridan aquifer system underlies a total area of about 100,000 square miles in southern Alabama, southeastern Georgia, southern South Carolina, and all of Florida. The Floridan aquifer system is defined on the basis of permeability: it is at least 10 times more permeable than its upper and lower confining units. It is composed of a thick sequence of carbonate rocks (limestone and dolomite) of Tertiary age that range in age from late

50

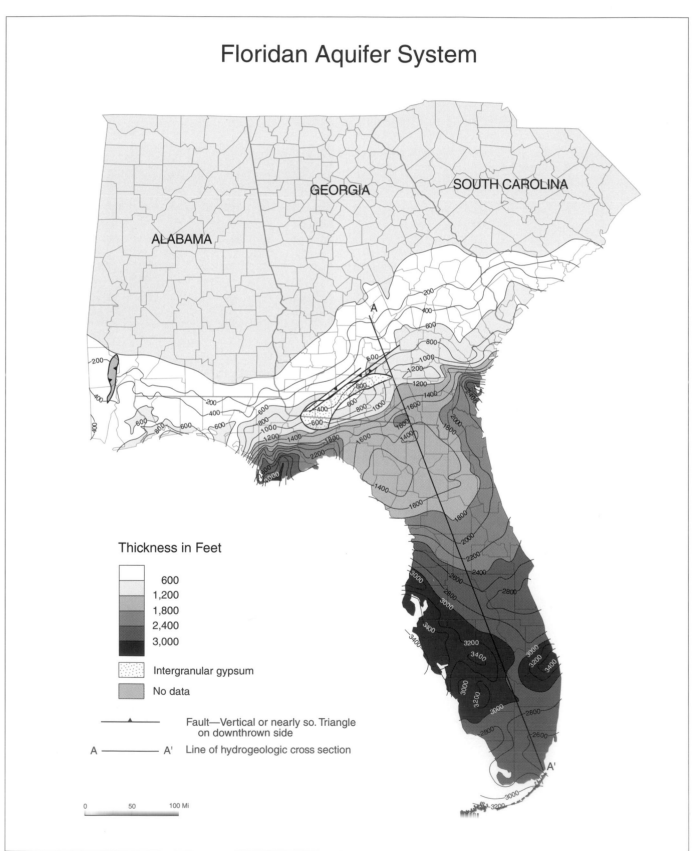

Floridan Aquifer System

Thickness in Feet

- 600
- 1,200
- 1,800
- 2,400
- 3,000

Intergranular gypsum

No data

Fault—Vertical or nearly so. Triangle on downthrown side

A ——— A' Line of hydrogeologic cross section

0   50   100 Mi

Paleocene to early Miocene. The aquifer system generally consists of the following geologic units, from oldest to youngest: Oldsmar Formation (lower Eocene age), Avon Park Formation (middle Eocene), Ocala Limestone (upper Eocene), Suwannee Limestone (Oligocene), Hawthorn Group (Miocene), and St. Marks Formation in northern Florida. The Hawthorn Group is part of the Floridan aquifer system where it contains permeable limestone units that are hydraulically connected to the underlying, older rocks. The thickest and most productive units are the Eocene age Avon Park Formation and Ocala Limestone. The Suwannee Limestone of Oligocene age is also a principal source of water, but it is thinner and much less areally extensive than the Eocene units.

The Floridan aquifer system generally thickens toward the south from a thin edge near its northern limit. In most places, the Floridan aquifer system can be divided into three units: the Upper Floridan aquifer, the middle confining unit, and the Lower Floridan aquifer. The middle confining unit restricts the movement of groundwater between the Upper and Lower Floridan aquifers and consists of several separate units. At some locations the confining unit is clay; at others it is a very fine-grained limestone; at still other places it is a dolomite with the pore spaces filled with anhydrite. In some places the middle confining unit yields several hundred gallons per minute to wells and thus may be considered an aquifer. Few supply wells penetrate

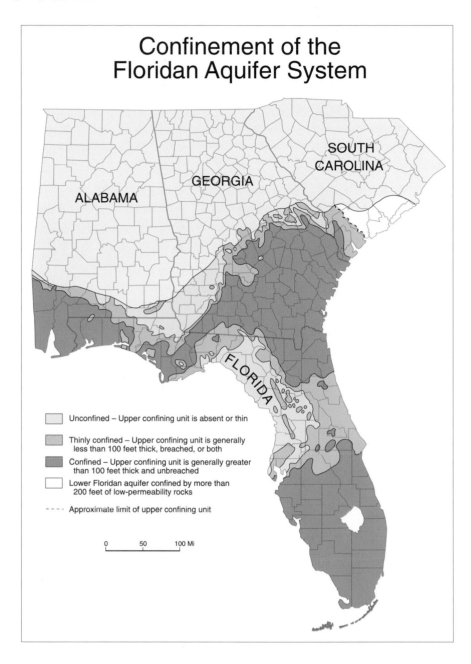

Confinement of the Floridan Aquifer System

- Unconfined – Upper confining unit is absent or thin
- Thinly confined – Upper confining unit is generally less than 100 feet thick, breached, or both
- Confined – Upper confining unit is generally greater than 100 feet thick and unbreached
- Lower Floridan aquifer confined by more than 200 feet of low-permeability rocks
- – – – Approximate limit of upper confining unit

0   50   100 Mi

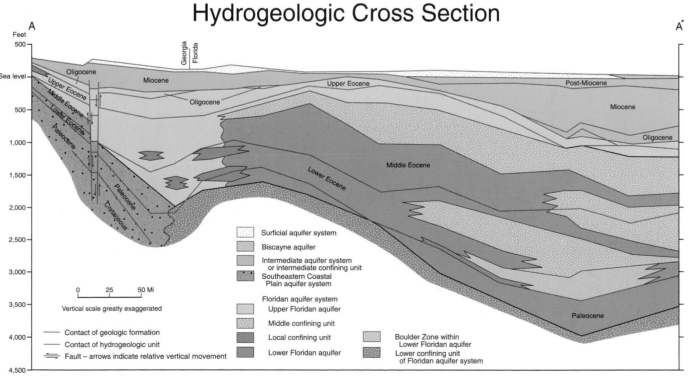

Hydrogeologic Cross Section

51

- Surficial aquifer system
- Biscayne aquifer
- Intermediate aquifer system or intermediate confining unit
- Southeastern Coastal Plain aquifer system
- Floridan aquifer system Upper Floridan aquifer
- Middle confining unit
- Local confining unit
- Lower Floridan aquifer
- Boulder Zone within Lower Floridan aquifer
- Lower confining unit of Floridan aquifer system

0   25   50 Mi

Vertical scale greatly exaggerated

——— Contact of geologic formation
——— Contact of hydrogeologic unit
≡≡≡ Fault – arrows indicate relative vertical movement

beyond the Upper Floridan aquifer because it is so productive and because much of the Lower Floridan aquifer contains mineralized or even saline water. South of Lake Okeechobee the entire aquifer system contains saltwater. In places, no middle confining unit exists and the aquifer system is highly permeable throughout its vertical extent.

Two highly permeable zones exist within the Lower Floridan aquifer: the Fernandina permeable zone in northeast Florida and southeast Georgia, and the Boulder Zone in southeast Florida. The Fernandina permeable zone contains large amounts of fresh to brackish water. The Boulder Zone, named not because it contains boulders but because it is difficult to drill into, contains saltwater and is used in the Miami-Ft. Lauderdale area to dispose of sewage and some industrial effluents through injection wells.

The degree of confinement of the Upper Floridan aquifer is the major hydrogeologic control on the distribution of recharge, discharge, and groundwater flow. Over most of Florida, the Upper Floridan aquifer is overlain by a sequence of sand, clay, limestone, and dolomite that ranges in thickness from a few feet in parts of west central and north central Florida to

hundreds of feet in southeastern Georgia, northeastern Florida, southeastern Florida, and the westernmost part of the panhandle of Florida. The overlying sand generally comprises the surficial aquifer system, and the clay and limestone generally comprise the intermediate aquifer system. Both of these aquifers act as confining units to the Upper Floridan aquifer because they are less permeable than the Upper Floridan. Unconfined portions of the Upper Floridan aquifer are located in western parts of north central Florida (north of Pasco County to Wakulla County).

Major (or general) features of the groundwater flow system in the Upper Floridan aquifer are illustrated by a map of its potentiometric surface. The altitude and configuration of the potentiometric surface in 1995 are shown on the map. The arrows show the direction of groundwater movement, which generally is perpendicular to the contours. In the past several decades groundwater withdrawals have had a pronounced effect on the potentiometric surface of the Upper Floridan aquifer in panhandle Florida, northeastern Florida, southwestern Florida, and in southeastern, coastal Georgia.

52

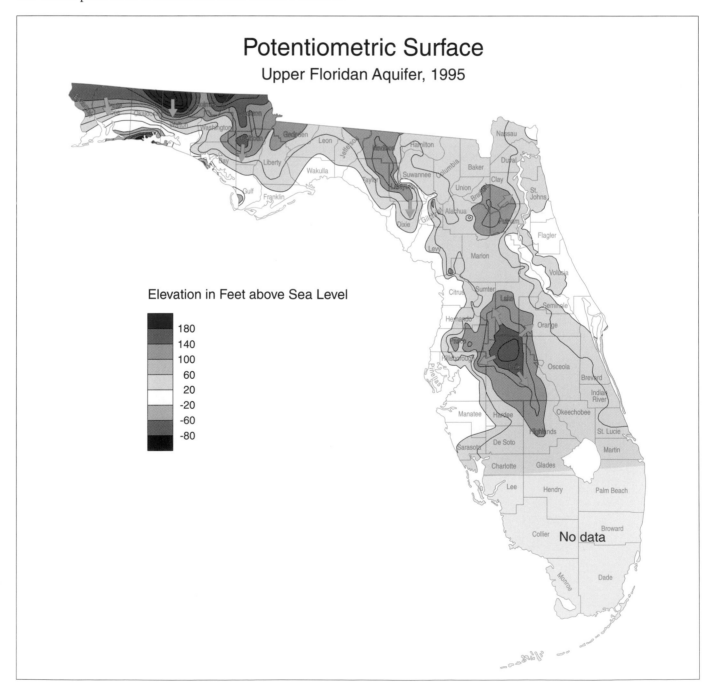

Potentiometric Surface
Upper Floridan Aquifer, 1995

Elevation in Feet above Sea Level

180
140
100
60
20
-20
-60
-80

No data

Water in the Upper Floridan aquifer moves from areas of high to low altitude on the potentiometric surface. The highest areas on the Upper Floridan aquifer's potentiometric surface are located where the aquifer is exposed at the land surface near its updip limit and in an area in central peninsular Florida. Water moves coastward from the outcrop area of the aquifer and outward in all directions from the potentiometric surface high in central Florida.

Recharge to the Upper Floridan aquifer (and other confined aquifers) does not occur everywhere but is restricted to places where the altitude of the water table is higher than the altitude of the potentiometric surface of the confined aquifers. Areas with little or no recharge under natural conditions typically occur where the potentiometric surface of the aquifer is above the land surface most of the time, that is, in areas of artesian flow. About 45 percent of the state falls within this classification, mostly in coastal areas and areas south of Lake Okeechobee. Areas of very low recharge occur where the Floridan is overlain by relatively impermeable confining beds that are generally more than 25 feet thick. In these areas recharge rates are estimated to be less than 2 inches per year. Areas of very low to moderate recharge (estimated to range

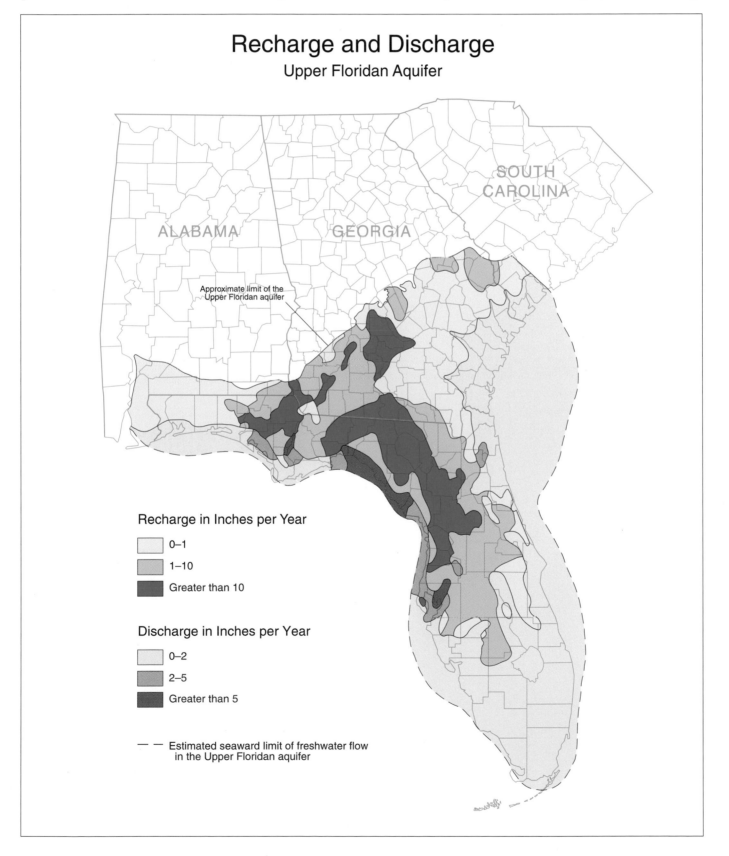

Recharge and Discharge
Upper Floridan Aquifer

SOUTH CAROLINA

ALABAMA

GEORGIA

Approximate limit of the Upper Floridan aquifer

Recharge in Inches per Year

- 0–1
- 1–10
- Greater than 10

Discharge in Inches per Year

- 0–2
- 2–5
- Greater than 5

— — Estimated seaward limit of freshwater flow in the Upper Floridan aquifer

between 2 inches and 10 inches per year) occur where the confining beds are generally less than 25 feet thick or are breached. Where the confining bed is breached or absent, but where the water table and the potentiometric surface of the Floridan aquifer are both close to the land surface, little recharge occurs. Areas of high recharge, which are primarily well-drained upland areas characterized by poorly developed stream drainage and many closed depressions, constitute about 15 percent of the state. Some examples of high recharge areas are the well-drained porous sand ridges of central and west central Florida, including parts of Orange, Lake, Polk, Pasco, and Hernando counties. Many areas where internal drainage through sinkholes connects the land surface to the Floridan aquifer also have high recharge rates, such as in central Polk, north central Pasco, south central Hernando, southwestern Clay, Marion, Sumter, Suwannee, and northwestern Putnam counties. Recharge rates in these areas are estimated to range from 10 to 20 inches per year (Stewart 1980). These natural recharge conditions in some of these areas have been significantly modified recently by pumping wells. In fact, recharge to the Floridan and other confined aquifers now occurs in some places that were formerly discharge areas.

Groundwater Quality

The natural water quality of groundwater in aquifers is related to the quality of recharge water, the mineralogy of soils and aquifer sediments, the residence time in the groundwater flow system, and the presence of nearby saline water. Groundwater moving through aquifers generally reaches chemical equilibrium with the aquifer sediments. Accordingly, natural groundwater quality at a given point changes very little over time. Also, groundwater generally contains higher concentrations of dissolved minerals than surface runoff and stream water because it remains in contact with the aquifer materials for much longer periods. Human activity also affects groundwater quality. Florida's unique hydrogeologic features of a thin soil layer, high water table, porous limestone, and large amounts of rainfall, coupled with its rapid population growth, result in a groundwater resource that is extremely vulnerable to contamination. In this chapter, groundwater quality is described in terms of naturally occurring chemical characteristics.

The sand and gravel aquifer, which is composed predominantly of quartz-rich sediments and is recharged by rainfall, typically has very good water quality and very low concentra-

Water Quality
1985–1988

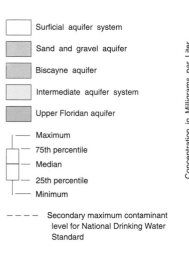

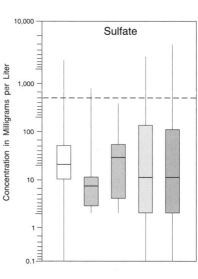

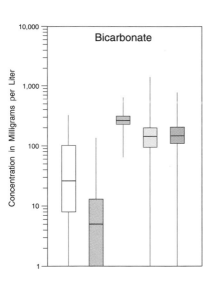

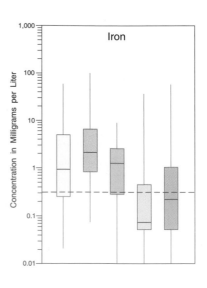

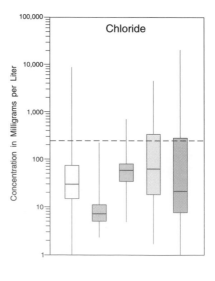

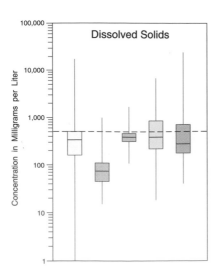

54

tions of most water-quality constituents. Groundwater in this aquifer is characterized by high acidity, low alkalinity, and low chloride and dissolved solids concentrations because of the sediment composition, the relatively low concentrations of inorganic constituents, and the low pH of rainfall. Groundwater in the sand and gravel aquifer has the lowest concentrations of sulfate, bicarbonate, chloride, and dissolved solids of all the aquifers in Florida. Dissolved solids concentrations in water represent the sum of all major inorganic constituents (cations and anions) in solution. Concentrations of iron are highest in the sand and gravel aquifer. Iron concentrations greater than the drinking-water standard of 0.30 mg/l are generally not a health concern, but can cause some damage to pipes and fixtures in the water distribution system. Concentrations of sul-

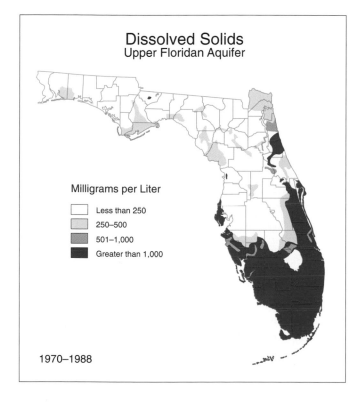

Dissolved Solids
Upper Floridan Aquifer

Milligrams per Liter

- Less than 250
- 250–500
- 501–1,000
- Greater than 1,000

1970–1988

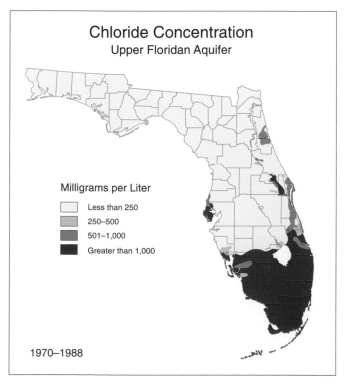

Chloride Concentration
Upper Floridan Aquifer

Milligrams per Liter

- Less than 250
- 250–500
- 501–1,000
- Greater than 1,000

1970–1988

fate, bicarbonate, chloride, and dissolved solids are higher in other parts of the surficial aquifer system than in the sand and gravel aquifer, probably due to the greater variety of sediments which comprise the surficial aquifer system throughout the state. Concentrations of sulfate, bicarbonate, chloride, and dissolved solids in the surficial aquifer system are lower than in the Biscayne, intermediate, and Upper Floridan aquifers.

The water quality in the Biscayne, intermediate, and Upper Floridan aquifers is similar. Bicarbonate concentrations are highest in groundwater from aquifers that contain predominantly carbonate rocks (limestone). Aquifers composed of readily dissolved limestone and that receive recharge from overlying aquifers (rather than directly from rainfall), such as the intermediate and Upper Floridan aquifers, also have higher dissolved solids concentrations. Chloride concentrations are also higher in the intermediate and Upper Floridan aquifers than in the surficial aquifer system probably because of longer residence times of water in the groundwater flow system and the presence of saline water near the coast.

The spatial distribution of chloride and dissolved solids concentrations in the Upper Floridan aquifer shows that most of the high concentrations are in the southern part of peninsular Florida and in areas along the coast. Chloride concentrations do exceed the recommended drinking water level in about 25 percent of the samples from the intermediate and Upper Floridan aquifers, but most of these high concentrations are probably in wells near the coast that are probably not used for drinking water. Water samples shown in these graphs and maps are from wells located throughout an aquifer's extent and do not necessarily reflect the water used for drinking water. In testing 91 public water supplies from various aquifers in Florida in 1983-84, concentrations of chloride were below 100 mg/l in nearly 90 percent of supplies, and only 4 percent exceeded the recommended drinking water level of 250 mg/l (Irwin et al. 1985). The extent of saltwater encroachment in aquifers in coastal areas is discussed in a later section of this chapter.

Groundwater and Surface-water Interaction

Virtually every surface-water feature in the state, including rivers, lakes, wetlands, and estuaries, interacts with adjacent groundwater. This interaction affects the water quality and quantity in both surface water and groundwater. Groundwater and surface-water interaction affects water chemistry, especially acidity, temperature, dissolved solids, dissolved oxygen, and reduction-oxidation potential. As land and water resource development increases in the state, it is becoming readily apparent that groundwater and surface-water interaction must be considered in establishing water management policies. This interaction can take many forms but the most common interactions are between aquifers and stream water, lakes, and wetlands. In coastal areas, interactions between aquifers and seawater occur. All of these interactions occur in Florida.

Streams interact with aquifers in two ways: either they receive water from groundwater inflow or they lose water to aquifers by seepage through the streambed. For many streams in Florida, the flow direction between the stream and aquifer can vary a great deal, sometimes over very short timeframes or distances in response to rapid rises in stream stage or stream flow, commonly from storm runoff. If the rise in stream stage is great enough to overtop the banks and flood large areas of land surface, widespread recharge to groundwater may occur throughout the flooded areas.

55

The presence of karst features sometimes makes stream and aquifer interaction even more obvious. Karst is a type of topography that is characterized by caves, sinkholes, springs, and other types of openings caused by dissolution of limestone. One of the largest karst environments in the country occurs from the central portion of the Florida peninsula to the big bend portion of the panhandle. In this area the Santa Fe River, a major tributary to the Suwannee River, completely goes underground, becoming part of the groundwater flow system before reemerging as a river three miles downgradient. Interaction between surface water and groundwater in this highly porous karst aquifer system is quite rapid and can significantly impact water quality. The water quality of streams flowing over this karst terrain can be improved or degraded by the addition of groundwater from large springs such as in the lower Suwannee River basin, depending upon the composition of the groundwater. In the Suwannee River a significant portion of the nitrogen load is being contributed from groundwater discharging to the river. During low flow periods in the river, groundwater is the predominant if not sole contributor of water to the river, introducing low dissolved oxygen concentrations which change the river's chemical conditions enough to significantly influence the movement of fish populations in portions of the river. In the St. Johns River basin, over half of the flow in the Ocklawaha River, a major tributary to the St. Johns, is groundwater from Silver Springs.

Aquifer and lake interaction frequently occurs when lakes receive groundwater inflow through part of their bed and have seepage to groundwater through other parts of their bed. Some lakes receive substantial amounts of their water from groundwater. The water levels in lakes generally do not change as rapidly as water levels in streams. Evaporation has a greater effect on lake levels than on stream levels because the surface area of lakes is greater and lake water is not replenished as readily as stream water.

Lake levels can be reduced by groundwater withdrawals and can be increased by groundwater return flows from irrigation and other applications of water to the land surface. The accounting of the groundwater components can be difficult and controversial. In the west central portion of the state, the drying of lakes has been attributed to excessive groundwater pumpage to meet the public water supply needs. As these needs increase in west central Florida, the possibility of transporting water from nearby watersheds is being considered, namely from the lower Suwannee River watershed. Concern for the Suwannee River and its direct connection with the Upper

Floridan aquifer is driving recent research to determine potential groundwater pumpage effects on stream flow in the Suwannee River.

Similar to streams, wetlands can receive groundwater inflow, recharge to groundwater, or do both. In Florida, wetlands have interactions with groundwater similar to streams and lakes. Many wetlands are present along streams, especially slow-moving streams. Wetlands along streams and in coastal areas have complex hydrological interactions because they are subject to periodic water level changes. Some wetlands in coastal areas are affected by predictable tidal cycles. Other coastal wetlands are more affected by predictable tidal cycles. Other coastal wetlands are more affected by seasonal water level changes and by flooding. A major difference between lakes and wetlands is that lakes commonly have a shallow zone around their perimeter, permitting waves to remove fine-grained sediments. In wetlands, fine-grained and organic sediments commonly extend to their shoreline (border), resulting in reduced transfer of water between groundwater and surface water in the wetlands.

In coastal areas in south Florida, rapid population growth has greatly increased the demand for water. If too much fresh water is pumped out of the Biscayne aquifer to meet this demand, sea water intrudes to replace the freshwater, contaminating the water supply. Canals constructed to prevent flooding in southern Florida rapidly remove excess surface water and groundwater from inland parts of the aquifer to coastal areas. Control structures near the mouths of canals allow groundwater levels near the canals in coastal areas to remain high enough to retard saltwater encroachment during periods of less than normal rainfall. However, this connection also means that pollutants in canal water from inland areas and saltwater from coastal areas can move through the canals and into the aquifer. The extensive canal system has also altered inland biologic communities dependent on shallow groundwater in the Everglades and wetland areas. Efforts are underway to better understand the interaction between groundwater and sea water in south Florida, so that further contamination can be prevented. This improved understanding can be applied to the management of the system of canals, levees, control structures, pumping stations, and water conservation (storage) areas to preserve the freshwater resources of southern Florida.

Springs

Springs have long been one of Florida's most valued natural and scenic resources. In 1513 the Spanish explorer Ponce de León came to Florida seeking a spring called the Fountain of Youth. Native Floridians used springs for water supply and fished in the streams formed by the springs. Many of Florida's springs are now tourist attractions. Several springs have been developed commercially, including Silver and Rainbow, while others have been incorporated into state parks, including Manatee, Homosassa, Wakulla, and Ichetucknee.

Numerous springs probably occur off the coast of Florida, but most are difficult to detect. Submarine springs sometimes can be detected by the appearance of a "boil" at the water surface. Many of these submarine springs are located near the coast, but a few are up to 20 miles offshore.

Springs are common in karst areas and are places where groundwater discharges through natural openings in the ground. Florida has about 320 known springs. The outflows from the springs range from less than 1 gallon per minute to 1.3 billion

Karst Features

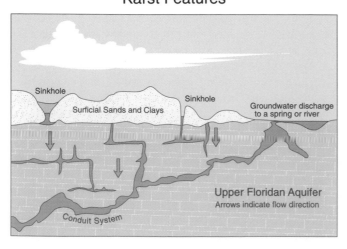

Sinkhole
Sinkhole
Surficial Sands and Clays
Groundwater discharge to a spring or river
Upper Floridan Aquifer
Arrows indicate flow direction
Conduit System

gallons per day at Spring Creek Springs, a group of submarine spring vents off the coast of Wakulla County. The known springs have a combined outflow of nearly 8 billion gallons of water per day. Florida has 27 first-magnitude springs or groups of springs (with flow greater than 64.6 million gallons per day) out of a total of 78 in the nation. All of the springs issue from the Upper Floridan aquifer, and nearly all of them are located in areas where the confining unit above the Upper Floridan aquifer is absent or is less than 100 feet thick. The distribution of large springs discharging from the Upper Floridan aquifer is the direct result of dissolution of carbonate rocks, which results in the development of large conduits and caves. Many of these conduits channel the groundwater to the land surface where they become the orifices of major springs.

The natural flow, water quality, and water temperature of large artesian springs remain relatively stable over long periods. Springs can serve as indicators of trends in hydrologic conditions. Records of spring flow are generally more repre-

sentative of the character of a large part of an aquifer than are records of well flow. Although spring flow is relatively stable over a long period, it does reflect long- and short-term variations in recharge from rainfall as well as changes in water quantity and quality brought about by human activities. Silver Springs, about 5 miles northeast of Ocala and the largest noncoastal spring in Florida, shows a remarkable long-term consistency in flow with short-term variations. The average flow since 1906 has been 530 million gallons per day (mgd), essentially the same as the earliest recorded flow of 531 mgd in 1898. Flow, however, has ranged from 348 to 833 mgd, reflecting variations in amount of rainfall (Heath and Conover 1981).

Large withdrawals of water from wells near a spring can reduce pressure in the aquifer to a level below the spring orifice and thus stop the flow. The only large spring in Florida known to have ceased flowing is Kissengen Spring, about 4 miles southeast of Bartow. The average discharge of the spring,

Springs

Rank	Name	County	Average Discharge mgd
1	Spring Creek Springs	Wakulla	1,293
2	Crystal River Springs	Citrus	567
3	Silver Springs	Marion	516
4	Rainbow Springs	Marion	459
5	Alapaha Rise	Hamilton	393
6	St. Marks Spring	Leon	334
7	Wakulla Springs	Wakulla	253
8	Wacissa Springs	Jefferson	251
9	Ichetucknee Springs	Columbia	233
10	Holton Spring	Hamilton	157
11	Homosassa Springs	Citrus	124
12	Blue Springs	Jackson	122
13	Manatee Spring	Levy	115
14	Weeki Wachee Springs	Hernando	112
15	River Sink Spring	Wakulla	106
16	Gainer Springs	Bay	103
17	Blue Spring	Volusia	102
18	Troy Spring	Lafayette	98
19	Kini Spring	Wakulla	97
20	Hornsby Spring	Alachua	96
21	Falmouth Spring	Suwannee	94
22	Chassahowitzka Springs	Citrus	90
23	Fannin Springs	Levy	73
24	Natural Bridge Spring	Leon	70
25	Blue Spring	Madison	68
26	Silver Glen Springs	Marion	68
27	Alexander Springs	Lake	66

57

prior to the onset of a progressive decline beginning about 1937, was about 19 mgd. As withdrawals from wells in the area increased, the decline in artesian pressure caused the spring to cease flowing in February 1950 (Peek 1951).

Water quality of Florida's freshwater springs is relatively constant. For example, the water quality of Wakulla Springs remains essentially the same as it was half a century ago. Although groundwater issuing from springs is usually clear, under certain conditions spring water can be turbid or contain brown organic matter, which is typical of many surface waters in Florida. Where turbid water recharges an aquifer near a spring, the water can move quickly, and minimally altered in quality, through solution channels and emerge at the spring. This is common for some springs in Florida, especially following heavy rainfall. The temperature of springs varies only about 4°C (7.2°F) and averages about 29°C (84°F) in southern Florida and 21°C (70°F) in northern Florida.

Sinkholes

Sinkholes are closed depressions in the land surface formed by the dissolution of near-surface rocks or by the collapse of the roofs of underground channels and caverns. Sinkholes are a natural, common geologic feature of limestone erosion (dissolution) in karst areas of Florida. Dissolution of rocks is enhanced where groundwater flow is concentrated and most vigorous. In the Floridan aquifer system, the greatest dissolution occurs where the confining unit above the system is thin or absent. Under natural conditions, sinkholes form slowly and expand gradually. Activities such as dredging, constructing reservoirs, diverting surface water, and pumping large amounts of groundwater can accelerate the rate of sinkhole expansion, resulting in the abrupt and dramatic formation of collapse-type sinkholes.

Vertical or near-vertical cracks or fractures in the limestone concentrate or control downward flow of groundwater. These fractures, called joints, commonly occur in intersecting sets. Some sinkholes occur randomly, but others are aligned along joints and at joint intersections. Groundwater can enlarge the pre-existing joints in the limestone and can eventually form caves, pipes, and other types of cavities and conduits, all of which collect and channel large volumes of water.

Sinkholes in Florida can be classified into three types, based on the manner in which they form: solution sinkholes, gradually subsiding sinkholes, and collapse sinkholes.

Solution sinkholes occur where the limestone surface is bare or thinly covered by soil or permeable sand. Solution is most active at the contact between the limestone surface and the overlying soil, and is usually concentrated at the intersection of a set of joints where fracturing of the limestone permits water to move easily to the subsurface. The most common type of sinkhole usually results from subsidence at the land surface at approximately the same rate as dissolution of the underlying limestone. The result is a gradual downward movement of the land surface, which develops into a depression that collects increasing amounts of surface runoff as its perimeter expands. This type of sinkhole usually forms as a bowl-shaped depression with the slope of its sides determined by the rate of subsidence relative to the rate of surface eroding into the depression. Surface runoff commonly carries sand, silt, and clay particles into the depression and thus forms a less permeable seal in the center of the depression where a marsh or intermittent lake may form.

Gradually subsiding sinkholes occur where the limestone is covered by 50 to 100 feet of permeable sand. Under these conditions, individual grains of sand move downward in se-

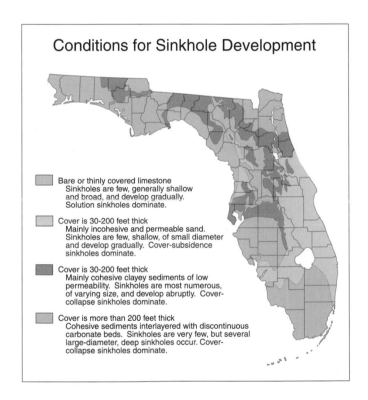

Conditions for Sinkhole Development

Bare or thinly covered limestone
Sinkholes are few, generally shallow and broad, and develop gradually. Solution sinkholes dominate.

Cover is 30-200 feet thick
Mainly incohesive and permeable sand. Sinkholes are few, shallow, of small diameter and develop gradually. Cover-subsidence sinkholes dominate.

Cover is 30-200 feet thick
Mainly cohesive clayey sediments of low permeability. Sinkholes are most numerous, of varying size, and develop abruptly. Cover-collapse sinkholes dominate.

Cover is more than 200 feet thick
Cohesive sediments interlayered with discontinuous carbonate beds. Sinkholes are very few, but several large-diameter, deep sinkholes occur. Cover-collapse sinkholes dominate.

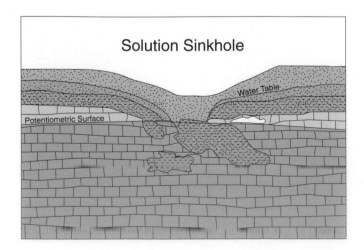

Solution Sinkhole

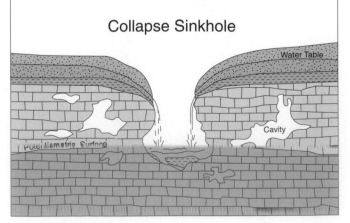

Collapse Sinkhole

58

quence replacing grains that have themselves moved downward to occupy space formerly held by the dissolved limestone. Spalling of incohesive sand into solution cavities along joints in the limestone can cause subsidence due to upward growth or migration of the cavities, and form holes at the land surface. Gradually subsiding sinkholes may be only a few feet in diameter and depth. Their small size is because cavities in the limestone cannot develop to appreciable size before they are filled with sand.

Collapse sinkholes occur where the limestone is covered by permeable sand and relatively cohesive clay. They occur where a cavity grows in size until its roof of sand and clay no longer supports its own weight. When this occurs, collapse is generally abrupt and sometimes catastrophic. Collapse sinkholes commonly occur where limestone is near the land surface but can also occur where the limestone is hundreds of feet below the surface. Locations of sinkholes are usually controlled by joints in the limestone that have influenced development of solution cavities. Collapse sinkholes commonly have vertical or overhanging walls and may be angular rather than round because of the positioning of joints. The large sinkhole that developed May 8, 1981, in Winter Park, Florida, illustrates the magnitude of a large cover-collapse sinkhole.

Formation of Gradually Subsiding Sinkholes

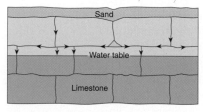

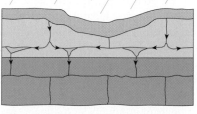

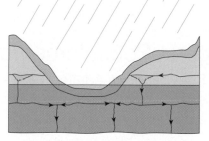

Water percolates through joints in limestone to the water table. The rock adjacent to the joints dissolves faster than elsewhere.

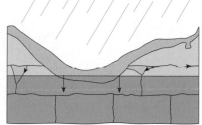

Differential solution of limestone is expressed by a depression at land surface that funnels water to the enlarged joints.

Sinkhole intersects the water table. Rate of dissolution is greatly reduced and may be less than that in surrounding area.

Sinkhole is expressed as a shallow, sand-filled depression because of clay and clayey sand filling, and subsidence of surrounding limestone.

59

Winter Park sinkhole, May 1981

Florida Geological Survey

Groundwater Use and Effects on Water Levels

Groundwater has long been a valuable source of plentiful, good-quality drinking water in Florida. About 93 percent of the state's population (14 million residents) relied on groundwater for their drinking water supply in 1995. Most of those people rely on the Upper Floridan aquifer, the Biscayne aquifer, and the surficial aquifer system for their water supplies. The sand and gravel aquifer and intermediate aquifer system are used much less, and only locally in northwestern and southwestern coastal parts of the state. The abundant supply of groundwater is vital to the state's important tourism and agricultural industries in addition to residential usage.

Because of differences in the distribution of population and agriculture, water use varies greatly around the state. The largest amounts of groundwater used were in southeastern and central areas: Dade, Polk, Broward, Orange, and Palm Beach counties. Dade and Broward withdrawals are from the Biscayne aquifer, Polk and Orange from the Upper Floridan aquifer, and Palm Beach from the Biscayne and other surficial aquifers. Most of the water used in these counties is for agriculture and

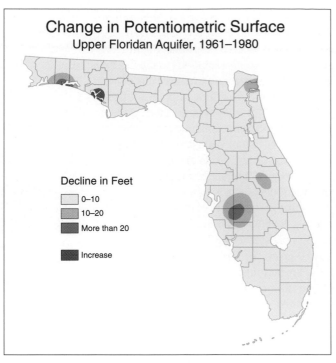

Change in Potentiometric Surface
Upper Floridan Aquifer, 1961–1980

Decline in Feet
- 0–10
- 10–20
- More than 20

- Increase

60

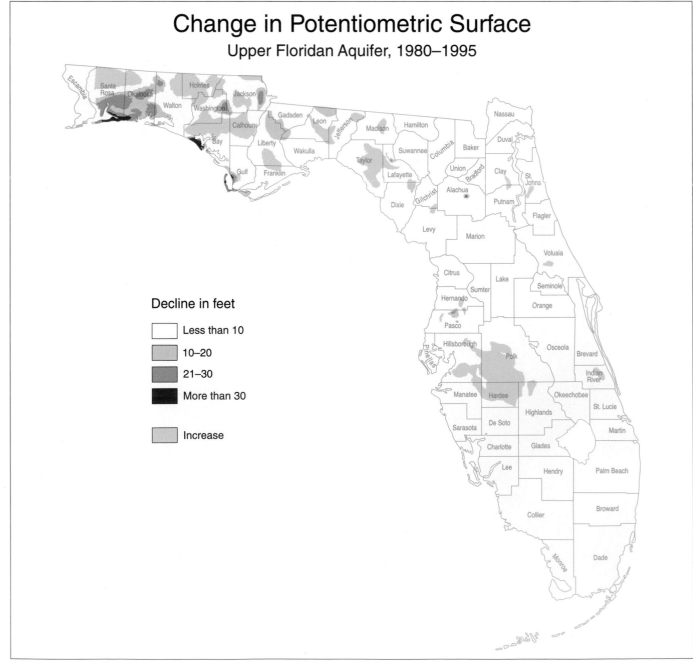

Change in Potentiometric Surface
Upper Floridan Aquifer, 1980–1995

Decline in feet
- Less than 10
- 10–20
- 21–30
- More than 30

- Increase

public supply, although Polk County withdrawals also include large amounts of water for phosphate mining.

To assess the impact of groundwater withdrawals and pumping on the water supply in an aquifer, periodic measurements are made of water levels in wells. These water levels are measured at various intervals, but measurements are made at least once every five years in a large group of wells in the Upper Floridan aquifer to assess current water levels and to monitor changes over time. In some wells, water levels are measured over long time periods, and graphs can be prepared showing long-term changes in water levels. Groundwater levels decline when wells are pumped and rise when pumping is reduced. Water levels also respond to recharge from rainfall, droughts, and seasonal changes in water demands for drainage, irriga-

tion, public supply, and industry. Irrigation is the largest user of groundwater in Florida and usage varies seasonally and annually in relation to the amount of rainfall. In areas with increased groundwater pumping, water levels have declined over time. When pumping ceases or is reduced substantially, water levels can recover to former levels.

Examples of seasonal variations and declines over time are seen in the series of graphs showing water levels in six wells, mostly in the Upper Floridan aquifer, from 1945 to 1995. Seasonal variations are seen in each of the water level graphs. In Columbia County, where water demand is not great, no long-term major declines in water level are apparent. Water levels vary by about 20 feet, probably in response to periods of high and low rainfall amounts, rather than in response to pumping.

Water Level Fluctuations in Selected Wells

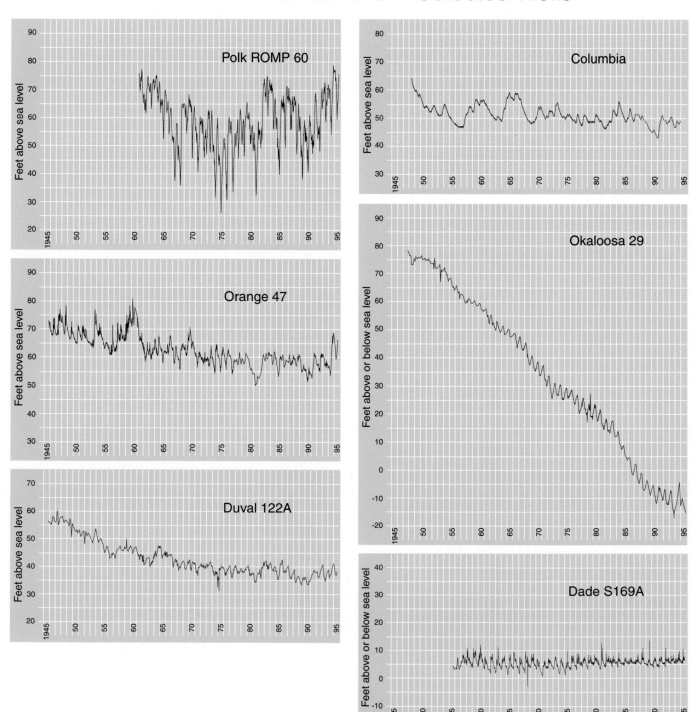

61

Long-term effects of pumping in northeastern Florida are shown in the graph for Duval County. Pumping there is primarily for public supply and industrial supply and has tended to increase over the last several decades. The water levels exhibited a long-term decline of about 20 feet with short periods of rise associated with recharge and reduction in pumping. Most of this decline occurred prior to 1980, and water levels have been relatively unchanged since that time. Pumping from the Upper Floridan aquifer was highest in northeastern parts of the state around 1970 but has declined since then. In Orange County, groundwater withdrawals are substantial and have continued to increase over the years because of agricultural irrigation and large increases in population in the Orlando metropolitan area. Water levels have declined about 10 feet in 50 years.

A different situation has occurred in Okaloosa County because of much lower transmissivity of the Upper Floridan aquifer and tighter confining units that overlie the aquifer. In the well shown in Okaloosa County, water levels have declined over 80 feet from 1945 to 1995 and the seasonal variation is apparent. This decline in long-term water levels has been the result primarily of a gradual increase in pumping. The decline appears to be leveling off in the 1990s.

Water use in Polk County has been dominated by withdrawals for commercial/industrial uses (phosphate mining) and agricultural irrigation. Overall water use peaked in the early 1970s, and recent use has been similar to the use in the mid-1960s. Groundwater levels shown in Polk County reflect these changes in water use: water levels declined about 20 feet from 1960 to about the mid-1970s and then have risen since that time.

Groundwater levels can fluctuate in response to groundwater management activities, such as control of the discharge in canals in southeastern Florida. The water levels in the Biscayne aquifer in Dade County near Homestead show seasonal changes of as much as eight feet in the early years before water-management control was fully effective, whereas in recent years seasonal changes have been about 4 feet. In general, construction and control of drainage canals have lowered the high seasonal groundwater levels and raised the low seasonal groundwater levels near the coast. Also, despite experiencing large withdrawals in a concentrated area, the Biscayne aquifer in Dade County has not exhibited noticeable declines in water levels. Management of water withdrawals and the extremely high permeability and high recharge rate for the Biscayne aquifer are probably responsible for the lack of decline in water levels.

Saltwater encroachment into groundwater supplies caused by large groundwater withdrawals is a concern in Florida, and of most concern in coastal areas. Saltwater encroachment into freshwater aquifers has several possible mechanisms, including the presence of pockets of relict seawater in the aquifers; lateral movement of saltwater in coastal areas; upconing of saltwater from deeper zones below the pumping zone; upward leakage of saltwater from deeper zones through uncased or improperly constructed wells; upward leakage of saltwater from deeper zones through breached confining units or through joints, faults, or collapse features; and through abandoned or improperly plugged exploratory holes drilled for testing for the presence of petroleum and other minerals and aggregates. These mechanisms are exacerbated by the pumping of large amounts of groundwater. Studies have been done to determine the extent of saltwater encroachment in northeastern, southeastern, southwestern, and west central parts of Florida. Construction of canals and control structures has helped control saltwater encroachment in southeastern Florida. Other parts of the state have not been as strongly impacted by saltwater encroachment.

Despite concerns about groundwater quality and quantity, declining water levels in some areas, and saltwater encroachment, the Upper Floridan aquifer has large areas that contain large quantities of high quality water for public supplies. This includes areas where the aquifer is thick, transmissivities are high, recharge amounts are large, and water quality is unaffected by saltwater encroachment. Because many of these areas include places where the aquifer is unconfined and karst features such as sinkholes and springs occur, these areas can be extremely vulnerable to contamination from surface sources. Potential sources of contamination include waste disposal impoundments, underground storage tanks, drainage wells, septic tanks, landfills, hazardous waste sites, and agricultural chemicals.

REFERENCES

A source for a map or figure has a number in parentheses following the entry. This number refers to the page in the atlas for which the source was used.

Allen, T.W. 1987. "Hydrogeology of the Holmes, Jackson and Washington Counties Area, Florida." Master's thesis, Florida State University, Tallahassee.

Berndt, M.P, and B.G. Katz. 1992. *Hydrochemistry of the Surficial and Intermediate Aquifer Systems in Florida*. U.S. Geological Survey Water Resources Investigations Report 91-4186. Tallahassee, Florida.

Bush, P.W., and R.H. Johnston. 1988. *Ground-water Hydraulics, Regional Flow, and Ground-water Development of the Floridan Aquifer System in Florida and Parts of Georgia, South Carolina, and Alabama*. U.S. Geological Survey Professional Paper 140 3-C. Reston, Virginia (map, 53)

Chen, C.S. 1965. *The Regional Lithostratigraphic Analysis of Paleocene and Eocene Rocks of Florida*. Florida Geological Survey Bulletin 45. Tallahassee, Florida.

Clark, M.W., and Schmidt, W. 1982. *Shallow Stratigraphy of Okaloosa County and Vicinity, Florida*. Florida Geological Survey Report of Investigations 92. Tallahassee, Florida.

Cooke, C.W. 1945. "Geology of Florida." *Florida Geological Survey Bulletin 29*.

Conover, C.S. 1973. *Florida's Water Resources*. Institute of Food and Agricultural Sciences, University of Florida. The Dare Report-1973, Pub 11. Gainesville.

Dall, W.H., and G.D. Harris. 1892. *Correlation Papers—The Neocene of North America*. U.S. Geological Survey Bulletin No. 84.

DuBar, J.R. 1974. *Summary of the Neogene Stratigraphy of Southern Florida*. Logan: Utah State University Press.

Florida Geological Survey. 1986. *Hydrogeological Units of Florida*. Special Publication No. 28. (chart, 39 modified from)

Franks, B.J., ed. 1982. *Principal Aquifers in Florida*. U.S. Geological Survey Water Resources Investigations Open-File Report 82-255. Tallahassee, Florida. (potentiometric surface map 1961–1980, 60)

Health, R.C., and C.S. Conover. 1981. *Hydrologic Almanac of Florida*. U.S. Geological Survey Open-File Report 81-1107. Tallahassee, Florida.

Healy, H.G. 1975. *Potentiometric Surface of the Floridan Aquifer in Florida, May 1980*. Florida Bureau of Geology Map Series 104. Tallahassee. (map, 60)

Heath, R.C. 1987. *Basic Groundwater Hydrology*. U.S. Geological Survey Water-Supply Paper 2220. Reston, Virginia.

Hendry, C.W., Jr., and Yon, J.W., Jr. 1967. "Stratigraphy of Upper Miocene Miccosukee Formation, Jefferson and Leon Counties, Florida." *American Association of Petroleum Geologists Bulletin* 51:250-256.

Hoffmeister, J.E. 1974. *Land from the Sea*. Coral Gables: University of Miami Press.

_____, K.W. Stockman, and H.G. Multer. 1967. "Miami Limestone of Florida and its Recent Bahamian Counterpart." *Geological Society of America Bulletin* 78.

_____, and H.G. Multer. 1968. "Geology and Origin of the Florida Keys." *Geological Survey of America Bulletin* 79:1487-1502.

Huddlestun, P.F. 1988. *A Revision of the Lithostratigraphic Units of the Coastal Plain of Georgia*. Georgia Geological Survey Bulletin 104.

Irwin, G.A., and J.L. Bonds. 1988. "Florida Groundwater Quality," In *National Water Summary 1986—Hydrologic Events and Groundwater Quality*. U.S. Geological Survey Water-Supply Paper 2325. pp. 205–214. Reston, Virginia.

Irwin, G.A., R.T. Kirkland, and J.B. Pruitt. 1985. *Quality of Groundwater Used for Public Supply in Florida, 1983–84*. U.S. Geological Survey Open File Report 84-804. 1 sheet. Tallahassee, Florida.

Katz, B.G. 1992. *Hydrochemistry of the Upper Floridan Aquifer, Florida*. U.S. Geological Survey Water Resources Investigations Report 91-4196. Tallahassee, Florida. (maps, 55)

Katz, B.G., and R.S. DeHan. 1996. *The Suwannee River Basin Pilot Study: Issues for Watershed Management in Florida*. U.S. Geological Survey FS080-96.

Katz, B.G., and A.F. Choquette. 1991. "Aqueous Geochemistry of the Sand-and-Gravel Aquifer, Northwest Florida." *Groundwater* 29:47–55.

Knapp, M.S., W.S. Burns, and T.S. Sharp. 1986. *Preliminary Assessment of the Groundwater Resources of Western Collier County, Florida*. South Florida Water Management District Technical Publication 86–1.

Maddox, G.L., J.M. Lloyd, T.M. Scott, S.B. Upchurch, and R. Copeland. eds. 1992. *Florida's Groundwater Quality Monitoring Program Background Hydrogeochemistry*. Florida Geological Survey Special Publication No. 34. Tallahassee, Florida.

Mahon, G.L., A.F. Choquette, and A.A. Sepulveda. 1997. *Potentiometric Surface of the Upper Floridan Aquifer in Florida, May 1995*. Florida Geological Survey Map Series No. 140. Tallahassee, Florida. (map, 60)

Marella, R.L. 1995. *Water-use Data by Category, County, and Water Management District in Florida, 1950–90*. U.S. Geological Survey Open-File Report 94-521. Tallahassee, Florida.

Marsh, O.T. 1966. *Geology of Escambia and Santa Rosa Counties*. Florida Geological Survey Bulletin 46.

McGuinness, C.L. 1963. *The Role of Groundwater in the National Water Situation*. U.S. Geological Survey Water-Supply Paper 1800. Reston, Virginia.

Miller, J.A. 1986. *Hydrogeologic Framework of the Floridan Aquifer System in Florida and Parts of Georgia, Alabama and South Carolina*. U.S. Geological Survey Professional Paper 1403-B.

Miller, J.A. 1990. *Groundwater Atlas of the U.S., Segment 6, Alabama, Florida, Georgia, and South Carolina*. U.S. Geological Survey Hydrologic Investigations Atlas 730-G. Reston, Virginia. (maps, 38, 48, 50, 51, 52; graphics, 45, 47, 48, 49; figures 59)

Parker, G.G. 1951. "Geologic and Hydrologic Factors in the Perennial Yield of the Biscayne Aquifer." *American Water Works Association Journal* 43:810-843.

Peek, H.M. 1951. *Cessation of Flow of Kissengen Spring in Polk County*. Florida Bureau of Geology Report of Investigations 7, Part 3. Tallahassee, Florida.

Puri, H.S., and R.O. Vernon. 1964. *Summary of the Geology of Florida*. Florida Geological Survey Special Publication 5 (Revised). Tallahassee, Florida.

Radell, M.J., and B.G. Katz. 1991. *Major-Ion and Selected Trace-Metal Chemistry of the Biscayne Aquifer, Southeast Florida*. U.S. Geological Survey Water-Resources Investigations Report 91-4009. Tallahassee, Florida.

Schmidt, W. 1984. *Neogene Stratigraphy and Geologic History of the Apalachicola Embayment, Florida*. Florida Geological Survey Bulletin 58. Tallahassee, Florida.

Schmidt, W., and C. Coe. 1978. *Regional Structure and Stratigraphy of the Limestone Outcrop Belt in the Florida Panhandle*. Florida Geological Survey Report of Investigation 86. Tallahassee, Florida.

Schroeder, M.C. 1954. "Stratigraphy of the Outcropping Formations in Southern Florida." Southeastern Geological Society, 8th Field Trip Guidebook:18-48.

Scott, T.M. 1988a. *The Lithostratigraphy of the Hawthorn Group (Miocene) of Florida*. Florida Geological Survey Bulletin 59. Tallahassee, Florida.

Sinclair, W.C., and J.W. Stewart, 1985. *Sinkhole Type, Development, and Distribution in Florida*. Florida Bureau of Geology Map Series 110. Tallahassee, Florida. (map, 58)

Sinclair, W.C., J.W. Stewart, R.L. Knutilla, A.E. Gilboy, and R.L. Miller, 1985. *Types, Features, and Occurrence of Sinkholes in the Karst of West Central Florida*. U.S. Geological Survey Water-Resources Investigations Report 85-4126. Tallahassee, Florida.

Smith, K.R., and K.M. Adams. 1988. *Ground Water Resource Assessment of Hendry County, Florida*. South Florida Water Management District Technical Publication 8812.

Southeastern Geological Society. 1986. *Hydrogeological Units of Florida*. Florida Geological Survey Special Publication 28.

Spechler, R.M. 1994. *Saltwater Intrusion and Quality of Water in the Floridan Aquifer System*. U.S. Geological Survey Water-Resources Investigations Report 92-4174. Tallahassee, Florida.

Spechler, R.M., and D.M. Schiffer. 1995. *Springs of Florida*. U.S. Geological Survey Fact Sheet FS-151-95. Tallahassee, Florida. (map, 57)

Stanley, S.M. 1966. "Paleoecology and Diagenesis of Key Largo Limestone, Florida." *American Association of Petroleum Geologists Bulletin* 50:1927-1947.

Stewart, J.W. 1980. *Areas of natural recharge to the Florida Aquifer in Florida*. Prepared by the U.S. Geological Survey in cooperation with the Florida Department of Environmental Regulation. Florida Geological Survey Map Series 98. Tallahassee, Florida.

Trapp, H. 1975. *Preliminary report November 1973, Hydrology of the Sand-and-Gravel Aquifer in Central and Southern Escambia County, Florida*. U.S. Geological Survey Open-File Report FL-74027. Tallahassee, Florida.

Vecchioli, J., and D.W. Foose. 1985. *Florida Groundwater Resources, in National Water Summary 1984—Hydrologic Events, Selected Water-Quality Trends, and Groundwater Resources*. U.S. Geological Survey Water-Supply Paper 2275. p. 173-178. Reston, Virginia.

Wagner, J.R. 1982. "Hydrogeology of the Northwest Florida Water Management District." In G. Fisher, ed. *Ground Water in Florida*. Proceedings of the First Annual Symposium on Florida Hydrogeology. Northwest Florida Water Management District. Public Information Bulletin 82-2.

White, W.A. 1970. "Geomorphology of the Florida Peninsula." *Florida Geological Survey Bulletin* 51.

Winter, T.C., J.W. Harvey, O.L. Franke, and W.M. Alley. In press. *Ground Water and Surface Water—A Single Resource*. U.S. Geological Survey Circular 1139. Reston, Virginia.

Wright, A.P. 1974. *Environmental Geology and Hydrology of the Tampa Area, Florida*. Florida Bureau of Geology Special Publication 19. Tallahassee, Florida. (figures, 58)

63

4

SURFACE WATER

Rivers, lakes, and wetlands are an integral part of the physical and human landscape. They are important for their resources, in addition to their relation to settlement, industry, navigation, and agriculture. Flow and form of rivers and lakes and adjacent wetlands vary spatially and temporally in response to both natural and human factors. Understanding these variations is essential for a variety of concerns, including flood control, engineering structure design, water supply, biotic habitat, navigation, hydroelectric power, and recreation.

Drainage Systems in Florida

A drainage basin is an area on the land surface from which water flows to a stream or lake. Drainage basins are separated from adjacent basins by topographic divides. Portions of drainage basins of several large rivers in Florida are in Alabama and Georgia. Local topography controls the drainage direction and patterns. For management purposes the state has been divided into five surface water regions: the Northwest,

Joann Mossa

Suwannee River, St. Johns River, Southwest, and Kissimmee-Everglades, generally corresponding to directions of surface water flow.

Geology as well as topography influences drainage systems and surface waters. Surficial sediments in Florida are both clastic (derived from weathering of rocks) and carbonate (derived from precipitation of carbonate minerals in solution and biologic processes). Where carbonate sediments are at or near the surface, karst topography typically develops. The landscape is characterized by sinkholes, caves, and underground drainage formed by dissolution of the carbonate sediments. Drainage patterns of karst landscapes are often characterized as disjointed, because rivers and creeks are not always continuous on the land surface and may disappear underground in local sinks or depressions. Karst areas generally have fewer large streams and tributaries than non-karst areas, but better developed underground drainage, such as caves and other underground conduits. Karst areas of Florida have more streams than karst areas elsewhere, partly because of high water tables, low topographic relief, and proximity to sea level. Geology also influences the subsurface drainage, and the groundwater basin contributing to a stream may be quite different from the topographic basin.

Some portions of Florida are poorly drained; that is, there are few or no channels, even though water flows across the surface. Extensive marsh or swamp areas, where the surface is almost flat, have poorly defined drainage. In Florida poorly defined drainage and disjointed drainage are commonly mixed and cannot be separated on a statewide map.

Joann Mossa

Hillsborough River

Topography

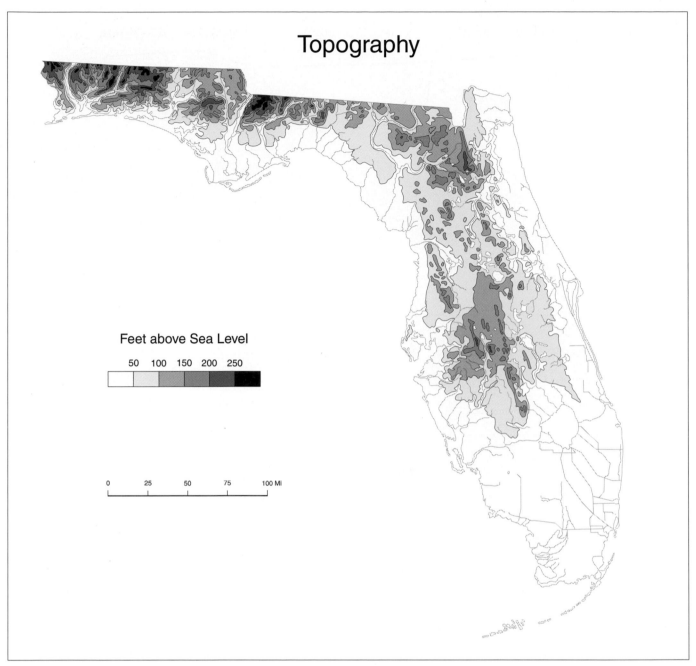

Feet above Sea Level

50 100 150 200 250

0   25   50   75   100 Mi

Soil type affects many aspects of drainage. Soil type is strongly influenced by geology, and different materials have differing drainage characteristics. Soils of the Central Ridge and Western Highlands are generally well drained, whereas soils of the Flatwoods and Coastal Lands and those of organic and recent limestone origin are somewhat poorly to very poorly drained, which causes differences in storage potential and the amount of ponding.

Climatic factors, especially inputs of precipitation and losses to evapotranspiration, are the most important influences on spatial and temporal variations in surface hydrology. Precipitation is strongly dominated by rainfall in Florida and contributes to flow in a stream through several pathways. Rainfall can be intercepted by vegetation and buildings, puddle, flow overland as a thin sheet of water, infiltrate the soil, or fall onto the surface of lakes and streams. A substantial proportion of precipitation is evapotranspired in Florida, especially in areas with dense vegetation. Water storage in puddles or depressions is generally temporary, as it ultimately evaporates or infiltrates the soil. Overland flow occurs when the soil is saturated or

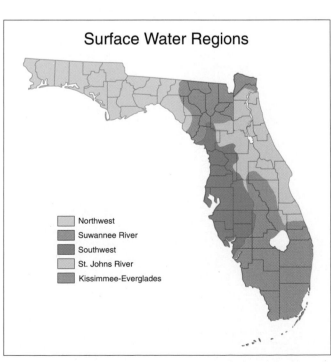

Surface Water Regions

- Northwest
- Suwannee River
- Southwest
- St. Johns River
- Kissimmee-Everglades

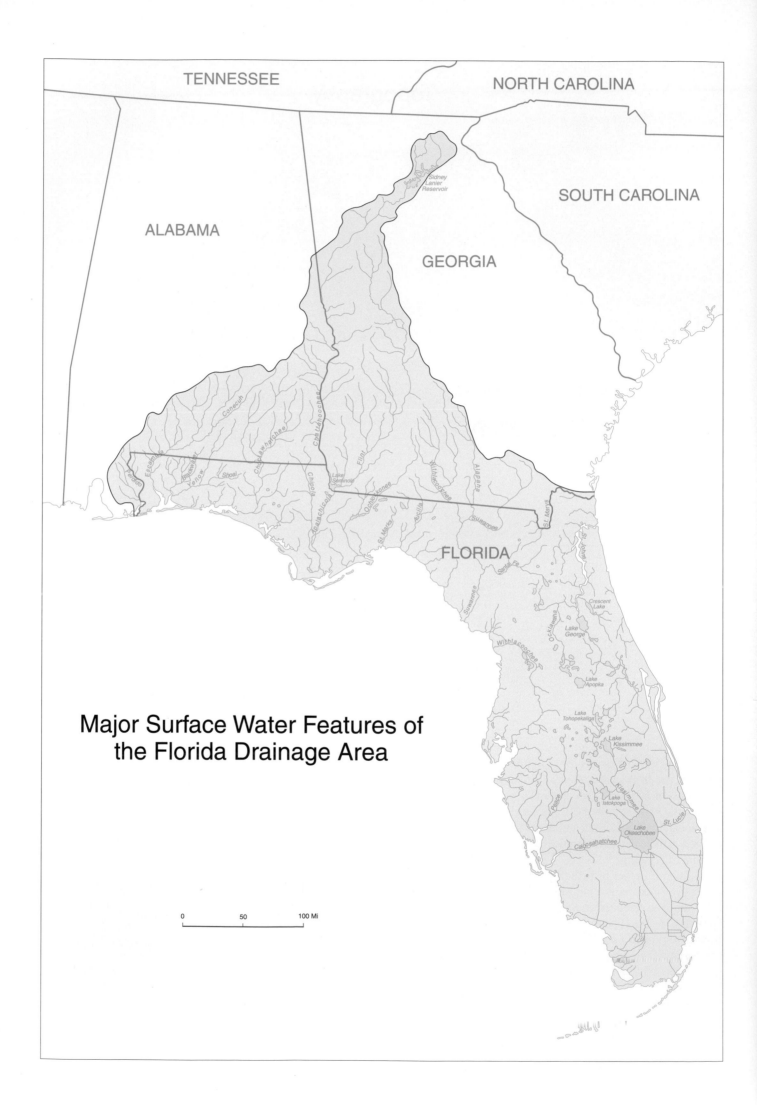

TENNESSEE

NORTH CAROLINA

ALABAMA

SOUTH CAROLINA

GEORGIA

Sidney Lanier Reservoir

Conecuh

Chattahoochee

Perdido

Escambia

Blackwater

Yellow

Shoal

Choctawhatchee

Chipola

Apalachicola

Flint

Lake Seminole

Ochlockonee

St. Marks

Aucilla

Withlacoochee

Alapaha

Suwannee

St. Marys

FLORIDA

Suwannee

Santa Fe

St. Johns

Withlacoochee

Ocklawaha

Crescent Lake

Lake George

Lake Apopka

Lake Tohopekaliga

Lake Kissimmee

Kissimmee

Peace

Lake Istokpoga

St. Lucie

Lake Okeechobee

Caloosahatchee

66

Major Surface Water Features of the Florida Drainage Area

0   50   100 Mi

Drainage Basins and Divides

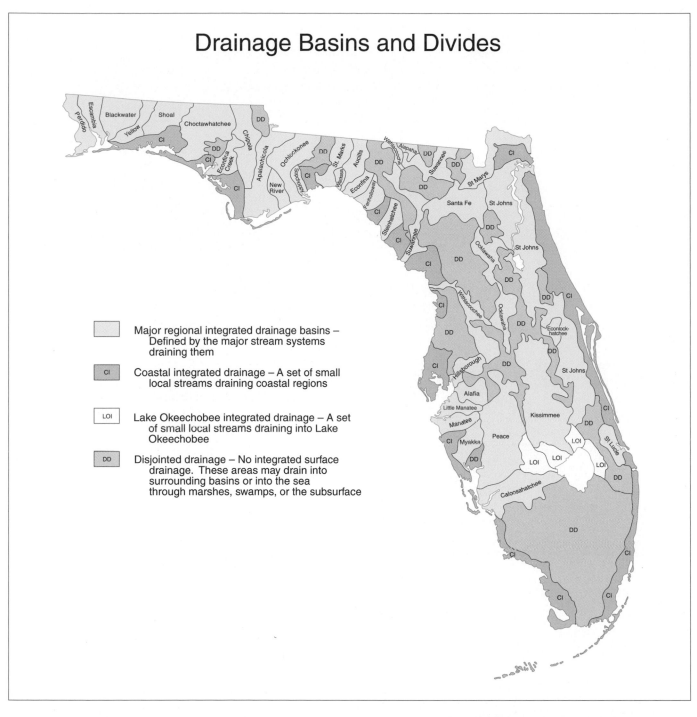

Major regional integrated drainage basins – Defined by the major stream systems draining them

CI — Coastal integrated drainage – A set of small local streams draining coastal regions

LOI — Lake Okeechobee integrated drainage – A set of small local streams draining into Lake Okeechobee

DD — Disjointed drainage – No integrated surface drainage. These areas may drain into surrounding basins or into the sea through marshes, swamps, or the subsurface

67

when the precipitation rate exceeds the infiltration rate. It usually lasts for a brief period during and following rainfall events, unless the ground surface is not very permeable. Soil permeability also influences percolation, or downward movement toward the water table. In permeable parts of the unsaturated zone, water moves downward, but in less permeable parts, infiltrated water will move horizontally, a process known as interflow.

Rainfall is generally abundant in Florida, but varies annually and seasonally. The details of these variations are discussed in the climate chapter. The statewide annual average is approximately 53 inches, and specific locations average from 40 inches in Key West to 69 inches at Wewahitchka in the panhandle. Seasonal distribution also varies, with the northern portion of the state having proportionately more winter precipitation associated with fronts and the southern part having proportionately more summer precipitation associated with thunderstorms.

Two ways in which the flow in streams is measured are discharge and runoff. Discharge is the volume of water pass-

Limestone banks, Suwannee River

Joann Mossa

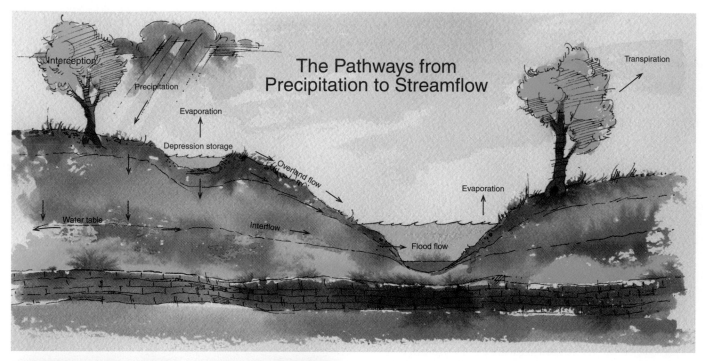

The Pathways from Precipitation to Streamflow

Interception

Precipitation

Transpiration

Evaporation

Depression storage

Overland flow

Evaporation

Water table

interflow

Flood flow

Silver River

Joann Mossa

ing through a particular cross section in a unit of time, generally measured in cubic feet or meters per second. Discharge is most often used to distinguish the size of rivers and to characterize temporal variations in flow. The stream flow is comprised of different sources: overland flow, interflow, and groundwater contributions or baseflow. Overland flow tends to produce a fairly rapid influence on stream flow, because water runs across the surface more quickly than though the ground. If the basin is small, rain falling on the basin surface might reach a stream via overland flow in minutes to hours. It could take days in a larger basin. Interflow has an intermediate response time, compared to overland flow and baseflow, be-

Major Rivers of Florida

River	Region	Length (mi.)	Basin Area (mi.[2])	Discharges to
Coastal				
Apalachicola[1]	Northwest	524	19,600	Apalachicola Bay
Suwannee[1]	Suwannee	80	9,950	Gulf of Mexico
St. Johns[2]	St. Johns	273	9,168	Atlantic Ocean
Choctawhatchee[3]	Northwest	230	4,646	Choctawhatchee Bay
Escambia[3]	Northwest	240	4,233	Escambia Bay
Peace[2]	Southwest	133	2,403	Charlotte Harbor
Ochlockonee[1]	Northwest	206	2,250	Ochlockonee Bay
Withlacoochee[2]	Southwest	138	2,035	Withlacoochee Bay
St. Marys[1]	Suwannee	127	1,480	Cumberland Sound
Yellow[3]	Northwest	110	1,365	Blackwater Bay
Perdido[3]	Northwest	68	925	Perdido Bay
St. Marks[2]	Northwest	37	871	Apalachee Bay
Blackwater[3]	Northwest	62	860	Blackwater Bay
Tributary				
Ocklawaha[2]	St. Johns	148	2,718	St. Johns River
Kissimmee[2]	Kissimmee-Everglades	170	2,300	Lake Okeechobee
Withlacoochee[1]	Suwannee	120	2,290	Suwannee River
Alapaha[1]	Suwannee	130	1,840	Suwannee River
Santa Fe[2]	Suwannee	87	1,384	Suwannee River
Chipola[3]	Northwest	115	1,237	Apalachicola River
Shoal[2]	Northwest	50	499	Yellow River

[1]Most distant source in Georgia
[2]Most distant source in Florida
[3]Most distant source in Alabama

Difference between Annual Rainfall and Annual Potential Evaporation

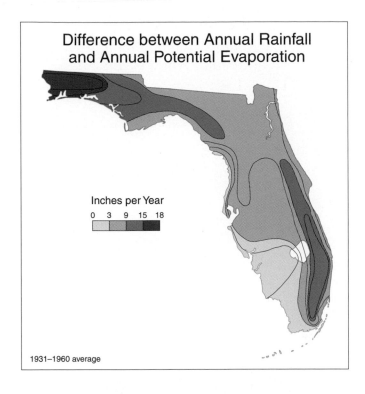

Inches per Year

0   3   9   15   18

1931–1960 average

Regional Runoff

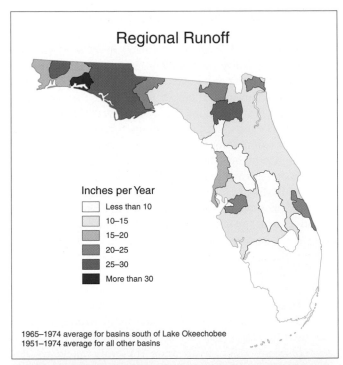

Inches per Year

- ☐ Less than 10
- 10–15
- 15–20
- 20–25
- 25–30
- More than 30

1965–1974 average for basins south of Lake Okeechobee
1951–1974 average for all other basins

Three Components to Stream Flow

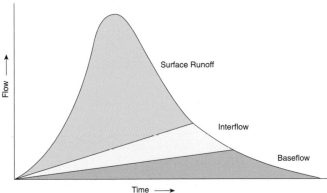

Surface Runoff

Interflow

Baseflow

Flow →

Time →

Channel bottom of the Santa Fe River   Joann Mossa

cause it generally has an intermediate length or pathway, with the response time being dependent upon the basin size, geology, and other factors. The baseflow or groundwater contributions tends to take longer to influence stream flow and is a relatively consistent source of water that allows streams to flow through extended periods of low rainfall. In rivers in karst terrain, groundwater is often contributed to streams via springs of varying sizes. In times of high river flow, springs may become sinks, drawing stream flow into the ground.

Runoff is depth of water uniformly distributed over a drainage basin, computed as the discharge divided by the drainage area. Runoff quantities and rates are influenced by climatic elements, slope, geology, land use, and other factors. Flat, poorly drained lands retain water and allow for more evapotranspiration and infiltration, thus yielding a low runoff per unit area. Permeability, soil moisture content, and the distribution of precipitation and evaporation also affect runoff. Long-term stream flow records show that local average annual runoff varies across the state, ranging from less than 10 to more than 30 inches (Hughes 1978).

Chassahowitzka River   Joann Mossa

69

Rivers and Their Classification

From a regional perspective, several rivers in Florida are moderate to large in terms of their discharge and drainage area. The largest rivers, as measured by discharge, are the Apalachicola, Suwannee, and St. Johns. Even the largest rivers in Florida have only a fraction of the flow of the continent's and world's largest rivers. Average runoff computations show regional variations throughout the state, with the northwest rivers having the highest discharge per unit of drainage area.

Planners, environmental scientists, and engineers require an understanding of the long-term and annual hydrology to be able to predict the likelihood of floods and droughts and their potential impact on humans and development. Long-term estimates of the seasonal variation in stream flow show considerable variation from the northern to southern part of the state. In the northernmost parts of the state, stream flow is highest in the winter and early spring months. In the southern part of the state, stream flow is highest in the summer and fall.

Several systems, developed primarily by ecologists, have been used for categorizing Florida rivers (Nordlie 1990). The most commonly used classification of Florida waterways, developed by Beck (1965), includes five categories: sand-bottomed streams, calcareous streams, swamp-and-bog streams, large rivers, and canals. Because of problems of mixing criteria, such as materials with size, setting, and human modification, this chapter characterizes Florida natural waterways as predominantly alluvial or predominantly karst. Canals and modified waterways are described separately. Yet this description is also general, as not all rivers in Florida are comprised exclusively of alluvium or carbonate bedrock. Some are transitional and have both materials.

Rivers are three-dimensional, but are typically displayed from various two-dimensional perspectives. Maps show a planform perspective, or comparison of width across the channel

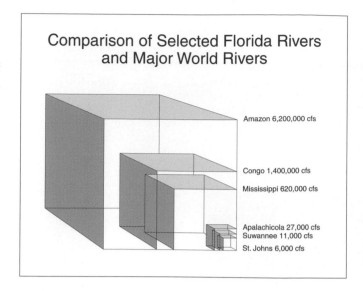

Comparison of Selected Florida Rivers and Major World Rivers

Amazon 6,200,000 cfs

Congo 1,400,000 cfs

Mississippi 620,000 cfs

Apalachicola 27,000 cfs
Suwannee 11,000 cfs
St. Johns 6,000 cfs

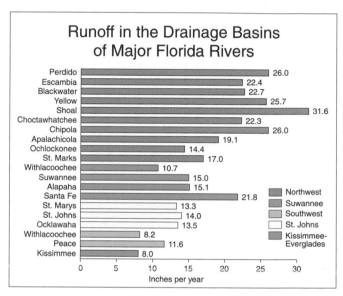

Runoff in the Drainage Basins of Major Florida Rivers

River	Inches per year
Perdido	26.0
Escambia	22.4
Blackwater	22.7
Yellow	25.7
Shoal	31.6
Choctawhatchee	22.3
Chipola	26.0
Apalachicola	19.1
Ochlockonee	14.4
St. Marks	17.0
Withlacoochee	10.7
Suwannee	15.0
Alapaha	15.1
Santa Fe	21.8
St. Marys	13.3
St. Johns	14.0
Ocklawaha	13.5
Withlacoochee	8.2
Peace	11.6
Kissimmee	8.0

Legend: Northwest, Suwannee, Southwest, St. Johns, Kissimmee-Everglades

Discharge of Major Florida Rivers

River	Gauging Site (Nearest Town)	Miles Above Mouth	Average Annual Discharge (cfs)	Average Annual Runoff (in.)	Drainage Area Above Site (sq. mi.)
Coastal					
Apalachicola	Blountstown	78	24,768	19.11	17,600
Suwannee	Wilcox	33	10,635	14.98	9,640
Choctawhatchee	Bruce	21	7,198	22.29	4,384
Escambia	Century	52	6,300	22.43	3,817
St. Johns	Deland	142	3,158	14.00	3,066
Ochlockonee	Bloxham	65	1,796	14.36	1,700
Yellow	Milligan	40	1,181	25.68	624
Peace	Arcadia	36	1,170	11.61	1,367
Withlacoochee	Holder	38	1,105	8.22	1,825
Perdido	Barrineau Park	27	754	25.99	394
St. Marys	Macclenny	100	683	13.25	700
St. Marks	Newport	14	669	16.96	535
Blackwater	Baker	35	342	22.66	205
Tributary					
Ocklawaha	Conner	51	1,186	13.46	1,196
Alapaha	Jennings	21	1,873	15.14	1,690
Withlacoochee	Pinetta	22	1,672	10.72	2,120
Santa Fe	Fort White	18	1,625	21.79	1,017
Chipola	Altha	54	1,495	25.98	781
Kissimmee	Okeechobee	8	1,409	8.00	2,300
Shoal	Crestview	7	1,104	31.60	474

Historic Mean Recurrence of High and Low Stream Flows

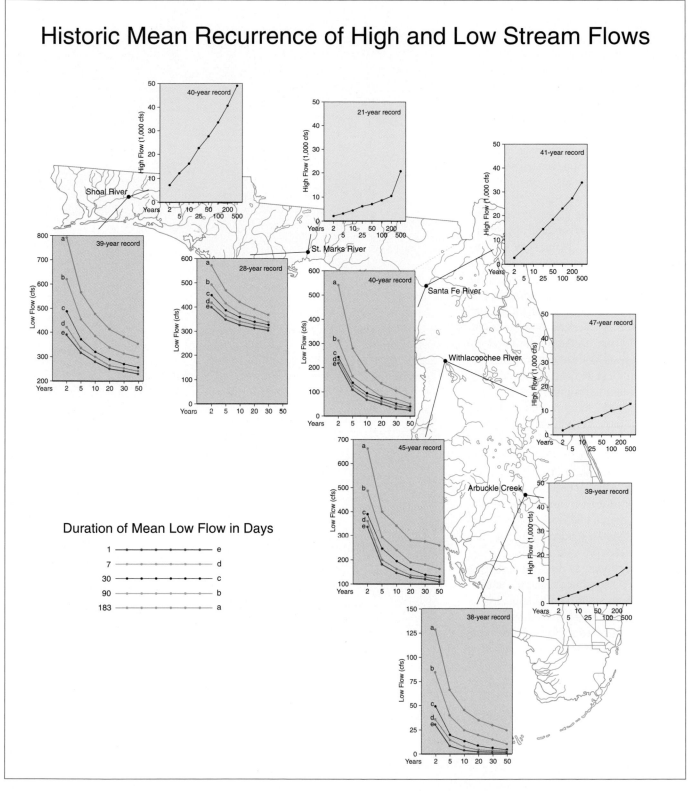

Duration of Mean Low Flow in Days

1	e
7	d
30	c
90	b
183	a

with distance along the valley or channel. A cross-section compares elevation (generally bed) with width or distance across the channel. Longitudinal profiles show the elevation of the water or bed surface with distance downstream. From the planform perspective, it is obvious that rivers have differing forms, varying in their sinuosity (ratio of channel length to valley length) and the number of channels.

Alluvial rivers occur in valleys surrounded by their own sedimentary materials and adjust their morphology according to discharges and the sediment sizes and loads present. Alluvial rivers typically develop features, such as meanders, channel bars, and islands, that are uncharacteristic of rivers exclusively in bedrock. Most alluvial rivers in sand and gravel have

a series of alternating deeps (pools) and shallows (riffles), with pool-to-pool spacing averaging six times the channel width. They typically are dominated by suspended load transport, especially in low gradient settings as Florida, and experience erosion and deposition along the channel, especially during and following floods. Alluvial rivers are common in the panhandle of Florida, traversing the geologic units comprised of clastic sediments. Some of the larger alluvial rivers in Florida include the Escambia, Choctawhatchee, Apalachicola, and Ochlockonee.

In Florida, alluvial rivers typically have meandering or anastomosing patterns, with multiple channels that are separated by densely vegetated islands. Because elevations in

Florida do not exceed 350 feet, rivers have low gradients and thus low energy. Most profiles are concave upward, with steeper headwaters that decrease in gradient approaching the bays or gulf, with local knickpoints associated with changes in geology. Some tributary stream profiles are locally quite pronounced, forming linear valleys with large gradients termed steepheads where some drainage networks have formed by groundwater seeping in highly permeable sands (Schumm et al. 1995).

Overland flow is generally very important in alluvial rivers and the stream hydrographs are relatively flashy (Escambia, Choctawhatchee, and Apalachicola). Even in large rivers, the crest occurs a few days following the precipitation event. Because of the limited delay caused by overland flow contributing much of the discharge during storm events, requests for evacuation in the event of flooding must be heeded immediately.

The stream hydrograph for karst rivers (for example, the Suwannee) is much flatter than those for alluvial rivers. Rivers in karst terrain typically have sinks and springs, and may disappear underground and reemerge for short or long distances. Groundwater input or baseflow contributes appreciably to stream flow, and the material load is dominated by dissolved materials rather than suspended sediments. Surface water-groundwater interactions are often bidirectional, as the river recharges the aquifer during floods, and the aquifer supplies the river during droughts. In rivers in karst terrain, groundwater input or baseflow contributes appreciably to stream flow. Because there is less direct runoff, it

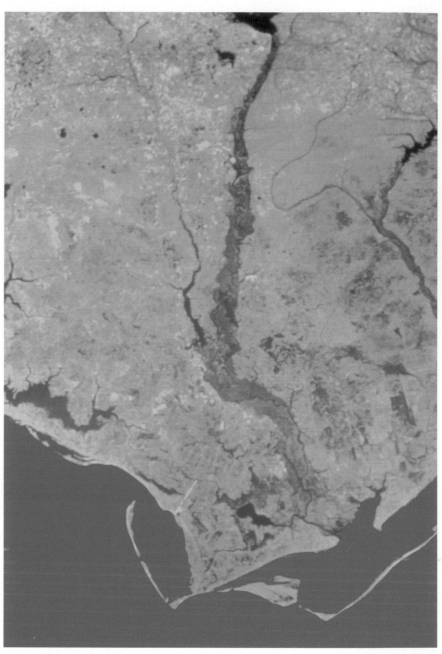

EROS Data Center

72

Flood along the Apalachicola River, February 6, 1977

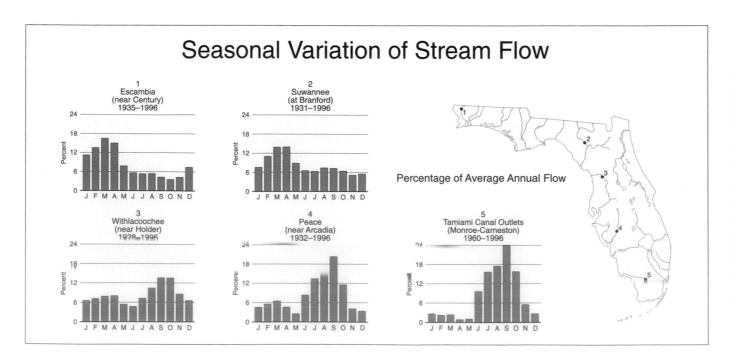

North Florida Rivers, 1990

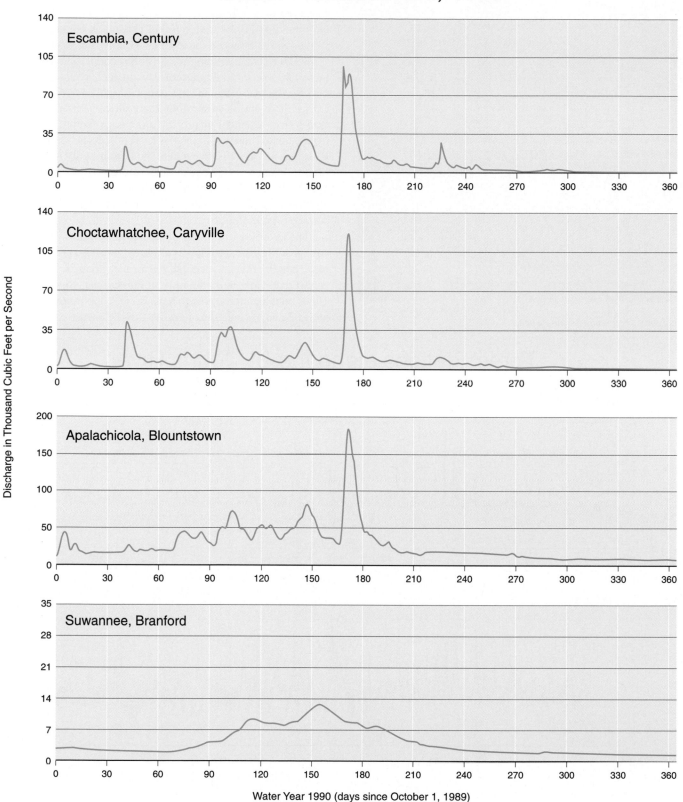

Discharge in Thousand Cubic Feet per Second

Escambia, Century

Choctawhatchee, Caryville

Apalachicola, Blountstown

Suwannee, Branford

Water Year 1990 (days since October 1, 1989)

may take several weeks and even months for a flood to rise and fall, generally allowing ample time for evacuation. However, the flows are also slow to recede, preventing floodplain residents from returning to their homes for weeks to months during periods of high water. Hydrology and valley evolution are strongly dependent upon subsurface voids and relative sea level changes. The larger karst rivers of the panhandle include the Chipola River and Holmes Creek. In peninsular Florida, karst rivers are best developed in the north and include the Suwannee, Alapaha, Withlacoochee, their tributaries, and a number of smaller rivers.

Sinks and springs of varying sizes, largely associated with the presence of carbonate rocks, are numerous along river corridors. Bed surface irregularities associated with springs and sinks occur on large rivers, such as the Suwannee River (U.S. Army Engineer District-Jacksonville 1974, Mossa and Konwinski 1998). Some rivers, such as the Silver and Ichetucknee, are predominantly spring-fed. Others, such as the

St. Johns River at Seminole Ranch

Santa Fe and Alapaha, have well-developed sinks that cause the river to disappear underground and springs that cause it to reemerge some distance downstream for all or part of the year. On the Santa Fe the underground channel is connected with wetland lakes between these points (Ellins et al. 1991).

Some rivers, including the St. Johns and Kissimmee, have large lakes or large depressions along their courses. Consequently, the hydrology of such rivers is highly varied along the river course and is sometimes more characteristic of a lake than a river. Channel offsets are a drainage feature which are in part created and maintained by karst processes. The St. Johns River has an offset course where the river initially turns to the west to reach a valley cut in older, higher terrain, then flows northward for a long distance, possibly in an ancestral valley, and then jogs back to the east to traverse a younger, lower surface (Pirkle 1971).

The hydrology of the St. Johns River is highly varied. Upstream at Melrose, the flow is unidirectional and generally not influenced by tides, with notable seasonal variation. Midstream at DeLand, flow is dominantly unidirectional. Since the late 1950s both locations seem to have smaller maxima and means, and DeLand has had more negative flows. Downstream at Jack-

74

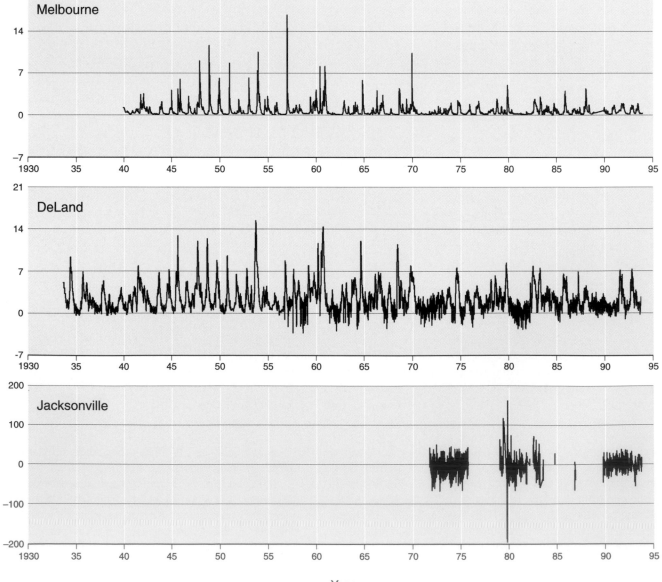

Three Stations along the St. Johns River

sonville, flow is bidirectional with a strong daily variation associated with tides.

Lakes

Florida has thousands of large and small lakes. Of the named lakes exceeding one acre in size, the great majority are less than 50 acres. Most of Florida's lakes average between 7 and 20 feet in depth, although a few sinkhole lakes are hundreds of feet deep (Heath and Conover 1981). About 35 percent of the lakes in Florida are concentrated in four counties of central Florida (Osceola, Orange, Lake, and Polk). Schiffer (1998) characterizes the hydrology and issues regarding lakes in these counties. In addition to Lake Okeechobee, one-fourth of all lakes in Florida are in the Kissimmee River drainage.

Most of the lakes are natural in origin, formed by solution processes where groundwater dissolves carbonate sediments to form cavities which collapse to form depressions. Some solution lakes are nearly circular at the surface and conical in cross section, others are somewhat irregular from several coalescing sinkholes, and others are elongated if formed in a valley where the sinkhole becomes plugged. Many of the solution lakes are enclosed by topographic divides, and drainage into them either evaporates or percolates downward to the groundwater system where it may emerge in an adjacent drainage basin. Lakes also originate from relict sea bottom depressions and erosion and sedimentation processes in rivers (Edminston and Myers 1983). Some Florida lakes have been formed through the emplacement of dams or impoundments to form reservoirs. Other human-made lakes or ponds include rock pits, sand pits, and cooling ponds for large power plants.

Natural lakes vary appreciably in their hydrology, depending on whether they only have subsurface connection, whether streams flow through them, whether streams only flow from the lakes, or whether streams flow into the lake. Lake levels

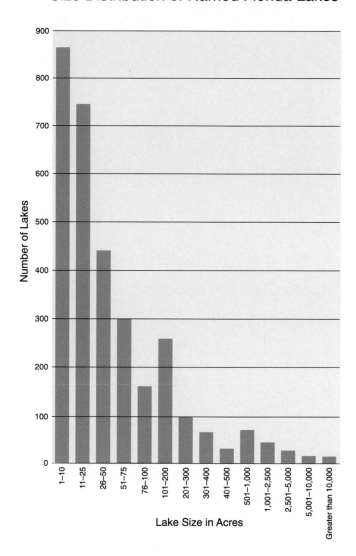

Size Distribution of Named Florida Lakes

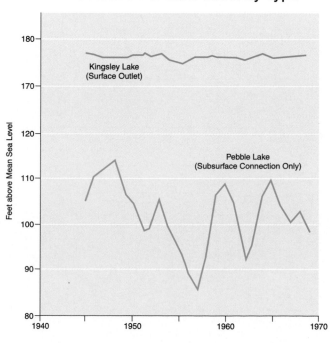

Fluctuation of Lake Level by Type

75

Natural Freshwater Lakes 10 Square Miles or Larger		
Lake	County	Surface area (sq. mi.)
Okeechobee	Glades, Hendry, Martin, Okeechobee, Palm Beach	681.0
George	Lake, Marion, Putnam, Volusia	73.0
Kissimmee	Osceola, Polk	54.2
Apopka	Orange	47.9
Istokpoga	Highlands	43.0
Tsala Apopka	Citrus	30.0
Tohopekaliga	Osceola	29.4
Harris	Lake	27.6
Crescent	Flagler, Putnam	26.8
Orange	Alachua, Marion	20.6
East Tohopekaliga	Osceola	18.7
Griffin	Lake	16.7
Monroe	Seminole, Volusia	13.8
Lochloosa	Alachua	13.7
Eustis	Lake	12.2
Jesup	Seminole	12.2
Weohyakapka	Polk	11.8
Newnans	Alachua	11.5
Hatchineha	Osceola	10.4
Blue Cypress	Indian River, Osceola	10.2

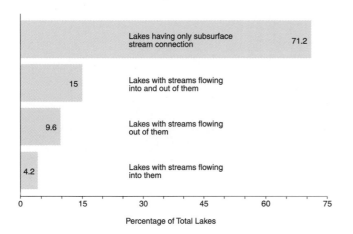

Man-Made Lakes or Impoundments
Six Square Miles or Larger

	County	Surface Area (sq. mi.)
Conservation Areas 3A and 3B	Broward, Dade	914.0
Conservation Area 1	Palm Beach	221.0
Conservation Area 2	Broward	210.0
Lake Seminole	Gadsden, Jackson, Decatur[1], Seminole[1]	58.6
Lake Ocklawaha	Marion, Putnam	16.9
Lake Talquin	Gadsden, Leon	10.7
Dead Lake	Calhoun, Gulf	10.5
Deer Point Lake	Bay	7.3
Lake Rousseau	Citrus, Levy, Marion	6.5

[1]Georgia counties

change in response to direct precipitation, runoff, evaporation, and the exchange between the lake and groundwater. In Florida, the more important influences include seepage by groundwater and, secondly, surface drainage. Most Florida lakes are seepage lakes, and some estimates suggest that as many as 70 percent of the lakes lack overland flows (Palmer 1984). Fluctuations in lakes dominated by seepage correlate with changes in the water table. Fluctuations in lakes that are dominated by drainage, with streams flowing through them, correlate with changes in stream flow. Lakes that are regulated show fairly consistent lake levels except for occasional breakages and stormwater inputs.

Lakes generally show variability annually and seasonally. During periods of below normal rainfall, lake levels begin to drop. They may do so for several years, causing concern for local residents with docks and lakeside businesses. Given time, lake levels generally rebound, and some lakeside residents may complain about too much water. Orange Lake has been through such cycles in recent years. Lake level is not actively regulated, but is influenced by a fixed crest weir on the outlet as there is no outflow, except from evaporation or seepage through the bottom when stages fall below 57.5 feet (Shuman, personal communication). Because slopes are gentle in Florida, vertical changes in water level of a few feet imply horizontal changes in water level of a few hundred feet. The St. Johns

Lakes Classified by Stream Connection

Percentage	Description
71.2	Lakes having only subsurface stream connection
15	Lakes with streams flowing into and out of them
9.6	Lakes with streams flowing out of them
4.2	Lakes with streams flowing into them

Percentage of Total Lakes

Nonregulated Lakes

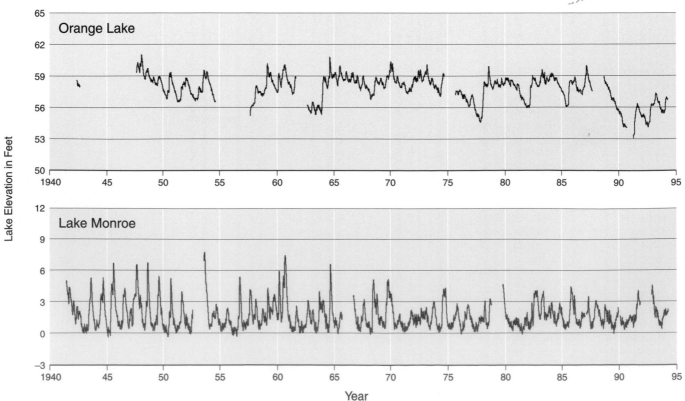

76

River flows through Lake Monroe and several other lakes. Lake levels within the river chain show seasonal fluctuations, related to stream flow variability.

Lakes that are regulated, or impounded for dams, show fairly consistent lake levels, especially in comparison with natural lakes. Variations are mostly associated with occasional breakages, stormwater inputs, and controlled management changes; for example, there was a breakage on Lake Talquin, a reservoir on the Ochlockonee River, in 1959.

Wetlands

Wetlands are the largest component of the state's surface waters in terms of total area. In wetlands, high water tables determine the nature of soil development and the types of plant and animal communities living in the soil and on the surface. The water table is at, near, or above the land surface for a significant part of most years. These ecosystems are complex transitional systems between aquatic and terrestrial environments.

South Florida Water Management District

East Lake Tohopekaliga

Wetlands are often classified as swamps or marshes, depending on whether the vegetation is dominated by trees (swamps) or by grasses (marshes).

Wetlands occur near the ocean and gulf, adjacent to rivers and lakes, in areas of poor soil drainage, and in relict lake valleys or river channels. River and lacustrine (lake) floodplains are periodically inundated and often remain partly wet because of their low topographic position in the proximity of high water tables. In karst areas, the valleys and lakes may become dry because of water-table changes associated with sea level changes, climate, vertical adjustments in the earth's crust, and cavern development. Specific examples reported include features associated with the Suwannee valley (White 1970) and a dry spring-fed tributary to the Santa Fe near High Springs (Edwards 1948). Paynes Prairie, a 19,000-acre wetland near Gainesville, is a relict lake bed.

Wetlands, like lakes, may be sites of internal drainage, exporting water only by infiltration and evapotranspiration, or they may be connected with streams along the stream corridor, transporting runoff as well. The dense vegetation and flat topography of bottomland wetlands in floodplains attenuates the flood peaks and provides greater detention storage (U.S. Environmental Protection Agency 1983).

Evapotranspiration in wetlands approximates the evaporation from open water bodies (Visher and Hughes 1975). Thus, changes in wetlands, usually a decrease in area from a reduction in hydroperiod, reduce the amount of water lost directly to the atmosphere. Some wetlands play a role in recharge, but most are situated in low-lying areas that are discharge areas of the groundwater system. Recharge results from the vertical movement of water through the soil. However, this vertical movement is often restricted because wetlands are often underlain by virtually impermeable clay and organic layers that severely restrict groundwater recharge.

77

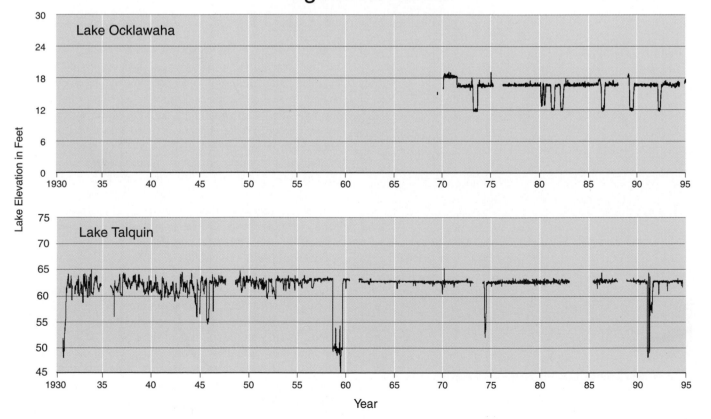

Wetlands are extensive and are found nearly everywhere in the state. Prior to development, wetlands, including open waters and seasonally flooded areas, covered about half the state's area. Based upon satellite imagery from the early 1970s, wetlands and their associated open-water areas accounted for almost a third of the total land area of the state (Hampson 1984). Over one-third of the wetlands had been drained for agriculture, flood control, and residential development, but many floodplain wetlands and coastal marshes are still largely undeveloped but are threatened by urban and agricultural land uses.

In southern Florida, extensive areas of wetlands include the Everglades and Big Cypress Swamp, where historically most surface flow moved slowly either as sheet flow through marshes or through broad sloughs. Extensive wetland areas in central Florida include the Green Swamp and parts of the Kissimmee basin. The Okeefenokee is an extensive swamp in the upper Suwannee Basin of northern peninsular Florida.

Human Modifications of Surface Waters

Humans created and modified waterways in Florida for a number of centuries, if not millennia, although the impacts, both indirect and direct, have been particularly severe within this past century. Most indirect changes are associated with human activities and land use changes within the basin, especially close to the channel and floodplain. Deforestation, agriculture, land drainage or flood protection, and urbanization have a number of effects on waterways. These activities typically increase the magnitude of peak flow and decrease the lag time, generally aggravating flooding. To minimize such impacts many communities in Florida have built retention and detention ponds in conjunction with development to increase the local storage and allow flood waters to behave more as they would under predevelopment conditions.

Direct modifications along the channel and floodplain are typically built to manipulate the spatial and temporal varia-

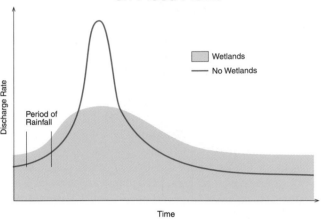

Joann Mossa

Great white heron, Everglades National Park

tions in surface waters. Structures such as dams and weirs, bridges and pipeline crossings, and activities such as channelization, dredging, and floodplain and in-channel mining are more direct impacts. Direct modifications have a long history, as building canals and modifying waterways dates well before European settlement (Leur 1989). Further changes have occurred in this century, when sections of waterways have been straightened and new artificial channels intertwine with the former natural one, especially along the Kissimmee. Some channels have been deepened or widened locally for navigation by dredging, and others have artificial cutoffs or shortcuts across meander bends. Blount Island on the St. Johns River is one of the larger artificial cutoffs, and several occur on the Caloosahatchee River and Upper St. Johns River as well.

Canals have been constructed in a number of places throughout peninsular Florida, especially the lowlands of south Florida in areas of urban and agricultural development. They have been constructed for a multitude of reasons, including flood control, water supply, navigation, wetlands drainage, and for control of water flow directions and elevations. Canalization results in either the straightening, widening, and/or deepening of an existing waterway or in the construction of a new waterway. Examples of canalization are so numerous that ca-

78

Wetlands
1989

Wetlands

nals are included in Beck's (1965) classification of Florida's waterways. Eight major waterways, including the Caloosahatchee and Kissimmee rivers, and the Tamiami, Miami, North New River, Hillsboro, West Palm Beach, and St. Lucie canals are classified as such. Furthermore, there is an extensive set of numbered rather than named canals. This extensive network of canals built for flood control and water supply has led Palmer (1984) to characterize south Florida as the "quintessence of surface water manipulation."

Two areas of considerable modification in Florida include the partially completed Cross Florida Barge Canal (St. Johns to southern Withlacoochee) and the Kissimmee River basin. The Cross Florida Barge Canal was to have connected the east and west coast via the Withlacoochee, Ocklawaha, and St. Johns rivers, resulting in the modification of a number of Florida waterways. Predecessors to this aborted project were first initiated in 1850. Construction on the canal was first halted in 1862 because of the Civil War, but resumed for a short time in 1935 and 1936. Later, work recommenced in the 1960s with

construction of major dams and locks on the Ocklawaha and Withlacoochee rivers (Southeastern Geological Society 1970). More recently, construction was halted in 1971, largely because of environmental opposition. Considerable controversy exists as to whether the modified system should be retained, whether the original conditions should be restored as much as possible, or whether a compromise involving partial restoration should be attempted. The Rodman Dam on the Ocklawaha River represents part of this controversy (Shuman 1995). Both the St. Johns River Water Management District (1994) and the Florida Department of Environmental Protection (1998) have conducted studies documenting problems resulting from the Rodman Dam. The Florida Defenders of the Environment (1998) have called for removal of the dam and restoration of the Ocklawaha, and the U.S. Fish and Wildlife Service (1997) has also issued a Biological Opinion in favor of restoration.

Construction of the project initially resulted in destruction of much bottomland forest. By changing the hydrology, the dam reduces productivity in the St. Johns River. The dam also

Joann Mossa

Inglis Spillway, Cross Florida Barge Canal

Joann Mossa

Pump structure at L-31

is harmful to migratory aquatic species, especially manatees, because structures block passage and reduce habitat of these and other species. In warm and nutrient-rich waters of the reservoir, aquatic weeds and algae have flourished, requiring the use of mechanical and chemical treatments to control undesirable water plants. Additionally, maintaining the structure has an annual cost which over a period of years exceeds the one-time cost of destruction. However, many local fishermen, supported by a powerful legislator, want it left in place because it has become a favorite spot for bass, and the fish and bird populations now accustomed to the dam would undergo a period of adjustment. Should the dam be removed, much planning and environmental assessment will be needed to minimize potential problems associated with sediments, channel instability, and ecological changes.

The Kissimmee River is in south-central peninsular Florida. The Lower Kissimmee flows about 100 miles from Lake Kissimmee to Lake Okeechobee. Congress authorized the Kissimmee River Flood Control Project in 1954 to facilitate the passage of floodwater, and it was constructed between 1962 and 1971 at a cost of $32 million. The project diverted flow from the 103 miles of meandering river channel and a 0.9- to 1.9-mile-wide floodplain to an excavated 56-mile-long, 210- to 345-foot-wide, 29.5-foot-deep canal named C-38. Included in the project were six water flow control structures with tie-back levees and navigation locks designed to allow passage of small boats. These maintain stable water levels in five stair-step impoundments or "pools" along the canal's length. Although remnants of the former river channel remain on either side of the canal, the flowing river ecosystem has essentially been replaced by a series of relatively stagnant reservoirs with a central deep canal (Toth et al. 1993). Inflows to C-38 occur through the uppermost structure and are regulated by a flood control operation schedule that was implemented in the Kissimmee's headwater lakes.

Loss of wetlands and water-quality problems were anticipated, but the project went ahead anyway (Pilkey and Dixon 1996). The drainage of 200,000 acres of floodplain wetlands caused a decline in water quality, water birds, commercially valuable fish species, and wildlife habitat. In the absence of flow, thick deposits of organic matter accumulated on the bottom of the remaining river channel and reduced depth and substrate diversity within these stagnant, remnant river courses (Toth 1993, Toth et al. 1993). One year after the canal's completion, there was much opposition calling for river restoration. In 1991, under a congressional mandate, the corps began restoring about one-third of C-38, which will cost over $400

million, more than ten times the cost of the entire original project (Pilkey and Dixon 1996). Little is known about appropriate strategies for river restoration since such efforts have only been attempted quite recently, so it is unknown how successful these efforts will be. To avoid repeating such mistakes, an increasing number of individuals are interested in seeking alternatives to river modification, such as land acquisition and other approaches.

Conclusions

The surface waters of Florida are both unique and important. The abundance, accessibility, and good quality of these waters and the recreational and industrial opportunities they provide will increasingly attract people and business to the state. The stress imposed by development, however, poses a great danger to the future well being of these waters and the state itself. The rivers have been important to humans for millennia, but within the last century they have been appreciably modified by human activities. Although much effort has been expended in some areas to minimize the effects of human activities in Florida, elsewhere these modifications have resulted in considerable environmental deterioration. Because of their importance to society, further understanding of the spatial and temporal variations of water resources will be useful to resource management and planning. Because of these mounting stresses, the preservation and protection of the state's surface waters must be a first-order priority for state and local governments and for private citizens.

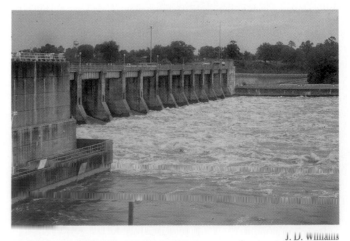

J. D. Williams

Apalachicola River, Jim Woodruff Dam

REFERENCES

A source for a map or figure has a number in parentheses following the entry. This number refers to the page in this atlas for which the source was used.

Bass, D.G., Jr. 1983. *Rivers of Florida and Their Fishes*. Completion Report for Investigation Project, Dingell-Johnson Project F-36. North Florida Streams Research Study III, Florida Game and Fresh Water Commission, 1980-1983. Tallahassee.

Beck, W.M., Jr. 1965. "The Streams of Florida." *Bulletin Florida State Museum Biological Science* 10:91-126.

Edminston, H.L., and V.B. Myers. 1983. *Florida Lakes*. Florida Department of Environmental Regulation. Tallahassee.

Edwards, R.A. 1948. "An Abandoned Valley Near High Springs, Florida." *Quarterly Journal of Florida Sciences* 11:125-133.

Ellins, K.K., R.A. Hisert, T. Kincaid. 1991. *Hydrogeology of the Western Santa Fe River Basin*. Field Trip Guide for the Southeastern Section of the Geological Society of America, Dept. of Geology, University of Florida, Gainesville.

Florida Defenders of the Environment. 1998. *Restoring the Ocklawaha River*. Gainesville.

Florida Department of Environmental Protection. 1998. *Environmental Impact Statement: Ocklawaha River Restoration Project, Marion and Putnam Counties Florida*. Submitted to U.S. Army Corps of Engineers.

Florida Game and Fresh Water Fish Commission. (Data for wetlands map, 79)

Hampson, P.S., 1984. *Wetlands in Florida*. Florida Bureau of Geology Map Series 109. Tallahassee. (wetlands map, 78)

Heath, R.C. 1983. *U.S. Geological Survey Flood Operations Plan for the Florida District*. Tallahassee.

Heath, R.C., and C. S. Conover. 1981. *Hydrologic Almanac of Florida*. U.S. Geological Survey Open-File Report 81-1107. Tallahassee. (table, 68; Comparison of Rivers graphic, 70; tables, 70, 75, 76)

Hughes, G.H. 1974. *Water Level Fluctuations of Lakes in Florida*. Florida Bureau of Geology Map Series 62, Tallahassee, Florida (line graph, 75).

Hughes, G.H. 1978. *Runoff from Hydrologic Units in Florida*. Florida Bureau of Geology Map Series 81. Tallahassee, Florida (runoff map, 69).

Hughes, G.H. 1981. *Low Flow Frequency Data for Selected Stream-gauging stations in Florida*. U.S. Geological Survey Water-Resources Investigations Open-File Report 8169. Tallahassee. (map, 71)

Kenner, W.E. 1975. *Seasonal Variation of Streamflow in Florida*. Florida Bureau of Geology Map Series 31. Tallahassee. (maps and graphs, 71-72)

Leur, G.M. 1989. "Calusa Canals in Southwestern Florida: Routes of Tribute and Exchange." *The Florida Anthropologist* 42:89-130.

Mossa, J., and J. Konwinski. 1998. "Thalweg Variability at Bridges Along a Large Karst River." *Engineering Geology* 49:15–30.

Nordlie, F.G. 1990. "Rivers and Springs." In R.L Myers. and J.J. Ewel, eds. *Ecosystems of Florida*. Orlando: University of Central Florida Press.

Palmer, S.L. 1984. "Surface Water." In E. A. Fernald and D. J. Patton, eds. *Water Resources Atlas of Florida*. Tallahassee: Florida State University.

Pilkey, O.H., and K.L. Dixon. 1996. *The Corps and the Shore*. Washington D.C.: Island Press.

Pirkle, W.A. 1971. "The Offset Course of the St. Johns River, Florida." *Southeastern Geology* 13:39-59.

St. Johns River Water Management District. 1994. *Environmental Studies Concerning Four Alternatives for Rodman Reservoir and the Lower Ocklawaha River*. 20 vols. Palatka.

Schiffer, D.M. 1998. *Hydrology of Central Florida Lakes–a Primer*. U.S. Geological Survey Circular 1137. U.S. Government Printing Office.

Schumm, S.A., K.F. Boyd, C.G.Wolff, and W.J. Spitz. 1995. "A Ground-Water Sapping Landscape in the Florida Panhandle." *Geomorphology* 12:281-97.

Shuman, J.R. 1995. "Environmental Considerations for Assessing Dam Removal Alternatives for River Restoration." *Regulated Rivers: Research and Management* 11:249-61.

Snell, L.J., and W.E. Kenner. 1974. *Surface Water Features of Florida*. Florida Bureau of Geology Map Series 66. Tallahassee (surface water regions map, 65).

Southeastern Geological Society. 1970. *Geology and Geohydrology of the Cross-Florida Barge Canal Area*. Southeastern Geological Society, Ocala.

Tanner, W.F., and L.D. Smith. 1981. "Natural Environment." In *Atlas of Florida*. E. A. Fernald, ed. Tallahassee, Florida: Florida State University Foundation. (map, 65)

Toth, L.A.1993. "The Ecological Basis of the Kissimmee River Restoration Plan." *Florida Scientist* 56:25-51.

Toth, L.A., J.T.B. Obeysekera, W.A. Perkins, and M.K. Loftin. 1993. "Flow Regulation and Restoration of Florida's Kissimmee River." *Regulated Rivers: Research and Management* 8:155-66.

U.S. Army Corps of Engineers Jacksonville District. 1974. *Special Flood Hazard Information: Suwannee River Floods-Florida and Georgia*. Report for the Suwannee River Water Management District.

U.S. Department of Agriculture. Soil Conservation Service. 1970. *Atlas of River Basins of the U.S.* Washington, D.C. (maps, 66, 67)

U.S. Environmental Protection Agency. 1983. *Freshwater Wetlands for Wastewater Management Phase I Report*. Atlanta, Georgia. (graph, 78)

U.S. Geological Survey. (data for hydrographs, 73, 74, 76, 77)

Visher, F.N., and G.H. Hughes. 1975. *The Difference Between Rainfall and Potential Evaporation in Florida*. Florida Bureau of Geology Map Series 32. Tallahassee. (rainfall and evap. map, 69)

White, W.A.1970. *The Geomorphology of the Florida Peninsula*. Florida Geological Survey. Bulletin 41. Tallahassee.

U.S. Fish and Wildlife Service. Biological Opinion, FWS Log No. 96-513c (January 6, 1997).

5

NATURAL
SYSTEMS

Water is the thread connecting all ecosystems on earth. An ecosystem can be defined as a community of organisms, including humans, interacting with one another and the environment in which they live. Ecosystems are the result of interactions among abiotic (non-living) factors, such as soils, water, nutrients, and climate; biotic (living) factors, such as plants, animals, fungi, and bacteria; and physical and chemical processes, such as fire, floods, drought, energy flow, and water acidification. The word ecosystem was coined by English botanist Sir Arthur Tansley in 1935 from the Greek root "oikos" meaning house. Ecosystems are earth and life functioning together.

Ecosystems may be conceived and studied in various sizes. An ecosystem can be as small as the community of bacteria, insects, and microscopic plants living in rainwater collected in the crook of a tree, or it can be as large as the Kissimmee River-Lake Okeechobee-Everglades-Florida Bay ecosystem, or it can be even larger. The size of an ecosystem, and often its boundaries, are arbitrary and depend on the needs and inter-

Randy S. Kautz, Kenneth Haddad, Theodore S. Hoehn, Thomas Rogers, Ernest D. Estevez, Tom Atkeson

ests of the scientist. Sometimes boundaries between ecosystems are relatively well demarcated. In other instances ecosystems blend gradually one into another. In Florida changes in moisture, soil fertility, fire frequency, and land-use history occur over very short distances and result in clear and striking changes in the landscape: a scrub community adjoins a cypress pond, a tropical hammock stands out from surrounding pineland (Myers and Ewel 1990).

Scientists do not agree on any one classification scheme for ecosystem types. Most ecosystem classifications are based on vegetation, the physical landscape, environmental factors, and successional status. Although animals are crucial components of ecosystems, it is easier to define a place by vegetation.

A common approach is to classify ecosystems based on potential natural vegetation. In 1927 Roland M. Harper published descriptions of 24 vegetation types in South Florida. In 1943 John H. Davis delineated 19 vegetation types in South Florida based on fieldwork and aerial photography. In 1967 Davis produced a vegetation map for the entire state. On this map he reduced his 19 original South Florida types to 10. The Florida Game and Fresh Water Fish Commission used Landsat imagery collected between 1985 and 1989 to map natural plant communities and disturbed lands. Myers and Ewel (1990) divided and roughly mapped 13 ecosystems based on Davis's vegetation types with the addition of aquatic systems. The Nature Conservancy and the Florida Natural Areas Inventory (1990) have distinguished 81 community types in Florida. The Florida Department of Environmental Protection, for the purpose of ecosystem management, has defined Ecosystem Management Areas primarily on the basis of drainage basins or watersheds.

In this chapter, we have basically used the Myers and Ewel (1990) scheme with finer distinctions for aquatic systems. We attempt to characterize the major abiotic conditions, biota, and processes that interact to form Florida's natural ecosystems. We also discuss some of the problems and management concerns facing ecosystems in Florida. Much of the information presented in this chapter appears in map form, which suggests that the boundaries of Florida's natural ecosystems have been accurately mapped; however, these boundaries are largely conceptual.

Upland ecosystems, as well as ecosystems of wetlands, streams, lakes, and coastal areas, have been included. Healthy uplands are essential for maintaining healthy aquatic ecosystems. The type and condition of uplands influence the amount and the quality of water reaching lakes, streams, and estuaries. Natural vegetation in uplands slows runoff and prevents soil from eroding. Many uplands are also groundwater recharge areas. Most wildlife use both uplands and wetlands. For example, the bald eagle nests in upland trees and feeds on fish and water fowl in wetlands and lakes.

Abiotic Components of Ecosystems

Florida spans 6.5 degrees of latitude and extends from the southern end of the temperate zone to the northern edge of the tropics. The climate of most of the state is humid subtropical. Most of the earth's land sharing Florida's latitude is desert, a fate spared Florida by the seas that surround it.

Rainfall and temperature vary seasonally, annually, and geographically, influencing the distribution of plants and animals. Annual rainfall is highest in the western panhandle and along the southeast coast and lowest in the western portion of the Florida Keys. Peninsular Florida receives most rain in the summer and fall from thunderstorms, whereas northern Florida also has a secondary rainfall maximum in the winter from the mixing of warm maritime and cold continental air masses. Normally, little rain falls in south Florida during the winter. Throughout the state droughts are most common in spring (April and May) and fall (October and November). In some years hurricanes arrive in the fall bringing excessive rainfall.

Temperatures, particularly hard winter freezes, play a strong role in the distribution of plants and animals in Florida. In north Florida freezing temperatures arrive earlier, last longer, and are lower; and plant species more common to the temperate zone predominate. As one moves south, the frequency of freezes decreases; plant species common in the temperate zone decrease; and plants more common to tropical climates increase. Proximity to the coast, particularly the Atlantic Ocean, further moderates the effects of freezing temperatures.

The modern-day Florida peninsula is the above-water portion of the Florida Platform, a 300-mile wide by 450-mile long, relatively flat deposit of carbonate sediments (Lane 1994). The sediments comprising the Florida Platform accumulated in warm, shallow seas similar to today's Bahama Banks. Until 25–30 million years ago, sedimentary processes were dominated by the biological activity of fossil marine life which deposited carbonates to the sea floor. From about 25 million years ago until about 5 million years ago, quartz sands, silts, and clays from the eroding Appalachian Mountains were added to the carbonate sediments being deposited on the Florida Platform.

Most of the landforms characterizing Florida's modern topography formed over the last 1.8 million years (Lane 1994).

The Pleistocene Epoch (i.e., Ice Ages), from about 1.8 million years ago to 10,000 years ago, was a time of world-wide glaciations and widely fluctuating sea levels. Huge ice sheets formed over the northern latitudes of the globe in at least four separate events, and sea levels around the world fell by as much as 400 feet, exposing most of the Florida Platform. During the warmer interglacial periods, sea levels rose as high as 150 feet above their current level, drowning most of the Florida Platform and leaving only the highest areas of Florida exposed as islands.

Repeatedly rising and falling sea levels during the Pleistocene dramatically affected Florida's modern topographic features and surficial sediments. As the Appalachian Mountains continued to erode, marine currents delivered a steady supply of sand to the portions of the Florida Platform below sea level. A blanket of sand was deposited over the underlying limestone, infilling the irregular rock surface and forming a relatively featureless sea bottom. These flat, shallow sea bottoms eventually emerged to became today's flatwoods ecosystems. In an environment of abundant sand and constant sea breezes, sand dunes and sand ridges formed along the coast lines of the various sea level stands. Many of these relict dune systems are the sites of today's scrub and sandhill ecosystems.

Prior to the Pleistocene, naturally acidic rain and groundwater flowed through and dissolved the limestone rock of the Florida Platform, forming a myriad of underground caverns and conduits. During low sea level stands in Pleistocene times, these conduits often collapsed, creating many of the sinkholes, springs, and lakes dotting the modern Florida landscape. The Western and Central Valleys of the central peninsula were formed by the dissolution and collapse of the underlying limestone over large areas.

83

Some rivers flow over limestone in areas of the state where limestone outcrops occur near the land surface.

The southern end of the Florida peninsula, south of approximately Lake Okeechobee, had a significantly different history during the Pleistocene. Most of the quartz sands from the eroding Appalachian Mountains never reached south Florida, but instead were funneled offshore (Lane 1994). As a result, a marine depositional environment dominated in south Florida, and calcium carbonate, in the form of broken shells and chemically precipitated particles, was the main source of sediments. These sediments eventually compacted into the jagged, craggy limestone rock underlying south Florida. The Florida Keys, which occur along the southeastern rim of the Florida Platform, formed from the accumulation of living and dead corals as sea levels rose and fell.

The beaches, barrier islands, and spits that constitute Florida's modern coastline, as well as most of the state's lakes, wetlands, and spring-fed river systems, developed during the last 10,000 years, a period known as the Holocene Epoch (Lane 1994). The Holocene began when Earth's climate gradually warmed following the last glaciation. At the beginning of the Holocene, sea level was as much as 100 feet lower than today, the land area of Florida was much larger, and the climate was generally arid. Surface water was scarce, and groundwater levels were much lower than today. The northern half of the peninsula was dominated by savanna vegetation, with mesic forests occupying favorable sites (Webb 1990). The southern half was limited to semiarid sandhill and scrub vegetation, and extensive mangrove swamps bordered the southern edge of the peninsula. Beginning about 9,500 years ago, wetter conditions began to prevail, and sea levels gradually rose. These changes led to higher groundwater levels, more abundant surface waters, and the development of more organized surface water drainage systems. In turn, these conditions allowed for the development of today's springs, swamps, bayheads, lakes, and many wetlands, including the famous Everglades. Many of these ecosystems are no more than several thousand years old.

The westernmost four counties of the panhandle are the only areas of Florida where sandy clay, clay, gravel, and coarse sand are found at the surface. Clayey sands cover most of the areas of highest relief in Florida, including the hills of north Florida extending from the panhandle to western Nassau and Duval counties and down the center of the Florida peninsula. Limestone rock is at or near the surface in the Big Bend region

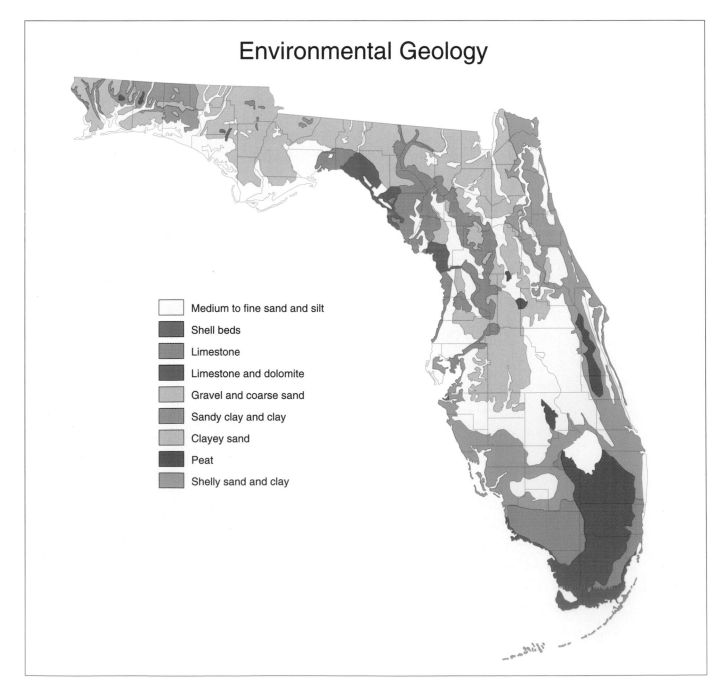

Environmental Geology

Medium to fine sand and silt

Shell beds

Limestone

Limestone and dolomite

Gravel and coarse sand

Sandy clay and clay

Clayey sand

Peat

Shelly sand and clay

of north Florida, in the Big Cypress region of southwest Florida, along the lower East Coast, and in the Florida Keys. Areas of fine sand, shelly sand, silt, and clay, which represent deposits from more recent geologic times, occur mostly inland from the East Coast and extend over to the West Coast in the south central portion of the state. Peat deposits are common in the Everglades and Ten Thousand Islands regions of south Florida and along the upper St. Johns River basin in east central Florida.

Soils in Florida vary from place to place but are generally sandy and low in fertility (Brown et al. 1990). Well-drained loamy soils (Ultisols) occur in the Western Highlands of the Florida panhandle extending approximately 30 miles south of the Alabama and Georgia borders. Soils of deep, excessively drained sands (Entisols), often referred to as sandhills, occur in the Western Highlands of the panhandle and on the Central Ridge from the vicinity of the Suwannee River in north central Florida south to south central Florida. Well-drained sandy soils with loamy subsoils underlain by phosphatic limestone (Alfisols and Ultisols) occur in the western portions of the Central Ridge in the northern half of the peninsula. Somewhat poorly to poorly drained sandy soils with a dark sandy subsoil layer (Spodosols) are the most common soils in the state. Spodosols occur in flatwoods, which are nearly level lands derived from ancient sea bottoms. Poorly drained organic soils

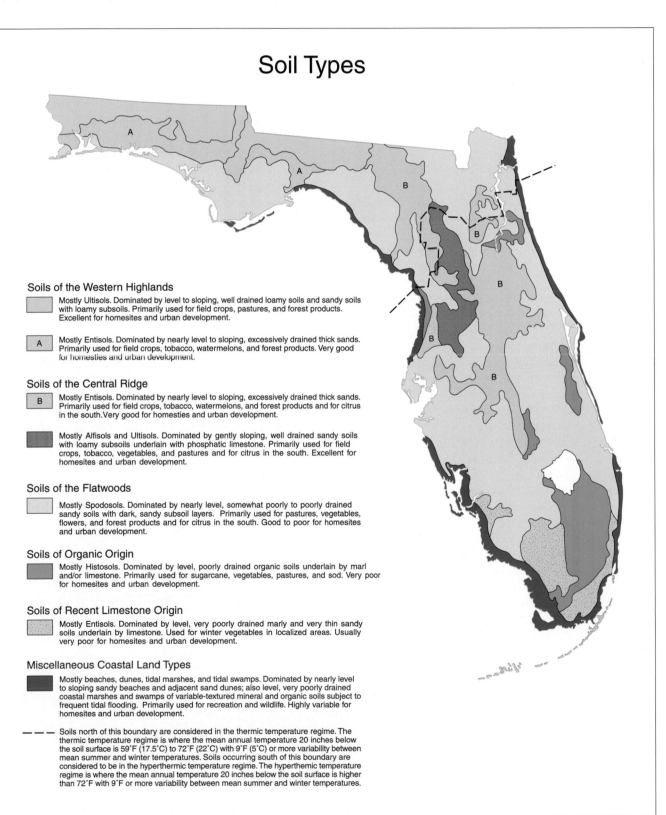

Soil Types

Soils of the Western Highlands

Mostly Ultisols. Dominated by level to sloping, well drained loamy soils and sandy soils with loamy subsoils. Primarily used for field crops, pastures, and forest products. Excellent for homesites and urban development.

A Mostly Entisols. Dominated by nearly level to sloping, excessively drained thick sands. Primarily used for field crops, tobacco, watermelons, and forest products. Very good for homesites and urban development.

Soils of the Central Ridge

B Mostly Entisols. Dominated by nearly level to sloping, excessively drained thick sands. Primarily used for field crops, tobacco, watermelons, and forest products and for citrus in the south. Very good for homesites and urban development.

Mostly Alfisols and Ultisols. Dominated by gently sloping, well drained sandy soils with loamy subsoils underlain with phosphatic limestone. Primarily used for field crops, tobacco, vegetables, and pastures and for citrus in the south. Excellent for homesites and urban development.

Soils of the Flatwoods

Mostly Spodosols. Dominated by nearly level, somewhat poorly to poorly drained sandy soils with dark, sandy subsoil layers. Primarily used for pastures, vegetables, flowers, and forest products and for citrus in the south. Good to poor for homesites and urban development.

Soils of Organic Origin

Mostly Histosols. Dominated by level, poorly drained organic soils underlain by marl and/or limestone. Primarily used for sugarcane, vegetables, pastures, and sod. Very poor for homesites and urban development.

Soils of Recent Limestone Origin

Mostly Entisols. Dominated by level, very poorly drained marly and very thin sandy soils underlain by limestone. Used for winter vegetables in localized areas. Usually very poor for homesites and urban development.

Miscellaneous Coastal Land Types

Mostly beaches, dunes, tidal marshes, and tidal swamps. Dominated by nearly level to sloping sandy beaches and adjacent sand dunes; also level, very poorly drained coastal marshes and swamps of variable-textured mineral and organic soils subject to frequent tidal flooding. Primarily used for recreation and wildlife. Highly variable for homesites and urban development.

– – – Soils north of this boundary are considered in the thermic temperature regime. The thermic temperature regime is where the mean annual temperature 20 inches below the soil surface is 59°F (17.5°C) to 72°F (22°C) with 9°F (5°C) or more variability between mean summer and winter temperatures. Soils occurring south of this boundary are considered to be in the hyperthermic temperature regime. The hyperthermic temperature regime is where the mean annual temperature 20 inches below the soil surface is higher than 72°F with 9°F or more variability between mean summer and winter temperatures.

85

underlain by limestone or marl (Histosols) occur on flat lands primarily in the Everglades of south Florida and a few other areas of smaller extent. Very poorly drained, marly, and very thin sandy soils underlain by limestone (Entisols) occur on flat lands in extreme south Florida, particularly in Big Cypress, at the southern end of the lower East Coast, and in the Florida Keys. Miscellaneous soil types occur in coastal areas of Florida. High energy coastlines are characterized by nearly level to sloping sandy beaches and adjacent sand dunes. Low energy coastlines support level, very poorly drained marshes and swamps of variable-textured mineral and organic soils subject to frequent tidal flooding.

Water is a non-living but absolutely essential component of natural ecosystems. Several aspects of water profoundly influence the distributions of plants and animals, the living components of ecosystems. The most significant aspects of water are temperature, salinity, dissolved oxygen content, color, and turbidity.

Water temperature influences the distribution of aquatic organisms, particularly in saltwater. Saltwater environments of north Florida are cooler in the winter than those of south Florida. As a result, marine species intolerant of the cooler waters are restricted from the shallow marine systems of north Florida.

Salinity refers to the salt content of water. Whereas freshwater generally has a salinity of around 0 ppt (parts per thousand), oceanic waters have salinities of about 35 ppt. Estuarine ecosystems, the coastal waters where freshwater draining from the land mixes with saltwater from the Gulf of Mexico and Atlantic Ocean, have salinities that range between these extremes. High salinities present osmoregulatory problems for marine life, and special adaptations are needed to allow marine life to retain bodily fluids. Freshwater aquatic life has the opposite problem. Osmoregulatory adaptations are needed to prevent freshwater species from swelling up and bursting from excess water. Organisms that inhabit estuaries typically have broader tolerances for varying salinity, a specialization which allows them to persist in an highly variable environment.

Since most aquatic organisms require oxygen in order to survive, the dissolved oxygen content of water is absolutely critical. Most forms of aquatic life exist in waters with dissolved oxygen content ranging from 2 to 3 mg/l (milligrams per liter) to 7 to 8 mg/l. Most species of finfishes and shell fishes will avoid waters with dissolved oxygen below 2 to 3 mg/l. Deeper waters and those subject to excess discharges of organic matter, whether of natural or human origin, typically are low in dissolved oxygen. Particulate organic matter in the water column or on the bottom is a food source for microbes that use oxygen to meet their own metabolic needs and deplete oxygen from the water column.

In Florida, water color generally is influenced by tannin and lignin content. Tannins and lignins are dark-colored substances that leach from plants, such as pine, cypress, and gum trees. Waters draining from pine flatwoods and cypress swamps often are referred to as "blackwater streams" due to their dark brown color. Generally speaking, blackwater streams and lakes are low in nutrients and high in acidity. Highly colored water reduces light penetration, and as a result, phytoplankton and submersed aquatic plant production is low in lakes and estuaries that receive heavy discharges from blackwater streams.

Turbidity refers to the suspended particulate content of water, whether of inorganic or organic origin. The rivers of the Florida panhandle are naturally turbid as their larger drainage basins deliver large volumes of eroded soil and their higher flows scour the bottom and suspend sediments in the water column. However, most Florida streams and lakes are characterized by low turbidity because the state is relatively flat, drainage basins are generally small in area, and flowing waters do not reach velocities sufficient to scour the bottom and suspend sediments. High turbidity affects aquatic life in three ways. First, similar to high color, high turbidity in the water column prevents sunlight from penetrating the water column, and photosynthesis by phytoplankton or submersed aquatic plants is inhibited. Second, when highly turbid waters reach calm areas, the suspended sediments settle out, smothering submerged grassbeds or bottom-dwelling organisms essential to the food chain. Third, very high levels of sediments in the water column can kill finfishes and shell fishes by clogging their gills and preventing respiration.

Ecoregions and Natural Communities

Ecoregions are broad geographic areas characterized by a relative homogeneity of ecological systems and relationships between organisms and their environment. Ecoregions are usually determined by similarities in a combination of factors such as climate, physiography, geology, soils, and vegetation. After reviewing numerous sources of information characterizing the ecosystems of Florida, Griffith et al. (1994) proposed a classification system for Florida that contained 3 major ecological regions and 13 subregions.

The Southeastern Plains ecological region encompasses the rolling hills of the Florida panhandle from the Alabama state line east to about the Suwannee River. In Florida, the Southeastern Plains is composed of three subregions: Southern Pine Plains and Hills, Dougherty/Marianna Plains, and Tifton Upland/Tallahassee Hills. The Southeastern Plains is the southern extent of the southeastern coastal plains extending from Texas through the Carolinas. By and large, the rolling hills of the panhandle mark the southern range limits for many species of plants and animals of temperate North America. In many respects, the Southeastern Plains ecological region marks the southern end of the temperate zone.

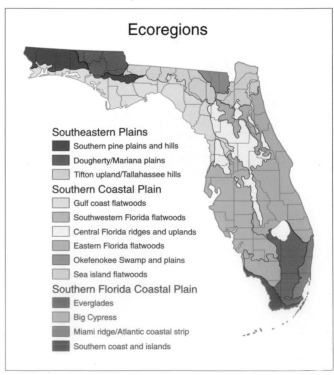

86

The Southern Coastal Plain ecological region extends from the flatwoods of the panhandle and northeast Florida down the peninsula to about Lake Okeechobee. The Southern Coastal Plain ecological region is transitional between the ecosystems of temperate North America and the subtropical climate of the Caribbean Sea. Though this ecological region is dominated by pine flatwoods ecosystems, it also includes the xeric uplands of the Central Ridge and the mesic limestone outcrops of the Brooksville Ridge. Hard winter freezes affect the Southern Coastal Plain ecological region with decreasing frequency as one moves down the peninsula.

The Southern Florida Coastal Plain ecological region extends from Lake Okeechobee south through the Florida Keys. This region marks the northern extent of the subtropics and is rarely affected by freezing temperatures. The Southern Florida Coastal Plain is characterized by the thick peat deposits of the Everglades and the limestone outcrops along the southeast coast and in the Florida Keys. Tropical species of plants and animals are common.

Davis's 1967 map of the potential distribution of Florida's major vegetation types prior to European settlement coincides

Randy Kautz

Pinhook Swamp, part of Okefenokee Swamp and plains ecoregion

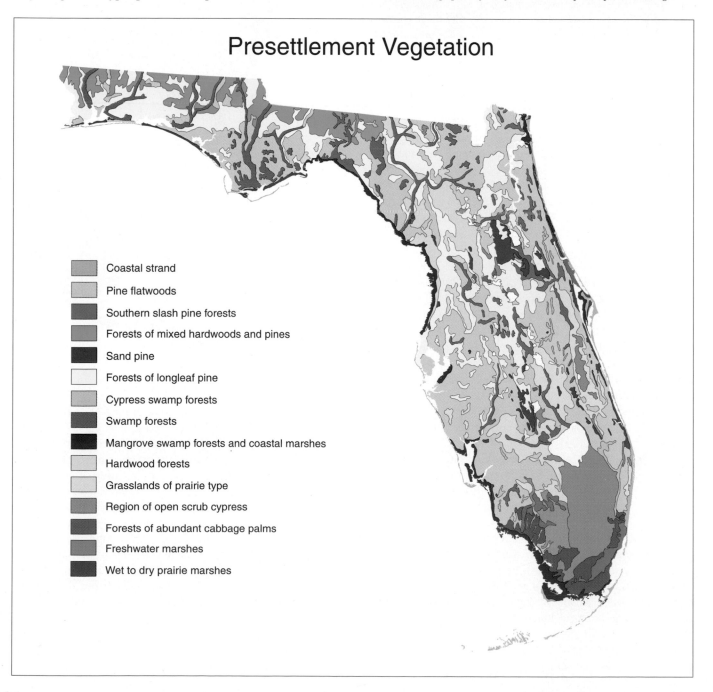

Presettlement Vegetation

Coastal strand

Pine flatwoods

Southern slash pine forests

Forests of mixed hardwoods and pines

Sand pine

Forests of longleaf pine

Cypress swamp forests

Swamp forests

Mangrove swamp forests and coastal marshes

Hardwood forests

Grasslands of prairie type

Region of open scrub cypress

Forests of abundant cabbage palms

Freshwater marshes

Wet to dry prairie marshes

87

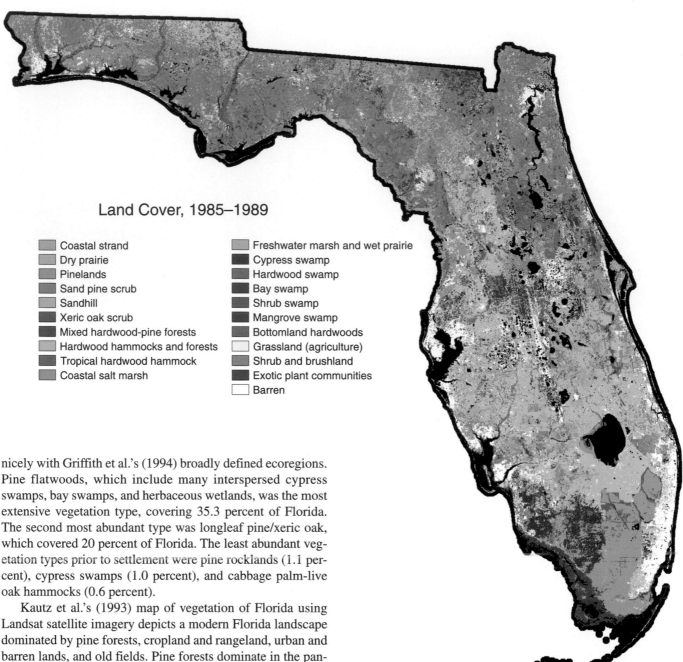

Land Cover, 1985–1989

- Coastal strand
- Dry prairie
- Pinelands
- Sand pine scrub
- Sandhill
- Xeric oak scrub
- Mixed hardwood-pine forests
- Hardwood hammocks and forests
- Tropical hardwood hammock
- Coastal salt marsh
- Freshwater marsh and wet prairie
- Cypress swamp
- Hardwood swamp
- Bay swamp
- Shrub swamp
- Mangrove swamp
- Bottomland hardwoods
- Grassland (agriculture)
- Shrub and brushland
- Exotic plant communities
- Barren

nicely with Griffith et al.'s (1994) broadly defined ecoregions. Pine flatwoods, which include many interspersed cypress swamps, bay swamps, and herbaceous wetlands, was the most extensive vegetation type, covering 35.3 percent of Florida. The second most abundant type was longleaf pine/xeric oak, which covered 20 percent of Florida. The least abundant vegetation types prior to settlement were pine rocklands (1.1 percent), cypress swamps (1.0 percent), and cabbage palm-live oak hammocks (0.6 percent).

Kautz et al.'s (1993) map of vegetation of Florida using Landsat satellite imagery depicts a modern Florida landscape dominated by pine forests, cropland and rangeland, urban and barren lands, and old fields. Pine forests dominate in the panhandle and the northern third of the peninsula. Cropland and pastureland dominate the south central portion of the peninsula. Urban areas are most common in coastal areas, especially along the lower East Coast and around Tampa Bay, Charlotte Harbor, and Pensacola Bay. Other large urban centers are found around Orlando and Jacksonville. Old field vegetation is most common in the panhandle and the northern third of the peninsula, usually on recently logged sites.

Among natural vegetation types, freshwater marshes and wet prairies are most abundant, dominating the Everglades of south Florida and the upper St. Johns River valley. Upland hardwood forests also are abundant, occurring largely along river bluffs, in coastal areas, and as small, scattered patches in north Florida. Other relatively abundant vegetation types include mixed hardwood swamps, cypress swamps, and dry prairies. Mixed hardwood swamps are most common along the floodplains of panhandle rivers, in the floodplain of the Wekiva River, and in the extensive wetlands systems of Dixie County. Cypress swamps are most abundant in the Big Cypress Swamp in south Florida, Green Swamp in central Florida, and the Pinhook Swamp region of north Florida. Dry prairies are found scatted throughout the south central portion of the peninsula.

88

Natural Communities of Rivers

Within Florida's boundaries are around 10,000 miles of rivers and streams. Florida rivers and streams can be classified as predominantly alluvial, blackwater, or spring-run. Alluvial rivers typically have large drainage basins and carry high sediment loads. Alluvial rivers have wide, forested floodplains characterized by sandbars, levees, old river channels or sloughs, and oxbow lakes. Annual floods inundate the floodplain, at which time much of the sediment load of the river is deposited, leaving behind rich, clayey soils. The only alluvial rivers in Florida are in the Florida panhandle. In-stream habitats are characterized by fallen logs, scoured bends, sand and silt deposits, and alternating reaches of pools and riffles. The bottom of the food chain is composed of macroinvertebrates as few plants can tolerate the turbid, high-flow conditions. Most of Florida's rare species of freshwater fishes, many of which are at the southern extent of their range in North America, are found in alluvial rivers and streams of the panhandle.

Blackwater streams are so named because their waters are darkly stained with tannins and lignins from decomposing plant materials. Blackwater streams typically drain Florida's flatwoods and cypress swamps, and as a result flows are sluggish and productivity is low. Blackwater streams are highly acidic, nutrient-poor, dark in color, and naturally low in dissolved oxygen. As a consequence of these conditions, submerged plants usually are absent, and in-stream productivity is low. Macroinvertebrates comprise the base of the food chain, and the fish community of blackwater streams is usually limited to relatively common species such as Florida gar (*Lepisosteus platyrhincus*), bowfin (*Amia calva*), mosquitofish (*Gambusia affinis*), and pygmy sunfish (*Elassoma* spp.).

Spring-run streams are most common in north central Florida where limestone outcrops allow groundwater to flow from springs. Spring-run rivers are clear, slightly basic, and very productive. Water clarity is such that sunlight can reach the stream bottom, and, as a result, most spring-run streams support submersed aquatic vegetation. Spring-run streams typically support abundant aquatic life, including alligators (*Alligator mississippiensis*), various turtles and water snakes, limpkins (*Aramus guarauna*), wading birds, and river otters (*Lutra canadensis*).

Many Florida rivers are a mixture of these three types. For example, the Suwannee River is a blackwater river in its upper reaches which drain the Okefenokee Swamp. Numerous springs discharge to the Suwannee in its middle reach, increasing water clarity and productivity. The lower reach of the Suwannee flows through a low, forested floodplain which floods annually, though the river lacks the sediment load of an alluvial river. While it is convenient to classify rivers into a few distinct types, riverine habitats are a complex result of the variety of inputs their tributaries receive and the types of landscapes through which they flow.

Natural Communities of Lakes

Florida has about 7,800 lakes within its boundaries. Lakes are relatively large bodies of standing water in which open water areas predominate over shallow vegetated areas. Ponds are distinguished from lakes by their smaller size and a predominance of shallow vegetated areas over deeper open water areas. Florida lakes may be classified into three types: acid clear, acid colored, or alkaline clear.

Acid clear lakes, sometimes referred to as sandhill lakes, have pH values ranging from 5 to 6, are very clear and nutrient-poor, are relatively low in productivity, and occur in areas of deep, well-drained, sandy soil. Acid clear lakes most often are closed basin lakes, meaning they have no outflowing streams. Lake levels are closely tied to groundwater levels of the surficial aquifer. Acid clear lakes typically are surrounded by a fluctuating zone of emergent vegetation and frequently support submersed grasses such as maidencane (*Panicum hemitomon*). Because they are nutrient poor, acid clear lakes support a low biomass of relatively common Florida fishes.

Acid colored lakes have pH values ranging from 4 to 6, are black or brown in color, relatively low in nutrients and productivity, and receive drainage from swamps, marshes, or flatwoods. Acid colored lakes are most common where flatwoods comprise the dominant ecosystem. Although acid colored lakes may exist in a closed basin, they often have streams flowing in, streams that flow out, or both. Acid colored lakes often are ringed by cypress and gum trees, but generally do not support submersed aquatic plants due to low levels of light penetration. Due to nutrient poor, acidic, and colored conditions, productivity is generally low, and fishes are restricted to relatively common Florida species.

Alkaline clear lakes have pH values ranging from 7 to 8, are very clear, highly productive, and either occur in areas of

89

Lake Habitats

Wetland　　Littoral Zone　　Limnetic Zone　　Profundal Zone

more fertile soils or receive inputs of spring water. Alkaline clear lakes typically are surrounded by a fluctuating zone of emergent vegetation, and often have extensive beds of floating aquatic vegetation, such as white water lily (*Nymphaea odorata*). Submersed aquatic vegetation may also be present. In today's Florida lakes, the non-native submersed weed hydrilla (*Hydrilla verticillata*) is an often-present but unwelcome inhabitant. Due to their nutrient rich conditions, clear alkaline waters, and shallow depths in a warm, subtropical climate, alkaline clear lakes are very productive. As a result, they support a large biomass of relatively common Florida fishes and an abundant wildlife fauna, including alligators, wading birds, and bald eagles (*Haliaeetus leucocephalus*).

Habitats within lakes can be divided into three separate zones: littoral zone, limnetic zone, and profundal zone. The littoral zone includes any area of the lake shallow enough to support rooted-emergent or floating-leaved vegetation. Littoral zones are the within-lake habitats that have the highest productivity and support the largest biomass and number of species of aquatic life. The vascular plants of the littoral zone not only produce plant materials important to the food chain of the lake, but they also provide shelter and hiding places for prey species. The richness of aquatic life in littoral zones naturally attracts predators.

The limnetic zone is that portion of a lake with depths too great to support rooted-emergent or floating-leaved vegetation. The limnetic zone occupies the largest portion of most lakes. Generally, plant life in the limnetic zone is limited to microscopic algae. As a result, productivity and species diversity is naturally low. The fish community of the limnetic zone typically is limited to species capable of feeding on algae in the water column, such as gizzard shad (*Dorosoma cepedianum*).

The profundal zone is below the level of light penetration. It is very low in productivity and species diversity owing to the lack of light, absence of primary producers (i.e., plants) and habitat structure, and generally low dissolved oxygen. The primary energy source of the profundal zone derives from dead plant and animal materials that reach the lower regions of a lake. The profundal zone includes the deep sediments of lake bottoms and is the site of decomposition. Due to the oxygen-demanding requirements of decomposer bacteria and macroinvertebrates that live within and on the sediment surface, dissolved oxygen content of the profundal zone is typically low, and only those organisms tolerant of low dissolved oxygen are found. The profundal zone also is the principal site of anaerobic decomposition, which recycles nitrogen and sulphur back to the atmosphere.

Natural Communities of Estuaries

In estuaries freshwater runoff from the land mixes with sea water to produce brackish waters. Florida's estuaries can be categorized into four major types: closed embayments, open bays, lagoons, and northeast Florida estuary.

Closed embayments are found along Florida's Gulf coast in regions of high wave energy that leads to the formation of barrier islands. Closed embayments receive freshwater inputs from rivers with relatively large drainage basins, and they are protected by barrier islands. Examples of closed embayments include Escambia Bay, Choctawhatchee Bay, St. Andrews Bay, and Apalachicola Bay in the Florida panhandle, and Tampa Bay and Charlotte Harbor on the west coast of the Florida peninsula. The closed embayments of the panhandle tend to be fresher and more turbid than those of the west coast due to larger drainage basins, larger volumes of freshwater reaching the bays, and naturally turbid waters of Florida's only alluvial rivers.

Open bays occur in the shallow waters of Florida's Gulf coast where wave energy is low. The shallow conditions, lower wind and wave energy, and lack of sediment prevent barrier island development such that open bays connect directly to the Gulf of Mexico. Florida's open bays include Apalachee Bay along the Big Bend Coast, the shallow seas off the Ten Thousand Islands region of southwest Florida, and Florida Bay in extreme south Florida. Because they are less confined, salinities in open bays tend to be higher than in closed embayments.

Lagoons are shallow and narrow embayments. Most lagoons in Florida are found along the east coast from approximately St. Augustine south to Ft. Pierce; however, St. Joseph Bay along the panhandle coast also qualifies as a lagoon. The principal lagoons in Florida are the Indian River Lagoon, Banana River, Mosquito Lagoon, Halifax River, Matanzas/Tolomato River, and St. Joseph Bay. Lagoons typically have small coastal drainage basins, and they are connected to the Atlantic Ocean via one or more inlets. Conditions in lagoons vary from high velocity currents and high salinities near inlets to low velocities and salinities at nodes between inlets.

The estuaries of the northeast coast from Jacksonville to the Georgia state line are a special case. These estuaries are semi-confined by a series of barrier islands that have formed in the presence of high wind and wave energy from the Atlantic Ocean. At the same time, these estuaries receive large volumes of freshwater from the St. Johns River, as well as the Amelia and Nassau rivers, but flows from these rivers are very sluggish. As a result, tidal and brackish conditions extend far upstream in the St. Johns River (which is itself actually a drowned lagoon from the geologic past), and expansive salt marshes occur behind the barrier islands of the region.

The major biological communities found in Florida's estuaries are: salt marshes, mangrove swamps, seagrass beds, oyster bars, and soft bottoms. Salt marshes are salt-tolerant herbaceous wetlands that occur in the intertidal zones of estuaries throughout Florida. However, the most extensive salt marshes in Florida are found along the Big Bend coast from the mouth of the Ochlockonee River south to New Port Richey, and in northeast Florida from St. Augustine north to the Georgia state line. Plant species diversity often is very low, with smooth cordgrass (*Spartina alterniflora*) occurring along tidal creeks and in areas receiving daily tidal inundation. Black needlerush (*Juncus roemerianus*) dominates high marshes inundated a couple of times each month. Various other marsh grasses, forbs, and shrubs are found in high transitional marshes subject only to inundation during high spring and storm tides. Despite low plant species diversity, salt marshes are among the most productive plant communities on earth (*see* Coultas and Hsieh 1997).

Mangrove swamps are forested wetlands found in the intertidal zones of Florida estuaries south of a line extending across the state from about Cedar Key to Daytona Beach (Odum and McIvor 1990). Mangrove swamps are typically low growing, reaching heights of no more than 10 to 15 feet, but in some locations, such as lower Biscayne Bay, mangroves may reach 65 to 80 feet in height. Like salt marshes, mangrove swamps are characterized by low plant species diversity. Red mangroves (*Rhizophora mangle*) dominate in the middle and lower portions of the intertidal and upper subtidal zone. Black mangroves (*Avicennia germinans*) are dominant in the upper part of the intertidal zone and into less frequently flooded areas of the higher elevations. White mangroves (*Laguncularia racemosa*) usually are found in patches throughout the intertidal zone but most frequently at irregularly flooded higher elevations. A fourth species, buttonwood *(Conocarpus erectus)*, although not a type of mangrove, often is found mixed with mangroves, but most often occurs at higher elevations than white mangroves. Also like salt marshes, mangrove swamps are tremendously productive and provide critical habitats to many estuarine and marine animals. Mangrove leaves fall into the water where they decompose and form the base of the estuarine food chain. Mangroves themselves provide nesting and roosting habitats for birds such as roseate spoonbills (*Ajaia ajaja*), brown pelicans (*Pelicanus occidentalis*), and mangrove cuckoos (*Coccyzus minor*), while mangrove roots provide shelter to many species of finfishes and marine invertebrates.

Seagrasses are vascular plants that live in shallow subtidal zones of estuaries and coastal regions. Seven species of seagrasses inhabit Florida waters. Turtle grass (*Thalassia testudinum*), manatee grass (*Syringodium filiforme*), shoal grass (*Halodule wrightii*), and widgeon grass (*Ruppia maritima*) are the most common shallow water species. Often less abundant and sparsely distributed are three species of a small delicate seagrass in the genus *Halophila*. It is estimated that 2.6 million acres of seagrass occur in Florida with the largest distributions in the Big Bend region (Anclote to Apalachee Bay) of northwest Florida and the Florida Bay/Florida Keys region of south Florida (Sargent et al. 1995). Seagrasses are found in almost all of Florida's estuaries with the exception of northeast Florida, and their distributions are often limited by turbid waters, lowered salinity, and lack of suitable substrate.

Seagrass meadows are one of Florida's most important submerged marine habitats. They provide structural shelter and food for fish and shellfish important to the fishery and ecosystem. Seagrasses provide a direct food source to herbivores, such as manatees and sea turtles, and to organisms dependent on the detrital matter produced from the seagrass leaves. They also form the basis for a complex food web that conserves biodiversity and sustains a healthy ecosystem. Seagrasses im-

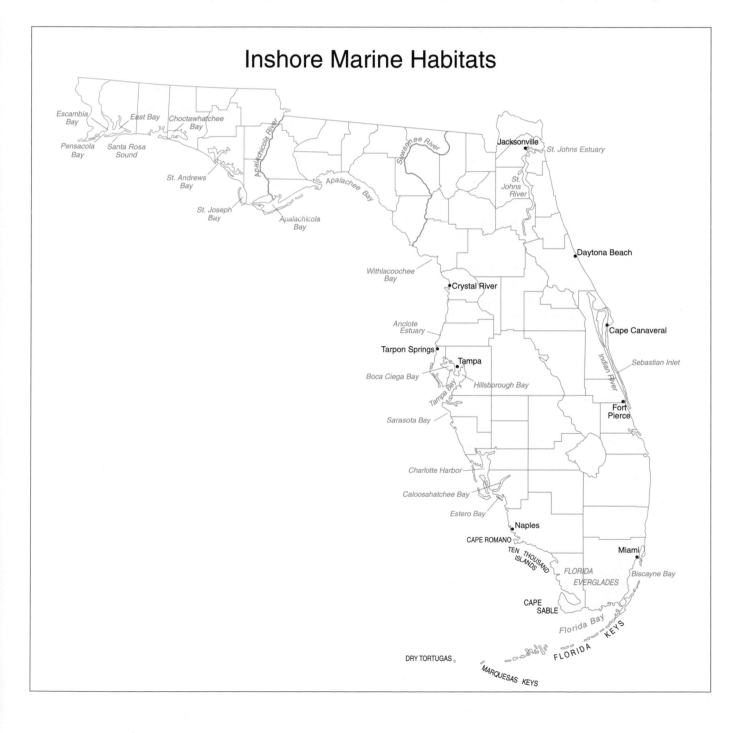

Inshore Marine Habitats

Ernest Estevez

Cockroach Bay, a small estuary near the Little Manatee River

Florida Department of Commerce

Tampa, a highly urbanized estuary

prove water quality by assimilating nutrients and by providing a baffle effect on waves and currents, which causes settling of suspended particles in the water column. Seagrasses also stabilize sediments by binding them with their root-like rhizomes.

Oyster bars are comprised of colonies of oysters (*Crassostrea virginica*), a filter-feeding, sedentary bivalve that feeds on unicellular algae and suspended particulate organic matter (Livingston 1990). Oyster bars occur in the estuaries of both coasts, especially near the mouths of rivers, in less than 35 feet of water, and on firm mud/shell substrates. Oysters provide food and habitat for a variety of estuarine species, including boring sponges, gastropod molluscs, polychaete worms, and decapod crustaceans (Livingston 1990). In turn, these species provide food for a variety of estuarine finfishes of economic significance.

Soft bottoms comprise the dominant benthic habitat of the estuaries along both Florida coasts (Livingston 1990). Soft bottoms are unvegetated soft sediments composed primarily of sand, sand-gravel, and shell. In extreme south Florida, mud-sand and coral rock bottom types are common. Soft bottoms are inhabited by a variety of animals living at or near the sediment-water interface and within the substrate. Typical organisms include polychaete worms, tubificid worms, amphipods, crustaceans, molluscs, and insect larvae. These species are largely detritivores, filter feeders, or predators. The faunal composition of soft bottoms plays a strong role in determining the macroinvertebrate and fish species composition in the overlying water column.

Natural Communities of Marine Ecosystems

Natural communities of the marine environment include: hard bottoms, tropical coral reefs, worm reefs, vermetid reefs, *Oculina* banks, deep coral banks, and artificial reefs (Jaap and Hallock 1990).

Hard bottoms are among the most widely distributed marine communities in Florida's coastal waters (Jaap and Hallock 1990). The principal requirement for hard bottoms is a solid substrate that provides attachment sites for species that live attached to hard bottoms. Hard bottom communities are found on reef limestone, rock outcrops on the sea floor, artificial reefs, seawalls, buoys, bridge pilings, and even boat bottoms. Once colonized by algae, sponges, octocorals, hard stony corals, and bryozoans, hard bottoms attract other marine life, including fishes. The Florida Middle Ground northwest of Tampa is the

best developed hard bottom community on the Florida Platform in the Gulf of Mexico. Species composition of hard bottom communities off the East Coast are similar to those off the Gulf Coast. East Coast hard bottom communities are more frequent south of Cape Canaveral. A notable hard bottom community is found on an extensive limestone outcrop off Jupiter Island at depths of 15 to 50 feet.

The most familiar of Florida's marine communities are the tropical coral reefs found in the shallow waters off the Florida Keys. Species composition and physiographic characteristics are similar to tropical reefs of the Bahamas and the Caribbean. Tropical coral reefs are characterized by high species diversity; rapid recycling of nitrogen and phosphorus; high gross primary productivity and low net primary productivity; highly transparent water; many species with specialized food requirements, narrow ecological niches, and complex life cycles; symbiotic relationships; and primary productivity by microscopic symbiotic algae. Tropical coral reefs are comprised of bank reefs, patch reefs, and Dry Tortugas reefs. Bank reefs are the primary reef systems occurring 4 to 8 miles seaward of the larger islands of the Florida Keys. Bank reefs consist of spurs, which are elongate limestone formations covered with living corals, and grooves, which are valleys of sand and rubble separating spurs. Patch reefs are smaller, roughly circular coral reefs. Most patch reefs are interspersed with grassbeds in waters 7 to 30 feet deep, often between the shore and bank reefs. Dry Tortugas reefs, where staghorn coral is common, occur about 75 miles west of Key West.

Worm reefs occur intertidally to depths of 30 feet along the east coast of Florida from Cape Canaveral to Key Biscayne, but they are best developed off of St. Lucie and Martin counties (Jaap and Hallock 1990). Worm reefs are formed by aggregations of the tropical marine worm *Phragmatopoma lapidosa*, which constructs low reefs of tubes comprised of sand grains cemented together by proteins. Worm reefs provide habitat for a diverse community of live-bottom plants and animals, serve as a nursery for numerous marine fishes, and support recreational fisheries for lobster and fish.

Vermetid reefs are found intertidally seaward of the outer islands of the Ten Thousand Islands region of southwest Florida (Jaap and Hallock 1990). Vermetid reefs were built by a worm-like gastropod mollusc of the genus *Petaloconchus* which grew on offshore shallow bars. Although *Petaloconchus* may be found living in the area, they are no longer forming reefs. Vermetid reefs provide habitat for estuarine live bottom species, including juvenile and adult stone crabs (*Menippe mercenaria*), as well as temporary refuge for a variety of fishes at high tide.

Oculina banks are found offshore of the east coast of Florida from Jacksonville to the St. Lucie Inlet in depths of 165 to 330 feet (Jaap and Hallock 1990). These little known reefs are banks constructed by ivory tree coral (*Oculina varicosa*), individuals of which may grow to 5 feet in height. Oculina banks often grow on limestone outcrops that parallel the coast at the margin of the continental shelf. As a result of extremely low light levels, the principal food source of *Oculina* banks is the primary production of phytoplankton in the overlying waters. A single coral colony may support hundreds of animals, including crabs, shrimps, molluscs, worms, anemones, small and large fish. *Oculina* banks are fragile and prone to damage by fishing gear.

Deep water coral banks are found offshore of the east coast of Florida along the margins of the continental shelf at depths of 1,300 to 2,600 feet (Jaap and Hallock 1990). Several species of fragile, branching corals create structures, sediment accumulations, and habitat similar to *Oculina* banks. Coral growth is relatively slow. The depths at which deep water coral banks occur suggest a dependence on planktonic and detrital food sources; however, little is known of the ecology of these reefs. Isopods and other crustaceans as well as a variety of fishes are associated with deep water coral banks.

Artificial reefs are comprised of all manner of materials accidentally or purposefully deposited in marine waters (Jaap and Hallock 1990). Examples of artificial reefs include shipwrecks, engineering structures, bridge pilings, piers, wrecked aircraft, pipelines, and navigation aids. Artificial reefs occur throughout Florida's coastal waters. The hard substrates of reef materials provide attachment sites for many epibiotic organisms, and the complexity of some structures can provide many hiding places for prey species. Artificial reefs often are colonized by algae, sponges, corals, tunicates, and bryozoans, and many mobile species, such as spiny lobsters, stone crabs, and reef fish, are attracted. The length of time required for an artificial reef to become viable habitat capable of supporting species important to marine fisheries depends on location, current patterns, local bottom type, and other factors. Typically, several years of biological community development are necessary before larger invertebrates and fishes take up residence (Jaap and Hallock 1990).

Species of Animals and Plants

Perhaps the most defining features of ecosystems and natural communities are the species of plants and animals that comprise them. Florida is widely recognized as one of North America's most important reservoirs of biological diversity. Millsap et al. (1990) reported that 668 terrestrial and freshwater vertebrate taxa occur regularly in Florida. This list includes 75 mammals, 283 birds (excluding some migratory species), 127 reptiles, 57 amphibians, and 126 fishes. About 115 (17 percent) of these are found nowhere else in the United States (Muller et al. 1989). Florida also contains approximately 3,500 species of vascular plants, of which about 8 percent are endemic (Ward 1979, Muller et al. 1989). The total number of invertebrate species inhabiting Florida is not known, but at least 410 invertebrates are thought to be endemic (Muller et al. 1989). The total number of marine species in Florida is unknown, but marine scientists estimate that there are more than 1,100 fish species and more than 5,000 invertebrate species.

The diversity of life in Florida has been shaped by many events. The Florida peninsula is a transitional area between temperate North America and the tropical West Indies, and the state contains faunal and floral elements of both. For example, American beech (*Fagus grandifolia*) and white oak (*Quercus alba*) reach the southern limits of their ranges in the Florida panhandle, whereas gumbo limbo (*Bursera simarubra*) and Bahama lysiloma (*Lysiloma latislaquum*) reach the northern limits of their ranges in extreme south Florida. Over geological time, high levels of ancient seas isolated populations of plants and animals on sandy scrub islands and allowed them to evolve into unique species endemic to Florida. Examples of scrub endemics include sand skink (*Neoseps reynoldsi*) and scrub plum (*Prunus geniculata*). In addition, over geologic time a number of species common elsewhere in North America and the tropics found their way to the state and managed to establish small disjunct populations in Florida. Species with disjunct populations include Florida scrub jay (*Aphelocoma coerulescens coerulescens*), Florida grasshoppper sparrow (*Ammodramus savannarum floridanus*), and eastern chipmunk (*Tamias striatus*).

93

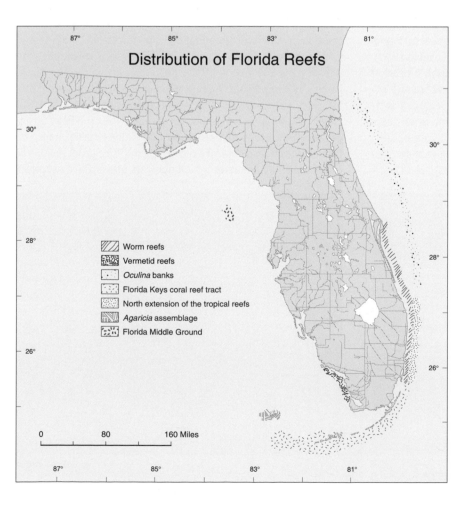

Distribution of Florida Reefs

Worm reefs
Vermetid reefs
Oculina banks
Florida Keys coral reef tract
North extension of the tropical reefs
Agaricia assemblage
Florida Middle Ground

0   80   160 Miles

Ecosystem Processes

Hydrological Cycles and Hydroperiods

In simplest terms, the hydrological cycle is the process by which water that rains on the land eventually flows to the sea, and water in the sea evaporates into the atmosphere, is blown over land, and falls on the land as rain, completing the cycle. In Florida, rainfall at times is torrential, leading to flood conditions in rivers, lakes, and wetlands. At other times, scarce rainfall leads to periods of drought when river, lake, and groundwater levels fall, and wetlands dry out. Floods and droughts both create stressful conditions to which the plants, animals, and natural communities of Florida have evolved a variety of adaptations. To a great extent, the locations of plants, animals, and communities are determined not only by seasonal rainfall patterns and geographic location but also by floods and droughts.

Florida is relatively flat with abundant rainfall and a water table that is near the soil surface in many places. As a result, wetlands are a common feature of the landscape. A factor which plays a strong role in determining the locations of wetland-adapted species, and therefore wetland communities in Florida, is hydroperiod (Ewel 1990). Hydroperiod refers to the depth and duration of standing water in wetlands following rain events. For example, the forested wetlands found in the floodplains of major rivers typically are inundated for 1 to 6 months each year. Hydric hammocks, which are usually found where limestone is very near the earth's surface and groundwater seepage is constant, typically are inundated for 3 to 6 months each year. Most forested wetlands typically are inundated for 5 to 9 months each year. Bay swamps and shrub bogs, both of which occur on sites that have constantly saturated soils that rarely flood, have hydroperiods of 9 to 11 months each year. Herbaceous freshwater wetlands are inundated 7 to 12 months each year to depths of less than 20 inches, and they dry out to depths of less than 12 inches below the ground surface (Kushlan 1990).

Hydroperiods are determined in part by wetland location and soil type. For example, river floodplains, obviously, extend landward from the banks of rivers. The species of wetlands plants typical of these areas tolerate frequent, often deep, inundation by flowing waters, but they are intolerant of still-water situations. On the other hand, wetlands found in flatwoods (e.g., cypress ponds, gum ponds, prairie marshes) are in environments where the water does not flow, but rather fluctuates up and down, and inundation may extend for longer periods of time. The species of plants adapted to flatwoods wetlands require adaptations that allow their roots to survive in soils that are low in oxygen for extended periods. Bay swamps often are found at the bases of sandy ridges where rainwater drains through the excessively drained soils, reaches the groundwater table, and then migrates to the base of the ridge where it constantly seeps out. In this situation, the soil remains constantly saturated but rarely floods. The bay swamp at the base of the southeastern end of the Lake Wales Ridge in Highlands County was formed in this manner.

Fire

Naturally occurring wild fires have played a defining role in shaping Florida's natural communities. Florida has one of the highest frequencies of lightning strikes of any region in the United States and more thunderstorm days per year than anywhere in the country (Abrahamson and Hartnett 1990). In response to thousands of years of frequent lightning-set wild fires, many natural communities in Florida actually are maintained in a stable, nonsuccessional state by frequent fires. Pine flatwoods, longleaf pine (*Pinus palustris*)-wiregrass (*Aristida stricta*) sandhills and clayhills, prairies, scrubs, and herbaceous wetlands all are maintained by regularly occurring fires. In the absence of fires, fire intolerant species, particularly hardwoods, invade a site, and over time the vegetation of a site will succeed to a hardwood forest.

Longleaf pine, formerly the dominant tree of sandhills, clayhills, and flatwoods in the northern two-thirds of the state, is well adapted to frequent wildfires. Longleaf pine is even credited with having adaptations that promote frequent fires. The bark of longleaf pines is highly fire-resistant such that the base of a tree will be scorched by a fire, but the entire tree rarely burns. Juvenile longleaf pines go through a "grass" stage in which the delicate growing bud is closely surrounded by densely packed needles that protect it from ground fires. Longleaf pines also drop their needles like a carpet on the forest floor or on any low-growing vegetation beneath them. Highly flammable when dry, the pine needles readily carry a ground fire of low intensity such that flames rarely reach the forest canopy. In a natural state, longleaf pines grow in a fairly open, park-like situation which does not allow a fire to spread

94

David LaHart

Pine flatwoods are maintained by regularly occurring fires.

through the canopy even if flames manage to reach the canopy of some trees. Ground cover species such as wiregrass and saw palmetto (*Serenoa repens*) also are highly flammable, promoting the spread of fires, but they rapidly send up new shoots from underground stems and roots after a burn.

Specific burn frequencies are necessary to maintain fire-adapted communities. Sandhills and clayhills burn every 2 to 3 years, pine flatwoods and prairies burn every 3 to 7 years, scrubs burn no more often than every 40 to 55 years, deep water marshes burn every 3 to 5 years, shallow water marshes burn on 1- to 3-year cycles (Kushlan1990), shrub bogs burn every 11 to 33 years, dwarf cypress savannas burn every 11 to 12 years, and cypress ponds and strands burn as often as once every 20 to 25 years (Ewel 1990). Almost all upland and wetland communities are affected by fire at one time or another. Even forested wetlands, such as river swamps, hydric hammocks, mixed hardwood swamps, gum ponds, lake fringe swamps, and bay swamps, are likely to experience fire once a century. Hardwood forests are about the only upland type of community that does not burn regularly. Fires that burn hardwood forests typically are catastrophic, and other types of communities are likely to vegetate a site after a hardwood forest has burned.

Historically, naturally occurring wild fires could burn over large areas, impeded only by water bodies or saturated wetlands. However, Florida is now crisscrossed with roads and fire lanes, urban developments have sprung up next to flatwoods and sandhills, and timber has been cleared. The net result of human intervention has been that naturally occurring wild fires no longer occur with their former frequency, and fire-maintained communities are no longer able to sustain themselves without help. Many forests must now be burned under controlled conditions in order to reduce fuel and eliminate hardwoods. Otherwise, unburned sites will either succeed to hardwood forests or will burn catastrophically due to over-accumulation of fuel. However, even controlled burning of fire-maintained communities is becoming more difficult as Florida continues to develop. Smoke from controlled fires may drift across an increasing number of roads, creating traffic hazards, or it may blow into urban neighborhoods where the residents are likely to have health or safety concerns.

A further issue with burning pertains to season of burn. Most natural wild fires occur in the summer months when thunderstorms and lightning are more likely. Summer is the growing season for most plants as well as the reproductive season for most animals. Plant ecologists, in particular, believe that the growing season is the appropriate time to conduct controlled burns of Florida's fire-maintained communities as many species of plants are stimulated to reproduce by fires. However, most controlled burns have been conducted in the winter when weather is cooler and plant materials are dead or dry and highly flammable. Many ecologists believe that the long history of winter burns has subtly shifted the composition of many plant communities away from that which occurred naturally. Land managers are experimenting with conducting controlled fires during the growing season in an effort to shift fire-maintained communities towards a more natural state.

Nutrient Cycling and Food Webs

The phrase "ashes to ashes, dust to dust" is an age-old acknowledgment of the existence and fundamental necessity of nutrient cycling. All plants and animals require nutrients in order to live and grow. Whereas plants require nutrients in elemental or ionic form, animals are more dependent on nutrients in organic form. The principal nutrients affecting life on earth are nitrogen, phosphorus, potassium, sulphur, oxygen, and carbon. Since the earth contains a finite quantity of the nutrients needed for life, plants, animals, and communities have evolved complex mechanisms for recycling nutrients for repeated use.

Plants obtain nitrogen, phosphorus, potassium, and sulphur from the soil, and they obtain carbon and oxygen from the air around them. These raw ingredients are used to capture sunlight energy and build plant tissues. The process of growing depletes nutrient reserves in the soil, and, in order for life to continue, mechanisms are needed to return nutrients to the soil. This is accomplished in several ways. Plants may die and fall to the ground where decomposing organisms, such as fungi and bacteria, slowly break organic materials down into inorganic form for reuse by plants. Fire is a more rapid way of recycling nutrients. Wild fires or prescribed burns quickly turn organic plant (and animal) materials into inorganic form, bypassing the decomposer organisms and making nutrients available to plants.

Another way that nutrients are recycled is through the food web. Most plants and plant parts are eaten by some type of animal. Animal species have evolved a tremendous variety of adaptations to take advantage of specific species of plant or particular parts of plants. For example, butterfly larvae eat leaves, aphids suck plant juices, sandhill cranes feed in part on plant roots, cedar waxwings prefer berries, and gopher tortoises eat grass. In turn, animals are eaten by other animals, which are eaten by still other animals. All along the way, all animals excrete dung, which usually ends up on the ground where it is reduced to inorganic form by decomposer organisms. Animals may also simply die of illness or old age and be recycled to the soil, again by decomposer organsims.

Nutrients often are exported from one ecosystem to another by water. Falling rain carries with it dilute quantities of dissolved nutrients which are readily available to plant life. As water from rainfall seeps into the soil or flows off the land, nutrients are leached from the soil and carried downstream, ultimately fueling life in rivers, lakes, estuaries, and the ocean.

A very special form of nutrient recycling without which life could not exist is anaerobic decomposition, the break down of organic materials in environments where oxygen is lacking. Such environments typically occur in sediments at the bottoms of lakes, wetlands, estuaries, or marine ecosystems. In these environments, specially adapted bacteria are capable of using the energy available in organic compounds to break organic materials into inorganic nutrients. In the process, these special decomposers release elemental nitrogen and hydrogen sulfide gases which bubble to the surface and are released into the atmosphere. Anaerobic decomposition is the only way that nitrogen and sulphur are recycled for reuse by plants and animals. In the absence of anaerobic decomposition, all dead organic materials would eventually end up in an anaerobic environment at the bottom of a water body, and life would cease to exist. Famed Florida limnologist Edward Deevy once wrote a brilliant essay entitled, "In Defense of Mud," in which he extolled the importance of mud, wetlands, and smelly estuarine sediments for their role in recycling nutrients essential to the very existence of life.

FLORIDA ECOSYSTEMS
Estuarine and Marine Ecosystems

Kenneth Haddad

Kenneth Haddad

Florida Game and Fresh Water Fish Commission

CORAL REEFS AND HARD BOTTOMS

SUBSTRATE: Limestone base created by skeletal deposits of dead corals and coralline algae.

TOPOGRAPHY: Bank reefs—three-dimensional, forest-like structures on continental margin seaward of larger islands of the Florida Keys; patch reefs—smaller, roughly circular structures in waters less than 10 meters deep; Hard bottom—limestone base with a variety of corals, plants, and sponges in depths of 1 to 100 meters.

VEGETATION/ALGAE: Microscopic algae live symbiotically in outer parts of coral polyps (i.e., coral bodies); calcareous algae also live among the corals and hard bottoms and secrete thin layers of limestone; microalgae are common on hard bottoms.

FAUNA: Over 100 species and subspecies of corals and algae; hundreds of fish and invertebrate species; numerous species of commercial and recreational value, including spiny lobster, grouper, snapper, parrotfish, and butterfly fish. Many reef species have specialized food requirements, narrow niches, and complex life cycles.

PROCESSES/DYNAMICS/ABIOTIC FACTORS: Highly transparent, warm, relatively nutrient-poor waters are favorable for coral reefs; hard bottoms are tolerant to a wide range of temperatures and water quality, but require salty waters; terrestrial vegetation, including mangroves along shoreline, filters sediments, organic debris, and nutrients that would otherwise be detrimental; waves generated by storms and hurricanes may erode and undermine the structure of reefs.

HUMAN IMPACTS: Impacts from ship groundings, certain fishing practices, overharvest, and excessive recreational use are problems. Nutrient pollution is a serious problem for coral reefs, but as long as nutrient levels remain favorable, communities may have the potential to recover.

SEAGRASS BEDS AND SOFT BOTTOMS

SUBSTRATE: Mixtures of sand, silt, mud, clay, and shell fragments.

TOPOGRAPHY: Coastal areas, covered by shallow water.

VEGETATION/ALGAE: Seven species of seagrass are found in Florida waters, of which turtle, shoal, and manatee grasses are predominant. Seagrass beds are one of the most productive and important vegetative habitats of inshore marine systems; these beds are also substrates for epiphytic (attached) algae, an important component of the seagrass food web.

FAUNA: Seagrass beds provide excellent habitat for many fishes, crustaceans, and shellfish and are critical to the younger marine animals as nursery areas. Bay scallops, blue crabs, and spotted seatrout are examples of especially important recreational and commercial species that depend on seagrass habitat. Manatees and sea turtles depend on seagrasses as a major part of their diet.

PROCESSES/DYNAMICS/ABIOTIC FACTORS: Good water clarity and estuarine to ocean salinities are the primary factors that allow seagrass beds to flourish. Seagrasses stabilize the bottom and filter the water.

HUMAN IMPACTS: Dredge and fill have historically impacted seagrasses. Today, degraded water quality and water clarity, changes in freshwater flow, and boat propeller scarring are responsible for declines.

MANGROVES AND SALT MARSHES

SUBSTRATE: Waterlogged, anaerobic, brackish sediment deposited by freshwater runoff and tides, and increased by organic matter from mangroves.

TOPOGRAPHY: Low-lying, intertidal zone, with some extensive to irregularly flooded higher fringe areas or sloping up slightly from permanent water edge.

VEGETATION/ALGAE: Red, black, and white mangroves grow in intertidal to high intertidal waters, respectively, and are often zoned by tidal regime; buttonwood (not a true mangrove) is often on upland fringe; prop roots serve as substrate for many algae. Salt marshes are nonwoody, salt-tolerant plants; principal species are smooth cordgrass and black needlerush; above mean high water level are numerous vascular plant species in addition to black neelerush; several hundred species of benthic microalgae and phytoplankton; a few species of large, multicellular seaweeds.

FAUNA: Valuable habitat for wide range of invertebrates and vertebrates; food and cover for resident and transient animals; nursery grounds for many fish and shellfish of commercial and recreational importance; many visiting birds and four exclusive salt marsh residents—clapper rails, long-billed marsh wrens, seaside sparrows, and endangered Atlantic salt marsh snake. Mangrove islands are important nesting habitat for many wading and diving birds.

PROCESSES/DYNAMICS/ABIOTIC FACTORS: Mangroves are limited by temperature to tropics and subtropics and outcompete salt marshes in those areas; salt marshes are cold tolerant and are dominant in northern Florida; fluctuations of water level necessary for proper development; salt water excludes potential plant competitors; stabilizes shorelines.

HUMAN IMPACTS: Thousands of acres have been destroyed and replaced with filled and developed land; can be seriously damaged by oil spills and herbicides; both sport and commercial fisheries decline when mangroves are destroyed.

OTHER SHALLOW WATER HABITATS

SUBSTRATE: Mud, sand, silt, clay, shell.

TOPOGRAPHY: Intertidal to subtidal and submerged.

VEGETATION/ALGAE: Microalgae can be transient (both attached and free) in bare bottom areas and attached to oyster reefs; algal mats can form in the sediments; benthic microalgae thrive.

FAUNA: Bare sediments are deceiving in that they host a variety of benthic fauna living in the sediments; a variety of fish and shellfish feed on the organisms living in bare sediments; oyster reefs are concentrated in inshore areas along the Gulf coast, particularly the Apalachicola estuary; oyster reefs provide habitat for many fauna including crabs and juvenile fish.

PROCESSES/DYNAMICS/ABIOTIC FACTORS: Bare sediments are found throughout the marine environment in a wide range of salinities and temperatures. Oyster reefs depend on freshwater flow and brackish salinities to survive. Hurricanes and storm events can significantly alter sediment characteristics and flora and fauna.

HUMAN IMPACTS: Dredge and fill; pollution can alter the biodiversity and composition of sediment organisms and close oyster and clam beds to fishing; alterations in freshwater flow.

Perry Oldenburg

DUNES AND MARITIME FORESTS

SUBSTRATE AND TOPOGRAPHY: Sandy, sometimes mixed with calcium carbonate; linear barrier islands and some other shorelines along coast; sandy capes; typically contain parallel zones of upper beach, undulating foredune, transition or "backdune," and stable dune, sloping upward and away from the water's edge.

VEGETATION: Foredunes contain grasses such as sea oats; a variety of forest vegetation is characteristic of stable dunes: going south from Cape Canaveral on the east and from Tampa Bay on the west, gradually changes from domination by temperate species to domination by tropical species; at least 22 species of endemic plants are found in dunes and maritime forests.

FAUNA: Beaches are the most important nesting site for loggerhead turtle in Western Hemisphere, as well as for several species of shore birds, including the endangered snowy plover; dunes and forests are wintering grounds for many other bird species, habitat for several special-interest species of small rodents, and habitat for migratory songbirds.

PROCESSES/DYNAMICS/ABIOTIC FACTORS: Wind- and wave-driven sand interact with pioneer grasses to build dunes; waves from hurricanes may destroy dunes.

HUMAN IMPACTS: Development of beachfront, with greatest impacts near Ft. Walton, Jacksonville, Daytona Beach, Palm Beach, Ft. Lauderdale, Miami, and Clearwater–St. Petersburg; by 1975 nearly 20 percent of Florida's barrier islands had been developed; heavy recreational use; exotic plants such as Australian pine, Brazilian pepper, and sisal are also a serious problem.

Florida Game and Fresh Water Fish Commission

Freshwater Wetlands and Aquatic Ecosystems

ALLUVIAL RIVERS

SUBSTRATE: Sand, silt, gravel, and exposed limestone are present.

TOPOGRAPHY/HYDROLOGY: These rivers typically have large drainage basins which result in the high bed load. Typically, alluvial rivers contain large forested floodplains, with sandbars, levees, old river channels or sloughs, and oxbow lakes.

VEGETATION: Floodplains contain a wide variety of hardwoods, shrubs, and woody plants. Tupelo-ash-cypress communities are found in the wetter areas of the floodplain. Oak-hickory communities are found on the drier levees or upslope areas. Oxbow lakes may contain a variety of aquatic and wetland vegetation like maidencane, rushes, *Nuphar* and *Nymphea*.

FAUNA: Alluvial rivers contain 100 to 152 species of fish, many mussel and invertebrate species. Floodplains are home to ducks and wading birds, otters, beavers, bear, and other mammals. The Apalachicola contains more rare and endangered species of plants and animals than any other river system in Florida.

PROCESSES/DYNAMICS/ABIOTIC FACTORS: Natural wide fluctuations in flow occur with very high flows usually in the spring and low flows in the summer and fall. These rivers have high sediment or bed loads which accumulate on the numerous sandbars or pointbars.

HUMAN IMPACTS: Channelization and dredging for navigation, dam construction, introduction of exotic species, water withdrawals and flow alterations, wetland filling, and pollution.

Florida Game and Fresh Water Fish Commission

SPRING-FED RIVERS

SUBSTRATE: Sand and exposed limestone are the primary bottom types.

TOPOGRAPHY/HYDROLOGY: Spring-fed rivers derive the majority of their flow from natural springs. The springs are natural connections to the aquifer. These rivers typically occur in karst or limestone areas.

VEGETATION: Submerged vegetation, like eelgrass, hornwort, and water lilies, are abundant in these rivers due to the clarity of the water.

FAUNA: Spring-fed rivers contain abundant populations of musssels and snails. Mussel- and snail-eating turtles, like Barbour's map turtle (*Graptemys barbouri*) and loggerhead musk turtle (*Sternotherus minor*), and mussel-eating fish, such as redbreast sunfish (*Lepomis auritus*), are typically found in spring-fed rivers and streams. The bluefin killifish (*Lucania goodei*) and redeye chub (*Notropis harperi*) are almost exclusively found in spring-fed systems.

PROCESSES/DYNAMICS/ABIOTIC FACTORS: Spring-fed rivers have high water clarity, low sedimentation rates, and slight changes in water level or flow conditions. Because there is minimal change in water levels, the river channel is very stable and does not create a large floodplain with the same features as an alluvial river.

HUMAN IMPACTS: Flow alterations due to groundwater withdrawals and dams, wetland filling, introduction of exotic plants and animals, and groundwater pollution.

Perry Oldenburg

BLACKWATER RIVERS

SUBSTRATE: Sand, silt, and some exposed limestone bottoms

TOPOGRAPHY/HYDROLOGY: Blackwater rivers drain acidic flatwoods and swamps. Typically the flow has low velocities and the streams and rivers are low gradient.

VEGETATION: Drainage basins are typically acidic flatwoods and cypress-gum swamps. Submerged vegetation is limited due to the highly colored and acidic water, which limits light penetration. However, some *Nupar* and *Nymphea* species may be present.

FAUNA: Blackwater rivers have lower fish and invertebrate species diversity than spring-fed or alluvial rivers due in part to the high acidity of the water. The three-lined salamander (*Eurycea longicauda guttolineata*), southern dusky salamander (*Desmognathus auriculatus*), and the mud salamander (*Pseudotriton montanus*) are commonly found in blackwater systems.

PROCESSES/DYNAMICS/ABIOTIC FACTORS: Blackwater rivers derive their name from the high amounts of tannin and humic acids which darkly color the water and are produced in the acidic flatwoods and swamps. Blackwater rivers may carry a high sediment load during high water because of the land runoff occurring upstream, and a low sediment load during low flow periods.

HUMAN IMPACTS: Wetland filling, flow alterations due to groundwater withdrawal and dams, and water pollution.

Perry Oldenburg

97

LAKES

SUBSTRATE: Predominantly sandy with beds of clay, phosphatic mudstone, and peat; usually underlain by limestone.

TOPOGRAPHY/HYDROLOGY: Most Florida lakes formed by dissolution of limestone bedrock, subsequent groundwater flow into subterranean caverns, and collapse of surface layers; 7,800 lakes greater than 1 acre; most are small, shallow, and in central, sandy ridge part of state; Okeechobee, produced by an uplifted sea-floor depression, is by far the largest.

VEGETATION/ALGAE: Density and diversity of microalgal species dependent on trophic level; aquatic plants, macroalgae, mosses, and floating flowering plants particularly important in Florida's numerous shallow lakes.

FAUNA: Molluscs, crustaceans, larval and adult insects common; about 40 species of native fishes.

PROCESSES/DYNAMICS/ABIOTIC FACTORS: Trophic (nutrient) status varies; most lakes are poorly to moderately supplied with nitrogen and phosphorus nutrients and have low to medium densities of microalgae and aquatic plants.

HUMAN IMPACTS: Discharge of nutrients and other pollutants from human activities; siltation from forest clearing; exotic plant species such as water hyacinth and hydrilla clog water bodies and change their chemical composition; native fish experience competition from 21 established exotic fish species.

SWAMPS

SUBSTRATE: Saturated with water for varying periods each year; amount of organic matter depends on length of saturation, source of water, and fire frequency.

TOPOGRAPHY: Low-lying; along drainages, around lakes, in small ponds, and on limestone outcrops.

VEGETATION: About 100 species of trees, shrubs, and woody vines commonly found; river swamps most diverse and productive; cypress usually dominates in swamps with frequent fires and fluctuating water levels; bays usually dominate in seepage swamps with little water-level fluctuation; high frequency of endemic epiphytes in south Florida swamps.

FAUNA: Many invertebrate species; large and diverse fish populations in swamps adjacent to rivers and lakes; many common amphibians and some reptiles depend on swamps for reproduction; considerable diversity of birds and mammals; rare and endangered birds and mammals most likely to occur in cypress swamps and mixed hardwood swamps.

PROCESSES/DYNAMICS/ABIOTIC FACTORS: Annual length of soil saturation, amount of organic matter accumulation in soil, source of water, and fire frequency determine major characteristics of Florida swamps.

HUMAN IMPACTS: Drainage, filling, mining, logging, water pollution, invasion of human-introduced exotic plants such as melaleuca; in south Florida, alteration of hydroperiod affects swamps rapidly and profoundly.

FRESHWATER MARSHES

SUBSTRATE: Peat in deep-water marshes with long hydroperiods; marl or sandy in marshes with moderate to short hydroperiods and seasonal drying.

TOPOGRAPHY: Low, flat, poorly drained.

VEGETATION: Dominant species are herbaceous plants such as water lily, cattail, maidencane, and pickerelweed; most are of temperate origin; the Everglades marsh, which is by far the largest, is dominated by saw grass.

FAUNA: Abundant animal life but not diverse, except for birds; both temperate and tropical birds abound; habitat for the endangered Cape Sable seaside sparrow, snail kite, and wood stork; the American alligator is an important animal in many Florida marshes; white-tailed deer use freshwater marshes extensively.

PROCESSES/DYNAMICS/ABIOTIC FACTORS: Shallow water at or above the soil surface for much of the year; fire is of crucial importance in limiting invasion of woody vegetation; fire period in deep-water marshes is every 3 to 5 years; shallow marshes tend to burn on a 1- to 3-year cycle.

HUMAN IMPACTS: Campaigns to drain wetlands throughout the history of Florida following European settlement; between mid-1950s and mid-1970s, 24 percent of Florida's remaining marshes were drained; many more have been severely altered by unnatural flooding.

Upland Ecosystems

PINE FLATWOODS

SUBSTRATE: Relatively poorly drained, acidic, sandy soils underlain by organic hardpan.

TOPOGRAPHY: Low, flat.

VEGETATION: Overstory of longleaf, slash, or pond pine dominates; shrub understory contains species such as saw palmetto, wax myrtle, gallberry, and wiregrass.

FAUNA: Diverse birds, mammals, reptiles, and amphibians are found in pine flatwoods, e.g., eastern diamondback rattlesnake, threatened red-cockaded woodpecker, white-tailed deer, threatened Florida black bear, endangered Florida panther.

PROCESSES/DYNAMICS/ABIOTIC FACTORS: Natural fires tend to maintain relatively stable stands of pine flatwoods.

HUMAN IMPACTS: Flatwoods were once the most extensive terrestrial ecosystem in Florida; they are now being converted to many uses, including agriculture, pasture for livestock, and urbanization; much of north Florida pine flatwoods has been converted to pine plantations; alteration of natural fire regimes can cause major changes in species composition, even when not accompanied by land-use conversions; 48 percent decline in pine flatwoods since settlement.

DRY PRAIRIES

SUBSTRATE: Relatively poorly drained, acidic, sandy soils underlain by organic hardpan.

TOPOGRAPHY: Low, flat.

VEGETATION: Similar to pine flatwoods but without trees. Herbaceous species include wiregrass, bottlebrush three-awn, arrowfeather, broomsedge, and love grasses. Sparse saw palmetto and other shrubs also may be present.

FAUNA: Primary habitat of threatened crested caracara and threatened sandhill crane.

PROCESSES/DYNAMICS/ABIOTIC FACTORS: Natural fires tend to maintain relatively stable stands of dry prairies.

HUMAN IMPACTS: Dry prairies are now being converted to many uses, including agriculture, pasture for livestock, and urbanization; alteration of natural fire regimes can cause major changes in species composition, even when not accompanied by land-use conversions; 32 percent decline in dry prairies since settlement.

Beth Stys

SCRUB

SUBSTRATE: Droughty, sandy, low-fertility soils.

TOPOGRAPHY: Hilly uplands, low sandy ridges in flatwoods, sandy ridges interior from coast.

VEGETATION: Shrubby evergreen oaks and/or Florida rosemary; may have sand pine overstory; contains 13 federally listed endangered or threatened plant species.

FAUNA: Several thousand species of arthropods; threatened Florida scrub jay, Florida scrub lizard, threatened sand skink, blue-tailed mole skink, gopher tortoise, white-tailed deer, bobcat, gray fox, spotted skunk.

PROCESSES/DYNAMICS/ABIOTIC FACTORS: Dependent on infrequent, high-intensity fires; species tolerant of very dry, low nutrient conditions.

HUMAN IMPACTS: Ecosystem rare, even prior to European settlement; after earlier losses to agriculture, now threatened primarily by real estate development; 56 percent decline since settlement.

Florida Game and Fresh Water Fish Commission

HIGH PINE

SUBSTRATE: Droughty, sandy, low-fertility soils; clay soils in panhandle.

TOPOGRAPHY: Hilly uplands.

VEGETATION: Longleaf pine interspersed with deciduous oaks, especially turkey oak, with an herbaceous layer usually dominated by wiregrass.

FAUNA: Many broadly distributed vertebrates; endangered red-cockaded woodpecker, bobwhite quail, Sherman's fox squirrel, gopher tortoise, Bachman's sparrow.

PROCESSES/DYNAMICS/ABIOTIC FACTORS: Dependent on frequent, low-intensity fires; species tolerant of very dry, low nutrient conditions.

HUMAN IMPACTS: 6.5 billion board feet of virgin longleaf pine removed in Florida in late 1800s and early 1900s; 87 percent loss since European settlement; does not regenerate well; very few good examples of old-growth longleaf pine remain.

99

Perry Oldenburg

Florida Game and Fresh Water Fish Commission

TEMPERATE HARDWOOD FORESTS
"HAMMOCKS"

SUBSTRATE: Soils generally contain more organic matter and moisture than adjacent, well-drained sandy soils.

TOPOGRAPHY: On slopes between upland pinelands and lake margins or floodplain forests and marshes; also in some uplands protected from fire.

VEGETATION: In typically narrow bands; varies from warm temperate, mixed deciduous-evergreen flora (e.g., oaks, hickories, beech, magnolia) in north to subtropical evergreen flora in south; many species of trees but few species of herbs, except for diverse ferns in peninsular hammocks; hammocks on the Apalachicola Bluffs contain *Torreya taxifolia*, a tree on the verge of extinction, as well as other endemic plant species.

FAUNA: Diversity of vertebrates, including bobcat, gray fox, white-tailed deer, southern flying squirrel, Mississippi kite, barred owl, pileated woodpecker, eastern diamondback rattlesnake.

PROCESSES/DYNAMICS/ABIOTIC FACTORS: Species composition continually being modified by changing and variable environment; combinations of species in some hardwood forests were not present before European settlement.

HUMAN IMPACTS: Composition of plant species has been affected by human disturbance; increasingly threatened by residential/commercial development, e.g., around Gainesville and Tallahassee.

Julie Hovis

Natural Ecosystems Management Issues

Atmospheric Deposition

Air pollution not only affects human health, but can also affect the quality of water in rivers, lakes, and estuaries. Air pollutants may fall as dry particles on land or water or may be deposited with rainfall. The process of deposition entails emissions of particulates and gases from air pollution sources, transport of these emissions by wind, potential chemical or physical transformations, and depositions to land and water surfaces. Deposition may be direct to the water body or indirect from runoff from the land surface.

Sources of pollutants reaching Florida may be global as well as regional and local. In Florida most air pollutants come from fossil fuel combustion, mostly from power plants and motor vehicles. Waste incineration, sulfuric acid production, cement manufacturing, pulp and paper production, and combustion of plant and animal biomass are also significant sources of air pollutants. Natural processes such as volcanic eruptions, forest fires, and suspension of eroded soil particles may contribute to air pollution.

The U.S. Environmental Protection Agency conducted a national surface water survey between 1984 and 1986 to identify the extent of acidification of lakes and streams in the United States. Of water bodies sampled in Florida, 23 percent of the lakes and 39 percent of the streams were found to be acidic. Further studies indicated that some lakes in the north central peninsula do have increased acidity due to atmospheric deposition. In most cases, however, naturally occurring organic acids are the dominant factor controlling the acidity in acidic streams. No widespread fish population losses or decreases in fish biomass have been documented because of acidic deposition in Florida.

The U.S. Environmental Protection Agency has identified eutrophication (nutrient enrichment) as one of the most serious pollution problems facing estuarine waters in the United States. Nitrogen compounds from atmospheric deposition exacerbate this problem. Eutrophication may result in oxygen depletion or reduced oxygen in the water, nuisance or toxic algae blooms, dieback of underwater plants due to reduced light penetration, and reduced populations of fish and shellfish.

In Florida coastal waters seagrasses provide shelter, and nursery and feeding habitat for many popular fish and shellfish. The quantity of seagrass is an important indicator of estuary health. In the Tampa Bay estuary, for example, seagrass losses have been attributed, in part, to reduced penetration of sunlight due to excess concentrations of phytoplankton and suspended solids in the water column. These excess concentrations are related to the increased nutrient loadings that have occurred in the past in the Tampa Bay estuary. Over the past

100

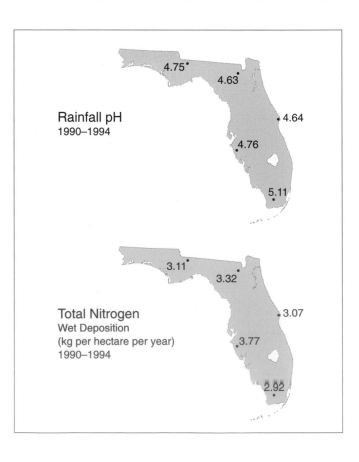

Rainfall pH
1990–1994

4.75
4.63
4.64
4.76
5.11

Total Nitrogen
Wet Deposition
(kg per hectare per year)
1990–1994

3.11
3.32
3.07
3.77
2.92

10 to 15 years, however, seagrass has increased by about 4,000 acres, largely as a result of improvements in sewage treatment and stormwater management. The current nitrogen loading to Tampa Bay is largely due to atmospheric deposition, either directly to the bay's surface or transported by stormwater from the bay's watershed. The Tampa Bay National Estuary Program has estimated that 27 percent of the bay's nitrogen loading is due to direct deposition to the bay. Atmospherically derived nitrogen from watershed runoff could increase the total to 50 to 60 percent.

In 1989 a joint monitoring project by the Florida Game and Fresh Water Fish Commission, Florida Department of Health and Rehabilitative Services, and the Florida Department of Environmental Protection found high levels of mercury in fish from the Everglades. Mercury is known to be neurotoxic to humans, and its consumption through contaminated food has caused substantial illness and mortality in several episodes elsewhere in the world. These and subsequent findings of high mercury levels in fish led the State Health Officer to issue a series of health advisories urging fishermen not to eat some species of fish caught in the Everglades, and to sharply limit consumption of largemouth bass taken from other fresh waters in Florida.

At the time of this writing, seven years after the initial findings, we know that approximately 1 million acres of the Everglades drainage system contain fish with markedly elevated mercury burdens. Largemouth bass (*Micropterus salmoides*) average over 1.5 parts per million mercury, which exceeds all health-based standards. More than another million acres of fresh waters of Florida contain largemouth bass with elevated, but lesser, levels of mercury. When sampling is complete, mercury problems in bass are expected to be found in one-half to two-thirds of Florida's lakes and streams. Excessive mercury levels are also found in some marine fish, particularly large, long-lived predators such as shark and king mackerel (*Scomberomerus cavalla*), and certain fish from limited areas of near-shore waters.

Excessive levels of mercury found in fish today is not limited to Florida. Thirty-seven states have issued health advisories restricting consumption of fish, and similar problems are

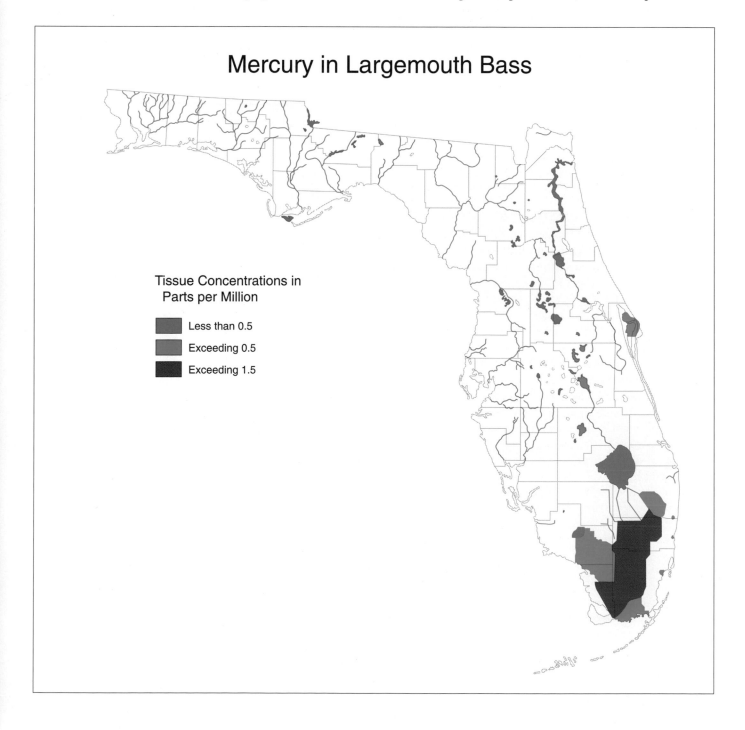

Mercury in Largemouth Bass

Tissue Concentrations in
Parts per Million

Less than 0.5

Exceeding 0.5

Exceeding 1.5

found widely in North America, Europe, and Asia. Many lakes in Canada and Scandinavia, for example, are affected.

It is generally accepted that the widespread mercury problem is caused by air pollution. Both long distance transport and localized deposition around certain types of sources may be important. Major sources to the atmosphere are metals mining and smelting, coal-fired utilities and industry, and the use and disposal of mercury in commercial products. The unusually severe problem in the Everglades has many unique features, and may be the result of a combination of other factors. Initial studies focused on the local effects of municipal incinerators and other emissions sources on the southeast coast of Florida, increased release of mercury from the soils of the Everglades Agricultural Area promoted by drainage and soil disturbance, or increased mercury mobilization from Everglades soils stemming from hydrological changes caused by the Central and South Florida Flood Control Project.

A four-year study by researchers at Florida State University and Texas A & M University funded by the U.S. Environmental Protection Agency, Florida Department of Environmental Protection, the Florida Electric Power Coordinating Group, Florida Power and Light, the Electric Power Research Institute, and the South Florida Water Management District found that mercury concentrations in rainfall increase in the summertime when rainfall is highest, whereas concentrations of other pollutants decrease. Researchers theorized that most of the air-borne mercury falling on the Everglades originates from heavy industry to the north both in the United States and abroad. Elemental mercury travels along with air currents from the U.S. east across the Atlantic until it reaches and mixes with air currents from the coast of Europe, which contain mercury not only from Europe but perhaps from Russia and China as well. The air mass now travels south where the trade winds carry it back across the Atlantic to Florida. Summer thunderstorms, with thunderheads up to 12 miles high, scour the mercury out of the upper atmosphere (Stephenson 1997).

Once mercury is in the surface water rapid geochemical transformations can occur beginning the process of bioaccumulation. Precise mechanisms are unknown, but mercury probably enters the food chain when plankton consume mercury containing bacteria. Understanding this initial step is critical because concentrations of mercury in plankton increase 10,000-fold over water concentrations (Krabbenhoft 1996). At each other trophic level the increase in concentration is 10-fold or less. The U.S. Geological Survey, the South Florida Water Management District, and the U.S. Environmental Protection Agency are co-funding a group of scientists to study mercury bioaccumulation in the Everglades. The overall objective of the study is to provide resource managers with information on the hydrologic, biologic, and geochemical processes controlling mercury cycling in the Everglades. Results of this study are expected to be available in the fall of 1999.

Loss and Degradation of Upland and Wetland Habitats

The land area of Florida supporting natural vegetation types has declined dramatically since European settlement. Florida's rapid population growth, particularly over the last 100 years, has resulted in the conversion of vast areas of the natural landscape to human uses. Today, agricultural, urban, and other uses account for 43 percent of the Florida landscape, and forests and herbaceous wetlands comprise the other 57 percent (Kautz, in press).

Most of the remaining 57 percent that is in some type of natural vegetative cover has been affected by human use to some extent. For example, nearly all forest lands in Florida have been logged at some time in the past. In 1995, 24 percent of all forest land was in densely stocked, single-species pine plantations (Kautz, in press), and wetland and upland hardwood forests increasingly are being logged for wood products. Many remaining natural areas are subject to intensive recreational uses including off-road vehicle and airboat operation. In addition, exotic species, such as melaleuca (*Melaleuca quinquenervia*) and Brazilian pepper (*Schinus terebinthefolius*), have invaded many natural areas, radically altering habitat values for native species of plants and animals.

In the course of conversion of the Florida landscape to human uses, some natural community types have been impacted more severely than others. Overall, forested lands have suffered the most with over 4.63 million acres having been cleared in the last 59 years (Kautz, in press). Of particular interest, south Florida pine rocklands have all but disappeared. Of the 375,000 acres of south Florida pine rockland habitats mapped by Davis (1967), only 6,000 acres remained (a 98 percent loss) in 1988. Large areas of herbaceous wetlands have been drained and converted to human uses. For example, herbaceous wetlands declined 51 percent between 1936 and 1995 (Kautz, in press) with over 700,000 acres having been lost in the Everglades ecosystem alone. Forested wetlands declined 17 percent between 1970 and 1987 despite aggressive wetlands protection programs (Kautz 1993).

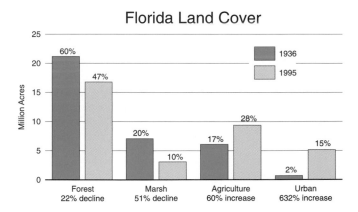

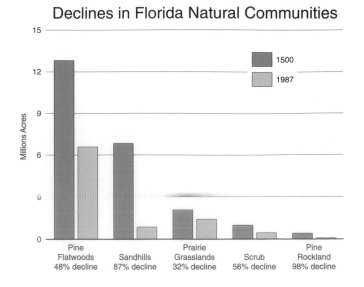

Construction of Tamiami Trail, 1924

Loss and Degradation of Riverine Habitats

The rivers throughout Florida are under stress from a number of factors. Many of the rivers have been channelized for navigation; flows have been stabilized by dams and reservoirs; floodplains have been converted to agricultural, development-related, or mining-related uses or have been destroyed by dams; and flows have been reduced due to water withdrawal for human use. These man-made alterations have resulted in loss of physical habitat and of aquatic species. For example, many species of mussels are in serious decline due to alterations of riverine habitats, siltation, deteriorating water quality, and flow stabilization throughout the United States.

The Apalachicola River system is an example of a river system that has been altered by navigation, reservoir management, and potential minimum flow level requirements. The river has a congressionally authorized 106-mile navigation channel, upstream dams, and a reservoir/dam located at the Florida state line. Navigation channel maintenance has led to substantial changes in shoreline and floodplain habitats (Ager et al. 1987). The shoreline has been converted from snag and natural bank habitat to unproductive sand piles due to spoil disposal practices. The Jim Woodruff Dam at the Florida state line impedes the migration and spawning of anadromous fish species, like the threatened Gulf sturgeon and striped bass. Striped bass eggs naturally float or bounce down the river prior to hatching into fry. Prior to the dam, striped bass could swim upstream far enough that, when spawning was complete, the eggs were in no danger of reaching the injurious brackish waters of Apalachicola Bay before hatching. However, now, with the dam in place, striped bass eggs float downstream into the estuary before they can hatch, effectively precluding striped bass reproduction from the Apalachicola River. During low flow periods, the management of the upstream reservoirs and dams is altered to create short-term flow pulses for navigation. These pulses have been observed to affect the spawning be-

havior of fish (Charles Mesing, personal communication) and may affect the ecology of the river and bay. Upstream users also are interested in the identification of minimum flow levels for the Apalachicola River such that in-stream biological resources are protected while water use needs of Georgia residents are met (U.S. Army Corps of Engineers 1992). If a single minimum flow level is established, the entire river and bay system ecology will change without the naturally occurring high and low flow conditions.

The introduction of non-native species has also placed riverine ecosystems under extreme stress. These species compete with the native species for habitat and food. Non-native species often will eliminate native species from their natural habitats. These introductions have occurred over the years due to intentional release by individuals, escapes from fish hatcheries, migration from upstream sources, inadvertent transport by shipping and boating interests, and escapes of ornamentals from landscaping projects. Several aquatic plants that were released into Florida's rivers, lakes, and streams, such as hydrilla, Eurasian water milfoil (*Myriophyllum spicatum*), and water hyacinth, require extensive control measures in order to keep the water bodies open and not completely covered by the vegetation. Non-native fish that have escaped from fish hatcheries or

103

Gulf sturgeon

Gray Bass

have been deliberately released are now found throughout central and south Florida streams and canals. Many of these fish have established breeding populations and are eliminating native fish populations. The National Biological Survey has documented over 100 non-indigenous species and over 750 specific location occurrences in Florida water bodies. The flathead catfish (*Pylodictis olivaris*) and several mussel species have migrated into Florida rivers from upstream sources. The appearance of the flathead catfish in several north Florida rivers corresponds to a decline in redbreast sunfish (*Lepomis auritus*) populations, which are a food source for the flathead catfish (Charles Mesing, personal communication).

Loss and Degradation of Lake Habitats

The principal problems experienced by Florida lakes are: lake level stabilization, dredge and fill, eutrophication, lowered lake levels from groundwater withdrawals, and invasion by non-native aquatic plants.

In their natural condition, water levels of Florida lakes fluctuated in response to rainfall. In many areas, the very flat landscape allowed lake margins to expand or contract over a large floodplain depending on whether flood or drought conditions prevailed. As a result, many lakes were characterized by broad, productive floodplains usually supporting herbaceous wetland vegetation. Fluctuating lake levels allowed fish populations to expand and contract, and permitted shallow margins to dry out and accumulated organic sediments to decompose. However, throughout central and south Florida, lakes have been connected by canals, and water levels have been stabilized by water control structures as a flood control measure. The consequences of lake level stabilization have been that large areas of floodplain habitat are no longer available to aquatic life in many lakes, and no opportunity exists for organic sediments that accumulate on the lake bottom to decompose. Under these conditions, habitat conditions for aquatic life have deteriorated. In an effort to rejuvenate conditions for aquatic life, many lakes are drawn down and dried out on 7- to 10-year cycles to allow organic accumulations to decompose. However, lakes never have the chance to flood their natural floodplain because those areas have been converted to housing developments that would flood if lake levels were raised.

The dredging of lake bottoms to create navigation canals, the filling of lake bottoms for building construction, or the removal of shoreline vegetation for beach development have all led to loss or degradation of lake habitats. Dredging of lake bottoms typically creates a zone that is too deep for light penetration. Moreover, deep areas of lake tend to accumulate organic sediments that rob the water column of oxygen as they decompose and render those areas of the lake bottom uninhabitable to most aquatic life, including sport fishes. Filling of lake bottoms for building construction eliminates wetland and aquatic plants. Similarly, the clearing of wetlands and aquatic vegetation from the shoreline for aesthetic purposes or to create a beach destroys plants and animals.

Eutrophication is the natural process of aging of lakes (and even estuaries). All lakes receive a steady supply of nutrients, particularly nitrogen and phosphorus, from rainfall and runoff. Nutrients stimulate the growth of algae and aquatic plants, which ultimately die, fall to the bottom, and decompose. Because decomposition is usually incomplete, lakes gradually fill in over long periods of time, eventually becoming wetlands. Today most Florida lakes receive excessive nutrients in stormwater runoff draining from agricultural fields, fertilized lawns, and other sources. Increased nutrient inputs have dramatically increased algal production in many Florida lakes. The higher numbers of algae not only reduce light penetration, rendering shallow habitats less suitable to submerged aquatic plants, but they also accumulate on the bottom. As a result, bottom habitats are deprived of oxygen by oxygen-demanding decomposer organisms and are rendered unsuitable for many forms of aquatic life. Although the early stages of lake eutrophication result in increased populations of sport fishes, continued inputs of nutrients accelerate the aging process, leading to poor habitat conditions and low fish populations. Examples of highly eutrophic lakes are Lake Apopka, Lake Jessup, Lake Hancock, and Lake Munson. Lake drawdowns also are used to rejuvenate eutrophic lakes, at least for 7 to 10 years, depending on nutrient input levels.

In some areas, such as the DeLand Ridge, excessive withdrawals of groundwater for human uses have dramatically lowered the level of the surficial aquifer. Since lakes typically occur where groundwater levels intersect the land surface, lowered groundwater levels have led to lowered lake levels. In some cases, lakes have dried up completely due to excessive groundwater pumping. Lakes that occur in regions of deep, sandy, excessively drained soils are especially susceptible to lowered levels in response to lowered groundwater levels.

Many Florida lakes are infested with non-native aquatic plants, the most familiar being hydrilla (*Hydrilla verticillata*) and water hyacinth (*Eichhornia crassipes*). Hydrilla, a rooted, submersed aquatic weed, is the most troublesome nuisance aquatic plant in Florida lakes (Nordlie 1990). Hydrilla, which spreads rapidly from both underground rhizomes as well as seeds, can quickly fill the water column and form dense mats at the surface. Dense growths of hydrilla reduce fish habitat, impede navigation, and accelerate eutrophication by overloading a lake with huge quantities of dead plant materials. Water hyacinth, a free-floating aquatic plant from Brazil, can double its biomass in two weeks in nutrient rich waters. Water hyacinths can completely cover the surface of small lakes or of embayments of larger lakes. Water hyacinths prevent sunlight from penetrating the water column and reaching submersed aquatic plants. They continually rain dead plant materials on the lake bottom, overloading the decompositional capabilities of lake sediments, depleting oxygen from the water column, and rendering the water column beneath water hyacinth mats uninhabitable to most fishes and other forms of aquatic life.

Loss and Degradation of Estuarine and Marine Habitats

Loss and degradation of estuarine and marine habitat from human impact has been prevalent ever since coastal development began in Florida. Habitat loss and degradation can be categorized into five broad categories: dredge and fill, mosquito control impoundments, water quality degradation, propeller scarring, and alteration of freshwater inflows.

In Florida dredging and filling typically refers to the practice of digging or filling areas classified as wetland or submerged lands. Historically, this has been the most prevalent type of direct impact on mangrove, salt marsh, seagrasses, and tidal river habitats. Major dredge and fill impacts have been from waterfront development and navigation channel construction and maintenance. In three case studies Durako et al. (1988) found that dredge and fill accounted for salt marsh losses of 36 percent, 20 percent, and 19 percent, respectively, in the Jacksonville, St. Augustine, and Daytona Beach regions since the 1940s. Boca Ciega Bay near Tampa is an example of extreme loss (over 90 percent) of estuarine habitat. Shallow seagrass beds were dredged into massive fill areas for residential and commercial development (Haddad 1989). Since the 1970s, loss of estuarine and marine habitat due to dredge and fill has been significantly reduced through regulation.

Mosquito control has been responsible for much of the impact to salt marshes and mangrove swamps in Florida. The salt marsh mosquito (*Aedes taeniorhynchus*) lays its eggs on tidally moist sediments, and small tidal pools and puddles within a marsh are necessary for successful larval hatching. One technique to control mosquitoes has been to build a dike around a marsh, cutting it off from the estuary. Salt water is then pumped into the impounded area to flood the marsh so that tidally moist sediments are not available for egg laying. In the Indian River Lagoon, over 85 percent of the salt marsh and mangrove swamp habitats have been impounded, effectively removing these habitats as functional components of the estuary. Salt marsh impoundments are no longer permitted, and active impoundment management and reconnection of the marshes to the estuary is taking place to try to reduce the extent of previous impacts.

Ditching has been the most widespread method of salt marsh mosquito habitat control. Ditches are dug to drain or to allow predatory fishes access to the small intramarsh tidal pools and puddles required for the five-day, aquatic larval stage of the salt water mosquito. Thousands of miles of ditches have been dug, crisscrossing virtually every major tidal marsh and wetland in Florida. Not only were ditches created, but also the spoil taken out of the ditch often became a dike that impeded sheet flow, altering the drainage patterns responsible for creating the marsh in the first place.

Degradation of water quality has been determined to be a significant factor in the loss of seagrass habitat and is potentially detrimental to the health of Florida's coral reefs. Seagrass health and distribution are primarily controlled by the amount of light available for photosynthesis. By changing upland and riverine drainage and land-use patterns, increased quantities of nutrients and silts have been introduced into estuaries, the result of which has been reduced water clarity. Coupled with discharges of treated sewage and industrial effluents, reductions in water quality have significantly impacted seagrass populations. For example, it has been estimated that Tampa Bay has lost 81 percent of its seagrass beds since the 1940s, Charlotte Harbor has lost 29 percent of its seagrass beds, and

Indian River Lagoon has lost 30 percent due to degraded water quality (Lewis et al. 1985, Haddad and Harris 1985).

Water quality degradation remains the most significant threat to seagrasses statewide. A costly and successful effort to ameliorate water quality problems in Tampa Bay has resulted in an increase in water clarity and a concurrent 10 percent increase in seagrass (Lewis et al. 1991). This demonstrates that many areas that have historically lost seagrasses can recover if water quality is improved.

There is considerable concern that degradation of water quality in the Everglades has led to deteriorating habitat conditions in Florida Bay and that degraded waters from the Florida Keys are impacting Florida's precious coral reefs. Smith-Vaniz et al. (1995) have suggested that Florida coral reefs are undergoing change due to water quality.

A phenomenon associated with the tremendous increase in the number of power boats coursing Florida's coastal waters is propeller scarring of seagrass beds. In many areas, seagrass beds are in estuarine and marine waters at depths less than 3.5 feet. When power boats move through such areas, their propellers often hit bottom, uprooting and killing seagrasses. In shallow waters that experience heavy boat traffic, seagrass beds can be badly damaged, seagrass productivity can be lowered, and the value of these waters as habitats for estuarine and marine life can be severely damaged.

Estuarine ecosystems have evolved into one of the most productive ecosystems in the world in response to naturally fluctuating, seasonal drainage patterns of freshwaters flowing to the sea. Freshwater delivers the needed nutrients and environmental conditions for sustaining habitat, and the life cycles of many of the marine species of recreational and economic importance are closely tied to natural freshwater inputs.

The flow of too much freshwater into an estuary can be catastrophic. In many areas of Florida, the practice of flood control has resulted in huge volumes of water being released into the estuarine environment over short periods of time. For example, water management practices in the upper Everglades result in excessive flood water releases into the St. Lucie estuary. The flood waters carry heavy loads of silt that have smothered some of the offshore hard bottom and reef communities in the area. Further south at the terminus of the Everglades, large volume releases of fresh water through the C-111 canal system into Barnes Sound have resulted in massive fish kills and loss of seagrass bed and other bottom habitats. Similarly, a flood control canal connecting the upper St. Johns River to the Indian River Lagoon occasionally releases huge quantities of freshwater through the Sebastian River, periodically devastating commercially cultured clams in the lagoon.

Too little freshwater can also be detrimental to estuaries. Perhaps Florida Bay at the southern tip of Florida represents the extreme results of reductions in water delivery. Since the late 1800s, the Everglades ecosystem, stretching from the Kissimmee River to Florida Bay, has been ditched and drained for farming and flood control. Now, about 80 percent of the water that formerly moved slowly through the Everglades and into southern estuaries, such as Florida Bay, today is discharged to east and west coast estuaries. As a result, conditions in the Everglades have changed in response to changes in water delivery and water quality, and reductions in freshwater inflows are believed to be a major reason for the ongoing problems with the biological systems of Florida Bay. It has been estimated that many thousands of acres of seagrass beds have been dying due to poorly understood changes in the Florida Bay

105

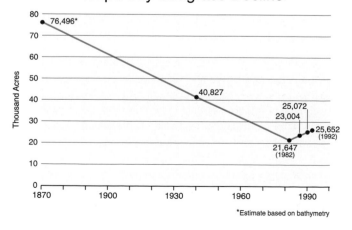

Tampa Bay Seagrass Decline

*Estimate based on bathymetry

ecosystem. In addition, persistent and harmful algal blooms, as well as mangrove and sponge die-offs, have been occurring in the bay. These changes appear to be linked to the overall problems in the Everglades. Reduced freshwater inflows also allow higher salinities to extend further upstream in tidal rivers, often killing plants and animals adapted to tidal freshwater environments.

With the exception of the Caloosahatchee River, the estuaries of the Florida Gulf coast have experienced decreasing inflows of freshwater, in part for climatological and in part for cultural reasons. In order to meet the demands of a growing population for water supply, flood control, and irrigation, further declines in freshwater inflows to Gulf coast estuaries are very likely in coming decades. Some river supplies already are tapped to the maximum, as is the case with the Manatee River near Bradenton, where impoundment and diversion of water for municipal supply reduces river flow by 90 percent for 80 percent of the time. In other streams, such as the Peace River, water use permits allowing for gradual, albeit monitored, increases in flow diversions to support a regional water supply system have been issued. Like their counterparts in the Apalachicola, estuarine scientists and resource managers working in the Suwannee River are bracing for claims from south Florida residents on that river's abundant supply of fresh water.

Ecological effects of reduced freshwater inflows are numerous and diverse, and depend on the nature of the changes. Inflow reductions promote higher salinities in estuaries. In some cases, flow reductions also can accelerate eutrophication by increasing retention times of nutrients in estuaries. In the Tampa bypass canal (formerly the Palm River), reduced flows create hypoxic (low-oxygen) zones harmful to larval and juvenile fishes. Sub-lethal harm to fisheries may result when changed inflows dislocate physiologically favorable salinity zones in rivers or estuaries from the preferred marsh, seagrass, oyster-reef, or other structural habitats preferred by particular life stages of individual species.

Some estuarine ecosystems have been or may be affected by multiple changes. In southwest Florida, for example, the connected estuaries of Faka Union, Fakahatchee, and Pumpkin bays have experienced freshwater inflow increases, decreases, changes in timing, and relocations of points of delivery, owing largely to drainage impacts caused by the Golden Gate Estates canal.

Slow progress is being made in methods for detecting ecological responses caused by inflow changes. It is clear from studies of panhandle oysters or south Florida shrimps that inflows at certain times of the year are more critical than other times. The same studies have shown that statistical relationships between flows and landings or catch-per-unit-effort must consider the maturation rate of particular species. Recent studies around the margin of Tampa Bay have shown that small changes in the riverine position of salinity zones can translate into large gains or losses of oligohaline (i.e., low salinity) habitat.

Impacts of flow alterations are worsened by the presence of instream barriers. Many Florida streams have dams, flood-control gates, salinity barriers, or other structures near, if not actually in, tidal waters. Numerous estuarine fishes historically moved far up into Florida's freshwater rivers due, in part, to the state's abundance of mineralized springs. Instream barriers prevent such movements. A single flood control structure in the tidal Sebastian River, for example, has reduced fish species diversity by 60 percent upstream of the barrier. Many valued species, such as the snook (*Centropomus undecimalis*), naturally extend into rivers. For example, some 3.4 percent of fishes at Fort Meade, 109 miles upstream of the mouth of the Peace River, are snook. However, snook no longer occur upstream of large barriers on other coastal rivers. Instream barriers that no longer serve their purpose need to be identified and either replaced by other structures or removed.

Loss of Biological Diversity

Extinction refers to the decline and eventual complete disappearance of all individuals of a species or subspecies. Extirpation refers to disappearance of all individuals of a species or subspecies from a particular region, even though the species or subspecies may persist elsewhere. Whereas extinction is forever, extirpation holds out the hope that a species or subspecies may be reintroduced into and persist in its former range.

Since the time of settlement, 12 vertebrates and 14 plants have either become extinct or have been extirpated from Florida. These species were lost as the result of wanton slaughter, overcollection, or conversion of Florida's natural ecosystems to human uses.

Plants and Animals Extinct or Extirpated from Florida	
Plants	
San Felasco spleenwort	*Asplenium monanthes*
Tamarindillo	*Acacia choriophylla*
Star-scale fern	*Pleopeltis revoluta*
Spider orchid	*Brassia caudata*
American chestnut	*Castanea dentata*
Balsam-apple	*Clusia rosea*
Beaked spike-rush	*Eleocharis rostellata*
Turk's-cap lilly	*Lilium superbum*
Sleeping-beauty water-lily	*Nymphaea blanda*
Coot Bay dancing-lady	*Oncidium carthagenense*
Ginseng	*Panax quinquefolius*
Mistletoe cactus	*Rhipsalis baccifera*
Edward's maiden fern*	*Thelypteris macilenta*
Scentless vanilla	*Vanilla inodora*
Animals	
Goff's pocket gopher*	*Geomys pinetis goffi*
Pallid beach mouse*	*Peromyscus polionotus decoloratus*
Chadwick Beach cotton mouse*	*Peromyscus gossypinus restrictus*
Florida red wolf*	*Canis rufus floridanus*
West Indian monk seal*	*Monachus tropicalis*
Plains bison	*Bison bison bison*
Carolina parakeet*	*Conuropsis carolinensis*
Passenger pigeon*	*Ectopistes migratorius*
Ivory-billed woodpecker	*Campephilus principalis*
Dusky seaside sparrow*	*Ammodramus maritimus nigrescens*
Zenaida dove	*Zenaida aurita zenaida*
Key West quail dove	*Geotrygon chrysia*
*Extinct	

Another measure of the status of biological diversity in Florida is the number of species listed as endangered, threatened, and species of special concern. Species listed as endangered have population sizes so low that they are in imminent danger of extinction. Species listed as threatened have declining populations and are in jeopardy of being listed as endangered if population trends are not reversed in the near future. The species of special concern category serves as an early warning system by recognizing species that are declining.

In part due to the rich variety of life in Florida and in part due to extent of development in the state, Florida is second only to California in the number of species listed by the federal government as endangered and threatened. Florida lists 110 vertebrates, 7 invertebrates, and 413 plants as endangered, threatened, and species of special concern (Logan 1997). These endangered and imperiled species include 13 percent of freshwater fishes, 9 percent of the amphibians, 19 percent of the reptiles, 12 percent of the birds, 33 percent of the mammals, and 12 percent of the vascular plants in the state. Overall, a relatively high percentage of the state's plants and animals are in sufficient jeopardy of extinction or extirpation that they are legally recognized as in need of conservation attention.

The populations of Florida's most endangered species are perilously low. The Florida panther (*Puma concolor coryi*) numbers 30 to 50 adults. The key deer (*Odocoileus virginiana clavium*) population is estimated to include only 250 individuals. The American crocodile (*Crocodylus acutus*) population includes no more than 500 juveniles and adults, of which only 30 are breeding females.

Although a few Florida species are already extinct or extirpated, and although many have already been listed as endangered or potentially endangered, many more are known or suspected to have declining populations. In a survey of experts in vertebrate biology in Florida, Millsap et al. (1990) found that 31 fishes, 12 amphibians, 59 reptiles, 151 birds, and 43 mammals have declining populations. Overall, this survey showed that 44 percent of all Florida vertebrates are known to have, or are suspected of having, declining populations. Loss of habitat to development is usually cited as the reason for the observed declines in the populations of most of these vertebrates.

Habitat Fragmentation

One consequence of the conversion of the natural Florida landscape to agricultural, silvicultural, mining, and urban uses has the been the fragmentation of remaining habitats. As development progresses, remaining habitat patches become smaller in size and increasingly isolated from one another (Wilcove et al. 1986).

The inevitable consequence of habitat fragmentation is the loss of biological diversity from a region. Remaining patches of habitat grow too small to support individual plants or animals of a given species, and those species are eliminated from the patch. When many habitat patches in a region become too small to support individuals, entire populations may disappear from a region even though remaining patches appear to contain suitable habitat in all other respects.

Small patches of habitat, particularly forests, also experience edge effects. Edge refers to a zone extending from the forest edge some distance into the interior where influences

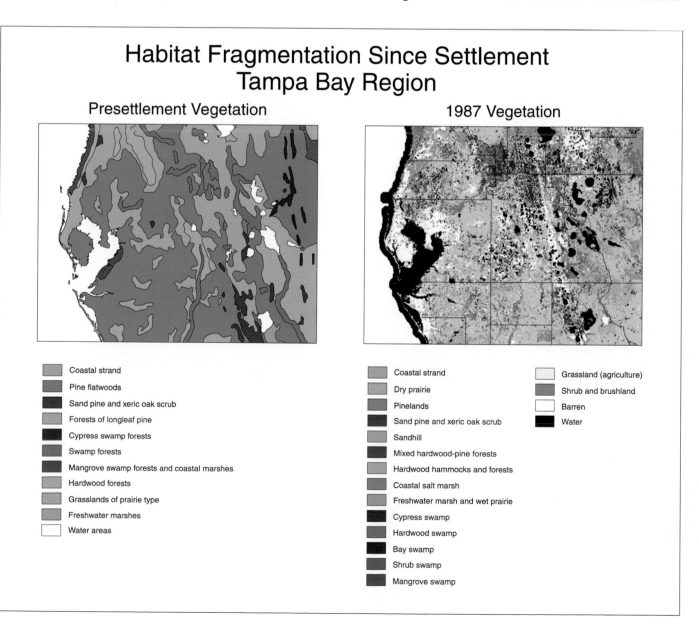

Habitat Fragmentation Since Settlement
Tampa Bay Region

Presettlement Vegetation

- Coastal strand
- Pine flatwoods
- Sand pine and xeric oak scrub
- Forests of longleaf pine
- Cypress swamp forests
- Swamp forests
- Mangrove swamp forests and coastal marshes
- Hardwood forests
- Grasslands of prairie type
- Freshwater marshes
- Water areas

1987 Vegetation

- Coastal strand
- Dry prairie
- Pinelands
- Sand pine and xeric oak scrub
- Sandhill
- Mixed hardwood-pine forests
- Hardwood hammocks and forests
- Coastal salt marsh
- Freshwater marsh and wet prairie
- Cypress swamp
- Hardwood swamp
- Bay swamp
- Shrub swamp
- Mangrove swamp
- Grassland (agriculture)
- Shrub and brushland
- Barren
- Water

Conservation Lands

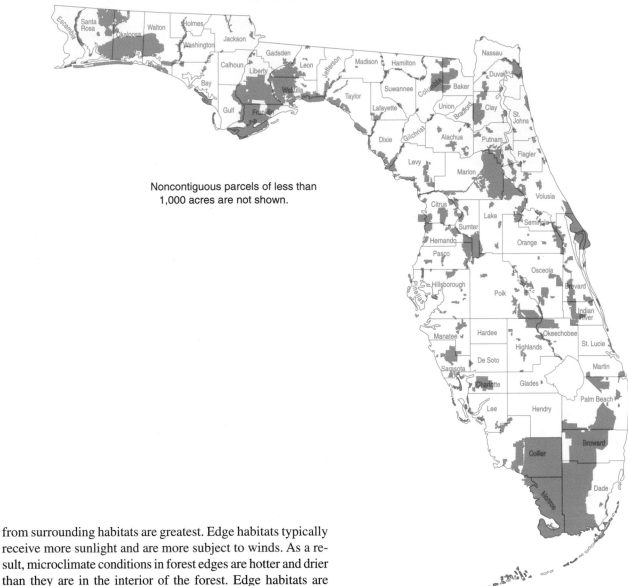

Noncontiguous parcels of less than 1,000 acres are not shown.

from surrounding habitats are greatest. Edge habitats typically receive more sunlight and are more subject to winds. As a result, microclimate conditions in forest edges are hotter and drier than they are in the interior of the forest. Edge habitats are dominated by common, weedy, early successional stage species of plants, whereas forest interiors are dominated by shade-tolerant climax species. As a general rule, forest interiors also support more rare species. The animals that inhabit edge habitats are subject to increased predation and nest parasitism. Moreover, small patches of forest habitat are comprised of entirely edge species and have no species typically found in forest interiors.

Another consequence of conversion of the landscape to human uses is the loss of natural connections among remaining patches of habitat. Linkages between habitat patches benefit many species by allowing for dispersal of juveniles away from their places of birth, for movement of animals within their home ranges, and for long distance range shifts (Noss and Cooperrider 1994). Landscape linkages, such as riparian forests, may also provide habitat directly for many species. Loss of connections among habitat patches can be particularly severe in the case of wide ranging species. The Florida black bear and Florida panther have become increasingly susceptible to collisions with automobiles as they cross busy highways trying to reach other patches of suitable habitat.

Many conservation biologists agree that the greatest hope for conserving Florida's biological heritage rests in the state's system of public lands. Lands in public ownership are less sub-

108

Size Distribution of Public Land Parcels

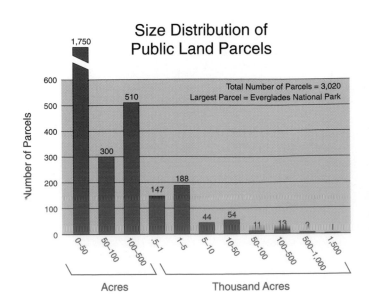

Total Number of Parcels = 3,020
Largest Parcel = Everglades National Park

Strategic Habitat Conservation Areas

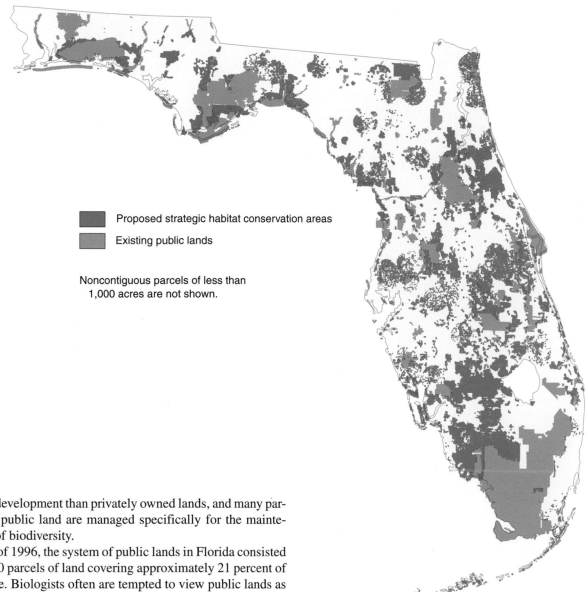

Proposed strategic habitat conservation areas

Existing public lands

Noncontiguous parcels of less than 1,000 acres are not shown.

ject to development than privately owned lands, and many parcels of public land are managed specifically for the maintenance of biodiversity.

As of 1996, the system of public lands in Florida consisted of 3,020 parcels of land covering approximately 21 percent of the state. Biologists often are tempted to view public lands as islands of natural habitat surrounded by a sea of human land uses. Over two-thirds of public lands are smaller than 100 acres in size, and approximately 90 percent are smaller than 1,000 acres. The largest parcel of public land in Florida is Everglades National Park, which is 1.5 million acres in size. This large-scale picture of the system of public lands in Florida is one of many very small, poorly connected patches of habitat with all of the problems associated with small patch sizes.

Priority Conservation Lands

In 1994, the Florida Game and Fresh Water Fish Commission published a technical report (Cox et al. 1994) which identified a set of lands referred to as Strategic Habitat Conservation Areas (SHCA). SHCAs are 4.82 million acres of privately owned lands that should be protected from development in order to ensure the long-term persistence of most elements of Florida's biological diversity. SHCAs are built around and intended to complement biodiversity conservation efforts on the existing system of public lands.

The lands identified as SHCAs include (1) the minimum area of habitat needed to maintain viable populations of 30

Florida Department of Commerce

Flamingo, Everglades National Park

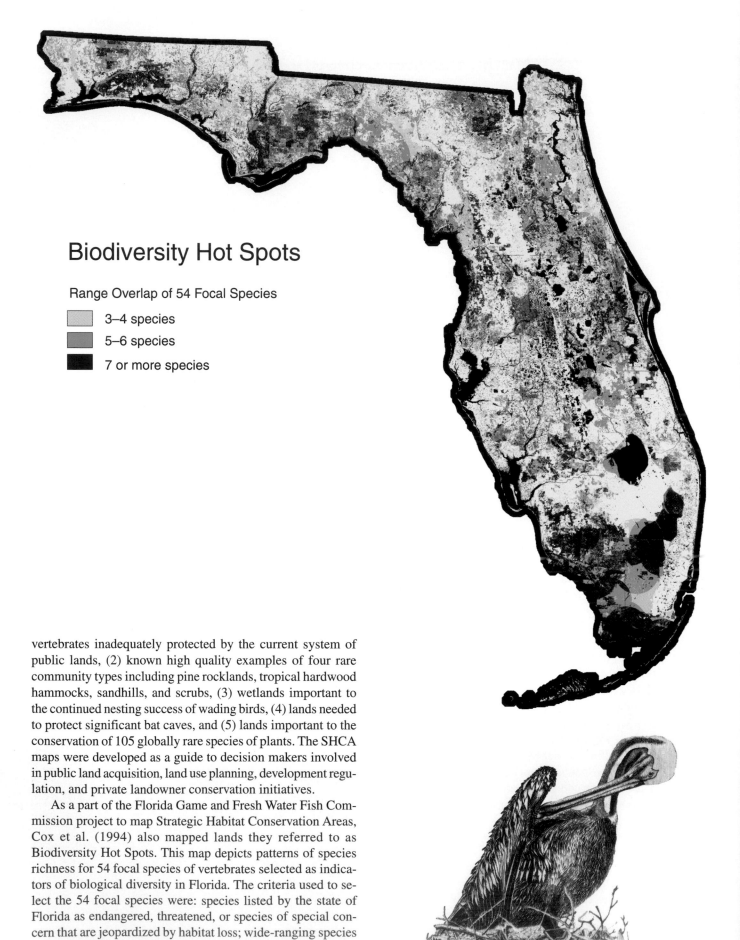

Biodiversity Hot Spots

Range Overlap of 54 Focal Species

- [ ] 3–4 species
- [ ] 5–6 species
- [ ] 7 or more species

vertebrates inadequately protected by the current system of public lands, (2) known high quality examples of four rare community types including pine rocklands, tropical hardwood hammocks, sandhills, and scrubs, (3) wetlands important to the continued nesting success of wading birds, (4) lands needed to protect significant bat caves, and (5) lands important to the conservation of 105 globally rare species of plants. The SHCA maps were developed as a guide to decision makers involved in public land acquisition, land use planning, development regulation, and private landowner conservation initiatives.

As a part of the Florida Game and Fresh Water Fish Commission project to map Strategic Habitat Conservation Areas, Cox et al. (1994) also mapped lands they referred to as Biodiversity Hot Spots. This map depicts patterns of species richness for 54 focal species of vertebrates selected as indicators of biological diversity in Florida. The criteria used to select the 54 focal species were: species listed by the state of Florida as endangered, threatened, or species of special concern that are jeopardized by habitat loss; wide-ranging species whose protection would also protect habitats for many species with smaller area requirements; species that are indicators of rare community types; and keystone species whose activities allow other species also to be present. Separate habitat distribution maps were created for each of the 54 focal species using a map of Florida vegetation derived from Landsat satellite

Drawing by Jonathan Miller

The brown pelican, a familiar element of the estuarine panorama

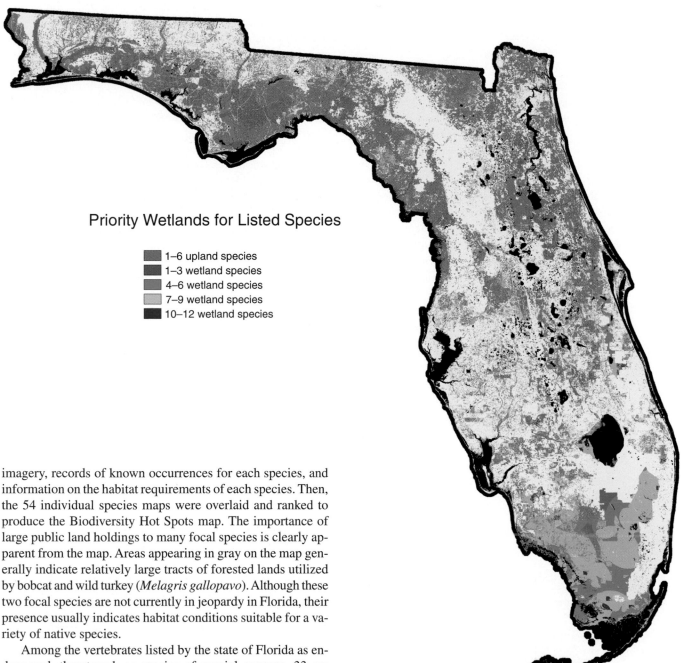

Priority Wetlands for Listed Species

- █ 1–6 upland species
- █ 1–3 wetland species
- █ 4–6 wetland species
- ░ 7–9 wetland species
- █ 10–12 wetland species

imagery, records of known occurrences for each species, and information on the habitat requirements of each species. Then, the 54 individual species maps were overlaid and ranked to produce the Biodiversity Hot Spots map. The importance of large public land holdings to many focal species is clearly apparent from the map. Areas appearing in gray on the map generally indicate relatively large tracts of forested lands utilized by bobcat and wild turkey (*Melagris gallopavo*). Although these two focal species are not currently in jeopardy in Florida, their presence usually indicates habitat conditions suitable for a variety of native species.

Among the vertebrates listed by the state of Florida as endangered, threatened, or species of special concern, 33 are wetland-dependent. That is, these species inhabit only wetlands, or they require wetlands during some time in their lives to survive (e.g., breeding, feeding, roosting).

Kautz et al. (1994) mapped and ranked Florida wetlands based on the number of wetland-dependent listed species likely to use each wetlands. The map was created by first developing a distribution map for each species using habitat maps and known occurrence information, and then overlaying the 33 separate species maps and ranking wetlands based on species use. The extensive wetlands ecosystems of south Florida, particularly in the regions of the Everglades and Big Cypress Swamp, provide habitat to the largest number of wetland-dependent listed species. Other notable wetlands include the marshes of Lake Okeechobee, the marshes of the upper St. Johns River, coastal wetlands around Pine Island in Charlotte Harbor, the wet prairies south of Gainesville, forested and shrub swamp wetlands in Dixie and Lafayette counties, and forested wetlands around Osceola National Forest. Also mapped by Kautz et al. (1994) were upland habitats used by some of the wetland-dependent listed species. The most extensive areas of upland use are the pine flatwoods ecosystems of north Florida

111

Florida Game and Fresh Water Fish Commission

Wading bird rookery (roseate spoonbills)

and the Florida panhandle. In many cases, these are the uplands that provide habitat for the Florida black bear.

Conclusions

Florida is one of the most biologically rich areas of North America due to geographic position between the temperate zone and the tropics, a warm and humid climate, and long coast line. Natural ecosystem types include a variety of uplands, wetlands, rivers, lakes, estuaries, and marine systems. Many of the species of plants and animals found in Florida occur nowhere else on earth.

Human population growth in Florida has been explosive, especially since the 1950s, and Florida is a popular tourist destination that receives over 40 million visitors annually. In accommodating the large numbers of people moving to or visiting Florida, most of the natural Florida landscape has been converted to agricultural, silvicultural, mining, urban, or other human uses. In the process, forest lands have been reduced by 22 percent in the last 60 years, and 51 percent of the state's herbaceous wetlands were converted to other uses during the

same period. Numerous species of plants and animals have been driven to extinction or have been extirpated from the state, and many more species are in imminent danger of extinction or have declining populations. Originally rare plant communities such as scrub, pine rocklands, and coastal strand have all but disappeared; and entire ecosystems, such as the Everglades, Florida Bay, and Upper St. Johns River, have been severely damaged by extensive water management systems. Most of Florida's lakes, rivers, and estuaries have experienced water quality degradation as a consequence of polluted stormwater runoff from agricultural and urban areas or alterations of freshwater inflows.

On the positive side, lands protected by public ownership now include about 22 percent of the state's ecosystems, and Florida's aggressive and far-sighted land acquisition programs are bringing new lands into public ownership every day. With careful planning and a commitment to ecological resource protection, there is a strong possibility that Florida will experience no further extinctions, previously damaged ecosystems can be restored, and Florida can maintain a productive and healthy environment.

REFERENCES

A source for a map or figure has a number in parentheses following the entry. This number refers to the page in this atlas for which the source was used.

Abrahamson, W.G., and D.C. Hartnett. 1990. "Pine Flatwoods and Dry Prairies." In R.L. Myers and J.J. Ewel, eds. *Ecosystems of Florida*. Orlando: University of Central Florida Press.

Ager, L.A., C.L. Mesing, R.S. Land, M.J. Hill, M. Spelman, R. Rosseau, and K. Stone. 1987. *Fisheries Ecology and Dredging Impacts on the Apalachicola River System*. Five-Year Completion Report. Florida Game and Fresh Water Fish Commission, Tallahassee.

Brown, R.B., E.L. Stone, and V.W. Carlisle. 1990. "Soils." In R.L. Myers and J.J. Ewel, eds. *Ecosystems of Florida*. Orlando: University of Central Florida Press.

Coultas, C.L., and Y. Hsieh, eds. 1997. *Ecology and Management of Tidal Marshes*. Delray Beach: St. Lucie Press.

Cox, J., R. Kautz, M. MacLaughlin, and T. Gilbert. 1994. *Closing the Gaps in Florida's Wildlife Habitat Conservation System*. Office of Environmental Services, Florida Game and Fresh Water Fish Commission, Tallahassee, FL. (maps, 109, 110)

Davis, J.H. 1967. *General Map of Natural Vegetation of Florida*. Institute of Food and Agricultural Sciences, Agriculture Experiment Stations, Circular S-178. University of Florida, Gainesville, FL. (map, 87; Presettlement vegetation map, 107)

Durako, M.J., M.D. Murphy, and K.D. Haddad. 1988. *Assessment of Fisheries Habitat: Northeast Florida*. Florida Marine Research Publications No. 45. Florida Department of Natural Resources, Bureau of Marine Research, St. Petersburg.

Ewel, K.C. 1990. "Swamps." In R.L. Myers and J.J. Ewel, editors. *Ecosystems of Florida*. Orlando: University of Central Florida Press.

Fernald, E.A., and E.D. Purdum, eds. 1992. *Atlas of Florida*. Gainesville: University Press of Florida. (map, 85)

Florida Game and Fresh Water Fish Commission. (map, 111)

Florida Natural Areas Inventory. Unpublished data. (map, 108)

Florida Natural Areas Inventory. 1990. *Guide to the Natural Communities of Florida*. Florida Natural Areas Inventory, Tallahassee, FL.

Griffith, G.E., J.M. Omernik, C.M. Rohm, and S.M. Pierson. 1994. Florida Regionalization Project. U.S. Environmental Protection Agency, Environmental Research Laboratory, unpublished report. Corvallis, OR. (map, 86)

Haddad, K. 1989. "Habitat Trends and Fisheries in Tampa and Sarasota Bays." In E.D. Estevez, ed. *Tampa and Sarasota Bays: Issues, Resources, Status, and Management. NOAA Estuary-of-the-Month Seminar Series No. 11*. U.S. Department of Commerce, National Oceanic and Atmospheric Administration, Washington, D.C.

Haddad, K., and B.A. Harris. 1985. "Use of Remote Sensing to Assess Estuarine Habitats." In *Proceedings of the Fourth Symposium on Coastal and Ocean Management*. "Coastal Zone '85" ASCE/Baltimore, MD.

Jaap, W.C., and P. Hallock. 1990. "Coral Reefs." In R. L. Myers and J. J. Ewel, editors. *Ecosystems of Florida*. Orlando: University of Central Florida Press. (map, 93)

Kautz, R.S. 1993. "Trends in Florida Wildlife Habitat 1936-1987." *Florida Scientist* 56(1):7-24.

Kautz, R.S. In press. "Land Use and Land Cover Trends in Florida 1936–1995." *Florida Scientist*. (Florida land cover graph, 102)

Kautz, R.S, D.T. Gilbert, and G.M. Mauldin. 1993. "Vegetative Cover in Florida Based on 1985-1989 Landsat Thematic Mapper Imagery." *Florida Scientist* 56(3):135-154. (map, 88; declines in Florida natural communities graph, 102; 1987 vegetation, 107)

Kautz, R.S., J.A. Cox, M.T. MacLaughlin, and J. Stys. 1994. Mapping Wetlands of High Priority to Vertebrates Listed as Endangered, Threatened, and Species of Special Concern in Florida. Unpublished report. Florida Game and Fresh Water Fish Commission, Tallahassee.

Krabbenhoft, D.P. 1996. *Mercury Studies in the Florida Everglades*. U.S. Department of the Interior, U.S. Geological Survey Fact Sheet FS-166-96. (map, 101)

Kushlan, J.A. 1990. "Freshwater Marshes." In R.L. Myers and J.J. Ewel, eds. *Ecosystems of Florida*. Orlando: University of Central Florida Press.

Lane, E., ed. 1994. *Florida's Geological History and Geological Resources*. Florida Department of Environmental Protection, Florida Geological Survey, Special Publication No. 35. Tallahassee.

Lewis, R.R., III, K.D. Haddad, and J.O.R. Johansson. 1991. "Recent Areal Expansion of Seagrass Meadows in Tampa Bay, Florida: Real Bay Improvement or Drought-Induced?" In S. F. Treat and P. A. Clark, eds. *Proceedings, Tampa Bay Area Scientific Information Symposium 2*. Tampa.

Lewis, R.R., III, M.J. Durako, M.D. Moffler, and R.C. Phillips. 1985. "Seagrass Meadows at Tampa Bay." In S. Treat, J. Simon, R. Lewis III, and R. Whitman Jr., eds. *Proceedings of the Tampa Bay Area Scientific Information Symposium*. Florida Sea Grant Report No. 65. Burgess Publishing Co., Minneapolis.

Livingston, R.J. 1990. "Inshore Marine Habitats." In R.L. Myers and J.J. Ewel, eds. *Ecosystems of Florida*. Orlando: University of Central Florida Press. (map, 91)

Logan, T.H. 1997. Florida's Endangered Species, Threatened Species, and Species of Special Concern. Official lists. Florida Game and Fresh Water Fish Commission, Tallahassee.

Millsap, B., J. Gore, D. Runde, and S. Cerulean. 1990. *Setting Priorities for the Conservation of Fish and Wildlife Species in Florida*. Wildlife Monographs 111.

Muller, J.W., E.D. Hardin, D.R. Jackson, S.E. Gatewood, and N. Caire. 1989. *Summary Report on the Vascular Plants, Animals, and Plant Communities Endemic to Florida*. Nongame Wildlife Program Technical Report No. 7, Florida Game and Fresh Water Fish Commission, Tallahassee.

Myers, R.L., and J.J. Ewel, eds. 1990. *Ecosystems of Florida*. Orlando: University of Central Florida Press.

National Atmospheric Deposition Program. Annual Data Summaries, Precipitation Chemistry in the United States. (maps, 100)

Noss, R.F., and A.Y. Cooperrider. 1994. *Saving Nature's Legacy: Protecting and Restoring Biodiversity*. Washington, D.C.: Island Press. (map, 110)

Nordlie, F.G. 1990. "Rivers and Springs." In R.L. Myers and J.J. Ewel, eds. *Ecosystems of Florida*. Orlando: University of Central Florida Press.

Odum, W.D., and C.C. McIvor. 1990. "Mangroves." In R.L. Myers and J.J. Ewel, editors. *Ecosystems of Florida*. Orlando: University of Central Florida Press.

Sargent, F.J., T.J. Leary, D.W. Crews, and C.R. Kruer. 1995. *Scarring of Florida Seagrasses: Assessment and Management Options*. FMRI Technical Report TR-1. Florida Marine Institute, Florida Department of Environmental Protection, St. Petersburg.

Smith-Vaniz, W.F., J.A. Bohnsack, and J.D. Williams. 1995. "Reef Fishes of the Florida Keys." In E.T. LaRoc, G.S. Farris, C.E. Puckett, P.D. Doron, and M.J. Mac, eds. *Our Living Resources*. U.S. Department of the Interior, National Biological Service, Washington, D.C.

Southwest Florida Water Management District. 1994. SWIM Plan, Tampa Bay, Southwest Florida Water Management District, Brooksville. (graph, 105)

Stephenson, F. 1997. "Florida's Mercury Menace." Florida State University Research in Review 8(2–3):10–21.

Tanner, W.F. 1992. "Natural Environment." In E. A. Fernald and E. D. Purdum, eds. *Atlas of Florida*. Gainesville: University Press of Florida. (map, 84)

U.S. Army Corps of Engineers. 1992. *Apalachicola-Chattahoochee-Flint and Alabama-Coosa-Tallapoosa River Basins Comprehensive Plan of Study*. USACOE, Mobile, AL.

Ward, D., ed. 1979. *Rare and Endangered Biota of Florida*. Volume five. *Plants*. Gainesville: University Presses of Florida.

Webb, S.D. 1990. "Historical Biogeography." In R.L. Myers and J.J. Ewel, eds. *Ecosystems of Florida*. Orlando: University of Central Florida Press.

Wilcove, D.S., C.H. McLellan, and A.P. Dobson. 1986. "Habitat Fragmentation in the Temperate Zone." In M.E. Soule, ed. *Conservation Biology: The Science of Scarcity and Diversity*. Sunderland, MA: Sinauer.

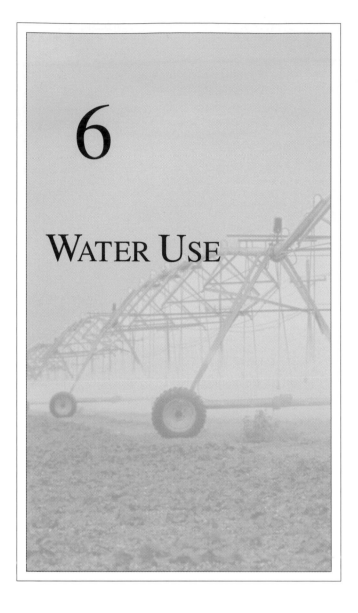

6

WATER USE

114   Water resources are one of the most valued assets in Florida. The state is underlain virtually everywhere by aquifers capable of yielding significant quantities of fresh groundwater to wells. Surface water resources include 1,700 streams and rivers and 7,800 lakes, providing water for natural and human needs in Florida.

In 1995 the resident population of Florida was 14.15 million and ranked fourth behind California, Texas, and New York, (University of Florida 1997). This is an increase of 410 percent from the 1950 population of 2.77 million, and a 9 percent increase from the 1990 population of 12.94 million (University of Florida 1997). The population is projected to be nearly 16 million by the year 2000 and more than 20 million by the year 2020 (University of Florida 1997). An estimated 41 million people visited the state in 1995, compared with 24 million in 1980 (Florida Department of Commerce 1996).

In addition to tourism, Florida's economy is also dependent on agricultural production. Florida accounted for more than 80 percent of the total citrus produced in the United States

Richard L. Marella; Reuse, David W. York

during 1995 and the state's total agricultural production ranked among the top ten in the nation for 1995 (University of Florida 1997). Agricultural production will continue to flourish because of the subtropical climate and demands from the increasing population.

Water needs from growth in population, tourism, seasonal residents, and agriculture are expected to increase demands on water resources. Scientific knowledge and assessment of water resources are vital to support the human and environmental needs of Florida. The U.S. Geological Survey (USGS), in cooperation with the Florida Department of Environmental Protection, estimates water withdrawn from groundwater and surface water sources for different uses by month by county and by water management district. Because rainfall varies greatly both seasonally and annually, it is important to know how much water is withdrawn for what purposes, where it is withdrawn, and when it is withdrawn.

Many factors affect water usage in Florida. Some of those factors include population (resident and seasonal), climate (temperature and precipitation), economics (income, manufacturing, market availability), water cost (capital infrastructure, production, distribution, treatment), and regulations (water availability, permitting restriction, discharge limitations). These factors can vary in effect on a local, regional, or national level and effects can be long lasting or very short term. As demands for water continue to increase, these factors will become more important and have a greater impact.

Water Withdrawn

There are two types of water usage, withdrawals and nonwithdrawals. Withdrawals include water pumped or diverted

Painting by Molly Mabe
Natural systems as well as people require adequate clean water.

for direct or indirect uses. This water can be fresh or saline and is available from ground or surface sources. Typically, a portion of the water withdrawn is consumptively used; however, most of the water is returned as wastewater or runoff and becomes available for further use. The portion of the water withdrawn that is consumptively used is either incorporated in a product, evaporated, or transpired into the atmosphere and later returns as rainfall. The amount of water withdrawn is generally measured, regulated, and managed. Nonwithdrawal uses of water include navigation or transportation, water-based recreation (boating, fishing, etc.), propagation of fish and wildlife and all other natural system needs, hydroelectric power generation, and dilution and conveyance of liquid or solid waste. Nonwithdrawal uses of water are not usually measured and little or no consumption is associated with these uses. All water-use values in this chapter are water withdrawals.

In 1995 the total amount of water withdrawn in Florida was 18,181 mgd (million gallons per day), of which 7,215 mgd was freshwater (40 percent) and 10,966 mgd was saline water

(60 percent). Total water withdrawals increased more than 520 percent (15,260 mgd) between 1950 and 1995, and more recently increased nearly 2 percent (283 mgd) between 1990 and 1995. Between 1955 and 1995, freshwater withdrawals increased 230 percent (5,030 mgd) while saline water withdrawals increased 1,600 percent (10,320 mgd). However, between 1990 and 1995, freshwater withdrawals decreased 5 percent (370 mgd) while saline water withdrawals increased 6 percent (652 mgd). The largest amount of freshwater withdrawn in 1995 was in Palm Beach County (960 mgd), followed by Dade (569 mgd), and Hendry (557 mgd) counties.

Nearly all of the saline water withdrawn in Florida is surface water used for once-through cooling at 22 thermoelectric power plants. Most of this water is withdrawn from bays or rivers along the coast, and nearly all of it is returned to these surface sources. Florida was the largest user of saline water (10,966 mgd) in the nation followed by California (9,640 mgd) in 1995 (Solley et al. 1998). The largest amount of saline water, most of which was obtained from Tampa Bay, was withdrawn in Hillsborough County (2,382 mgd) during 1995.

Florida, the largest user of groundwater east of the Mississippi River, ranked fifth in the nation in fresh groundwater withdrawals in 1995 (Solley et al. 1998). Groundwater is vir-

Total Freshwater Withdrawals
1995

Million Gallons per Day

- [ ] 1–10
- [ ] 10–50
- [ ] 50–100
- [ ] 100–200
- [ ] Greater than 200

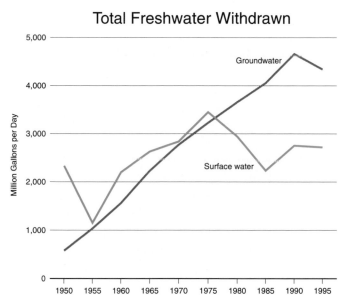

Total Freshwater Withdrawn

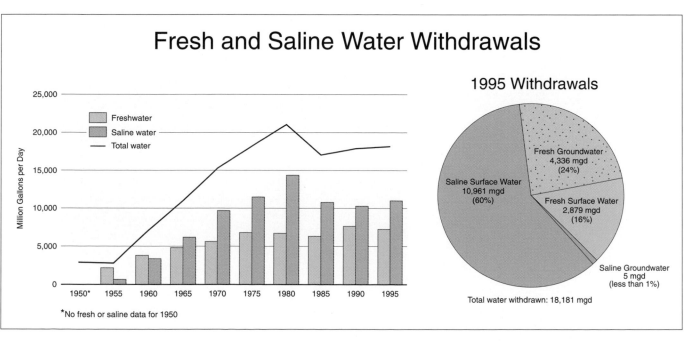

Fresh and Saline Water Withdrawals

1995 Withdrawals

*No fresh or saline data for 1950

Total water withdrawn: 18,181 mgd

tually available anywhere throughout the state and generally needs no treatment for immediate use. In 1995 groundwater accounted for 60 percent (4,336 mgd) of the freshwater withdrawn. Nearly 93 percent of the state's population (13.1 million people) relied on groundwater for their drinking water needs, far more than any other state in the nation (Solley et al. 1998). Since 1970 groundwater has supplied most of Florida's freshwater (Marella 1995). Groundwater withdrawals steadily increased between 1950 and 1990, but show a decrease between 1990 and 1995. The majority of groundwater withdrawn in Florida is obtained from the Floridan aquifer system, which underlies most of the state and parts of Alabama, Georgia, and South Carolina. About 57 percent (2,480 mgd) of the total groundwater withdrawn in Florida was obtained from the Floridan aquifer system in 1995. The Biscayne aquifer, which underlies southeastern Florida only, accounted for about 20 percent (872 mgd) of the groundwater withdrawn in 1995. The remaining groundwater withdrawn in the state was from un-

named surficial aquifers (622 mgd), the intermediate aquifer (255 mgd), and the sand and gravel aquifer (107 mgd). The surficial aquifers (water table aquifers), present throughout much of the state, are primarily used for small self-supplied household wells (domestic self-supplied) or in places where water from the Floridan aquifer system is nonpotable. Florida accounted for 78 percent of the total water withdrawn from the Floridan aquifer system in the southeastern U.S. during 1995. The largest amount of fresh groundwater was withdrawn in Dade County (550 mgd) during 1995, followed by Broward (268 mgd), Polk (243 mgd), Orange (229 mgd), and Palm Beach (220 mgd) counties.

Florida ranked relatively low, thirtieth in the nation, in fresh surface water withdrawals in 1995 (Solley et al. 1998), primarily due to the abundant availability of fresh groundwater and the use of saline surface water. Surface water accounted for 40 percent of the freshwater withdrawals (2,879 mgd) in Florida during 1995. Fresh surface water withdrawals peaked in 1975

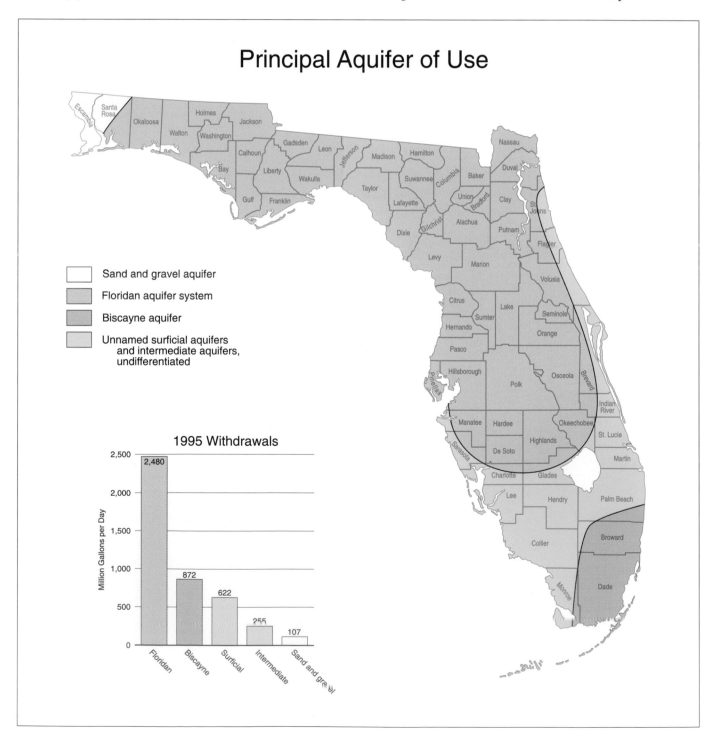

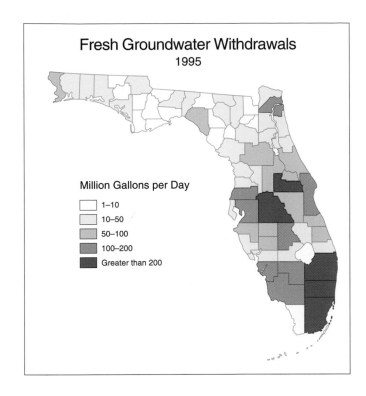

Fresh Groundwater Withdrawals
1995

Million Gallons per Day

- 1–10
- 10–50
- 50–100
- 100–200
- Greater than 200

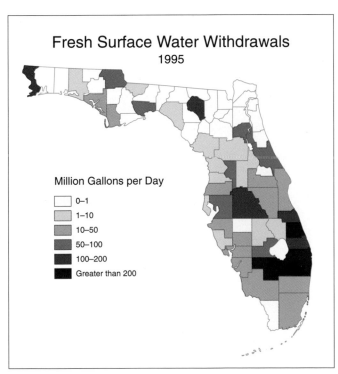

Fresh Surface Water Withdrawals
1995

Million Gallons per Day

- 0–1
- 1–10
- 10–50
- 50–100
- 100–200
- Greater than 200

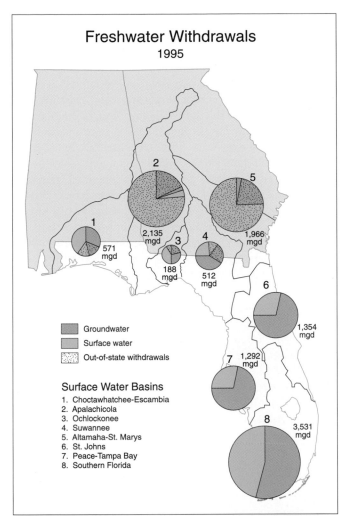

Freshwater Withdrawals
1995

2,135 mgd
1,966 mgd
571 mgd
188 mgd
512 mgd
1,354 mgd
1,292 mgd
3,531 mgd

- Groundwater
- Surface water
- Out-of-state withdrawals

Surface Water Basins
1. Choctawhatchee-Escambia
2. Apalachicola
3. Ochlockonee
4. Suwannee
5. Altamaha-St. Marys
6. St. Johns
7. Peace-Tampa Bay
8. Southern Florida

South Florida Water Management District

Surface water canals used for irrigation, Palm Beach County

117

and remained about the same in 1990 and 1995. The primary users of surface water throughout Florida are irrigators and power producers. The surface water used in Florida comes from either managed and maintained surface water systems or large natural water bodies. Major sources of fresh surface water for irrigation purposes include Lake Okeechobee and associated canals, Lake Apopka, the Caloosahatchee River, and the marshlands associated with the headwaters of the St. Johns River. Surface water used for irrigation from these sources is usually diverted through canals or ditches, then pumped or gravity-fed onto cultivated fields or groves. A large percentage of the water that is flooded onto fields or groves is unused and returned to canals or ditches for further use. Throughout the rest of

Florida, surface water used for irrigation purposes is obtained from other canals or ditches, local lakes or ponds, and small rivers, creeks, or tributaries. Often, many of the canals, ditches, or ponds that are used for irrigation are filled or augmented with groundwater. Most of the fresh surface water used in the state is in the Southern Florida Basin and associated with Lake Okeechobee and the Everglades Agricultural Area. This area is intensively irrigated (sugarcane and vegetables) and accounted for nearly 60 percent of the surface-water withdrawals during 1995. The largest amount of fresh surface water was withdrawn in Palm Beach County (550 mgd) during 1995, followed by Hendry (401 mgd) and St. Lucie (229 mgd) counties.

Water Use by Category

For 1995 withdrawal data were collected and compiled in Florida for the following water use categories: public supply, domestic self-supplied, commercial-industrial self-supplied (including mining), agricultural self-supplied (including livestock), recreational irrigation, and power generation (thermoelectric). Public supply accounted for the largest portion (43 percent) of the groundwater withdrawn in 1995, followed by agricultural self-supplied (35 percent), commercial-industrial self-supplied (10 percent), domestic self-supplied (7 percent), recreational irrigation (4.5 percent), and power generation (0.5 percent). Agricultural self-supplied accounted for the largest amount (60 percent) of fresh surface water withdrawn in 1995, followed by power generation (21 percent), commercial-industrial self-supplied (9 percent), public supply (7 percent), and recreational irrigation (3 percent). Power generation accounted for nearly all (99.5 percent) of the saline water withdrawals, with commercial-industrial self-supplied accounting for the remaining 0.5 percent.

Water-use values for the following sections were compiled using data from the USGS water use program. Water use data are obtained from the five water management districts and the Florida Department of Environmental Protection as well as from various utilities, industries, and power companies. Most of the reported values for 1995 are published in "Water withdrawals, use, and trends in Florida, 1995" (Marella 1998) and

"Estimated use of water in the United States in 1995" (Solley et al. 1998). Data for previous years are published in USGS reports by Marella (1992, 1995).

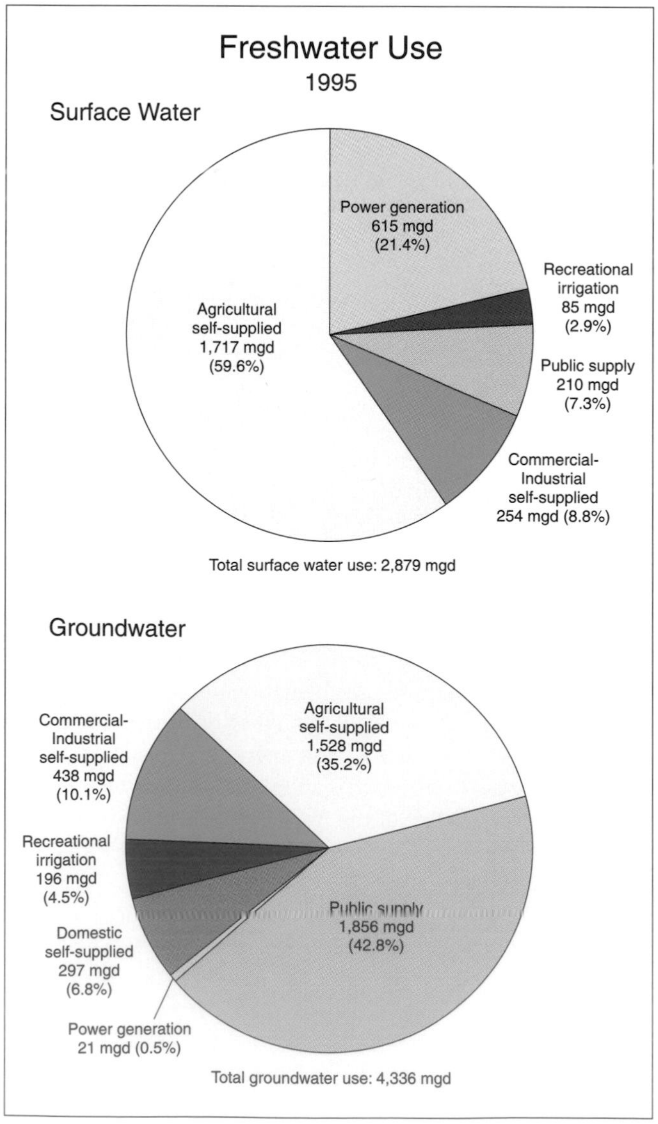

Public Supply

In 1995 about 2,065 mgd of water was withdrawn for public supply, an increase of 135 percent from 1970 and 7 percent from 1990. Nearly 90 percent of the water withdrawn for public supply in 1995 was groundwater.

More than 86 percent of the resident population or about 12.2 million people obtain their drinking water from a public-supply water system. Furthermore, groundwater was the source of public supply drinking water for 11.2 million residents; surface water was the source of 1 million residents.

Of the nearly 2,141 public water supply systems in the state, 1,100 (51 percent) supplied 99.5 percent of the water; only 1 percent relied on surface water as their primary water source.

Public supply per capita use for Florida in 1995 was 169 gallons per day (gd) and was below the national average of 179 gd. The public supply per capita usage in Florida has remained between 160 and 170 gd since 1970, with the excep-

118

Freshwater Use
1995

Surface Water

Power generation
615 mgd
(21.4%)

Recreational
irrigation
85 mgd
(2.9%)

Public supply
210 mgd
(7.3%)

Commercial-
Industrial
self-supplied
254 mgd (8.8%)

Agricultural
self-supplied
1,717 mgd
(59.6%)

Total surface water use: 2,879 mgd

Groundwater

Commercial-
Industrial
self-supplied
438 mgd
(10.1%)

Recreational
irrigation
196 mgd
(4.5%)

Domestic
self-supplied
297 mgd
(6.8%)

Power generation
21 mgd (0.5%)

Agricultural
self-supplied
1,528 mgd
(35.2%)

Public supply
1,856 mgd
(42.8%)

Total groundwater use: 4,336 mgd

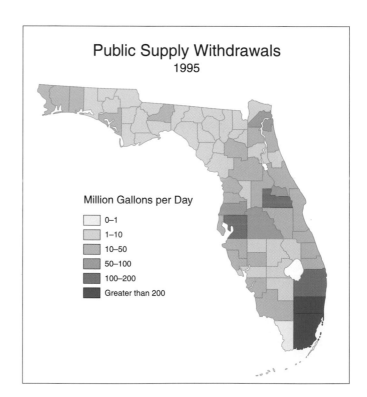

Public Supply Withdrawals
1995

Million Gallons per Day

- 0–1
- 1–10
- 10–50
- 50–100
- 100–200
- Greater than 200

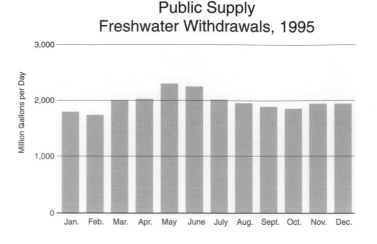

Public Supply
Freshwater Withdrawals, 1995

Richard Marella

Public supply surface water intake, Palm Beach County

U.S. Geological Survey

Public supply well, Leon County

tion of 1980 when per capita usage peaked at 181 gd due to a lengthy statewide drought.

Of the 2,065 mgd withdrawn for public supply use in 1995, 61 percent was delivered for residential (domestic) purposes, 19 percent for commercial uses, 5 percent for industrial uses, and 15 percent for public uses (including system maintenance, firefighting, and irrigation) or was lost or unaccounted for.

Nearly 30 percent of water for public supply was withdrawn during April, May, and June of 1995. Rainfall in Florida during these months is typically low, and as a result, lawn watering and other outdoor uses tend to increase during these months.

The largest amount of water withdrawn for public supply in 1995 was in Dade and Broward counties. Withdrawals totaled 387 mgd, and 1.95 million people were served in Dade County. In Broward County withdrawals totaled 222 mgd and 1.35 million people were served. These two Florida counties accounted for nearly 30 percent of the public water-supply withdrawals and 27 percent of the population served in 1995.

A relatively small amount of water (60 mgd) was withdrawn from brackish or saline ground sources for public supply and treated through a desalination process or diluted with

fresher water to meet drinking water standards. This is an increase of 250 percent since 1985, when the amount of water treated through desalination or diluted for public supply was 17 mgd. This practice is expected to increase throughout Florida, especially in coastal areas.

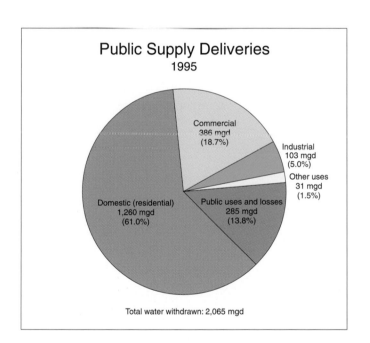

Public Supply Deliveries
1995

Commercial
386 mgd
(18.7%)

Industrial
103 mgd
(5.0%)

Other uses
31 mgd
(1.5%)

Domestic (residential)
1,260 mgd
(61.0%)

Public uses and losses
285 mgd
(13.8%)

Total water withdrawn: 2,065 mgd

119

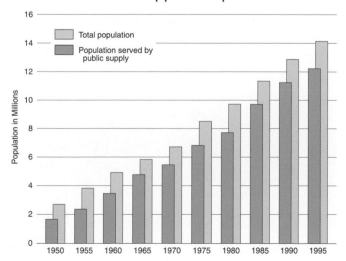

**Total Population and
Public-Supplied Population**

Total population

Population served by
public supply

Population in Millions

1950 1955 1960 1965 1970 1975 1980 1985 1990 1995

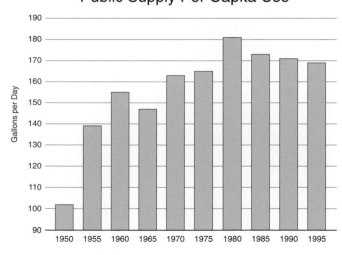

Public Supply Per Capita Use

Gallons per Day

1950 1955 1960 1965 1970 1975 1980 1985 1990 1995

Domestic Self-Supplied

Domestic self-supplied water use includes withdrawals by residential and small commercial users (churches, convenience stores, restaurants) that are not served by a public water supply. This category also includes 1,040 small public supply systems (less than 0.01 mgd) not inventoried under public supply.

It is assumed that all water withdrawn for domestic self-supplied is groundwater due to its widespread availability and general good quality. About 52 percent of the water is obtained from the Floridan aquifer system, while the remaining 48 percent is obtained from local surficial aquifers.

In 1995 an estimated 297 mgd of water was withdrawn for domestic self-supplied use. Water withdrawn for domestic self-supplied use increased by 42 percent from 1970, but remained nearly constant from 1990 to 1995.

According to the U.S. Bureau of Census, an estimated 795,600 households in Florida used an individual well as their source of drinking water in 1990. Assuming the number of households with wells increased between 1990 and 1995 at the same rate as the population (9 percent), the number of households with wells increased to 867,000 in 1995.

Based on the water withdrawn for this category in 1995 and the estimated 867,600 households with wells, average use per well would be about 340 gd.

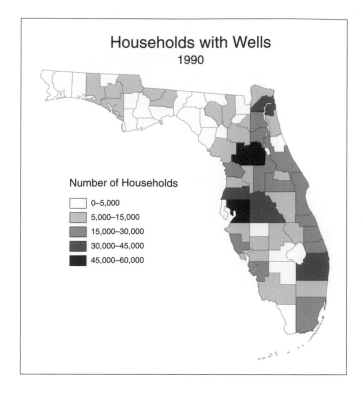

Households with Wells
1990

Number of Households

- 0–5,000
- 5,000–15,000
- 15,000–30,000
- 30,000–45,000
- 45,000–60,000

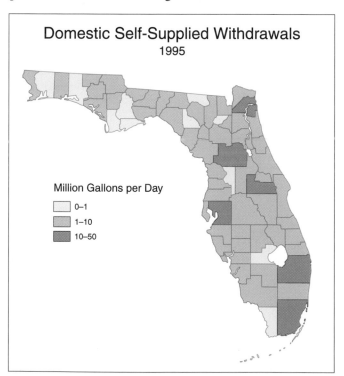

Domestic Self-Supplied Withdrawals
1995

Million Gallons per Day

- 0–1
- 1–10
- 10–50

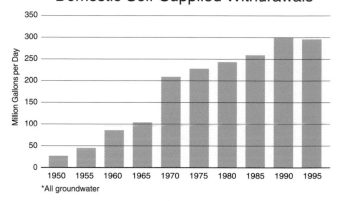

Domestic Self-Supplied Withdrawals*

*All groundwater

In 1995, an estimated 1.94 million people in Florida used domestic self-supplied water, of which 97 percent of this population used an individual well for drinking water and 3 percent were served by the 1,040 small public supply water systems.

The largest amount of freshwater withdrawn for domestic self-supplied purposes in 1995 was in Marion County (20 mgd), followed by Palm Beach (17 mgd), Dade, Hillsborough, and Orange counties (13 mgd each). These five counties accounted for 25 percent of the water withdrawn in this category.

120

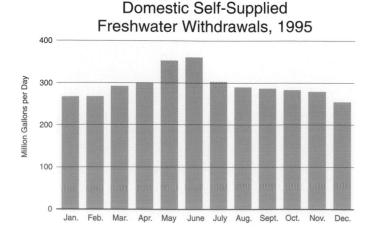

Domestic Self-Supplied
Freshwater Withdrawals, 1995

Richard Marella

Domestic household well and tank, Putnam County

Commercial-Industrial Self-Supplied

Commercial-industrial self-supplied water use includes withdrawals at commercial facilities (recreation, schools, prisons, and military or civilian institutions), industrial facilities (manufacturing or processing), and mining facilities. Water obtained from public supply for these users is not included in this category.

In 1995 nearly 692 mgd of freshwater was withdrawn for commercial-industrial self-supplied use, a decrease of 23 percent from 1970 and 10 percent from 1990. About 63 percent of the water withdrawn for commercial-industrial self-supplied use was groundwater, while the remaining 37 percent was surface water.

A combination of water-use conservation and water recycling efforts, combined with restrictions on industrial wastewater discharges, are largely responsible for the downward trend in this category. In addition, many once self-supplied facilities now obtain water from public supply water systems.

The largest quantity of water withdrawn in this category was used for mining (43 percent), followed by pulp and paper manufacturing (27 percent), chemical manufacturing (13 percent), commercial (7 percent), food production (7 percent), and all other manufacturing (3 percent).

Monthly withdrawals for commercial-industrial self-supplied use fluctuated very little during 1995. January through April generally have the highest withdrawals, primarily because the demand increases as citrus and vegetables are harvested and produced, while mining and pulp and paper production withdrawals remain steady throughout the year.

The largest amount of freshwater withdrawn for commercial-industrial self-supplied purposes in 1995 was in Polk County (92 mgd), followed by Escambia (59 mgd), and Sumter (54 mgd) counties. These three counties accounted for nearly 30 percent of the water withdrawn in this category. Other counties with substantial amounts of commercial-industrial self-supplied water withdrawals include Taylor, Putnam, Dade, and Hamilton.

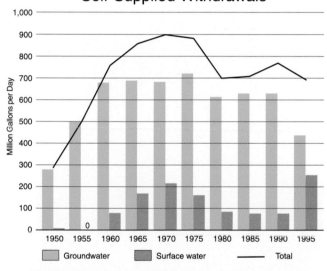

Commercial-Industrial Self-Supplied Withdrawals 1995

Million Gallons per Day
- 0–1
- 1–10
- 10–50
- 50–100

Commercial-Industrial Self-Supplied Freshwater Withdrawals, 1995

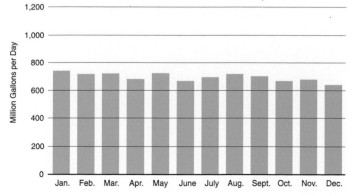

U.S. Geological Survey

Phosphate mining and processing, Hamilton County

121

Agricultural Self-Supplied

Agricultural self-supplied water use consists of withdrawals for both irrigation and nonirrigation purposes. Irrigation is defined as the artificial application of water on lands to assist in the growing of crops or pasture or to prevent damage to crops due to freezing conditions. Nonirrigation includes water withdrawn for livestock needs (watering, feedlots, and washdown), fish farming, and other uses associated with farm operations.

Water withdrawal values for this category are usually estimated based on crop acreage multiplied by a coefficient generated from selected irrigation models for each crop. Factors for these models include growing season, soil type, rainfall, and temperature. A small percentage of water use estimates for this category were derived directly from measured (metered) data.

In 1995 nearly 3,245 mgd of freshwater was withdrawn for agricultural irrigation and nonirrigation purposes in Florida. This is an increase of 55 percent from 1970, but a decrease of 7 percent from 1990. Nearly 53 percent of the water withdrawn for agricultural irrigation and nonirrigation in 1995 was surface water while the remaining 47 percent was groundwater.

Water conservation efforts, changes in irrigation systems from flood or sprinkler to more efficient micro or drip, and other changes in farm practices and management have contributed to the decrease in water withdrawals since 1990. In

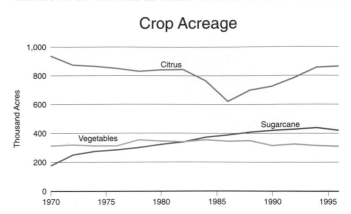

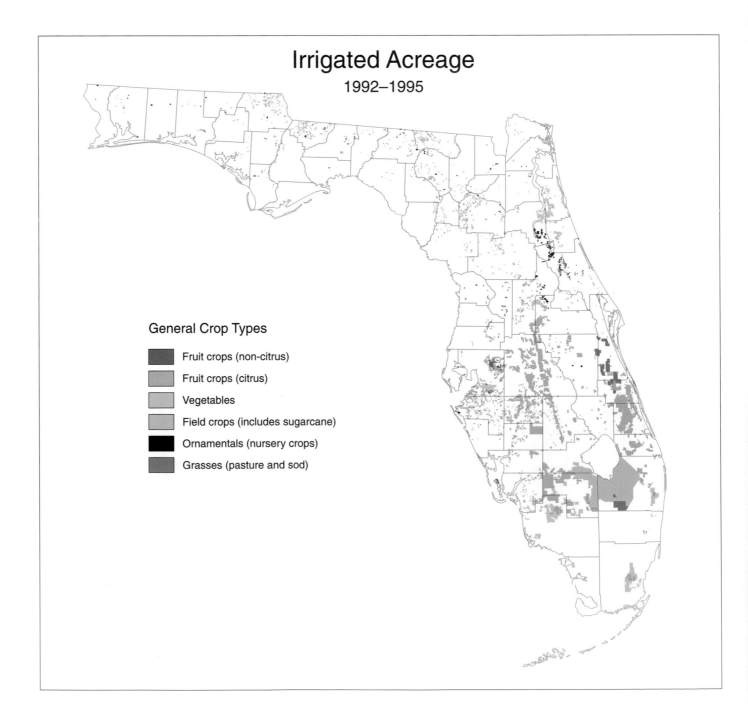

122

Agricultural Self-Supplied Withdrawals
1995

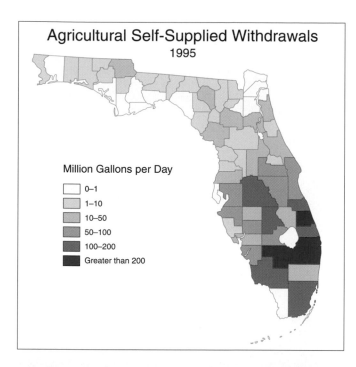

Million Gallons per Day

- 0–1
- 1–10
- 10–50
- 50–100
- 100–200
- Greater than 200

Agricultural Self-Supplied Freshwater Withdrawals
1995

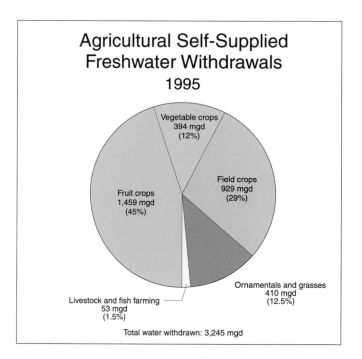

Vegetable crops
394 mgd
(12%)

Field crops
929 mgd
(29%)

Fruit crops
1,459 mgd
(45%)

Ornamentals and grasses
410 mgd
(12.5%)

Livestock and fish farming
53 mgd
(1.5%)

Total water withdrawn: 3,245 mgd

South Florida Water Management District

Lateral-moving irrigation, southern Florida

U. S. Geological Survey

Center pivot irrigation, northern Florida

123

St. Johns River Water Management District

Fern freeze protection, Volusia County

Agricultural Self-Supplied Withdrawals
1995

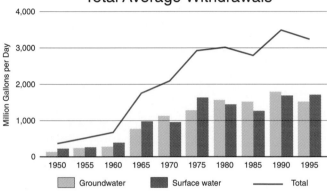

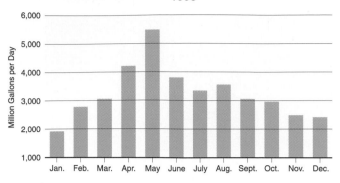

Subsurface flood irrigation, Putnam County

Richard Marella

Agricultural Self-Supplied Total Average Withdrawals

South Florida Water Management District

Traveling gun irrigation, southern Florida

addition, 1990 was considered a drier than normal year, so the values for the year reflect higher than normal demands.

The largest use of freshwater in Florida was agricultural self-supplied, accounting for 45 percent of the total freshwater withdrawn in 1995. Even though Florida ranked thirteenth in the nation for irrigation and nonirrigation withdrawals in 1995, it still accounted for the largest withdrawals of any state east of the Mississippi River.

Monthly withdrawals for agricultural self-supplied use had the largest variation of any category in 1995. A seasonal fluctuation of more than 3,000 mgd is a result of intense crop production during early spring (April and May) and a relatively dormant time during late fall (November and December). This seasonal fluctuation is normal.

Estimated acres farmed in 1995 totaled 3.66 million, of which 1.97 million acres (54 percent) were irrigated. Most of the crop acreage was irrigated by flood or subsurface systems (52 percent), while the remaining acreage was irrigated by micro or drip systems (30 percent) or sprinkler systems (18 percent). This is a substantial change from 1985, when flood or subsurface acreage accounted for 58 percent, micro or drip for 16 percent, and sprinkler for 26 percent.

Citrus accounted for the largest amount of acreage irrigated (820,000 acres), followed by sugarcane (440,000 acres), and vegetable crops (270,000 acres). About 98 percent of the citrus acreage was irrigated, while nearly all of the sugarcane and vegetables acreage was irrigated in 1995.

Citrus acreage has increased steadily since the losses of acreage due to freezes during the mid-1980s. Nearly all of the

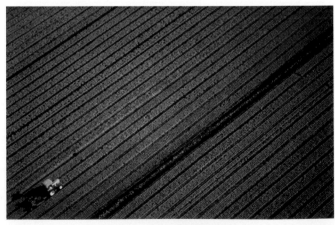

South Florida Water Management District

Subsurface flood irrigation, southern Florida

citrus acreage that was lost to freezes was in central Florida while most of the replanting has occurred in southern Florida.

The largest amount of water withdrawn for agricultural self-supplied use in 1995 was in Palm Beach County (672 mgd), followed by Hendry (550 mgd), and St. Lucie (274 mgd) counties. These three counties accounted for more than 45 percent of the agricultural self-supplied water withdrawn in 1995. Other counties with substantial amounts of agricultural self-supplied water withdrawn include Indian River, Collier, and Martin.

124

Recreational Irrigation

Recreational irrigation water use includes withdrawals for the artificial application of water on lands to assist in the growing of turf grass or shrubbery. Turf grass includes golf courses, nonresidential lawns, cemeteries, and parks or playing fields. Water withdrawal amounts for this category are estimated based on acreage irrigated multiplied by a crop coefficient generated by selected irrigation models. A small percentage of the water use estimates for this category were derived directly from measured (metered) data.

Recreational irrigation is a new water use category for 1995. In previous years, recreational irrigation was accounted for under the agricultural self-supplied category. Prior to 1985 water withdrawals and acres irrigated for turf grass were included under other crops, but for 1985 and 1990 turf grass values were specifically identified under agricultural self-supplied.

In 1995, 281 mgd of freshwater was withdrawn for recreational irrigation with an additional 154 mgd being obtained from reclaimed water. Withdrawals increased 54 percent from 1985, but decreased 9 percent from 1990. Nearly 70 percent of the water withdrawn for recreational irrigation was groundwater, while 30 percent was surface water.

An estimated 93,000 acres were irrigated at nearly 1,100 golf courses throughout Florida in 1995. This is an increase in acreage of about 26 percent from the 74,000 acres irrigated in 1985. The average 18-hole golf course in Florida irrigated about 80 acres or about 4.5 acres per hole in 1995.

Golf course irrigation is the largest user of water in this category, accounting for 67 percent of the withdrawals and 64 percent of reclaimed wastewater used.

The largest amount of water withdrawn for recreational irrigation in 1995 was in Palm Beach (67 mgd) and Broward (53 mgd) counties. Pinellas County used 40 mgd of reclaimed water for recreational irrigation purposes in 1995.

Monthly withdrawals for recreational irrigation had a large seasonal variation in 1995. Withdrawals were greatest in March through October and lowest in December through February.

Recreational Irrigation Withdrawals
1995

Million Gallons per Day
- 0–1
- 1–10
- 10–50
- 50–100

Recreational Irrigation Withdrawals

Groundwater   Surface water   —— Total water

Combined with agricultural self-supplied before 1985

Recreational Irrigation Freshwater Withdrawals, 1995

Richard Marella

Golf course irrigation, Putnam County

125

Power Generation

Power generation water use includes withdrawals at thermoelectric power generating facilities (fossil fuel or nuclear) and water used at hydroelectric facilities. In 1995, 54 thermoelectric (4 were on standby use only) and 2 hydroelectric power generating facilities were in operation statewide.

In 1995, 11,596 mgd of water was withdrawn for power generation purposes. This represents about 66 percent of the total water withdrawn in the state. An additional 10 mgd of public supplied or reclaimed water was used directly for power generation in 1995.

Both nuclear and fossil fuel plants require massive amounts of water for cooling. However, of the total water withdrawn, only about 0.5 percent was consumptively used, as the remaining 99.5 percent was returned to its source.

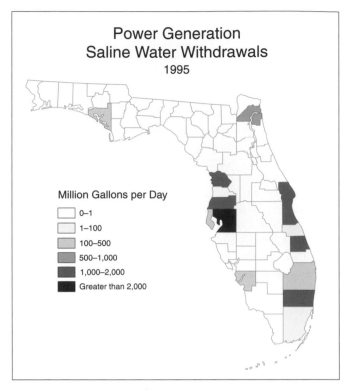

Power Generation
Saline Water Withdrawals
1995

Million Gallons per Day
- 0–1
- 1–100
- 100–500
- 500–1,000
- 1,000–2,000
- Greater than 2,000

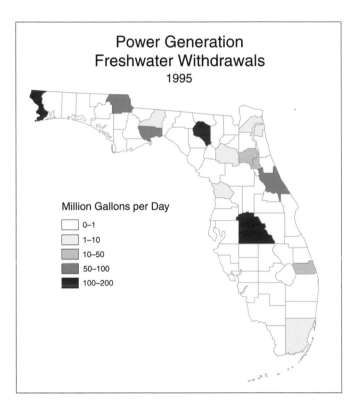

Power Generation
Freshwater Withdrawals
1995

Million Gallons per Day
- 0–1
- 1–10
- 10–50
- 50–100
- 100–200

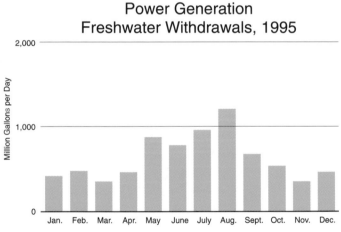

Power Generation
Freshwater Withdrawals, 1995

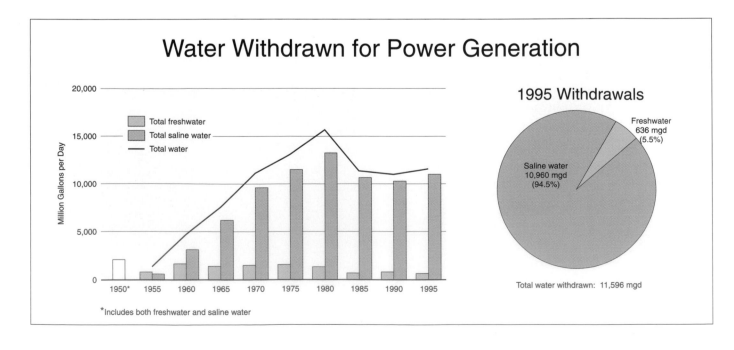

Water Withdrawn for Power Generation

Total freshwater
Total saline water
Total water

*Includes both freshwater and saline water

1995 Withdrawals

Freshwater
636 mgd
(5.5%)

Saline water
10,960 mgd
(94.5%)

Total water withdrawn: 11,596 mgd

126

Nearly 95 percent of the water withdrawn for power generation in 1995 was saline water. The remaining 5 percent was withdrawn from freshwater sources (of which 97 percent was surface water and 3 percent was groundwater). Saline withdrawals increased 15 percent from 1970 and 7 percent from 1990, whereas freshwater withdrawals decreased 58 percent from 1970 and 19 percent from 1990.

Total gross power generated by the 56 power generating facilities in 1995 was estimated at 149,200 megawatt hours. This is an increase of more than 160 percent since 1970, despite only a 5 percent increase in total water withdrawn during this period. Between 1970 and 1995, several facilities have been modernized with increased capacity and efficiency, while several older inefficient facilities have been taken out of service or operated on standby use only.

Monthly freshwater withdrawals for power generation fluctuated substantially during 1995. May through August have the highest withdrawals, primarily because air conditioning demands increase during the hot summer months.

The largest amount of freshwater withdrawn in 1995 was in Escambia County (162 mgd), and the largest amount of saline water withdrawn was in Hillsborough County (2,382 mgd). Gadsden and Leon counties had the only active hydroelectric facilities in 1995.

Most of the surface water is withdrawn from bays or rivers along the coast, and nearly all of it is returned to these sources. Major saline surface water sources include the Caloosahatchee River, Crystal River, Indian River, St. Johns River, and Tampa Bay. Several of the rivers are freshwater rivers; however, at the point of withdrawal for most of the power plants the water is brackish or saline due to tidal flows.

Thermoelectric power plant, Orange County

David York

127

Thermoelectric power plant, Suwannee County

U.S. Geological Survey

Water Management Districts

In 1995 the largest amount of freshwater withdrawn was in the South Florida Water Management District. The total amount of water withdrawn was 3,571 mgd, nearly one-half (49.5 percent) of the state's total freshwater withdrawn in 1995.

South Florida Water Management District accounted for the largest amount of water withdrawn for public supply (47 percent), agricultural self-supplied (68 percent), and recreational irrigation (67 percent). St. Johns River Water Management District accounted for the largest amount of water withdrawn for domestic self-supplied (32 percent). Southwest Florida Water Management District accounted for the largest amount of water withdrawn for commercial-industrial self-supplied (34 percent). Northwest Florida Water Management District accounted for the largest amount of freshwater withdrawn for power generation (45 percent).

Forty percent of the state's 1995 population lived in the South Florida Water Management District, 25.5 percent in the Southwest Florida Water Management District, 25 percent in the St. Johns River Water Management District, 8 percent in the Northwest Florida Water Management District, and 1.5 percent in the Suwannee River Water Management District.

Water withdrawals in the Northwest Florida, St. Johns River, Southwest Florida, and Suwannee River water management districts remained about the same or decreased slightly between 1975 and 1995. However, as a result of increases in irrigated acreage and population, water withdrawals in the South Florida Water Management District increased substantially between 1985 and 1995.

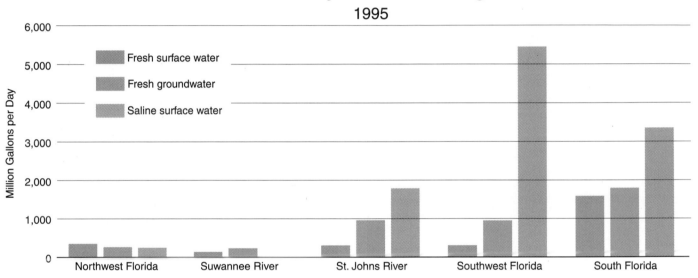

Water Withdrawals by Water Management District
1995

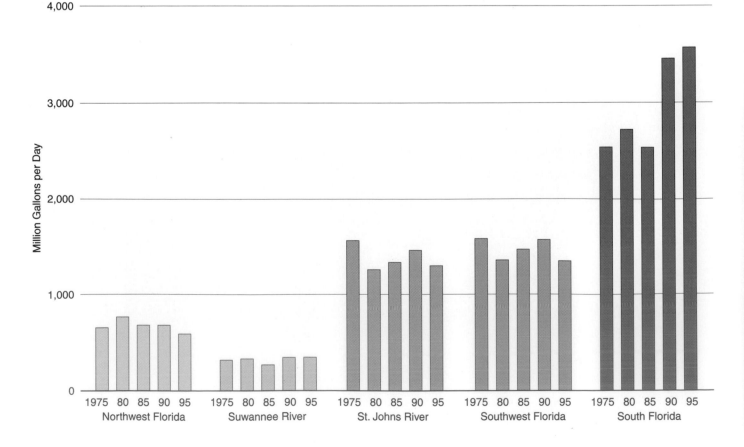

Freshwater Withdrawals by Water Management District

128

Fresh Surface Water Withdrawals

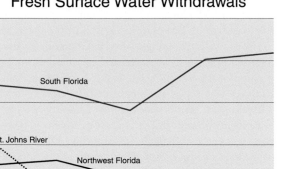

Fresh Groundwater Withdrawals

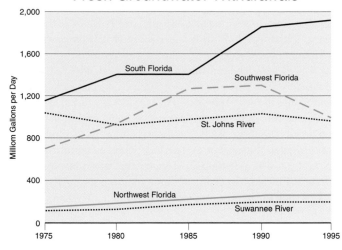

Water Withdrawals by Water Management District
1995

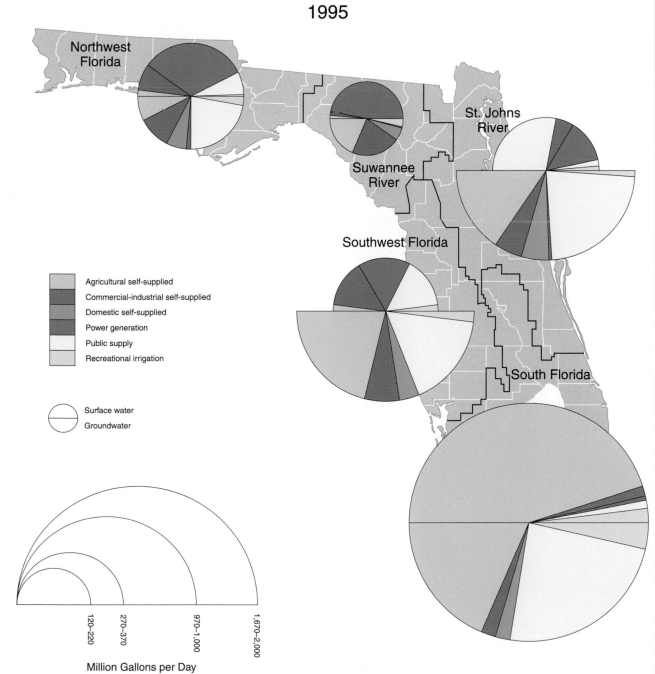

Northwest Florida

Suwannee River

St. Johns River

Southwest Florida

South Florida

Agricultural self-supplied
Commercial-industrial self-supplied
Domestic self-supplied
Power generation
Public supply
Recreational irrigation

Surface water
Groundwater

120–220
270–370
970–1,000
1,670–2,000

Million Gallons per Day

129

Consumptive Water Use and Treated Discharges

For 1995, an estimated 2,783 mgd or 39 percent of the freshwater withdrawn in Florida was consumptively used, while the remaining 4,432 mgd or 61 percent was returned for use again as wastewater. The consumptive use is basically lost for immediate use as it is either incorporated into products or transpired into the atmosphere and later enters as rainfall. The largest amount of consumptive use occurs in agricultural and recreational irrigation and is due to large amounts of acreage that are irrigated during hot dry periods when evapotranspiration is highest. The percentage of water that was consumptively used in Florida has changed some over the past 20 years. In 1975, statewide consumptive use was about 33 percent, and in 1985 consumptive use was about 43 percent of the freshwater withdrawn. All consumptive use values are estimated, primarily based on irrigation models or industry standards.

Wastewater includes water discharged or released from treatment facilities, septic tanks, or runoff from agricultural, mining, or urban lands. The water discharged from treatment facilities and septic tanks generally is treated to some level, whereas most runoff water is not. Treatment can be as simple as a settling process or as complex as advanced treatment. Discharge data are collected for domestic (municipal) and industrial facilities since these discharges are generally regulated and metered, whereas records of the amount of water released from septic tanks or that runs off of agricultural and urban lands are generally not available.

130

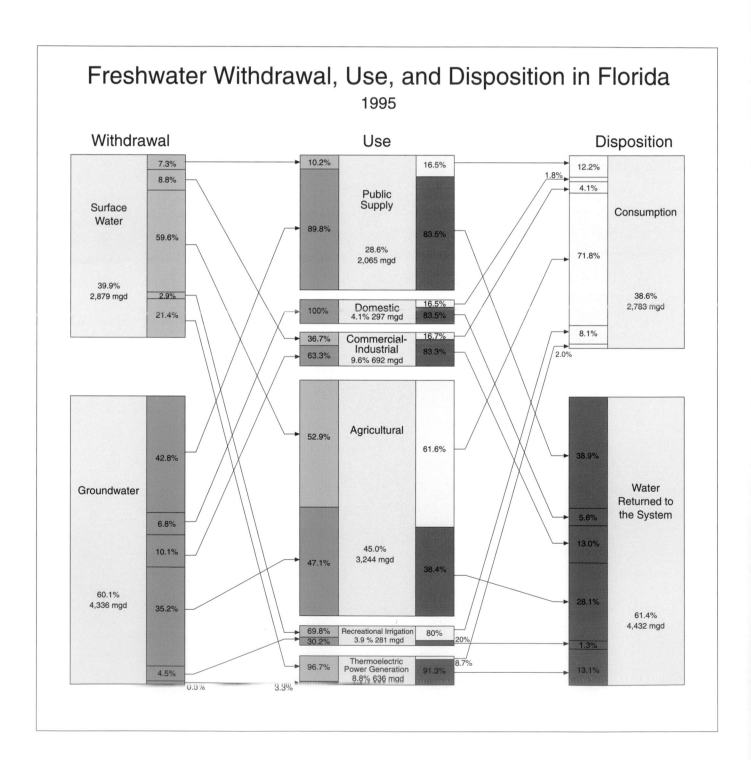

Domestic Wastewater

Domestic wastewater facilities (includes municipal) are those systems that receive or dispose of wastewater derived principally from residential dwellings, businesses or commercial establishments, institutions, and some industrial facilities. According to the Florida Department of Environmental Protection 3,034 domestic wastewater systems were in operation during 1995.

Estimated discharge from these domestic wastewater systems in 1995 was 1,566 mgd. Of this total, nearly 98.5 percent was from 561 systems that discharged 0.10 mgd or more. The remaining 1.5 percent was from the 2,473 systems that discharged less than 0.10 mgd.

The estimated population served by the 561 larger systems in 1995 was 9.47 million, while the population served by the 2,473 smaller systems was estimated at about 0.82 million. The remaining 3.86 million people in Florida discharged domestic wastewater to septic tanks.

Domestic wastewater discharge increased 37 percent between 1985 and 1995 and 14 percent between 1990 and 1995. Capacities of the 561 large systems totaled 2,054 mgd, of which 75 percent (1,544 mgd) was used in 1995.

In 1995 the 1,544 mgd of domestic wastewater discharge represents about 75 percent of the 2,065 mgd of the public supply water withdrawn. This indicates that about 25 percent was not returned for treatment and was consumptively used. This compares with consumptive-use rates of 30 percent in 1990 and 33 percent in 1985.

Of the 1995 total domestic wastewater, 53 percent (817 mgd) was discharged to surface water, 24 percent (372 mgd) was discharged to deep aquifers through injection wells, and 23 percent (355 mgd) was discharged to the land through drain fields, percolation ponds, spray fields, and land application systems.

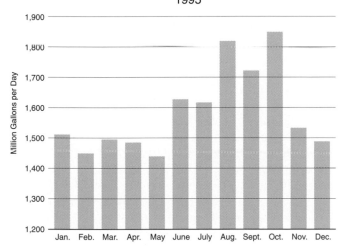

U.S. Geological Survey

Domestic wastewater plant, Leon County

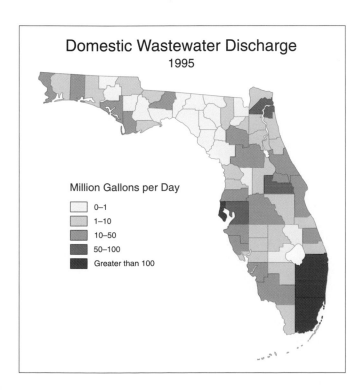

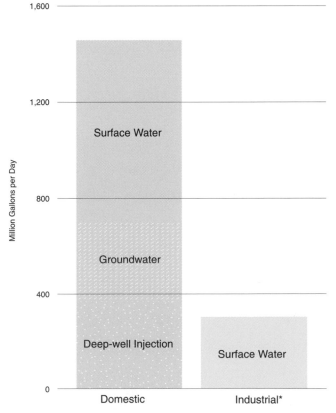

131

The largest amount of domestic wastewater discharge in 1995 was in Dade and Broward counties. Treated domestic wastewater discharged in Dade County totaled 324 mgd, of which 70 percent was released to the Atlantic Ocean; in Broward County discharges totaled 191 mgd, of which nearly 60 percent was released to deep well injection. Other counties that had discharges over 100 mgd of domestic wastewater in 1995 include Pinellas (122 mgd) and Palm Beach (108 mgd).

Monthly domestic wastewater discharges in Florida fluctuated substantially during 1995. June through October had the highest discharges, primarily due to infiltration into wastewater collection systems from summer rains. This seasonal fluctuation is normal.

Industrial Discharges

Industrial wastewater facilities include those that produce, treat, or dispose of wastewater not otherwise defined as domestic wastewater. This includes runoff and leachate from areas that receive pollutants associated with industrial or commercial storage, handling, or processing. According to the Florida Department of Environmental Protection, 1,650 industrial facilities were in operation during 1995.

Estimated discharge from the 54 industrial wastewater systems inventoried in 1995 was 292 mgd. This represents those systems that treated and discharged 0.10 mgd or more. Many of the larger systems that do not treat wastewater are not included, such as power plant discharge of once-through cooling water that is neither altered or treated, water discharged for dewatering purposes, and the discharge of stormwater from retention ponds. Additionally, many permitted systems only discharge periodically during the year.

Industrial wastewater discharge increased 7 percent between 1985 and 1995 and 2 percent between 1990 and 1995.

More than 96 percent (282 mgd) of the industrial wastewater was discharged to surface water in 1995. The remaining 4 percent (10 mgd) was discharged to land application systems or injection wells.

The largest amount of industrial wastewater discharge in 1995 was in Escambia and Taylor counties (49 mgd each), fol-

U.S. Geological Survey

Industrial wastewater lagoon, Taylor County

lowed by Nassau County (36 mgd) during 1995. These three counties accounted for 46 percent of the state's total industrial discharge in 1995.

Septic Tanks

Septic tanks are buried, watertight receptacles constructed to promote the separation of solids, grease, and liquid components of wastewater in the absence of oxygen. The liquid fraction from the septic tank is usually discharged to a drain field for disposal.

According to the Florida Department of Health and the U.S. Bureau of Census, an estimated 1,753,300 households in Florida were on septic tanks in 1995. This is a 87 percent increase from the 938,350 households on septic tanks in 1970, and a 13 percent increase from the 1,559,100 households on septic tanks in 1990. Dade and Polk counties had the largest number of septic tanks in 1995 with more than 124,400 and 90,960, respectively.

Based on a discharge of 135 gd per tank, the total discharge from these tanks in 1995 would be about 237 mgd. Most of this water is discharged to the local surficial (water table) aquifer through drain fields or boreholes.

132

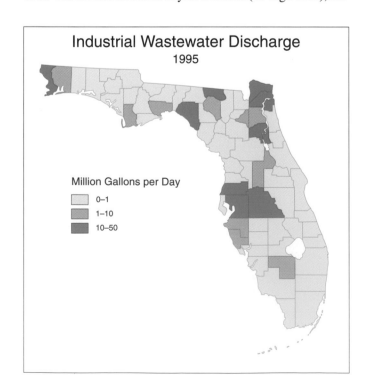

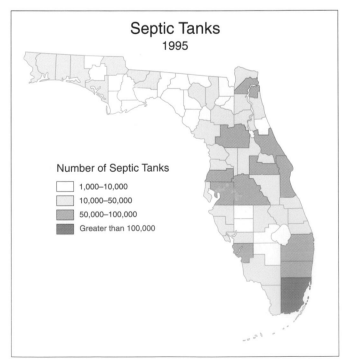

Water Reuse

Each day 60 gallons of wastewater per person flows out of the home and into the sewers. As the wastewater travels miles through the collection system, relatively large amounts of groundwater infiltrate through the joints and defects in the sewers. By the time wastewater reaches the treatment facility, the volume has increased to about 100 gallons per person per day. Wastewater is relatively dilute. In fact, based on weight wastewater normally is about 99.9 percent water and only 0.1 percent pollutants. However, effective treatment and disinfection are still needed to ensure protection of environmental quality and public health.

Secondary treatment is the minimum level of treatment allowed in Florida. Preliminary treatment may include screening, pulverizing, grit removal, and flow measurement. Primary sedimentation allows relatively large solid materials to settle while floatable scum is removed at the surface. Secondary treatment involves biological treatment using activated sludge (most common in Florida), trickling filters, or rotating biological contactors. In an activated sludge system, microorganisms are used to stabilize organic materials in the wastewater. The secondary sedimentation process allows the microorganisms produced in the biological treatment process to settle and be removed. Disinfection, most commonly chlorination, is provided to destroy disease-causing organisms.

David York

Forty percent of reclaimed water is used for landscape irrigation.

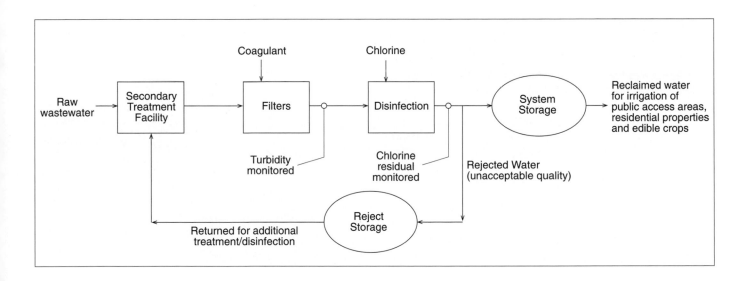

133

Domestic Wastewater Characteristics

	Untreated Wastewater	Secondary Treatment	Advanced Treatment	Reclamation Facility[a]
Total suspended solids	200	20	5	5
CBOD5[b]	200	20	5	5
Total dissolved solids	500	500	500	500
Total nitrogen	25	15	3	15
Total phosphorus	10	8	1	5
Fecal coliform (number/100ml)	1,000,000	200	ND[c]	ND

[a] a treatment facility providing reclaimed water for irrigation of public access areas, residential properties, or edible crops
[b] Carbonaceous biochemical oxygen demand (a measure of organic content)
[c] ND = not detected
All measurements mg/l except fecal coliform

Advanced wastewater treatment provides for the removal of nutrients and greater removals of suspended solids and organic materials. Advanced wastewater treatment plants can be designed and operated to provide effluent quality tailored to the discharge or reuse requirements. Florida Statutes require advanced wastewater treatment for discharges in the Tampa Bay and Indian River Lagoon areas and define advanced wastewater treatment for these areas as a final effluent quality of 5 milligrams per liter (mg/l) carbonaceous biochemical oxygen demand, 5 mg/l total suspended solids, 3 mg/l total nitrogen, and 1 mg/l total phosphorus. Other advanced wastewater treatment processes (such as reverse osmosis, ion exchange, and activated carbon) may be added to the treatment processes to produce a drinking-water-quality product.

Between 1985 and 1996 Florida became a leader in the reuse of reclaimed water. Reuse is required within the state's water resource caution areas. In 1996 the Department of Environmental Protection identified 416 reuse systems using 402 mgd of reclaimed water. The total capacity of these facilities was 826 mgd, which is nearly 40 percent of the total domestic wastewater treatment capacity in Florida.

Reclaimed water is being used for landscape irrigation (including golf courses, parks, highway medians, playgrounds, and residential properties), agricultural irrigation (including irrigation of edible crops), aesthetic uses (decorative ponds, pools, and fountains), groundwater recharge, industrial uses (for cooling, process, or wash waters), wetlands creation, restoration, and enhancement, and fire protection (use in hydrants or sprinklers).

134

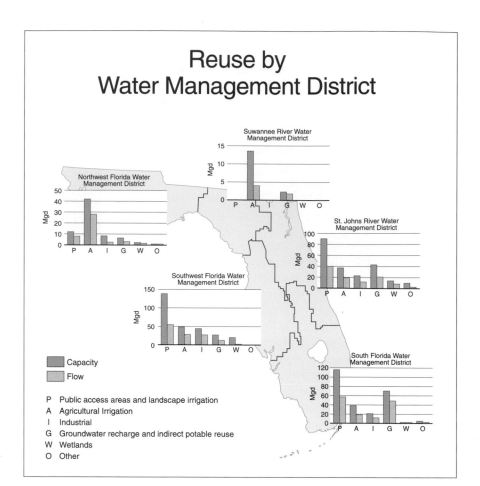

Reuse by Water Management District

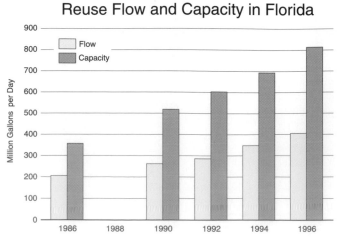

Reuse Projects in Florida

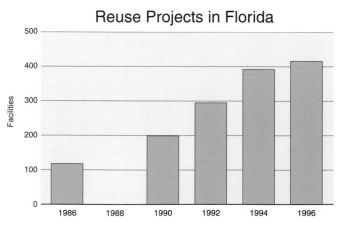

Reuse Flow and Capacity in Florida

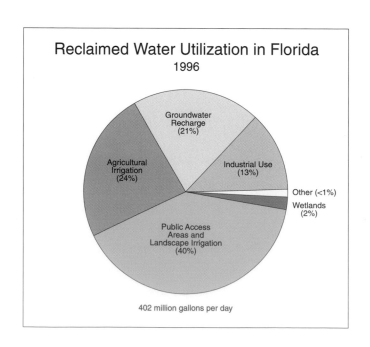

Reclaimed Water Utilization in Florida
1996

402 million gallons per day

REFERENCES

Unless otherwise indicated, data are from U.S. Geological Survey water-use program.

Florence, B.L., and C. Moore. 1997. *Annual Water Use Survey, 1995*. St. Johns Water Management District Technical Publication SJ 97-4. Palatka.

Florida Agricultural Statistics Service. 1996. *Citrus Summary 1994-1995*. Florida Department of Agriculture and Consumer Services. Orlando.

Florida Agricultural Statistics Service. 1996. *Field Crop Summary 1995*. Florida Department of Agriculture and Consumer Services. Orlando.

Florida Agricultural Statistics Service. 1996. *Vegetable Summary 1994-1995*. Florida Department of Agriculture and Consumer Services. Orlando.

Florida Department of Commerce. 1996. *Florida Visitor Study, 1995*. Bureau of Economic Analysis. Office of Tourism Research. Tallahassee.

Florida Department of Environmental Protection. 1997. *1996 Reuse Inventory*. Tallahassee. (map and graph, 134)

Florida Department of Environmental Regulation. 1990. *Drinking Water Standards, Monitoring, and Reporting*. Chapter 17-550. Tallahassee.

Florida Department of Environmental Regulation. 1991. *Domestic Wastewater Facilities*. Chapter 17-600. Tallahassee.

Florida Department of Health. 1997. In *Florida Assessment of Coastal Trends, Onsite Sewage Program*. Florida Department of Community Affairs. Tallahassee.

Florida Sports Foundation. 1994. *Fairways in the Sunshine, Official Florida Golf Guide*. Florida Sports Foundation. Tallahassee.

Izuno, F.T., and D.Z. Haman. 1987. *Basic Irrigation Terminology*. Agricultural Engineering Fact Sheet AE-66. University of Florida. Institute of Food and Agricultural Sciences. Gainesville.

Marella, R. L. 1992. *Water Withdrawals, Use and Trends in Florida, 1990*. U.S. Geological Survey Water-Resources Investigations Report 92-4140.

Marella, R. L. 1994. *Estimated Discharge of Treated Wastewater in Florida, 1990*. U.S. Geological Survey Open-File Report 93-364.

Marella, R. L. 1995. *Water-Use Data by Category, County, and Water Management District in Florida, 1950–90*. U.S. Geological Survey Open-File Report 94-521.

Marella, R.L. 1997. *Irrigated Crop Acreage and Water Withdrawals in Florida, 1990*. Florida Geological Survey Map Series 143. Florida Department of Environmental Protection. Tallahassee.

Marella, R. L. 1998. *Water Withdrawals, Use, Discharge, and Trends in Florida, 1995*. U.S. Geological Survey Water-Resources Investigations Report.

Seaber, P.R., F.P. Kapinos, and G.L. Knapp. 1984. *State Hydrologic Unit Maps*. U.S. Geological Survey Open-File Report 84-708.

Smajstrla, A.G., B.J. Boman, G.A. Clark, D.Z. Haman, D.S. Harrison, F.T. Izuno, and F.S. Zazueta. 1988. *Efficiencies of Florida Agricultural Irrigation Systems*. Bulletin 247. University of Florida, Institute of Food and Agricultural Sciences. Gainesville.

Solley, W. B., R. R. Pierce, and H. A. Perlman. 1998. *Estimated Use of Water in the U.S. in 1995*. U.S. Geological Survey Circular 1200.

Southwest Florida Water Management District. 1997. *1995 Estimated Water Use in the Southwest Florida Water Management District*. Resource Projects Department, Conservation Projects Section. Brooksville.

U.S. Bureau of Census. 1993. *1990 Census of Housing, Detailed Housing Characteristics: Florida*. U.S. Department of Commerce, Bureau of Census. Washington, D.C.

U.S. Soil Conservation Service. 1982. Florida Irrigation Guide. U.S. Department of Agriculture, Soil Conservation Service. Gainesville.

University of Florida. 1997. *1997 Florida Statistical Abstract*. University of Florida, Bureau of Economic and Business Research. Gainesville.

Vecchioli, J. and D.W. Foose. 1985. "Florida Ground-Water Resources." In the *National Water Summary, 1984–Selected Water Quality Trends and Ground-Water resources*. U.S. Geological Survey Water-Supply Paper 2275.

7
WATER QUALITY

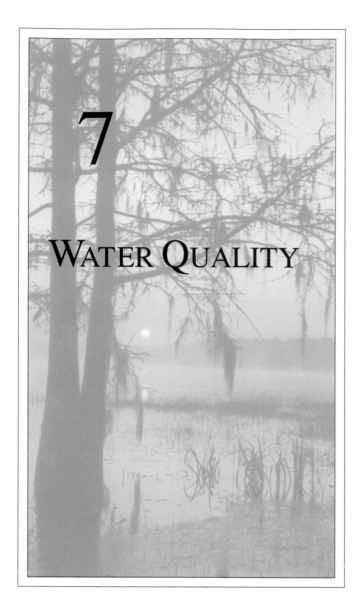

Florida Photographic Collection, Florida State Archives

Juan Ponce de Léon at the Fountain of Youth

Florida Photographic Collection, Florida State Archives

136

According to some accounts, Ponce de Léon, the European discoverer of Florida, was seeking a Fountain of Youth. Water from the fountain would have provided the ultimate standard of comparison for good water quality. Ponce de Léon never found the rejuvenating spring, but strong confidence in the healthful qualities of Florida's waters persisted. In 1901, mineral water from Suwanee (now Suwannee) Springs, near Live Oak, was advertised as producing benefits to health almost as wonderful as a Fountain of Youth. Not everyone agreed, however, that the water from underground sources was so healthful. A physician from this era advised that underground water had passed through rotten limestone and that "the deeper the well, therefore, the cooler and more dangerous the water" (Little 1870:423). In the 1990s we recognize the fundamental importance of clean water, but we also have a better understanding of water quality and water pollution.

Good water quality is indispensable, of course, for the water we drink, but it is also essential for many other uses. We can-

Eric Livingston, Joe Hand, Mary Paulic, Tom Seal, Tom Swihart, Gary Maddox, Jay Silvanima, Charles Coultas, Kenna Study, Michael Scheinkman, Tricia McClenahan, Bob Fisher, Donnie McClaugherty, Steve Partney, Rich Deuerling

not safely swim or fish in polluted waters, nor can Florida's many ecosystems long prosper without good water quality. Clearly, we have a well-justified interest in protecting water quality. This chapter briefly describes some of what is known about the quality of Florida's surface water and groundwater. It also describes some major pollution sources and pollution control techniques.

The most limited definition of water quality is the chemical and physical state of a water sample or water body. Many indicators of water quality, such as nutrient levels, temperature, transparency, and levels of dissolved oxygen, are routinely measured in the field and in laboratories. Others are measured infrequently and techniques for measuring additional indicators are being developed. A broader definition of water quality includes biological and sediment measures. It is useful in and of itself to know what forms of life inhabit a river or lake, especially in the bottom sediments where many pollutants accumulate. They are as characteristic of a body of water as is its chemistry. The biological community of a water body also integrates the cumulative effects of all of the pollutants that enter a water body. As discussed later in this chapter, the concentrations and distribution of pollutants in bottom sediments also help assess cumulative effects and can be used to pinpoint areas where management activities should be focused.

Causes and Sources of Water Pollution

Pollution problems vary in Florida. In the past, most identifiable water-quality problems were derived from industrial and domestic point source discharges. By implementing new technologies, better treating wastes, and putting into place regulatory controls, point source pollution has diminished. Still, there are many water bodies that are adversely affected by point source pollution. Most are located near urban centers.

Nonpoint sources now account for most water quality problems. Nonpoint sources are diffuse and driven by rainfall, runoff, and leaching of pollutants into groundwaters. They include stormwater runoff, septic tanks, and erosion from construction sites, unpaved roads, and farm fields.

Because Florida is so populous and has grown so rapidly, an important source of pollution is urban stormwater. This runoff carries many different pollutants, from nutrients to toxic pollutants, and adds biological oxygen demand. Urban stormwater and siltation and turbidity from construction are major sources of impairment for all waterbody types. Problems concentrate around the state's urban centers. As a major nutrient source, stormwater accelerates lake eutrophication. Although current stormwater rules and growth management laws restrict pollution from new sources, regulations are difficult to monitor and enforce.

Runoff from agriculture and silviculture includes nutrients, sediments (increased turbidity), bacteria, and pesticides. These generally do their worst damage in lakes, slowly moving rivers and canals, and sometimes receiving estuaries. Problems are concentrated in central and southern portions of the state and in several rivers entering Florida from the north. Nonpoint pollution from agriculture, both croplands and animal husbandry operations such as dairies and chicken farms, also has impacted

groundwater quality as the pollutants move through Florida's sandy soils and limestone geology. Problems are concentrated in the Middle Suwannee Basin and along the Central Florida Ridge. Although agricultural operations have traditionally been less regulated than point sources, the need is increasingly realized for improved treatment of runoff and better implementation of best management practices. Significant restoration projects to treat stormwater by marsh filtration or retention are

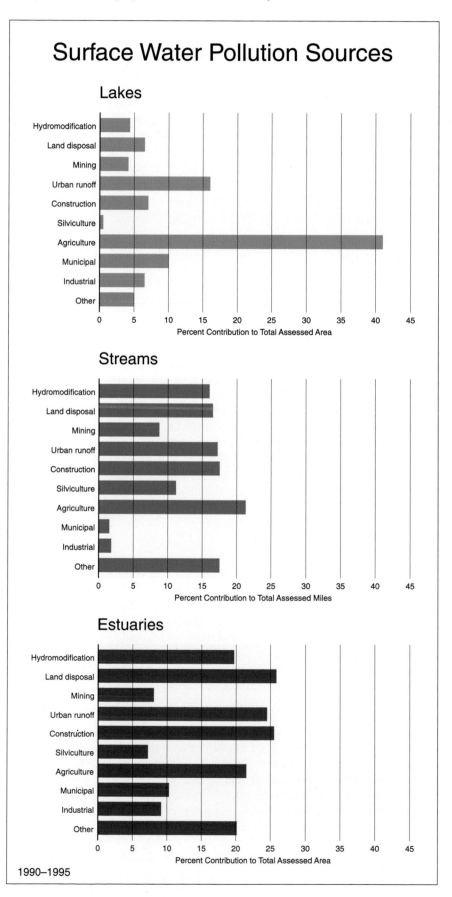

137

underway in the Everglades, Upper St. Johns River basin, and Upper Ocklawaha River basin.

Wastewater, which contributes primarily nutrients and pathogens, can also be a source of toxins. Sources include municipal wastewater treatment plants, package plants, septic tanks, and runoff from land application. In particular, septic tank leachate contributes to the degradation of many water bodies, including many lakes and tributaries into Sarasota Bay. Treatment by domestic wastewater plants has improved significantly since the early 1980s. In fact, most improving water quality trends can be traced to plant upgrades or the elimination of these surface water discharges. Further advancements are being encouraged using design innovations such as wetland treatment systems, water reuse, and advanced treatment. A problem still exists in rural areas, however, where septic tanks are used widely and where limited financial and technological resources have allowed poorly operating facilities to continue to pollute relatively pristine waters.

Most notably, industrial sources include pulp and paper mills. Because of the volume and nature of their discharges, all pulp and paper mills operating in Florida seriously degrade their receiving waters. The phosphate and fertilizer industries generate major point and nonpoint pollution in several basins, and phosphate mining also creates hydrologic modifications in surface waters and land.

Hydrologic modifications include damming running waters; channeling slowing moving waters; or dredging, draining, and filling wetlands for flood control, agriculture, drinking-water supplies, and urban development. While such modifications are not strictly pollution sources, in most cases where natural hydrologic regimes are modified, water quality problems ensue. Rating the effects of hydrologic modifications is difficult. Dredging and filling destroy habitats. Disrupting wetlands and causing a net loss in their areas reduces buffering and filtering capacities and biological potential. This is a particularly important problem in estuaries. Losses of seagrasses, which provide crucial juvenile habitat for many commercial and recreational species, and other marine habitat losses can seriously affect the long-term viability of fisheries.

Quality of Surface Water

Florida's surface waters are comprised of more than 51,000 miles of streams (about half are identified as canals), 3,000 square miles of lakes, and 4,000 square miles of estuaries. These waters support diverse habitats, plants, and animals as well as agriculture, recreation, and industry. More than 50 agencies and governments at the federal, state, and local level monitor surface waters.

The primary source of Florida's water quality data is the Environmental Protection Agency's computerized water-quality database (STORET). Several thousand stations are sampled annually statewide for water quality. Most monitoring networks contain fixed or targeted stations. Stations are selected at particular locations for specific reasons. In many cases they monitor pollution sources or are integrator sites in larger watersheds.

Data are usually collected in the field for pH, specific conductance, dissolved oxygen, Secchi depth, and temperature. Typical laboratory analyses are for color, total suspended solids, biological oxygen demand (BOD), bacterial contamination, nutrients, chlorophyll a and less often major ions (calcium, magnesium, sodium, potassium, chloride, and sulfate).

Fewer agencies regularly collect water column trace metals, biological, or sediment contaminant data making the distribution across the state spatially patchy. The only contaminant collected statewide in an organized fashion is mercury in fish tissue.

Overall Quality and Trends

The last complete statewide assessment was performed in 1996. For that assessment, 2,500 of the state's 4,534 watersheds were evaluated. Waters were assessed to determine their support or nonsupport of their designated use. The state of Florida recognizes five use classifications for surface water: Class I (potable water supplies), Class II (shellfish propagation or harvesting), Class III (recreation and fish and wildlife propagation), Class IV (agricultural water supplies), and Class V (navigation and utility and industrial use).

For the 1996 Water Quality Assessment, the state assessed 11,858 miles of streams, 2,004 square miles of lakes, and 3,939 square miles of estuaries. Of the stream miles, 61 percent fully supported their designated use. Another 32 percent of stream miles partially supported use. About half the area of lakes (45 percent) and estuaries (54 percent) fully supported designated use while 41 percent of lakes and 49 percent of estuaries partially supported use.

Some areas repeatedly fail to fully support designated use. Water bodies that only partially or do not meet use are found with higher frequency in the southeast, in the central region near Orlando, in the St. Johns River basin particularly around Jacksonville, in Pensacola Bay and its tributaries, in the Peace River basin, and along the west coast between Tampa and Naples. Though it is difficult to discern direct cause and effect relations from these patterns, water bodies whose watersheds include large urban areas and those with intensive industrial and agricultural activities appear to have the poorest water quality.

The state of Florida has developed an index to categorize surface water quality. The index is based on water quality data in the STORET database and biological data from the state's biology and rapid bioassessment sampling programs. Information on nonpoint source pollution and data on fish consumption advisories are combined with the water quality and biological data to assess the health of each watershed as either good, fair, or poor.

Changes or trends in water quality are an important indicator of the long-term health of surface waters. A simple nonparametric correlation analysis (Spearman's Ranked Correlation) of changes in 12 water quality variables plus the Water Quality and Trophic State Indices was calculated for 627 water bodies from 1986 to 1995. The number of trends detected for each water quality variable was counted. If two or more showed a change, than that waterbody was classified according to the direction of the change. Because of nonsystematic monitoring data and the simplicity of the analysis, this technique only detects large alterations in water quality, such as are anticipated from removal of point sources. Most waterbodies (71 percent) showed no trend, while 20 percent improved and 9 percent worsened.

Two areas show improved water quality, because of better pollution control. Near Orlando, Lakes Jesup, Howell, and Harney and the Econlockhatchee River have improved as a result of better wastewater treatment and improved point source controls. Another 59 waterbodies showed worsening trends related to increased nonpoint source pollution.

138

Surface Water Quality Status
1995

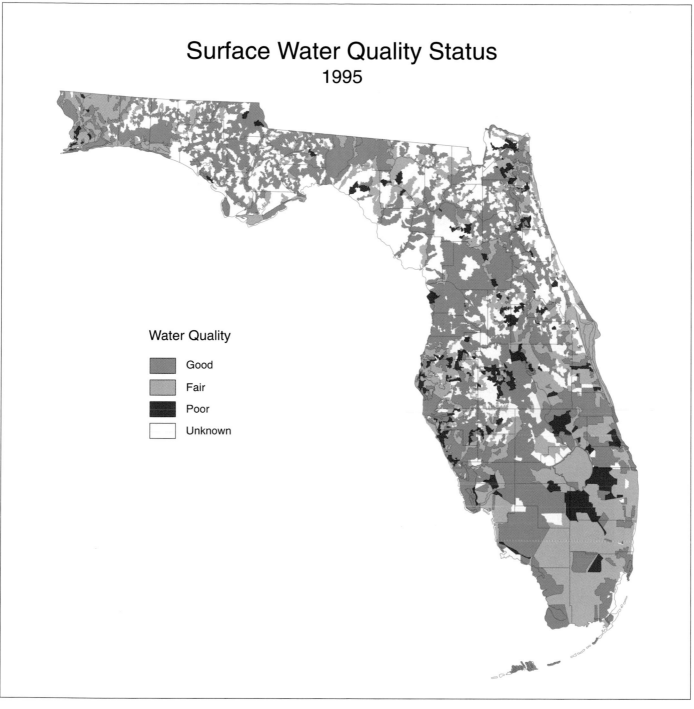

Water Quality

- Good
- Fair
- Poor
- Unknown

Improvements in water quality have provided major benefits to Tampa Bay. Historically, excess nutrients entering the bay created an overabundance of phytoplankton with resultant increased turbidity and reduced light penetration. As a result as much as 81 percent of the bay's seagrass beds have been lost. Legislative and regulatory actions required that wastewater treatment facilities upgrade their discharge to advanced treatment and implement reuse where practical. Analysis of 17 years of nitrogen and phosphorus data from 70 baywide monitoring stations indicates that as a result of these actions nitrogen concentrations have decreased by one-third in most areas and phosphorus concentrations decreased an average of 67 percent. The results of improved water quality have been an increase in seagrass acreages and potential for reestablishment of the scallop fishery in the bay.

In 1988 when the 256-acre Banana Lake was listed as a SWIM waterbody, it was hypereutrophic with poor water quality, almost perpetual algal blooms and extensive muck deposits on the bottom. Wastewater effluent was diverted from the lake and muck deposits were removed. As a result chlorophyll a concentrations have dropped from a mean of 220 $\mu g/l$ to 85 $\mu g/l$ and total nitrogen has dropped from 9.14 $\mu g/l$ to 0.8 $\mu g/l$. The fishery has improved from one comprised almost exclusively of rough fish to one that in 1992 had a 34 percent composition of sport fish.

Sarasota Bay has also benefitted from regulatory actions. Improved wastewater handling by the city of Sarasota and Manatee County has reduced nitrogen concentrations to the central bay by 43 percent and baywide by 25 percent. This resulted in improved water quality (particularly clarity) and has led to an increase of 125 acres of seagrasses in the central bay.

Toxicity in Surface Waters

Traditionally toxic substances have been regulated by limiting the introduction of certain specific chemicals in certain concentrations. The weakness of this method, however, lies in

Unreclaimed land from phosphate mining

Bryant's Branch Reclamation, 1995

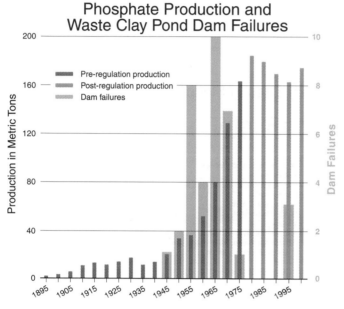

Phosphate Production and Waste Clay Pond Dam Failures

Production in Metric Tons

Dam Failures

Pre-regulation production
Post-regulation production
Dam failures

Bars are cumulative for five year period preceeding date.

wastes may include hazardous wastes (as defined by state and federal laws) such as pesticides and toxic chemicals or other wastes including chemicals of unknown toxicity, petroleum fuels, radioactive substances, explosives, and flammable substances.

Many of the chemical contamination sites in Florida are hazardous waste sites under the terms of the Comprehensive Environmental Response Compensation and Liability Act of 1980, popularly known as "Superfund." Because of the hydrogeology of the state, which facilitates the movement of pollutants in groundwater and surface waters, nearly all the sites have experienced both groundwater and surface water contamination.

Phosphate Mining

Florida is the largest producer of phosphate rock in the United States and second only to Morocco as the largest producer in the world. All of this material is extracted by surface mining at a rate of 5,000 acres per year. Water quality, as well as land and air quality, can be significantly degraded by phosphate mining. The process leaves long, deep parallel pits, separated by spoil piles of overburden, and disrupts water quality soils, drainage patterns, and wetlands. It also leaves mining and processing wastes, such as sand, clays, and gypsum. If mine sites are unreclaimed, moonscapes and permanent ecosystem degradation are the result.

The Mining Reclamation Act of 1975 required that all land mined after July 1, 1975, be reclaimed. All land mined before 1975 (about 150,000 acres) was deemed "nonmandatory" or "old lands" and a trust fund was established to reclaim some of this land via a voluntary grant program. Since 1972 about 125,000 additional acres have been mined. To date about 54 percent of the lands mined since 1975 have been reclaimed and about 35 percent of the old lands have been reclaimed.

Waste clay ponds are a necessary part of phosphate mining. They are large (averaging 1 square mile) and often protrude 20 to 50 feet above natural grade. In 1963 a dam failed at a clay pond outside Brandon sending brownish white water via the Alafia River 2 miles into the Gulf. In 1971 a clay pond spill flowed into Whidden Creek, down the Peace River turning Charlotte Harbor the color of chocolate milk.

Florida has adopted a specific rule (62-672, F.A.C.) regarding the configuration and design of earthern dams for waste clay ponds but has not addressed the height of the dams. In addition, Florida has enforced several policies since 1978 that appear to have resulted in a decrease in waste pond failures and dam failures. Most recently Florida has required additional dam design and operational criteria for new clay settling areas as recommended by a special technical advisory forum established following three dam failures in 1994.

Phosphogypsum, a waste product of phosphoric acid manufacturing, is also a concern. Phosphogypsum is piled in large mounds called stacks to over 200 feet in height. High contaminant levels in phosphogypsum stacks pose potential threats to groundwater as rain water and process water wash over the mounded phosphogypsum and then soak into the ground. In 1994 a portion of a phosphogypsum stack collapsed through a sinkhole into the underlying aquifer, and in 1997 a phosphogypsum impoundment was breached spilling millions of gallons of acidic waste water into a tributary of the Alafia River, resulting in one of the largest fish kills ever documented in a Florida river. As a result, the 1998 Florida legislature directed the Florida Department of Environmental Protection to write regulations governing the construction of phosphogypsum impoundments.

Underground Injection

An injection well is any well used to place fluids into an underground formation. Injection wells have been used in Florida for lake level control and stormwater drainage since the early 1900s. There are more than 10,000 injection wells in Florida ranging from small wells used for air conditioning re-

152

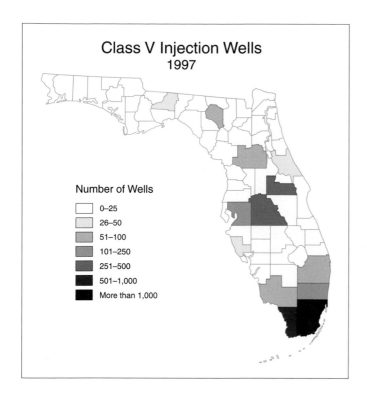

Class V Injection Wells
1997

Number of Wells
0–25
26–50
51–100
101–250
251–500
501–1,000
More than 1,000

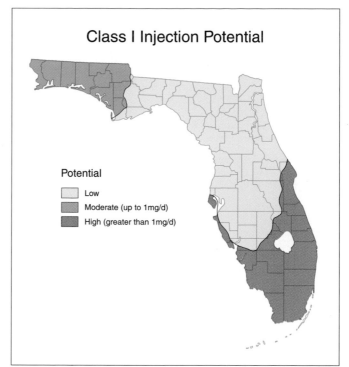

Class I Injection Potential

Potential
Low
Moderate (up to 1mg/d)
High (greater than 1mg/d)

turn flow to large diameter wells used to inject domestic and industrial wastewater.

Injections wells, if not properly constructed and operated, can contaminate underground drinking water supplies. In order to protect potable water sources, Chapter 62-528 of the Florida Administrative Code was adopted in 1982. This rule categorizes injection wells into five classes based on quality of the injected fluid, the use of the well, and the depth of the injection zone with respect to drinking water aquifers.

Class I wells are generally used to inject industrial wastes, reclaimed water, or desalination process concentrate below all aquifers that can be used for drinking water supply. In a Class I well, the injected fluids are isolated from the drinking water aquifer by at least one confining unit so that the injected fluids will remain in the injection zone. Water quality in aquifers overlying the injection zone is monitored to provide assurance that injected fluids are not migrating into, or in the direction of the drinking water aquifer. There are currently 116 Class I wells in the state. Most of the Class I wells have been drilled in the southern half of the peninsula where suitable injection and confining zones are present.

Class II wells are used to inject fluids related to the production of oil and gas. In Florida these include brine injection wells and enhanced recovery wells. Approximately 50 Class II wells are found in the oil fields of the western Panhandle and southern peninsula. There are no Class III wells (those intended for the extraction of minerals) in Florida. Class IV wells, used to inject hazardous wastes into or above drinking water aquifers, have been banned in Florida. The three Class IV wells known to exist have ceased operation.

Class V wells are the most common type of injection wells found in Florida. There are more than 10,000 Class V wells in Florida. These wells are generally used to inject fluids by gravity flow directly into drinking water aquifers or below drinking water aquifers where no confinement is present. Class V wells include those used for lake level and stormwater control, swimming pool drainage, air conditioning return flow, reclaimed water disposal, laundry drainage, and connector wells

used to lower the water table for mining. Class V wells may also be used for beneficial purposes such as aquifer storage and recovery, or as part of an aquifer remediation project. Fluids injected through Class V wells into drinking water aquifers must meet drinking water standards.

Also included in the Class V well category are aquifer storage and recovery (ASR) wells. ASR wells are used to place fluids into an underground formation for the purpose of storage and later recovery. The recovered fluids are used for irrigation or as drinking water. These systems are generally seasonal in nature with injection occurring during either high rainfall periods or periods of low water usage and recovery taking place during periods of little rainfall or during periods of high water usage. At this time, 27 ASR systems are either planned or operational in Florida.

Conclusion

Although analysis of water quality and water pollution is complex, we all understand the need for clean water. Some major water quality problems of the past, particularly waterborne epidemics, are now well controlled. Unfortunately, a fast-growing population and an industrial economy have been accompanied by some old pollution problems and some entirely new ones. Our new capacity to measure minute quantities of substances dissolved in water, to assess sediment contamination, and to measure biological community health have revealed possible new hazards. Some pollutants are being found today, not because they are new, but because we have developed an ability to detect them. What danger these substances pose and what response should be made are two of the most pressing contemporary questions about water quality and water pollution.

No one today believes that the Fountain of Youth ever existed. We no longer hope to find water with such miraculously healthful qualities. We can, however, reasonably ask that our water be at least safe to drink and pure enough to protect Florida's unique ecosystems.

153

REFERENCES

A source for a map or figure has a number in parentheses following the entry. This number refers to the page in this atlas for which the source was used.

Baker, B. 1994. *Ground Water Guidance Concentrations*. Bureau of Drinking Water and Ground Water Resources. Florida Department of Environmental Protection. Tallahassee.

Florida Department of Health. 1997. *Nitrates and Newborns: the "Blue Baby" Disease*. Florida Department of Health. Bureau of Environmental Toxicology. Tallahassee.

Griffith, G., D. Canfield, C. Horsburgh, J. Omernik, and S. Azevedo. 1997. *Lake Regions of Florida*. Final report and poster submitted to Florida Department of Environmental Protection under an Interagency Agreement with EPA.

Harper, H.H. 1994. *Stormwater Loading Rate Parameters for Central and South Florida*. Report prepared by Environmental Research and Design. Orlando, Florida. (table, 148)

Little, J.P. 1870. "Florida." *Lippincott's Magazine* 5 (April 1870):423. Quoted in *Land into Water—Water into Land* by Nelson M. Blake, p. 62. Tallahassee, Florida: University Presses of Florida, 1980.

MacDonald, D., B. Charlish, M. Haines, and K. Brydges. 1994. *Approach to the Assessment of Sediment Quality in Florida Coastal Waters*. MacDonald Environmental Sciences for the Florida Department of Environmental Protection. Vol. 3.

National Oceanic and Atmospheric Administration. Mussel Watch Program. (map, 144)

Paulic, M., J. Hand, and L. Lord. 1996. *Water-Quality Assessment for the State of Florida*. Section 305(B) Main Report. Florida Department of Environmental Protection. Tallahassee, Florida. (graph, 137; map, 139; map and graphs, 140; table, 151)

Seal, T., G. Sloane, F. Calder, S. Schropp, and H. Windom. 1994. *Florida Sediments Contaminants Atlas*. Florida Department of Environmental Protection. Tallahassee.

Schropp, S., and H. Windom. 1988. *A Guide to the Interpretation of Metal Concentrations in Estuarine Sediments*. Florida Department of Environmental Protection.

154

III

MANAGEMENT
AND
REGIONAL DIVERSITY

In response to the federal Water Quality Act and growing concerns by the state's citizens, the Florida Air and Water Pollution Control Act was adopted in 1967. The new state law repealed most of the existing environmental statutes and replaced them with the first real statewide pollution control law (Chapter 403, Florida Statutes). This act remains the keystone of Florida's pollution control efforts, although it has been much expanded. The act contains a declaration by the legislature of its determination to prevent the pollution of Florida's air and water. It also consolidated pollution control authority in a new Florida Air and Water Pollution Control Commission consisting of the governor, secretary of state, attorney general, commissioner of agriculture, and two "discrete" citizens. Day-to-day functions were carried out by the staff of the old State Board of Health. The act granted authority to the commission to classify all the waters of the state and to require permits for the construction or operation of any installation that could be a source of water pollution. In 1968, in response to requirements of the federal Water Quality Act, the commission adopted Florida's first statewide water quality standards and criteria.

The Air and Water Pollution Control Commission was abolished in 1969 as part of a major reorganization of state government. Absorbing some of the responsibilities of the former Board of Health, the commission reappeared as the Department of Air and Water Pollution Control. One year later the agency's name was shortened to the Department of Pollution Control (DPC). As part of the reorganization, the State Board of Conservation, which previously was charged to protect Florida's mineral, water and marine resources, was also abolished and the Department of Natural Resources (DNR), headed by the governor and cabinet, took its place. While most of these changes emphasized protection of public health, they also reflected widespread public concern that, in Florida's relentless push for economic development, many of the state's most valuable natural assets were needlessly being squandered.

First Calls for Statewide Management

During the 1940s, water resource problems were becoming more widely apparent, and a call for statewide water re-

source management was beginning to be made. In 1944, Governor Holland and Governor-elect Caldwell established the State Committee on Water Resources to study Florida's freshwater situation and to frame proposed legislation embodying corrective measures. In its report to the 1945 Legislature, the committee stated: "The fundamental point seems to be for the State, its various sub-divisions and the people to bear in mind that there are many angles making up the general subject of fresh water in this state. We must immediately take into consideration not only the primary angles of water supply and use, but also the conservation, storage, drainage, flood control and all other angles must be considered collectively for the future welfare of all concerned. Every Agency or group, in planning or executing any of its direct functions or undertakings, should analyze them fully and carefully as to possible beneficial or detrimental effect on fresh water.... Based on what we have heard and seen the Committee feels that the State must make an immediate start on a vigorous program to conserve, protect, develop, control, and utilize its water resources for the public welfare."

The legislature did not directly address the committee's concerns, but in 1945 it established the State Board of Conservation, with general responsibility for protecting the state's mineral, water, and marine resources. In 1947 the legislature created the Water Survey and Research Division within the Board of Conservation to function as the state agency responsible for matters of conservation of water and control of floods. This agency was dissolved in 1955, and its files turned over to the Florida Geological Survey.

At the urging of another study committee appointed by Governor Leroy Collins in 1954, the 1955 legislature established the Florida Water Resources Study Commission to again evaluate the state's water resource problems and to determine the need for a comprehensive Florida water law administered by a state-level board. The act which created this commission (Senate Bill Number 377) also contained Florida's first official expression of state water policy. Heeding the recommendations of the commission, the legislature enacted the 1957 Florida Water Resources Act, which created the Department of Water Resources as a division of the State Board of Conser-

1920s South Florida real estate boom; Carl Fisher transforms wet, mangrove-fringed island to resort of Miami Beach; saltwater intrusion in St. Petersburg's municipal wellfields.

1923 "The only attraction belonging to the state that we do not ruin is the climate."—Naturalist Charles Torrey Simpson

Miami flood after hurricane, 1926   FSA

1926 Hurricane kills 400 in Lake Okeechobee area.

1929 Okeechobee Drainage District formed; In *From Eden to Sahara: Florida's Tragedy*, John Kunkel Small predicts that, once drained, Florida will become a desert. Southern Sugar Company accumulates 130,000 acres south of Lake Okeechobee.

1931 Gulf Intracoastal Waterway extended from Pensacola to Carrabelle.

1920 — 1925 — 1930

1919 Florida Legislature creates the Winter Haven Lake Region Boat District to construct a navigation canal through the Winter Haven Chain Of Lakes.

1916 Royal Palm State Park established; construction of the Tamiami Trail begins.

1928 Hurricane kills 2,000 south of Lake Okeechobee when earthen dike fails to contain Lake Okeechobee: "The monstropolous beast had left his bed. The two hundred miles an hour wind had loosed his chains. He seized hold of his dikes and ran forward until he met the quarters; uprooted them like grass and rushed on after his supposed-to-be conquerors, rolling the dikes, rolling the houses, rolling the people in the houses along with other timbers. The sea was walking the earth with a heavy heel."—Zora Neale Hurston, *Their Eyes were Watching God*

1930 Federal Rivers and Harbors Act authorizes project for Caloosahatchee and Lake Okeechobee drainage areas.

1931–45 Drought, saltwater contamination in wells along the coast, fires in dry muck soils.

FSA

vation. The department's authority included issuing permits for withdrawal and use of excess surface water and groundwater and initiating water conservation activities in areas threatened with saltwater intrusion. "Excess" was defined as surface water in excess of average minimum flows and groundwater in excess of mean low flow.

Modern Water Management

In the 1970s a series of landmark laws intended to address Florida's environmental protection, water resource, and growth management problems was enacted. Expanding on earlier pollution control initiatives, the 1970 legislature passed the Pollutant Spill Prevention and Control Act, which established the DNR as the state's oil spill control agency and required terminal facilities around the state to maintain oil spill control equipment. Also in 1970, voters approved the issuance of up to $200 million annually in full faith and credit bonds to finance local sewage treatment facilities. In 1971, the legislature banned sewage discharges that provided less than secondary waste treatment, including discharges through the ocean outfalls along Florida's coast, and allowed the DPC to impose stricter requirements if necessary. The legislature enacted the Environmental Protection Act of 1971, allowing Florida citizens to sue the state for failure to enforce environmental law.

Although Florida had experienced a surge of environmental protection legislation in the previous two years, 1972 is often referred to as Florida's "Year of the Environment." The worst drought on record had occurred during 1970-71, and it was becoming evident that broader statewide approaches were needed to protect water resources and restore degraded areas. The Governor's Conference on Water Management, convened by Governor Reuben Askew in September 1971, concluded that land use, growth policy, and water management could not be separated. Following the conference, the Task Force on Resource Management appointed by Governor Askew drafted four major pieces of legislation that were enacted by the 1972 legislature: the Environmental Land and Water Management Act, which created the Development of Regional Impact and the Area of Critical State Concern programs; the Comprehen-

---

1972
Year of the Environment

• Federal Clean Water Act sets "swimmable" and "fishable" goal for all U.S. waters

• First public hearing on the restoration of the Kissimmee River

• Florida Water Resources Act creates regional water management districts and establishes permit system for regulating the consumptive use of water, calls for establishment of minimum flows and levels

• Environmental Land and Water Management Act creates Development of Regional Impact and Area of Critical State Concern Programs

• State Comprehensive Planning Act creates Division of State Planning within the Department of Administration

• Land Conservation Act authorizes sale of state bonds to purchase environmentally endangered lands

• Florida citizens approve a constitutional amendment authorizing some $240 million in state bonds for the Department of Natural Resources to purchase environmentally endangered lands.

---

sive Planning Act, which required development and legislative adoption of a state comprehensive plan and created the Division of State Planning within the Department of Administration; the Land Conservation Act, which authorized the sale of state bonds to raise revenues to fund the state's first concerted effort toward acquiring environmentally endangered lands; and the Water Resources Act.

The Florida Water Resources Act, Chapter 373 of the Florida Statutes, combined aspects of eastern and western United States water law into a comprehensive new Florida water law. It established a permit system regulating consump-

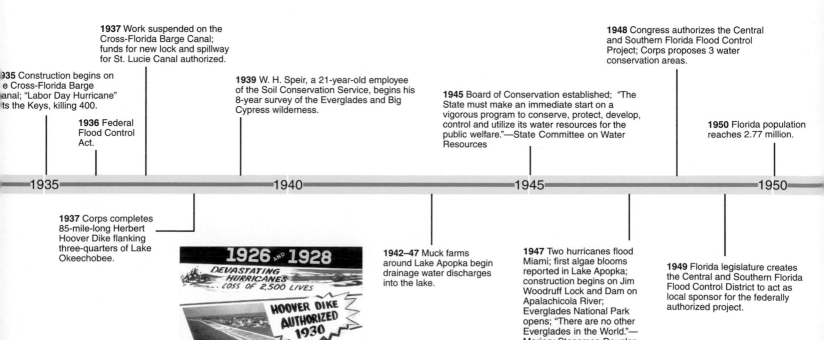

1937 Work suspended on the Cross-Florida Barge Canal; funds for new lock and spillway for St. Lucie Canal authorized.

1948 Congress authorizes the Central and Southern Florida Flood Control Project; Corps proposes 3 water conservation areas.

935 Construction begins on e Cross-Florida Barge anal; "Labor Day Hurricane" ts the Keys, killing 400.

1939 W. H. Speir, a 21-year-old employee of the Soil Conservation Service, begins his 8-year survey of the Everglades and Big Cypress wilderness.

1945 Board of Conservation established; "The State must make an immediate start on a vigorous program to conserve, protect, develop, control and utilize its water resources for the public welfare."—State Committee on Water Resources

1936 Federal Flood Control Act.

1950 Florida population reaches 2.77 million.

1935 — 1940 — 1945 — 1950

1937 Corps completes 85-mile-long Herbert Hoover Dike flanking three-quarters of Lake Okeechobee.

1942–47 Muck farms around Lake Apopka begin drainage water discharges into the lake.

1947 Two hurricanes flood Miami; first algae blooms reported in Lake Apopka; construction begins on Jim Woodruff Lock and Dam on Apalachicola River; Everglades National Park opens; "There are no other Everglades in the World."— Marjory Stoneman Douglas, *The Everglades: River of Grass*

1949 Florida legislature creates the Central and Southern Florida Flood Control District to act as local sponsor for the federally authorized project.

1926 AND 1928 DEVASTATING HURRICANES ... LOSS OF 2,500 LIVES HOOVER DIKE AUTHORIZED 1930 .... COMPLETED 1937

tive use of water based on reasonable-beneficial use. The law provided a two-tiered administrative structure headed at the state level by the Department of Natural Resources (now the Department of Environmental Protection) and at the regional level by five water management districts mainly based on hydrologic rather than political boundaries. Two of the districts—the Southwest Florida District and the South Florida District—covered the same territory and took on many of the same functions as earlier flood control districts. Each water management district, except Southwest Florida, is governed by a nine-member board appointed by the governor and confirmed by the senate. Southwest Florida has an eleven-member board. Board members, who must be members of the district, serve four-year terms. The governing board of each district also employs an executive director and a legal and technical staff. Funding for the water management districts comes from four sources: direct state appropriations, permit fees, bonds, and ad valorem taxes assessed by each district. The maximum millage rate for each district is established by the legislature within limits imposed by the Florida Constitution. Northwest Florida Water Management District has a constitutional ad valorem millage cap of .05 mills, which limits the northwest district's taxing capability to only 5 percent of the amount authorized for the state's four other water management districts.

The law required each water management district to formulate a water shortage plan and to establish minimum flows and levels for surface waters and minimum levels for groundwater.

In 1972 Florida's citizens also approved a constitutional amendment authorizing some $240 million in state bonds for the Department of Natural Resources to purchase environmentally endangered and recreation lands. Under the Environmentally Endangered Lands (EEL) program the state acquired approximately 350,000 acres, including such areas as Tosohatchee State Preserve, Big Cypress National Preserve, Three Lakes Wildlife Management Area, Paynes Prairie State Preserve, Cayo Costa State Park, and Cape St. George State Reserve. Other less heralded 1972 laws strengthened the enforcement capability of the Department of Pollution Control and established a

pollution restoration fund, which allowed fines to be used for environmental restoration. The 1972 legislature also passed a law requiring that domestic wastes discharged into Tampa Bay receive advanced waste treatment.

In 1973 the Power Plant Siting Act established a one-stop siting process for electrical generating facilities. Also in that year, the first guidelines and standards for Developments of Regional Impact were ratified by the legislature, and water resource concerns led the Florida Cabinet to designate the Big Cypress Swamp as an Area of Critical State Concern.

The legislature in 1974 imposed a 2-cent tax on each barrel of oil coming into Florida and earmarked these funds for oil spill cleanup. Also in 1974, the legislature authorized local governments to form Regional Water Supply Authorities.

The legislature continued its environmental protection and growth management agenda through the latter half of the 1970s. In 1975, the legislature again reorganized the state's environmental agencies, combining the Department of Pollution Control, several functions of the Board of Trustees of the Internal Improvement Trust Fund, and parts of the DNR into the Department of Environmental Regulation (DER). The new department was assigned statewide responsibility for controlling pollution, regulating dredging and filling, and providing general supervision over the five regional water management districts. The 1975 legislature also passed the Aquatic Preserves Act, beginning a statewide system of aquatic areas to receive special state protection and management. Public concerns about environmental impacts of the recently completed Kissimmee River project spurred the 1975 legislature to create the Kissimmee Coordinating Council to study ways to restore the channelized river.

During 1977 and 1978, legislative actions concentrated on fine-tuning existing pollution control laws, addressing dredge and fill permitting, fines and penalties, restoration of polluted areas, deep well injection, and delegation of programs.

The 1979 legislative session took new steps to address the continuing need for acquisition of environmentally important and recreational areas by creating the Conservation and Recreation Lands (CARL) program. Funding for this program came from several sources, including bond proceeds, severance taxes

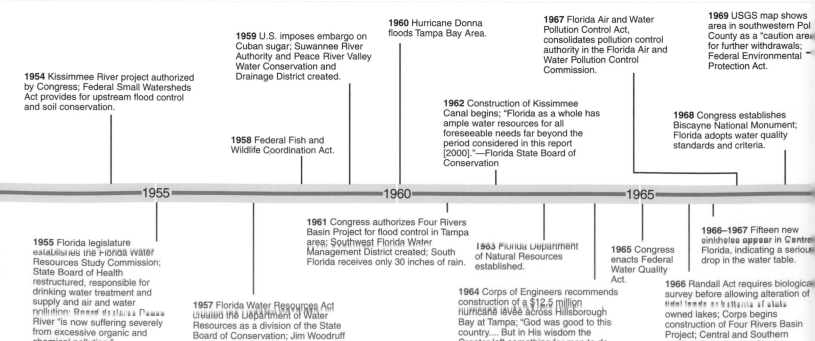

1954 Kissimmee River project authorized by Congress; Federal Small Watersheds Act provides for upstream flood control and soil conservation.

1959 U.S. imposes embargo on Cuban sugar; Suwannee River Authority and Peace River Valley Water Conservation and Drainage District created.

1960 Hurricane Donna floods Tampa Bay Area.

1967 Florida Air and Water Pollution Control Act, consolidates pollution control authority in the Florida Air and Water Pollution Control Commission.

1969 USGS map shows area in southwestern Pol County as a "caution area for further withdrawals; Federal Environmental Protection Act.

1962 Construction of Kissimmee Canal begins; "Florida as a whole has ample water resources for all foreseeable needs far beyond the period considered in this report [2000]."—Florida State Board of Conservation

1958 Federal Fish and Wildlife Coordination Act.

1968 Congress establishes Biscayne National Monument; Florida adopts water quality standards and criteria.

1955 — 1960 — 1965

1955 Florida legislature establishes the Florida Water Resources Study Commission; State Board of Health restructured, responsible for drinking water treatment and supply and air and water pollution; Board declares Peace River "is now suffering severely from excessive organic and chemical pollution."

1957 Florida Water Resources Act created the Department of Water Resources as a division of the State Board of Conservation; Jim Woodruff Lock and Dam on Apalachicola River becomes fully operational.

1961 Congress authorizes Four Rivers Basin Project for flood control in Tampa area; Southwest Florida Water Management District created; South Florida receives only 30 inches of rain.

1963 Florida Department of Natural Resources established.

1964 Corps of Engineers recommends construction of a $12.5 million hurricane levee across Hillsborough Bay at Tampa; "God was good to this country.... But in His wisdom the Creator left something for men to do for themselves."—Lyndon B. Johnson, Groundbreaking for the Florida Cross-State Barge Canal

1965 Congress enacts Federal Water Quality Act.

1966–1967 Fifteen new sinkholes appear in Central Florida, indicating a serious drop in the water table.

1966 Randall Act requires biological survey before allowing alteration of tidal lands or bottoms of state owned lakes; Corps begins construction of Four Rivers Basin Project; Central and Southern Florida Flood Control District pumps excess water from farmlands into water conservation areas, drowning hundreds of deer.

on phosphate mining, excise taxes on real estate and financial documents, and revenues from the sale of surplus state lands. In 1979 the governor and cabinet designated the Green Swamp an Area of Critical State Concern because of its regional water resource importance.

During the 1970s the need for restoring damaged natural systems was gaining attention. The Upper St. Johns River Basin Project, originally designed by the Army Corps of Engineers in the 1960s as a flood control project, was completely redesigned in 1977 as a cooperative project between the Corps of Engineers and the St. Johns River Water Management District. About 65 percent of the floodplain marsh had been drained for cattle range and for the production of citrus and row crops, causing major environmental impacts. The redesigned project marked the beginning of the state's first major attempt at ecosystem restoration—a 20-year effort to address the interrelated basin management issues of water supply, flood control, water quality improvement, environmental preservation, and recreation. This project is slated for completion in 1998.

Efforts to protect water quality and natural systems continued into the 1980s. Chemical contamination of Florida's groundwater, the state's primary source of drinking water, was of particular concern. The 1980 legislature enacted legislation providing "cradle to grave" regulation of hazardous wastes from the day of generation to the day of treatment, disposal, or shipment out of the state for safe disposal elsewhere. The 1981 legislature passed the Save Our Rivers Act (SOR), authorizing the water management districts to purchase land along rivers using funds derived from an increase in the documentary stamp tax. DER adopted the State Water Policy Rule in 1981, which for the first time provided water policy goals, objectives, and guidance for the development and review of programs, rules, and plans related to water resources.

In the late 1970s and early 1980s protection of Florida's groundwater, the primary source of drinking water in the state, became a major issue. The Task Force on Water Issues, appointed by the Speaker of the House of Representatives in 1983, reported that the threat of contamination of groundwater and related surface waters from hazardous wastes, sewage, industrial wastes, and pesticides was "the most significant water

Suwannee River Water Management District

Poorly maintained landfills such as this one photographed in 1975 provided impetus for legislation and other actions.

problem facing Florida today." In response to the report of the task force, the legislature passed the Water Quality Assurance Act of 1983, levying a tax on pollutants entering the state, and improving the ability of DER to protect groundwater and to clean up contaminated resources. The act also created the Pesticide Review Council to review and comment on restricted

163

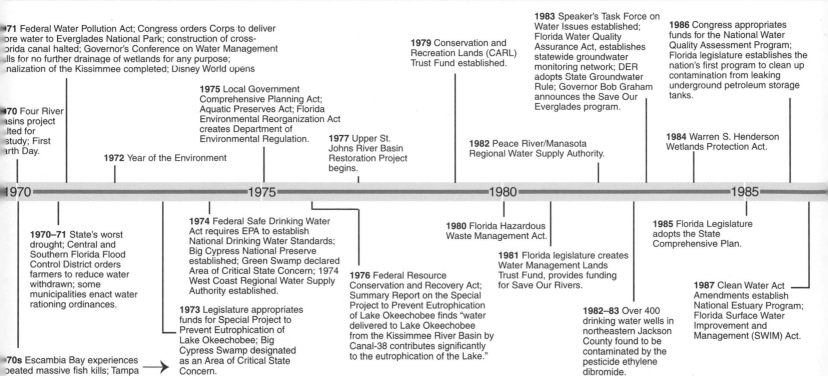

1971 Federal Water Pollution Act; Congress orders Corps to deliver more water to Everglades National Park; construction of cross-Florida canal halted; Governor's Conference on Water Management calls for no further drainage of wetlands for any purpose; channelization of the Kissimmee completed; Disney World opens

1970 Four River Basins project halted for study; First Earth Day.

1975 Local Government Comprehensive Planning Act; Aquatic Preserves Act; Florida Environmental Reorganization Act creates Department of Environmental Regulation.

1972 Year of the Environment

1977 Upper St. Johns River Basin Restoration Project begins.

1979 Conservation and Recreation Lands (CARL) Trust Fund established.

1983 Speaker's Task Force on Water Issues established; Florida Water Quality Assurance Act, establishes statewide groundwater monitoring network; DER adopts State Groundwater Rule; Governor Bob Graham announces the Save Our Everglades program.

1982 Peace River/Manasota Regional Water Supply Authority.

1986 Congress appropriates funds for the National Water Quality Assessment Program; Florida legislature establishes the nation's first program to clean up contamination from leaking underground petroleum storage tanks.

1984 Warren S. Henderson Wetlands Protection Act.

1970 — 1975 — 1980 — 1985

1970–71 State's worst drought; Central and Southern Florida Flood Control District orders farmers to reduce water withdrawn; some municipalities enact water rationing ordinances.

1974 Federal Safe Drinking Water Act requires EPA to establish National Drinking Water Standards; Big Cypress National Preserve established; Green Swamp declared Area of Critical State Concern; 1974 West Coast Regional Water Supply Authority established.

1973 Legislature appropriates funds for Special Project to Prevent Eutrophication of Lake Okeechobee; Big Cypress Swamp designated as an Area of Critical State Concern.

1976 Federal Resource Conservation and Recovery Act; Summary Report on the Special Project to Prevent Eutrophication of Lake Okeechobee finds "water delivered to Lake Okeechobee from the Kissimmee River Basin by Canal-38 contributes significantly to the eutrophication of the Lake."

1980 Florida Hazardous Waste Management Act.

1981 Florida legislature creates Water Management Lands Trust Fund, provides funding for Save Our Rivers.

1982–83 Over 400 drinking water wells in northeastern Jackson County found to be contaminated by the pesticide ethylene dibromide.

1985 Florida Legislature adopts the State Comprehensive Plan.

1987 Clean Water Act Amendments establish National Estuary Program; Florida Surface Water Improvement and Management (SWIM) Act.

70s Escambia Bay experiences repeated massive fish kills; Tampa v Water Wars.

use pesticides. DER adopted the state Groundwater Protection Rule in 1983. The movement to protect Florida's groundwater continued into 1986, when the legislature created a fund for cleaning up groundwater contaminated by leaking underground petroleum storage tanks.

In 1983, concerns for ecosystem restoration were bolstered by Governor Bob Graham's Save the Everglades program. This initiative recognized that the entire Everglades ecosystem was in jeopardy of being lost, and established a goal that "by the year 2000, the Everglades would look and function more like it did in 1900 than in 1983." This initiative ultimately led to establishment of a federal-state-regional partnership to restore the natural functions of the Kissimmee River-Lake Okeechobee-Everglades system, and laid the foundations for major federal and state actions in the 1990s.

During the 1980s the Florida legislature also moved to further protect natural systems. The Warren S. Henderson Wetlands Protection Act of 1984 expanded criteria for evaluating dredge and fill permits to include a broad range of public interest factors, including the extent to which a proposed project would adversely affect fish and wildlife habitat. In 1985 the legislature adopted the state comprehensive plan as Chapter 187, Florida Statutes, containing a Water Resources Policy statement that "Florida shall assure the availability of an adequate supply of water for all competing uses deemed reasonable and beneficial and shall maintain the functions of natural systems and the overall present level of surface and groundwater quality. Florida shall improve and restore the quality of waters not presently meeting water quality standards."

In 1987 the Florida legislature passed the Surface Water Improvement and Management Act (SWIM), which initiated the first statewide program for protecting or restoring priority surface water bodies of regional or statewide significance. This program provided general revenue funding for the water management districts to assess overall restoration or protection needs of individual water bodies, and to implement restoration or protection strategies tailored to the specific needs of the water body. The initial legislation identified six specific water bodies that would fall under SWIM: Lake Apopka, Tampa Bay, Lake Okeechobee, Biscayne Bay, Indian River Lagoon,

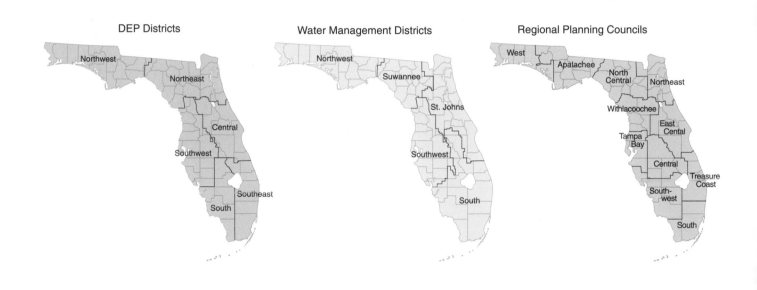

DEP Districts — Water Management Districts — Regional Planning Councils

1990 Florida's population reaches 12.9 million; Governor's Commission on the Future of Florida's Environment calls for expanded land acquisition program; Preservation 2000 provides $3 billion over 10 years to purchase ecologically valuable lands; legislation requires elimination of existing discharges of treated effluent into the Indian River Lagoon before July 1, 1995.

1994 Everglades Forever Act; Tropical Storms Alberto and Beryl and Hurricane Opal flood panhandle; Environmental Resource Permitting Program consolidates most land development permitting within the water management districts; water management districts complete comprehensive District Water Management Plans.

1996 Water management districts required to submit priority lists and schedules for establishment of minimum flows and levels; Florida Legislature establishes an Ecosystem Management and Restoration Trust Fund and assesses $75,000 per wetland acre impacted by DOT transportation projects to fund regional wetlands mitigation projects.

1997 Florida legislature defines regional water supply planning responsibilities of the five water management districts, local governments, and utilities; legislature approves an agreement with Alabama and Georgia establishing the basis for an interstate compact on the Apalachicola/ Chattahoochee/Flint River system; reclassification of Fenholloway River (the last-remaining industrial stream in Florida) from Class V to Class III; approximately 38 percent of flow from Florida's domestic wastewater treatment plants is reused.

1990 — 1995 — 2000

1988 St. Johns River Water Management District begins restoration of Lake Apopka.

1992 Hurricane Andrew strikes southern Dade County, causing $16 billion in damages; Congress directs Corps to undertake restoration of the Kissimmee.

1993 Florida Environmental Reorganization Act merges DNR and DER into the Department of Environmental Protection; new wetland delineation rule defining wetlands by soils, vegetation, and hydrology; DCA estimates 1.3 million Floridians live in areas subject to flooding.

1995 Florida Water Plan adopted by DEP declares "water must be managed to meet the water needs of the people while maintaining, protecting, and improving the state's natural systems."; Governor Chiles creates Commission on a Sustainable South Florida.

1996–97 St. Johns River Water Management District receives $91 million in state and federal funds to begin restoration of wetlands on former muck farms around Lake Apopka.

1990 Florida population reaches 14 million. Solid Waste Management Trust Fund review commission recommends $25 million be provided annually for the SWIM program.

and Lower St. Johns River. As of 1997, restoration or protection plans for 29 water bodies have been approved under the SWIM Act.

In 1987 Congress began a national initiative to restore degraded estuaries by establishing the National Estuary Program (NEP) through amendments to the Water Quality Act. These amendments provided federal funding to develop and implement Comprehensive Conservation and Management Plans for restoring estuaries of regional or national significance. The Tampa Bay, Indian River Lagoon, Sarasota Bay, and Charlotte Harbor systems have been designated as NEP water bodies.

In 1989 Governor Martinez signed Executive Order 89-74, creating the Governor's Water Resource Commission, and directing it to analyze the current state of Florida's water resources, including the quantity of available water, its continued viability as a source of drinking water, and steps necessary to ensure that Floridians may continue to enjoy these resources. The commission's report in December 1989 made recommendations regarding the need for integrated land and water use plans, water needs and sources assessments, identification of critical water supply problem areas, completion of district water management plans, areawide water supply authorities, and developing better public awareness of the value of Florida's water resources. Many of these recommendations were subsequently incorporated into the DER Water Policy Rule.

Water Management in the 1990s

In 1990 continuing public support for earlier land buying initiatives (EEL, CARL, and SOR) spurred the legislature to adopt Governor Martinez's Preservation 2000 (P2000) proposal, which provided for a $3 billion bond program to finance various land acquisition programs over a ten-year period. Fifty percent of funds from these bonds were earmarked for the Conservation and Recreation Lands Trust Fund (CARL), and thirty percent for Save Our Rivers Trust Fund (SOR). The SOR

is the primary source of funding for environmental land purchases by the water management districts, and has been used in conjunction with other federal, state, and local sources to acquire lands for protection or restoration of water resources.

Through these programs Florida has carried out the largest sustained public land acquisition effort in the nation. Over the past 25 years, Florida has spent $2.8 billion to purchase 2.1 million acres of conservation and recreation land. In combination with land protected by local and federal programs or under private conservation management, these purchases place some 7.6 million acres of land (about 22 percent of the land in Florida) under protection. The continuing support for public land acquisition as a way of protecting Florida's remaining natural systems has stirred legislative debate for reauthorizing P2000.

In 1990 the Florida legislature heeded recommendations contained in the Indian River Lagoon SWIM Plan, and enacted legislation prohibiting new discharges or increased loadings from existing sewage treatment plants, and requiring the removal of existing discharges of treated effluent into the Indian River Lagoon system by July 1, 1995. All direct discharges except stormwater discharges receiving advanced treatment have stopped. Much of the flow from previous discharges is now reused for irrigation and other beneficial purposes.

Based on the results of earlier studies and a demonstration project by the South Florida Water Management District, Florida's recommended plan for restoring the Kissimmee River ecosystem was submitted to the Corps of Engineers in 1990. In 1991 the corps completed a feasibility analysis, and as part of the Water Resources Development Act of 1992, Congress authorized the Corps of Engineers to undertake restoration of the Kissimmee River.

In 1988 continuing water quality problems in federal areas of the Everglades led the federal government to sue the State of Florida and the South Florida Water Management District over water quality. In 1991 the Florida legislature passed the Everglades Protection Act in an unsuccessful attempt to end

165

Molly Mabe

Detail from the painting At the Round Earth's Imagined Corners

the federal lawsuit. Two more years of legal wrangling finally led to a settlement and to passage by the 1994 Florida legislature of the Everglades Forever Act. Also, as part of the Water Resources Development Act of 1996, Congress passed the Everglades and South Florida Ecosystem Restoration Act. The federal act streamlined and accelerated the federal government's participation in restoring the Everglades, including authorization for the federal government to share 50 percent of the costs of restoration projects with the State of Florida. The project has evolved into a comprehensive attempt to restore the water quality and basic hydrologic patterns for the entire south Florida ecosystem (Kissimmee River-Lake Okeechobee-Everglades-Florida Bay) in a way that meets the water supply needs of both humans and natural systems.

In 1993 the Florida legislature combined the Departments of Natural Resources and Environmental Regulation into a single agency called the Department of Environmental Protection (DEP), and empowered this new department to focus its resources on managing entire ecosystems through voluntary interagency cooperation and "team permitting," public/private partnerships to protect environmentally important areas while keeping them on the tax rolls, and citizen participation in place-based (Ecosystem Management Area) projects. In 1996 the legislature established an Ecosystem Management and Restoration Trust Fund, and required the Florida Department of Transportation to contribute $75,000 for each acre of wetlands anticipated to be impacted by planned transportation projects. DEP administers the fund to pay for regional wetland mitigation projects conducted by the water management districts.

As the year 2000 approaches, the basic water management framework established by the 1972 Water Resources Act has remained intact. DEP and the water management districts jointly implement a broad range of interrelated planning, regulatory and management programs pertaining to water supply, flood protection, water quality, and protection of natural systems. Pursuant to legislative intent expressed in Chapter 373, Florida Statutes, DEP regulatory functions increasingly have been delegated to the water management districts, but regulation of point source pollution discharges remains primarily at the state level.

In an effort to streamline the permitting process, the 1993 legislature passed the Florida Environmental Resource Act, which combined permitting for "management and storage of surface waters" and "wetlands resource management" into a single "environmental resource permit" (ERP). The act also transferred most related land development permitting responsibility from DEP to the water management districts. Because of financial constraints, the Northwest Florida Water Management District does not currently participate in the ERP process.

Water supply and water allocation have emerged as paramount issues for the late 1990s and beyond. In some areas of the state, demands for water are beginning to exceed the capacity of aquifers and surface waters to meet these demands without significant harm to natural systems. Competition for water is increasingly a source of conflict between agricultural, industrial and urban interests, and between these user groups and the needs of natural systems. The effects of groundwater overwithdrawals (saltwater intrusion into municipal water supplies, reduced base flows of springs and streams, lowered lake levels, drying marshes and swamps, and increasing salinity in estuaries) are becoming more common. For some areas, the

prospects for new, easily developed, clean sources of water no longer exist. Adequate sources can be developed, but usually at higher costs than in the past. These increasing water scarcity problems are compounded by the continuing risk that existing and potential new supplies may experience contamination from a variety of sources such as saltwater intrusion, municipal landfills, septic tanks, industrial wastes, and agricultural practices.

In 1988, DEP and the water management districts began a coordinated statewide water resource planning initiative involving broad participation by federal, state, and local agencies and private interests. In 1994, comprehensive District Water Management Plans (DWMPs) were completed for each region of the state. These plans provided for the first time a regional view of each district's water resources, focusing on bringing together programs relating to water supply, flood protection, water quality, and natural systems.

In 1995 DEP adopted the Florida Water Plan, which builds upon the regional plans and provides intergovernmental strategies for addressing priority statewide issues. The legal basis for these efforts was strengthened in 1995 when, after two years of administrative challenges, major revisions became effective for the Water Resources Implementation Rule, Chapter 62-40, F.A.C. The purpose of this rule is "...to provide water policy goals, objectives, and guidance for the development of programs, rules and plans relating to water resources, as expressed in Chapters 187, 373, and 403, Florida Statutes." Collectively, these planning and rule advancements established the practical administrative and program management tools needed to ensure consistent statewide implementation of Florida's water laws along with the flexibility needed to address regional problems.

As competition for water increases, the decisions confronting water managers become increasingly complicated and controversial. Not surprisingly, they have spurred increased legislative scrutiny of water management programs. From 1994 to 1996 Florida's system of water management was subjected to in-depth review by several executive and legislative forums, including the Water Management District Review Commission, Governor's Commission on a Sustainable South Florida, and Governor's Land Use and Water Planning Task Force. While major changes were not recommended regarding Florida's basic water management framework, the need to accelerate regional water supply planning was recognized as a priority issue.

In 1996 concerns about the environmental impacts of groundwater overwithdrawals, particularly in the Tampa Bay region, redirected attention to the establishment of minimum flows and levels for surface waters and minimum levels for aquifers. On October 30, 1996, Governor Chiles issued Executive Order 96-297, requiring the water management districts to send DEP a priority list and schedule for establishment of minimum flows and levels by November 15, 1997; to work with interested and affected parties to ensure regional water supply planning; and to recommend water supply development that sustains water resources and related natural systems.

In amendments to Chapter 373, the 1997 legislature built upon many of the directives of Governor Chiles's 1996 Executive Order, reiterating the need to establish minimum flows and levels for priority surface waters and aquifers and requiring water management districts to implement water resource recovery strategies where water withdrawals cause flows or

Agencies Responsible for Water Management*
1997

FEDERAL

Department of Commerce
National Oceanic and Atmospheric Administration
  Weather forecasting and climate change
  Coastal ecosystems
  Fisheries

Environmental Protection Agency
Implementation of programs under the Clean Water Act and the
  Safe Drinking Water Act, Superfund, and the Resource Conser-
  vation and Recovery Act

Department of the Interior
U.S. Geological Survey
  Assessment of quantity and quality of the nation's water resources,
    includes NAWQA (National Water-Quality Assessment) Program
  Biological Resources Division, includes National Wetlands Research
    Center
U.S. Fish and Wildlife Service
  Endangered species, migratory birds, certain marine mammals, and fresh-
    water and anadromous fish

U.S. Army Corps of Engineers
River and harbor navigation
Flood control
Hydroelectric power
Environmental restoration
Wetland permitting

Department of Agriculture
Natural Resources Conservation Service
  Programs to reduce erosion
    and to conserve and protect water
  National Resources Inventory
  Wetlands Reserve Program

Federal Emergency Management Agency
Flood zone mapping
National Flood Insurance Program
Disaster Relief

STATE

Executive Office of the Governor
Coordination of interagency review of development projects and grant
  applications
Review of water management district budgets
Appointment of water management district governing board members

Department of Environmental Protection
Water Resources Implementation Rule
Florida Water Plan
Pollution control permitting and monitoring
Ecosystem management and restoration
Water quality standards
Solid and Hazardous waste management
Aquatic weed control
Administration SWIM and Preservation 2000 funds
Mine reclamation management
Marine resources

Department of Community Affairs
Areas of Critical State Concern
Developments of Regional Impact review
Coastal management
Emergency management coordination and disaster relief

Game and Fresh Water Fish Commission
Research and manage freshwater habitats
Assess development impacts on habitats

Department of Health
Protect public health related to solid waste disposal, septic tanks,
  drinking water

Public Service Commission
Private water and sewage utility rate structures and approval

Department of Agriculture and Consumer Services
Development of agricultural and silvicultural BMPs for protection of
  water resources
Regulation of pesticide and fertilizer use

REGIONAL

Water Management Districts
District water management plans
Regional water supply plans
Water resource development
Water supply assistance to local governments
Flood protection and emergency response
Stormwater management
Natural system protection and restoration
Consumptive use permitting
Water well construction
ERP (Environmental Resource Permitting Program)
SWIM plans
Land acquisition for conservation and recreation
Water shortage orders

Regional Planning Councils
Developments of Regional Impact review
Growth Management coordination
Surface water quality planning and studies
Development of regional policy plans that provide guidelines for local com-
  prehensive plans
Hurricane evacuation planning and mapping

Water Supply Authorities
Water distribution
Development of regional sources

LOCAL

City and County Governments
Water supply development
Local environmental controls and monitoring
Building codes, zoning, land use
Drinking water and waste water services
Growth management and comprehensive planning
Land acquisition and management
Emergency preparedness
Public utility provision (water, sewer, solid waste)
Stormwater management
Water conservation programs
Emergency water restrictions

Special Districts
Operation, maintenance of local surface water management systems
  (Chapter 298 districts, others)

*This is not intended as a comprehensive or definitive list. It is meant to
give the reader an idea of the agencies involved in water management
and their responsibilities.

levels to drop below established minimums. The water management districts are now assigned primary responsibility for water resource development projects. Local governments and private utilities have primary responsibility for water supply and water distribution systems.

The 1997 legislature also approved an agreement by the governors of Florida, Georgia, and Alabama on the basic aspects of an interstate compact for future water allocations in the Apalachicola-Chattahoochee-Flint River basin. Congress ratified the agreement setting the stage for establishing limits on water withdrawals or diversions by Georgia and Alabama, and for reserving downstream flows needed to maintain the environmental health of the lower river system and Apalachicola Bay National Estuarine Reserve.

Future Prospects

Florida's water challenge in the 21st century will be to meet increasing human demands for finite water resources in a sustainable way. The 1997 amendments to the Water Resources Act, for the first time, clearly established as state policy that cumulative impacts on water resources must be taken into account; that water resources must be managed in a manner which sustains those resources; and that the adverse impacts of competition for water should be avoided.

In regard to meeting human demands for water, expected population growth will place added stress on Florida's water resources. Providing adequate water supply for the 20 million residents that are expected by the year 2020 will require careful planning and large capital investments. And water will cost more. In regard to meeting the water needs of natural systems, very long-term management perspectives will be needed.

Florida's system of water management has served the state for a quarter century, and has been widely acclaimed as a national model. But in spite of these merits, deterioration of the state's environment continues. Water resource management must compete for limited funding with education, law enforcement, health care and other social services. New environmental justice issues have emerged, with greater activism by minority and religious organizations. The public is demanding a new relationship with government. Water management, and environmental protection programs in general, are faced with the question of how to reverse the continuing decline in environmental quality in the face of continued growth, without significant increases in funding, and in ways that include citizens as full partners.

To cope with such complexities, Florida's water resources programs must continue to emphasize comprehensive, long-range planning and coordinated intergovernmental efforts. They must provide better understanding of statewide and regional needs, and provide clear strategies for meeting those needs in a cost-effective manner. Special emphasis must be placed on developing and maintaining close coordination between land and water planning programs. And the currently embraced principle of managing water resources to meet the needs of people while maintaining, protecting, and improving the state's natural systems must continue to be supported. How well these water stewardship responsibilities are carried out will in large part determine Florida's economic future and quality of life.

REFERENCES

A source for a map or figure has a number in parentheses following the entry. This number refers to the page in this atlas for which the source was used.

The authors drew upon Chapter 9 by Wayne C. Huber and James P. Heaney (1984) and Chapter 11 by Bram D. E. Canter and Donna R. Christie (1984) in the writing of this chapter.

Blake, N. M. 1980. *Land into Water–Water into Land: A History of Water Management in Florida.* Tallahassee, Florida: University Presses of Florida.

Boesch, D. F., N. E. Armstrong, C. F. D'Elia, N. G. Maynard, H. W. Paerl, and S. L. Williams. 1993. *Deterioration of the Florida Bay Ecosystem: An Evaluation of the Scientific Evidence-Report to the Interagency Working Group on Florida Bay.*

Canter, B. D. E., and D R. Christie. 1984. Water policies and regulations. In E. A. Fernald and D. J. Patton, eds. *Water Resources Atlas of Florida.* Tallahassee: Florida State University.

Carter, L. J. 1974. *The Florida Experience: Land and Water Policy in a Growth State.* Baltimore and London: Johns Hopkins University Press.

Central and Southern Florida Flood Control District. 1952. Comprehensive Plan for Flood Control and Water Conservation. (map, 157)

Derr, M. 1989. *Some Kind of Paradise: A Chronicle of Man and the Land in Florida.* New York: William Morrow.

Fernald, E. A., and E. D. Purdum, eds. 1996. *Atlas of Florida.* Gainesville: University Press of Florida. (map, 158)

Florida Department of Environmental Protection, Division of State Lands, Office of Environmental Services. 1997. *Conservation and Recreation Lands (CARL) Annual Report.* Tallahassee.

Florida Department of Environmental Protection, Office of Water Policy. 1995. *Florida Water Plan 1995.* Tallahassee.

Florida Department of Environmental Protection, Office of Water Policy. 1995. *Water Resources Implementation Rule* (Chapter 62-40, Florida Administrative Code). Tallahassee.

Florida Department of Environmental Protection, Office of Environmental Education. 1997. *An Environmental State of the State of Florida...Earth Day 97.* Tallahassee.

Florida Executive Office of the Governor. 1997. *Save Our Everglades Update: Summary of Progress From July 1 December 31, 1997.* Tallahassee.

Florida Water Resources Study Commission. 1956. *Florida's Water Resources-A Study of the Physical, Administrative, and Legal Aspects of Water Problems and Water Management, Agricultural-Industrial-Municipal-Recreational. Report to the Governor of Florida and the 1957 Legislature.* Gainesville.

Huber, W. C., and J. P. Heaney. 1984. "Drainage, Flood Control, and Navigation." In E. A. Fernald and D. J. Patton, eds. *Water Resources Atlas of Florida.* Tallahassee: Florida State University.

Lewis, J. 1993. *From Earth Day 1 to Earth Day 25: Twenty Five Years of Environmental Lawmaking in Florida.* Florida Department of Environmental Protection. Tallahassee.

St. Johns River Water Management District. 1994. *District Water Management Plan.* Palatka.

St. Johns River Water Management District. 1995. *Upper Ocklawaha River Basin SWIM Plan.* Palatka.

Smith, L. 1980. *The Challenge of Water Management.* In-Depth Report, Vol. 5, No. 1. South Florida Water Management District. West Palm Beach.

South Florida Water Management District. 1995. *South Florida Ecosystem Restoration Plan.* West Palm Beach.

South Florida Water Management District. 1996. *Everglades 1996 Annual Report.* West Palm Beach.

Tebeau, C. W. 1974. "Exploration and Early Descriptions of the Everglades, Lake Okeechobee and the Kissimmee River." In *Environments of South Florida: Present and Past.* P. J. Gleason, ed. Miami: Miami Geological Society.

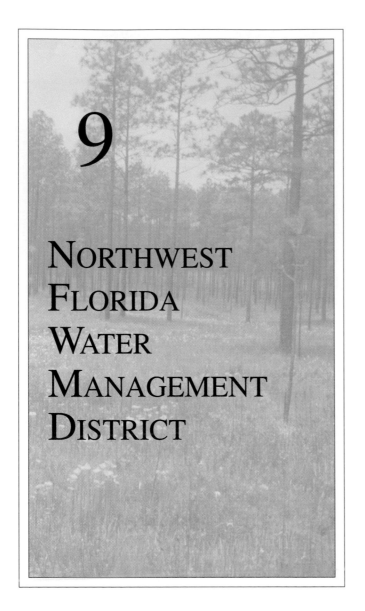

9

NORTHWEST FLORIDA WATER MANAGEMENT DISTRICT

Northwest Florida has more rivers and streams than any other region in the state. Seven major rivers (Escambia, Blackwater, Yellow, Choctawhatchee, Chipola, Apalachicola, Ochlockonee) cross the district on their way to the coast. By volume of flow Northwest Florida has three of the five largest rivers in the state: the Apalachicola, Choctawhatchee, and Escambia. The Apalachicola, the largest river in the state, derives its flow from the extensive basins of the Flint and the Chattahoochee in Georgia, which converge at Lake Seminole, an impoundment created by the Jim Woodruff Dam.

Northwest Florida Water Management District is participating in a multiyear comprehensive study of the Apalachicola-Chattahoochee-Flint river system with the states of Alabama and Georgia and the U.S. Army Corps of Engineers. This study includes a freshwater needs assessment of the Apalachicola River and Bay to identify minimum flows of freshwater needed to sustain the current productivity of the river and bay. In 1997 the legislatures of Florida, Georgia, and Alabama adopted the Apalachicola-Chattahoochee-Flint River Basin Compact creating the Apalachicola-Chattahoochee-Flint River Basin Commission. The U.S. Congress ratified the compact in November 1997 and President Clinton signed the compact into law on November 20, 1997.

Most of the region's rivers are in their natural state and have few man-made structures that alter their floodplains and channels or control their flow rates. Rainfall, runoff, and groundwater discharge into the streams determine variations in flow. In the western portion of the region the rivers are generally highly colored with little sediment and few nutrients. Those in the eastern portion of the district are generally alluvial and nutrient rich.

Flooding can and does occur along major rivers, although damages are not usually widespread because of relatively sparse development and public ownership within floodplains. Caryville on the Choctawhatchee River, however, has experienced several disastrous floods during this century. Blountstown and a few other communities on the Apalachicola River flooded during the summer of 1994 from tropical storms Alberto and Beryl. Local flooding also occurs in some urban areas as a result of inadequate stormwater drainage.

Although surface water is plentiful, the Floridan and sand and gravel aquifers supply about 77 percent of the potable water needs in the region. For the most part the Floridan yields water of excellent quality that requires little or no treatment. In Escambia, Santa Rosa, and parts of Okaloosa counties, however, water from the Floridan is saline, and potable supplies are obtained from the sand and gravel aquifer overlying the Floridan. Only Bay County (Panama City metropolitan area) and Quincy (Gadsden County) use surface water for public supply. In Bay County, Deer Point Lake, a reservoir created in 1961, supplies about 19 million gallons of potable water per day. The city of Quincy depends on Quincy Creek for its potable water supply.

Both surface-water and groundwater quality are generally good in Northwest Florida, although localized problems do exist. Several rivers originate in Alabama and Georgia making them vulnerable to water quality degradation caused by actions in those states. The sand and gravel aquifer, like other surficial aquifers, is very susceptible to contamination. Investigations have found instances of groundwater contamination in southern Escambia County. In Jackson County, domestic wells in the Floridan aquifer were found to be contaminated with the agricultural pesticide ethylene dibromide (EDB). Sev-

The Northwest Florida Water Management District (NWFWMD) stretches from the St. Marks River basin in Jefferson County to the Perdido River in Escambia County. The district encompasses all of 15 counties as well as the portion of Jefferson County within the St. Marks River basin. Within its 11,305 square miles of land are parts of five major drainage basins: the Perdido-Escambia, the Blackwater-Yellow, the Choctawhatchee, the Apalachicola-Chipola, and the Ochlockonee-St. Marks. When areas of water are combined with land areas, the square miles within the district total 13,264. Tallahassee, the state capital, with an estimated 1990 population of 124,773, is the largest city. All of the other major urbanized areas—Pensacola, Destin, Ft. Walton Beach, Panama City—are on the coast. Small towns dot the interior of the region where most of the land is in agriculture or forestry. Within Northwest Florida are several large government land holdings including Eglin Air Force Base, the Apalachicola National Forest, the Blackwater River State Forest, and the St. Marks National Wildlife Refuge.

Elizabeth D. Purdum and Georgann Penson

eral public water supply wells in Leon and Escambia counties were shut down because of contamination with dry-cleaning solvent. Continuing large withdrawals of groundwater in coastal areas have the potential to degrade groundwater quality by inducing saltwater intrusion. Abandoned wells pose an additional groundwater contamination threat. Between 1990 and 1995, over 4,700 abandoned wells were identified and plugged in the district.

Wellhead protection is an area of increasing concern and activity in the district, especially in the westernmost portions such as Escambia and Santa Rosa counties, which rely on the sand and gravel aquifer. Other places where wellhead protection is critical include recharge areas where the Floridan aquifer is at or near the surface such as in Leon, Wakulla, Jefferson, Jackson, Holmes, and Washington counties.

Pollution of bays, rivers, and lakes from stormwater runoff is a serious problem in the region and throughout Florida. For example, Lake Jackson in Leon County, once a pristine lake famous for its trophy-size largemouth bass, has been adversely affected since the early 1970s by stormwater runoff. The Pensacola Bay system has also been affected by stormwater runoff as well as by point-source pollution. By the late 1960s and early 1970s the system experienced decreased fish landings, fish kills, and severe reductions in seagrass beds. The water management district is working with local governments to monitor stormwater and to develop stormwater management plans.

Before human alteration, most of Northwest Florida was open pine woods on rolling hills and flat lands. In the valley bottoms and along creeks were hardwood forests. Since 1984, the district has acquired approximately 150,000 acres through Save Our Rivers and Preservation 2000 for preservation and, in many cases, for restoration to more natural conditions. Included are river floodplains, headwater wetlands, coastal marshes, first-magnitude springs, and bottomland hardwood and associated upland forests. Within the region are eight first-magnitude springs, most of which are popular recreation spots. Wakulla Springs, the most notable, has an annual average discharge of 250 million gallons per day. More than 85 percent of the floodplains along the Choctawhatchee and Escambia rivers have been acquired by the district.

Although an adequate supply of water is, for the most part, available for existing and future demands throughout most of the region, the district's governing board has designated two Water Resource Caution Areas: the coastal portion of Santa Rosa, Okaloosa, and Walton counties and the Upper Telogia Creek drainage basin in Gadsden County. By 1980, Floridan aquifer water levels in the Ft. Walton Beach area in southern Okaloosa County had declined as much as 100 feet below sea level. Large amounts of water are withdrawn from the upper Telogia Creek basin for irrigation.

Water management activities in Northwest Florida are limited by the current taxing structure. All of the state's five water management districts have the authority to levy ad valorem (property) taxes. Four of the five districts are allowed by the Florida Constitution to levy up to one mill. NWFWMD is limited to 1/20th (.05) of a mill, which is 5 cents for every $1,000 of taxable property value. Most of the district's funding comes from cooperative projects, grants, and legislatively funded programs such as Save Our Rivers and Preservation 2000.

171

Lake Jackson, Leon County

Georgann Penson

Topography

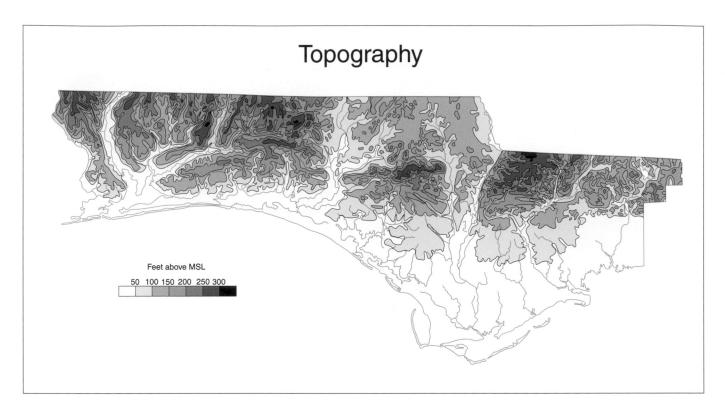

Feet above MSL

50 100 150 200 250 300

Physiographic Regions

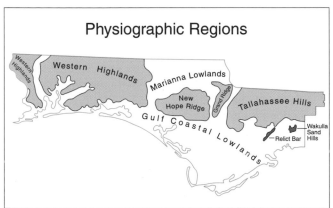

Topography, Physiographic Features, and Climate

172

Streams and waves acting upon the land's surface over the last 10 to 15 million years have sculpted Northwest Florida's landscape. During this time, sea level oscillated considerably from its present level and created much of the present topography in the region. More recently, dissolution by groundwater has played a role in shaping the landscape.

The major topographic divisions are the Northern Highlands, the Marianna Lowlands, and the Gulf Coastal Lowlands. The Western Highlands, the New Hope and Grand ridges, and the Tallahassee Hills make up the Northern Highlands. They are underlain by ancient delta deposits of clays, clayey sands, and gravel and range in elevation from 50 to 345 feet above sea level. The Marianna Lowlands, produced by stream erosion and karst dissolution, have elevations on average 100 to 200 feet lower than the highlands to the west, south, and east. The lowlands have well-developed karst features that include the Marianna Caverns. The Coastal Lowlands are primarily ancient coastal features and include beach ridge plains, ancient shorelines, and marine terraces with elevations ranging from sea level to 100 feet.

Northwest Florida's climate is humid subtropical with temperatures that average 81°F in the summer and 54°F in the win-

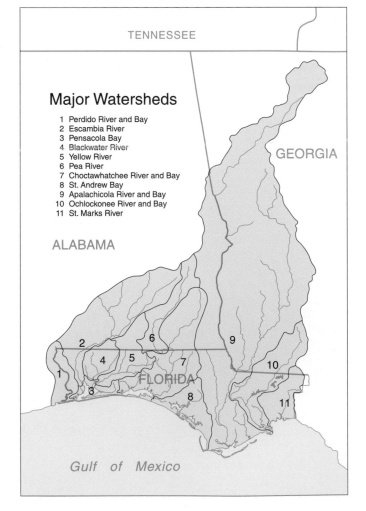

Major Watersheds

1 Perdido River and Bay
2 Escambia River
3 Pensacola Bay
4 Blackwater River
5 Yellow River
6 Pea River
7 Choctawhatchee River and Bay
8 St. Andrew Bay
9 Apalachicola River and Bay
10 Ochlockonee River and Bay
11 St. Marks River

ter. During the year there are two prominent wet periods. The first occurs in the winter and early spring and is the result of major fronts moving from the northwest. The second occurs from thunderstorms during the summer.

Temperature

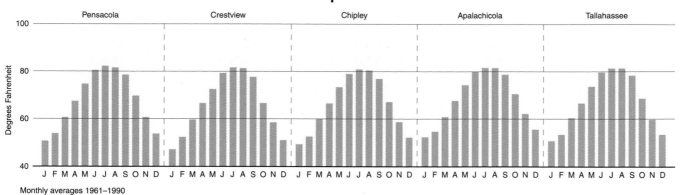

Pensacola　　　　Crestview　　　　Chipley　　　　Apalachicola　　　　Tallahassee

Degrees Fahrenheit

J F M A M J J A S O N D　J F M A M J J A S O N D　J F M A M J J A S O N D　J F M A M J J A S O N D　J F M A M J J A S O N D

Monthly averages 1961–1990

Rainfall

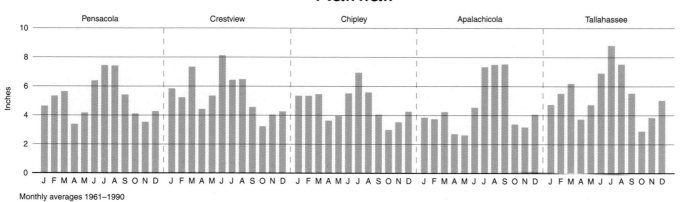

Pensacola　　　　Crestview　　　　Chipley　　　　Apalachicola　　　　Tallahassee

Inches

J F M A M J J A S O N D　J F M A M J J A S O N D　J F M A M J J A S O N D　J F M A M J J A S O N D　J F M A M J J A S O N D

Monthly averages 1961–1990

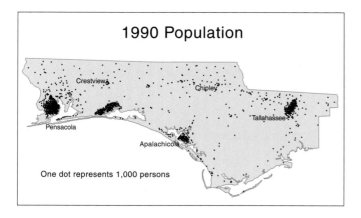

1990 Population

Crestview

Chipley

Tallahassee

Pensacola

Apalachicola

One dot represents 1,000 persons

Land Use and Population

Over 60 percent of Northwest Florida is forests, and an additional 10 percent of the region is forested wetlands. Timber companies own about 2 million acres, or 25 percent of the total land in the region. Much of this land is planted in fast-growing slash or sand pine, the raw material for paper mills scattered throughout northern Florida. The federal government owns 745,000 acres of predominately forested land including the 550,000-acre Apalachicola National Forest, and the state owns over 450,000 acres. Four military bases occupy another 500,000 acres in the region.

Farms are scattered across the north and comprise 16 percent of the land area. These farms are smaller, more diverse, and less energy intensive than those in other parts of the state. Farmers usually grow peanuts, soybeans, corn, and cotton and raise beef cattle and hogs. They commonly irrigate crops with large center-pivot systems, particularly in Jackson and central Walton counties. In Gadsden County the more efficient drip irrigation systems are being used. Water bodies and urban ar-

eas each cover approximately 6 percent of the total land in the region. The remaining 2 percent of the land is divided between nonforested wetlands and barren land such as mines, quarries, and beaches.

In 1990, 1,008,780 persons lived in Northwest Florida, a 27 percent increase over the 1980 population. Approximately three-fourths of this increase resulted from in-migration. Most of this growth occurred within the metropolitan statistical areas (MSAs) of Pensacola, Ft. Walton Beach, Panama City, and Tallahassee. The fastest growing MSA was Ft. Walton Beach (31 percent increase). However, the population of Santa Rosa County (part of the Pensacola MSA) increased by 46 percent. The coastal counties also host large numbers of seasonal residents who are not included in the population counts. Outside the MSAs the region is still very lightly populated. Liberty County, for example, in 1990 had the lowest population density in the state with seven persons per square mile. The Bureau of Economic and Business Research at the University of Florida predicts that the region's population will increase to 1,305,780 by 2010 with the highest growth in Bay, Leon, Okaloosa, and Walton counties. Migration is expected to remain the predominant source of population growth.

Agriculture and forestry are still important components of the economy, particularly in rural areas. Fishing is locally important along the coast, especially from Panama City to Pensacola. Apalachicola Bay supports Florida's largest commercial oyster fishery. The region's beaches attract thousands of tourists and provide jobs in the services and construction sectors. Naval and Air Force bases located near Ft. Walton Beach, Pensacola, and Panama City are major civilian as well as military employers. Since Tallahassee is the state capital and home to two state universities, state government is the largest employer in the city.

173

Water Resources

Surface Water

Northwest Florida has larger drainage basins and a greater stream density than any other region of Florida. Major river basins, if portions outside the state are included, range in size from 133 square miles for the New River to 21,794 square miles for the Apalachicola, Flint, and Chattahoochee system. The rivers in the district have few man-made structures to modify their channels or control their rates of flow. Variations in local flow are determined by rainfall and its resultant runoff or by groundwater discharge into the stream channel. In general, average annual rainfall decreases to the east. West of the Choctawhatchee River, average rainfall is about 64 inches per year, whereas to the east it ranges from 64 inches to less than 56 inches along the Alabama and Georgia borders. The annual surface runoff from this rainfall ranges from 24 to 38 inches in stream basins in the western portion of the district and from less than 15 to 24 inches in the eastern basins. Basin yields of runoff to streams are thus greater west of the Choctawhatchee than they are to the east.

The groundwater contribution is also a very important factor in determining the flow of most streams in Northwest Florida. The Shoal, Big Coldwater, Perdido, and Blackwater rivers and the Big Coldwater Creek in the western part of the district receive large and fairly uniform discharges of groundwater from the sand and gravel aquifer that tend to moderate

their annual variations in stream flow. The Chipola River and Econfina Creek exhibit even greater regularity of flow as a result of receiving constant contributions of groundwater, primarily from the Floridan aquifer. At the other extreme, the Ochlockonee River receives insignificant groundwater contributions and depends almost entirely on runoff. The flow of the Ochlockonee is, accordingly, highly variable throughout the year and from year to year.

Several of the largest and most productive estuaries in the state are in Northwest Florida. Estuaries are places where freshwater meets saltwater and are most commonly formed at the mouths of rivers. Major estuaries are the Pensacola Bay, the Choctawhatchee Bay, the St. Andrew Bay, the Apalachicola Bay, the Ochlockonee Bay, and the Apalachee Bay systems.

A diversity of wetland types is found in Northwest Florida, including bogs, freshwater marshes, saltmarshes, swamps, wet prairies, and wet flatwoods.

Eight first-magnitude springs are found within the region, and most are used for recreation. The most notable is Wakulla Springs, which has an annual average discharge of 250 million gallons per day.

Because less water-bearing limestone is near the ground surface, the panhandle of Florida has fewer natural lakes than the neighboring Big Bend region or the central peninsula (Wolfe et al. 1988). Most of the lakes are on the sandy uplands between the Choctawhatchee River and Econfina Creek in Bay and Washington counties.

174

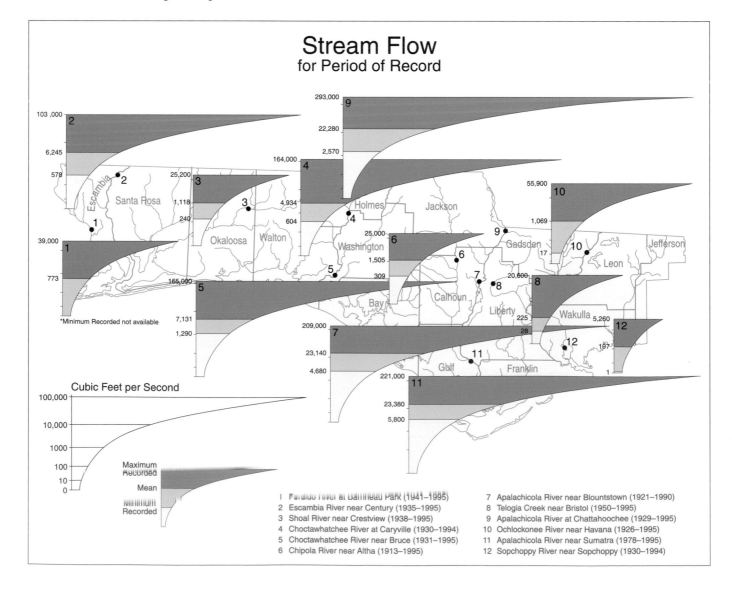

Stream Flow
for Period of Record

1 Perdido River at Barrineau Park (1941–1995)
2 Escambia River near Century (1935–1995)
3 Shoal River near Crestview (1938–1995)
4 Choctawhatchee River at Caryville (1930–1994)
5 Choctawhatchee River near Bruce (1931–1995)
6 Chipola River near Altha (1913–1995)
7 Apalachicola River near Blountstown (1921–1990)
8 Telogia Creek near Bristol (1950–1995)
9 Apalachicola River at Chattahoochee (1929–1995)
10 Ochlockonee River near Havana (1926–1995)
11 Apalachicola River near Sumatra (1978–1995)
12 Sopchoppy River near Sopchoppy (1930–1994)

Mean Stream Flow

for Period of Record

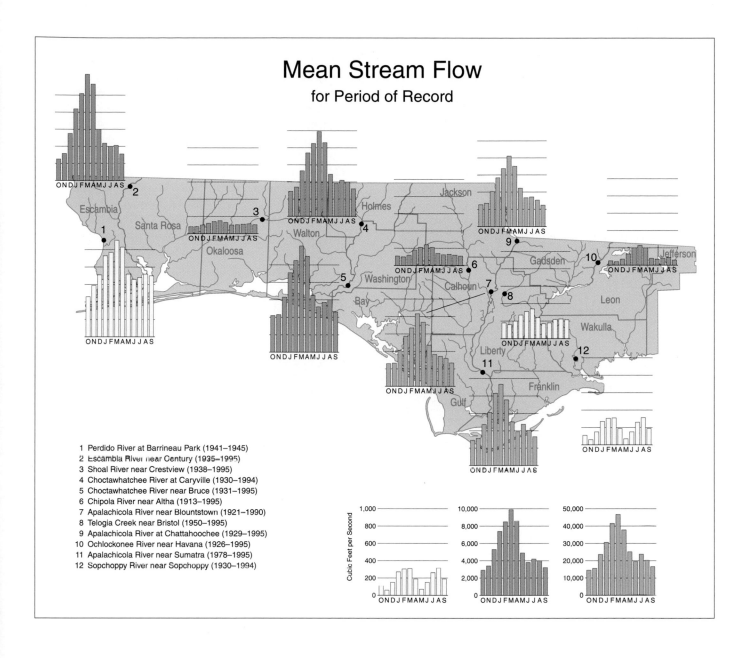

1 Perdido River at Barrineau Park (1941–1945)
2 Escambia River near Century (1935–1995)
3 Shoal River near Crestview (1938–1995)
4 Choctawhatchee River at Caryville (1930–1994)
5 Choctawhatchee River near Bruce (1931–1995)
6 Chipola River near Altha (1913–1995)
7 Apalachicola River near Blountstown (1921–1990)
8 Telogia Creek near Bristol (1950–1995)
9 Apalachicola River at Chattahoochee (1929–1995)
10 Ochlockonee River near Havana (1926–1995)
11 Apalachicola River near Sumatra (1978–1995)
12 Sopchoppy River near Sopchoppy (1930–1994)

175

Surface Water

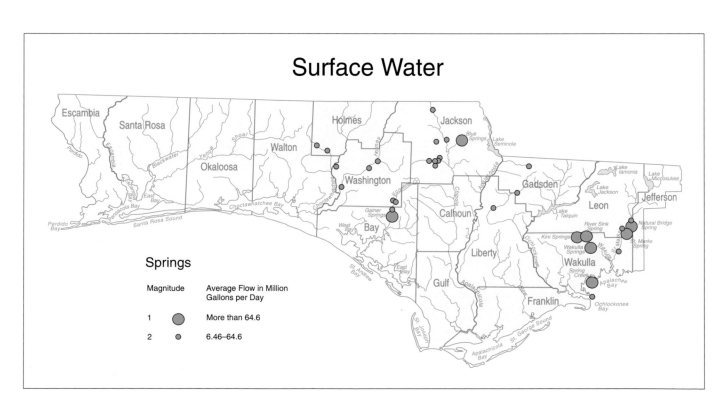

Springs

Magnitude		Average Flow in Million Gallons per Day
1	●	More than 64.6
2	●	6.46–64.6

Groundwater

In Northwest Florida the sand and gravel aquifer and the Floridan aquifer system are the principal sources of groundwater. The sand and gravel aquifer is part of the surficial aquifer system and is the primary source of potable water in all of Escambia County and most of Santa Rosa County. The Floridan aquifer system is the most productive water-bearing unit in Northwest Florida. The Floridan aquifer system is primarily composed of limestone and ranges in thickness from 100 feet to more than 1,000 feet. In many areas of the region, highly mineralized water occurs at the bottom of the aquifer, resulting in a reduced productive or usable thickness.

Groundwater tends to flow from areas of high potentiometric surface to areas of low potentiometric surface. In Northwest Florida the potentiometric surface of the Floridan aquifer system ranges from 210 feet above sea level to 100 feet below sea level. The potentiometric surface decreases toward the coast and towards streams or springs where water from the aquifer is discharged. Well pumping from the aquifer also affects potentiometric surface.

Groundwater in Northwest Florida is replenished by local recharge with minimal out-of-state contributions. Most of the area overlying the sand and gravel aquifer is a recharge area, and discharge areas are almost always near areas being recharged. In two principal areas (northern Jackson County and

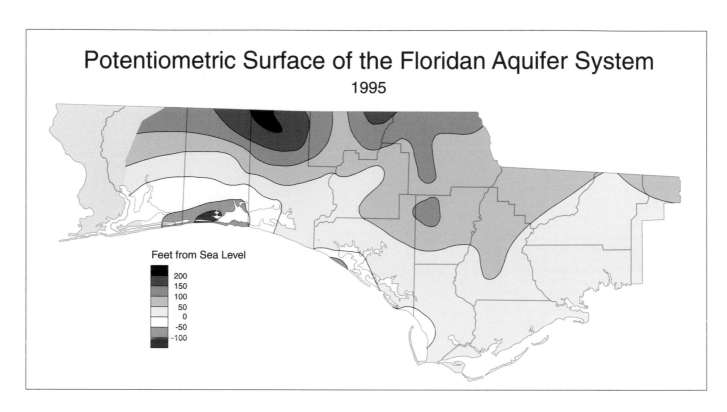

Potentiometric Surface of the Floridan Aquifer System
1995

Feet from Sea Level

200
150
100
50
0
-50
-100

176

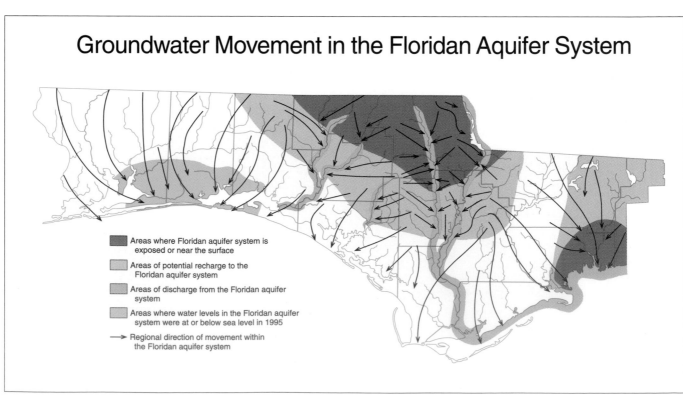

Groundwater Movement in the Floridan Aquifer System

Areas where Floridan aquifer system is exposed or near the surface

Areas of potential recharge to the Floridan aquifer system

Areas of discharge from the Floridan aquifer system

Areas where water levels in the Floridan aquifer system were at or below sea level in 1995

Regional direction of movement within the Floridan aquifer system

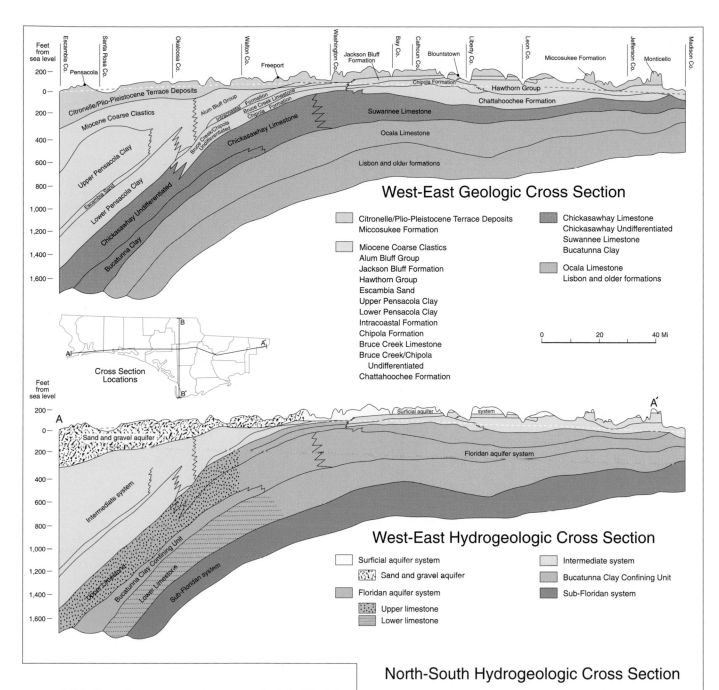

West-East Geologic Cross Section

Citronelle/Plio-Pleistocene Terrace Deposits
Miccosukee Formation

Miocene Coarse Clastics
Alum Bluff Group
Jackson Bluff Formation
Hawthorn Group
Escambia Sand
Upper Pensacola Clay
Lower Pensacola Clay
Intracoastal Formation
Chipola Formation
Bruce Creek Limestone
Bruce Creek/Chipola
  Undifferentiated
Chattahoochee Formation

Chickasawhay Limestone
Chickasawhay Undifferentiated
Suwannee Limestone
Bucatunna Clay

Ocala Limestone
Lisbon and older formations

Cross Section Locations

0   20   40 Mi

West-East Hydrogeologic Cross Section

Surficial aquifer system
Sand and gravel aquifer
Floridan aquifer system
Upper limestone
Lower limestone

Intermediate system
Bucatunna Clay Confining Unit
Sub-Floridan system

177

eastern Wakulla and southeastern Leon counties) the Floridan is at or near land surface. Recharge to the aquifer in these areas is higher than in areas where the aquifer is confined. In areas with relatively low recharge rates, recharge often occurs indirectly via leakage from the surficial aquifer system that overlies the Floridan aquifer system. In Okaloosa and Walton counties, because of the tight confinement of the Floridan aquifer system, recharge rates are extremely low. Water availability from the aquifer is quite limited in this area and saltwater intrusion is a major concern. High recharge areas generally produce abundant water, but the water is also more easily contaminated.

Transmissivity is one component of groundwater availability. Regionally, the highest transmissivities in the Floridan aquifer system occur in the Woodville and Dougherty karst regions. Vertically, the most prolific zones generally coincide with the Suwannee and Ocala limestones. The availability of groundwater from the sand and gravel aquifer generally increases from east to west. This is, in part, due to the thickening of the aquifer that occurs in this direction.

North-South Hydrogeologic Cross Section

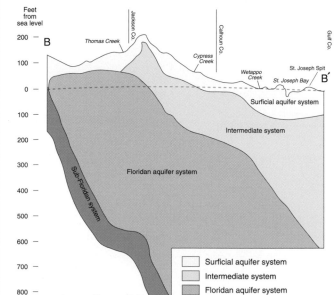

Surficial aquifer system
Intermediate system
Floridan aquifer system
Sub-Floridan system

0   10   20 Mi

Water Supply Planning and Use

In the early 1980s the Northwest Florida Water Management District identified the coastal areas of Walton, Okaloosa, and Santa Rosa counties to be of highest priority for water supply planning because of population growth and limited potable water sources in the immediate area. Since 1940 the potentiometric surface of the Floridan aquifer has shown a marked decline in Ft. Walton Beach, Niceville, and Destin.

Walton, Okaloosa, and Santa Rosa counties and the cities of Freeport, Destin, Ft. Walton Beach, Gulf Breeze, and Mary Esther established the Walton/Okaloosa/Santa Rosa Regional Utility Authority in 1986. The regional utility authority is working with the Northwest Florida Water Management District and local utilities to develop new sources of potable water. Alternatives include piping water from inland wellfields and desalination. The district is also working with the Escambia County Utilities Authority to address water supply concerns in southeastern Escambia County.

Gadsden County has water supply problems because of limited availability of groundwater and large withdrawals from Telogia Creek for agricultural irrigation. In most of Gadsden County the lower portion of the Floridan aquifer is highly mineralized and its use for potable supply limited. In the central portion of the county, water yields from the aquifer are low. The city of Quincy depends on Quincy Creek for its water supply.

The district has designated both Telogia Creek drainage basin and the western coastal areas as Water Resource Caution Areas (WRCA). Permittees within a WRCA have increased water use reporting requirements, must implement water conservation measures, and must improve water use efficiencies. The district requires permittees to evaluate the technical, environmental, and economic feasibility of providing reclaimed water for reuse. The WRCA designation for coastal areas of Santa Rosa, Okaloosa, and Walton counties prohibits new or expanded use of the Floridan aquifer for nonpotable supplies.

The district has also applied stringent consumptive use permit thresholds to the St. Joseph Peninsula and St. George Island, both high-growth coastal regions.

In 1996 the district began a new water supply planning initiative. Recognizing that Florida has an abundance of water resources and related natural systems that are vital to the economic and environmental health of the state, the governor issued an Executive Order (96-297) that called for the implementation of comprehensive water supply planning by all of the water management districts for at least a 20-year period, district water supply assessments, and establishment of minimum flows and levels for surface watercourses, aquifers, and surface waters. In 1997, the Florida legislature approved similar legislation.

Through this extensive long-term water supply planning effort, the district will identify alternative sources to meet expected future water supply needs.

Several steps in this planning process have already been taken. The district has identified Areas of Special Concern and divided the district into water supply planning regions. Seven planning regions have been identified for purposes of water supply assessment.

Region I (Escambia County). Virtually all the water used for public supply is obtained from the sand and

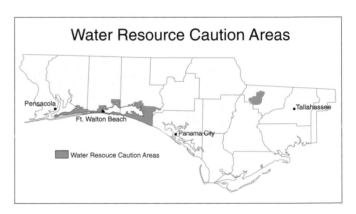

Water Resource Caution Areas

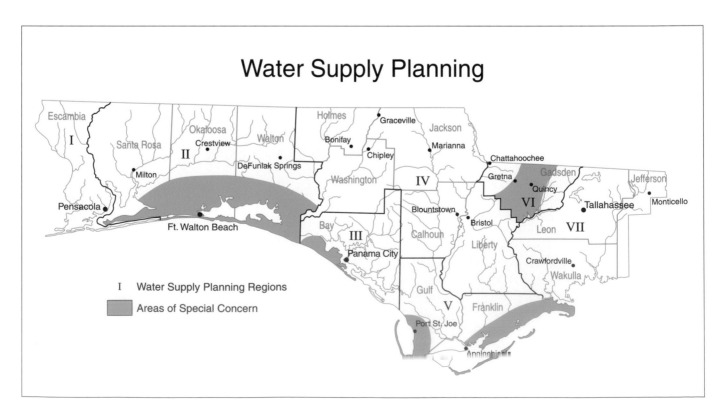

Water Supply Planning

I Water Supply Planning Regions

Areas of Special Concern

178

Potentiometric Surface of the Floridan Aquifer

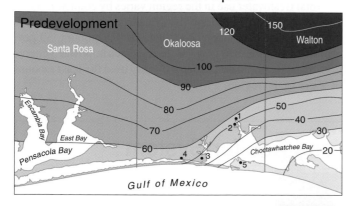

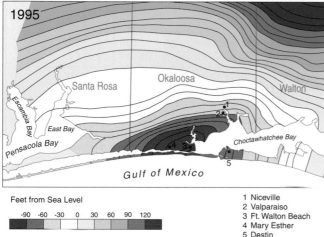

Feet from Sea Level

-90 -60 -30   0   30   60   90 120

1 Niceville
2 Valparaiso
3 Ft. Walton Beach
4 Mary Esther
5 Destin

gravel aquifer. Quantity of freshwater is not likely to be an issue, but water quality is expected to be a concern. The aquifer is highly susceptible to contamination because of its proximity to the land surface.

Region II (Santa Rosa, Okaloosa, and Walton counties). Most of the public supply is withdrawn from the Floridan aquifer. The coastal area is a Water Resource Caution Area and population growth continues at a relatively high rate.

Region III (Bay County). The majority of public supply is withdrawn from the Deer Point Lake reservoir. Panama City Beach relies in part on the Floridan aquifer. Most of the growth in this area has been in Panama City Beach. A cone of depression has formed in the aquifer.

Region IV (Holmes, Washington, Jackson, Calhoun, and Liberty counties). The Floridan aquifer is the primary source of public supply. Quantity of freshwater is not a concern. In some areas the aquifer has been contaminated with agricultural chemicals.

Region V (Gulf and Franklin counties). Public supply is withdrawn from the Floridan aquifer. Growth has been concentrated in the coastal area and especially on St. George Island in recent years. The possibility exists of saltwater intrusion into water supplies.

Region VI (Gadsden County). Surface water from Quincy Creek is the primary source of public supply

for the city of Quincy. Agricultural withdrawals have reduced flows on Telogia Creek and its upper basin has been designated a Water Resource Caution Area.

Region VII (Leon, Wakulla, and Jefferson counties). The Floridan aquifer supplies all of the public supply and the area contributes high recharge to the aquifer, which makes the aquifer susceptible to contamination. Hundreds of sinkholes are direct conduits to the aquifer. Growth rates are high.

In 1995 about 660 million gallons of freshwater were withdrawn each day in the Northwest region. Surface water accounted for 390 million gallons per day (mgd) or 59 percent of the freshwater withdrawn, and groundwater accounted for 270 mgd or 41 percent of the freshwater withdrawn. Since 1980, surface water withdrawals have been steadily decreasing in Northwest Florida. Much of this decrease can be attributed to a decrease in withdrawals of freshwater by thermoelectric power generation facilities, which still have the largest withdrawal of surface water (71 percent of total surface water use in 1995). Commercial-industrial-mining use of fresh surface water decreased from 1975 until 1985 and has since remained relatively stable. Surface water is used for public supply in Bay County (44 mgd) and Gadsden County (1.4 mgd).

Panama City Beach, Bay County

179

Flood Protection and Floodplain Management

Flooding is a natural occurrence and becomes a problem when development takes place in floodplains or other floodprone areas. Floodplains are associated with streams and rivers. Most of the flooding in the region occurs along the Choctawhatchee and Apalachicola rivers and their tributaries. Wetlands, land surrounding lakes, closed basins, and coastal areas are potential floodprone areas. Land clearing and filling, levee construction and adding impervious surfaces aggravate flooding.

Natural vegetation along rivers acts like a sponge, absorbing excess water and gradually releasing it over a prolonged period. Wetlands also help filter nutrients and impurities such as pesticides and other toxic agents from runoff. Natural floodplain vegetation is extremely important for modifying both the quality and the quantity of freshwater entering rivers and estuaries. These ecosystems or floodplain systems are also a source of food and habitat for both terrestrial and aquatic organisms.

No major flood control structures exist in Northwest Florida. Dams in Northwest Florida were constructed for water supply, hydropower, recreation, or navigation and have limited flood storage capacity. Structural responses to flooding such as dams, dikes, detention or storage facilities, culvert enlargements, channel modifications, canals, and floodgates are expensive, and they modify natural systems and bring greater risks as floodplain development intensifies. NWFWMD implements nonstructural flood protection measures including floodplain acquisition, and discouragement of development in floodplain areas. The district also requires that wells located in floodprone areas be elevated. Some development has occurred in floodprone areas of Northwest Florida, most notably in recently developed parts of Leon County, and in the older towns of Caryville and Blountstown.

Flooding of rivers in Northwest Florida usually occurs in association with low pressure centers and with cold fronts most common during the winter or early spring, whereas low flow conditions are most common in the fall. Flooding might be expected to be greater in the summer when total rainfall is much greater than in the winter and early spring. However, in the summer, surface temperatures are much higher, and far more rainfall evaporates from warm surfaces. More rainfall is also transpired from lush summer foliage. The chance of summer flooding is also reduced because the drainage basins of many Northwest Florida rivers extend into Georgia and Alabama,

Georgann Penson

Flooding along the Apalachicola River, 1990

182

Floodplain, Florida River Island

Diane Sterling

where rainfall from summer thunderstorms is less than in Northwest Florida. Reduced foliage in the winter and decreased evaporation allow more of the rain falling during the winter rainy season to the north to run off and flood panhandle rivers.

Although river stages are usually higher in the winter and early spring, hurricanes and tropical storms can result in severe flooding in the summer and fall. Tropical storm Alberto made landfall near Destin on July 3, 1994, moved slowly across the panhandle through Alabama and Georgia and then back-tracked to the panhandle leaving behind 15 inches of rain in some areas. The Choctawhatchee River rose 15 feet above flood stage at the towns of Westville and Caryville. Houses, businesses, and public facilities were damaged in Caryville. The Apalachicola River crested at its highest level in 65 years, causing extensive damage in Blountstown, Wewahitchka, and New Hope. Inadequate storm drainage systems resulted in flooding in Leon and Wakulla counties. Additional flooding occurred in August when tropical storm Beryl took a similar path dumping large amounts of rain on a still-saturated watershed. In October another tropical depression inundated the same area.

Through Preservation 2000 and Save Our Rivers the district has acquired 150,000 acres of predominantly floodplain land. The district purchased these lands specifically to protect water resources. It manages these lands as natural systems and is restoring some disturbed lands to their natural state.

District staff reviews local government comprehensive plans, plan amendments, developments of regional impact, and other projects and recommends floodplain management strategies to be implemented by other governmental agencies and private landowners. Only local governments, however, can institute regulatory actions such as zoning, performance standards, and establishment of buffers or other development restrictions.

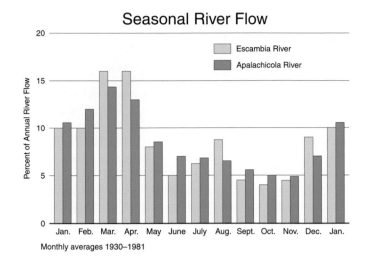

Seasonal River Flow

Monthly averages 1930–1981

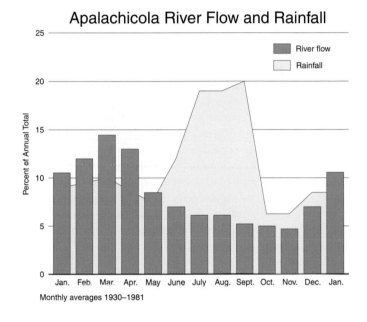

Apalachicola River Flow and Rainfall

Monthly averages 1930–1981

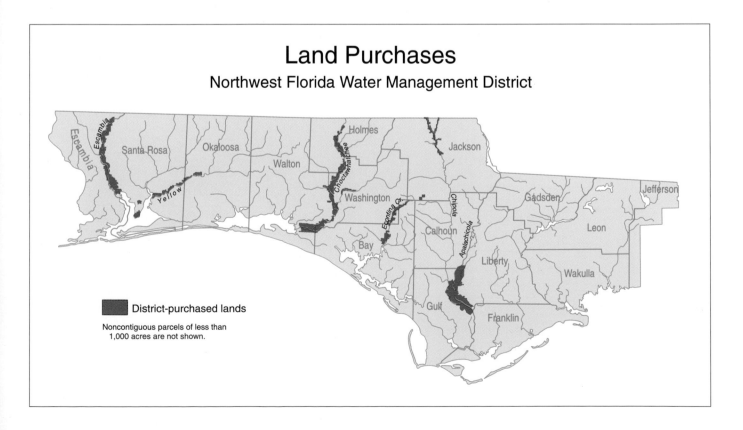

Land Purchases
Northwest Florida Water Management District

■ District-purchased lands

Noncontiguous parcels of less than 1,000 acres are not shown.

183

Water Quality

Surface Water

The physical, chemical, and biological characteristics of surface waters in Northwest Florida are variable and highly complex. Streams that receive most of their flow from a surficial source, such as direct runoff from rainfall or from the sand and gravel aquifer, have waters that are acidic (with a pH of less than 6) and low in dissolved minerals. Many of the smaller streams that drain swamplands are also acidic, as well as highly colored as a result of decomposing organic materials. In the central and easternmost portions of the district, where the carbonate Floridan aquifer contributes heavily to stream flows, the pH is more often neutral and dissolved mineral concentrations are relatively high.

In general, water quality is good, and a number of water bodies throughout the region are nearly pristine. There are, however, continued concerns about maintaining the water quality. Rapid coastal development is threatening bays and lagoons. Agricultural, silvicultural, and construction practices also can result in nonpoint source pollution and direct discharges from some business enterprises can result in point source pollution.

A major source of surface-water pollution in Northwest Florida is nonpoint source pollution from agricultural, silvicultural, and construction runoff. Several poorly operating or overloaded wastewater treatment plants in rural areas as well as the use of septic systems have also degraded water quality in some areas. Rapid coastal development threatens several bays and lagoons, and high-volume discharges from paper mills have had an adverse effect on local water quality. Stormwater runoff is a major concern for the more developed urban areas and their receiving water bodies.

In the Perdido Bay basin, Eleven-Mile Creek and Bayou Marcus Creek have degraded water quality. Fish from Eleven-Mile Creek have dioxin levels 8.1 to 25.7 parts per trillion, which exceed the U.S. Environmental Protection Agency (EPA) recommended maximum of 7 parts per trillion, and Bayou Marcus Creek receives urban runoff and wastewater discharges. The northernmost Escambia River is affected by domestic discharges and the southern reaches are degraded by industrial discharges. Violation of discharge standards to the Trammel Creek in the Yellow River basin by a wastewater treatment plant resulted in a large fish kill. Enough mercury has been found in largemouth bass in the Escambia, Blackwater, Yellow, and Perdido rivers to warrant limited-consumption advisories. The Pensacola Bay basin is affected by treated wastewater and urban runoff, and Escambia Bay has industrial discharges. Fish kills have occurred in both Pensacola and Escambia bays and their tributary bayous.

The Choctawhatchee River has been moderately degraded by agricultural runoff, a large portion of which is from Alabama, and several tributaries have been polluted by domestic or industrial discharges. Choctawhatchee Bay has good water quality, but is threatened by increasing development in its watershed.

Water quality in St. Andrew Bay is good, except around a paper mill discharge. High concentrations of lead, mercury, DDT, chlordane, polychlorinated biphenyls, and polycyclic aromatic hydrocarbons have been found in sediments in Watson Bayou. Deer Point Lake has problems with aquatic weeds and elevated nutrient levels. Largemouth bass limited-consumption advisories have been issued for both Econfina Creek and Deer Point Lake. Water quality in St. Joseph Bay is excellent except around a paper mill discharge.

The Chipola River generally has good water quality except for local areas impacted by agriculture and silviculture. Dry Creek, a tributary to the Chipola contaminated by heavy metals from a battery-salvage operation, has been cleaned up under the Superfund program.

184

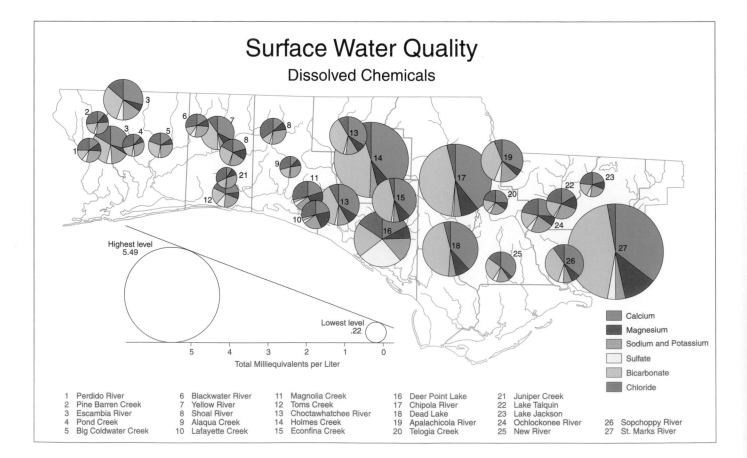

Surface Water Quality
Dissolved Chemicals

Highest level 5.49

Lowest level .22

Total Milliequivalents per Liter

Calcium
Magnesium
Sodium and Potassium
Sulfate
Bicarbonate
Chloride

1 Perdido River	6 Blackwater River	11 Magnolia Creek	16 Deer Point Lake	21 Juniper Creek	26 Sopchoppy River
2 Pine Barren Creek	7 Yellow River	12 Toms Creek	17 Chipola River	22 Lake Talquin	27 St. Marks River
3 Escambia River	8 Shoal River	13 Choctawhatchee River	18 Dead Lake	23 Lake Jackson	
4 Pond Creek	9 Alaqua Creek	14 Holmes Creek	19 Apalachicola River	24 Ochlockonee River	
5 Big Coldwater Creek	10 Lafayette Creek	15 Econfina Creek	20 Telogia Creek	25 New River	

Surface Water Quality Characteristics
1990–1995

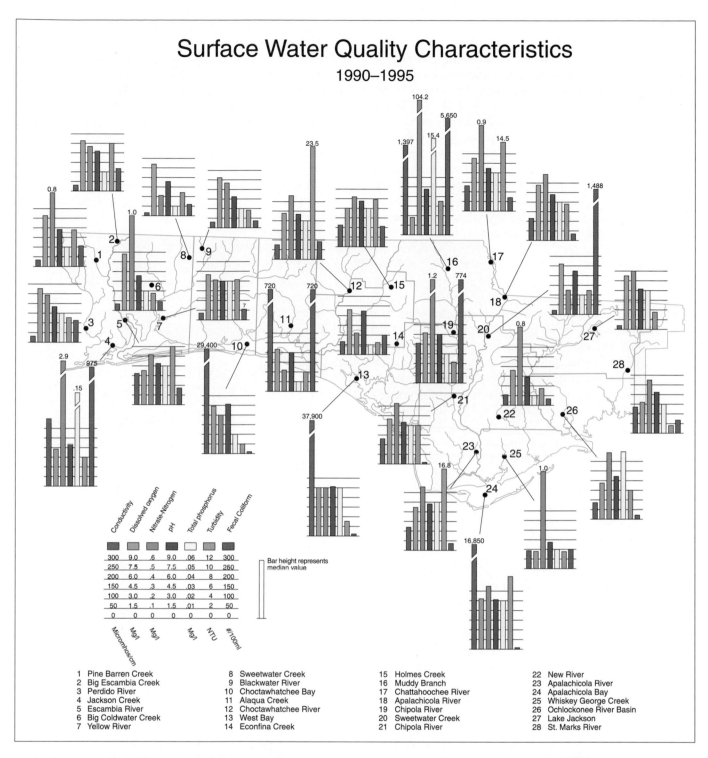

Legend:

	Conductivity	Dissolved oxygen	Nitrate-Nitrogen	pH	Total phosphorus	Turbidity	Fecal Coliform
	300	9.0	.6	9.0	.06	12	300
	250	7.5	.5	7.5	.05	10	250
	200	6.0	.4	6.0	.04	8	200
	150	4.5	.3	4.5	.03	6	150
	100	3.0	.2	3.0	.02	4	100
	50	1.5	.1	1.5	.01	2	50
	0	0	0	0	0	0	0
	Micromhos/cm	Mg/l	Mg/l		Mg/l	NTU	#/100ml

Bar height represents median value

1 Pine Barren Creek	8 Sweetwater Creek	15 Holmes Creek	22 New River
2 Big Escambia Creek	9 Blackwater River	16 Muddy Branch	23 Apalachicola River
3 Perdido River	10 Choctawhatchee Bay	17 Chattahoochee River	24 Apalachicola Bay
4 Jackson Creek	11 Alaqua Creek	18 Apalachicola River	25 Whiskey George Creek
5 Escambia River	12 Choctawhatchee River	19 Chipola River	26 Ochlockonee River Basin
6 Big Coldwater Creek	13 West Bay	20 Sweetwater Creek	27 Lake Jackson
7 Yellow River	14 Econfina Creek	21 Chipola River	28 St. Marks River

185

In the Apalachicola River basin water quality is good in most places and degraded in others. At the river mouth, Scipio Creek is impaired by shrimping and marina activities and by wastewater discharges. Sutton Creek has been adversely affected by discharges from the City of Blountstown Wastewater Treatment Plant.

Apalachicola Bay has very good water quality with the exception of local pollution from fish houses and marinas. The New River basin remains largely undeveloped and has very good water quality.

The upper Ochlockonee River has high nutrient levels and turbidity from agricultural runoff and out-of-state point sources. As a result, fisheries have declined. The lower Ochlockonee River, Lake Talquin, and the Sopchoppy River still maintain good water quality, although limited fish-consumption advisories have been issued for Lake Talquin and the Ochlockonee River and may be issued for the Sopchoppy River. Telogia

Creek has low dissolved oxygen and high nutrient levels from the city of Gretna's wastewater spray fields.

The St. Marks and Wakulla rivers both have excellent water quality, except for a small stretch in the lower St. Marks impacted by an electric utility plant and oil storage facilities. Historically, Munson Slough and Lake Munson were polluted by wastewater discharges and are currently affected by stormwater runoff. Lake Munson has improved markedly since city of Tallahassee wastewater discharges have been diverted to spray irrigation. Concern continues over Lake Jackson in Leon County, as runoff from residential development, construction, roads, and parking lots continues to threaten the lake. A stormwater treatment system was developed by NWFWMD in the early 1980s as a U.S. EPA demonstration project. This system was expanded and improved in the late 1980s and early 1990s.

Groundwater

Throughout Northwest Florida, groundwater is the primary source of the region's drinking water. Approximately 77 percent of the region's drinking water comes from groundwater. Its quality is generally good and requires little or no treatment.

Groundwater is monitored through background network wells and VISA (Very Intensive Study Area) wells. Wells in the background network are selected as representative of the general groundwater quality of a region and are used to define baseline groundwater quality. VISA wells monitor specific areas thought to be highly susceptible to groundwater contamination from surface sources. Water from these wells is tested for an extensive array of industrial contaminants as well as pesticides and herbicides.

The natural chemical quality of groundwater in Northwest Florida derives from the chemistry of the geologic sediments. The concentrations of naturally occurring dissolved minerals in water from the sand and gravel aquifer are much lower than those found in the Floridan aquifer. Water from the sand and gravel aquifer has a low pH, which tends to corrode metals. Mineral content in water from the Floridan aquifer system is much higher because of the greater solubility of the limestone that makes up the aquifer. In areas with lower recharge rates, dissolved mineral concentrations increase, especially with depth. For much of Gadsden, Liberty, Calhoun, Bay, Gulf, and Franklin counties, the Floridan aquifer is thick but contains highly mineralized water in its lower portions. Consequently the productive thickness of the aquifer for this region is limited. As the Floridan dips deeper beneath the land surface in the western part of the panhandle, the water within the aquifer increases in mineral content. As a result, in much of Escambia and Santa Rosa counties the Floridan aquifer is so saline that it is not used for potable water.

The surficial aquifer system is universally susceptible to contamination. Throughout much of the panhandle the depth to the water table is between 20 and 40 feet. Rarely is this depth more than 60 feet; in many places it is 10 feet or less. The vulnerability of the sand and gravel aquifer in Escambia County is typical of the surficial aquifer system. A long history of urban, commercial, and industrial land use in the southern half of the county has resulted in numerous instances of groundwater contamination. Groundwater has been affected by inorganic fertilizer manufacturing, wood preservation waste, landfilling, leaking underground storage tanks, and uncontrolled releases of dry cleaning solvents. Throughout urbanized Pensacola, a large number of public supply wells have been found to be contaminated by solvents, hydrocarbon derivatives, and pesticides.

The Floridan aquifer system is most susceptible to contamination in the Woodville and Dougherty karst regions where the aquifer is at or near the land surface and where karstic and erosional processes have removed some (or all) of the overlying confining unit. Some public supply wells in the Woodland karst region in Tallahassee were contaminated with the dry cleaning solvent perchloroethylene (PCE). In Jackson County

186

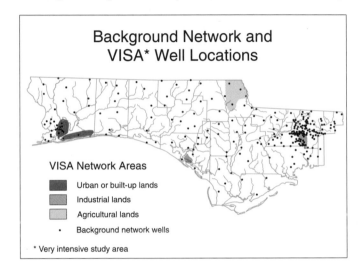

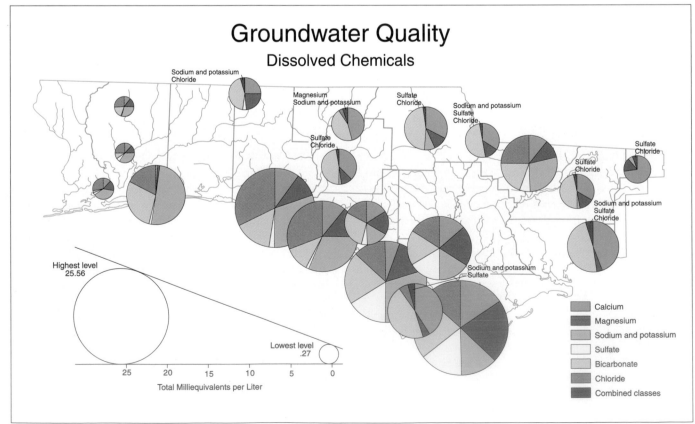

Profile of Coastal Groundwater Chloride Concentrations

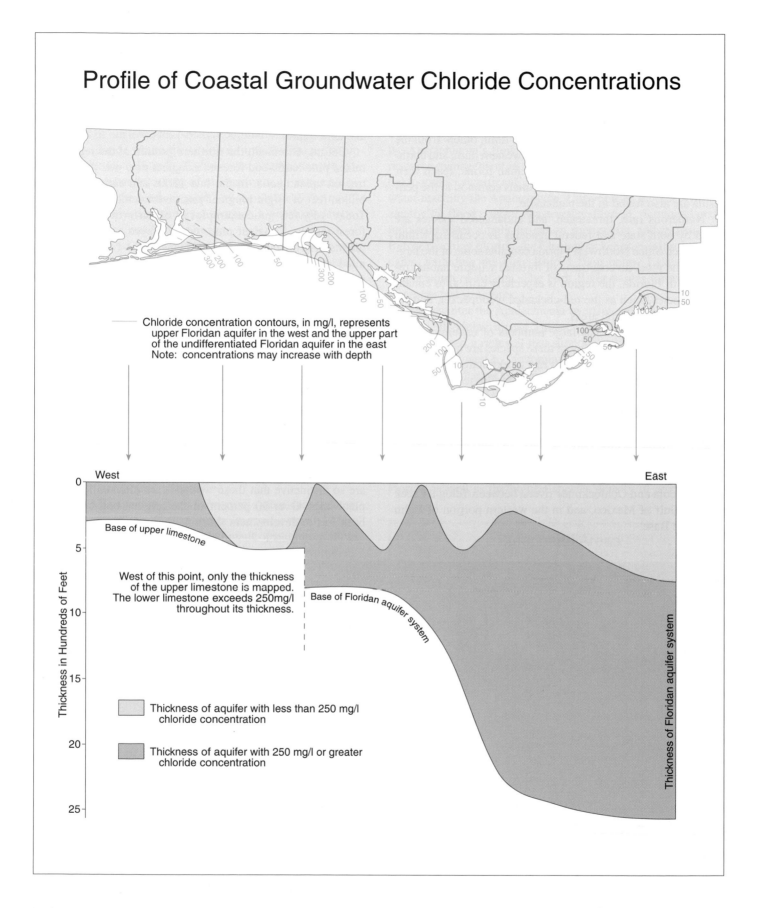

Chloride concentration contours, in mg/l, represents upper Floridan aquifer in the west and the upper part of the undifferentiated Floridan aquifer in the east
Note: concentrations may increase with depth

West

Base of upper limestone

West of this point, only the thickness of the upper limestone is mapped. The lower limestone exceeds 250mg/l throughout its thickness.

Base of Floridan aquifer system

East

Thickness in Hundreds of Feet

Thickness of Floridan aquifer system

Thickness of aquifer with less than 250 mg/l chloride concentration

Thickness of aquifer with 250 mg/l or greater chloride concentration

187

in the Dougherty karst region the agricultural pesticide ethylene dibromide has contaminated over 400 wells.

The Floridan aquifer system throughout coastal portions of the panhandle is susceptible to saltwater intrusion. When pumpage exceeds recharge, water levels can be depressed for many years before a significant change in water quality is seen. Generally, a well tapping a deeper portion of the aquifer will experience saltwater intrusion earlier than will a well open to a shallower depth. Once water quality deteriorates, even if pumpage is discontinued or reduced, water quality problems persist. Once saltwater intrusion occurs, it takes many years without pumpage for the aquifer to return to preexisting geochemical conditions.

Suspension bridge over the Suwannee River near Luraville

Lying to the south and east of the lower Suwannee River is the Waccasassa River basin. The Waccasassa River and its small tributary system form the major drainage system in a 924-square-mile area. The Waccasassa begins as a poorly defined watercourse connecting swamps and ponds along the Gilchrist County-Levy County border. Moving southward through Levy County the river is augmented by discharge from Blue and Wekiva springs, which help maintain flow during the drier times of the year. The Waccasassa, like all rivers in the district that empty into the Gulf of Mexico, is influenced in its lower reaches by tidal fluctuations, and stream flow may reverse depending on discharge and tidal heights.

The Aucilla is the westernmost river system in the district. Its headwaters are in southern Georgia and it drains approximately 880 square miles. The spring-fed Wacissa River, its primary tributary, joins the Aucilla in the lower coastal plain. Southeast of the Aucilla basin is the Coastal Rivers basin, a generally poorly drained region in Taylor, Dixie, and Lafayette counties with numerous lakes, ponds, swamps, and creeks. Principal drainage to the Gulf of Mexico is provided by the Econfina, Fenholloway, and Steinhatchee rivers.

There are over 150 known springs in the district. An accurate survey and count of all springs would be difficult since most are in the streambeds and visible only during very low flow. Although there are many springs in the Wacissa, Waccasassa, and Coastal Rivers basins, most springs are in the

Suwannee and Santa Fe River basins. Of the 27 first-magnitude springs (average flow, 64.6 mgd or more) in Florida, 10 are in the district.

The types of lakes in the district range from landlocked to those with streams running both in and out of them. Most of the lakes are shallow and small in surface area although a few are large, such as the Santa Fe Lakes (5,856 acres), Lake Sampson (2,042 acres), and Ocean Pond (1,774 acres). Madison County has the most lakes and ponds in the district, although most are small, shallow, and ephemeral. Numerous small lakes and ponds exist in the Waccasassa Flats area and to the west of the Suwannee River in Lafayette and Dixie counties. Many lakes and ponds have close connections to the surficial, intermediate, or Floridan aquifer systems where these aquifers are under water table conditions. Alligator Lake, in Columbia County, periodically drains to the Floridan aquifer system through a series of sinkholes.

Groundwater

Three different aquifers can be described in the region. When they occur together in a vertical overlap sequence, a surficial water table aquifer overlies an intermediate artesian aquifer, which, in turn, overlies the artesian Floridan aquifer system. The cross sections show details of variations in geologic conditions in the district. The Floridan aquifer system may be divided into three classes. In Class I, it is unconfined and is the sole source for groundwater supplies. In Class II—which may be thought of as a transitional area—a semiconfined Floridan is overlain by a water table aquifer. In Class III, the Floridan aquifer system is confined and may be overlain by a water table aquifer and/or intermediate artesian aquifers.

The boundary at the edge of the Class III (confined) area generally represents the Cody Scarp, an escarpment between the Northern Highlands and the Gulf Coastal Lowlands. The Cody Scarp separates distinct hydrogeological provinces. Surficial aquifers and intermediate artesian aquifers may underlie the Highlands side of the scarp. The Floridan aquifer system is confined (artesian) on the Highlands side and unconfined (nonartesian) on the Lowlands side. The scarp represents the area containing the most mature karst features in the district (artesian springs, steep-sided sinkholes, disappearing

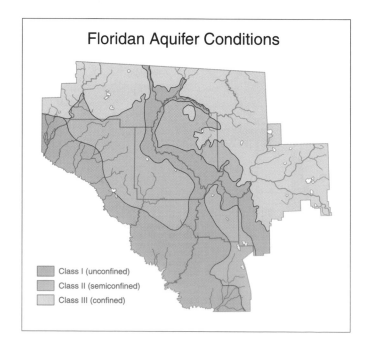

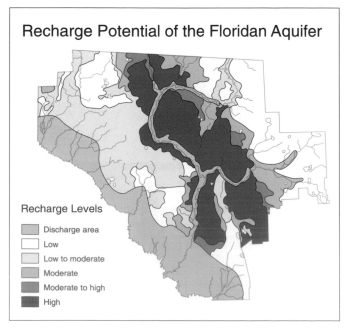

streams, lakes that periodically drain downward, and resurgences of disappearing streams).

Although little data are available on the depth of the potable portion of the Floridan aquifer system within the region, Klein (1975) has inferred that the potable portion of the aquifer increases in thickness from 250 feet near the coast to 1,500 feet beneath the Northern Highlands.

Groundwater within the Floridan aquifer system flows from confined to unconfined regions. The main recharge areas are the potentiometric highs (100 feet above msl) in Brooks and Lowndes counties in Georgia and the lakes region in the border area of Alachua, Bradford, Clay, and Putnam counties in Florida. Locally important recharge areas include the interior-drainage basins of Suwannee, Columbia, Gilchrist, Levy, and Alachua counties where deep sands overlying the Floridan aquifer system enhance aquifer recharge.

Groundwater within the region flows toward the Suwannee and Santa Fe river corridors or to the coast, the major discharge areas for the Floridan aquifer system. Groundwater is discharged from the Floridan aquifer system via springs and seeps in the sides or bottom of streams when the potentiometric surface is higher than the stream stage.

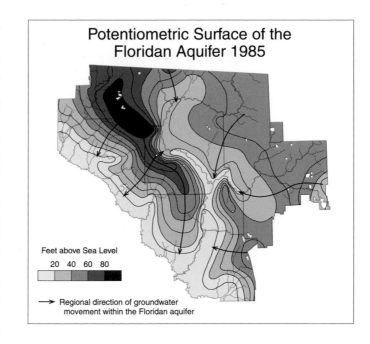

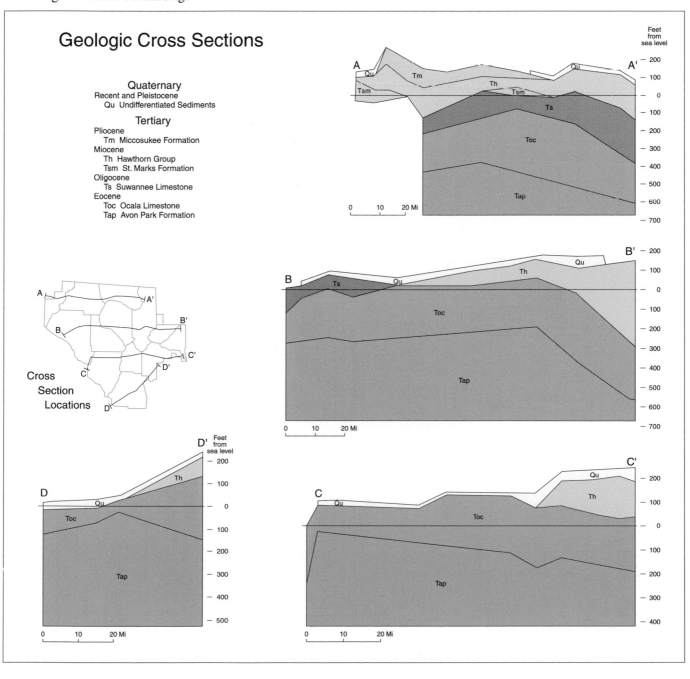

Water Supply and Use

In the mid 1990s the Suwannee River Water Management District is still chiefly rural. The district's available water supply appears sufficient to meet current and projected demand; however, water use is continuously increasing due to a growing population, increased use of water for irrigation, and industrial development. An ever-increasing demand upon the finite resource requires planning today to ensure adequate water supplies for the future. Although large-scale impacts from water withdrawal are not likely to occur, significant localized impacts from high-volume withdrawals are a possibility unless preventive and/or remedial measures are taken.

Total water use for 1995 within the district is estimated at 335.01 mgd. Three major water users account for 60 percent of the district's total water use. All the remaining 1995 water uses total 135.057 mgd.

Most of the water used in the district is from the Floridan aquifer system. Intermediate aquifers exist in several locations in the region, but are used as a water source only in Baker, Bradford, and Union counties. The more productive Floridan aquifer system is the preferred water source. Most wells provide adequate water at depths less than 200 feet.

Surface water is used only for irrigation (2.93 mgd), mining (3.98 mgd), and for cooling water at the power plant on the Suwannee River at Ellaville (113 mgd). The power plant uses water only for once-through cooling, and then returns it to the river.

202

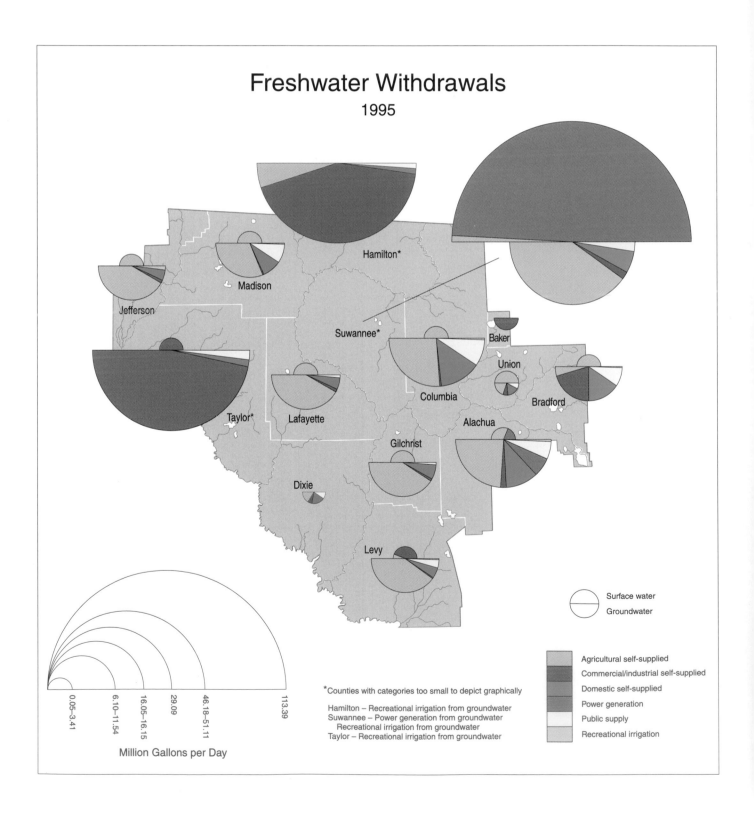

Freshwater Withdrawals
1995

*Counties with categories too small to depict graphically

Hamilton – Recreational irrigation from groundwater
Suwannee – Power generation from groundwater
    Recreational irrigation from groundwater
Taylor – Recreational irrigation from groundwater

Surface water
Groundwater

Agricultural self-supplied
Commercial/industrial self-supplied
Domestic self-supplied
Power generation
Public supply
Recreational irrigation

0.05–3.41   6.10–11.54   16.05–16.15   29.09   46.18–51.11   113.39

Million Gallons per Day

Water Use Trends

Total water use has not changed appreciably in the district over the last two decades, due largely to the consistent water use of the three major users. Potable and irrigation uses account for most of the increase. Commercial, industrial, and mining uses have changed little, and power generation uses (for cooling water) have decreased. This trend is likely to continue, with potable and irrigation uses increasing, commercial uses staying about the same, and decreasing use in the power generation category.

The demand for potable water has increased in direct proportion to population increases. In rural, unincorporated areas water use has increased along with population. Between 1975 and 1995 domestic self-supplied use increased 150 percent, compared with a 51 percent increase in public water supplies. The proliferation of rural subdivisions, where each lot is served by private onsite water and septic disposal systems, is the primary cause of this trend.

Despite the slow growth of many communities, some are reaching the point where public water supply and wastewater systems are becoming economically feasible and even necessary. Fanning Springs, Fort White, High Springs, Archer, and Bronson are developing urban infrastructure to accommodate growth and development, while trying to protect and conserve water resources. The town of Suwannee, at the river's mouth, recently developed a central wastewater treatment facility to improve water quality conditions in the river's estuary.

Few water resource issues generate citizen concern more than the possibility of transporting water from the Suwannee region to water-thirsty areas to the south. Throughout the past several decades, local citizens and elected officials have resisted suggestions to pipe water from the Suwannee River or from inland wellfields to the Tampa Bay area, where rapid population growth has placed increased demands on regional water supplies. Regional water managers statewide are committed to developing other "local source" alternatives such as desalination, conservation, and use of reclaimed water before

any consideration is given to transferring water across regional boundaries. In order for a long-distance transfer of water to take place, the present and future water needs of the sending area must be protected (including natural systems' needs) and the receiving area must have first exhausted all reasonable local sources or options.

Suwannee River Water Management District

Traveling gun irrigation

Freshwater Withdrawals

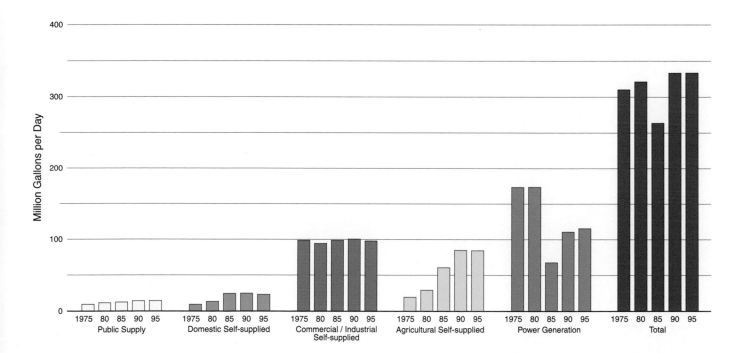

Flooding and Floodplain Management

Flooding, which can occur in all seasons, is the partial or complete inundation of normally dry land from the overflow of inland surface-water bodies or from abnormally high tidal water or rising coastal waters resulting from severe storms or hurricanes. Flooding also occurs within closed basins (areas with no surface-water outfall), in areas with poorly drained soils, or where development has adversely impacted natural drainage patterns. Depending on natural conditions and human influences, floods vary in volume, frequency, duration, and extent. The natural conditions that affect flooding are total quantity, intensity, and geographical distribution of rainfall, storm patterns, antecedent moisture conditions, temperature, and season of the year, as well as physical features of the watershed, such as topography, soils, geology, and drainage patterns. Human influences include urban and rural land uses, storage, diversions, and regulation of stream flow as well as changes in drainage and other factors that affect stormwater runoff.

Rivers flood when flow is in excess of channel capacity. The geometry of a river channel and its ability to accommodate discharge is governed by the erosive power of moderate flood flows, which occur more frequently than do the peak flows of large floods. Most of the time, river flow is readily contained within a river channel. Because rivers do not form passageways that will accommodate all sizes of flow events, the greater flow volumes overflow the channel and spread onto the floodplain. A river floodplain is formed by fluvial deposi-

Suwannee River Water Management District

Suwannee River at Dowling Park, April 1973 flood

204

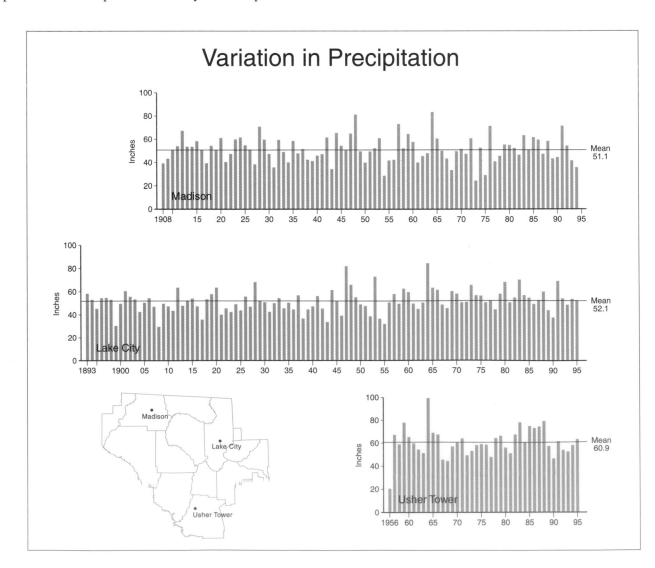

Suwannee River Monthly Mean Discharge

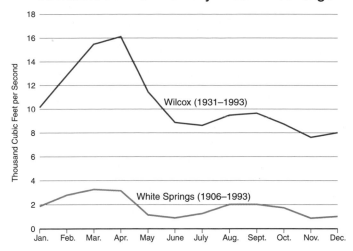

Suwannee River Monthly Elevation

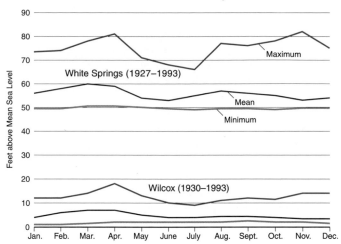

tion on the inside (point bars) of river bends and by a thin mantle of sediment deposited outside the channel when overflow occurs. Floodplains are integral parts of river systems. By furnishing room for water that cannot be conveyed in the entrenched river channel, they are, as described by Waananen et al. (1977), "the high-water channels of rivers."

Although a portion of the region is subject to coastal flooding, most flooding is associated with the overflow of inland surface water bodies or with the accumulation of water in closed basins. The maximum annual surface water stages in the district usually occur from February through April and are associated with frontal-type rainfall. Since 1948 three major floods

have occurred in the region. During the flood of March-April 1948, 500 square miles were inundated along the Suwannee River and its principal tributaries. The Suwannee River was out of its banks from the Gulf of Mexico to north of the Florida-Georgia state line. In March 1959, flood waters covered an estimated 350 square miles along the Suwannee River and its tributaries with some ponding up to 5 miles wide. In comparison with the 1948 flood, peak stages in 1959 were 2 to 4 feet lower on the major tributaries and middle and upper reaches of the Suwannee River. Peak stages in the lower reaches of the Suwannee River were 6 to 9 feet below the 1948 flood. The flood of April 1973 was the result of prolonged rainfall in the

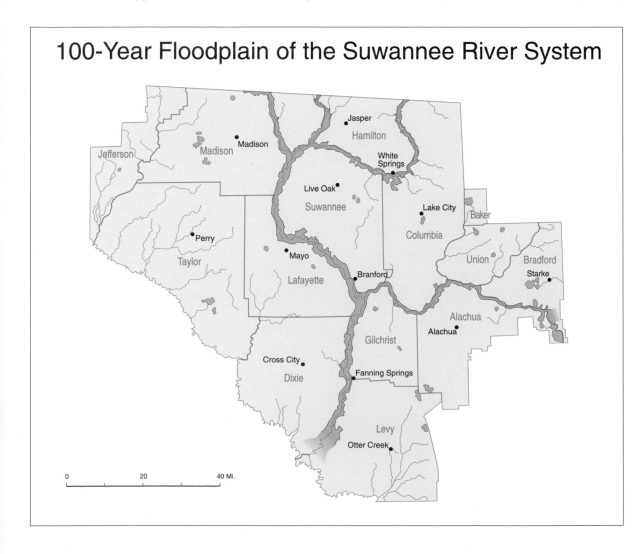

100-Year Floodplain of the Suwannee River System

basin during March and April. The flood of record for the upper reaches of the Suwannee occurred in 1973 and exceeded the 1948 flood by roughly 3 feet at White Springs. At Ellaville, the 1973 flood was about 3 feet lower than the 1948 event (U. S. Army Corps of Engineers 1974).

Two recent minor floods characterize the variability of stream flow in the region. Following three years of near record low surface-water and groundwater levels in the Suwannee basin, a prolonged winter frontal system in early 1991 caused a 10-year flood event in the upper and middle Suwannee River. During 1990, river levels at Ellaville (at the confluence with the Withlacoochee River) were very low, including the lowest discharge, 835 cfs, recorded at the station on November 8. By March 12, 1991, the river was discharging approximately 53,100 cfs and the river had risen over 25 feet.

During the normally dry season in October 1992, 11 to 13 inches of rain fell in one weekend on the upper Santa Fe River basin and the Santa Fe approached flood stage. The river actually flowed over the land bridge at O'Leno State Park for the first time in recent history. Shortly afterwards the river returned to normal stage.

Generally, for rainfall distributed equally throughout a basin, flooding increases downstream. In the Suwannee region, however, groundwater/surface-water interaction may actually decrease flooding in some areas by providing substantial subsurface storage when rivers are high. Springs discharging into rivers may reverse flow and temporarily become sinks. On the Suwannee River flooding decreases between Luraville and Branford due in part to the increase in channel size downstream. A substantial part of the decrease, however, is thought to occur because at high stream levels, springs become sinks. This same phenomenon is thought to occur on the Santa Fe River between Worthington Springs and High Springs (Giese and Franklin 1996).

The district has a policy of nonstructural floodplain management. Research, public education, land acquisition, and regulations are actively pursued as a means to protect water resources and lives in floodprone areas. Major areas of concern are the floodplains of the Suwannee River and its tributaries.

206

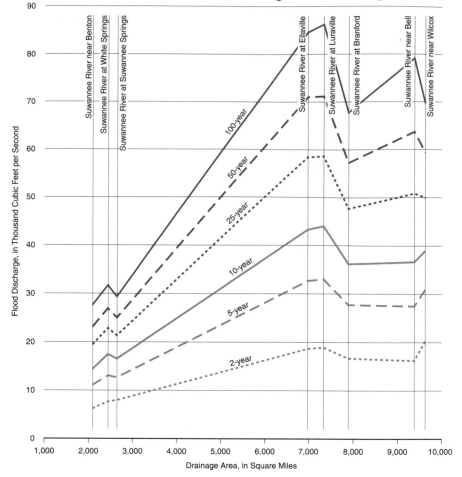

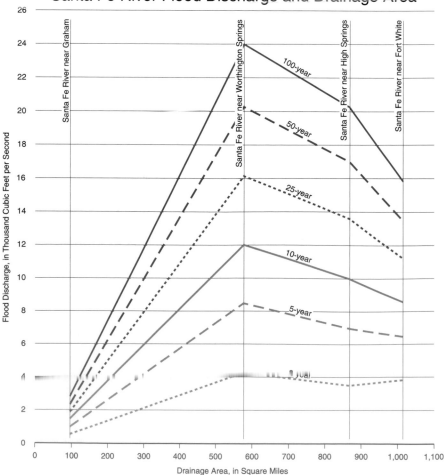

Water Quality

Surface Water

The district collects, tests, and evaluates water samples at many stations and at regular intervals to measure the physical and chemical state of surface water. Some sites are monitored for biological as well as chemical parameters. Benthic invertebrate diversity describes the composition of the bottom-dwelling invertebrate community in terms of the number of taxa present and the extent to which the community has few or many taxa. Low diversity usually indicates some type of human disturbance. These data are compared, both spatially and temporally, and trends established.

In 1996 SRWMD rated as good all monitored surface water bodies with the exception of Lake Rowell, Alligator Creek, Camp Branch, Pareners Branch, Hunter Creek, New River, Olustee Creek, and Swift Creek, which are rated as fair, and

Fenholloway River, which is rated as poor. In the Coastal Rivers basin, the Fenholloway receives effluent from a large cellulose fiber plant. Although the quality of discharges improved in the early 1970s, the river still has high levels of nutrients and color and low dissolved oxygen and biological diversity. Previously Florida's only Class V industrial river, recent reclassification to Class III is intended to provide for improvements to the river. Mill effluent will receive additional treatment and the outfall relocated to the lower river, where it can be more easily assimilated by river flow and tidal action.

Surface water in the uppermost portion of the Suwannee River basin is primarily derived from runoff, and water quality at stations near the headwaters reflects the influence of a poorly drained, heavily vegetated sedimentary environment. Characteristically, the water is acidic, low in dissolved inorganic constituents, high in concentrations of organic material, and highly colored. Farther downstream in the vicinity of White Springs, the Floridan aquifer system outcrops in the river corridor and

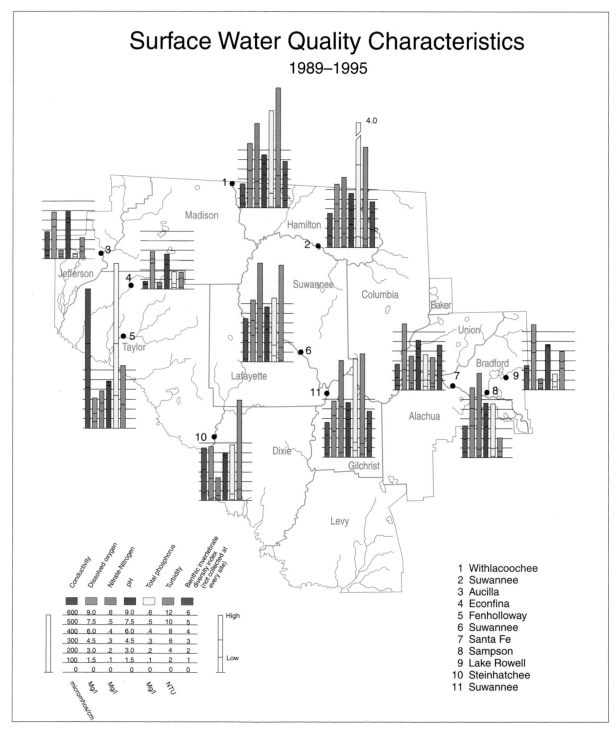

Surface Water Quality Characteristics
1989–1995

Conductivity
Dissolved oxygen
Nitrate-Nitrogen
pH
Total phosphorus
Turbidity
Benthic invertebrate diversity index (not collected at every site)

600	9.0	.6	9.0	.6	12	6
500	7.5	.5	7.5	.5	10	5
400	6.0	.4	6.0	.4	8	4
300	4.5	.3	4.5	.3	6	3
200	3.0	.2	3.0	.2	4	2
100	1.5	.1	1.5	.1	2	1
0	0	0	0	0	0	0

High
Low

micromhos/cm
Mg/l
Mg/l
Mg/l
NTU

1 Withlacoochee
2 Suwannee
3 Aucilla
4 Econfina
5 Fenholloway
6 Suwannee
7 Santa Fe
8 Sampson
9 Lake Rowell
10 Steinhatchee
11 Suwannee

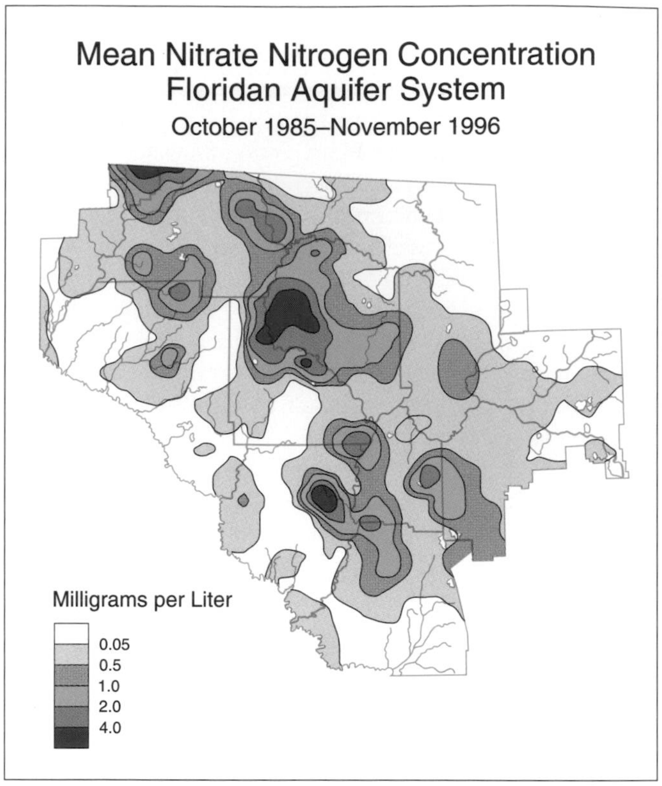

Prometon Concentration

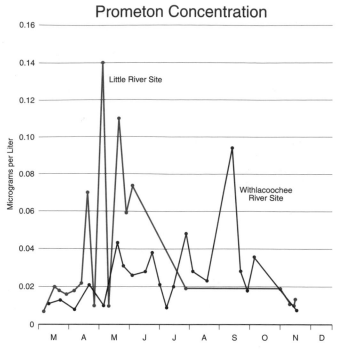

Mean Nitrate Nitrogen Concentration
Floridan Aquifer System
October 1985–November 1996

Milligrams per Liter

0.05
0.5
1.0
2.0
4.0

surface water becomes a mixture of runoff and groundwater discharge from springs and seeps. A trend of increasing pH and specific conductivity and decreasing total organic carbon (TOC) begins in this stretch of the river as a result of the influence of the carbonate aquifer. Along the entire river, water quality at times of high flow tends to approach the character of the high organic surface water of the headwater areas. Downstream from White Springs low or base flow takes on groundwater characteristics.

The middle reaches of the Suwannee River are increasingly being impacted by nutrients. During February 1995 (high flow conditions) concentrations of nitrate plus nitrite ranged from 0.05 to 0.38 mg/l. In June 1995 (low flow conditions), they ranged from 0.07 to 1.05 mg/l. Highest concentrations were observed at Branford. The most likely source of elevated nutrients is groundwater contaminated from a combination of croplands, poultry operations, dairies, and septic tanks. Groundwater rather than surface water is thought to be the most likely source because there is no significant surficial stream inputs to the Suwannee between Luraville and Branford and because as stage decreases, nitrate-nitrogen concentration increases.

A 1993 study of surface water quality in the Suwannee River watershed found the presence of three herbicides (prometon, metolachlor, and atrazine) in the Little River in Georgia at the headwaters of the Suwannee basin (Oaksford 1994). These herbicides were generally detected in low concentrations, but concentrations were somewhat elevated during the spring of 1993. Prometon concentrations were also elevated in samples from the Withlacoochee River site, but were higher in the fall than in the spring. Had the Little River not been dry during the fall of 1993, prometon concentrations at the Little River site also might have exceeded concentrations measured in the spring. These chemicals are typically applied to croplands from February through June.

Increases in the mean concentrations of some inorganic chemical constituents and nutrients such as phosphorus, total nitrogen, and nitrate in the Suwannee River below White Springs are the result of inflow from tributaries receiving discharges from a phosphate mining operation in Hamilton County. From Wilcox downstream water quality shows little variation because the effects of any local activities are diluted by discharges from other parts of the basin.

208

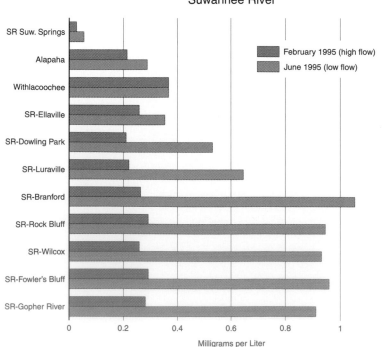

February 1995 (high flow)
June 1995 (low flow)

Groundwater

Different rock formations, water residency times, and human influences can impart particular chemical "flavors" to groundwater. Water from the Floridan aquifer system is slightly alkaline and is characterized by high relative values for specific conductivity, alkalinity, pH, magnesium, and calcium. This is typical of groundwater that occurs in a limestone aquifer that is undergoing dissolution.

Total sulfate in groundwater results from natural and human-induced activities. Acid rain, natural rock weathering, sea water, and agricultural, waste disposal, and industrial activities can all increase total sulfate. In SRWMD, high sulfate levels are found along the coast and in the confined sluggish portion of the Northern Highlands in the northeastern portion of the district. Chloride concentrations are generally low in the Floridan aquifer except for a narrow band along the coast. An inland high occurs at Ichetucknee Springs.

Surficial aquifer water is acidic and has high relative values for sodium, chloride, and nitrate. The surficial aquifer and the unconfined portions of the Floridan aquifer system are more susceptible than the confined portions of the Floridan aquifer system to human influence because the water table is near land surface.

Groundwater quality is good throughout most of the district. Areas with poorer quality water are due to both natural and human-induced causes. Along the Suwannee and other river corridors, the high degree of interaction between surface water and groundwater limits the reliability of the aquifer as an untreated water supply. During higher river stages and floods, springs and seeps reverse flow and river water enters the aquifer—often up to several miles inland. This occurs in Branford, Fanning Springs, and other riverside communities where mixed river water and groundwater is pumped and treated for public supply.

Elevated nitrate-nitrogen has been recorded in the Middle Suwannee River watershed (western Suwannee and western Lafayette counties). Croplands, dairies, and poultry operations are the dominant land use. In this area, the Floridan aquifer is unconfined, allowing water soluble contaminants to leach into the aquifer. The state has designated part of this area a very intensive study area (VISA) for groundwater monitoring. The district has one of the largest expanses of elevated nitrate nitrogen concentrations in the Floridan aquifer system in the state. Springs in the middle Suwannee River watershed have nitrate nitrogen concentrations ranging from 1.2 to 19.2 mg/l. Groundwater from the watershed flows toward the Suwannee and is affecting surface water via springs and seeps in the riverbed. Current efforts to address this problem to protect public health and natural systems are aimed at installing waste treatment systems to properly treat and dispose of animal wastes.

Water quality in the Floridan aquifer system generally declines with depth because the deeper water has usually been there longer and is more mineralized than the upper-level water. Although little data are available on the depth of the potable portion of the Floridan aquifer system,

Klein (1975) has inferred that within the Suwannee district the potable portion of the aquifer increases in thickness from 250 feet near the coast to 1,500 feet beneath the Northern Highlands.

Anthropogenic (human-caused) impacts to groundwater quality include increased nutrients from fertilizers and farming operations, septic tanks, pesticides and herbicides, discharge from industrial facilities, and untreated stormwater runoff from cities and streets. Leaking underground storage tanks have caused localized groundwater quality problems, particularly in older communities that lack a public water-supply system, and residents rely on untreated water from private wells.

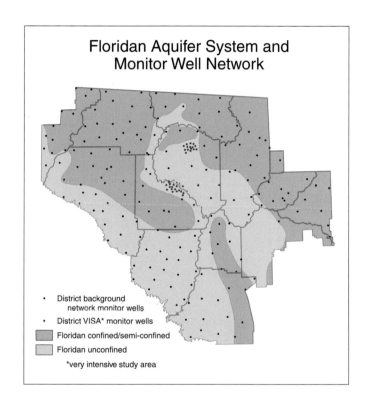

Floridan Aquifer System and Monitor Well Network

·   District background network monitor wells

·   District VISA* monitor wells

   Floridan confined/semi-confined

   Floridan unconfined

*very intensive study area

Chemical Characterization of the Floridan Aquifer System 1992

Parameter	Units	Minimum	Maximum	Median
pH		4.9	12.5	7.1
Calcium	mg/l	0.6	1000.0	82.0
Magnesium	mg/l	<0.1	430.0	6.3
Sodium	mg/l	0.2	3200.0	6.3
Potassium	mg/l	0.1	320.0	1.1
Total Iron	mg/l	<0.01	17.0	0.61
Mercury	µg/l	<0.2	2.0	<0.2
Lead	µg/l	<10.0	100.0	<10.0
Bicarbonate	mg/l	<1.0	770.0	150.0
Total Carbonate	mg/l	<1.0	650.0	<1.0
Sulfate	mg/l	<1.0	2200.0	6.7
Chloride	mg/l	<1.0	5200.0	8.9
Orthophosphate (as P)	mg/l	<0.01	21.0	<0.1
Fluoride	mg/l	<0.02	2.5	<0.2
Nitrate-Nitrogen	mg/l	<0.01	8.4	<0.05
Total Dissolved Solids	mg/l	40.0	10,200.0	220.0
Specific Conductivity	µmhos/cm	50.0	15,000.0	310.0
Total Organic Carbon	mg/l	<1.0	34.0	2.0

Natural Systems

The Suwannee River Water Management District includes extensive tracts of pinelands, upland hardwood forest, hardwood swamp, cypress swamp, and coastal saltmarsh. The wetlands of northeast Levy County are habitat for the federally listed endangered wood stork and other rare wading birds as well as the Florida sandhill crane. Much of the region has been affected by commercial timber operations, but these large forested areas are still habitat for wide-ranging species such as black bear, bobcat, American swallow-tailed kite, and wild turkey. A few patches of rare, xeric upland communities such as sandhill and oak scrub remain scattered throughout the region and are home to the federally listed endangered Florida scrub jay.

Of the 300 springs identified statewide, 90 are in the Suwannee River basin. Recent surveys by the district have identified many springs previously unidentified. Four of the largest, Manatee, Fanning, Troy, and Blue, contribute 368 mgd to the Suwannee River. One small spring along the Ichetucknee River is the only place in the world the sand grain snail is found. Peacock Spring near Mayo features one of the most extensive and spectacular caves in the world with more than 35,000 feet of passageways mapped and explored.

The federally endangered Gulf sturgeon travels from the coastal estuary up the Suwannee River to spawn. The Suwannee is the only river system in the eastern Gulf of Mexico that supports a healthy functioning population of Gulf sturgeon.

Although the region contains relatively little urban, commercial, or industrial development, the proportion of land in conservation in this region is less than in other regions in Florida. Only 6.4 percent of the total land is in conservation, compared with 19.6 percent statewide (Cox et al. 1994).

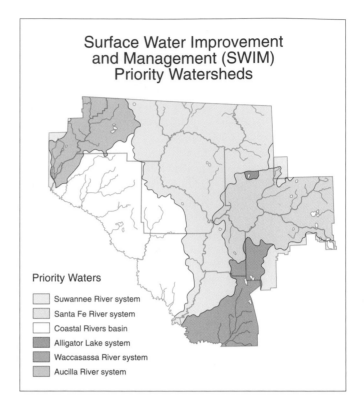

Surface Water Improvement and Management (SWIM) Priority Watersheds

Priority Waters

- Suwannee River system
- Santa Fe River system
- Coastal Rivers basin
- Alligator Lake system
- Waccasassa River system
- Aucilla River system

SRWMD's primary tools for natural system management and protection are the Surface Water Improvement and Management (SWIM) program, establishment of minimum flows and levels, land acquisition, intergovernmental coordination and technical assistance, and special projects and grants.

In the Suwannee region, determining minimum flows and levels is complicated by the fact that surface water and groundwater intermingle freely throughout much of the region. This

210

Little River Spring

Suwannee River Water Management District

Conservation Lands 1997

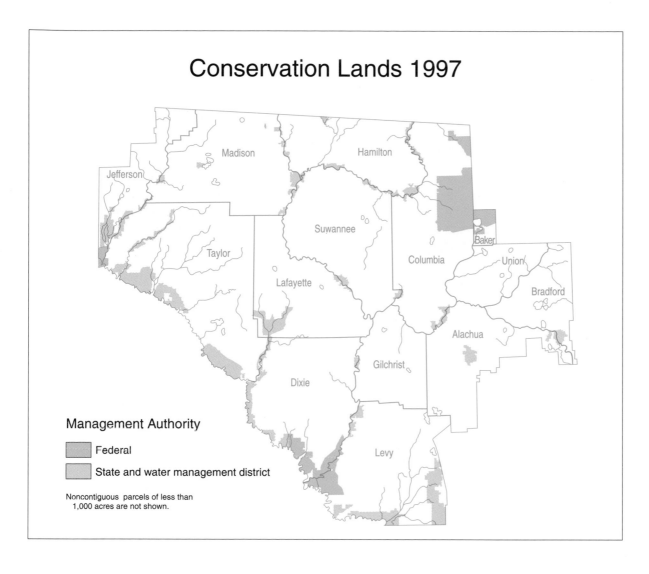

Management Authority

Federal

State and water management district

Noncontiguous parcels of less than
1,000 acres are not shown.

is best shown by the springs along the Suwannee and its tributaries, which provide base flow to the river during low river stages, yet take in surface water during floods.

A large-volume withdrawal of groundwater has the potential to reduce down-gradient spring flow, particularly if wells tap into an underground conduit system that provides a spring's flow. Reduced spring flow, in turn, has an adverse impact on river flow especially during low flow conditions. Reduced stream flow has the effect of decreasing the amount of freshwater in coastal estuaries, disrupting the delicate salinity balance that estuarine organisms depend on.

Another concern is the potential for water withdrawals to alter natural hydrologic fluctuations that the ecological communities along the river system have adapted to and depend on. Just as water withdrawals have the potential to reduce critical low flows, significant reduction of high flow can cause adverse impacts. The river's floodplain ecosystems depend on periodic and frequent inundation to introduce and recycle nutrients, transport seeds, and provide forage and breeding areas for aquatic organisms.

The basic components of the minimum flows and levels program for the lower Suwannee River include assessing the

211

Suwannee River Water Management District

Endangered West Indian manatee

Suwannee River Water Management District

River otter

relationships between the natural system and river hydrology, and integrating the results into regulatory, monitoring, and other management programs. Because the primary use of the minimum flows and levels standards will be in a regulatory capacity, an adequate scientific basis for the program is important.

Other applications of minimum flows and levels standards apply to lakes and streams that may be pursued as a water source, usually for agricultural irrigation. Setting limits on such consumptive uses to prevent seasonally low water levels from being further decreased due to water withdrawals assures the protection of important natural system functions. In some cases it may be necessary to prohibit any withdrawal if the lake or stream reaches a critical low stage. Not many such permits are requested in the district, due in large part to the uncertainty of surface-water sources and the relative ease of developing groundwater sources.

The Suwannee was one of the first rivers considered for study and designation in the federal Wild and Scenic River legislation approved in 1968. However, due to local opposition, the Suwannee was removed from the list. Although the Suwannee's status as a Wild and Scenic River was never achieved, many objectives of the program have been accomplished. Through the Save Our Rivers and Preservation 2000 programs, the public is now the largest landowner along the river, local ordinances require streamside setbacks and buffers, and interstate coordination is at an all-time high.

A committee formed by the North Central Florida Regional Planning Council in 1977 to study management issues and possible solutions gradually led to the Suwannee River Resource Planning and Management Committee, formed by Governor Bob Graham in 1979. This group developed a set of recommendations for improving river protection. Issues included floodplain mapping and management, maintaining or improving water quality, protecting the river's flow from being diminished, interstate coordination, protecting springs and spring runs, and managing recreational use of the river—particularly the need for boating controls.

Most of the issues were addressed or resolved during the 1980s by the agencies and local governments represented on the committee. Some, however, continue to the present. Boating controls have long been a difficult issue to address, and represent one of the more direct user conflicts that must be resolved. Recreational boating on the river has increased considerably. Boat wakes have become an increasing problem, causing damage to riverbanks and adjacent private property. Several fatal accidents on the river in recent years have increased awareness of the need to more actively manage use of the river. Also, manatees use the river, having been seen as far upstream as Rum Island Spring on the Santa Fe River near High Springs. Although no manatees have been reported injured or killed on the Suwannee recently, the potential for such accidents increases in direct proportion to boat traffic. The challenge now is to meet the competing needs of recreational boaters, private property owners, and the environment.

The issue of interstate coordination is important because half the river's watershed is in Georgia, and drains into Florida. Recent activities by the district and the Department of Environmental Protection, and counterpart agencies in Georgia, have led to the formation of the Suwannee Basin Interagency Alliance. This group is working to develop a basin-wide manage-

212

Fishing boat at Steinhatchee

ment planning and river protection program that, for the first time, will address the entire watershed.

A precursor to the latest of these management planning efforts was in response to a 1989 Governor's Executive Order, in which the Suwannee River Task Force recommended a series of controls to protect the Suwannee River. Over 40,000 platted lots have been identified in the 100-year floodplain, and concern was raised that the ultimate buildout of these lots—each on an individual septic tank and well—would threaten the river's water quality. Estimates of current buildout on these lots range from 20 to 30 percent.

Two important results of agency work towards implementing the task force recommendations will help protect water quality in the river system. Onsite wastewater treatment and disposal systems in the 10-year floodplain of the river and its tributaries must meet more stringent standards to ensure water quality protection. More intensely developed areas along the river were studied for the feasibility of central wastewater treatment facilities, and two areas in particular—the town of Suwannee and the city of Fanning Springs—were given top priority. Over 900 onsite systems in the town of Suwannee were identified as deficient and a primary cause of the closed oyster harvesting areas in Suwannee Sound. Through the work of local, regional, state, and federal agencies, a new wastewater treatment plant serving the community is being constructed.

REFERENCES

A source for a map or figure has a number in parentheses following the entry. This number refers to the page in this atlas for which the source was used.

Ceryak, R. 1977. *Alapaha River Basin*. Information circular no. 5. Suwannee River Water Management District. Live Oak.

Cox, J., R. Kautz, M. MacLaughlin, and T. Gilbert. 1994. *Closing the Gaps in Florida's Wildlife Habitat Conservation System*. Florida Game and Fresh Water Fish Commission, Tallahassee.

Florida Department of Environmental Regulation. 1980. *Report to the Environmental Regulation Commission on the Proposed Redesignation of the Suwannee River Between State Road 6 (Hamilton and Columbia Counties) and Suwannee Springs (Hamilton and Suwannee Counties) as an "Outstanding Florida Water."* Tallahassee.

Florida Natural Areas Inventory. Tallahassee. (map, 211)

Franklin, M.A., G.L. Giese, and P.R. Mixson. 1995. *Statistical Summaries of Surfacewater Hydrologic Data Collected in the Suwannee River Water Management District, Florida, 1906–93*. U.S. Geological Survey Open-file Report 94-709. Tallahassee, Florida. (map, 198; Mean Stream Flow map, 199)

Garrett, A.A., and C.S. Conover. n.d. *River Basins of the U.S.: The Suwannee*. Washington, D.C.: U.S. Geological Survey.

Giese, G.L., and M.A. Franklin. 1996. *Magnitude and Frequency of Floods in the Suwannee River Water Management District, Florida*. U.S. Geological Survey Water Resources Investigations Report 96-4176. Tallahassee. (graphs, 207)

Hand, J., J. Col, and L. Lord. 1996. *Northeast Florida District Water Quality*. 305(b): Technical appendix. Florida Department of Environmental Protection. Tallahassee.

Katz, B.G., and R.S. DeHan. 1996. *The Suwannee River Basin Pilot Study: Issues for Watershed Management in Florida*. U.S. Geological Survey Fact Sheet FS-080-96. Tallahassee, Florida.

Klein, H.F. 1975. *Depth to Base of Potable Water in the Floridan Aquifer System*. Florida Bureau of Geology Map Series 42. Rev. ed. Tallahassee.

Leach, S.D. 1983. *Source, Use, and Disposition of Water in Florida, 1980*. U.S. Geological Survey Water-Resources Investigations 82-4090. Tallahassee.

Oaksford, E.T. 1994. *Preliminary Results: Agricultural Chemicals in the Suwannee River Basin*. Georgia-Florida Coastal Plain Study Unit Open File Report 94-103. Tallahassee. (Prometon Concentration graph, 208)

Puri, H.S., and R.O. Vernon. 1964. *Summary of the Geology of Florida and a Guidebook to the Classic Exposures*. Florida Geological Survey Special Publication 5. Tallahassee.

Rosenau, J.C., and G.L. Faulkner. 1975. *An Index to Springs of Florida*. Florida Bureau of Geology Map Series 63. Rev. ed. Tallahassee, Florida. (Surface Water map, 199)

Rosenau, J.C., G.L. Faulkner, C.W. Hendry, Jr., and R.W. Hull. 1977. *Springs of Florida*. Florida Bureau of Geology Bulletin 31. Rev. ed. Tallahassee.

Suwannee River Water Management District. 1993. *Surface Water Quality and Biological Monitoring Network Annual Report*. WR-96-02. Live Oak, Florida. (map, 207; Nitrate plus Nitrite Concentration graph, 208)

Tanner, W.F. 1960. "Florida Coastal Classification." Transactions of the Gulf Coast Association of Geological Society 10: 259-226.

U.S. Army Corps of Engineers. Jacksonville District. 1974. *Suwannee River Floods*. Special Flood Hazard Information. Jacksonville, Florida.

U.S. Geological Survey. Water Resources Division. Tallahassee, Florida. (map, 202; graph, 203)

University of Florida. Bureau of Economic and Business Research. 1995. *Florida Statistical Abstract*. Gainesville.

Waananen, A.O., J.T. Limerinos, W.J. Kockelman, W.E. Spangle, and M.L. Blair. 1977. *Flood-Prone Areas and Land Use Planning*. U.S. Geological Survey Professional Paper 942. Washington, D. C.

White, W.L. 1970. *The Geomorphology of the Florida Peninsula*. Florida Bureau of Geology Bulletin 51. Tallahassee.

Yon, J.W., Jr. 1966. *Geology of Jefferson County, Florida*. Florida Bureau of Geology Bulletin 48. Rev. ed. Tallahassee.

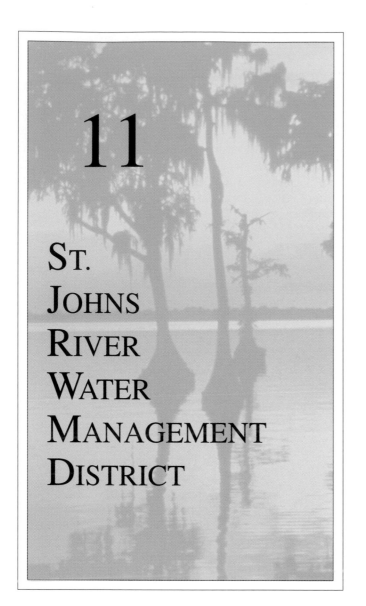

11

ST. JOHNS RIVER WATER MANAGEMENT DISTRICT

estuaries in North America (shared with the South Florida Water Management District).

This district contains the longest river in the state, over one-third of the state's lakes including the second largest, and 12 of the 20 lakes exceeding 10 square miles, one of four National Estuary Programs, and numerous springs and spring runs, most notably Silver Springs with outflow among the largest in the world. Florida's most popular tourist attraction in the late 1800s was a steamship tour up the St. Johns and Ocklawaha rivers to Silver Springs.

In the 1960s, as part of construction of the Cross-Florida Barge Canal, the lower Ocklawaha was dammed and about 20 miles of the river were flooded, creating Rodman Reservoir. Upstream portions of the Ocklawaha had been channelized earlier in the century, and marshlands along the river and lakes in the Ocklawaha chain had been drained for farming. The district has purchased large tracts of these drained marshes, stopped the pumping of polluted water from farms and reflooded the fields. The marshes are returning and with them wintering waterfowl, wading birds, and other wildlife.

Major efforts are underway to restore Lake Apopka, one of the most polluted lakes in the state and the main headwater for the Ocklawaha river and chain of lakes. Removal of excess nutrients presently in the lake is being addressed through harvest of gizzard shad and construction of a marsh filtration system on former muck farmland. Direct discharges from sewage treatment plants and citrus processing plants have stopped.

For further reduction of nutrient inputs to Lake Apopka and restoration of its wetlands, funding has been provided by the Florida legislature and the federal Wetland Reserve Program for acquisition of the remaining muck farms. To encourage the return of game fish populations, native aquatic vegetation species that were originally in the lake are being planted in the shallow water near the shoreline. The plants provide food, protection from predators, and spawning sites for fish

214   St. Johns River Water Management District is located in northeastern and east central Florida, extending south from the Georgia border to cover 12,400 square miles, almost 21 percent of the state's total area. Within its boundaries are the entire St. Johns and Nassau River basins, the Indian River Lagoon and Northern Coastal basins, and the Florida portion of the St. Marys basin. The district includes all or part of 19 counties and has a population of approximately 3.7 million, or 25 percent of the state's total.

It is a diverse region, with rural counties dominated by pine plantations in the Nassau and St. Marys river basins, major urban areas including Jacksonville and large portions of the Gainesville and Orlando metropolitan areas, and world-famous Atlantic coast beaches. It has the oldest continuously occupied European settlement in the U.S. and the first National Audubon Sanctuary; a major citrus-producing region and one of the largest cattle-producing areas in the nation; the largest stand of sand pine and one of the most biologically diverse

Linda McGrail, Kenneth Berk, Donald Brandes, Douglas Munch, Clifford Neubauer, William Osburn, Donthamsetti Rao, John Thomson, David Toth

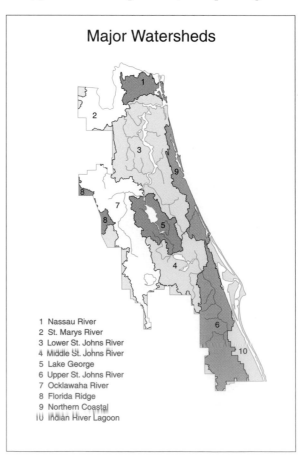

Major Watersheds

1 Nassau River
2 St. Marys River
3 Lower St. Johns River
4 Middle St. Johns River
5 Lake George
6 Upper St. Johns River
7 Ocklawaha River
8 Florida Ridge
9 Northern Coastal
10 Indian River Lagoon

and other wildlife, and their root systems help stabilize the loose sediments on the lake bottom, improving water clarity.

As in the Ocklawaha basin, the upper St. Johns River floodplain was diked and drained. One of the largest wetland restoration projects in the world is repairing the resulting environmental damage. The Upper St. Johns River Basin (USJRB) Project is a cooperative effort with U.S. Army Corps of Engineers that encompasses 235 square miles and incorporates flood control, habitat, and water quality components, restoring 150,000 acres of floodplain wetlands.

The USJRB Project also benefits the Indian River Lagoon (IRL) by reducing the amount of upper basin runoff diverted there. That runoff carries excess freshwater that changes the salinity of the lagoon, affecting animals such as oysters and clams, and delivers nutrients (nitrogen and phosphorus) that can cause the overgrowth of algae, resulting in the death of seagrasses. Protection and restoration of seagrass beds and reconnection of mangroves and marshes diked off from the lagoon for mosquito control are major IRL issues being addressed by the district.

Many restoration projects are made possible by the district's land acquisition program. Highest priority in the 1980s was given to purchase of the land needed for the upper basin project, where the most severe loss of floodplain had occurred. SJRWMD now owns property in all its major basins except Florida Ridge, most of which is in the Southwest Florida Water Management District. These lands are acquired for flood protection, water supply protection, water body preservation, restoration, and habitat protection. They provide the added benefit of public recreation, with 98 percent open to the public.

Joint purchases and management agreements with local governments and other agencies supplement funds available to the district. Less-than-fee acquisitions, or purchase of con-

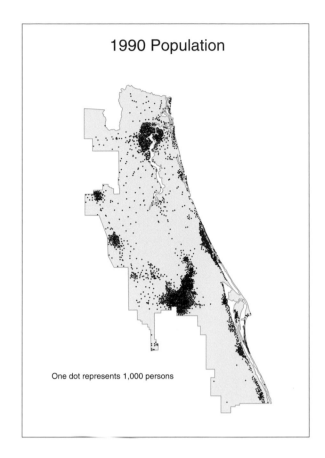

1990 Population

One dot represents 1,000 persons

servation easements, have been used to stretch those funds where the cost of the development rights is significantly less than the total purchase price of the land.

Passage of the Bluebelt Act by the 1996 Legislature recognized the importance of land owner agreements to refrain from developing significant recharge areas. The Floridan aquifer is

215

Egrets in flight at Lake Jesup Conservation Area, Seminole County

St. Johns River Water Management District

SJRWMD's main source for public supply, and the district will delineate significant recharge areas for any of its counties willing to offer reduced tax assessments in exchange for their protection, as authorized by the act. Orange County was the first county in Florida to offer this opportunity to its residents.

In some parts of the district, use of the Floridan aquifer is limited because of poor quality. High chloride content generally occurs east of the St. Johns River where intensive agricultural, industrial, and urban uses as well as abandoned free-flowing wells have reduced groundwater supplies and contributed to saltwater contamination. In those areas the surficial aquifer is tapped as a potable water source, and in some cases blended with water from the Floridan. In addition, reverse osmosis is increasingly being used to provide drinking water.

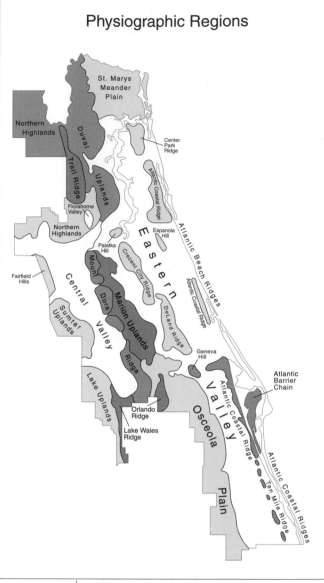

Physiographic Regions

Topography

Feet above MSL

50 100 150 200

Physiography, Topography, and Climate

The topography of SJRWMD is generally flat to gently rolling and rises to elevations slightly over 200 feet above sea level. Highest elevations and greatest relief occur in the western part of the district, in the central part of the Florida peninsula. The northern part of SJRWMD is generally flat and low near the Atlantic coast and rises inland to the Duval Uplands, Trail Ridge, and Northern Highlands. The southern two-thirds is characterized by alternating uplands and lowlands, parallel to the coast. Two types of features typify the physiography and topography of the district: marine terraces and karst.

During the Pleistocene geological period, fluctuating sea levels created marine terraces at approximately 10, 30, 100, and 150 feet above the present sea level. These terraces are relatively flat areas separated

by bluffs. They tend to parallel the current coast and are often associated with wind-built sand dunes. While the land was covered by the sea, deposits of Pleistocene alluviums, marls, and marine sediments settled over Eocene limestones and Miocene phosphatic clays. Later geological uplift of the peninsula left the terraces above sea level.

Subterranean erosion by groundwater solution of limestone also shapes the land surface in many parts of the district. Limestone is found at the ground surface or underlying shallow strata of other sediments across the entire SJRWMD area. Karst landforms such as sinkholes and basins, resulting from limestone solution, appear in many locations. Closed drainage patterns and disappearing streams are found in areas where the limestone is exposed or close to the ground surface, particularly in central Marion and southern Alachua counties. Underground streams, caverns, and springs in the region also result from limestone solution.

Average annual rainfall for SJRWMD is about 52 inches per year, varying from about 50 to 60 inches per year for different parts of the district. Rainfall for individual years, however, may deviate substantially from these averages. Annual rainfall totals for stations within the district are known to vary from less than 40 inches to more than 80 inches (NOAA 1919-94). About half of SJRWMD's annual rainfall typically falls between mid-June through mid-September (Winsberg 1990).

Summer temperatures generally reach daytime highs from 90 to 95°F throughout the district. Overnight low temperatures in the summer are usually about 70 to 75°F, with a slight tendency for warmer temperatures to the south. High temperatures rarely exceed 100°F.

Winter temperatures exhibit slightly greater spatial variation. The mean daily January high temperature varies from 68°F in the northwestern part of SJRWMD to 74°F in the southeastern part. The mean daily January low temperature varies from 42°F in the northwest to 60°F in the southeast. During most years, overnight temperatures will drop below freezing for a few nights in the northern two-thirds of the district.

Population and Land Use

Most of the region's population is found in a few counties that contain large urban concentrations, notably Duval and Orange. SJRWMD's population has grown rapidly in recent decades and is expected to continue growing at a comparable rate in the future. The total SJRWMD population increased by almost 900,000 people, or 39 percent, during the period from 1980 to 1990. The greater Orlando urban area experienced the largest part of that growth.

From 1990 to 1996 the highest percentage growth in the district was in unincorporated portions of the more rural counties. Flagler County experienced the greatest percentage increase in the state (36.1 percent). The county's unincorporated development of Palm Coast alone had a 1990 population of over 14,000. Other high-growth areas were the unincorporated portions of neighboring St. Johns County and the intersection of Marion, Lake, and Sumter counties.

The most prominent economic activities in SJRWMD are tourism, agriculture, forestry, and paper manufacturing. Tourist attractions include beaches along the Atlantic coast and commercial developments such as Silver Springs and Marineland. Amelia Island, St. Augustine, Daytona Beach, and

217

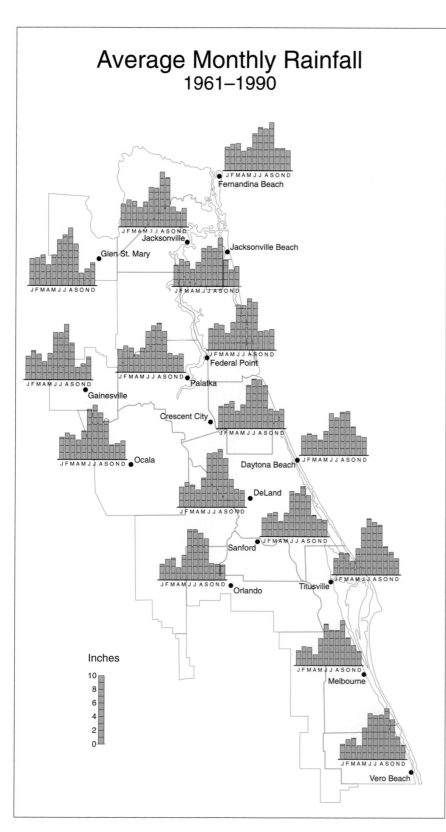

Average Monthly Rainfall
1961–1990

Kennedy Space Center are widely known tourist destinations. Aerospace and electronics firms are prominent in Brevard County near the space center.

The region's primary agricultural products are dairy and beef cattle, citrus, cabbage, potatoes, and other vegetables, and ornamental ferns. Processing of dairy products is concentrated primarily in Clay and Duval counties but is also significant in Alachua, Indian River, Lake, Marion, Orange, and Osceola counties. Production of beef cattle is spread throughout SJRWMD, with inland counties tending to be the primary production areas. Citrus is found mainly in the south. Cabbage, potatoes, and other vegetables are grown mainly in Orange, Putnam, and St. Johns counties. Ornamental ferns are important in parts of Lake, Putnam, and Volusia.

Forestry is prominent in the northern half of SJRWMD. Much of this forest is pine plantation owned by paper and lumber companies. The wood is primarily used for paper manufacturing. Approximately half of the state's paper mills are located in SJRWMD.

Water Resources

Surface Water

The St. Johns is the longest river located entirely in Florida. A slow-moving river, it drops less than 2 inches per mile in altitude from its headwaters at the south end of the district to its mouth at Mayport, east of Jacksonville. Tidal effects normally extend as far as Lake George, a distance of about 106 miles. In periods of low water, tides may cause a reverse flow as far south as Lake Monroe, 161 miles upstream from the river's mouth. The very low gradient also results in many wide, shallow lakes along much of its length, leading the Timucuans to call it "Welaka" or "river of lakes."

The 310-mile journey of the St. Johns begins in broad marshy areas of Indian River and Brevard counties, where thousands of acres of ditched, diked, and drained floodplain wetlands have been restored and water quality improved by a joint project of SJRWMD and the U.S. Army Corps of Engineers. Because it is the headwaters, this southern portion of the river's drainage area is the upper basin. This basin contains the district's two surface water sources for potable water, Lake Washington, which is used by the city of Melbourne and portions of south Brevard County, and Taylor Creek, used by the city of Cocoa.

Continuing through lakes Winder and Poinsett and into the middle basin, the St. Johns is joined by the Econlockhatchee River, its second-largest tributary, and by the spring-fed Wekiva River. Both these river systems are near Orlando, in areas of intense development pressure. To protect their natural attributes, special regulatory criteria have been adopted by SJRWMD for activities within their hydrologic basins.

North and downstream of its meeting with the Econlockhatchee, the St. Johns broadens to form lakes Harney and Monroe. Between them is Lake Jesup, connected to the river by an outlet channel that is constricted by the SR 46 bridge. A restoration effort led by the district is addressing Lake Jesup's problems of excessive nutrients, extensive muck deposits, and lack of fish habitat. Beyond Lake Monroe and the Wekiva River, the St. Johns widens into Lake George, the second largest lake in Florida.

West and northwest of the middle St. Johns and Lake George basins lies the Ocklawaha basin. Principal tributary to the St. Johns, the Ocklawaha River is fed by Silver Springs, which produces the largest spring outflow in the U.S. Surface

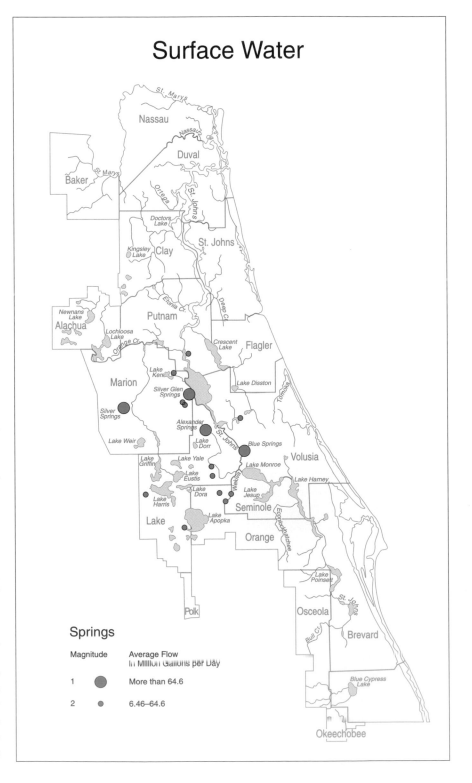

Surface Water

Springs

Magnitude	Average Flow In Million Gallons per Day
1	More than 64.6
2	6.46–64.6

waters in this basin have been heavily modified for farming, navigation, flood control, and construction of the Cross-Florida Barge Canal. The district is restoring thousands of acres of muck farms to aquatic and wetland habitat along the river and adjacent to lakes in the Ocklawaha chain and Lake Apopka. Water quality and quantity issues in Orange, Lochloosa and Newnans lakes, Paynes Prairie, and Gainesville streams that drain to Paynes Prairie or the Floridan aquifer are being addressed through a surface water management plan for the Orange Creek sub-basin.

Downstream of the barge canal the St. Johns River becomes larger, averaging two miles in width between Palatka and Jack-

sonville. Because this river flows so slowly, pollutants remain in the river an average of two months. Wastewater treatment upgrades and reuse projects, improved treatment of stormwater runoff from urban areas, implementation of agricultural best management practices, and replanting of aquatic grass beds will help to improve water quality and restore aquatic habitat.

At Jacksonville the river turns east to empty into the Atlantic. The coastal waters surrounding the mouth of the St. Johns serve as calving grounds for the right whale. Just to the north is the mouth of the Nassau River, and above it the St. Marys. The Nassau River flows eastward to form part of the boundary between Nassau and Duval counties; the St. Marys, with more

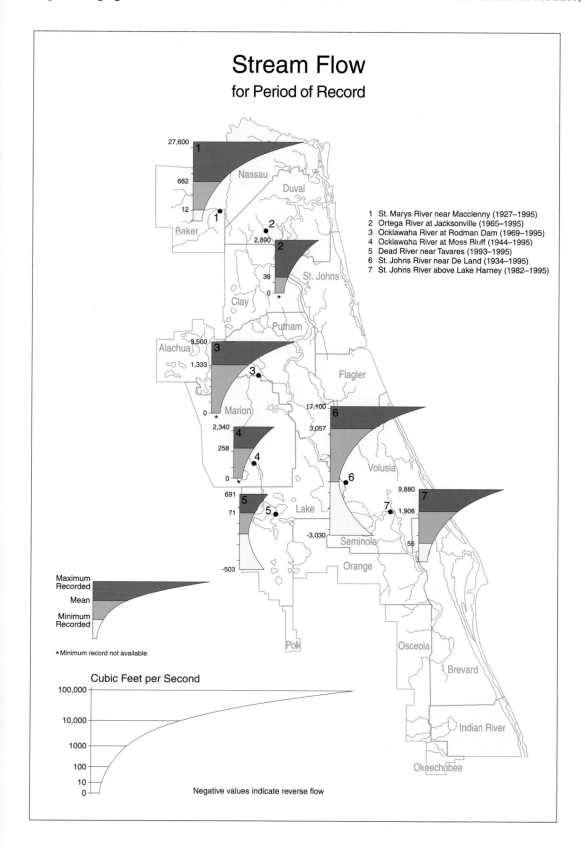

Stream Flow
for Period of Record

1 St. Marys River near Macclenny (1927–1995)
2 Ortega River at Jacksonville (1965–1995)
3 Ocklawaha River at Rodman Dam (1969–1995)
4 Ocklawaha River at Moss Bluff (1944–1995)
5 Dead River near Tavares (1993–1995)
6 St. Johns River near De Land (1934–1995)
7 St. Johns River above Lake Harney (1982–1995)

Maximum Recorded
Mean
Minimum Recorded

*Minimum record not available

Cubic Feet per Second

Negative values indicate reverse flow

219

than one-third of its drainage area in Georgia, defines the boundary between Florida and Georgia for almost the entire length of the river. An interstate committee coordinates management of the St. Marys watershed to preserve its ecological health and scenic beauty.

The Northern Coastal basins stretch from northern St. Johns County south to Ponce de Leon Inlet in Volusia County. Shellfish harvesting areas in St. Johns County have been closed because of an increase in bacteria levels. Suspected sources are septic systems and wastewater treatment facilities, stormwater runoff, and boating activities. At the southern end of the basins, Rose Bay, an estuary on the Halifax River, has been degraded by stormwater runoff, septic system leachate, and restricted water flow. Restoration activities include sediment removal, stormwater quantity and quality improvements, central sewer service, and replacement of a bridge and removal of two causeways.

The Indian River Lagoon system extends 156 miles from Ponce de Leon Inlet in Volusia County south to Jupiter Inlet in Palm Beach County in the South Florida Water Management District. With a climate ranging from temperate to sub-tropical it is one of North America's most diverse estuaries, home to several thousand plant and animal species. However, large areas of wetlands and seagrass beds, critical components of biological productivity and species diversity, have been lost.

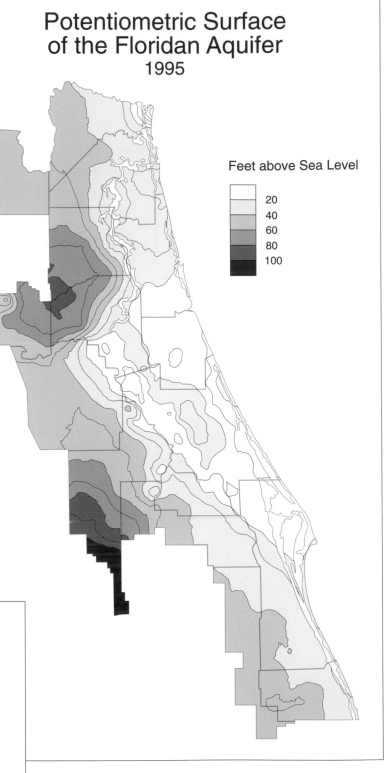

Potentiometric Surface of the Floridan Aquifer
1995

Feet above Sea Level

20
40
60
80
100

220

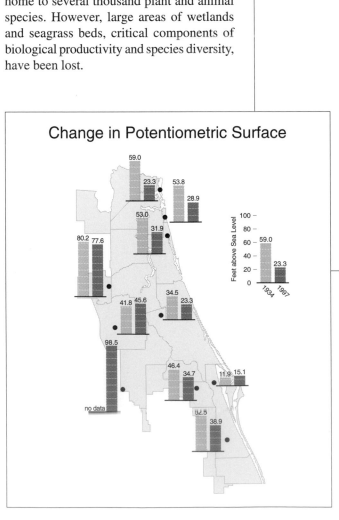

Change in Potentiometric Surface

Toward sustaining a healthy ecosystem, the district has reconnected to the Indian River Lagoon thousands of acres of wetlands formerly diked to control mosquito breeding. The Upper Basin Project is re-diverting runoff to the St. Johns River floodplain and away from the lagoon, where excess stormwater has upset salinity levels and added nutrients and sediment that foster algal growth and destroy seagrass beds. Sewage treatment plant discharge to the lagoon has been significantly reduced. Accumulated muck is being removed from tributary creeks, and projects throughout the basin are reducing sediment, improving stormwater treatment, and planting shoreline vegetation.

Groundwater

Water is drawn from three aquifers in the St. Johns River Water Management District: the surficial non-artesian or unconfined aquifer, the secondary artesian aquifer, and the Floridan aquifer. The surficial non-artesian or unconfined aquifer consists mainly of late Miocene, Pleistocene, and Recent sands and clayey sands. Permeable shell beds and limestone beds of these ages are locally significant sources of water in Alachua, western Clay, St. Johns, eastern Volusia, Seminole, Brevard, and eastern Indian River counties.

The secondary artesian aquifer in the district is part of the Hawthorn Group. Generally, these zones consist of sandy phosphatic limestone beds. Flagler and eastern Orange counties have secondary artesian aquifers capable of supplying varying quantities of potable water. In the lower portion of the Hawthorn Group, these carbonate beds, usually brown to gray sandy phosphatic dolostone, may provide water of sufficiently low salinity for withdrawal from individual wells.

The Avon Park and Ocala Formations and, in some areas, the Suwannee Limestone make up the Floridan aquifer. The confining beds are usually Miocene clay and clayey sand of the Hawthorn Group and vary in thickness from 0 to 500 feet. The base of the Floridan aquifer is considered to be within the Avon Park Formation. This formation becomes progressively less porous with depth. Generally along the coast and in the southern portion of SJRWMD, the Avon Park Formation contains saline water. The Avon Park Formation consists mainly of alternating limestone and dolomite beds with disseminated peat and carbonized plant material. The most widely used formation within the Floridan aquifer is the Ocala Limestone, which consists of an upper level of white, very pure, loose to partially lithified, foraminiferal coquina and a lower level of more lithified, white to tan, fine grained, slightly dolomitic foraminiferal limestone.

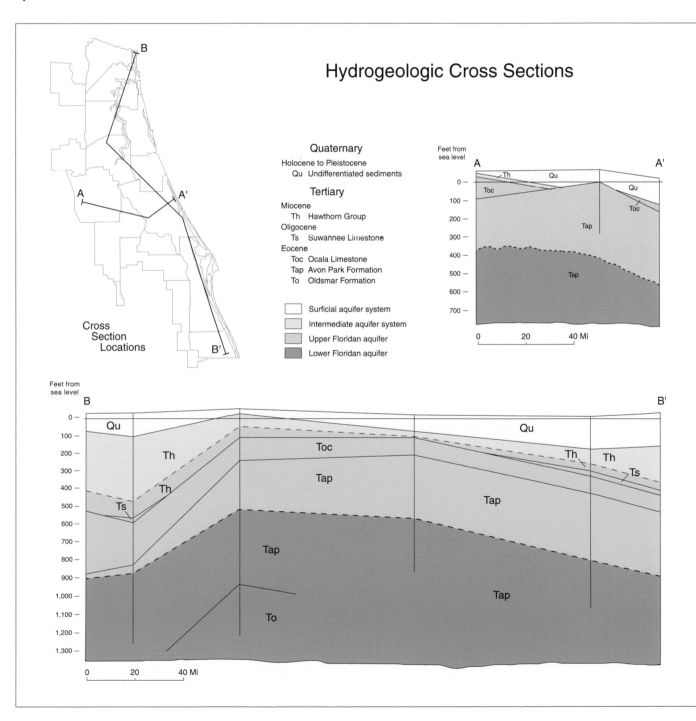

221

Water Supply and Use

The 1998 Water Supply Assessment addresses the ability of water sources to meet present and anticipated needs. This assessment is necessary because land development and population growth have resulted in rapidly increasing water use within SJRWMD. The increasing demand for water poses potential threats to water sources and creates the risk of possible water supply shortfalls.

The primary procedure used for the assessment compared projected groundwater table and potentiometric surface changes with water level thresholds for various impact criteria developed by the district. Mathematical models were used to project groundwater responses to proposed water withdrawals to the year 2020. The resultant water levels were then compared to thresholds for the impact criteria to ascertain whether significant harm would occur to water resources or associated natural systems or existing legal users as a result of the projected withdrawals. Locations where water resource problems were projected were designated Priority Water Resource Caution Areas.

The models used in the Water Supply Assessment simulate changes to groundwater flow and water quality. These models were developed on regional scales for areas that have experienced or are expected to experience significant groundwater development during the next 20 years. In addition to evaluations using these regional models, analytical techniques have been used to evaluate proposed withdrawals from several public supply wellfields that were not covered by the modeled areas or were located in areas where regional models are considered too coarse to adequately predict water level changes in the vicinity of the well fields.

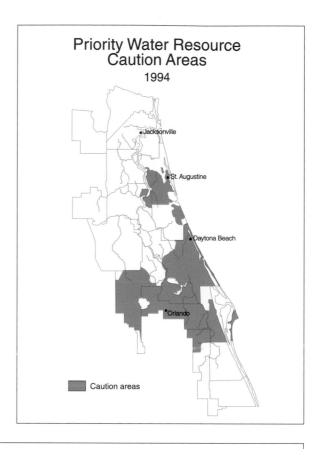

Freshwater Withdrawals (mgd) 1995

Category	Ground-water	Surface Water	Total
Public Supply	441.33	12.15	453.48
Domestic self-supplied	71.98	0.00	71.98
Agricultural self-supplied	363.58	223.39	586.97
Recreational irrigation	68.78	30.35	99.13
Commercial/Industrial self-supplied	96.03	38.13	134.16
Power generation	7.66	14.50	22.16
Total	1,049.36	318.52	1,367.88

Projected 2020 Total Freshwater Demand (mgd) for an Average and Dry Rainfall Year

Category	2020 Average Rainfall Year			2020 Dry Rainfall Year			Percent Change from 1995	
	Ground-water	Surface Water	Total	Ground-water	Surface Water	Total	2020 Average Rainfall Year	2020 Dry Rainfall Year
Public Supply	702.48	16.81	719.29	744.63	17.82	762.45	59	68
Domestic self-supplied	64.84	0.00	64.84	68.73	0.00	68.73	-10	-5
Agricultural self-supplied	368.45	220.69	589.14	430.76	267.55	698.31	0	19
Recreational irrigation	107.77	48.67	156.44	110.51	49.89	160.40	58	62
Commercial/Industrial self-supplied	102.48	44.01	146.79	102.48	44.31	146.79	9	9
Power generation	11.13	16.42	27.55	11.13	16.42	27.55	24	24
Total	1,357.15	346.90	1,704.05	1,468.24	395.99	1,864.23	25	36

Freshwater Withdrawals
1995

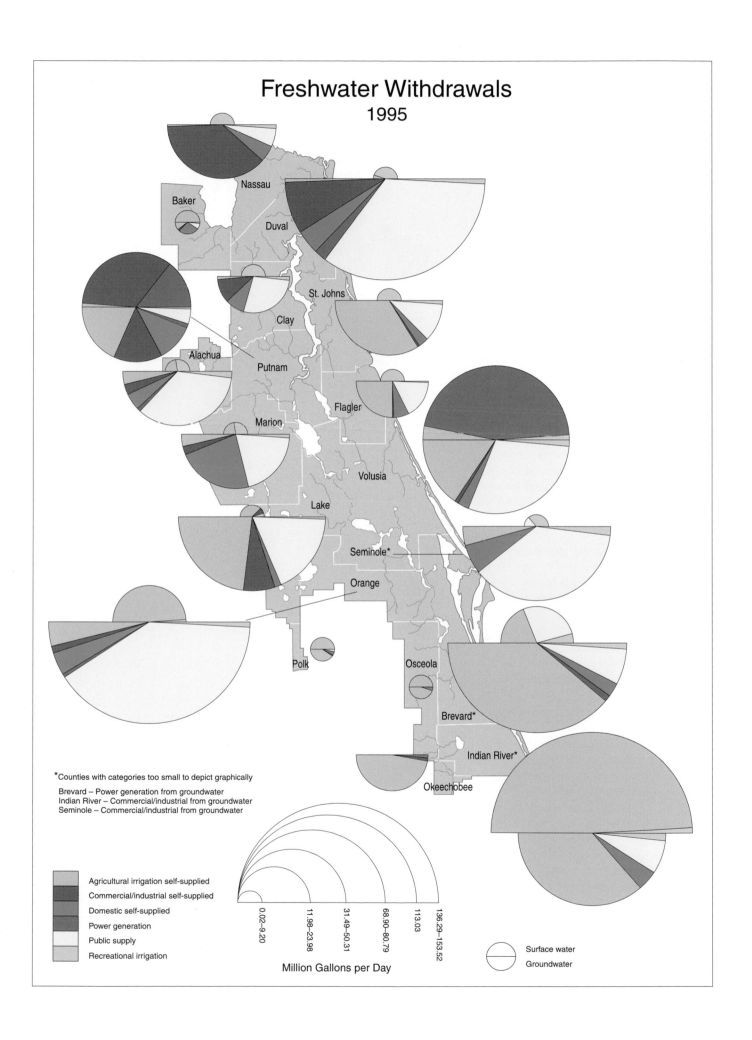

Nassau

Baker

Duval

St. Johns

Clay

Alachua

Putnam

Flagler

Marion

Volusia

Lake

Seminole*

Orange

Polk

Osceola

Brevard*

Indian River*

Okeechobee

*Counties with categories too small to depict graphically

Brevard – Power generation from groundwater
Indian River – Commercial/industrial from groundwater
Seminole – Commercial/industrial from groundwater

Agricultural irrigation self-supplied
Commercial/industrial self-supplied
Domestic self-supplied
Power generation
Public supply
Recreational irrigation

0.02–9.20
11.98–23.98
31.49–50.31
68.90–80.79
113.03
136.29–153.52

Million Gallons per Day

Surface water
Groundwater

223

Water supply is considered to be inadequate in any location where water withdrawal to meet existing or projected demand causes or is projected to cause water supply problems as defined by the following criteria:

• Impacts to natural systems— harm to native vegetation and excessive reduction in spring flows;

• Impacts to groundwater quality—unacceptable levels of saltwater intrusion and upconing;

• Impacts to existing legal users—new users affecting the supplies of existing legal users.

In addition to locations where the impact criteria are exceeded, SJRWMD defines water resource problems as occurring in public water supply service areas where a long-term supply source has not been identified.

About three-fourths of the freshwater used in SJRWMD is taken from groundwater sources. Groundwater is the most common source for uses that require higher quality water, such as public supply, domestic self-supply, and most commercial applications. Surface water sources are more commonly used where lower water quality will suffice, such as for agriculture and power generation.

Current water use is inventoried annually for several use categories to provide baseline data. Water use projections for the needs assessment were derived by several methods, depending on the type of use. Public supply and domestic self-supply projections were based on population growth. For agricultural and golf course irrigation, the Blaney-Criddle model, an agricultural water use projection model, was used. Other types of uses were projected by SJRWMD staff using numerical methods that extended current trends into the future. Additional details concerning water use projection methods are available in the SJRWMD *Water Supply Assessment 1998*.

A two-year water supply planning process was initiated by the district in the fall of 1997. Work groups were established for locations where impacts to water quality, natural systems, or existing legal users are predicted. Work groups consist of representatives of major water suppliers, local governments, environmental organizations, public interest groups, and developers. Working closely with the district, each group will develop an area plan that will be integrated into the district's regional water supply plan. Results of SJRWMD investigations of the technical, environmental, and economic feasibility of various alternative water supply strategies are provided for use in identifying sources that will assure the availability of adequate future water supplies while avoiding the projected impacts.

224

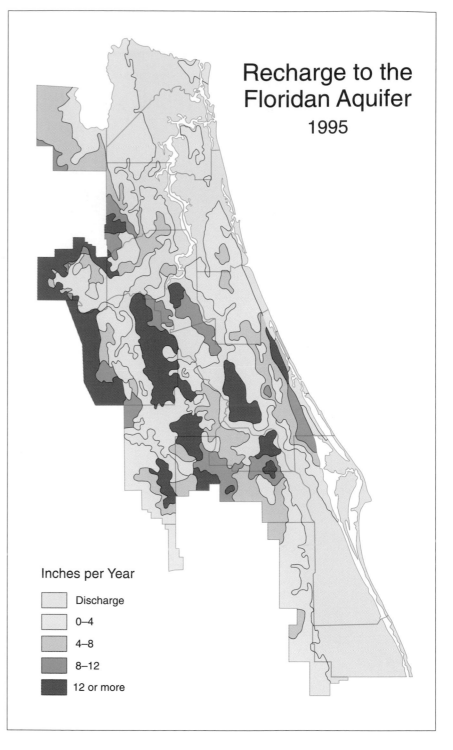

Recharge to the Floridan Aquifer
1995

Inches per Year

Discharge
0–4
4–8
8–12
12 or more

Source Protection

Source protection is accomplished through the identification and protection of aquifer recharge areas and capture zones for public supply well fields, plugging or repair of abandoned artesian wells, and protection of surface water sources.

Sixty percent of SJRWMD contributes recharge to the Floridan aquifer; discharge occurs in the remaining 40 percent (Boniol et al. 1993). Areas of high rates of recharge to the Floridan occur in the Crescent City–DeLand Ridge in Putnam and Volusia counties; the Casselberry, Oviedo, Geneva, and Chuluota Hills in Seminole County; the Mount Dora Ridge, Lake Wales Ridge, Apopka Hills, and Orlando Hills in Orange and Lake counties; the Interlachen Hills and Trail Ridge in Putnam and Clay counties; the Ocala Scrub in eastern Marion County; and those areas in central and western Alachua and Marion counties where the limestones of the Floridan aquifer are at or near land surface. In general, discharge occurs in areas along the St. Johns, Wekiva, and Ocklawaha river systems, in most of Brevard and Indian River counties, in parts of northeastern SJRWMD, and along the Atlantic coast.

Potential protection areas for public supply wells have been delineated by the district for local governments that requested this service. These capture zones indicate the distance contaminants on the land surface would travel within the aquifer to reach the well within a specified period of time, usually between two and ten years. Their size and shape is determined by the aquifer characteristics and the pumping rate of the wells. The local government can decide how large an area to protect on the basis of the amount of time it needs to respond to a contamination threat.

Possible protection measures are similar for well fields and aquifer recharge areas. Examples are public acquisition of the land, conservation easements, land use designations restricting potentially polluting activities (e.g., landfills, wastewater treatment plants), and performance standards for the design and operation of such activities (e.g., extra precautions for containment of hazardous material spills). An additional option to protect recharge areas is provided by the Bluebelt Act (193.625, F.S.). The 1996 Florida legislature authorized counties to reduce property tax assessments on significant aquifer recharge lands in exchange for owner agreement not to develop the land for a specified time. SJRWMD delineates significant recharge areas for counties that choose to adopt this program.

The district has special basin criteria for maintaining at least pre-development recharge capacity within the Wekiva River hydrologic basin and for protecting the Floridan aquifer from inadequately treated stormwater within the Sensitive Karst Areas basin. Sensitive karst areas have been designated in parts of two counties, Alachua and Marion, where the Floridan is unconfined and exists within 20 feet of land surface. The district's rule is designed to lessen the likelihood of sinkhole formation beneath stormwater treatment ponds.

Free-flowing, abandoned artesian wells waste millions of gallons of water each day. Older wells that tapped deeper portions of the aquifer where the water quality has since deteriorated can contaminate upper drinking water zones through corroded casing or seepage from the land surface. The loss of freshwater can induce saltwater intrusion.

Wells that are capped and not reported become increasingly difficult or impossible to locate and properly close. The district's current inventory of approximately 500 free-flowing wells is estimated to represent 50 to 60 percent of the actual number. SJRWMD encourages reporting of these wells by sharing the cost of plugging or reconstructing them. Some counties provide supplemental funding so there is no cost to the well owner. Special assistance for agricultural wells may also be available. The district's Abandoned Artesian Well Plugging Program has plugged or repaired more than 1,100 wells, resulting in water savings of over 250 million gallons per day.

The district has two surface water sources for potable water and may have more in the future. Protection of their water quality requires careful attention to type, density, and intensity of land use throughout their watersheds in addition to buffers and setbacks adjacent to the water bodies.

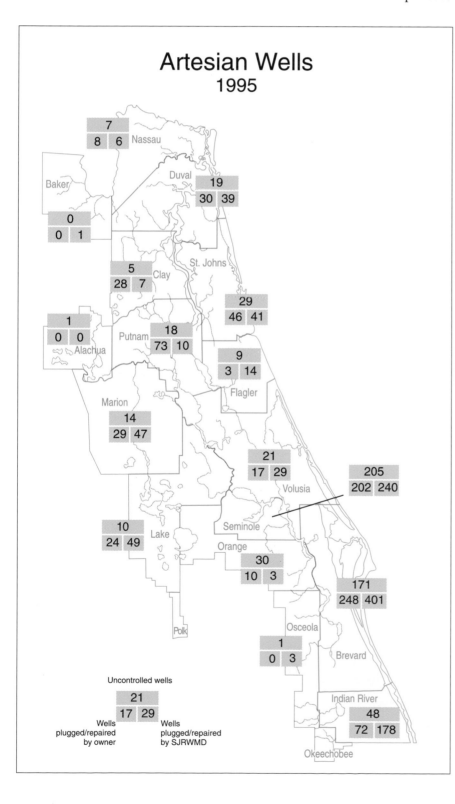

225

Flood Protection

Flooding is a natural and beneficial process that only becomes a problem when people and property are adversely affected. Floodplains provide a variety of benefits, including water storage and filtration, erosion control, natural habitat, and recreation.

The State Comprehensive Plan supports the use of natural water systems in lieu of structural approaches for flood protection. The Water Resources Implementation Rule (62-40, F.A.C.) requires agencies engaged in water management to provide both floodplain protection and flood protection. Thus, SJRWMD's goal for this area of responsibility is "to minimize the potential for damage from floods by protecting and restoring the natural water storage and conveyance functions of flood-prone areas, with preference given to the use of non-structural surface water management methods."

District regulations for new development provide for water storage and conveyance for the 25-year storm but do not prevent flooding of yards, driveways, or local streets. Prospective buyers of property in flood-prone areas should be aware of potential inconvenience from 25-year and smaller storms, and risk from larger storms and cumulative storm events.

The major source of information on flood elevation for SJRWMD is the Federal Emergency Management Agency (FEMA). Under the National Flood Insurance Act of 1968 and the Flood Disaster Protection Act of 1973, FEMA developed flood insurance rate maps (FIRM) showing areas of inundation for the 100- and 500-year floods. Accompanying reports include flood stage profiles for the 10-, 50-, 100-, and 500-year events.

For some areas more detailed studies are needed. In some cases the FEMA results are based on approximate methods; also, the information can become outdated because of development in the basin. SJRWMD conducts special floodplain studies for basins with flooding problems. Some of the intensively studied areas are the Upper and Middle St. Johns River

226

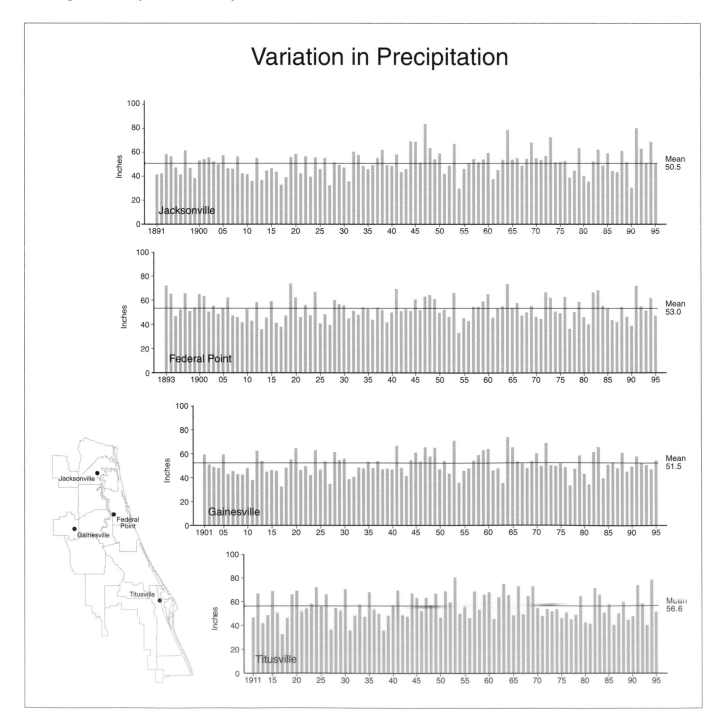

Water Control Structures
in the Upper Ocklawaha River Basin

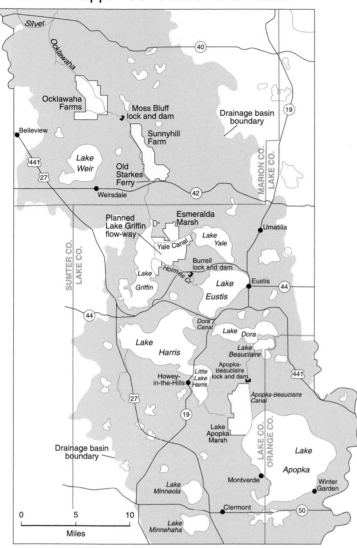

basins, the Ocklawaha River basin, and the Indian River Lagoon basin.

Results of these studies are commonly used in revising the FEMA FIRM maps. The district uses them in regulating urban development and agricultural activities and in developing floodplain management plans. Calculations of expected flood damages in the basin are used in conjunction with environmental issues and criteria to evaluate alternative flood mitigation plans. Local governments select an appropriate plan for implementation in the case of urban areas (e.g., the Little Wekiva River and Howell Creek basins in Orange and Seminole counties). In the case of larger regional problem areas, SJRWMD takes the responsibility of implementing a management plan (e.g., the Upper St. Johns and Ocklawaha River basins).

In November 1994 east central Florida suffered widespread flooding as Tropical Storm Gordon churned through the area dumping up to 10 inches of rain (Garver et al. 1996). Saturated soil conditions at the time of this early winter storm produced severe runoff, flooding several homes and business communities in Volusia, Brevard, and Indian River counties. Winter rains also caused severe flooding of Paynes Prairie and Kanapaha Prairie in Alachua County in 1997-98.

Although the district emphasizes nonstructural flood management, some structures were inherited and must be maintained, and others are built as a necessary part of restoration projects. Water control structures are operated by drainage districts, counties, cities, and private concerns as well as the water management district. SJRWMD structures are primarily in the Upper St. Johns River and the Ocklawaha River basins. The goal of their operation is to minimize flooding while meeting basin-specific environmental criteria. Water is discharged according to pre-established regulation schedules. Special flow releases are also made in anticipation of major storm events, as occurred when these structures were successfully operated to minimize the impacts of Tropical Storm Gordon.

227

St. Johns River Water Management District

St. Augustine Flood, September 1995

Water Quality

Surface Water

SJRWMD maintains districtwide surface water quality and sediment monitoring networks. Water quality is assessed using the district's own sampling networks and data acquired by other agencies. Assessments are directed toward establishing background conditions, determining trends over time, and identifying areas of poor or impacted water quality.

Water quality has been improving in the Upper St. Johns River basin (USJRB). Cattle and citrus are the primary land uses in the basin. Nutrient loads to the river have been reduced through the implementation of best management practices by farms and the restoration of large tracts of formerly drained agricultural lands. The completion of the Army Corps of Engineers/SJRWMD flood control project with its associated environmental goals in the southern portion of the basin should further improve water quality throughout the area. Nevertheless, naturally occurring, low concentrations of dissolved oxygen in some areas may occasionally cause fish kills. Exotic aquatic weeds also pose a problem in several of the river lakes, requiring expensive control measures.

The Indian River Lagoon (IRL) system, consisting of the Mosquito, Banana River, and Indian River lagoons, receives inputs of saltwater from the ocean through inlets, and freshwater from direct precipitation, groundwater seepage, surface runoff, and discharges from tributary streams and drainage canals. Healthy seagrass beds, which are important for biological productivity and diversity, are found where water quality and water clarity are good.

Factors affecting water quality in various portions of this system are urbanization, agriculture, historical wastewater treatment plant discharges, proximity to inlets, and flows from canals draining the upper basin floodplain. The C-1 rediversion project will eliminate much of the polluted freshwater discharge from the upper basin. Wastewater treatment plant discharges have been substantially reduced.

In Mosquito Lagoon and the northern portion of the Banana River Lagoon near the Kennedy Space Center, good water quality is attributable to the absence of intense development or agriculture. However, south of Cape Canaveral the land is highly urbanized, and water quality and seagrass coverages are lower.

North of Titusville, in the Indian River lagoon proper, development is very limited and water quality is good to excellent. Between Titusville and Cocoa, the somewhat poor water quality along the developed western side is due to urban runoff and, perhaps, the lingering effects of a long history of wastewater discharges.

In the Melbourne area, water quality is fair except for the immediate vicinities of Turkey Creek, Crane Creek, and Eau Gallie River. More than 80 percent of seagrass acreage has been lost in this area over the last 50 years. These tributaries discharge large amounts of urban runoff, interbasin flows, and huge amounts of soil and muck sediments to the IRL. Water quality improves further south in the vicinity of Sebastian Inlet because of oceanic flushing.

In the south segment of the IRL (Sebastian to Vero Beach), large inflows

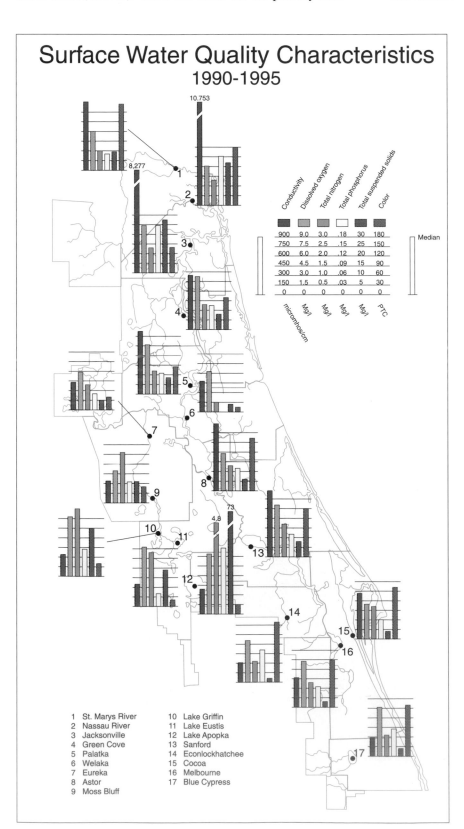

Surface Water Quality Characteristics
1990-1995

Conductivity	Dissolved oxygen	Total nitrogen	Total phosphorus	Total suspended solids	Color
900	9.0	3.0	.18	30	180
750	7.5	2.5	.15	25	150
600	6.0	2.0	.12	20	120
450	4.5	1.5	.09	15	90
300	3.0	1.0	.06	10	60
150	1.5	0.5	.03	5	30
0	0	0	0	0	0
micromhos/cm	Mg/l	Mg/l	Mg/l	Mg/l	PTC

Median

1 St. Marys River	10 Lake Griffin
2 Nassau River	11 Lake Eustis
3 Jacksonville	12 Lake Apopka
4 Green Cove	13 Sanford
5 Palatka	14 Econlockhatchee
6 Welaka	15 Cocoa
7 Eureka	16 Melbourne
8 Astor	17 Blue Cypress
9 Moss Bluff	

of phosphorus from urban and agricultural land appear to be linked to a trend toward increasing phytoplankton levels. These microscopic, one-celled plant organisms in high concentrations block light that is needed for seagrass growth.

Water quality in the Econlockhatchee River, which flows into the St. Johns just south of Lake Harney, has improved with the operation of a wetland treatment facility that now receives effluent from Orlando's Iron Bridge sewage treatment plant, removing that discharge from the river. Lake Jesup, a few miles downstream of Lake Harney, is one of the most polluted lakes directly connected to the St. Johns River. The lake receives urban runoff from Orlando, Winter Park, Casselberry, and Maitland, as well as agricultural runoff from adjacent farms. Restoration efforts by SJRWMD are ongoing for this lake.

The Ocklawaha chain of lakes, stretching from Lake Apopka downstream to Lake Weir, generally has severely degraded water quality. Nutrient runoff from rapid urbanization and intensive agricultural development has dramatically increased productivity of the lakes and Ocklawaha River. Stabilization of water levels by the operation of water control structures may have augmented the accumulation of nutrients and sediments. Lakes Yale and Weir, with no major tributaries, are exceptions exhibiting good water quality.

Cleanup of Lake Apopka will benefit the downstream lakes. Pilot operation is underway for a marsh flow-way for Lake Griffin similar to the filtration system being constructed for Apopka. Agricultural runoff is being curtailed with district acquisition of thousands of acres of muck farms in the basin.

The Orange Creek sub-basin of the Ocklawaha River basin includes Newnans, Lochloosa, and Orange lakes and Orange Creek. Orange and Lochloosa have fair water quality and healthy fish and wildlife populations. Newnans is a very shallow, hypereutrophic, algal-dominated lake that has been targeted for restoration. The causes for its condition are being evaluated. Orange Creek has high quality water. Paynes Prairie State Preserve, a wet prairie that is a major feature of this sub-basin, receives urban runoff from both Sweetwater Branch

St. Johns River Water Management District

Great blue heron, Sunnyhill Wetlands, restoration site in the Upper Ocklawaha River basin

and Tumbling Creek, and wastewater treatment plant effluent from Sweetwater Branch. A study is in progress to determine the cause of the spread of woody vegetation over a part of the prairie.

The lower St. Johns River has three distinct "ecozones" based on patterns of water residence time and salinity. From Palatka to the Duval County line the river is predominantly fresh, with a wide channel and low-velocity, lake-like conditions that are conducive to the growth of free-floating algae. From the Duval County line to the Fuller Warren Bridge in Jacksonville, mixing with marine waters produces a mildly salty zone. The river here is at its widest and slightly deeper than upstream. Light penetration is at a minimum because of both natural conditions and algal blooms. From the Fuller Warren Bridge to the river's mouth the channel is relatively narrow, deep, and characterized by fast tidal currents and increasing salinity.

Major pollution sources for the lower St. Johns are runoff from the vegetable-producing area in the southeast portion of the basin, responsible primarily for nutrients and suspended solids, sewage treatment and industrial effluents, responsible primarily for nutrients but in some instances color and biochemical oxygen demand, and urban runoff carrying toxic metals and organic chemicals. The latter two sources are concentrated in the northern portion of the basin.

Water quality in the Northern Coastal basins is generally fair to good with more stressed conditions occurring around some of the heavily urbanized areas in St. Augustine and Daytona Beach. Impact from urban areas is somewhat mitigated by the three ocean connections at the St. Augustine, Matanzas and Ponce de Leon inlets. Major local initiatives to reduce or eliminate sewage effluent discharges into the Halifax River have corresponded with an improvement in water quality in that river, while actively developing watersheds for upper Spruce Creek and the Tolomato River have shown a gradual decline in water quality.

At the northern end of the district, shellfish beds have been closed in the estuary and tidal lagoon area of the Nassau River. Monitoring station data indicate elevated levels of phosphorus in Alligator Creek, a tributary to Mills Creek that flows into the Nassau River. The City of Callahan has upgraded its wastewater treatment plant, which discharges into Alligator Creek, to provide a higher level of treatment. Within the St. Marys River basin, high levels of ammonia have been found in the Amelia River.

Groundwater

The upper part of the Floridan aquifer is the primary source of water for public supply water use in the district. This aquifer is a source of water for public supply in the northern and central portions of the district where the aquifer contains water that generally meets primary and secondary drinking water standards. This aquifer is also a source of water for public supply in the southern portion of the district where water withdrawn from it is treated by reverse osmosis. Portions of the Lower Floridan aquifer are also tapped as a source of water for public supply in Duval, central and western Orange, and southern and southwestern Seminole counties. The Floridan aquifer system in the southern portion of the district, where the aquifer generally contains water that exceeds secondary drinking water standards for chloride, sulfate, and total dissolved solids, is widely used as a source of irrigation water.

Water quality in the upper part of the Floridan aquifer varies depending on its location in the district. Water quality in this aquifer is generally good in the northern and western portions of the district where chloride, sulfate, and TDS concentrations are below the secondary drinking water standard of 250, 250, and 500 mg/l respectively. Chloride and TDS concentrations in the upper part of the Floridan aquifer generally exceed the secondary drinking water standards throughout most of Brevard and Indian River counties, in southern St. Johns and most of Flagler counties, in areas bordering the St. Johns River south of Clay County (i.e., in parts of Putnam, Marion, Lake, Volusia, Seminole, Orange, and Osceola counties), and in eastern Volusia County. Sulfate concentrations also exceed the secondary drinking water standards in many of these areas.

Water quality in the lower part of the Floridan aquifer also varies depending on its location in the district. Water quality in this aquifer is generally good in the northern and western portions of the district where chloride and TDS concentrations are below the secondary drinking water standards. Chloride concentrations in the lower part of the Floridan aquifer generally exceed the secondary drinking water standards throughout all of Flagler, Brevard, and Indian River counties, in eastern Nassau and Volusia counties, and in areas bordering the St. Johns River in Putnam, Marion, Lake, Volusia, Seminole, Orange, and Osceola counties (Sprinkle 1989). TDS concentrations in the lower part of the Floridan aquifer generally exceed the secondary drinking water standards throughout all of St. Johns, Flagler, Brevard, and Indian River counties, in most of Nassau and Duval counties, in eastern Clay and Volusia counties, and in areas bordering the St. Johns River in Putnam, Marion, Lake, Volusia, Seminole, Orange and Osceola counties (Sprinkle 1989).

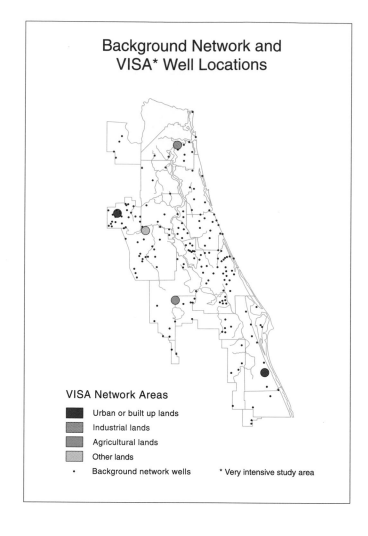

Background Network and VISA* Well Locations

VISA Network Areas

- Urban or built up lands
- Industrial lands
- Agricultural lands
- Other lands
- Background network wells
- * Very intensive study area

230

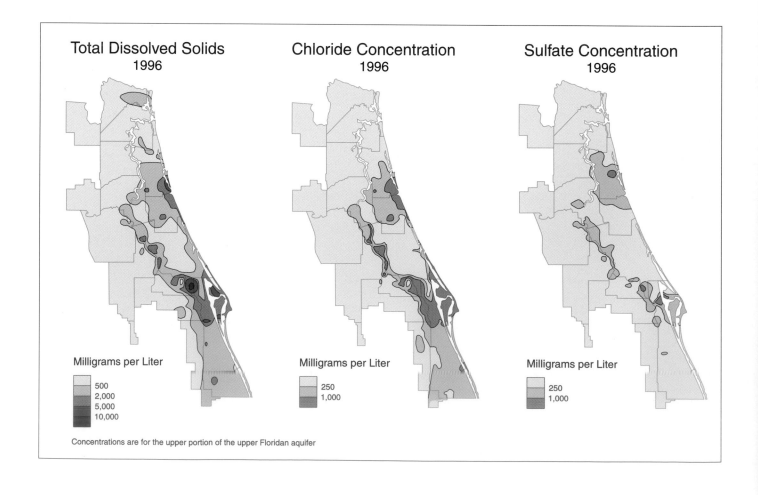

Total Dissolved Solids
1996

Milligrams per Liter

500
2,000
5,000
10,000

Chloride Concentration
1996

Milligrams per Liter

250
1,000

Sulfate Concentration
1996

Milligrams per Liter

250
1,000

Concentrations are for the upper portion of the upper Floridan aquifer

SJRWMD maintains a permanent observation well network and carries out additional monitoring programs in cooperation with DEP. Besides the background network wells shown on the map, the district samples approximately 160 wells quarterly and anticipates increasing that number. USGS collects long-term data that supplement the district's data base. The DEP program has two major components: (1) The Background Network monitors representative areas to establish baseline conditions and detect changes. (2) The Very Intensive Study Area (VISA) Network monitors areas thought to be highly susceptible to contamination to try to ascertain the effects of different types of land use on groundwater quality.

Natural Systems

Within the St. Johns region is some of the state's most significant wildlife habitat, including freshwater marshes, forested wetlands, mesic pinelands, and dry prairies (Cox et al. 1994). Patches of sand pine scrub, sand hill, and oak scrub are still found around Deltona, and the largest natural stand of sand pines in the world is found in the Ocala National Forest in Marion County (Grow 1981). Tosohatchee State Reserve, 25 miles east of Orlando, contains 200 acres of virgin cypress, a remnant of once rich stands. John James Audubon came to paint birds in what is now Tomoka State Park, one of the finest coastal hammocks in Florida.

Several large forested areas support rare, wide-ranging species such as Florida black bear, bobcat, wild turkey, and American swallow-tailed kite. Merritt Island National Wildlife Refuge (part of the Indian River Lagoon system) is one of the richest wildlife areas in Florida and home to more endangered and threatened species than any other refuge outside of Hawaii (Grow 1981), including bald eagles, wood storks, and giant sea turtles.

Xeric uplands in Clay County support the Florida scrub jay and red-cockaded woodpecker. Anastasia Island in St. Johns County is home to the endangered Anastasia Island beach mouse. Found in coastal areas of Volusia County are the Atlantic salt marsh snake and winter concentrations of piping plover and other shorebirds. West of Blue Cypress Lake are found Audubon's crested caracara and wood stork.

Just south of Gainesville is Paynes Prairie State Preserve, formerly a lake that drained in 1823, 1870, and 1892. From approximately 1870 to 1892 boats operated on the lake, including a ferry and a steamboat that carried oranges, vegetables and passengers to the railroad that ran from Jacksonville to Cedar Key (Lauter 1950). Now a wet prairie, it provides home to nesting sandhill cranes and a population of round-tailed muskrats among many other species.

Bird Island, a combination of floating marsh and shrub swamp in Orange Lake, is the oldest National Audubon Sanctuary in the world. Floating wetlands in the lake provide very productive habitat for many species of reptiles, amphibians, and birds.

Blue Spring on the St. Johns River is a winter congregation area for the endangered West Indian manatee. Numerous springs feed the surface waters in the central part of the district, including the largely undeveloped Wekiva River. Florida black bears move between the public lands of the Wekiva sub-basin and the Ocala National Forest, and disperse through forested areas north of Crescent Lake to St. Johns, Flagler, and Volusia counties. Protecting habitat for the district's bear populations will have multiple natural system benefits.

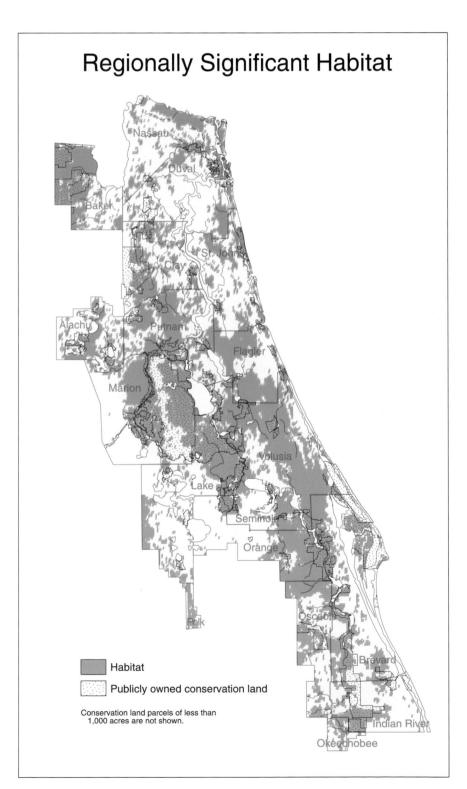

231

Ecosystem Protection

The district's goal for natural systems is to maintain native biological diversity and productivity by protecting ecosystems and restoring altered systems to a naturally functional condition. Maintaining and restoring ecological communities helps to preserve native plants and wildlife and also safeguards water supply sources, floodplain functions, surface water quality, and groundwater quality. Ecosystem protection at the district integrates surface water, groundwater, and natural systems on a watershed basis. Management of these resources is implemented through numerous programs, including land acquisition, restoration, research, regulation, and technical assistance.

SJRWMD has identified regionally significant habitat by combining the results of the Florida Game and Fresh Water Fish Commission's statewide habitat assessment (Cox et al. 1994) with the district's land use/land cover data base. Riparian habitat zones are designated in rules adopted by the district for the Wekiva and Econlockhatchee river basins (Chapter 40C-41, F.A.C.). These rules provide a standard for the avoidance of adverse impacts to aquatic and wetland-dependent species within the habitat protection zones.

The Wekiva River basin and the Lower St. Johns River basin were pilot project areas for the Department of Environmental Protection's (DEP) ecosystem management initiative. Ecosystem management areas identified by DEP within SJRWMD are the Upper St. Johns River basin, Indian River Lagoon, Ocklawaha River basin, Lower St. Johns River basin, Northeast Coast lagoons, and St. Marys/Nassau River basins.

SJRWMD's land acquisition and restoration programs, described in following sections, are designed to protect and enhance a wide range of ecosystem functions. Local governments also have the ability to protect whole systems through their authority to designate land use. Land use patterns have a profound impact on the health of water resources. The district's technical assistance to local governments program is designed to integrate land use and water resource planning by providing data, reports, maps, and staff expertise to local planners for determining land uses compatible with ecosystem protection.

Minimum Flows and Levels

Lakes, streams, and rivers and their associated wetlands are dynamic ecosystems that are dependent upon fluctuating water levels or flows. Minimum Flows and Levels (MF&L) is a legislatively mandated project (373.042, F.S.) designed to prevent

significant harm to the water resources or ecology of surface waters (streams, rivers, ponds, lakes, and springs) and groundwater aquifers of Florida.

SJRWMD staff have developed a multiple MF&L approach that defines three or five minimum flows or levels that protect different parts of the system. Each minimum level or flow is composed of an elevation in feet NGVD or a flow in cubic feet per second, and a temporal component. The temporal component specifies how long and how often a designated level or flow can or must occur without causing significant harm, and may be expressed as a duration and a return interval or as one

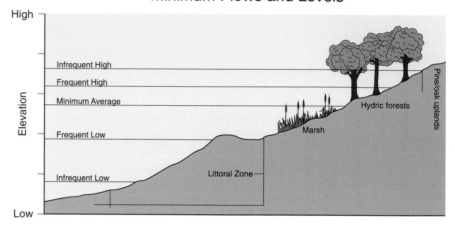

Minimum Flows and Levels

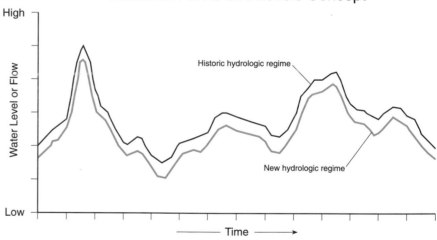

Minimum Flows and Levels Concept

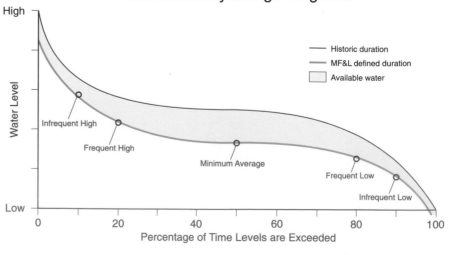

Comparison of Historic and Minimum Flows and Levels Hydrologic Regimes

of the following hydroperiod categories: Intermittently Flooded, Temporarily Flooded, Seasonally Flooded, Typically Saturated, Semipermanently Flooded, Intermittently Exposed, and Permanently Flooded.

MF&Ls describe a hydrologic regime that is less than the historic or optimal one but allows for prudent water use while protecting critical ecosystem structure and functions. MF&L durations and return intervals may be graphed as the percentage of time each given flow or level is exceeded. The historic flows or levels are analyzed and plotted in the same manner. The upper curve then shows percentage of time that the lake or stream is above each corresponding historic level or flow; the lower curve, which is defined by the MF&Ls, shows the hydrologic regime needed to avoid significant harm. The difference between the two curves defines the amount of water that can be withdrawn without causing significant harm.

Minimum flows and levels are used to declare water shortages, to issue consumptive use permits and management and storage of surface water permits, to manage water levels of restored wetlands and floodplains, to construct and operate water resource projects, and to assess potential water supply sources. Surface water and groundwater computer simulation models will be used to evaluate the potential impacts from existing and new consumptive uses, providing a cumulative approach. New water uses that would cause a minimum level or flow to be violated should not be permitted. In addition, existing uses that cause such a violation can be modified upon permit renewal. Long-term hydrologic and biologic data collection and monitoring will be done to ensure that modeled predictions reflect actual conditions.

The district plans to determine MF&Ls for at least 20 systems each year, including one or two large systems (e.g., Wekiva river system, Lake Washington, or the St. Johns River downstream from Lake Washington), and 18 to 19 lakes at the rate of one every three weeks.

Land Acquisition

As of May 1998, the St. Johns River Water Management District held some form of interest in approximately 450,000 acres of land. Much of that land is jointly managed through cooperative agreements with other agencies. Increasingly the district is involved in less-than-fee acquisitions, also known as purchase of development rights or conservation easements. In those cases the property title remains in the name of the private owner and public access may or may not be part of the agreement.

The first land acquisitions in the district were associated with restoration of

the historic floodplain of the upper St. Johns River. As the acquisition phase of that 200,000-acre project has approached completion, the district has been able to focus attention towards significant purchases in the nine other major surface water drainage basins within the 19-county district.

Acquisition for major restoration projects in the Ocklawaha River basin has occurred at Lake Apopka, Emeralda Marsh, Sunnyhill Farm, and Ocklawaha Prairie. As in the Upper St. Johns River basin, much of the historic floodplain and wetlands along the Ocklawaha River and chain of lakes had been converted to agricultural use. The Ocklawaha River basin presently contains about 42,000 acres of fee simple district ownership and 17,000 acres of a less-than-fee conservation easement over commercial forest lands connecting Paynes Prairie

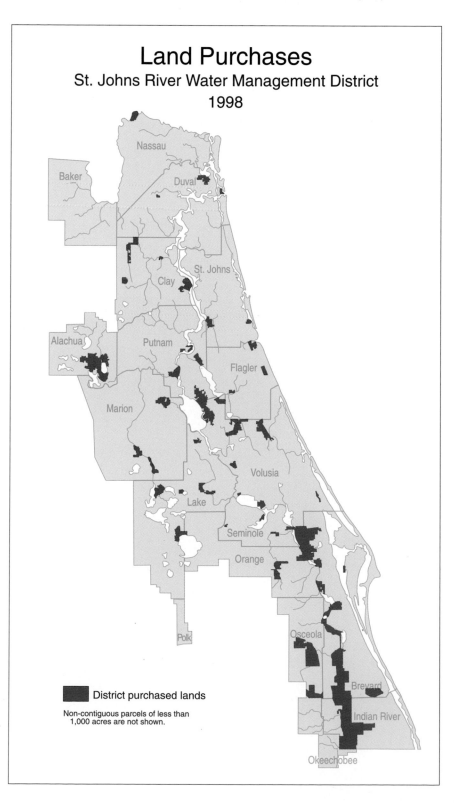

Land Purchases
St. Johns River Water Management District
1998

District purchased lands

Non-contiguous parcels of less than 1,000 acres are not shown.

233

Major Surface Water Programs

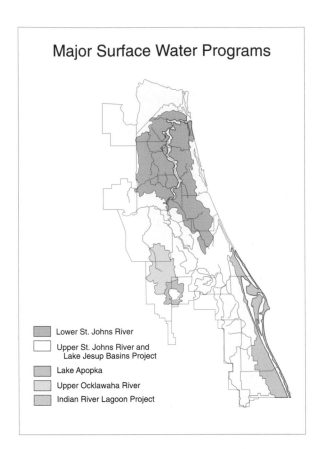

- ◼ Lower St. Johns River
- ☐ Upper St. Johns River and Lake Jesup Basins Project
- ▦ Lake Apopka
- ☐ Upper Ocklawaha River
- ▨ Indian River Lagoon Project

State Preserve with the district's 10,333-acre Lake Lochloosa property in Alachua County.

The Middle St. Johns River basin spans part of the Orlando urban area as well as some unique natural areas. Within an hour's drive of Orlando the district has acquired a total of over 35,000 acres along the Econlockhatchee River, Wekiva River, Lake Jesup, Lake Monroe, and the St. Johns River.

The Lake George basin contains approximately 34,000 acres of district land. A large portion of this land was purchased with Volusia County as part of the Lake George CARL Project on the lake's eastern shore.

Close to 56,000 acres have been acquired in the Lower St. Johns River basin, which stretches from Volusia County to northern Duval County. Opportunities for maintaining large natural corridors or regional ecological linkages still exist within the lower basin. Major projects include Haw Creek, Dunns Creek, Deep Creek, Caravelle Ranch, Bayard Point, Jennings State Forest, and Pumpkin Hill Creek. Less-than-fee acquisitions are pending with more planned for the future.

The Nassau River basin shares the Pumpkin Hill Creek CARL Project with the Lower St. Johns River basin. The 3,800 acres that have been acquired form a Buffer Preserve for the adjacent Nassau River–St. Johns River Aquatic Preserve and the federal Timucuan Ecological and Historic Preserve. State

234

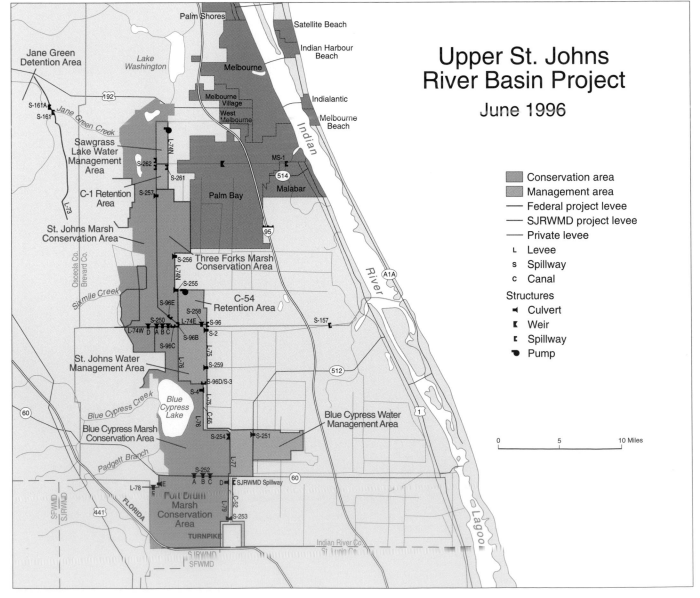

Upper St. Johns River Basin Project
June 1996

- ◼ Conservation area
- ▨ Management area
- — Federal project levee
- — SJRWMD project levee
- — Private levee
- ʟ Levee
- s Spillway
- c Canal

Structures
- ◄ Culvert
- ĸ Weir
- ɛ Spillway
- ● Pump

0   5   10 Miles

acquisition efforts on Fort George Island and the Talbot Islands have received assistance from the district. The upper reaches of the relatively undisturbed Nassau River are under study for future public purchase.

Florida shares the St. Marys River basin with the state of Georgia. The district has purchased 3,638 acres along the St. Marys River adjacent to the Nassau County boat ramp east of U.S. 1 on the state line. Less-than-fee arrangements with some of the large property owners in the basin are under consideration.

SJRWMD encompasses two coastal basins. The Indian River Lagoon basin contains almost 12,000 acres of district-acquired land. Much of that land is in the Sebastian Creek CARL Project, a joint effort of the district and the state that will protect 22,000 acres when completed. Another CARL project called the IRL Blueway is co-sponsored by SJRWMD, SFWMD, the five IRL counties, and The Nature Conservancy to acquire the remaining impounded wetlands and natural shoreline areas along the lagoon.

The Northern Coastal basins have seen close to 10,000 acres of district acquisition in recent years. Pellicer Creek and Moses Creek, key tributaries of the highly productive Matanzas River estuary, have been protected.

Restoration Projects

Major restoration activities in the upper basin of the St. Johns River and in the four Surface Water Improvement and Management (SWIM) areas (Lower St. Johns River basin, Lake Apopka, Indian River Lagoon, and Upper Ocklawaha River basin) are described below. Additional restoration efforts are ongoing for the Orange Creek sub-basin, the Northern coastal basins, and Lake Jesup.

A major flood control and wetland restoration effort is nearing completion in the headwaters area of the St. Johns River. The Upper St. Johns River Basin Project stretches for 85 miles through Indian River and Brevard counties. In the early 1900s, thousands of floodplain acres were diked and drained for agricultural use. After a series of floods in the 1940s Congress authorized a flood control project, and dikes and canals were built to funnel water to the Indian River Lagoon. Environmental concerns stopped construction in the early 1970s.

In 1977 SJRWMD took over local sponsorship and developed a new plan that will achieve the flood control objectives while also providing significant environmental benefits. Under the current design, the marsh areas that remain in the basin become marsh conservation areas where flood waters are held for gradual release to the river. These areas have been enlarged through district

purchase and restoration of drained farmlands. Polluted agricultural discharge is diverted into water management areas for reuse by farmers.

Flood protection is provided to the land in private ownership by a system of levees. Environmental benefits include decreased stormwater discharge to the lagoon, improved water quality, and restoration and enhancement of 150,000 acres of wetlands. Furthermore, recreational opportunities are provided in the restored and preserved wetlands.

In 1987, the SWIM Act declared that a number of Florida water bodies were seriously degraded and in need of restoration and management to ensure the protection of their natural systems. Of the six water bodies originally addressed in the act, three are in the St. Johns River Water Management Dis-

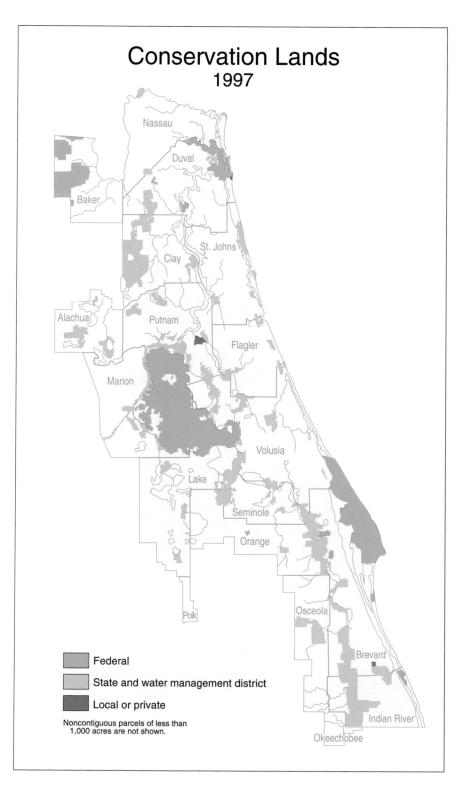

Conservation Lands
1997

Nassau
Duval
Baker
St. Johns
Clay
Alachua
Putnam
Flagler
Marion
Volusia
Lake
Seminole
Orange
Polk
Osceola
Brevard
Indian River
Okeechobee

Federal

State and water management district

Local or private

Noncontiguous parcels of less than 1,000 acres are not shown.

trict: the Indian River Lagoon, Lake Apopka, and the Lower St. Johns River basin. The district added its own fourth SWIM area, the Upper Ocklawaha River basin.

The restoration component of the SWIM plan for the Indian River Lagoon focuses on wetland and seagrass habitat restoration and management. The lagoon's salt marshes and mangrove swamps naturally provide food and protection for fish and other aquatic animals. However, most of those wetlands were isolated from the lagoon and vegetation was killed by diking and flooding to prevent mosquitos from laying eggs in the mud. It is now known that only a few inches of water during the summer are needed to control mosquito breeding. The district has reconnected over 18,000 acres of impounded wetlands while maintaining effective mosquito control.

Additionally, a mangrove planting program is underway in the southern portion of the lagoon. Seagrass beds have been mapped every 2 to 3 years since 1986 (pre-SWIM), to identify healthy and stressed areas. Linkage between seagrass distribution and water quality is being analyzed. In 1995, the Legislature approved issuance of the Indian River Lagoon license plate to raise money for protection and restoration efforts.

St. Johns River Water Management District

Slough and cypress head in Upper St. Johns River Basin, April 1995

Lake Apopka has a 100-year history of alteration by human activity. The fundamental changes began with construction of the Apopka-Beauclair Canal in 1888, which lowered the level of the lake and changed its drainage path. Subsequent population growth resulted in the introduction of raw and primarily treated sewage to the lake after the turn of the century. In 1941 a levee was built along the north shore to drain about 20,000 acres of shallow lake bottom for farming. The discharge of nutrient laden waters from those farms provided the conditions that created an algal bloom in 1947 that persists to this day. Because of those alterations, the lake lost its recreational value along with its game fish populations.

Restoration efforts include muck farm acquisition and restoration to reduce the amount of phosphorus entering the lake, wetland filtration and harvest of gizzard shad for nutrient removal from the lake, and planting of littoral zone vegetation for encouragement of game fish populations.

Wetland filtration was initiated with a 530-acre experimental marsh treatment system, which has tested engineering design and operation methods for a 3,500-acre marsh flow-way to filter and clean the lake water. This marsh flow-way will be located on former muck farms purchased by the district. Prior to conversion to farming, this land was part of a marsh habitat on the north shore of the lake. The Florida legislature appropriated a total of $65 million for acquisition of the remaining muck farms and an additional grant of $26 million has been awarded from the federal Wetland Reserve Program.

Algal blooms, fish lesions and fish kills, and declining aquatic plant beds are indicators of water quality problems in the Lower St. Johns River basin. Algal blooms lower the levels of dissolved oxygen, block sunlight from reaching the submerged vegetation that provides shelter and food for fish and manatees, and can produce toxins. Studies will investigate possible connections between the algal blooms and problems affecting fish in the river.

Algae growth is fed by excessive nutrients from sewage treatment plant and industrial wastewater discharges and from urban and agricultural runoff. Planned or ongoing actions to reduce nutrient input include wastewater treatment plant upgrades, wastewater reuse projects, construction of stormwater treatment facilities, and implementation of best management practices for row crops and dairy farms. The 1998 legislature appropriated $10.5 million for river restoration projects that complement and expand the efforts of the district's SWIM program.

The Upper Ocklawaha River basin has been modified extensively by draining marshland for farming and constructing channels and dams to improve navigation and flood control. To keep the land dry enough for crop production, large amounts of water polluted with fertilizer and pesticides were pumped into the river and lakes. The dams have kept water levels in the lakes from naturally fluctuating, limiting the normal flushing of nutrients and sediments and reducing aquatic habitat.

SJRWMD has acquired and reflooded over 17,000 acres of drained farmland, or muck farms, to restore wetlands, improve water quality, provide for expanded flood storage and increase recreational opportunities. At Sunnyhill Farm and Ocklawaha Prairie a total of 16 miles of the historic river channel are being restored. New schedules being developed for seasonal water levels in the Ocklawaha chain of lakes will improve the health of the lakes while meeting flood control and navigation needs.

Land Management and Education

SJRWMD owns over 414,000 acres of land and holds conservation easements on an additional 35,000 acres. The majority of these lands are wetlands, historically wet areas, or areas that are vitally important to water quality. District-owned uplands adjacent to wet areas provide habitat for wetland-dependent species as well as critical buffer zones between developed lands and sensitive wetlands and waterways.

Management of district lands focuses on protection of water and related land resources while providing for public recreational and educational uses. In many cases management responsibilities are shared with local governments or agencies such as the Division of Forestry and the Game and Fresh Water Fish Commission. Ninety-eight percent of district land is open to the public, with the remaining 2 percent temporarily closed because of construction or restoration projects. The *Recreation Guide to District Lands* provides maps and lists of activities available at each property.

In recent years, district lands have been increasingly used as outdoor classrooms. District staff and high school teachers and students have begun a program entitled "Legacy," which seeks to promote a sense of land ethic or stewardship. The program encourages students to assist in land management activities that protect natural resources, enhance fish and wildlife habitat, and provide appropriate educational and recreational opportunities on district land. Legacy helps participants to understand how today's decisions and actions determine tomorrow's quality and quantity of natural resources.

REFERENCES

A source for a map or figure has a number in parentheses following the entry. This number refers to the page in this atlas for which the source was used.

Boniol, D., M. Williams, and D. Munch. 1993. *Mapping Recharge to the Floridan Aquifer Using a Geographic Information System*. St. Johns River Water Management District. Palatka.

Cox, J., R. Kautz, M. MacLaughlin, and T. Gilbert. 1994. *Closing the Gaps in Florida's Wildlife Habitat Conservation System*. Office of Environmental Services, Florida Game and Fresh Water Fish Commission, Tallahassee.

Florida Geological Survey. 1991. *Florida's Ground Water Quality Monitoring Program Hydrogeologic Framework*. Florida Geological Survey Special Publication No. 32. Tallahassee. (map background network, 230)

Florida Natural Areas Inventory. Tallahassee. (map, 235)

Garver, R., M. Ritter, D. Dycus, T. Ziegler, and D. Clapp. 1996. Tropical Storm Gordon. Technical Memorandum No. 16. St. Johns River Water Management District. Palatka.

Grow, G. 1981. *Florida Parks*. Tallahasssee: Longleaf Publications.

Hand, J., J. Col, and L. Lord. 1996. *Northeast Florida District Water Quality 1996*. 305(b) Technical appendix. Florida Department of Environmental Protection. Tallahassee. (map, 228)

Lauter, F. 1950. *Steam-boating in Alachua County 1870-1905*. Publisher unknown.

National Oceanic and Atmospheric Administration. 1919-1994. Monthly Climatological Data. (graph, 217; graph, 226)

Sprinkle, C.L. 1989. *Geochemistry of the Floridan Aquifer System in Florida and in Parts of Georgia, South Carolina, and Alabama*. USGS Professional Paper 1403-I.

U.S. Geological Survey. 1996. *Water Resources Data, Florida, Water Year 1995*. Vol. 1A: Northwest Florida Surface Water. U.S. Geological Survey Water Data Report Fl-95-1A. (map, 219)

U.S. Geological Survey, Water Resources Division. Tallahasssee, Florida (map, 223)

Winsberg, 1990. *Florida Weather*. Orlando: University of Central Florida Press.

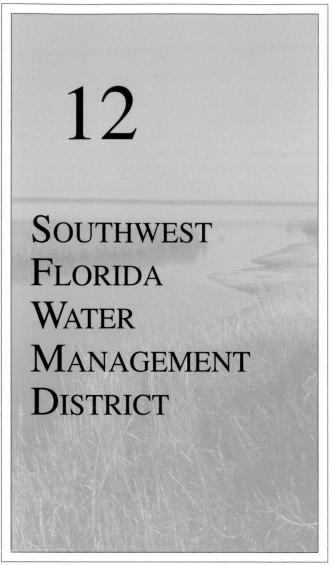

12

SOUTHWEST FLORIDA WATER MANAGEMENT DISTRICT

The district's primary funding source is ad valorem taxes, although revenues are also derived from state and federal appropriations, permit fees, interest earnings, and other sources. The taxing capabilities of the district are established by the legislature within the limits set by the Florida Constitution. The limit for SWFWMD is one mill, or one dollar per thousand dollars of assessed value.

SWFWMD is further divided into nine hydrologic subdistricts, or basins, eight of which have separate basin boards. Activities within the Green Swamp Basin are the responsibility of the governing board. Members of the basin boards are also appointed by the governor, confirmed by the senate, and serve three-year terms. These boards identify water-related issues and problems in their basins, and provide programs and budgets to address these concerns. At present, SWFWMD is the only water management district with this form of basin system.

The one-mill taxing capability of the district is divided evenly between the governing board (0.5 mill) and the district's eight basin boards (0.5 mill).

SWFWMD includes all or part of 16 counties on the west-central coast of Florida, from Charlotte County on the south to Levy County on the north. It extends from the Gulf of Mexico east to Polk and Highlands counties. Several major and rapidly growing urban areas lie within this area, as does much of Florida's most productive agricultural lands (especially for citrus) and major phosphate areas. The region also contains the Green Swamp, headwaters for the Peace, Hillsborough, Withlacoochee, and Ocklawaha rivers, and many lakes, springs, and streams.

The significance of Tampa Bay, Sarasota Bay, and Charlotte Harbor estuaries has been recognized through the National Estuary Programs. These vital estuarine systems have also been designated as state priorities through the Surface Water Improvement and Management Program (SWIM). It is often along, and in, these very sensitive ecosystems that development pressure and population growth have been most demanding and have had adverse environmental impacts.

238   The Florida legislature created the Southwest Florida Water Management District (SWFWMD) in 1961 to be the local sponsor of the Four River Basins, Florida Project. The U.S. Army Corps of Engineers initiated this major flood control project after Hurricane Donna severely damaged southwest Florida in 1960. The project includes flood control structures and 6,000 square miles of water detention areas. SWFWMD continues to cooperate with the corps in maintaining and operating portions of this flood control system.

The district's responsibilities expanded in the mid to late 1960s when regulatory programs for regional wellfields serving the Tampa Bay metropolitan area were initiated, and again in 1972 when the Florida legislature passed the Water Resources Act. This act significantly furthered the transition from strictly flood control to a more broad-based policy of resource management and service to the public.

SWFWMD is governed by an 11-member board appointed by the governor and confirmed by the senate. Board members, who must live in the district, serve staggered four-year terms.

Wes Whedon, Richard Owen, and Terry Johnson

Basin Board Boundaries

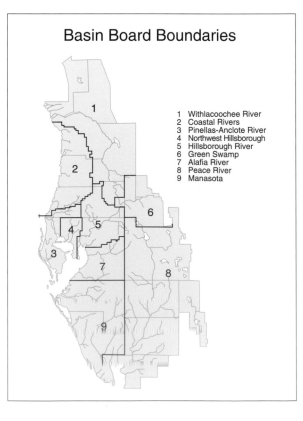

1   Withlacoochee River
2   Coastal Rivers
3   Pinellas-Anclote River
4   Northwest Hillsborough
5   Hillsborough River
6   Green Swamp
7   Alafia River
8   Peace River
9   Manasota

Physiography and Topography

Land in the region ranges in elevation from sea level along the Gulf coast to more than 290 feet above mean sea level at several places along the Lake Wales Ridge. Higher elevations are associated in particular with three ridges, the Brooksville, Lakeland, and Lake Wales ridges, aligned with the Florida peninsula. The Polk Upland region has gently rolling, sometimes hilly, terrain. The Tsala-Apopka Plain is part of the Withlacoochee River valley. The Withlacoochee River originates in the Green Swamp and flows northward before turning west through the Dunnellon Gap.

The high sandy ridges are remnants of ancient sand dunes, the only portion of peninsular Florida not inundated in a series of advancing and receding ocean levels. This unique isolation created and supports ecosystems not found anywhere else in the world. The high sandy soils are also a high recharge area for the Floridan aquifer. In the northern part of the region, the Floridan rises close to, and is often exposed at, the surface. This exposed aquifer is the source of the several first-magnitude springs in Hernando and Citrus counties.

The Gulf Coastal Lowlands and the DeSoto Plain are flat areas with wetlands interspersed with pine-palmetto flatwoods. In the southern part of Southwest Florida, soils in these flat areas are typically acidic because of the dominant types of vegetation and the lack of underground drainage. Rivers in this area are characterized as "black water," so called because the acidic soil causes a high tannic content (tea-colored water) in the surface water runoff.

The northern part of Southwest Florida has karst geology. In karst areas, water-soluble limestone below the earth's surface may dissolve, causing the land surface to sink or collapse, and often, to fill with water. This condition, most common in the northern and eastern regions of the district, produces sinkholes. They can range from 20 feet in diameter to half a square mile or more.

Under karst conditions, surface water and groundwater are closely interrelated. Lake levels are often a direct reflection of

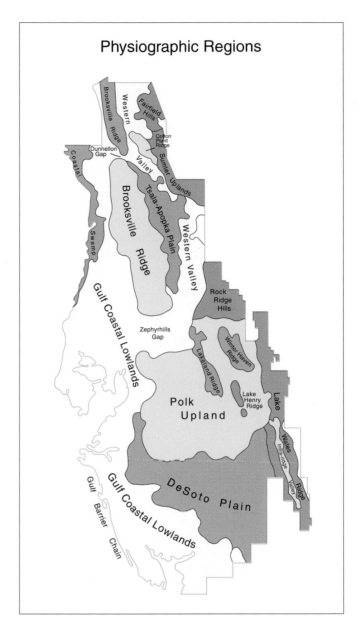

Physiographic Regions

239

Tampa Bay, E. G. Simmons Area

Michael Crow

groundwater levels; spring flow and seepage constitute the base flow of many streams; freshwater wetlands slow and store floodwaters and enhance infiltration to groundwater; and stream discharges to estuaries are critical for maintenance of salinity regimes. As development increases on the sandy ridges and karst areas of this region, so to has nutrient loading to the groundwater. This nutrient loading is thought to be a factor in increased algal blooms occurring in the northern coastal springs.

Land Use

Land use within Southwest Florida is a strong indicator of water needs. Agricultural, industrial, commercial, residential, and other uses have particular requirements for freshwater.

In 1994, agriculture accounted for the greatest percentage of land use area (31.3 percent) in Southwest Florida. This was

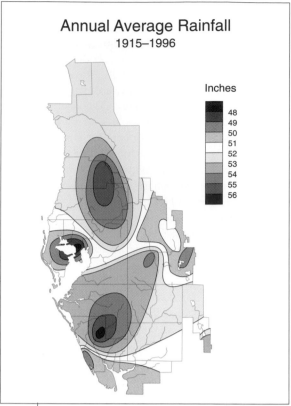

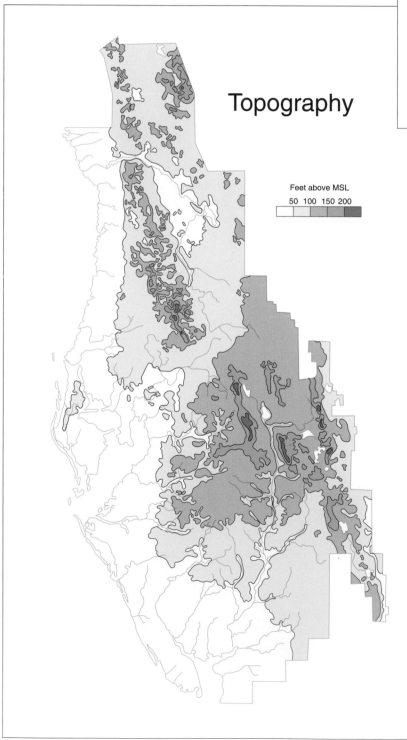

240

followed by urban uses, such as residential, commercial, and industrial, that accounted for approximately 21.5 percent of the total land area. More than 18.8 percent of the region was in upland forest, while wetlands occupied 18.6 percent. Other land use categories included rangeland, water, beaches, and transportation.

In the last several decades, urban growth and development have increased dramatically throughout Southwest Florida. Much of this growth has occurred along the Gulf of Mexico coastline, severely taxing coastal communities' ability to accommodate rapid expansion while maintaining the quality of life that initially generated it.

These coastal zones have, in many cases, little or no existing local freshwater supplies. Fragile dune systems have been damaged by excessive recreational use and residential development. Estuarine systems have been overloaded with nutrients and other pollutants, primarily from wastewater from sewage treatment plants, surface water runoff, industrial emissions, and auto exhaust. Nutrient-laden waters have become cloudy, blocking light to the underlying seagrass beds. Coastal waters have also, in some cases, been subjected to extensive commercial use and industrial toxic waste disposal. Tidally influenced flooding has led to widespread property damage. Many coastal communities are vulnerable to potentially catastrophic impacts from major storm events, such as hurricanes.

Climate

Most of Southwest Florida shares a humid subtropical climate with the rest of the southeastern United States. The more southerly parts of the district, however, have climatic characteristics that mark a transition zone between that climate and the tropical savanna climate of southernmost Florida. Frost and freezing temperatures may occur once a year north of Tampa Bay and at most inland locations south of Tampa Bay. Average annual rainfall in SWFWMD is approximately 53 inches, but is highly variable both seasonally and from year to year. About 60 to 65 percent of annual rainfall typically occurs between June and September when evaporation rates are highest. These rains are generally associated with thunderstorms, and can cause widespread flooding. Although some water supplies in northern Florida originate from rainfall in Georgia or Alabama, Southwest Florida is primarily dependent on local rainfall.

The pronounced difference between the rainy season (June to September) and the dry winter, early spring months produces a significant change in water use demands. On urban and agricultural lands, drainage systems have been developed to move the water away quickly. Oftentimes these drainage systems do not adequately treat the stormwater runoff. Localized flooding occurs when parts of the drainage system fail or at the "downstream" end of the system. Often the very effectiveness of the extensive drainage systems works against water users in the dry months. During these months, users want to hold back water to maintain existing flows or levels. At this time of the year irrigation needs for agricultural, recreational, and residential users are often met through extensive groundwater withdrawals.

Population

Southwest Florida is home to one-fourth of the state's population, or approximately 3.6 million people (1995), with the largest concentration in the Tampa Bay metropolitan area. SWFWMD contains 98 local governments spread over approximately 10,000 square miles. The region is diverse and includes some of the state's most productive agricultural lands as well as high growth urban areas along the Gulf coast. Phosphate and other mining, industry and power generation, and tourism and recreation are significant components of the region's economy.

Most of Southwest Florida's population growth has been due to net migration (more people moving to an area than leaving), as opposed to natural increase (births minus deaths). Approximately 2.5 million people lived within SWFWMD in 1980. By 1995 the population had increased to approximately 3.6 million permanent residents, a net increase of about 44 percent for the 15-year period.

Southwest Florida has a substantial seasonal population, predominantly retirees, who also have a home outside the area. These visitors create a seasonal water use effect that complicates water management, especially in coastal counties and other communities that attract many retirees. During these periods, daily peak demands on water supply systems may increase, creating localized capacity or pressure problems.

Southwest Florida's average population density was 383 permanent residents per square mile in 1996. Pinellas County had the highest population density in the region and in the state (3,146 persons per square mile), and Lake County had the lowest in the region (20 persons per square mile). In 1990, the

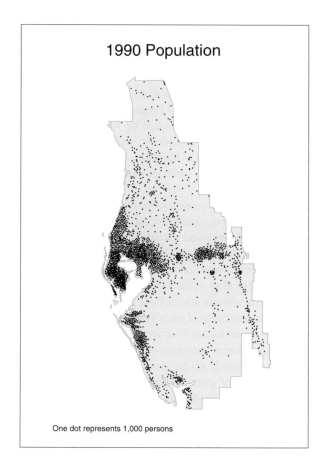

1990 Population

One dot represents 1,000 persons

region's average population density was 346 persons per square mile.

Southwest Florida is expected to have approximately 4.6 million permanent residents by the year 2010. This represents a 37 percent increase during a 20-year period, or roughly 1,179 new permanent residents each week. The predominant source of population growth will remain net migration.

The largest projected increase in population for the year 2010 will occur in the developed areas surrounding Tampa Bay (Hillsborough, Pasco, Manatee, and Pinellas counties). More than 53 percent of the region's increase (or nearly 650,000 additional residents) is expected in these counties. Hernando County is expected to be the fastest growing county with an estimated population increase of 92 percent between 1990 and 2010.

241

Southwest Florida Water Management District

Canals, City of Northport

Groundwater

Approximately 80 percent of the water used in Southwest Florida is groundwater. This region has three different aquifer systems: the water table or surficial, the intermediate, and the Floridan, the deepest and most productive of the three.

Withdrawals from the surficial aquifer are usually small but are significant along the central ridge. Here the thickness of sands is substantial and so the aquifer is more productive than in most areas. The surficial aquifer is also used in the southwestern part of the district.

The intermediate aquifer occurs only in the southern part of the region. Polk, Sarasota, Highlands, Hardee, and DeSoto counties rely on the intermediate primarily for public supply,

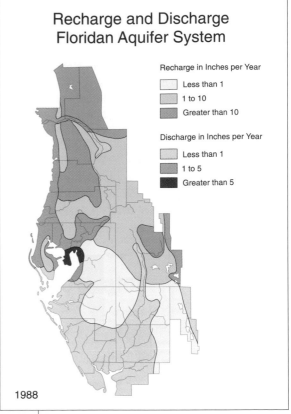

Recharge and Discharge
Floridan Aquifer System

Recharge in Inches per Year

- Less than 1
- 1 to 10
- Greater than 10

Discharge in Inches per Year

- Less than 1
- 1 to 5
- Greater than 5

1988

domestic self-supply, and agricultural water use.

The Upper Floridan aquifer system supplies more than 10 times the amount of water pumped from either the surficial or intermediate aquifer systems. Most groundwater is pumped from the Upper Floridan aquifer and exhibits a fairly constant temperature and dissolved solids content.

In the coastal areas, a zone of transition from fresh to saline water occurs. Under the southwestern part of the region, the Floridan has moderate to relatively high concentrations of sulfate, which limit its use. These concentrations increase with depth and also increase toward the coast, where higher chloride concentrations also occur. In these areas the importance of the Floridan system as a source of potable water diminishes. Concentrations of dissolved solids, chlorides, and sulfates exceed maximum recommended drinking water standards and require more expensive treatment technologies.

Groundwater recharge to the Upper Floridan aquifer is generally high in the northern and easternmost portions of the region and varies to the south. These areas are also more susceptible to groundwater contamination. The southern portions of the Upper Floridan aquifer are less susceptible to pollution primarily due to the thickening of overlying clay units. The surficial aquifer system, however, is very vulnerable to contamination throughout the region.

244

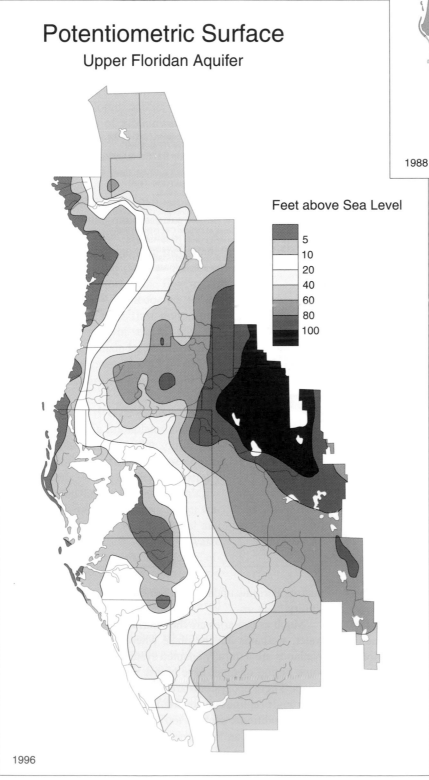

Potentiometric Surface
Upper Floridan Aquifer

Feet above Sea Level

- 5
- 10
- 20
- 40
- 60
- 80
- 100

1996

Geologic Cross Sections

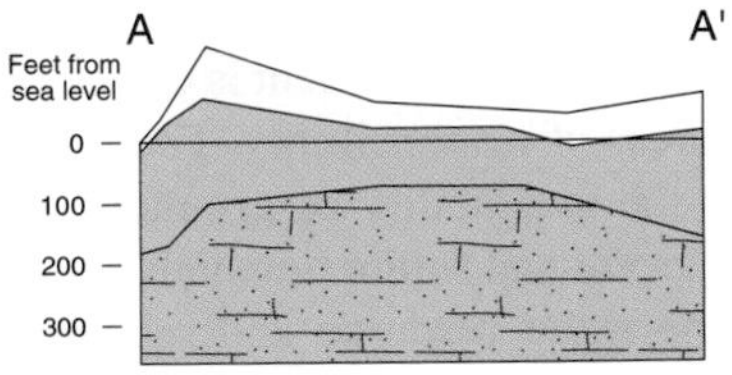

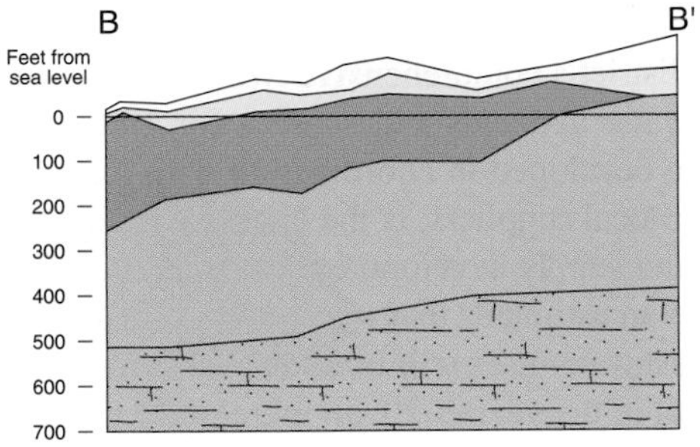

Quaternary

Plio-Pleistocene
☐ Surficial sediments

Tertiary

Miocene
Hawthorn Group

Oligocene
Suwannee Limestone

Eocene
Ocala Limestone

Avon Park Formation

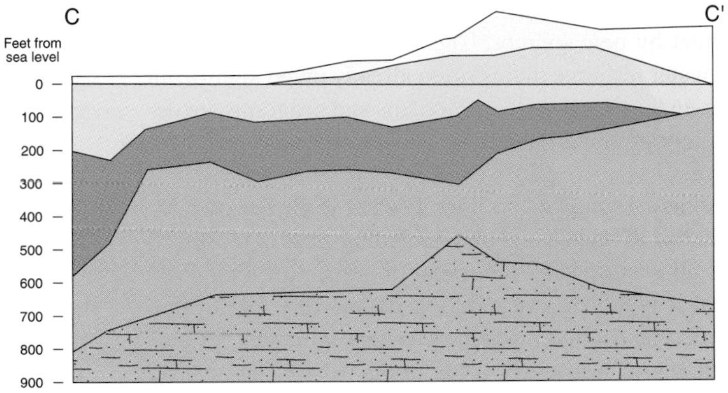

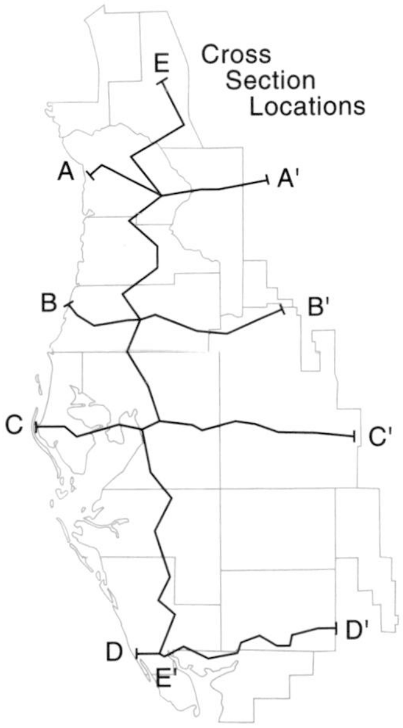

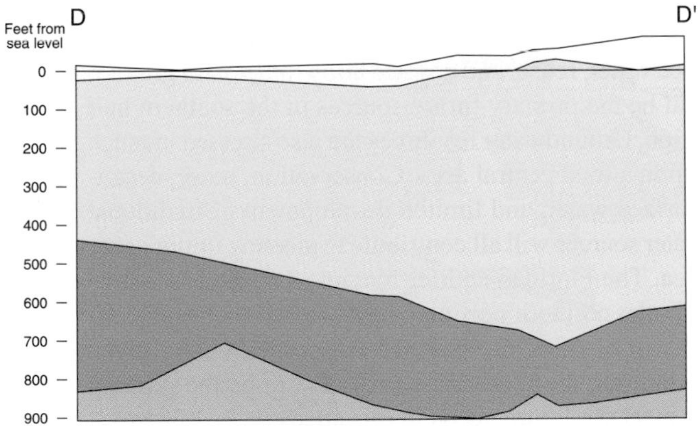

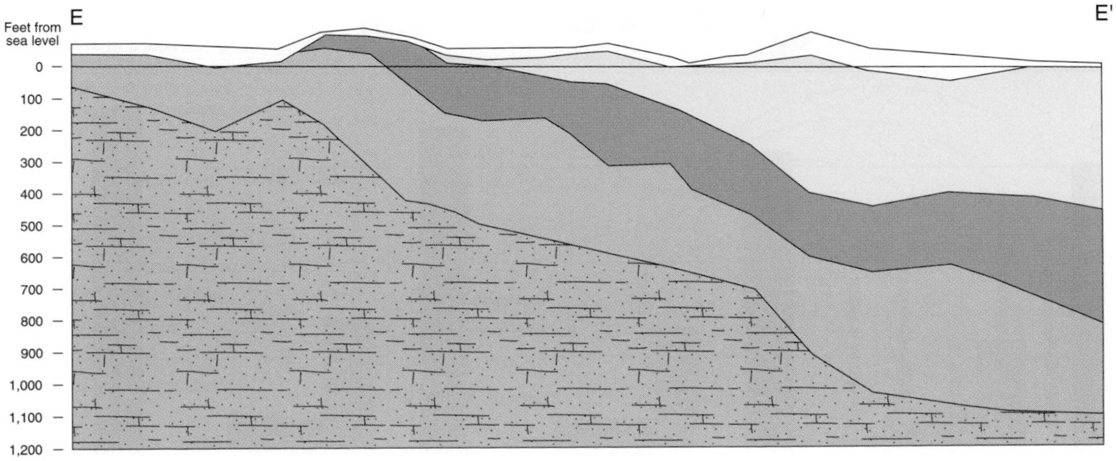

Cross Section Locations

245

Water Resource Assessment Projects and Water Use Caution Areas

The district's Water Resource Assessment Projects (WRAPs) and Water Use Caution Areas (WUCAs) are generally directed at source protection, and specifically at assuring human use of the resource does not exceed nature's ability to replenish our supply (or sustainable yield).

Increasing water withdrawals and below normal rainfall in some areas have created regional impacts. These impacts include lowered lake levels, impacts to wetlands, water quality deterioration in coastal areas and the lower part of the aquifer, and decreased pumping efficiencies for existing legal users.

WRAPs provide the technical basis to determine the quantity of water that could ultimately be permitted. Once deter-

mined, WUCA management plans are developed to ensure appropriate management of the resource. This approach emphasizes the close relationship between water supply quantity and quality, where overuse can degrade a good quality water source.

By 1989, the district recognized three distinct areas in which groundwater resources were stressed (Northern Tampa Bay, Eastern Tampa Bay, and Highlands Ridge). Specific use factors, as well as long-term drought impacts, were identified in each area. These "critical water resource problem areas" were designated as WUCAs by the district governing board the same year. In 1992, the district's entire Southern Ground Water Basin was designated the Southern Water Use Caution Area (SWUCA) as a first step toward achieving resource protection. State Water Policy now refers to these areas as Water Resource Caution Areas (WRCAs).

248

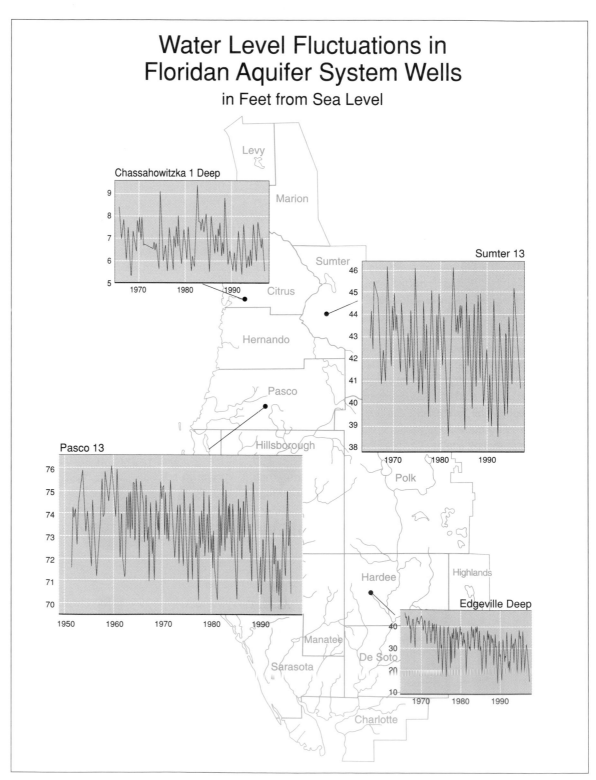

Water Level Fluctuations in Floridan Aquifer System Wells
in Feet from Sea Level

Financial and Technical Assistance

The district financially assists water users to help accomplish water management objectives. In the recent past this assistance has focused on complementing the district's water supply regulatory programs, such as implementing reuse and conservation projects and supporting water resource development projects of the regional water supply authorities.

The primary source of funding for this assistance has been the district's basin boards through the Cooperative Funding program. For the past several years, basin boards have identified water conservation and reuse assistance as priorities within their respective basin plans. Basin boards which have WRCAs designated in all or part of their jurisdictions have assisted water users in meeting the conservation requirements identified in the WRCA management plans and rules. In addition, the district has modified its funding assistance program to require that a local government's comprehensive plan must be consistent with the district's Needs and Sources Plan in order for that local government to be recommended for funding assistance.

In 1994, the district governing board initiated a major financial assistance/incentive program, called the New Water Sources Initiative (NWSI). The impetus for creating the NWSI was the fact that within the SWUCA, both permitted and actual water use from the confined aquifer must be reduced from current levels to achieve sustainable yield. The NWSI is designed to complement the various regulatory initiatives of the SWUCA management plan.

Although the SWUCA provided the impetus for NWSI, projects throughout the district may qualify for participation. NWSI creates an opportunity for the district to play a part in implementing solutions to water supply problems through alternative sources such as conservation, desalination, reuse and other projects.

The district provides technical assistance to the various water use sectors to help achieve resource management objectives. This includes a significant agricultural technical assistance program. Agriculture occupies a position of major importance in the region. In 1990, agriculture withdrew an estimated daily average of 628 million gallons, or about 42 percent of total freshwater withdrawn. Nearly four of every 10 acres in the district is used for agriculture. More than 95 percent of the strawberries grown in Florida come from within the district. Polk County is one of the largest citrus growing counties in Florida, and more tropical fish are raised in Hillsborough County than any other county in the United States.

Since 1977, the district has maintained continuous annual funding of programs with the Institute of Food and Agricultural Sciences (IFAS) aimed at better use of the water resource. Other cooperative efforts have been undertaken with the Natural Resource Conservation Service (NRCS) of the U.S. Department of Agriculture. The district has funded a mobile irrigation lab program with the NRCS which provides irrigation system efficiency assistance directly to farmers. The district also has an agricultural metering assistance program to improve the reliability of water use information and to allow quantification of conservation efforts.

The district similarly provides technical assistance to local governments in developing and implementing future water supplies, including conservation programs. Many basin boards, for example, have funded water conservation initiatives, which include water resource analysts who help local governments in developing and implementing conservation programs tailored to their local communities. This assistance includes developing appropriate water and sewer rate structures, plumbing retrofit programs, xeriscape promotion, public education, local landscape and plumbing codes, and other techniques.

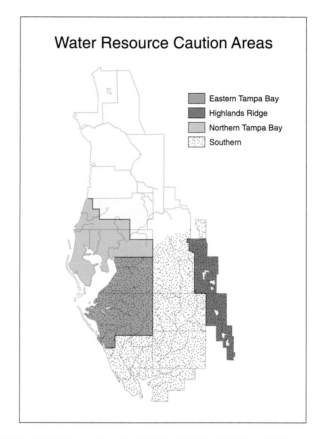

Water Resource Caution Areas

- Eastern Tampa Bay
- Highlands Ridge
- Northern Tampa Bay
- Southern

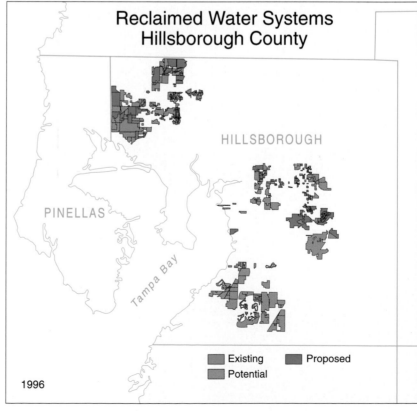

Reclaimed Water Systems
Hillsborough County

HILLSBOROUGH

PINELLAS

Tampa Bay

1996

- Existing
- Potential
- Proposed

Flood Protection

Flood Protection Facilities

The largest flood control project undertaken in Southwest Florida is the U.S. Army Corps of Engineers' Four River Basins, Florida Project. This project is designed to protect 6,000 square miles of urban and agricultural lands from severe flooding. Its name is derived from the four major rivers that flow from the Green Swamp: the Ocklawaha, Withlacoochee, Peace, and Hillsborough. The project is jointly administered by the U.S. Army Corps of Engineers and the district, with the corps responsible for design and construction. The district purchases necessary rights-of-way, approves project designs, and operates and maintains completed portions of the project.

Several major flood detention areas are strategically located in the upper reaches of the Hillsborough, Withlacoochee, and Little Withlacoochee rivers and their tributaries. Through a system of levees, canals, and water control structures, flood waters can be temporarily detained in these areas until the rivers recede. The excess water may then be discharged safely downstream.

A major portion of the Four River Basins Project is the Tampa Bypass Canal, which works with the Lower Hillsborough Flood Detention Area. Designed to divert flood waters around Tampa and Temple Terrace, both of which were extensively flooded by Hurricane Donna in 1960, this canal extends about 12.5 miles south and southwest from Cow House

Southwest Florida Water Management District

Water control structure on the Tampa Bypass Canal, Four Rivers Basin Project

250

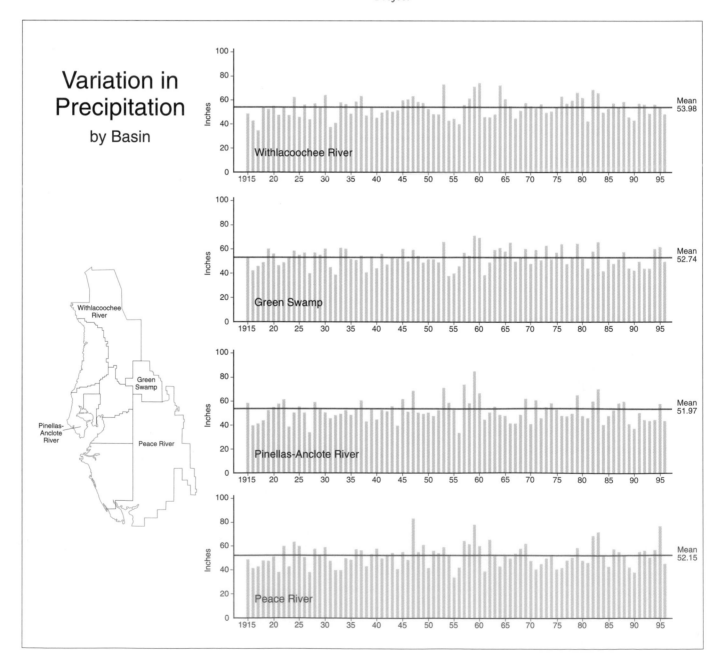

Creek in the lower Hillsborough to its outlet at McKay Bay. Another important element in the overall canal system is the Harney Canal, which provides a direct link between the main canal and the Hillsborough River. It is designed to intercept flood waters from the river and divert them into the main canal from which they can be released safely into McKay Bay. The district operates and maintains Four Rivers Basin Project facilities following Corps guidelines and continues to cooperate with the Corps and Hillsborough County in the completion of public recreational amenities associated with the project.

Other completed works in the Four River Basins Project include the Lake Tarpon Outfall Canal and Masaryktown Canal. Due to increased environmental impacts, the project has been significantly scaled back in favor of nonstructural strategies in flood control.

The district presently operates and/or maintains more than 70 surface-water management structures; however, only a few of these structures are designed for flood protection. The majority are basic water management structures whose primary function is to manage the level of a lake for environmental purposes, i.e., to mimic natural cycles. Though often misinterpreted as flood control structures, they provide very limited flood protection benefits.

The district is not responsible for the improvement or maintenance of local surface water management facilities. Examples of these facilities include those constructed for a local purpose by agricultural concerns, land developers, other state agencies, special interest districts, or local governments. Flood protection is a shared responsibility among many entities and requires careful coordination and clear role definitions. The district does assist local governments in addressing these problems through cooperative floodplain mapping projects, surface water management master planning, technical review of local projects, and other activities.

Floodprone Areas

Areas naturally subject to periodic flooding provide a host of water management functions that have only recently become fully recognized. These flood-prone areas are typically found along streams and rivers, next to ponds and lakes, in coastal areas, and in isolated low-lying areas. Floodprone lands temporarily store runoff from upland areas and overflow from water bodies. By temporarily detaining surface waters, floodprone lands regulate the timing, velocity, and levels of flood discharges. In addition, floodprone lands maintain water quality and provide habitats for fish and wildlife. Those lands that are most frequently flooded (i.e., wetlands) are the most important in terms of these functions, but less frequently flooded areas are also important for handling more severe floods.

Maintenance of natural storage areas is extremely important for regional water management. Runoff in southwest Florida is usually intercepted by wetlands or topographic depressions. When these areas are full, the overflow moves slowly through shallow swales and water bodies. Obstructions to flow, such as logs, rocks, trees, undergrowth, and meanders in watercourses, reduce the rate of flow and help to minimize the level and velocity of downstream flooding.

Recharge of the water table aquifer depends directly on the levels of water in such low-lying areas as cypress heads, sinkholes, swales, and floodplains. When these areas are flooded, they may help recharge the water table aquifer. Then, during dry periods,

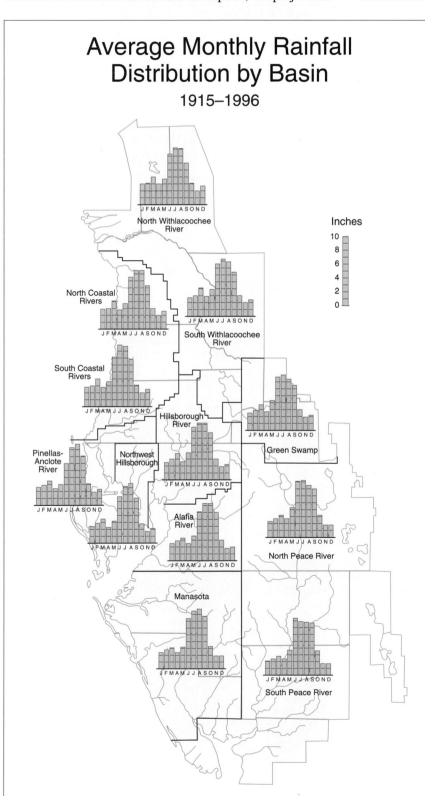

Average Monthly Rainfall Distribution by Basin
1915–1996

Inches
10
8
6
4
2
0

North Withlacoochee River
North Coastal Rivers
South Withlacoochee River
South Coastal Rivers
Hillsborough River
Pinellas-Anclote River
Northwest Hillsborough
Green Swamp
Alafia River
North Peace River
Manasota
South Peace River

251

the water table aquifer may provide part or all of the base flow to streams. Water stored in the water table aquifer also serves to recharge the Floridan aquifer by percolating downward along passageways through impermeable layers.

Past development practices in Southwest Florida paid little heed to naturally floodprone lands, and much of the growth that has occurred in recent decades has been in or near these areas. These floodprone areas are near the very water features that have attracted people to move to Florida. Much of Southwest Florida's growth has occurred in coastal areas, or next to rivers, streams, and lakes. The most evident impacts of building in floodprone areas have been damages to the development itself during flood events. Property losses and injury to inhabitants during flood events have resulted in the construction of the flood control facilities that exist today.

Richard Gant

Residential flooding near Bird Lake, Pasco County, January 1998

We now better understand the importance of floodprone areas and how development within these areas can result in a wide range of detrimental impacts. In addition, we know all too well such development has required costly structural solutions to flood problems and that these flood control facilities themselves can decrease water quality and harm natural systems. Based upon this greater knowledge, the district has many initiatives designed to prevent future development from causing these same impacts. Local governments, and not the water management district, control land use planning and development, making a land and water partnership a necessity.

The Department of Environmental Protection's (DEP) 1984 delegation of responsibilities under Chapter 17-25, F.A.C., was the beginning of the district's involvement with water quality management. These regulations provided design criteria for stormwater systems to lessen water quality degradation from stormwater runoff, and became the district's comprehensive Management and Storage of Surface Waters (MSSW) Rule. In 1987, the district began providing technical assistance cooperatively to address water quality issues of local governments upon request.

Responding to legislative changes in 1993, the district revised its surface water permitting rules. To streamline environmental permitting, the Florida legislature directed the water management districts and the Department of Environmental Protection to develop new regulations that would combine several types of permits into one Environmental Resource Permit.

The new rules combine existing MSSW rules and the Wetlands Resource Management permitting rules of the DEP. As stipulated in the Environmental Reorganization Act of 1993, these rules include a single definition for wetlands, a unified methodology for wetland delineation, and criteria for the establishment and use of mitigation banks.

252

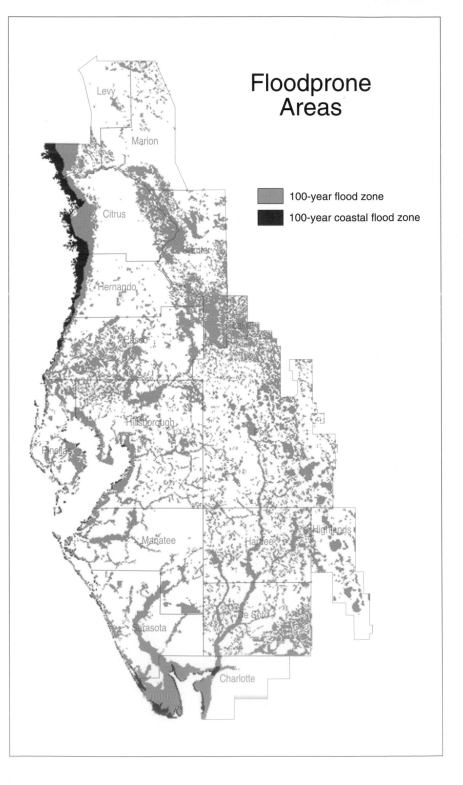

Floodprone Areas

- 100-year flood zone
- 100-year coastal flood zone

Water Quality

Surface Water

The district's early emphasis regarding surface water was to control its quantity and move it away from human habitation as quickly as possible. Years of striving to enhance and control drainage have resulted in concern with the impacts this fast moving water has on rivers, lakes, and estuaries.

Florida has experienced significant population growth in the last several decades. This growth has increased discharge of man-made pollutants to surface water bodies from impacted watersheds. This typically is followed by a decline in the value of the natural habitat. Public awareness of the degradation of many lakes and rivers in the state has increased. This aware-

ness has fostered a strong public desire to restore degraded waterbodies and preserve those that are still relatively pristine.

The district has established a waterbody monitoring network for selected surface water bodies. The project initially targeted Surface Water Improvement and Management (SWIM) priority waterbodies and waterbodies for which the district has completed diagnostic/feasibility studies. It will eventually encompass other significant waterbodies in the district. The network will establish a baseline for long-term water quality and biological monitoring. Most of the selected water bodies are in Citrus and Highlands counties because no local government agencies currently monitor water quality in these counties. Selected sites will not duplicate the monitoring efforts of other agencies. It is vitally important, however, that a single, unified monitoring system be employed.

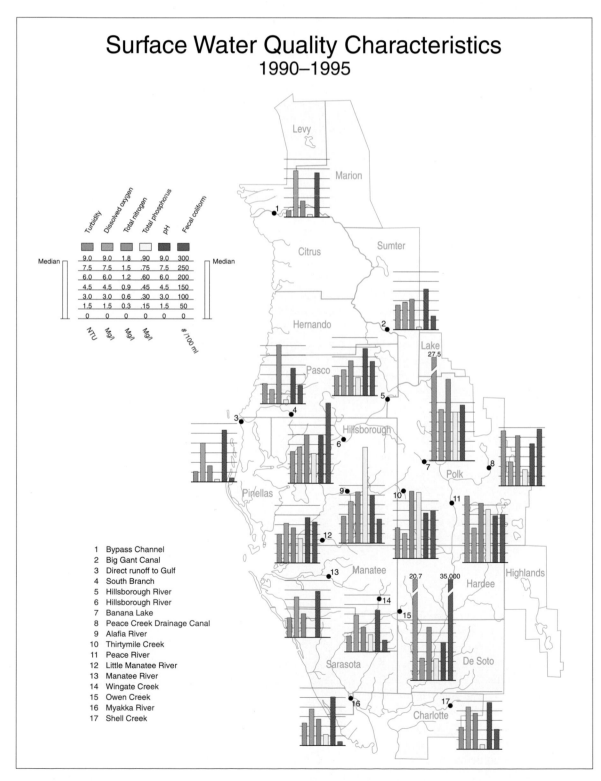

253

The Department of Environmental Protection, in cooperation with the Environmental Protection Agency, has begun a biological assessment project, Rapid Bioassessment Sampling, that will create an extensive database on near-pristine water bodies statewide, within a regional framework. District staff works with DEP staff to select representative sites within the district, and to coordinate the collection of biological assessment data from some sites.

According to the 1996 Southwest Florida District Water Quality Assessment, 305 (b) Technical Appendix, prepared by the Florida Department of Environmental Protection for the U.S. Environmental Protection Agency, Southwest Florida has many good water quality coastal rivers, often with significant spring flow. Major pollution sources are associated with urban land uses around Tampa Bay and phosphate mining and processing operations in central Florida.

The rivers along the west coast of Florida from the Wacasassa River to the Anclote River are mostly small, spring-fed streams and generally have good water quality, although many have high nutrient and bacteria levels. The upper portion of Boca Ciega Bay (Pinellas County) and its tributaries have fair to poor water quality. The Hillsborough River has a considerable number of problems in its upper reaches and tributaries to these reaches. The Alafia River is degraded by phosphate mining activities in the eastern portion of its basin. The Hillsborough and Alafia rivers flow into Tampa Bay.

Tampa Bay, which has recently improved, has had a loss of vegetation in coastal areas, dredge and fill activities, destruction of submerged habitat, and increased pollutant loading. Tampa Bay also receives water from the Hillsborough, Manatee, Little Manatee, and Alafia rivers, which contribute nutrients or toxins to the bay and nonpoint sources around the bay.

Sarasota Bay has fair to good water quality, with major pollution sources including urban runoff, historic wastewater treatment plant discharges, and septic tank loading. Wastewater treatment is being upgraded. Peace River has eutrophic lakes that feed river tributaries in the upper reaches. Discharges to the Peace River have included phosphate mining, fertilizer and other chemical manufacturing, wastewater treatment plants, citrus processing, and runoff from agricultural and urban land uses.

The Peace and Myakka rivers flow into Charlotte Harbor. The Myakka River has good water quality although it has naturally low DO concentrations from swamp drainage and has nutrient loading from agricultural runoff and natural phosphate-rich soils. The Charlotte Harbor estuary system generally has good water quality and still supports healthy estuarine habitat although the Peace River contributes water degraded by phosphate mining, and the Myakka and Caloosahatchee contribute nonpoint nutrient pollution.

Groundwater

Sources of potential groundwater contamination include nitrates from crop fertilization, injection wells, drainage wells, underground storage tanks, pesticides, septic tanks, landfills, industrial waste sites, lawn and landscape maintenance, polluted surface waters and chemical spills. The Floridan aquifer is most susceptible to contamination in the northern half of the district where it is not protected by a continuous, overlying impermeable layer. District monitoring studies indicate an increase in nutrient loading, particularly nitrates, in this part of the aquifer. These studies also indicate increasing concentra-

tions of chlorides and total dissolved solids from saltwater intrusion in the southern part of the aquifer.

Rehabilitation of contaminated aquifers can be exceedingly difficult and costly. Prevention, therefore, is the appropriate emphasis of groundwater policy. Local wellhead protection programs, recharge area protection, and management of known or potential groundwater pollution sources are the major initiatives needed to protect a continued supply of high quality groundwater.

In Southwest Florida, groundwater quality is protected through several means. The district has aggressive proactive groundwater quality identification and monitoring programs. These programs are coupled with well permitting, managing "delineated areas," and abandoned well plugging and capping that protect both groundwater and the users withdrawing that water.

The Water Quality Assurance Act of 1983 initiated a cooperative effort between the Department of Environmental Protection and the five water management districts to determine the quality of groundwater in the major aquifers of Florida. A Background Monitor Well Network, a Coastal Monitor Well Network, a Seasonal Variability Monitor Well Network and the Very Intensive Study Areas Network were established.

The district has increased the density of its groundwater monitoring network since the mid-1970s by constructing additional wells. The data from these monitoring sites are used to evaluate seasonal and long-term changes to the groundwater system, and the interaction and connectivity with surface water bodies.

Impacts from increased water demand over the past 30 years have been documented and assessed through analysis of groundwater data. These impacts directly affect the district's planning, regulatory policies, and programs. For example, groundwater data are used during the permitting process to model potential impacts of new uses. This information is also used to monitor existing permittees to prevent them from creating significant detrimental changes in areas surrounding

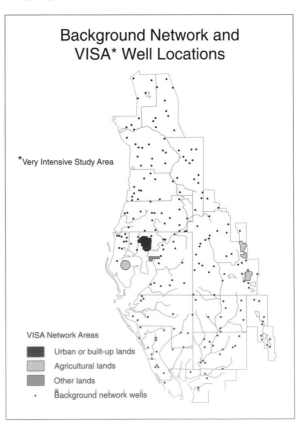

Background Network and VISA* Well Locations

*Very Intensive Study Area

VISA Network Areas
- ■ Urban or built-up lands
- ▨ Agricultural lands
- ▨ Other lands
- · Background network wells

254

groundwater withdrawals. If these impacts do occur, the district can respond by imposing regulatory fines or other actions.

Constructing new monitor wells also provides valuable technical information, recorded as the core is recovered from various depths (e.g., lithology, water quality, and potentiometric levels). From these data, aquifers and confining units are delineated, the freshwater-saltwater interface is determined, and water quality within aquifers is characterized. For the next few years most long-term monitoring wells will be installed in Water Resource Caution Areas.

Well construction permitting is one of the primary regulatory means by which the district protects groundwater (and surface water) from degradation while protecting the quality of water for potable uses. District rules on well construction practices and water well contractor licensing are contained in Chapter 40D-3, F.A.C.

The district also regulates well construction in "delineated areas" (known as areas of contamination) on behalf of the Department of Environmental Protection. This program assures appropriate well construction techniques to protect public health and safety while containing interaquifer contamination.

The Quality of Water Improvement Project (QWIP) was established in 1974 through Chapter 373, Florida Statutes (F.S.), to restore groundwater conditions altered by well drilling. QWIP's primary goal is to preserve groundwater and surface-water resources through proper well abandonment. Plugging abandoned artesian wells eliminates the waste of water at the surface and the degradation of groundwater from interaquifer contamination. Wells constructed before current well construction standards are often deficient in casing and expose several aquifers of varying water quality to one common wellbore. These wells are estimated to exist by the thousands and allow potable water supplies to be contaminated with mineralized water from deeper exposed aquifers. Contaminated water and potable water are allowed to flow to the surface, wasting potable water and contaminating surface water from the flow of mineralized water. Section 373.207, F.S., requires that all abandoned artesian wells be plugged.

Plugging wells consists of pumping cement from the abandoned well's total depth back to the surface. Confinement is thus reestablished, and mixing of varying water qualities and free-flowing are stopped. Prior to plugging, an abandoned well is geophysically logged to determine the proper plugging method and to provide background water quality and geologic data for inclusion in the district's data base. The district uses these data to determine changes in water quality since the well was constructed.

The emphasis of this program is in the southern half of the SWFWMD, where intact confining layers are pressurized, creating an artesian effect. Chapter 373, F.S., requires that artesian systems be specifically addressed.

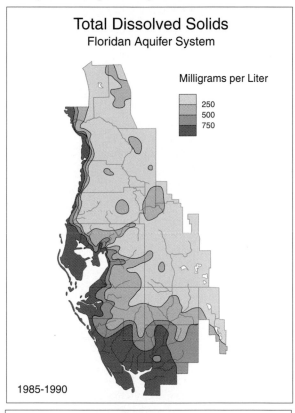

Total Dissolved Solids
Floridan Aquifer System

Milligrams per Liter

250
500
750

1985-1990

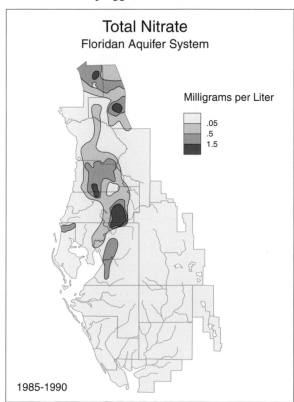

Total Nitrate
Floridan Aquifer System

Milligrams per Liter

.05
.5
1.5

1985-1990

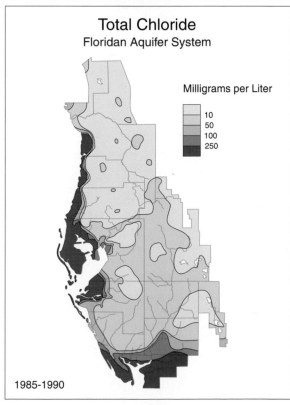

Total Chloride
Floridan Aquifer System

Milligrams per Liter

10
50
100
250

1985-1990

255

Natural Systems

The Environmental Resource Permitting program protects receiving watersheds, including vital wetlands and surface water ecosystems, from potential contamination or undue destruction. Wetlands protection, restoration, and mitigation standards provide an important means of preserving these ecosystems.

Public ownership is one of the most effective means of preserving Florida's remaining natural systems and their associated water resource benefits. The district, through its local and regional water management activities, has acquired lands for a broad spectrum of water resource protection and management benefits. These benefits have included flood protection, water quality protection and improvement, water supply development, protection of recharge areas, protection of wetland systems (such as headwater swamps and floodplains), and restoration and management of uplands.

Land acquisition at the district is guided and funded by two major statewide initiatives: the Save Our Rivers (SOR) and the Water Management Lands Trust Fund Preservation 2000 (P2000) programs. These programs target the protection of natural resources at the local and regional level. Lands important to water resources and water management are acquired along with lands of unique environmental values endangered by development activities. The district owns more than 260,000 acres, most of which were purchased through the SOR and P2000 programs.

The legislative inception of the Surface Water Improvement and Management (SWIM) program in 1987 established a broader district approach to surface water quality for selected, regionally significant water bodies.

The legislature enacted the SWIM Act in response to water quality declines and associated natural systems degradation in surface-water bodies of statewide or regional significance. The act mandated that priority be given to Tampa Bay and its tributaries, as one of the eight water bodies identified in the enabling legislation. The act also mandated that each of the five water management districts prepare and submit a prioritized list of water bodies of regional or statewide significance within their boundaries.

In addition to Tampa Bay, the district originally identified seven other ranked priority water bodies. Subsequent to that initial ranking, the district had added Winter Haven Chain of Lakes and Sarasota Bay as priority water bodies. Banana Lake, which DEP identified as "the most polluted lake in the state" prior to its restoration, was a successfully completed priority water body project.

The SWIM process calls for preparation of management plans for each priority water body. SWIM plans are action-oriented documents, not summaries of issues or policy. The plans are intended to serve as a guide to district staff and local governments in restoration and protection efforts for the priority water bodies. Management plans have been adopted for all nine of the priority water bodies.

Tampa Bay has been the focal point of the district's SWIM program activities, having been identified as the number one priority water body for preservation and restoration. Significant research, resources and remedial actions have also been directed at the district's other ranked priority water bodies. The SWIM Program has undertaken many activities, including en-

256

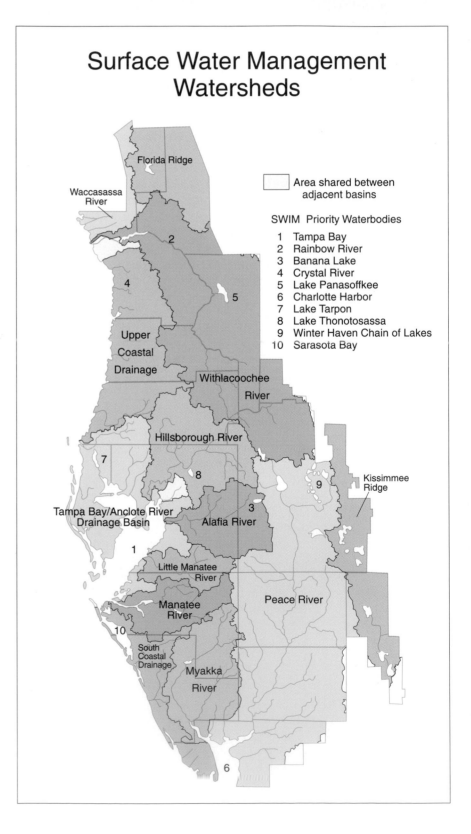

vironmental assessments, urban stormwater analyses, seagrass mapping and habitat restoration, model ordinance development, wildlife assessments, and lake rehabilitation.

Funding for the program was initially based on a funding formula of 80 percent state and 20 percent district match. This has since been altered to a 60-40 arrangement. Levels of state funding support have varied over time, and future program viability may well depend on assuring a dedicated funding source. The district's basin boards have provided solid funding support for SWIM and related programs for several years. These water quality projects have been funded at the request of, and with matching funds from, various local governments.

Maintaining minimum flows and levels is a statutory charge for Florida's water management districts. The district's programs on minimum flows and levels originate in Section 373.042, F.S., and from the district's desire to treat the environment as a rightful "user" of water. If water resources and associated natural systems are to be protected and maintained, the identification and the establishment of water levels and flows are essential. Such activities will also serve to balance water withdrawals for human needs with protection of surface-water levels for navigation, recreation, and related functions.

Through its statutory authority and by exercise of its rules in Chapter 40D-8, the district establishes minimum levels for selected lakes within its boundaries. Once officially adopted, levels are used as guidelines for the operation of district control structures, as advisory information to other regulatory and planning bodies, and, where relevant, in the district permit evaluation process. These levels are designed to allow for the natural stage fluctuations characteristic of Florida lakes and are based upon a study of each lake. This study includes an examination of all existing records and considerable field study of actual lake conditions.

Green Swamp

James Phillips

257

Cypress Dome

Southwest Florida Water Management District

E. G. Simmons Area   Michael Crow

The SWFWMD approach to managing withdrawal-related impacts to streams and other flowing watercourses involves two management components.

1. Allowable withdrawal rates are established in water use permits that specify volumes of water that can be removed from a stream or other surface watercourse over various times. These quantities are typically expressed as average daily and maximum daily rates of withdrawal.

2. Regulatory minimum flows are established at which withdrawals must cease so as not to cause any reduction in flow. Essentially, withdrawals may not reduce flows in a watercourse below its minimum flow.

The district has addressed the first component (allowable withdrawal rates) by establishing a 10 percent threshold for stream withdrawals. This threshold requires that cumulative withdrawals greater than 10 percent of daily flow at any point in a drainage basin will not be permitted unless it can be shown that such withdrawals will not cause unacceptable environmental impacts. The 10 percent threshold, which was based on several years of study of streams and estuaries in the district, does much to protect the natural flow characteristics of streams. The threshold is applied to all new withdrawals from watercourses in the district.

The chief threats to the groundwater resource are overdraft and contamination. The district's water supply source protection and water quality programs address both overdraft and contamination. Local governments, regional water supply authorities, and other water suppliers also play a significant role in protecting groundwater resources.

Overdraft occurs when groundwater withdrawals consistently exceed recharge, causing a long-term decline in groundwater levels. This human-induced imbalance results in going beyond sustainable yield, or exceeding the natural carrying capacity of the resource. Overdraft may lead to saltwater intrusion if the freshwater in an aquifer is reduced enough to allow saltwater to move upward from underlying sources or laterally from coastal areas. Excessive groundwater withdrawals may also cause the lowering of surface-water levels and flows and the shortening of wetland hydroperiods. Establishment of minimum aquifer levels is an important district tool in resource protection.

Other Programs

The district has an aggressive public communications initiative designed to support district activities, including water conservation efforts. Conservation initiatives have involved a variety of themes over the past several years, including "Turn It Off," "Know Your Day," "Plant It Smart," "Do Your Part," and "This Land is Your Land."

The district has also actively supported xeriscape, and the "Florida Yards Program."

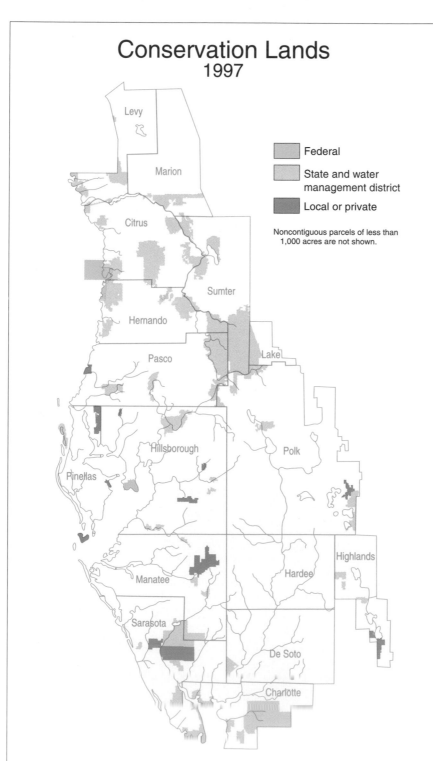

Conservation Lands
1997

Levy

Marion

Citrus

Sumter

Hernando

Pasco

Lake

Hillsborough

Polk

Pinellas

Highlands

Manatee

Hardee

Sarasota

De Soto

Charlotte

☐ Federal

☐ State and water management district

☐ Local or private

Noncontiguous parcels of less than 1,000 acres are not shown.

Communication efforts include television, radio and newspaper public service announcements, media relations, direct mailings, the district's speaker's bureau, feature length television programs, and publication in industry and trade journals. Many of these efforts have been coordinated on a statewide basis with the other water management districts and often with local governments within the district. An in-school education program provides curricula and materials to school systems, along with teacher training and other education programs. Public education programs target groups, organizations, and the public.

The district has a comprehensive Local Government Planning Assistance program. Overall, this program is intended to assist local governments in incorporating sound water management principles and the best available water resource information into their comprehensive plans. This assistance deals with all aspects of water management, including water supply, flood protection, water quality management, and natural systems management, as these issues are addressed by local governments in their plans.

For water supply needs and sources, the district cooperates with local governments to develop consistency and compatibility in water supply planning programs. This includes consistent projections of future demands and identification of sources to meet these demands, including alternative sources such as conservation, reuse and desalination, etc.

Planning assistance also includes the review of local government comprehensive plans. Between 1988 and 1991, the district provided comments on the plans of its 98 local governments as part of the review process outlined in Chapter 163, F.S. The district reviews plan amendments and provides advisory comments to the Florida Department of Community Affairs. The district also assists in the preparation, and subsequent review, of the regional planning councils' strategic regional policy plans.

James Phillips

Weekiwachee River

REFERENCES

A source for a map or figure has a number in parentheses following the entry. This number refers to the page in this atlas for which the source was used.

Coffin, J.E., and W.L. Fletcher. 1996. *Water Resources Data, Florida, Water Year 1995. Vol. 3A: Southwest Florida Surface Water.* U.S. Geological Survey Water-Data Report Fl-95-3A. (map, 243)

Florida Geological Survey. 1991. *Florida's Groundwater Quality Monitoring Program Hydrogeologic Framework.* Florida Geological Survey Special Publication No. 32. Tallahassee. (map, 255)

Florida Natural Areas Inventory. Tallahassee. (map, 258)

Hand, J., J. Col, and L. Lord. 1996. *Southwest Florida District Water Quality 1996.* 305(b) Technical Appendix. Florida Department of Environmental Protection. Tallahassee. (map, 253)

Sarasota Bay National Estuary Program. 1995. *Sarasota Bay: The Voyage to Paradise Reclaimed, 1995 Comprehensive Conservation and Management Plan for Sarasota Bay.* Sarasota, Florida.

Snell, L.J., and W.E. Kenner. 1974. *Surface Water Features of Florida.* Florida Bureau of Geology Map Series 66. Tallahassee. (map, 242)

Southwest Florida Water Management District. 1992. Draft Water Supply Needs and Sources, 1990–2020. Brooksville.

Southwest Florida Water Management District. 1993. Eastern Tampa Bay Water Resource Assessment Project. Brooksville.

Southwest Florida Water Management District. 1994. Draft Southern Water Use Caution Area Management Plan. Brooksville.

Southwest Florida Water Management District. 1995. *Southwest Florida District Water Management Plan, Volumes 1 and 2.* Brooksville.

Southwest Florida Water Management District. 1996. *Northern Tampa Bay Water Resources Assessment Project, Volumes 1 and 2.* Brooksville.

Southwest Florida Water Management District. 1997. *Five-Year Basin Board Plans, FY 1997–FY 2002.* Brooksville.

Southwest Florida Water Management District. 1997. *Southwest Florida Water Management District's Save Our Rivers/Preservation 2000 Five-Year Plan, 1997.* Brooksville.

Southwest Florida Water Management District. 1997. *Water Use Demand Estimates and Projections, 1996–2020.* Brooksville.

Southwest Florida Water Management District. Various years. *Southwest Florida Water Management District's Surface Water Improvement and Management Plans.* Brooksville.

Tampa Bay National Estuary Program. 1996. Charting the Course: The Comprehensive Conservation and Management Plan for Tampa Bay. St. Petersburg, Florida.

U.S. Geological Survey, Water Resources Division. Tallahassee, Florida. (map, 247)

Waldron, P.W., L.R. Cannon, G.S. Comp, P.M. Dooris, R.P. Evans, A.E. Gilboy, J.W. Heuer Jr., L. Miller, R.P. Morberg, R.S. Owen, D.K. Parkin-Welz, D.L. Slonena, R.W. Schultz, J.R. Whalen, D.A. Wiley, and B.C. Wirth. 1984. "Southwest Florida Water Management District." In E.A. Fernald and D.J. Patton, eds. *Water Resources Atlas of Florida.* Tallahassee, Florida: Institute of Science and Public Affairs.

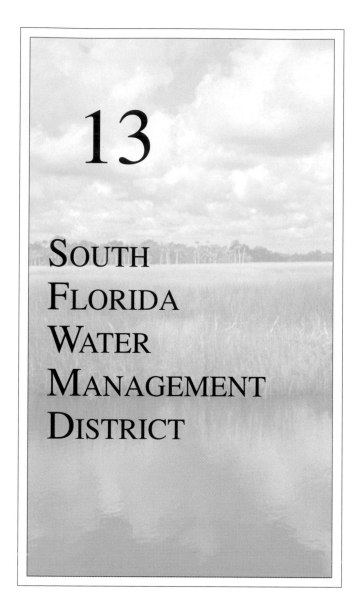

13

SOUTH FLORIDA WATER MANAGEMENT DISTRICT

The 17,000-square-mile South Florida Water Management District encompasses all or portions of 16 counties. Forty percent of the population and 31 percent of the land area of the state are within its boundaries. The district contains two watersheds or drainage basins: the Big Cypress Basin (Collier County and part of Monroe County) and the larger Okeechobee Basin, which begins at the headwaters of the Kissimmee River and ends in Florida Bay.

In its natural state, South Florida can be described in one word—wet. Rainfall occurs at an annual average rate of about 54 inches; 67 percent of that amount, or about 36 inches, occurs between May and September. The combination of concentrated periods of rainfall and flat terrain produces a continually swampy, flooded condition throughout much of the region during the wet season, a subtropical characteristic which, for a long time, made South Florida a less-than-desirable spot for human settlement. Over the last 100 years or so the South Florida environment has been substantially modified to accommodate urban, residential, and agricultural development, of-

Joel VanArman, Winnie Park, Patti Nicholas, Patricia Strayer, Agnes McLean, Barry Rosen, Jim Gross

ten to the detriment of the remaining areas of subtropical wilderness.

The first large-scale regional drainage project in South Florida began in 1881, when Hamilton Disston bought 4 million acres of land from the state for twenty-five cents per acre. In 1882, a Lake Okeechobee outlet to the Gulf coast, via the Caloosahatchee River was completed. In the same year, Southport Canal was cut between Lake Tohopekaliga and Lake Cypress. The St. Cloud Canal, which connects Lake Tohopekaliga to East Lake Tohopekaliga, was completed next. By fall of 1883, Disston's company had drained land and opened navigation channels from the Kissimmee Lakes to the Gulf of Mexico.

Disston's land reclamation project revived the depressed railroad industry in Florida which, in turn, brought new settlement, new industry, and new growth. The region's development, however, proceeded in a very haphazard manner—a reflection of the variety of private interests trying to make a profit from South Florida. Funding to sustain large land reclamation projects became harder to acquire as the nineteenth century drew to a close, and drainage efforts by private business ended as well.

In 1907, the state legislature created the Everglades Drainage District. From 1913 to 1927, six major canals and several smaller waterways, 440 miles of levees, and 16 locks and dams were constructed. Hurricanes in 1926 and 1928 halted construction by the Everglades Drainage District, but gave rise to the Okeechobee Drainage District (1929). The Okeechobee district was created to prevent a recurrence of the flooding produced by wind tides on Lake Okeechobee and constructed floodway channels, control gates, and major levees along the lake's shores.

Droughts occurred between 1931 and 1945, bringing saltwater intrusion along the coasts and causing extensive fires in the muck soils of the Everglades. This period came to a dramatic end with the hurricane of 1947. In 1948, Congress authorized the Central and Southern Flood Control Project to provide flood protection and adequate water supply, prevent saltwater intrusion, encourage agricultural and urban development, and preserve fish and wildlife. The Central and Southern Florida Flood Control District (CSFFCD) was established in 1949 by the Florida legislature to act as local sponsor for the federal project. The CSFFCD acquired lands for, and assumed operation and maintenance of, each section of the project as it was completed.

From 1949 through 1969, the U.S. Army Corps of Engineers and the CSFFCD built and operated the project works. At the same time, South Florida's population surged, and industrial and residential consumption became significant components, in addition to the existing agricultural demands, of water use within South Florida.

The National Environmental Protection Act, passed in 1969, requires the corps and the CSFFCD to consider damage to the environment when making management decisions. Growing concern for preservation of the environment prompted, in 1971, a Governor's conference on Florida's water management issues. The conference produced legislative action, the Water Resources Act of 1972, which broadens the authority and responsibility of the CSFFCD, and requires control and regulation of water supplies and their use. In 1976 the CSFFCD became the South Florida Water Management District (SFWMD), to reflect the changing scope of the district's responsibilities.

Planning Boundaries

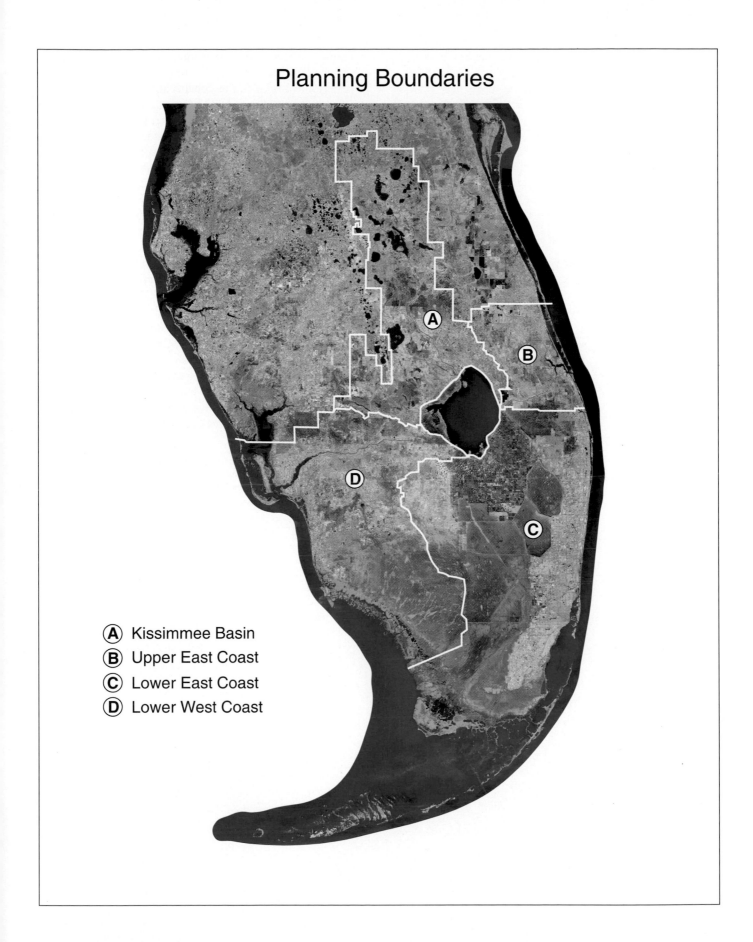

(A) Kissimmee Basin
(B) Upper East Coast
(C) Lower East Coast
(D) Lower West Coast

Excavation, construction of barriers, and other mechanical means to channel and retain water have been supplemented by the use of improved planning, operational, and regulatory processes to control human use of water. Recent efforts have focused on developing water management plans for four planning districts within the SFWMD and for Lake Okeechobee to address water supply, water quality, flood control, and environmental issues. Land acquisition programs place environmentally sensitive areas in public ownership and protect these resources from degradation and development. Major efforts began in the 1980s, and will continue well into the next century, to restore and enhance South Florida's remaining natural ecosystems.

Topography, Physiographic Features, and Climate

Nearly all the land in South Florida is less than 100 feet above mean sea level (msl). Land surface generally slopes from north to south. The coastal regions and most of the peninsula south of Lake Okeechobee are very flat and lie below 25 feet msl, except near Immokalee and parts of the Atlantic Coastal Ridge. North of Lake Okeechobee, the Lake Wales Ridge juts down the center of the peninsula and is mostly above the 100-foot contour. East of this ridge, the Okeechobee Plain rises from approximately 20 feet at the lake to 30 to 40 feet at the edge of the Osceola Plain, which rises in elevation from 60 feet to 90 feet.

Two major physiographic features, Lake Okeechobee and the Everglades, are discussed separately in this chapter. The Kissimmee River valley (also discussed separately) crosses the Osceola and Okeechobee plains and is a major source of surface water to Lake Okeechobee and the Everglades. Rainfall in the northern portion of the Osceola Plain recharges the Floridan aquifer. The Immokalee Rise provides recharge to the water table and sandstone aquifers in Lee and Collier counties. Water from the Atlantic Coastal Ridge and Everglades recharges the Biscayne aquifer in Dade and Broward counties and provides surface water flows to Florida Bay. The Big Cypress Swamp in eastern Collier and southern Hendry counties contributes primarily to surface-water flow to coastal estuaries along the southwest coast of Collier County and Everglades National Park. The Florida Keys have no major source of freshwater except for rainfall and limited storage in the shallow aquifer of the larger islands. Coastal marshes and mangrove swamps, which are subject to tidal influx of saltwater, border the southern end of the peninsula.

South Florida, with its distinct wet and dry seasons, is the only savanna climate in the continental United States. Within this region, rainfall varies considerably. Average wet season (May 1–October 31) rainfall ranges from 46 inches near the southeast coast to 36 inches in the Kissimmee valley. Average dry season rainfall varies from 17 inches along the south-

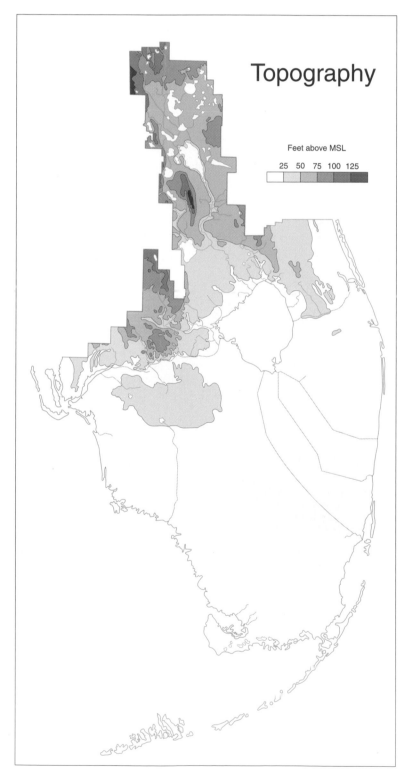

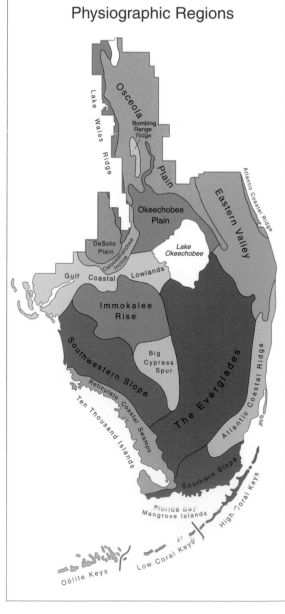

262

east coast to 10 inches on the southwest coast. The driest month is December, when average monthly rainfall ranges from less than 1.25 inches near Everglades City to 2.50 inches near West Palm Beach. The wettest month is September, when average rainfall ranges from 9.5 inches at West Palm Beach and Homestead to 6 inches near Okeechobee. The area occasionally experiences extended periods of below average rainfall, such as occurred during the drought of 1988–91. South Florida is also subject to tropical storms and hurricanes, which can produce significant amounts of rain. During such years, rainfall for the year can total over 80 inches.

Analysis of rainfall data by the South Florida Water Management District indicates four primary trends:

1. substantially less rainfall occurs over Lake Okeechobee than occurs over adjacent land areas;
2. much of the rainfall that occurs during the wet season along the southeastern coast results from convection due to differences in temperature between land and water;

3. precipitation on the mainland is therefore higher than in coastal waters or over the barrier islands; and
4. the lowest annual average amounts of rainfall generally occur in the Kissimmee River valley and in the Florida Keys

Researchers at the SFWMD are also studying long-range trends in weather conditions. Studies conducted by the University of Florida, the National Hurricane Center, the National Weather Service, and others show that a significant decline in tropical storm and hurricane incidence occurred in South Florida from 1960 until 1992, when Hurricane Andrew hit. Recent data, however, suggest that the frequency of hurricanes may be increasing. The SFWMD is developing methods to predict droughts and excessive rainfall periods based on time-sequence analyses and relationships to global climate trends. Major droughts have occurred at roughly ten-year intervals since the 1940s, whereas excessive rainfall has occurred in cycles of approximately six years. Some significant relationships are apparent between weather patterns in other parts of

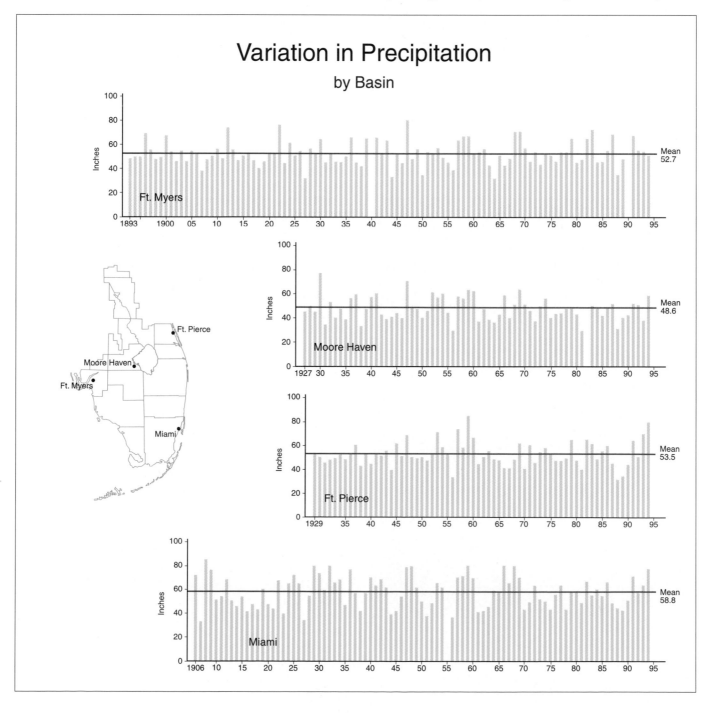

263

the globe, such as El Niño events in the tropical Pacific Ocean and rainfall in sub-Saharan Africa, and conditions in South Florida.

Land Use and Population

In 1990, South Florida had an estimated population of 5.2 million and was home to one of every three Floridians. Population is concentrated in the Orlando area, along the Atlantic coast, and along the Gulf Coast from Marco Island to Ft. Myers.

Agriculture is a major feature of the economy of South Florida. Unlike urban development, most of the agricultural development has occurred near the center of the state. The area north of Lake Okeechobee includes dairy and beef cattle farms. The Everglades Agricultural Area (EAA), located immediately south of Lake Okeechobee, is one of the most productive farming regions in the country. The primary crops include sugarcane, rice, truck crops, and sod. Citrus is grown extensively throughout the region, but is especially concentrated in the Upper East Coast and Lower West Coast planning areas. In spite of intense urban development along the coast, agriculture is still an important land use in western areas of Dade, Broward, and Palm Beach counties.

A large portion of the land in southern Florida remains natural, though much of it is disturbed. The dominant natural features are the Kissimmee River floodplain, Lake Okeechobee and the extensive marshes in the lake's littoral zone, the water conservation areas, the Big Cypress National Preserve and adjacent areas in Collier and Lee counties, and Everglades National Park at the southernmost tip of the peninsula.

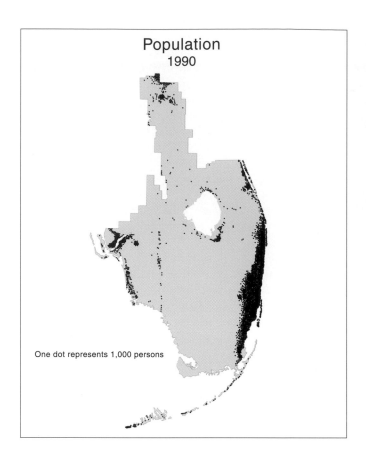

Population
1990

One dot represents 1,000 persons

Water Resources

Surface Water

The natural surface-water hydrology of much of South Florida is characterized by low topography and generally poor drainage. Much of the excess surface water flowed for short distances and collected in one of the region's numerous shallow lakes or wetlands. During extremely wet periods, these basins overflowed and large quantities of water moved to the south or to the coast and ultimately discharged to tide. This drainage pattern is still apparent in the northern and western parts of the district where many of the basins are named for the receiving water bodies

In order to make South Florida more acceptable for human habitation, the natural water courses were channelized and interconnected to expedite movement of water away from urban or agricultural lands. South Florida presently has an extensive, heavily managed canal network; a series of high-capacity, low-head pumping installations; and several surface-water impoundments totaling more than 1,000 square miles. These same canals and structures can be operated either for flood control or water supply purposes.

The basins of Lower East Coast and Upper East Coast planning areas are primarily named for the canals and structures that control their water movement. The heart of this modern surface water management system consists of Lake Okeechobee and the interconnected major features of the Central and Southern Florida Flood Control Project. These include the Kissimmee Lakes and River; Lake Okeechobee and outlets; the water conservation areas; Everglades National Park and Florida Bay; and the coastal canal networks of Dade, Broward, Palm Beach, Martin, and St. Lucie counties.

Lake Okeechobee functions as a primary storage reservoir for excess (flood) waters from lands adjacent to and north of

264

South Florida Water Management District

Residential development on edge of agricultural lands

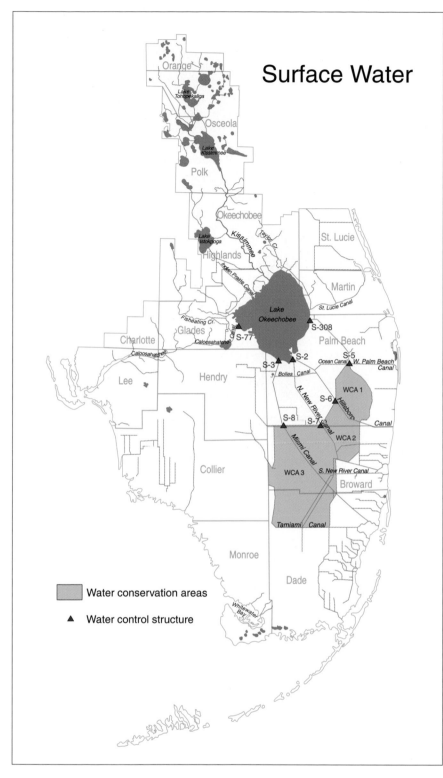

Surface Water

sionally used to pump water into the lake for emergency flood relief. Stations S-5, S-6, S-7, and S-8 pump excess water from the southern portion into the water conservation areas. Additional downstream structures provide for transfer of this water through the water conservation areas to east coast canals and to the sloughs and wetlands of Everglades National Park.

Groundwater

Three major aquifer systems have been identified in South Florida. The Floridan aquifer system is a deep, regionally extensive, artesian limestone system with generally high transmissivity. The Floridan aquifer system is the primary source of water supply in the northern counties of the district and is used as a source of supplemental irrigation water as far south as Martin County. This system receives direct recharge along a structural high, which occurs in the central part of the state. From these recharge areas, the Floridan dips southward and becomes confined by the clays and silts of the younger Hawthorn Group. The potentiometric surface is highest at the point of primary recharge and decreases to the south. Near Lake Okeechobee the potentiometric surface of the aquifer exceeds land surface, causing Floridan wells to freely flow up to 1,000 gals/min.

The intermediate aquifer system is developed within the Hawthorn Group, mainly in the southwestern part of the state and includes several aquifers. These leaky artesian aquifers consist of moderately transmissive sandstone or sandy and shelly limestone beds and produce water of fair to poor quality. In most other parts of the state, the Hawthorn Group is a major confining unit, separating the surficial aquifer system from the Floridan aquifer.

The surficial aquifer system consists of sands, sandy and shelly limestone, sandstone, and silts and contains water table and semi-confined aquifers. One of the major

265

aquifers in this system is the Biscayne aquifer in Dade, Broward, and southern Palm Beach counties. This water table aquifer generally contains water of potable quality, and wells in it can yield in excess of 10 mgd. Other surficial aquifers have water quality that varies from potable to nonpotable. Yields to wells may vary from a few gals/min to over 2,000 gals/min.

Three hydrogeologic regions have been identified within SFWMD. In the northern region, generally north of Lake Okeechobee, water in usable quantity and quality is available from the surficial aquifers and the Floridan aquifer system. The Floridan aquifer system yields in excess of 2,000 gal/min at the northern limits of the SFWMD and at various points in its recharge area along the central ridge. The district has conducted studies of this aquifer in the general vicinity of Lake Okeechobee and in Martin and St. Lucie counties. These stud-

the lake. In addition, the lake provides water supply to downstream basins. Most of the water enters the lake from rainfall, local runoff, and discharge from the Kissimmee River, Fisheating Creek, and Taylor Creek. Water is lost from the lake by evaporation and by discharge to the EAA through structures S-2 and S-3, to the Caloosahatchee River through S-77, and to the St. Lucie River through S-308.

The Everglades Agricultural Area, located south and east of Lake Okeechobee, has very little natural drainage and therefore depends on the canals and large pump stations to provide protection from flooding. Four major canals traverse the area from north to south.

Structures and pumps at stations S-2 and S-3 let water out of Lake Okeechobee to the north end of the EAA for irrigation during the dry growing season. These facilities are also occa-

ies have shown that water from the Floridan aquifer generally has high levels of dissolved solids that can be a source of contamination to the surficial aquifers. Use of water from the Floridan aquifer in these areas should be discouraged in favor of the better-quality water available from shallow aquifers.

In the southeastern region, only the surficial aquifers are suitable as potable groundwater supply sources. The Biscayne aquifer has extremely high transmissivities along the coast and is moderately thick in these areas. Wellfields in this aquifer can generally yield in excess of 2,000 gal/min. The operation of wellfields near the coast may be constrained by saltwater

intrusion. This aquifer tends to thin out toward the western portions of Dade and Broward counties, underneath the Water conservation areas and total groundwater yields in these areas may be limited. Wellfields in the Biscayne aquifer can be rapidly and effectively recharged from the water conservation areas and the coastal canal system.

The southwestern part of the state is characterized by a complex sequence of hydrostratigraphic units representing all three aquifer systems. In this region, water availability is constrained both by high mineralization and low transmissivities in some aquifers. The most productive aquifers in this area are

266

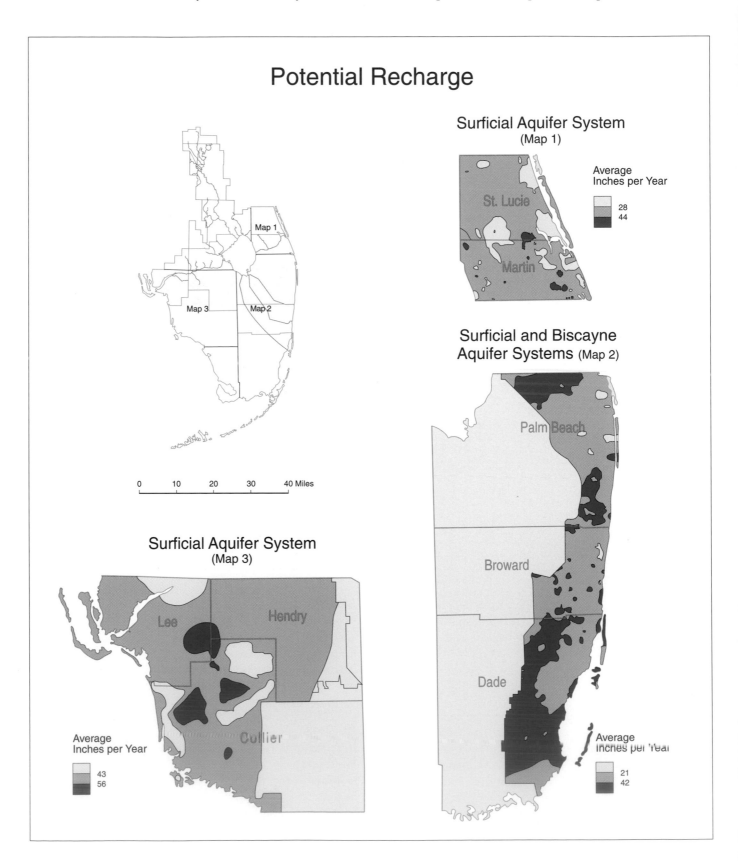

Potential Recharge

Surficial Aquifer System
(Map 1)

Average Inches per Year

28
44

Surficial and Biscayne Aquifer Systems (Map 2)

Palm Beach

Broward

Dade

Average Inches per Year

21
42

Surficial Aquifer System
(Map 3)

Lee
Hendry
Collier

Average Inches per Year

43
56

0 10 20 30 40 Miles

located in the surficial and Hawthorn aquifer systems in northeastern Collier and southwestern Hendry counties. These aquifers are recharged locally by rainfall in the Immokalee Rise.

The district has conducted surveys of groundwater resources of Collier and Lee counties that have identified a number of potential areas for future wellfield development.

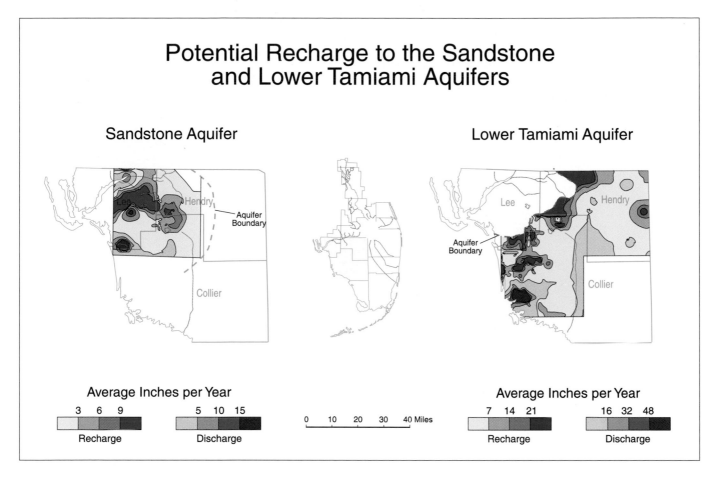

Potential Recharge to the Sandstone and Lower Tamiami Aquifers

Sandstone Aquifer

Lower Tamiami Aquifer

Average Inches per Year

3 6 9   5 10 15

Recharge   Discharge

0 10 20 30 40 Miles

Average Inches per Year

7 14 21   16 32 48

Recharge   Discharge

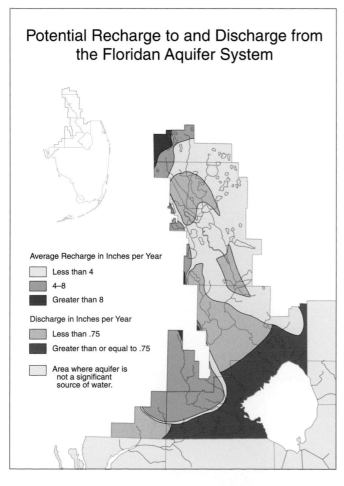

Potential Recharge to and Discharge from the Floridan Aquifer System

Average Recharge in Inches per Year
- Less than 4
- 4–8
- Greater than 8

Discharge in Inches per Year
- Less than .75
- Greater than or equal to .75

- Area where aquifer is not a significant source of water.

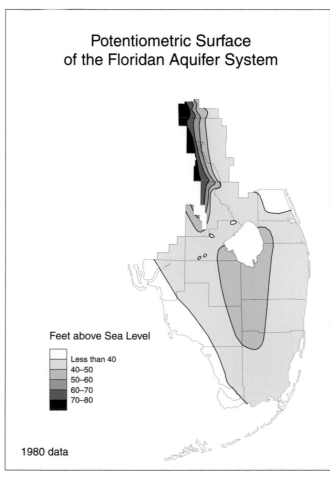

Potentiometric Surface of the Floridan Aquifer System

Feet above Sea Level
- Less than 40
- 40–50
- 50–60
- 60–70
- 70–80

1980 data

267

Hydrogeologic Cross Sections

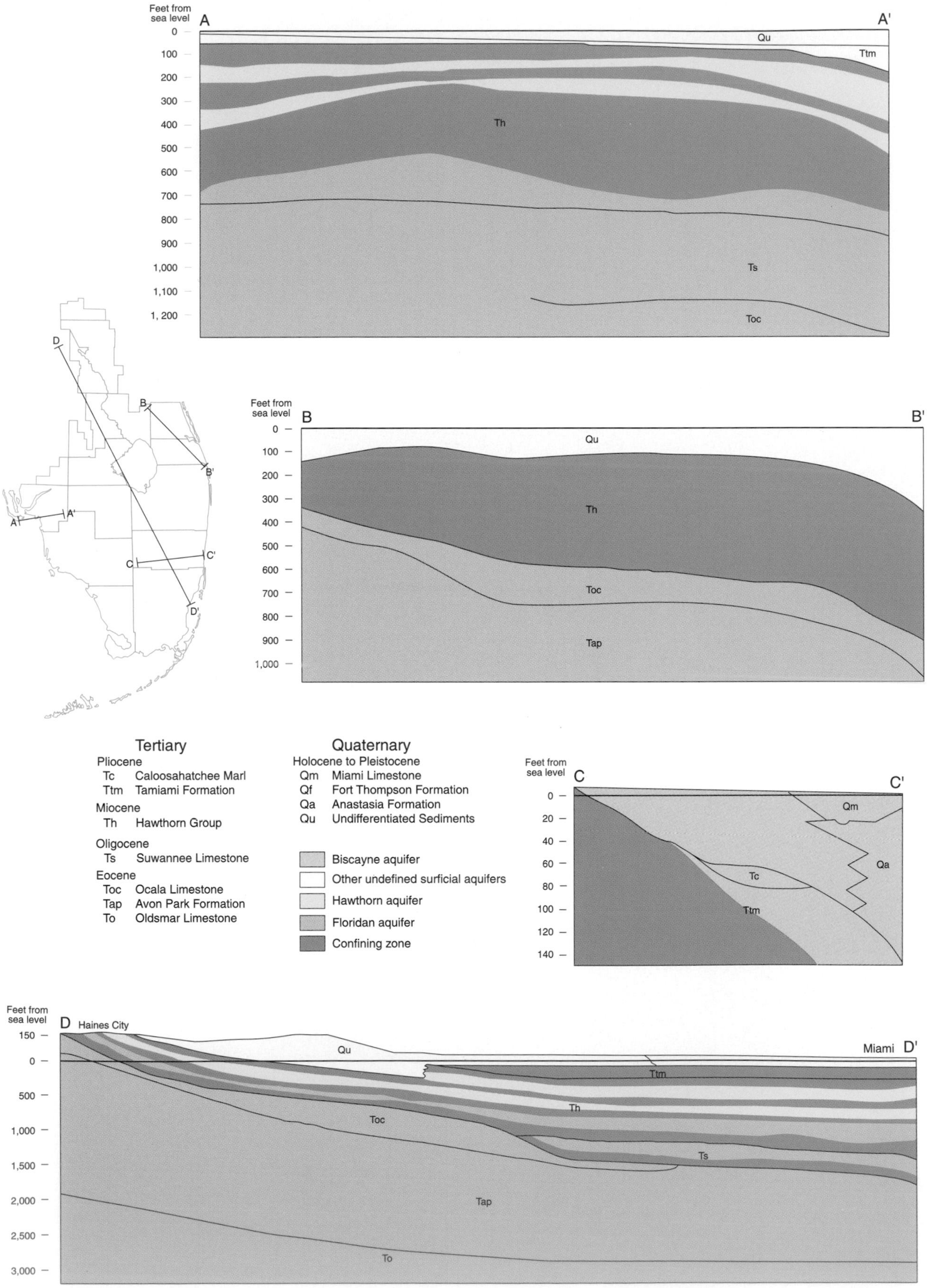

Feet from sea level
A
A'
Qu
Ttm
Th
Ts
Toc
0
100
200
300
400
500
600
700
800
900
1,000
1,100
1, 200
B
B'
Qu
Th
Toc
Tap
C
C'
Qm
Qa
Tc
Ttm
0
20
40
60
80
100
120
140
D Haines City
Miami D'
Qu
Ttm
Th
Toc
Ts
Tap
To
150
0
500
1,000
1,500
2,000
2,500
3,000
Tertiary
Pliocene
Tc Caloosahatchee Marl
Ttm Tamiami Formation
Miocene
Th Hawthorn Group
Oligocene
Ts Suwannee Limestone
Eocene
Toc Ocala Limestone
Tap Avon Park Formation
To Oldsmar Limestone
Quaternary
Holocene to Pleistocene
Qm Miami Limestone
Qf Fort Thompson Formation
Qa Anastasia Formation
Qu Undifferentiated Sediments
Biscayne aquifer
Other undefined surficial aquifers
Hawthorn aquifer
Floridan aquifer
Confining zone

Water Supply, Use, and Management

Demands for water vary seasonally. During the winter, the seasonal tourist population is at its peak, while irrigation demands are relatively low. In late spring, when irrigation demands are at their peak, tourist populations are declining. Overall, water demand for urban water systems remains fairly constant. However, the supply is primarily replenished from May to October when approximately 75 percent of the region's annual rainfall occurs. In extremely dry years, this can translate to low water availability during the late winter and spring. In areas where groundwater sources have limited storage capacity, water shortages may be declared, with associated economic and social hardships.

In addition to water that is processed for human uses, a great deal of water remains in the system and is set aside to protect the resource from significant harm. This water is needed to support natural systems by maintaining acceptable water levels and flows in lakes, rivers, streams, and wetlands; to protect groundwater resources; and to provide adequate freshwater flow to estuaries and coastal waters. South Florida's water supply is allocated to provide an equitable distribution of the resource between environmental water needs and other reasonable and beneficial uses.

In many cases, the exact amount of water required to maintain natural systems in their original or historical condition is unknown. Scientists are forced to estimate, extrapolate, or infer these needs based on historical data and the performance and characteristics of the remaining natural systems that exist today.

The SFWMD is working cooperatively with other agencies and groups to develop scientifically sound approaches for managing the quality, timing, distribution, and volume of water supply to remaining natural systems within the district. These studies are attempting to determine:

1. Water supply needs of lakes and wetlands in terms of water levels, duration, timing, and distribution of water deliveries;
2. Minimum water levels and the amount of time that these levels need to be sustained to protect groundwater systems from overuse or from saltwater intrusion; and
3. Minimum flows and levels for rivers and estuaries that are needed to maintain streamflow characteristics and biological communities.

Areas of the SFWMD where water resources are critical or are anticipated to become critical over the next 20 years are required by Florida law to be designated as Water Resource Caution Areas. Within these areas, a reasonable amount of use of reclaimed water from domestic wastewater treatment facilities is required. In the past the SFWMD designated these areas as Critical Water Supply Problem Areas.

Much of South Florida has been designated as a Water Resource Caution Area. This designation encompasses all of the Lower East Coast and the Upper East Coast Planning Areas, as well as the Lower West Coast, with the exception of Charlotte County. Within the Kissimmee Basin Planning Area, only those portions of Glades, Martin, and Okeechobee counties adjacent to Lake Okeechobee and southern Highlands County have been designated as Water Resource Caution Areas.

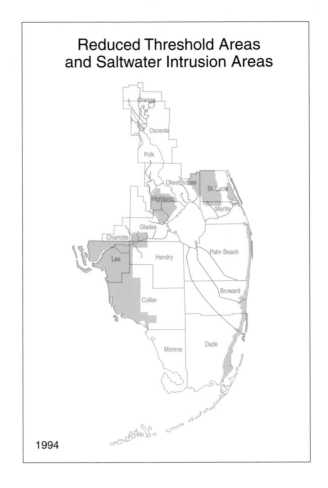

Reduced Threshold Areas and Saltwater Intrusion Areas

1994

Certain areas within the Water Resource Caution Areas have also been designated as reduced threshold areas for obtaining consumptive use permits. In these areas the normal daily withdrawal threshold is reduced from 100,000 gallons per day to 10,000 gallons per day.

Saltwater intrudes in groundwater in South Florida in three ways. The first, coastal seepage, is caused by the difference in density between saltwater and freshwater. The Ghyben-Herzberg principle, which relates the specific gravity of the two fluids with the elevation of the freshwater head above sea level, is used to approximate the position of the interface in coastal regions. In general, the ratio of the freshwater head above sea level to the depth to saltwater below sea level is 1 to 40. While this relationship has limited application to large land masses, the lowering of the freshwater head in a coastal region facilitates landward migration of seawater and limits the yields of coastal wellfields.

The 1904 map of coastal Dade County on p. 271 indicates the condition of the area prior to the construction of major drainage projects. As drainage systems were built, groundwater elevations were reduced and seawater moved landward. By 1953, several saltwater control structures had been built in order to control the inland extension of seawater. By 1962, the system had stabilized with significant rollback of the freshwater-saltwater interface along the Little River and Biscayne canals. The effects of the 1971, 1981, 1985, and 1990 droughts, prior to recovery, are shown in the more recent maps. Comparison of the 1984 map with recent data from 1995 indicates that conditions remain relatively stable and in some areas the line has moved further seaward.

A second source of saltwater is residual seawater trapped in an aquifer during deposition or as the result of high sea levels during interglacial periods or the effects of storm tides. Such

269

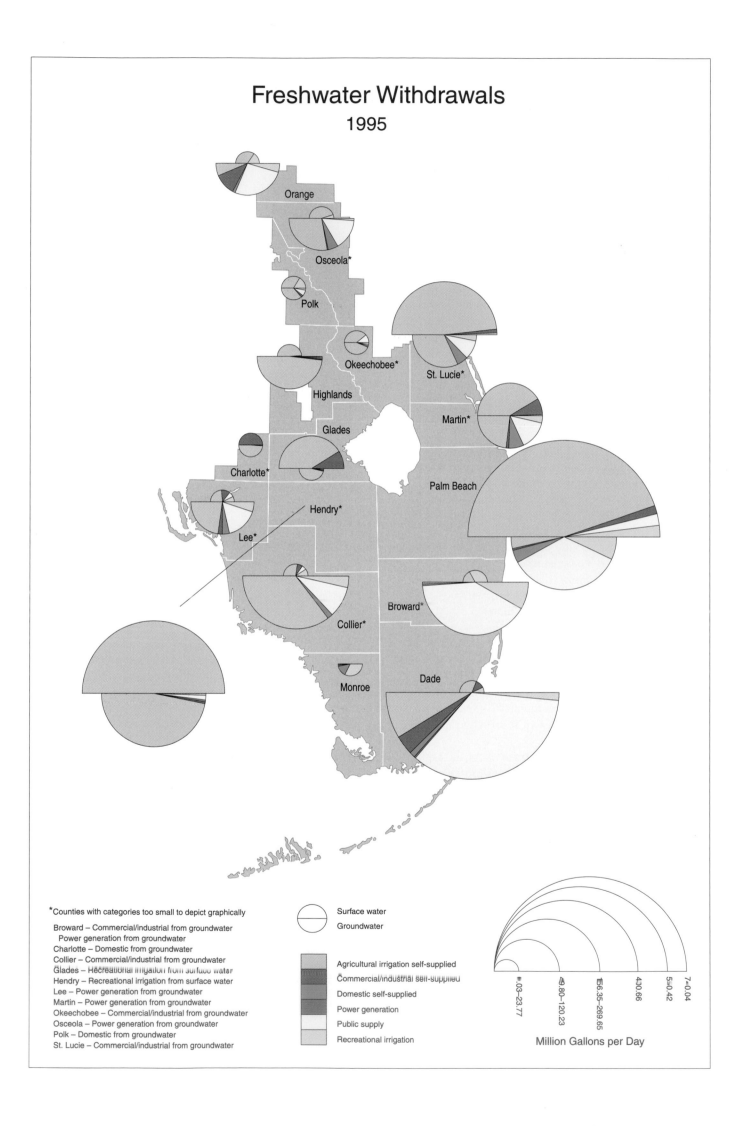

Freshwater Withdrawals
1995

Orange

Osceola*

Polk

Okeechobee*

St. Lucie*

Highlands

Martin*

Glades

Charlotte*

Palm Beach

Hendry*

Lee*

Collier*

Broward*

Monroe

Dade

*Counties with categories too small to depict graphically

Broward – Commercial/industrial from groundwater
  Power generation from groundwater
Charlotte – Domestic from groundwater
Collier – Commercial/industrial from groundwater
Glades – Recreational irrigation from surface water
Hendry – Recreational irrigation from surface water
Lee – Power generation from groundwater
Martin – Power generation from groundwater
Okeechobee – Commercial/industrial from groundwater
Osceola – Power generation from groundwater
Polk – Domestic from groundwater
St. Lucie – Commercial/industrial from groundwater

Surface water
Groundwater

Agricultural irrigation self-supplied
Commercial/industrial self-supplied
Domestic self-supplied
Power generation
Public supply
Recreational irrigation

0.03–23.77
9.80–120.23
56.35–269.65
430.66
550.42
7–0.04

Million Gallons per Day

Saltwater Intrusion

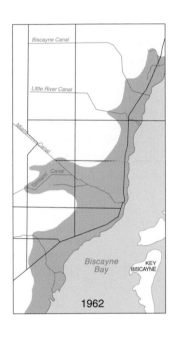

Extent of intrusion at base of Biscayne Aquifer in the greater Miami area

0   4   8 Mi

1904

1943

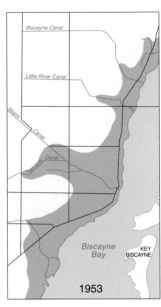

1953

1962

1971

1984

1995

relic saltwater occurs in low-permeability sediments or confined aquifers, which are not readily influenced by direct freshwater recharge. Saltwater anomalies of this type occur in Water Conservation Area 3, beneath Lake Okeechobee, and in coastal Collier County.

Uncontrolled discharge from thousands of abandoned wells, which tap the brackish waters of the Floridan aquifer system, is the third source of saltwater contamination. This problem was most acute in South Florida, where an estimated 6,500 wells discharged 359 mgd of saline water into freshwater aquifers. The Water Quality Assurance Act of 1983 required the permanent plugging of abandoned saline wells.

Flood Protection and Floodplain Management

The need to protect human settlements from flooding and to drain wetlands for agricultural development were driving forces behind construction of the original canal system in South Florida. Improvements to the system have been made to provide further protection from high water conditions. Today, the SFWMD operates many facilities for flood control, including the works of the C&SF Project as well as canals and structures within the Big Cypress Basin. These facilities collect runoff from local drainage systems and route it to the coast or to large

regional storage facilities. Local drainage systems are operated by a variety of special districts, private property owners, and local governments. The local systems typically convey water from individual projects, developments or sub-basins to the regional facilities.

The SFWMD's management efforts are directed at preventing or reducing damage from floods while protecting or enhancing the SFWMD's water supply and environmental resources. The importance of maintaining flood protection facilities within South Florida cannot be minimized. A significant percentage of the SFWMD's annual capital budget (approximately 7.6 percent, or $7.7 million, in FY 1994) is committed to routine maintenance of the C&SF Project.

The C&SF Project was designed in the 1940s and built in the 1950s and early 1960s. The system design was based on projected land uses, which were primarily agricultural. In many watersheds, actual land uses are more intensive than design projections. These watersheds typically generate more runoff than projected and the existing system, in some cases, provides less than adequate flood protection.

Since the C&SF Project was first designed, the SFWMD's responsibilities have expanded from flood control to water resource management; the knowledge of, and concern for, environmental issues have increased; and the operational goals of

271

the system have changed to reflect the SFWMD's multiobjective responsibilities. Attempting to meet these broader and more complex goals has pushed the C&SF Project beyond its original design objectives and revealed its limitations as a multifunctional system.

Most of the C&SF Project is in the Lower East Coast and consists of three water conservation areas (WCAs), about 1,400 miles of canals and levees, 181 major water control structures, over 2,000 minor water control structures, and 18 major pump stations. The same facilities that provide water supply to South Florida can also provide drainage and control floods.

The WCAs were created through construction of levees and the canals to divide the former Everglades into areas that were designated for development and areas that were established for water storage, natural system preservation, and fish and wildlife benefits.

The Kissimmee River was channelized to improve navigation and aid in flood protection. This modification has caused degradation of the river's ecological integrity and has led to the Kissimmee River Restoration Project discussed later in this chapter. Other elements of the C&SF system in the Kissimmee basin include canals linking the Kissimmee Chain of Lakes and canals providing drainage and water supply for the Indian Prairie basin.

A central element of the C&SF Project is Lake Okeechobee. With a surface area of 730 square miles, it has a maximum storage capacity of 1.05 trillion gallons. Although Lake Okeechobee is operated as a water supply reservoir, its regulation schedule is also intended to provide flood protection benefits. Lower water levels are maintained in the summer wet season to protect the levees from wave damage during hurricanes.

The St. Lucie Canal was constructed for navigation and as a flood control outlet for Lake Okeechobee. It also receives runoff from numerous secondary systems and plays a limited role with regard to water supply in the region. A primary canal system and an extensively developed network of secondary canals also occur in western St. Lucie County.

Many of the developed areas in southeastern Florida were formerly part of the Everglades. These areas depend on the C&SF system for flood protection. The canal network immediately south of Lake Okeechobee provides both drainage and irrigation water for the Everglades Agricultural Area. Farms in this area pump water from the canals into a network of irrigation ditches during the dry season; during the wet season this process is reversed with water pumped from irrigation ditches into the primary canal system for drainage.

The regional canal system also provides flood protection to developed areas in eastern Dade, Broward, and Palm Beach counties. Local stormwater management systems collect and route stormwater to the regional canals, which then discharge to the ocean via estuaries. Increased drainage for flood protection has modified the volume and distribution of freshwater flows to estuaries. In addition, pollutants from agricultural and urban activities are washed into stormwater and eventually discharge to receiving waters such as wetlands, lakes, and estuaries.

Levees and canals divide the former Everglades into areas designated for development and areas set aside for fish and wildlife benefits, natural system preservation, and water storage. The natural areas are further divided into the three water conservation areas and Everglades National Park. The water conservation areas store excess surface water during wet periods and are a primary source of recharge during the dry season for the coastal aquifers along the Lower East Coast.

The only element of the original C&SF system within the Lower West Coast region is the Caloosahatchee River. This canal was designed primarily for navigation and as a flood control outlet for Lake Okeechobee. However, it also provides flood protection, urban water supply and supplemental agricultural water supply within its watershed.

In Collier County, the SFWMD, through the Big Cypress Basin Board, has assumed responsibility for, operates, and maintains the Big Cypress Basin system, including 161 miles of canals and 34 water control structures. Local interests and landowners had originally constructed these water control facilities to provide drainage for agricultural and urban development.

Surface Water Management Permitting

Since 1975, the SFWMD has regulated the management and storage of surface waters within its boundaries. Generally, permits are required for construction, alteration, operation, or maintenance of local surface water management systems. In order to obtain a permit, landowners must demonstrate that a system will: provide adequate flood protection; not cause adverse water quality and quantity impacts on receiving waters and adjacent lands; not violate state surface water criteria; and not cause adverse impacts to public health and

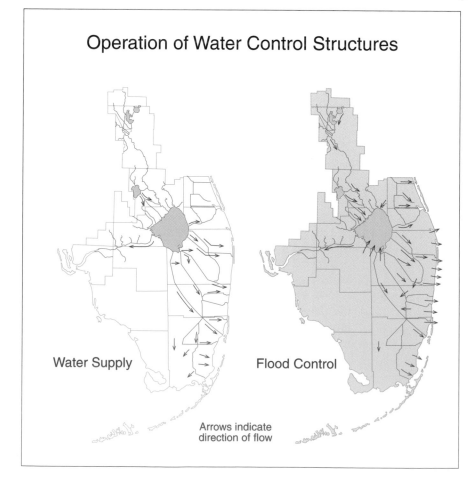

Operation of Water Control Structures

Water Supply

Flood Control

Arrows indicate direction of flow

Water Control Structures

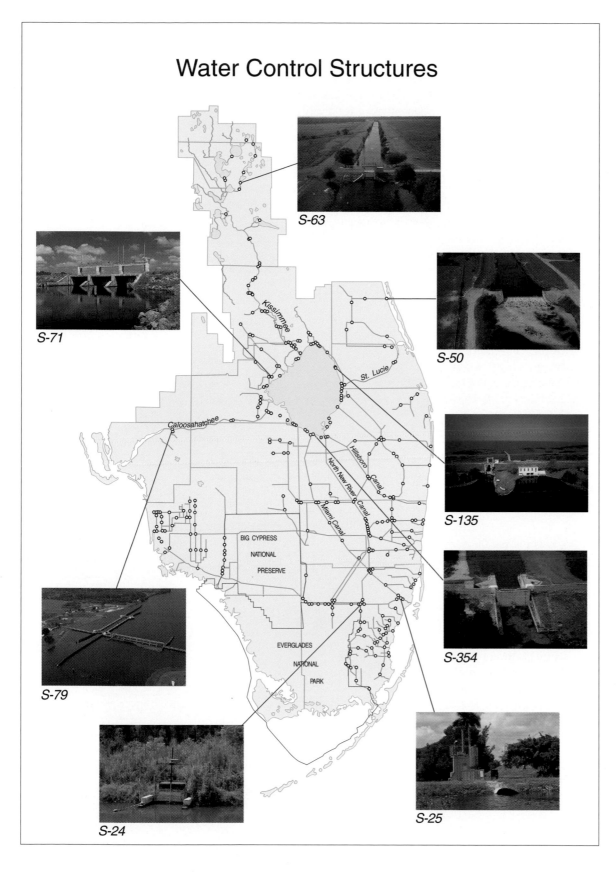

S-63

S-71

S-50

St. Lucie

Kissimmee

Caloosahatchee

Hillsboro Canal

North New River Canal

Miami Canal

S-135

BIG CYPRESS

NATIONAL

PRESERVE

S-354

S-79

EVERGLADES

NATIONAL

PARK

S-24

S-25

273

safety, the environment, or surface water and groundwater levels and flows. New development must meet minimum criteria under this program; however, development predating this program is not normally subject to regulation unless substantive alterations are proposed.

The SFWMD seeks to address existing stormwater management deficiencies by providing technical and financial assistance to local governments. Projects that are designed to retrofit existing surface water management systems are also subject to regulation. Typically, there are few economically

feasible approaches to solve the problems of existing floodprone developments. Retrofit projects frequently have difficulty meeting SFWMD flood protection and water quality permitting criteria.

South Florida's sustained high growth rate since the 1950s has reduced the availability of land suitable for new development. Landowners are applying increasing pressure to develop floodprone and environmentally sensitive areas. Growth has also placed a greater than anticipated demand on existing water management systems, exacerbating present flooding problems and limiting the ability of those systems to sustain additional growth.

The SFWMD looks to local governments, which are required by the Growth Management Act (163.3177, F.S.) to adopt level of service (LOS) standards for stormwater management as part of their comprehensive plans, to address local flooding problem areas.

The SFWMD works with local governments and other agencies to encourage integration among land use, watershed management, and other stormwater master plans. The SFWMD is encouraging local stormwater master planning through technical and financial assistance to local governments. Local governments that have received technical and financial assistance for development of stormwater management master planning include Dade, Lee, Okeechobee, and Osceola counties and the cities of St. Cloud and Kissimmee.

Under flood conditions, the focus of stormwater management becomes rapid and efficient removal of floodwaters, regardless of impacts on water supply and natural systems. However, the removal process takes time. The SFWMD's public education program is to provide the public with an understanding of how the system works, whom to contact for assistance, and the time frames that may be involved.

Water Quality

Good-quality water is essential for the survival of all life. Ultimately, damaged or polluted natural systems affect humans because we are at the top of the food chain. The recent discovery of elevated mercury levels in several water bodies in Florida illustrates this relationship. Invertebrates consume mercury in their food and accumulate it in their bodies. Fish eat invertebrates and build up mercury in their tissues; then humans eat the fish. The higher up the food chain, the greater the potential for accumulating toxic levels of mercury. As a result, restrictions have been placed on consumption of fish from these waters.

The primary causes of pollution can be traced to land and water uses. When vegetation is cleared from the land to make room for development, the nutrient absorption capability of the vegetation is lost. Agricultural and urban development also introduce pollutants in the form of fertilizers, car exhaust, industrial and sanitary waste, and general debris. If these pollutants are not adequately handled, they are washed into surface water bodies by stormwater runoff, or seep into the underlying aquifers, polluting the groundwater.

Surface Water Quality

The district routinely monitors water quality conditions within each of the major basins, at appropriate control points, and in the major conveyance channels. Parameters sampled are divided into six major groupings: physical, nutrients, major ions, trace metals, pesticides, and priority pollutants. The frequency of sampling for each parameter varies for each sampling station.

The monitoring network comprises almost 1,000 sampling stations that encompass a wide variety of South Florida ecosystems, agricultural and urban land uses including lakes, rivers, estuaries, canals, wetlands, dairies, and cattle ranches. Data collected from routine monitoring programs are often used to supplement more specific water quality studies. The SFWMD also has archived data from historical stations in the water quality database. Sampling frequencies and period of record are generalized for each program. Each sampling station has a specific period of record, and sampling frequency and list of parameters.

274

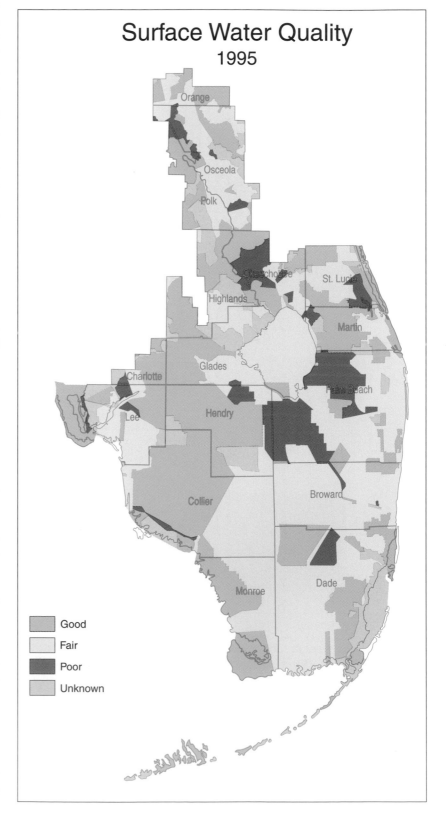

Surface Water Quality 1995

Good
Fair
Poor
Unknown

The quality of South Florida's surface waters has been most heavily impacted by inadequately treated stormwater runoff. Nonpoint pollution from runoff is generated from agricultural and urban land uses and includes sediments, nutrients from fertilizers, heavy metals and hydrocarbons from vehicles, herbicides and pesticides. Other nonpoint sources include leachate and seepage from landfills and hazardous waste disposal sites. Point sources of pollution generally include discharges from wastewater treatment plants and commercial or industrial facilities that discharge to a water body. Virtually all point source discharges to surface waters have been eliminated in recent years.

In addition to the routine monitoring of background water quality in the system, a number of special water quality studies have been conducted within the district, especially with regard to the Kissimmee River, Lake Okeechobee, and the Everglades. Special sampling programs have also been initiated in SWIM Priority water bodies, including water quality monitoring in Martin and St. Lucie counties as part of the Indian River Lagoon SWIM program and in Dade County as part of the Biscayne Bay SWIM program.

Groundwater Quality

The SFWMD maintains a network of stations to monitor groundwater quality. The major parameters examined include conductivity and chloride levels, which are necessary to analyze the extent of saltwater intrusion. The network used for monitoring groundwater quality includes wells located in areas where human activities are believed to have affected groundwater quality, as well as some wells developed for monitoring groundwater levels. As a routine procedure, groundwater quality samples are also collected from test wells drilled by the SFWMD.

Water quality within the Biscayne aquifer complies with State Drinking Water Standards and is suitable for all urban demands. Poor water quality exists in some coastal areas that are impacted by chemical contamination or saltwater intrusion. Areas that are affected by saltwater intrusion tend to be localized in linear extent due to the constant recharge (high water-levels) maintained at the various water control structures which exist throughout South Florida.

Because the Biscayne aquifer is close to the surface and highly permeable, groundwater in the Lower East Coast is vulnerable to contamination. Rapid urbanization combined with growth of agricultural areas continues to threaten contamination of the shallow groundwater supplies from a variety of man-made sources. Because of seasonal heavy rainfall combined with dilution, levels of contamination within the Biscayne aquifer are reduced in magnitude.

Water quality within the surficial aquifer system along the Lower West Coast generally meets State Drinking Water Standards, although localized areas display degraded water quality. Zones of increasing mineralization tend to occur locally along the coast, due to saltwater intrusion, and inland toward the Everglades area where residual seawater or Floridan aquifer system irrigation water has left high total dissolved solids concentrations.

As with all shallow aquifers, the proximity of the surficial aquifer system to the surface increases its susceptibility to contamination from a variety of man-made sources. In addition, because of large demands placed on this system, it has been endangered by saltwater intrusion along the coast and is frequently included in water shortage restrictions.

Water quality within the surficial aquifer system along the Upper East Coast meets State Drinking Water Standards, however, localized areas of poor water quality do exist. As in the Lower West Coast, zones of increasing mineralization tend to occur locally along the coast, due to saltwater intrusion, and inland where residual seawater or Floridan aquifer system irrigation water has left high total dissolved solids concentrations. The proximity of the surficial aquifer system to the surface in this region increases its susceptibility to contamination from a variety of man-made sources. In addition, because of increasing demands being placed on the system, saltwater intrusion is a constant threat along the coast.

Throughout most of the Kissimmee basin, the surficial aquifer produces good quality water of low mineral content, although it does not yield sufficient quantities of water for many applications. The proximity of the surficial aquifer system to the surface in the Kissimmee basin increases its susceptibility to contamination from a variety of man-made sources. Lack of confining layers, high recharge, relatively high permeability, and a high water table in most areas where this unit exists, all increase contamination potential.

In general, the water quality of the Floridan aquifer system in the Kissimmee basin meets or exceeds State Drinking Water Standards; however, regional mineralization within the aquifer system gradually increases to the south, due to the presence of residual seawater. The Floridan aquifer system (where confined) is protected from surficial contamination due to the presence of the Hawthorn confining layers. This does not eliminate the potential for contamination from the upconing of poorer quality water from deeper producing zones caused by excessive pumping. The Floridan is particularly susceptible to contamination in recharge areas and where sinkholes provide direct connections to the aquifer.

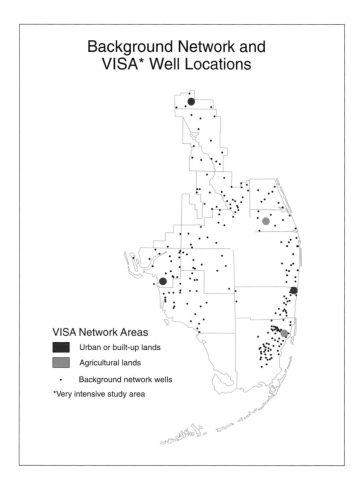

Background Network and VISA* Well Locations

VISA Network Areas
- ■ Urban or built-up lands
- ▨ Agricultural lands
- · Background network wells

*Very intensive study area

Natural Systems

South Florida contains unique natural resources of international significance. The centerpiece of these resources, and the basis for defining district boundaries, is the Kissimmee/Lake Okeechobee/Everglades system of interconnected lakes, rivers, wetlands, and estuaries. Historically this was a single system. Construction of the Central and Southern Florida Project artificially channelized and divided this system. In recent years, the district, the U.S. Army Corps of Engineers and other agencies have initiated efforts to protect and restore the ecological integrity of major features within this system.

The district's primary tools for natural system management and protection are land acquisition and management, the Surface Water Improvement and Management (SWIM) program, establishment of Minimum Flows and Levels, development of Water Supply Plans and cooperative regional restoration efforts. Through its land acquisition and management program the district preserves rare and unique resources, protects areas of special local interest, and provides the basis to meet water management needs of the 21st century. Lands are selected for purchase based on a number of criteria, including manageability, presence of surface water or groundwater systems, formation of corridors for the critical interaction of wildlife populations, and the need to support critical water management activities. Large areas of South Florida are already protected from development through ownership by state or federal agencies or private conservation interests. Other areas, many of them within and adjacent to the Kissimmee River valley, Lake Okeechobee, and the Everglades, are identified for acquisition and management by the district's during the coming years.

The state's SWIM program has been a highly effective means to identify problems and proposed solutions for water management problems. From 1987 until state funding declined in 1994, SWIM provided unique opportunities to leverage state funds with monies from the district, other agencies and local interests to develop solutions for problems that were too large for any single entity to address. The district has developed highly successful SWIM programs in Biscayne Bay, Indian River Lagoon, and Lake Okeechobee. In 1991, the Everglades Protection Act added the Everglades as a SWIM priority water body. The Everglades SWIM Plan was completed in 1992 but was superseded by the Everglades Forever Act (373.4592, F.S.) in 1994. Lakes of the Kissimmee chain are listed as priorities for development of SWIM Plans, when appropriate funding and support become available.

Water management districts are required to determine Minimum Flows and Levels to protect water resources within their jurisdiction from incurring significant harm. The district has developed a priority list and schedule for development of Minimum Flows and Levels. Minimum water level criteria have been proposed for Lake Okeechobee, the Everglades, and the Biscayne aquifer and will be formally adopted in 1999. Criteria for the Caloosahatchee River are scheduled to be established by 2000; the St. Lucie

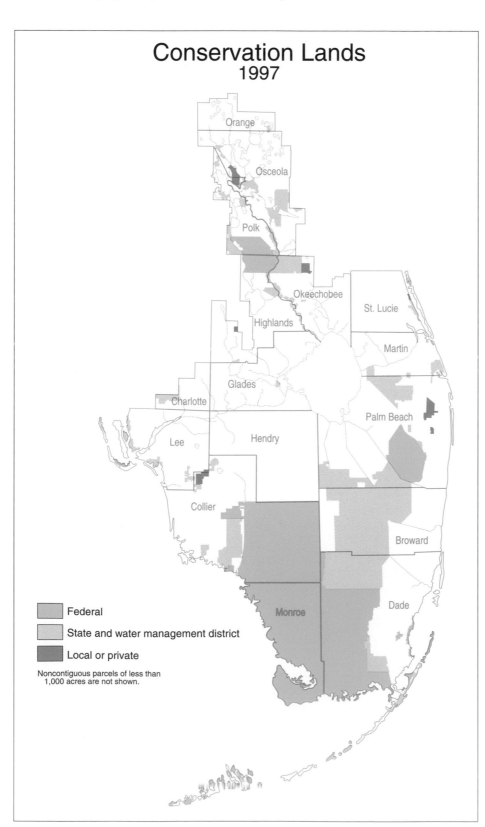

Conservation Lands
1997

Federal

State and water management district

Local or private

Noncontiguous parcels of less than 1,000 acres are not shown.

276

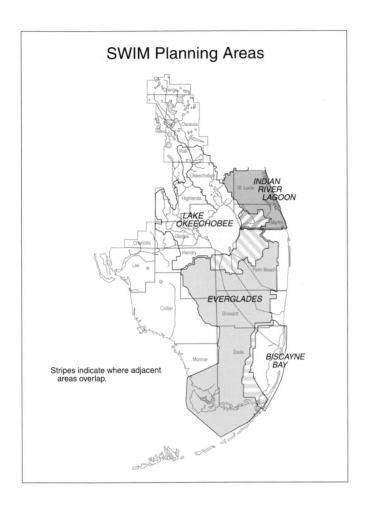

SWIM Planning Areas

Stripes indicate where adjacent areas overlap.

The Everglades

Historical Conditions

The Everglades is a resource of global significance—an extensive system of highly productive wetlands, habitat for numerous species of tropical and subtropical plants and animals, and a vast reservoir of freshwater. The term "Everglades" refers to the swamps, marshes, sloughs, prairies, tree islands and forests that covered most of southeastern Florida, west of the Atlantic coastal ridge.

Vegetation at the landscape level and extent of the historic Everglades are shown on the map on p. 278. During very wet periods, water overflowed the southern banks of Lake Okeechobee and continued in sheetlike fashion across the Everglades. The area immediately south of Lake Okeechobee con-

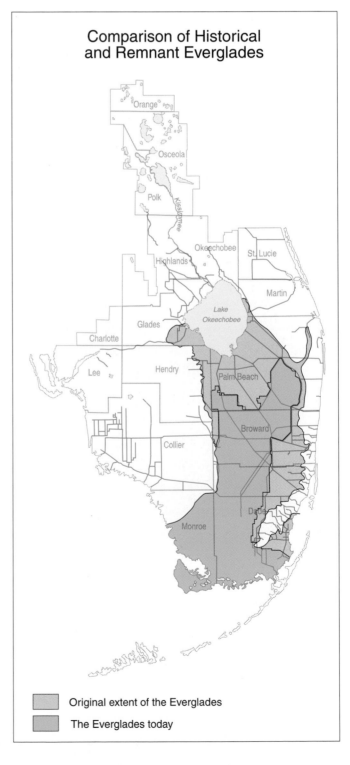

Comparison of Historical and Remnant Everglades

Original extent of the Everglades

The Everglades today

canal and estuary by 2001; Florida Bay and Biscayne Bay by 2004; and the Kissimmee River and lakes in the Kissimmee chain by 2004-2006.

Water supply plans have been or are being developed for the Upper East Coast, Lower East Coast, Lower West Coast and Kissimmee planning areas. Since Lake Okeechobee is the primary reservoir for most of South Florida, each of these plans, to some extent, will impact the amount of water that flows into or out of the Lake. These plans include opportunities for development of additional regional and local storage facilities, technologies, and new sources of water that can be used to expand the capacity and flexibility of the regional system and meet water needs throughout South Florida.

The district is participating in a number of ongoing restoration efforts. The largest such program is restoration of the Everglades. One of the primary components of Everglades restoration, the Central and Southern Florida Project Comprehensive Review Study (Restudy), under joint leadership by the Army Corps of Engineers and the district, will examine structural or operational changes to restore Everglades ecosystems and meet regional water supply needs.

The second major effort is occurring in the Kissimmee River watershed. One component of this program is to recreate the form and hydrology of the historic river/floodplain so that natural ecosystem functions can be restored along a major segment of the river. Another component is Headwater Revitalization, where the primary focus is the storage/release of water from the upper basin lakes to the Kissimmee River in a manner that more closely simulates historic conditions.

The following sections discuss historic, present, and possible future conditions in the major parts of Kissimmee/Lake Okeechobee/Everglades system.

277

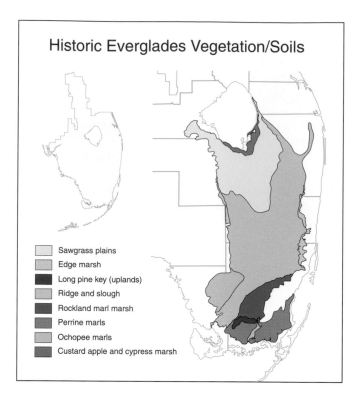

Historic Everglades Vegetation/Soils

- Sawgrass plains
- Edge marsh
- Long pine key (uplands)
- Ridge and slough
- Rockland marl marsh
- Perrine marls
- Ochopee marls
- Custard apple and cypress marsh

sisted of custard apple and cypress forest. Further south, in what is now the Everglades Agricultural Area (EAA), sawgrass was the dominant species. The area that is now water conservation areas (WCAs) consisted of a mixture of sawgrass, flag marsh, sloughs, ridges and tree islands. The deeper peat soils of the WCAs eventually gave way to shallower peat and marl soils of Everglades National Park (ENP). The uplands of southern Dade County and ENP were dominated by pine/palmetto flatwoods and oak/hardwood hammocks. Two primary flowways, Taylor Slough and Shark River Slough, moved water through ENP to the fringing marshes and mangroves along Florida Bay and the Gulf of Mexico.

The original Everglades had four primary physical characteristics that enabled the system to support unique plant and animal communities.

1. The Everglades covered about 3 million acres.

2. It was called a "river of grass," because water flowed from north to south as a continuous sheet, during wet periods.

3. The topography was very flat—water was distributed across broad areas and moved very slowly.

4. During dry periods, wildfires were common. Fire was a vital force that helped maintain the balance of communities.

The extent, distribution, and structure of major Everglades features were determined by soil and water conditions and the

278

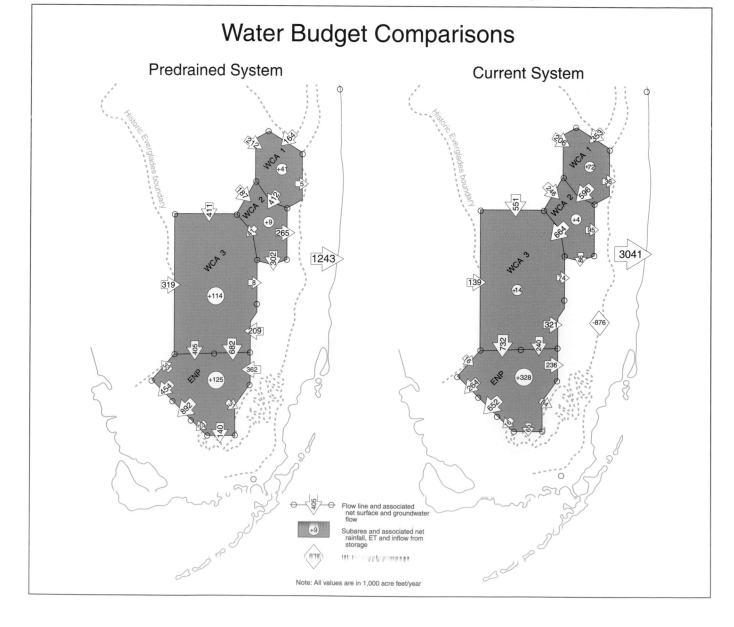

Water Budget Comparisons

Predrained System

Current System

Flow line and associated net surface and groundwater flow

Subarea and associated net rainfall, ET and inflow from storage

Note: All values are in 1,000 acre feet/year

frequency, duration, and severity of fires. Because water levels were high, fires generally only removed vegetation. The organic soils remained moist, were largely protected, and accumulated in some areas for thousands of years.

Present Conditions

The boundaries of the present Everglades are outlined on the map on p. 277. Historical conditions have been altered by human activities, including construction and operation of canals, levees, pump stations, and structures to provide drainage, flood control, and water supply. The total size of the Everglades has been reduced by about 40 percent. The former continuous expanse of wetlands is now divided into a series of management areas. The northern portion, includes about 1,000 square miles that have been primarily developed for sugarcane farming. The Holeyland and Rotenberger wildlife management areas, located just above the northwest corner of WCA-3, consist of sawgrass, brush, and tree islands and are being restored as Everglades habitat. The northernmost WCA (WCA-1) is managed as a national wildlife refuge. WCA-2 and WCA-3 are managed by the state for wildlife benefits. All three are used to detain flood waters, provide water storage and distribute water to coastal basins. Construction of levees isolated the central Everglades wetlands from adjacent areas that were seasonally flooded. Many of these peripheral wetlands were developed for urban and agricultural use. The finest remaining Everglades habitat is managed as an environmental preserve in the 1,400,000 acres of ENP. Florida Bay is a shallow estuary at the southern tip of Florida that has extensive mangrove and saltmarsh shorelines; submersed seagrasses; macroalgae, mud bottom, and hard bottom communities. The bay supports highly productive fisheries and provides habitat for large numbers of birds and other wildlife.

More water flow now occurs through canals to the east and less to ENP and Florida Bay than occurred historically. In general, the Everglades receives too much water during wet periods and too little during droughts. Everglades wetlands now compete with urban and agricultural interests for water. The need to protect developed lands from flooding has resulted in overdrainage of remaining wetlands. In wet periods, water is impounded in the WCAs and later discharged to ENP or coastal canals. During dry periods, water can flow through the canals to coastal areas and bypass the wetlands. Runoff from adjacent urban and agricultural lands threatens Everglades water quality, since water that is delivered during dry periods may contain unwanted nutrients, dissolved minerals, and pesticides.

Changes in hydrology have altered Everglades topography due to drainage, soil oxidation, subsidence, and burning. Large areas remain unnaturally flooded for long periods while other areas are almost continuously dry. The timing of wet and dry cycles has also been altered, resulting in water conditions that do not correspond to life cycles of native species. Fires are often destructive because water levels are well below the soil surface.

Florida Bay also has problems that may be related to lack of freshwater inflows during dry periods and poor water quality. These problems were very apparent in the 1980s and 1990s

Monitoring Stations in Florida Bay

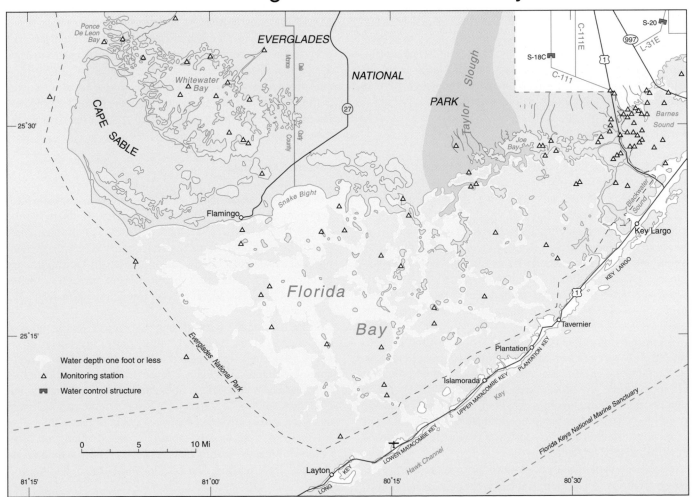

when phytoplankton blooms and massive seagrass die-offs occurred. In response to public concern, extensive research and monitoring studies were initiated to gain an understanding of Florida Bay features, hydrology, hydrodynamics and ecosystems.

The Everglades Forever Act (373.4592, F.S.) was passed in 1994 to improve the quantity and quality of water reaching the Everglades, urban and agricultural areas, and Florida Bay. Four major program elements are underway to implement this legislation:

> Construction of six stormwater treatment areas, occupying about 43,000 acres in the EAA, to remove nutrients and other pollutants.
>
> Reestablishment of appropriate depth, duration of flooding, timing, and distribution of freshwater flows.
>
> Conducting research and monitoring to describe water quality, document changes, and establish standards.
>
> Implementing changes to rules that govern water quality permits, standards and enforcement procedures.

The Lower East Coast Regional Water Supply Plan (LECRWSP) currently being developed will analyze water supply needs and sources for southeastern Florida. This plan will help managers and others predict impacts of development, evaluate strategies, and make decisions concerning public, agricultural and environmental water supply requirements, including the needs of Everglades ecosystems, through 2020. An interim plan will be available in 1998 and a final plan by 2000.

The Central and Southern Florida Project Comprehensive Review Study (the Restudy) consists of two phases. The reconnaissance phase (completed in 1994) defined problems and opportunities, Corps of Engineers and local roles in solving problems, and conceptual solutions. The feasibility phase (initiated in 1995) evaluated alternative plans to address problems and realize opportunities. A recommended comprehensive plan and feasibility report will be completed by 1999.

Future Conditions

Restoration of the Everglades is the most important water quality and natural system issue facing the SFWMD. In 1983, Governor Bob Graham announced a plan to save the Everglades that had four objectives: a) avoid further destruction or degradation; b) reestablish natural ecological functions; c) improve management of water, fish and wildlife, and recreation; and d) measure success by how much more the Everglades looks like it did in 1900 than it did in 1983. Since that time, significant progress has been made by state and federal agencies, local interests, and concerned citizens to achieve this goal.

A primary objective is to recreate historic hydrologic conditions. If hydrologic conditions are restored, over time soils, vegetation, and wildlife may return through natural processes of repopulation, growth, and succession. Various management options are tested in the field or with mathematical models to determine effects of different operational rules and adding or removing different features, on water conditions and natural systems in the Everglades.

The Restudy will analyze the need for modifications of existing facilities to protect or enhance environmental quality,

water supply, and other purposes in the Lake Okeechobee, the Everglades, Lower East Coast urban areas, and Florida Bay. A comprehensive, coordinated ecosystem study will be performed, including hydrodynamic modeling of Everglades hydrology, wetlands plant and animal communities, and connections to coastal ecosystems. Once these studies are complete, federal funds may then be provided by Congress, with matching funds from the state, to purchase land and begin construction. The Restudy and the LECRWSP are the primary means to analyze future options, achieve long-term restoration of the Everglades, and meet urban and agricultural water supply needs until the middle of the 21st century.

The Kissimmee River

Historical Conditions

The Kissimmee watershed is comprised of areas drained by the Kissimmee chain of lakes and the Kissimmee River valley. Water from the chain of lakes flowed into Lake Kissimmee and out to the Kissimmee River. The river channel was generally 10 feet deep or less and meandered for approximately 103 miles over a 1-to-2 mile wide floodplain to Lake Okeechobee. During wet periods, water overflowed the river banks and covered the floodplain. The surface of the river and floodplain sloped a vertical distance of approximately 36 feet, from 52 feet above sea level at Lake Kissimmee to 16 feet near Lake Okeechobee. The floodplain contained extensive and diverse wetland habitats that supported at least 320 species of fish, birds, mammals, and other animals. Upland vegetation occurred along ridges, islands, and at the floodplain boundary.

Slow movement of water through the narrow channels and wetlands caused water to back up in the rainy season. Occasional but extensive flooding occurred in the river valley, lakes, and watersheds as far north as Orlando. Maximum discharges occurred in October and minimum discharges occurred in May. Water flowed through the Kissimmee valley more than 90 percent of the time — ceasing to flow only during severe droughts. Sediments continually migrated within the basin, forming new channels, ridges, islands, and ponded areas as the river meandered across the floodplain.

Present Conditions

The river channel and channels between lakes were dredged, beginning in the 1880s. When the Central and Southern Florida project was formed in 1947, these channels were further modified to improve flood control and navigation. Regulation schedules were established for the major lakes to provide high water levels for irrigation during the dry season, enough water for navigation, and low lake levels for flood protection during the wet season.

The Kissimmee River Waterway Project was authorized by Congress in the 1960s. A 60-mile long, 33 feet deep, channel (C-38 Canal) was dredged through the floodplain. Water control structures and tieback levees were built to create five impoundments. Floodplain boundaries were still distinct, but 54 square miles of wetlands were lost. With the establishment of regulation schedules in the upper chain of lakes, the valley receives flow from the lakes about 10 percent of the time. Most of this flow occurs within the C-38 Canal. The remaining river channels have no flow and are clogged with silt and vegetation.

At the north end of each impoundment, wetlands are drained and replaced by terrestrial vegetation, farmland, and pasture. In the south end, wetlands are permanently flooded and have changed to ponds or sloughs. Impacts on wildlife were substantial and populations of many desirable species, especially birds and fishes, declined dramatically. Various management

Kissimmee River Restoration

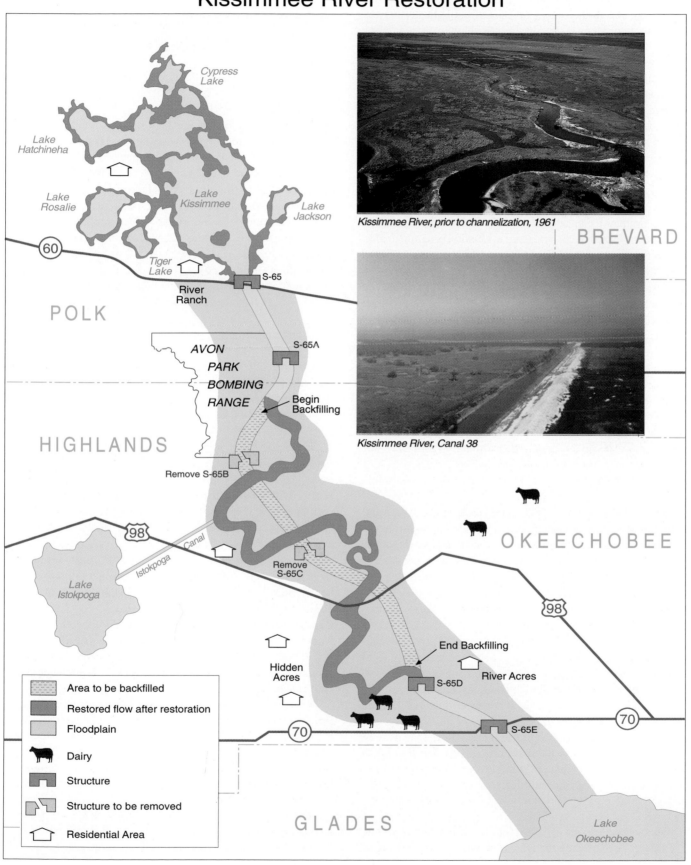

Kissimmee River, prior to channelization, 1961

Kissimmee River, Canal 38

Legend:
- Area to be backfilled
- Restored flow after restoration
- Floodplain
- Dairy
- Structure
- Structure to be removed
- Residential Area

Cypress Lake

Lake Hatchineha

Lake Rosalie

Lake Kissimmee

Lake Jackson

Tiger Lake

BREVARD

POLK

60

River Ranch

S-65

AVON PARK BOMBING RANGE

S-65A

Begin Backfilling

HIGHLANDS

Remove S-65B

98

Istokpoga Canal

Lake Istokpoga

OKEECHOBEE

Remove S-65C

98

Hidden Acres

End Backfilling

River Acres

S-65D

70

70

S-65E

GLADES

Lake Okeechobee

281

methods for impounded wetlands were studied and evaluated during the 1970s and 1980s before it was concluded that the only means to regain lost ecosystem values of the river and floodplain was to restore their physical form and hydrology.

The SFWMD and other agencies have initiated studies to address environmental problems of the Kissimmee system. Water quality and limnological investigations indicate that the productivity of lakes in the Kissimmee chain increased due to the influx of nutrients from adjacent agricultural and urban areas. Many symptoms of eutrophication can be alleviated by controlling the inflow of nutrients from wastewater and stormwater and by periodic drawdowns to consolidate and oxidize accumulated organic materials. Elimination of wastewater discharges and the use of improved farming practices and upland detention/ retention systems to manage flows from tributary watersheds have reduced the influx of nutrients to the Kissimmee lakes and river.

Large-scale efforts are presently underway, by the Army Corps of Engineers, SFWMD, and state agencies to restore the Kissimmee River and floodplain. Success of restoration will be determined by an extensive evaluation program to analyze ecosystem response. Results from this evaluation will be used to determine whether hydrologic and biological attributes have been restored. An adaptive management approach is used so that restoration activities can be modified, in response to data collected, to avoid adverse effects or enhance system performance.

Mathematical models and a physical model of the Kissimmee River were developed during 1986-1989 to simulate flow characteristics of the system, evaluate different back-filling options, and select the most feasible restoration methods. These models indicated that the restored system could provide adequate water movement during flood periods without causing excessive sediment deposition downstream.

Future Conditions

The area around Orlando is rapidly developing. Urban and agricultural water use are expected to increase significantly during the next 20 years. Restoration activities in the upper basin lakes will add 10,000 acre-feet of seasonal water storage by raising lake levels. This additional water will provide additional flow to simulate historic discharges to the valley. In addition, increased water level fluctuations in the lakes will more closely resemble historic conditions.

Kissimmee River and floodplain restoration involves management of two primary features — form and hydrology — to restore ecosystem integrity. Changes in form are required to restore natural river/floodplain interactions, including connectivity, continuity, and water level recession rates. A 22-mile segment of the channel will be filled, and 43 miles of river and 26,500 acres of floodplain will be restored during the next 10 years. These changes to the form of the river and floodplain will create conditions that are suitable for repopulation by native plant and animal communities, reestablishment of benthic invertebrates, improved distribution of fishes and enhanced use by birds.

The second aspect of restoration is to create hydrologic conditions that simulate the flow of a natural river. Filling of the dredged channel will increase flow and improve oxygen levels in the remaining oxbows. More water will be forced to flow across the floodplain, establish higher water levels, and ultimately support a natural river/floodplain ecosystem.

Finally, ongoing evaluation efforts will be used to demonstrate that observed responses are due to restoration efforts, document that these efforts are fiscally responsible, and determine better ways to manage the system. In addition, the evaluation program provides a basis to justify future construction and funding and to ensure that the people of South Florida receive the benefits they expect.

Lake Okeechobee

Historical Conditions

Lake Okeechobee, located in the heart of south Florida, is the second largest freshwater lake in the United States. The lake was formed about 6,000 years ago and is the central component of South Florida's interconnected Kissimmee River/ Lake Okeechobee/ Everglades ecosystem. Historically, water entered the lake primarily from rainfall, flow across adjacent wetlands, and discharge from Fisheating Creek, Taylor Creek, and the Kissimmee River. Water flowed south from the lake into the Everglades. Prior to construction of canals and levees, Lake Okeechobee was larger, water levels were higher, and surrounding marshes covered large areas to the north, west, and south of the existing lake. Maximum water levels ranged from 20 to 21 feet above sea level.

Present Conditions

Construction of channels into and out of the lake began in the late 1800s. Two major outlets, the Caloosahatchee and St. Lucie canals, were completed by the 1920s. Construction of levees around the lake began in the early 1900s and was completed in the 1960s. Maximum water levels were reduced to 16.75 feet to prevent hurricane flooding of lakeside communities. A new littoral zone/marsh community formed inside the levee and covers 98,000 acres. This important regional wetland provides habitat for a wide variety of plants and animals, including rare, threatened, and endangered species.

Lake Okeechobee covers 730 square miles with an average depth of 8.6 feet. The lake stores 2.7 million acre feet of water between water levels of 10.5 and 17.4 feet. Due to the large surface area, about 70 percent of this water is lost to evaporation annually. Water is released through the West Palm Beach, Hillsboro, North New River, Miami, St. Lucie and Caloosahatchee canals. Although the Caloosahatchee and St. Lucie estuaries depend on receiving some freshwater flow throughout the year, occasional massive discharges during high rainfall conditions, severely impact these estuaries and adjacent coastal waters.

Lake Okeechobee is South Florida's primary reservoir and provides drinking water for lakeside communities; recharge for coastal aquifers during drought; irrigation for agricultural crops; and water deliveries to the Everglades. The littoral zone provides critical wildlife habitat. Recreational and commercial fisheries have an estimated annual value of more than $22 million.

The integrity of the Lake Okeechobee levee is protected through use of a regulation schedule — a theoretical curve or graph that indicates the maximum allowable lake stage for each month. The present schedule is designed to maintain a level of 15.6 feet when the hurricane season begins (June 1) and 16.75 feet at the beginning of the dry season (October 1). The Corps of Engineers initiated a review in 1995 to determine whether a more ecologically beneficial schedule could be developed. A new schedule was proposed that incorporates long-range climate forecasting to make more efficient use of water resources and to meet C&SF Project objectives without requiring modifications to the levees.

A critical component of water supply management is allocation of water during droughts. When water levels in Lake Okeechobee fall below critical levels (which vary during the year), a regional drought is declared. The district implements a supplyside management plan that determines how much water can be released from the lake as needed to protect regional resources such as agricultural crops, Everglades wetlands, and major wellfields.

Water quality declined in Lake Okeechobee in the early 1970s due to nutrient loading from adjacent agricultural lands. As a result, the legislature, in 1987, identified the need to develop a Surface Water Improvement and Management (SWIM) plan. The most recent update of this plan (1997) supports five types of projects, to: help landowners achieve permitted discharge limits; monitor and document current condition of the resource; improve quality of water entering the lake; improve water quality in, and remove nutrients from, the lake; and improve ecological conditions.

Future Conditions

Lake Okeechobee will continue to provide South Florida with a wide range of benefits—as a reservoir, navigational waterway, recreation area, and important environmental resource. New sources of water and additional large storage facilities are needed to meet South Florida's growing water needs. Restoration efforts in the Kissimmee basin will provide more storage and help contain excess floodwaters. Everglades restoration will require more water from the regional system but will also provide support to construct new facilities. Lake water quality will improve as the influx of nutrients from tributary basins is controlled and existing nutrients are removed. The effects of large regulatory discharges on downstream estuaries will continue to be a problem, but a new regulation schedule and additional storage should reduce the frequency and volume of such discharges.

The most important changes may occur in communities surrounding the lake. Large areas of agricultural land will be displaced by construction of water storage and treatment facilities to protect the Everglades. Residents of surrounding towns and cities hope to develop tourism and recreational opportunities and improve the quality of living conditions. At a series of meetings and workshops in 1996, plans were developed for recreational and tourist facilities, and to improve the appearance of streets and surrounding landscapes. The intent is to promote redevelopment of urban areas as traditional communities, creating a unique rural/urban environment rather than the more typical suburban sprawl that has occurred along much of Florida's coastline.

Lake Okeechobee Water Control Structures

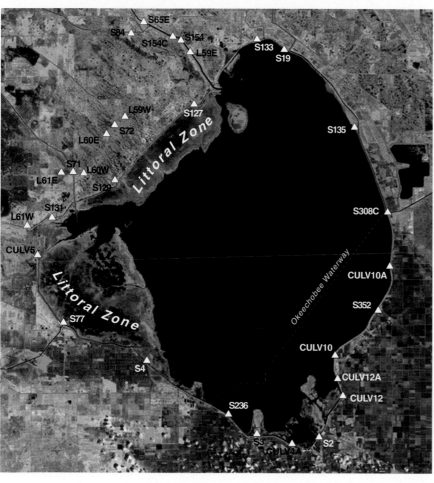

Lake Okeechobee

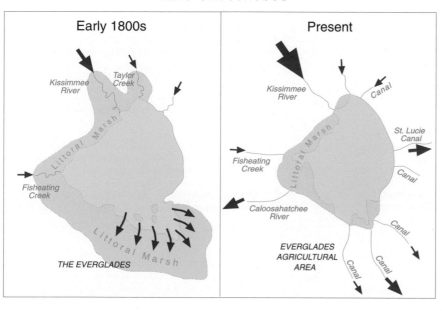

283

REFERENCES

A source for a map or figure has a number in parentheses following the entry. This number refers to the page in this atlas for which the source was used.

Aumen, N. G., and R.G. Wetzel, eds. 1995. "Ecological Studies of the Littoral and Pelagic Systems of Lake Okeechobee, Florida (USA)." Archiv fur Hydrobiologie, *Advances in Limnology* 45.

Brooks, H.K. 1984. "Lake Okeechobee." In P.J. Gleason ed. *Environments of South Florida: Present and Past II*. Coral Gables, FL: Miami Geological Society.

Chin, D. 1993. *Analysis and Prediction of South Florida Rainfall*. Final Report to the United States Department of Interior and South Florida Water Management District. University of Florida. Gainesville.

Dahm, C.N., K.W. Cummins, M. Valett, and R.L. Coleman. 1995. "An Ecosystem View of the Restoration of the Kissimmee River." *Restoration Ecology* 3(3):225-238.

Davis, S.M. and J.C. Ogden. 1994. "Toward Ecosystem Restoration." In S.M. Davis and J.C. Ogden, eds. *Everglades — The Ecosystem and its Restoration*. Delray Beach, FL: St. Lucie Press.

Florida Geological Survey. 1992. *Florida's Ground Water Quality Monitoring Program Background Hydrogeochemistry*. Special Publication No. 34. Florida Geological Survey. Tallahassee. (map, 275)

Florida Natural Areas Inventory. Tallahassee. (map, 276)

Germain, G. 1998. *Surface Water Quality Monitoring Network*. Technical Memorandum, Report #356. South Florida Water Management District. West Palm Beach, FL.

Greater Lake Okeechobee Tourism Alliance. 1997. *Second Draft Report on the Upper and Lower Lake Okeechobee Tourism Development Workshops*. Treasure Coast Regional Planning Council. Stuart, FL.

Hand, J., J. Col, and L. Lord. 1996. South Florida District Water Quality 305(b) Technical Appendix. Florida Department of Environmental Protection. Tallahassee. (map, 274)

Koebel, J.W. 1995. "An Historical Perspective on the Kissimmee River Restoration Project." *Restoration Ecology* 3(3):149-159.

Kushlan, J. 1990. "Freshwater Marshes." In R.L. Myers and J.J. Ewel eds., *Ecosystems of Florida*. Orlando: University of Central Florida Press.

Light, S.S. and J.W. Dineen. 1994. "Water Control in the Everglades: A Historical Perspective." In S.M. Davis and J.C. Ogden eds., *Everglades — The Ecosystem and its Restoration*. Delray Beach: St. Lucie Press.

Loftin, M.K., L.A. Toth, and J.T.B. Obeysekera. 1990. *Kissimmee River Restoration Alternative Plan Evaluation and Preliminary Design Report*. South Florida Water Management District, West Palm Beach.

McVoy, C.W., W.A. Park, and J. Obeysekera. (in prep.) *Landscapes and Hydrology of the Everglades, circa 1850*. (draft manuscript), South Florida Water Management District, West Palm Beach. (SWIM map, 277)

Milleson, J.F., R.L. Goodrick, and J.A. VanArman. 1980. *Plant Communities of the Kissimmee River Valley*. Technical Publication No. 80-7. South Florida Water Management District, West Palm Beach.

Niedrauer, C.J., P.J. Trimble and E.R. Santee. 1998. *Final Report of Alternative Operational Schedules for Lake Okeechobee*. South Florida Water Management District, West Palm Beach.

Parker, G.G. 1984. Hydrology of the Pre-Drainage System of the Everglades in Southern Florida. In P.J. Gleason ed. *Environments of South Florida: Present and Past II*. Coral Gables: Miami Geological Society.

Pesnell, G., and R. Brown. 1977. *The Major Plant Communities of Lake Okeechobee, Florida, and their Associated Inundation Characteristics as Determined by Gradient Analysis*. South Florida Water Management District, West Palm Beach.

Robinson, G.B., S.C. Robinson, and J. Lane. 1996. *Discover a Watershed: The Everglades*. The Watercourse, Montana State University, Bozeman, MT and South Florida Water Management District, West Palm Beach.

Rudnick, D.T., F.H. Sklar and S.P. Kelly. 1995. *An Overview of SFWMD Re-search in the Florida Bay-Everglades Ecotone*. Florida Sea Grant and University of Florida, Institute of Food and Agricultural Science, Gainesville.

Smith, T.J., J.H. Hudson, M.B. Robblee, G.V.N. Powell, and P.J. Isdale. 1989. "Freshwater Flow from the Everglades to Florida Bay: A Historical Reconstruction of Based on Fluorescence Banding in the Coral Solenastrea Bournoni." *Bulletin Marine Science*. 44(1): 274-282.

South Florida Water Management District. 1992a. *Surface Water Improvement and Management Plan for the Everglades*. West Palm Beach.

South Florida Water Management District. 1992b. *Water Supply Needs and Sources 1990-2010*. West Palm Beach.

South Florida Water Management District. 1994. *Lower West Coast Water Supply Plan*. West Palm Beach, FL.

South Florida Water Management District, 1995a. *Surface Water Improvement and Management (SWIM) Plan for Biscayne Bay*. West Palm Beach.

South Florida Water Management District, 1995b. *District Water Management Plan*. Planning Department. West Palm Beach.

South Florida Water Management District and St. Johns River Water Management District, 1995. *Indian River Lagoon Surface Water Improvement and Management (SWIM) Plan for Biscayne Bay*. West Palm Beach.

South Florida Water Management District. 1996a. "Redesigning the Water Management System." *Everglades Connection* V(2):1.

South Florida Water Management District. 1996b. *Kissimmee Basin Water Supply Plan Draft Background Document*. West Palm Beach.

South Florida Water Management District, 1997a. *Surface Water Improvement and Management (SWIM) Plan — Update for Lake Okeechobee*. West Palm Beach.

South Florida Water Management District, 1997b. *District Water Management Plan: 1997 Annual Report*. West Palm Beach.

South Florida Water Management District, 1997c. *1997 Everglades Annual Report*. West Palm Beach.

South Florida Water Management District. 1998a. *Upper East Coast Water Supply Plan*. West Palm Beach.

South Florida Water Management District. 1998b. *Save Our Rivers 1998 Land Acquisition and Management Plan*. West Palm Beach.

South Florida Water Management District, 1998c. *Interim Plan for Lower East Coast Regional Water Supply*. West Palm Beach.

South Florida Water Management District, 1998d. *1997 Annual Reuse Report*. West Palm Beach.

Tebeau, C.W. 1984. "Exploration and Early Descriptions of the Everglades, Lake Okeechobee and the Kissimmee River." In P.J. Gleason, ed. *Environments of South Florida: Present and Past II*. Coral Gables: Miami Geological Society.

Toth, L.A., D.A. Arrington, M.A. Brady, and D.A. Musick. 1995. "Conceptual Evaluation of Factors Potentially Affecting Restoration of Habitat Structure Within the Channelized Kissimmee River Ecosystem." *Restoration Ecology* 3(3):160-180.

U.S. Army Corps of Engineers. 1991. *Environmental Restoration of the Kissimmee River: Final Integrated Feasibility report and Environmental Impact Statement*. USACE, Jacksonville District.

U.S. Geological Survey. (Various Years). Water Resources Data — Florida. Volume 2A: South Florida Surface Water. U.S. Geological Survey. Miami.

U.S. Geological Survey, Water Resources Division. Tallahassee. (map, 270)

Working Group of the South Florida Ecosystem Restoration Task Force. 1998. Success in the Making. An Integrated Plan for South Florida Ecosystem Restoration. National Park Service, Denver Service Center, Denver CO.

IV

ISSUES AND CONFLICTS

285

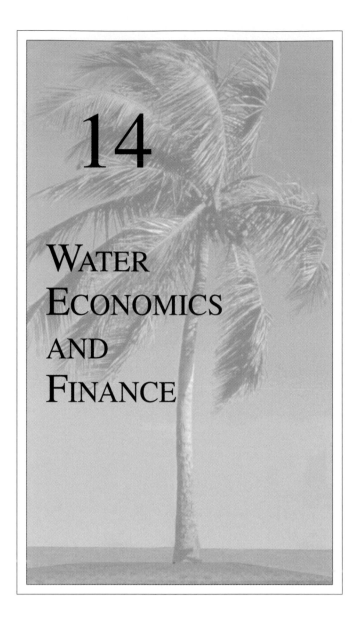

14

WATER
ECONOMICS
AND
FINANCE

286   Economics is about scarcity and about how scarce resources are used to satisfy competing demands. Freshwater can be a scarce resource even in water-rich Florida. When water is put to a specific use (e.g., manufacturing), it may no longer be available for other uses (e.g., households or agriculture). The quality of water also usually declines as it is used, which may render it unsuitable for further use without treatment. Both uses of water and alterations of water have costs associated with them. This chapter focuses on the costs of water supply and water use to major categories of water users and how they respond to changes in these costs. To some degree all water users face the same costs. Some costs are more relevant than others depending on the source of water and the intended use. In this chapter we also examine the relationship between water price and water use as well as options (including regulated markets) for water allocation under scarcity.

Jay W. Yingling, Grace M. Johns, William Hutchinson, Richard A. March, C. Donald Rome, Jr.

The Cost of Public Supply Water

The accompanying table displays monthly water charges estimated by national consulting services for utilities across the nation and in Florida in 1992 and 1998 for several customer classes. Caution should be exercised in comparing monthly water bills in Florida to the national averages since the number of Florida utilities surveyed is a very small subset of the hundreds of Florida water utilities. Because bills were estimated at different levels of usage in 1992 and 1998 for all categories of customers with 5/8-inch meters, it is more appropriate to compare the average cost of water per thousand gallons over time rather than the estimated monthly bills.

Several factors may cause Florida water prices to be higher than the national average. Florida water law is generally more protective of water-related environmental features than water law in other states. Many water systems in the state were built before water resource and environmental protection rules were fully developed and implemented and are undergoing modification to comply with current regulations. New systems must be built to accommodate Florida's rapidly growing population. New water supply systems built in compliance with more modern water resource and environmental protection standards add capital costs that must be recovered through water rates or other means. Florida also has one of the greatest concentrations of higher cost water treatment systems of any state due to naturally occurring poor water quality in some areas, particularly coastal areas, where the majority of Florida's population lives. It should not be surprising, therefore, that water costs in Florida might be higher than the national average.

Comparing "average" costs in the table, it appears that water becomes less expensive the more is used. Water professionals are often asked, "What incentive is there for me to conserve if water is cheaper for those who use more?" The appearance that the average cost of water declines as more is used is misleading. The phenomenon of declining average price occurs because the typical water bill is composed of both fixed and usage-related charges. The fixed charges are typically composed of meter reading, billing, and administrative costs that do not change on a per bill basis regardless of the amount of water used. Costs that vary significantly with usage, such as pumping and chemical costs are typically recovered in the usage-related portion of the bill. Capital costs that do not change with usage may be recovered in both the fixed and usage-related portions of the bill. The fixed portion of the bill is reflected in monthly charges for the 5/8-inch meter residential customer at 0 usage. Other customer classes pay these fixed charges as well. They were not, however, reported as "0" usage charges for other customer classes in the surveys. When the total bill is averaged over total water use, the fixed charges are "spread" over the gallons used, giving the appearance of water becoming cheaper the more is used. In reality, the per unit usage charge may be constant or increasing. Several water management districts require public water supply utilities to adopt water conserving rate structures in all or part of their districts. Inclining block rates, where the per unit charge increases with increases in water use, is a commonly used water conserving rate structure.

A survey of 91 water utilities was conducted within the Southwest Florida Water Management District at approximately the same time as the 1998 national survey. For single-family residential customers with a 5/8-inch meter, bills were estimated at 7,480 gallons consumption per month. The average

Monthly Water Charges
1992 Ernst and Young National Water and Wastewater Rate Survey

		Residential 5/8-inch meter		Non-Manufacturing/ Commercial 5/8-inch meter	Commercial/ Light Industrial 2-inch meter	Industrial 4-inch meter	Industrial 8-inch meter
	0 gal	4,000 gal	7,000 gal	22,000 gal	374,000 gal	7,480,000 gal	11,220,000 gal
Total Utilities (N=120)							
National Average Bill ($)	3.99	7.62	12.32	32.68	468.36	8,203.15	12,339.96
Average Cost ($)/1000 gal		1.91	1.76	1.49	1.25	1.10	1.10
Florida Utilities (N=7)							
Florida Average Bill ($)	3.47	5.71	8.97	23.28	373.38	7,377.43	11,363.45
Average Cost ($)/1000 gal		1.43	1.28	1.06	1.00	0.99	1.01

1998 Raftelis Environmental Consulting Group
National Water and Wastewater Rate Survey

		Residential 5/8-inch meter		Non-Manufacturing/ Commercial 5/8-inch meter	Commercial/ Light Industrial 2-inch meter	Industrial 4-inch meter	Industrial 8-inch meter
	0 gal	3,740 gal	7,480 gal	22,000 gal	374,000 gal	7,480,000 gal	11,220,000 gal
Total Utilities (N=150)							
National Average Bill ($)	5.58	10.13	16.50	43.97	639.78	11,434.23	17,233.85
Average Cost ($)/1000 gal		2.71	2.21	1.96	1.71	1.53	1.54
Florida Utilities (N=8)							
Florida Average Bill ($)	6.77	10.67	17.62	45.97	767.77	15,262.16	23,080.84
Average Cost ($)/1000 gal		2.85	2.36	2.05	2.05	2.04	2.06

Winter rates used where applicable

monthly bill for the 91 utilities was $17.93 compared with $17.62 for the Florida utilities and $16.50 for all utilities in the national survey. The majority of the SWFWMD utilities surveyed, however, have service area populations well below the median service area population of the smallest system size category sampled in the national survey (10,000 versus 60,000). All other factors aside, larger utilities can provide water at a lower per unit cost than smaller facilities.

The most comprehensive survey of *residential* water rates in Florida was conducted in 1995 for the Florida League of Cities. Water charges were calculated at 0, 5,000, 10,000, 15,000, 20,000 and 25,000 gallon intervals for 198 utilities. The 10,000 gallon charge can be compared to two previous surveys conducted in 1978-79 and 1988-89 in the table below.

Russell and Woodcock (1992) surveyed 30 utilities nationwide and found that the average cost of water per thousand

gallons increased from $.82 to $1.61 per thousand gallons from 1979 to 1989, an increase of 96.75 percent or an annual average growth rate of 7.01 percent. About half of the increase is attributed to inflation. Most of the balance of the increase was attributed to six factors: growth-induced expansion of capital facilities; replacement of old and deteriorating facilities; added facilities and processes required by more stringent environmental regulations; higher costs of borrowing to finance capital improvements (the average interest rate on high grade municipal bonds rose from 6.5 percent in the 1970s to 9 percent in the 1980s); increasing number of municipal systems switching to self-sustaining operations (primarily moving from property tax financing to rate and fee revenue financing); and rates designed in order to induce conservation.

Based primarily on the impacts of the Safe Drinking Water Act (SDWA), Russell and Woodcock estimated that 1999 water rates would average from $3.22 to $4.03 per thousand gallons. The 1998 Raftelis nationwide survey found the average cost per thousand gallons had only increased to $2.36 per thousand gallons (for a 5/8-inch residential connection at 7,480 gallons per month). Either the impacts of the SDWA projected to occur in the late 1990s have not yet been fully realized or the expected cost impacts were overestimated.

A factor that may have slowed the increase in water and sewer rates in Florida in the late 1980s and early 1990s was the passage of the 1985 Growth Management Act. A key provision of the act was that utilities of all kinds were required to impose impact fees for a number of infrastructure items, including water and sewer utility services. This requirement shifted some of the cost of meeting growth-related needs from existing and future utility customer rates to property develop-

287

Florida Monthly Residential Water Charges at 10,000 Gallons 1978–1995

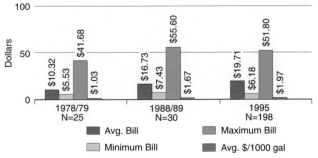

Marella 1992; David M. Griffith & Associates, Ltd. 1995

ers and ultimately, to the occupants of newly developed property.

Water costs vary significantly among utilities within Florida and the nation. In a 1995 survey of 153 utilities in Florida, monthly residential water bills at 5,000 gallons of usage ranged from a low of $3.85 to a high of $31.00 with a sample average of $12.07 (David M. Griffith & Associates, 1995). Similarly, monthly water bills for 8,000 gallons of usage from the 91 utilities surveyed in the SWFWMD in 1997 ranged from a low of $8.00 per month to a high of $61.94 with a sample average of $18.81. The median bill was $16.31 per month.

The causes of variance in utility rates was described by Metzler and Peterson in 1994 and are listed below:

Investment-related factors
Level of reserve or unused capacity contained in existing facilities
Proportion of net plant investment financed from grants
Age of major treatment and transmission facilities
Proportion of planned investment financed from debt proceeds
Level of annually recurring capital expenditures

Operating expense related factors
Complexity of treatment processes
Cost of electric power and chemicals per unit volume treated

Factors unique to individual utilities
Portion of annual impact fee receipts used to make principal and interest payments on long term debt obligations
Level of distribution system losses of water systems and the level of infiltration/inflow of wastewater systems
Outside city rate differential and relative level of sales to outside city customers, if applicable
Percentage of utility revenues transferred to the general fund as payment in lieu of taxes
Density of customers and percentage of total sales to large customers

Many of these components of water cost apply to self-supplied water users as well.

Investment-Related Factors

There are considerable economies of scale in water supply. That is, the larger the capacity of the water supply system, the cheaper the per unit cost of water. Economies of scale vary by the component parts of water supply systems and vary according to the source of water and treatment required. This does not mean that if the demand for a given utility or factory is only 5 mgd for the next ten years that a 10-mgd plant should be built simply to lower per unit cost of water. If the water is not used, then the effective per unit cost of water to end users will increase because the fixed costs of the plant are being divided among a smaller number of customers and gallons used. The choice of system size must be based on a combination of current and expected average daily demand and the need to meet peak demands such as peak irrigation demand. The more that the ratio of peak to average demand can be reduced, the cheaper the unit cost of water. The concept of economies of scale is demonstrated in the water supply component cost table. As can be seen, the economies of scale can be fairly dramatic. For example, the per 1000 gallon cost of a 30-mgd facility is about one-third the cost of a 1 mgd facility.

The relationship between the price of water, the size of the system, and unused capacity highlights the importance of accurate water demand projections (usually based on population projections and per capita water use) and the impact of water price on water demand in sizing public water supply facilities. If water demand is projected too low and the facility is sized smaller than optimal, economies of scale will not be fully exploited. If demand is projected too high, there may be significant under-utilization of plant capacity and water price will be unnecessarily high. If the development of new water supplies is expected to increase water price significantly, then the negative relationship between water price and water use (what economists call water price elasticity) should be taken into consideration. In general, as the price of water goes up, per capita water use goes down. If this relationship is ignored, the facilities may be sized too large resulting in under-utilization of capacity and higher than necessary water rates.

The direct impact of water supply grants on the price of water depends on the proportion of total water costs that will be subsidized by grants. Assume the annualized distribution and overhead costs of a utility are $.50 per thousand gallons. Assume that existing source and treatment facilities will provide 75 percent of future water needs at $.50 per thousand gallons capital cost. A new water supply facility will supply 25 percent of future water supply at a per thousand gallon capital cost 100 percent more than that provided by the existing facilities ($1.00). Without a grant, the new water rate, all other factors equal, would be:

$$\$.50 + .75(\$.50) + .25(\$1.00) = \$1.13$$

If a 25 percent construction grant lowered the cost of the new water supply to $.75, the new water rate would be:

$$\$.50 + .75(\$.50) + .25(\$.75) = \$1.06$$

The new water rate did not increase by 100 percent without the grant, nor did the new rate decrease by 25 percent because of the grant. The point of this simple exercise is that there is not usually a direct proportional relationship between the cost of a new source of water and the price of water, nor is there a direct proportional relationship between the percentage of new source costs covered by grants and postconstruction water rates. New costs are blended with existing costs and a less than proportional impact on rates occurs.

The age of major water supply facilities can have the impact of either increasing or decreasing water costs. On the one hand, the debt on older facilities may be paid off or the treatment process may be simpler than would be required of a new facility, incurring lower costs. It could also be that system maintenance is being deferred. All of these factors tend to result in lower rates. On the other hand, newer technologies may be more energy efficient or require fewer costly repairs than an aging system. For example, membrane treatment technology has been evolving rapidly and costs have been falling. As older reverse osmosis plants in the state are replaced, water rates are likely to decline even though the source water quality remains the same. Several years ago, desalination water costs were estimated to be in the range of $4.00 and up per thousand gallons. Recent proposals (1997) for a 20-mgd desalination plant for the West Coast Regional Water Supply Authority in the Tampa Bay area are in the $2.00 to $4.00 per thousand gallon range with the majority of proposals falling below $3.00 per thousand gallons.

Financing new facilities from a sinking fund rather than debt proceeds (bonding construction costs) avoids interest costs.

288

Facility expansion or new facility construction financed through debt simply costs more in the long run. Interest payments can add about 50 percent to the cost of a $10 million facility when financed from debt proceeds (assuming a 20-year bond at 5 percent interest). The difficulty in establishing a sinking fund is the potential resistance of utility customers to pay more now even though costs over the long run will be lower. Current customers are also resistant to the notion of paying for "growth."

A significant cost difference between government-owned utilities and private utilities is the cost of debt financing. The income from municipal bonds is generally tax exempt and therefore the bonds can be offered with a lower rate of return to bond investors. Privately owned utilities must compete for capital without the tax- exempt advantage. The borrowing costs for a municipal utility are therefore lower than for a private utility. For example the total financed cost of a $10 million facility is $15.8 million at an assumed 5 percent interest rate and $19.9 million at an 8 percent assumed interest rate (assuming 20-year financing). Furthermore, private utilities are essentially prohibited from charging more than the actual cost of service plus a regulated rate of return on investment. A sinking fund is not a feasible option for private utilities. Relative to other water-using industries, the borrowing costs for water utilities tend to be lower. Utilities tend to be monopolies within their service areas and have a greater ability to set prices to meet revenue requirements. This lower risk translates into lower costs of borrowing.

Source Development and Treatment-Related Factors

Source development and treatment costs vary significantly by water source as demonstrated in the water supply component cost table. The lower the source water quality and the higher the quality water desired, the higher the costs. The costs listed for wastewater reuse include treatment to irrigation quality, not potable quality. They are not directly comparable ex-

cept where potable quality water is being used for irrigation purposes. Due to seasonal and drought cycle fluctuations in stream flow, storage is more of an important factor for surface water sources than for groundwater sources. The most significant capital cost associated with surface water development, relative to other sources of water, is storage. Surface water is typically stored in either surface reservoirs or aquifers. In aquifer storage and recovery, water is withdrawn from the surface water source, treated, pumped into a suitable aquifer for storage, and then withdrawn when needed.

In other states where there is a higher degree of topographic relief, reservoirs require little excavation and consume relatively little land. In Florida, the land surface is flat and the construction of a reservoir requires significantly higher excavation and/or land costs to store the same amount of water that could be stored in an area with high topographic relief. These higher construction costs coupled with environmental impacts to estuaries, navigational impacts and high evaporative losses have made instream (dam) reservoirs less cost-effective in Florida than in other states. Off-stream reservoirs are more environmentally feasible than in-stream reservoirs but still suffer from high construction costs and evaporative losses.

The more cost-effective alternative to surface reservoirs is aquifer storage and recovery. Aquifer storage and recovery can also reduce raw water supply and treatment capacity requirements by meeting seasonal peak demands through storage. Storage costs for an off-stream reservoir have been estimated to range from $.80 to $3.20 per thousand gallons. The storage costs for aquifer storage and recovery ranged from $.18 to $.29 per thousand gallons (Hazen and Sawyer 1994). These capital costs for storage must be added to the source development costs for surface water sources in the water supply component cost table. The use of aquifer storage and recovery can be constrained by aquifer media and the aquifer ambient water chemistry.

Water Supply Component Cost

mgd	$/1000 gal Capital Treatment	$/1000 gal O&M Treatment	$/1000 gal Total Treatment	$/1000 gal Capital Source	$/1000 gal O&M Source	$/1000 gal Total Source	$/1000 gal Capital 10-Mi Pipe	Total System
Membrane Softening (Groundwater Source, Deep Well Disposal)								
1	$2.25	$1.01	$3.26	$0.16	$0.03	$0.18	$0.67	$4.12
10	$0.95	$0.60	$1.55	$0.10	$0.02	$0.12	$0.21	$1.87
20	$0.83	$0.57	$1.40	$0.09	$0.02	$0.12	$0.14	$1.66
30	$0.59	$0.52	$1.12	$0.09	$0.02	$0.11	$0.12	$1.35
Reverse Osmosis (Groundwater Source, Deep Well Disposal)								
1	$2.36	$0.93	$3.29	$0.16	$0.03	$0.18	$0.67	$4.15
10	$0.97	$0.78	$1.75	$0.10	$0.02	$0.12	$0.21	$2.08
20	$0.84	$0.76	$1.60	$0.09	$0.02	$0.12	$0.14	$1.86
30	$0.60	$0.72	$1.32	$0.09	$0.02	$0.12	$0.12	$1.56
Coagulation and Filtration (Surface Water Source, Surface Water Disposal—Does not include storage cost)								
1	$1.24	$0.70	$1.94	$0.10	$0.14	$0.23	$0.67	$2.84
10	$0.66	$0.29	$0.94	$0.07	$0.14	$0.20	$0.21	$1.36
20	$0.58	$0.25	$0.83	$0.06	$0.14	$0.19	$0.14	$1.17
30	$0.54	$0.21	$0.75	$0.05	$0.14	$0.19	$0.12	$1.06
Lime Softening (Groundwater Source, Surface Water Disposal)								
1	$1.26	$0.85	$2.10	$0.16	$0.02	$0.18	$0.67	$2.96
10	$0.57	$0.42	$0.98	$0.10	$0.02	$0.12	$0.21	$1.31
20	$0.47	$0.38	$0.86	$0.09	$0.02	$0.11	$0.14	$1.12
30	$0.41	$0.35	$0.76	$0.09	$0.02	$0.11	$0.12	$0.99
Wastewater Reuse (Effluent Source, Surface Water Disposal)								
1	$0.91	$0.57	$1.48	$0.00	$0.00	$0.00	$0.67	$2.15
10	$0.43	$0.21	$0.63	$0.00	$0.00	$0.00	$0.21	$0.84
20	$0.32	$0.18	$0.51	$0.00	$0.00	$0.00	$0.14	$0.65
30	$0.25	$0.17	$0.42	$0.00	$0.00	$0.00	$0.12	$0.54
Disinfection Only (High Quality Groundwater Source, Surface Water Disposal)								
1	$0.24	$0.06	$0.30	$0.16	$0.08	$0.23	$0.67	$1.21
10	$0.14	$0.05	$0.19	$0.10	$0.07	$0.17	$0.21	$0.57
20	$0.13	$0.05	$0.18	$0.09	$0.07	$0.16	$0.14	$0.49
30	$0.12	$0.05	$0.17	$0.09	$0.07	$0.16	$0.12	$0.45

Southwest Florida Water Management District 1992

Six proposals were recently submitted to the West Coast Regional Water Supply Authority for various sizes of desalination plants. The costs are relatively low compared to expectations. A primary reason for the lower than expected costs are that most of the plants are able to utilize water intake and discharge facilities at existing power plants in the Tampa Bay area.

Conservation can also be thought of as a source of water. Conservation is typically less expensive than new source development.

Factors Unique to Individual Utilities

The growth of public water and wastewater systems is sometimes financed, in part, from utility connection and impact fees.

Desalination Water Price/1,000 Gallons as a Function of Plant Capacity, 1997

Proposal	20 MGD	35 MGD	50 MGD
A	$2.29	$2.15	$2.06
B	$2.49	$2.35	NA
C	$3.03	$2.50	$2.07
D	$3.20	$3.40	$2.30
E	$2.76	NA	NA
F	$2.80	NA	$2.30

PB Water 1998

Conservation Program Costs

Program	Cost per 1,000 Gallons Saved
Metering Multifamily Residences, Including Mobile Homes	$0.06 – $0.18
Residential Water Audits	$0.22 – $0.45
Residential Shower Head/Toilet Dam Retrofit	$0.17 – $0.23
Residential Toilet Retrofit	$0.50 – $1.59
Apartment Plumbing Retrofit	$1.98
Institutional (Jr. High School) Leak Repair/Plumbing Retrofit	$1.05

Hazen and Sawyer 1998

290

The names used by utilities to describe such fees vary widely but commonly include connection, tapping, system development, and reserve capacity charges. Few utilities itemize the components of the system (distribution, source development, etc.) that the particular fee or portion of a fee finances.

Water distribution costs are likely to be more significant in public supply residential use and agriculture than in other types of uses, such as self-supplied industrial/commercial. In general, distribution costs vary with the "density" of customers and the percentage of total sales to large customers.

For the development of new public water supply service areas, housing density has been shown to be a significant factor in water distribution costs. The State of New Jersey estimated that distribution system costs comprise 42 percent of total water infrastructure costs. By clustering 15 percent of new single-family homes, rather than large lot development, distribution system costs could be reduced by 15 percent

Nationwide Residential Water and Wastewater Impact Fees, 1997

	Residential Connection Charges or Tap Fees		Residential System Development Charges	
	Water (N=95)	Wastewater (N=70)	Water (N=56)	Wastewater (N=54)
Average	$501	$577	$1,381	$1,229
Median	$356	$350	$683	$884

Raftelis Environmental Consulting

Residential Water and Wastewater Impact Fees in the Southwest Florida Water Management District, 1997

	Residential Connection Charges or Tap Fees		Residential System Development Charges	
	Water (N=16)	Wastewater (N=12)	Water (N=16)	Wastewater (N=16)
Average	$571	$808	$993	$1,403
Median	$310	$435	$616	$957

SWFWMD 1997 unpublished

(Burchell 1992). The savings are due to the shorter pipe length needed to serve the same population. Higher density development may reduce water demand as well due to typically smaller lawns. In a larger state with a much higher population growth rate than New Jersey, increased residential densities could substantially reduce both distribution and overall water infrastructure costs. There may be a considerable range in distribution system costs relative to total water supply costs. An analysis of investor-owned water utility data indicated that transmission and distribution costs averaged 18.8 percent of total costs (Beecher et al. 1993). This is significantly lower than Burchell's estimate of 42 percent. Distribution system losses, such as under-registering meters, leaks, and illegal hookups, also raise rates for paying customers.

According to the Raftelis Environmental Consulting Group 1998 Water and Wastewater Rate Survey, municipal water utilities sell water to customers outside their municipal boundaries at a price that is, on average, 42 percent higher than the price charged within their municipal boundaries. The median differential was 30 percent. Although there were 86 responding utilities nationwide, too few Florida water utilities responded to this question to calculate a meaningful Florida average. "Outside" customers may be more expensive to serve, depending on the development density in outlying areas and distance from the treatment plant. Florida law allows a municipality to charge customers outside a city between 25 and 50 percent more than the in-city charge (Section 180.191 F.S.).

Administration or overhead costs (wages, benefits, insurance, etc.) can be a significant portion of public water supply cost and presumably the price to the consumer. Although no data are available on Florida utilities, a study of internal rates of return for 14 California utilities indicated that overhead costs average 21.4 percent of total expenditures for the 7 lower performing utilities and 14.7 percent for the 7 higher performing utilities (Mercer and Morgan 1986). A 1991 national survey of investor-owned water utilities indicated that administrative and general costs comprised 20.2 percent of total costs (Beecher et al. 1993). Accounting classifications vary by utility so it is not known whether the public and investor-owned survey data are comparable.

Government-owned utility revenues may be transferred to non-utility funds for payment in lieu of taxes, as overhead for personnel, facilities and accounting services provided by general government, as subsidies to other government-provided services. Transfers may also be made from non-utility funds as a subsidy to the utility. No published data are available on the types or relative amount of transfers. A common perception is, however, that utilities are revenue generating enterprises for local governments and provide subsidies to other government services, keeping taxes lower than they would be otherwise. The transfer of utility revenues, however, is a prerogative of local governments.

Utilities can apportion the costs of reclaimed water systems to reclaimed water customers, wastewater customers, or potable water customers. In general, the more independent the water and wastewater divisions are and the more that the reclaimed water is considered a disposal problem rather than a resource, the more likely that the cost of the system will be apportioned to wastewater rather than potable water customers. Conversely, if the water utility faces rising costs to develop new sources of water, it is more likely that a portion of the cost of reclaimed water will be apportioned to reclaimed and potable water customers.

Wastewater Rates

A significant cost associated with the use of utility-supplied water is the treatment and disposal or reuse of wastewater. The cost of the disposal of wastewater in accordance with environmental regulations can vary significantly. For public water systems the cost of disposal increases from low-cost disposal methods, such as percolation ponds and surface water discharge, to high-cost disposal methods such as reuse. All of the factors that affect the cost of delivered water, such as economies of scale, used capacity, treatment and distribution (collection in this case), also affect the cost of wastewater disposal. To increase water use efficiency and minimize the harmful impacts of surface water discharges, wastewater utilities are increasingly being required to reclaim wastewater for non-potable irrigation and cooling use. While the cost of reclaiming water is significantly higher than other disposal methods, the water quality benefits in water bodies such as Tampa Bay have been dramatic. The use of reclaimed water for irrigation and other non-potable uses also preserves high quality groundwater and surface water. Again, the number of Florida utilities in the nationwide survey in the wastewater charge table is small. A larger survey of 64 utilities in the SWFWMD in 1997 found an average single-family residential bill (at 8,000 gallons per month) of $29.18 with the median bill being $26.38. Wastewater costs for some industrial users may be higher than reflected in the rates. Some production process by-products can disrupt the wastewater treatment process and require pre-treatment before discharge into the public wastewater system.

Regulatory Costs

Water supply utilities face a variety of regulatory costs. Two examples are those associated with the U.S. Environmental Protection Agency's Safe Drinking Water Act, and the Florida water management districts' withdrawal impact avoidance and mitigation rules.

A considerable amount of concern has been generated in association with the requirements of the Federal Safe Drinking Water Act (SDWA). The U.S. Environmental Protection Agency recently released the results of a community water systems "needs" survey to address these concerns (U.S. EPA 1997).

The table divides the 20-year needs according to their relationship to existing and proposed requirements. The Total Coliform Rule (TCR) -related distribution system costs reflect

Monthly Wastewater Charges
1992 Ernst and Young National Water and Wastewater Rate Survey

	(0 gal)	Residential (5/8-inch meter) (4,000 gal)	Residential (5/8-inch meter) (7,000 gal)	Non-Manufacturing/ Commercial (5/8-inch meter) (22,000 gal)	Commercial/ Light Industrial (2-inch meter) (374,000 gal)	Industrial (4-inch meter) (7,480,000 gal)	Industrial (8-inch meter) (11,220,000 gal)
Total Utilities (N=120)							
National Average Bill ($)	4.47	8.53	13.79	38.55	612.14	11,937.58	18,043.95
Average Cost ($)/1000 gal		2.13	1.97	1.75	1.64	1.60	1.61
Florida Utilities (N=7)							
Florida Average Bill ($)	4.84	10.66	18.02	50.73	836.54	16,431.33	24,737.72
Average Cost ($)/1000 gal		2.67	2.57	2.31	2.24	2.20	2.20

1998 Raftelis Environmental Consulting Group National Water and Wastewater Rate Survey

	0 gal	Residential 5/8-inch meter 3,740 gal	Residential 5/8-inch meter 7,480 gal	Non-Manufacturing/ Commercial 5/8-inch meter 22,440 gal	Commercial/ Light Industrial 2-inch meter 374,000 gal	Industrial 4-inch meter 7,480,000 gal	Industrial 8-inch meter 11,220,000 gal
Total Utilities (N=120)							
National Average Bill ($)	6.09	11.59	18.93	53.79	825.23	16,297.89	24,416.73
Average Cost ($)/1000 gal		3.10	2.53	2.40	2.21	2.18	2.18
Florida Utilities (N=7)							
Florida Average Bill ($)	9.28	19.42	31.18	88.17	1,456.54	28,506.58	42,959.43
Average Cost ($)/1000 gal		5.19	4.17	3.93	3.89	3.81	3.83

Winter rates where applicable

a widespread state of deterioration of distribution systems that should be addressed by routine repair and replacement programs.

20-Year Total SDWA and SDWA-Related Needs (in millions of 1995 dollars)			
	Existing Regulations	Proposed Regulations	Distribution System SDWA TCR-Related
Florida	346.5	340.5	1135.3
U.S.	16,219.8	13,989.4	35,463.5

U.S. EPA 1997

It is often said that we don't pay the full cost of water in Florida. Most commonly, people perceive this to mean that we are not paying for the forgone environmental services provided by in situ water (water stored in surface water features or water stored in aquifers). While this is the case in most other states and typical around the world, Florida water law provides very comprehensive protection for water dependent environmental systems and aquifer systems. The permit applicant may have to incur the costs of a number of impact avoidance actions. The regulations potentially affect water costs for all water users, whether utility or self-supplied. Self-supplied residences and water users below specific withdrawal quantity or withdrawal facility size thresholds are generally exempt from regulation.

The costs of these actions vary significantly from one applicant to another depending on site specific conditions and the size of the withdrawal request. For example, a regional water supply authority examined the regulatory costs of new wellfields under different capacity scenarios.

As the intensity of withdrawals increases from 4 to 40 mgd at wellfield A, the ratio of mitigation cost to total project cost increases rather than remaining constant. Comparing the 8 mgd withdrawals at wellfields A and B, the difference in impact sensitivity is reflected in the much higher mitigation/total cost ratio for wellfield B. In the area where these wellfields were to be located, the Floridan aquifer is not well confined and withdrawals have the potential to impact environmental features such as lakes and wetlands in the overlying surficial aquifer. Domestic and other permitted withdrawals also could be adversely impacted by the proposed withdrawals in the absence of impact avoidance regulations.

The Cost of Agricultural Water Use

There is a common misperception that utility-supplied individuals and businesses "pay" for water but self-supplied individuals and businesses do not. The reality is that neither group really pays for the raw water resource in Florida. However, both pay similar types of costs related to water use. The cost of water use to agricultural and other self-supplied uses varies with pumping depth, treatment, withdrawal impact avoidance and mitigation, transmission, distribution, and disposal requirements, just as it does for utility-supplied water. The misperception occurs because the costs that self-supplied water users pay are not commonly researched or published. Because it is not readily observable, it is perceived by many not to exist. No published data are available comparing the cost of water use among various agricultural uses or other self-supplied uses such as mining, thermo-electric, or other manufacturing uses. This is often considered proprietary data protected by the individual water user or trade group. The greatest amount of information available is for agriculture. However, the data are incomplete, generally focusing on a particular crop and irrigation system or group of systems and may not include the cost of pumping or withdrawal impact mitigation.

Two agricultural examples illustrate the cost of water to self-supplied water users. The first is based on the cost of irrigating 100 acres of tomatoes in the Ruskin producing area using three different irrigation systems: fully enclosed, semi-closed, and drip (Prevatt et al. 1992). Semi-closed is typically the least efficient, in terms of water used, and drip the most efficient. Due to saltwater intrusion concerns, tomato produc-

Estimated Efficiencies of Irrigation Systems	
System Type	Efficiency (percent)
Subsurface	
Seepage (Semi-closed)	20–60
Flood (Open Ditch)	20–50
Sprinkler	
Solid-set	70–85
Gun	60–75
Pivot	65–80
Microirrigation	75–90

Pitts and Smajstrla 1989

ers in this area face regulatory pressure to increase water use efficiency. Discounting potential benefits of increased yields, reduced disease, and fertilizer costs, which have not been well documented, the most water efficient irrigation system of the three is also the most expensive for this particular crop. The annualized costs per net production acre for the three systems are $587 for drip, $445 for fully enclosed, and $334 for semi-closed. Not surprisingly, semi-closed irrigation is the most popular system. The costs include wells, pumps, power source, treatment (drip and fully enclosed only), transmission (water source to field), dis-

Annual Withdrawal Impact Mitigation Cost Estimates ($1000)				
	Wellfield A			Wellfield B
	4 mgd	8 mgd	40 mgd	8 mgd
Repair or replace private wells	20	100	500	50
Environmental mitigation	100	200	1,500	250
Evaluation and monitoring	50	100	200	100
Total impact mitigation costs	170	400	2,200	400
Total annual project cost	1,627	3,135	9,936	1,174
Ratio of mitigation cost to total	.10	.13	??	.34

Law Environmental , Inc. in association with Havens and Emerson, Inc. 1994

tribution (within the field), energy, and irrigation-related labor taxes and insurance. Assuming that the grower is using the quantity permitted for spring tomatoes by the SWFWMD and this is the only crop grown on the field that year, the cost per thousand gallons used for the two most popular systems were calculated by the authors to be $.51 for drip and $.19 for semi-closed (1997 dollars). These agricultural water use costs do not include the potential regulatory costs of avoiding or mitigating withdrawal impacts to environmental systems or nearby water users, which may increase overall costs.

The low cost of groundwater use often associated with agriculture is likely the variable or marginal cost of pumping displayed below. Florida marginal pumping costs are akin to those for the Southern Plains. The marginal cost is *only* that cost associated with pumping the water out of the ground and into the field such as fuel and labor costs. It does not include the amortized fixed costs of water supply such as the well, pumps, treatment and monitoring equipment (if necessary), piping to the field and in-field distribution costs (such as microirrigation tubing which is fixed as least in the short run). The cost of water for the example tomato farm above includes both fixed and variable costs.

Irrigation of crops using surface water is less common in Florida than in other states, particularly in the West. No documented surface water irrigation cost estimates could be located for Florida. An example from a 10,000-acre irrigation district in California's San Joaquin Valley may illustrate the costs associated with surface water irrigation (Wichelns, 1991). The variable costs of obtaining 25,000 acre feet of water from the U.S. Bureau of Reclamation and transmission within the district are $16.00 per acre foot. The fixed costs of the district are recovered through an annual assessment of $42 per acre. Drainage costs average $3.08 per acre foot (325,848 gallons) delivered. When converted to cost per thousand gallons, the total average cost to the grower is $.14 per thousand gallons ($1997). The amount of subsidy provided by the U.S. Bureau of Reclamation, if any, is not indicated nor are field distribution costs.

Investment-Related Factors

Capacity utilization is also a cost factor in agricultural water use. A second crop planted on the same field reduces the cost of water used by spreading the fixed costs of the irrigation system over two crops. Using tomato irrigation system costs (updated to 1997 dollars) for a 100 acre drip microirrigation system (Prevatt et al. 1992) and assuming that the second crop has the same supplemental irrigation requirements as tomatoes, the cost of water used drops from $.51 per 1000 gallons for a spring tomato crop alone to $.32 per 1000 gallons if a second crop is added. The more likely a second crop can be profitably marketed, the more likely that investment will be made in a more expensive, efficient irrigation system.

For water using industries other than public supply, the choice between debt and revenue or sinking fund financing of water facilities is more a matter of risk and interest rates. The more volatile the market price for the goods being produced with water, the more likely that water-related capital investment will be made out of revenues rather than debt. This is particularly true of agriculture where market product prices tend to be very volatile. From the lender's perspective, the riskier the venture, the higher the interest rate charged. From the borrower's perspective, the more volatile the market product price, the more likely that debt cannot be repaid in low product price years.

Source Development and Treatment Costs

The cost of physically withdrawing groundwater from an aquifer varies by the depth of the well, the diameter of the well and the pressure required at the point of delivery into the transmission/distribution system.

The efficiency of use and operating pressures required can also affect well and well equipment costs. In the case of a 100-

Marginal Pumping Costs and Relevant Variables for Agriculture

	Northwest	Central Plains	Southwest	Southern Plains
Mean ($/ac-ft)	18.99	16.81	23.81	23.32
Std. Dev.	8.57	7.18	18.16	9.78
Mean ($/1,000 gal)	.06	.05	.07	.07
Std. Dev.	.03	.02	.06	.03
Mean Pump Depth (ft.)	151	99	153	179
Std. Dev.	131	69	142	98
Mean Pump Pressure (lbs./sq. in.)	59	39	18	25
Std. Dev.	17	20	21	17
Mean Wage Rate ($/hr.)	4.02	4.07	4.71	3.88
Std. Dev.	.72	.78	.88	.38
Mean Gasoline Cost ($/gal)	1.05	1.05	1.02	1.01
Std. Dev.	.11	.10	.08	.08

Moore et al. 1994

Well Equipment Cost Estimates

Component Capacity (mgd)	Construction Costs ($)	Non-Construction Costs ($)	Total Capital ($)	O&M Costs ($)	Equivalent Annual Costs ($)	Unit Costs Energy ($/1000 gal)	Set Up Costs ($)
1	39,229	17,653	56,882	21,297	26,823	0.052	7,961
2	47,676	21,409	68,985	34,310	40,219	0.047	6,268
3	55,387	24,924	80,311	51,130	58,016	0.046	7,897
4	63,843	28,729	92,572	68,497	76,468	0.046	9,014
5	72,100	32,445	104,545	82,090	91,128	0.044	10,291

Well equipment costs include pumps, valves, fittings, metering, a well house structure, and electrical controls.
Construction costs include all equipment, installation, and taxes.
O&M costs include normal maintenance of the well equipment, energy, and labor.

Law Engineering and Environmental Services, Inc. 1997

acre tomato field, the pumping head required to pressurize a drip irrigation system (46 feet) is significantly higher than that required for a semi-closed irrigation system (20 feet.) While this requires a more powerful and energy consuming pump for the drip system, the drip system is more water efficient, when properly operated, and requires only one well and pump while the semi-closed system requires two (Pitts et al. 1990).

There are considerable economies of scale for capital well equipment. Well equipment costs include pumps, valves, fittings, metering, well house structure and electrical controls. The data in the well equipment cost table show that the cost for a 5 mgd capacity well can be less than twice the costs for a 1 mgd well even though five times the amount of water is delivered. Pumping energy cost economies of scale for a given depth, quantity, and pressure requirement are less dramatic.

Well Drilling Cost Estimates in Dollars per Foot Depth

Diameter (inches)	10	12	16	18	24
Construction Costs ($)	77	97	125	140	199
Non-Construction Costs ($)	35	43	56	63	90
Total Costs	112	140	181	203	289

Law Engineering and Environmental Services, Inc. 1997

In the past, water treatment was not a major concern of agricultural producers. With the growing use of microirrigation, the need to filter and treat raw water for irrigation use has increased. The smaller emitter sizes in microirrigation systems have a greater potential to clog due to particulates such as sand or other debris, biological fouling such as the growth of algae, and precipitate fouling (such as calcium, magnesium and iron). Filtration is necessary to reduce particulate clogging. Anti-fouling chemicals (such as chlorine) are injected into the distribution system to control biological clogging and phosphoric acid is injected to control precipitate scaling (Boman and Ontermaa 1994). By way of example, filtration, chemical injection and related controller costs necessary for water treatment constitute approximately 8 percent of the capital cost of a drip irrigation system for a 100-acre tomato field (Pitts et al. 1990). Chemicals required for treatment increase operation and maintenance costs as well. Treatment costs are not typically incurred on less technologically advanced irrigation systems.

The increasing use of microirrigation to achieve water use efficiency is also causing distribution costs to be a significant portion of water supply costs for some agricultural uses. A primary reason that a microirrigation system is more efficient is that the water supplied is enclosed in the distribution system to the point of discharge at the plant rather than being open to percolation and evaporation. This protection from distribution losses, however, can increase distribution costs. Again, using a 100-acre tomato field as an example, distribution costs in the form of PVC piping and fittings have been estimated to be $37,000 for a microirrigation system (55 percent of total capital costs), compared to $23,500 for the less efficient semiclosed irrigation system (39 percent of total capital costs). Drip tubing adds another $10,750 in annual costs for the 100-acre microirrigation system. The additional distribution costs for drip irrigation are, in part, offset by lower pumping costs for drip irrigation systems since more water is delivered to the plant and less is lost to evaporation and percolation.

For citrus, the advent of microirrigation has led to a decline in distribution costs over the most popular previous system (solid set). The pressures needed to operate a solid set irrigation system required the use of more expensive steel piping. Distribution system costs for the microirrigation system represent about 46 percent of total system capital costs while the distribution system costs for the solid set overhead system represent about 73 percent of total system capital costs. The distribution system costs for a microirrigation system are approximately half of the cost for a solid set system. Some of this cost difference is offset by higher labor costs and or water treatment costs for microirrigation systems (Harrison et al. 1983).

Regulatory Costs

Agricultural and other self supplied water users face the same types of withdrawal impact avoidance and mitigation costs as public supply water utilities. Because agricultural water users face a more competitive market than monopolistic utilities, regulatory costs are more difficult to pass on to buyers of agricultural products. Therefore, agricultural users are more likely to pursue avoidance of impacts or forgo potential income rather than pursue the typically more expensive impact mitigation. The choice between impact avoidance and mitigation for other self-supplied users will likely depend on the competitive nature of the market in which they operate.

The Cost of Manufacturing Water

Total water costs by component are not available for manufacturing in Florida. However, a very extensive survey of manufacturing water use costs was conducted for Environment Canada in 1986 (Tate et al. 1992). Data on water use cost components were collected for approximately 5,000 manufacturing plants. Although the data in the manufacturing cost table are from Canada and the costs are reported in Canadian dollars, there is no *a priori* reason to believe that the proportion of total water use costs by component would be significantly different for manufacturing plants in Florida. Canada has a modern environmental regulatory program and climatic differences are assumed to have a minimal difference on water use costs for manufacturing. A similar survey was conducted in 1981. Between 1981 and 1986, water intake quantities fell by 20 percent and gross water use, including recirculated water, decreased by 24 percent. Yet, employment in the surveyed plants increased by 4 percent. The reduction in use is in part explained by a 110 percent increase in water acquisition costs over the same period.

The Relationship between Water Price and Water Use

The demand for water, like most other purchased items, is responsive to price. Where sewer charges are related to water use, water demand is related to the sum of water and sewer price. "Price elasticity" is the term economists use to describe this relationship. Price elasticity measures the percentage change in quantity demanded due to a one percent change in price, all other factors held constant. "All other factors held constant" is an important thing to remember. Water price elasticity is almost always negative. As price goes up, water use goes down—an inverse or negative relationship. The magnitude of response is the absolute value of the price elasticity. A

294

Manufacturing Water Costs
Components in Canada 1986*

Industry group	Water acquisition	Intake treatment	Recirculation	Discharge treatment	Total
Food	30,308	4,375	4,811	6,516	46,010
Beverage	9,836	2,449	759	504	13,548
Rubber	1,819	766	759	504	3,455
Plastics	2,516	515	1,162	261	4,454
Primary textiles	3,007	1,355	441	777	5,580
Textile products	2,113	350	226	77	2,766
Wood products	2,603	309	265	81	3,258
Paper and allied products	22,700	20,338	8,400	38,058	89,406
Primary metals	100,757	9,857	26,960	33,746	171,320
Fabricated metal products	3,949	583	625	3,125	8,282
Transportation equipment	13,908	2,650	2,503	12,106	31,167
Nonmetallic mineral products	5,761	825	1,685	490	8,761
Refined petroleum and coal products	6,347	6,157	3,685	8,744	24,933
Chemicals and chemical products	22,899	18,429	14,892	12,067	68,287
Total	228,424	68,958	67,160	116,673	481,215

*thousands of Canadian dollars

Tate et al. 1992

price elasticity of -.7 results in a larger reduction response than -.2 even though we typically think of -.7 as a "smaller" number.

Many water professionals overestimate or underestimate the impact of price changes on water use. This is where the "all other factors held constant" part is important. A good price elasticity estimation isolates the impact of price changes from other factors that affect demand such as rainfall for residential demand or higher wastewater treatment costs for industrial users. If water prices increase but water demand per household shows little or no decline in the following year, it may be thought that the price increase had no impact. In reality, the following year may have been a drier than normal and increased household irrigation demand. The impact of the price change is that the irrigation demand did not likely increase as much as it would have without the price change. The reverse is true as well. If it were to rain cats and dogs the year following the price increase, household demand may show a precipitous drop in demand. Again, other factors affecting demand were at work and only a portion of the reduction in use is likely attributable to the price change.

When demand is termed "price inelastic," this does not mean that there is no response to changes in price. It means that the absolute value of the price elasticity is less than one (e.g., -.75) and that the reduction in water demand is less than proportional to the change in price. "Price elastic" means that the absolute value of the price elasticity is greater than one (e.g., -1.25) and the reduction in demand is more than proportional to the change in price. A price elasticity of -1 is called "unitary" and means that the reduction in demand is proportional to the change in price.

There is another factor to consider when viewing the estimated price elasticities for various water users contained in this section. Estimated price elasticities are usually "long run" price elasticities unless otherwise noted. This means that the full impact of the price change may not be realized for several years. It takes time for water users to fully respond to price changes. Water using habits can change slowly. For homeowners, water conserving plumbing fixtures, irrigation systems and landscaping may take some time to budget for and install. Water conserving technology feasibility may have

to be investigated and planned for by commercial and industrial water users. Agricultural users may want to wait for a good product price year. However, dramatic changes in water using habits can occur if price changes are dramatic such as when pricing is used to control demand during droughts.

Why is it important to know how water users respond to price? If the development of more expensive water supply becomes necessary and results in significant changes in water costs, disregard for price elastic effects can result in the construction of excess capacity—resulting in higher than necessary rates. Price can also be used to reduce peak demand. Peak demand drives the size of water facilities. By charging higher prices for peak driven uses, such as irrigation, less capacity may be required. The use of price elasticities can help to estimate reduction in peak demand.

Price elasticity is, in some cases, a proxy measure of how important the cost of water is relative to overall costs, particularly where water is an input of production, and whether there are technological or labor substitutes for water use. Low price elasticities, such as −.2, can have two meanings. If the price elasticity estimate were based on analysis of data with very little range in water prices, it could be that 1) the cost of water relative to all other costs is very small and little effort was expended to reduce use, or 2) water is an integral part of production and few if any feasible substitutes for water use exist. Where the data used in the estimation contained a wide range of prices, a low price elasticity is more likely to mean that few feasible substitutes for water use exist. A water user with a truly low price elasticity will be relatively more adversely affected by a price increase than one with a relatively high price elasticity, say -.80, because there are likely fewer feasible opportunities to reduce water use. Well-researched price elasticities can therefore be used to determine where price increase impacts will have the most financial impact and where conservation research and funding can be best directed. In general, the reported elasticities appear to be well researched. However, the wider the range of price data and the greater the number of observations in the research data set, the more reliable the elasticity. The range of prices and number of observations generally were not included in the following tables due to space limitations. Before using the reported elasticities for analysis purposes, readers are urged to refer to the referenced studies and compare the data used.

Residential Response to Price

Several residential water price elasticity studies have been conducted in Florida over the years. Water demand during high irrigation demand seasons is typically more price elastic. The higher outdoor elasticities in the SJRWMD and SFWMD studies in the table are notable. It is generally accepted that outdoor single-family residential water use is more responsive to price than indoor water use because it is more of discretionary use than, for example, bathing and cooking. Studies conducted outside of Florida have estimated even higher outdoor water use price elasticities in the range of -1.38 (Danielson 1979) to -1.57 (Howe and Linaweaver 1967). It may be that with higher year-round evapotranspiration rates in Florida, which drive irrigation demand, that outdoor use in Florida is somewhat less responsive to price than in other areas of the country. The differential may also be the result of the imprecise method usually used to calculate outdoor use in most studies. Typically, outdoor water use is not separately metered from indoor use.

The degree of response varies by the type of industry depending on such factors as the relative share of water-related cost to total costs, and the economic and technical feasibility of substituting capital (different process technology, recirculation) or labor for water use. Again, one of the most comprehensive recent analyses of industrial water use was performed for Environment Canada (Tate et al. 1992). Water use and cost data were analyzed for approximately 5,000 manufacturing plants. Whereas residential and agricultural elasticities for Canada and Florida would likely be very different because of very different weather-related components of water demand, price elasticities for manufacturing in Canada and Florida are not as likely to be significantly different. Canada has a modern environmental regulatory program and production technologies are likely to be very similar. In the study, water price elasticities were estimated using two different equations. For elasticities in the columns with the heading "Intake," only the cost of intake water was included in the calculation of water price. The "Intake" price elasticity results are more applicable as a measure of response to a change in the price of purchased water. For elasticities in columns with the heading "Total," gross water use (the sum of intake plus recirculation water) is treated as a function of total water cost (i.e., expenditures for intake, pretreatment, recirculation, and waste treatment). As in the U.S., wastewater treatment costs are rising for manufacturers that are likely to produce hazardous wastewater discharges due to more stringent environmental regulation. This is evident in the

Comparison of Price and Output Elasticities in Canada, National Two Digit SIC Industries, 1986

Industry	Intake Water Price Elasticity	Intake Water Output Elasticity	Total Water Price Elasticity	Total Water Output Elasticity
Food (10)	-0.562	0.527	-0.877	0.546
Beverage (11)	-0.570	0.925	-0.891	0.866
Plastic products (16)	-0.600	0.316	-0.805	0.393
Primary textiles (18)	-0.645	1.024	-0.899	1.144
Textile products (19)	-0.683	0.837	-1.13	0.761
Wood products (25)	-0.912	0.700	-0.898	0.724
Paper and allied (27)	-0.702	1.166	-0.981	1.225
Metal fabricating (30)	-0.795	0.536	-0.493	0.601
Transportation equipment (32)	-0.352	0.621	-0.824	0.774
Nonmetallic mineral products (35)	-0.690	1.060	-0.781	1.186
Chemical and chemical products (37)	-0.877	0.703	-1.048	0.829

Tate et al. 1992

large "Total" elasticities for industries such as paper and chemicals. As their cost of water use and wastewater treatment increases, they tend to reduce water use more relative to other industries. In most cases, the water use reduction response to changes in total cost is much greater than that for "Intake" cost alone. It is this greater response to total water costs that make industrial water audits a successful conservation tool. When all water use costs are accounted for by a trained auditor, the potential savings of reducing water use become much more attractive to the manufacturer. The demand equations for both sets of estimates are highly statistically significant. The "Total" water price elasticity demand equations perform better in explaining overall variance in water use. For the interested water professional, water price elasticities were also estimated and reported at the three-digit SIC code level. Space limitations preclude their inclusion in this chapter.

Output elasticity was estimated as the relationship between the total value of product shipments and water use. As opposed to price elasticity, output elasticity is positive and measures the unit increase in water use in relation to a unit increase in the value of product shipped. For example, under the "Total water output elasticity" scenario, a one percent increase in the value of product shipped results in a gross water use increase of .546 percent for the average food manufacturer.

Water Allocation under Scarcity

When water is abundant, the existing water allocation system in Florida is very effective in allocating water supplies. As water withdrawals from freshwater sources approach or exceed safe yield estimates, it becomes essential to design and implement methods that guide the allocation and use of limited freshwater supplies and that encourage alternative water source development. The goal is to design methods so that the regional economy and its people can enjoy the greatest possible net benefits from water use while maintaining the sustainability of water and related natural resources. To this end, alternate methods may be evaluated with respect to (1) maximizing the efficiency in allocating water to permittees, (2) improving the efficiency of water use by permittees, and (3) promoting the development of economically feasible alternative water sources.

The Florida Water Resources Act addresses the allocation of water under scarcity in Chapter 373.233, Florida Statutes. This section titled, "Competing Applications" states: "(1) If two or more applications which otherwise comply with the provisions of this part are pending for a quantity of water that is inadequate for both or all, or which for any other reason are in conflict, the governing board or the department [of Environmental Protection] shall have the right to approve or modify the application which best serves the public interest. (2) In the event that two or more competing applications qualify equally under the provisions of subsection (1), the governing board or the department shall give preference to a renewal application over an initial application."

Water transfer mechanisms should efficiently and equitably reallocate water from constrained freshwater sources in a manner that encourages the efficient use of water and alternative source development. The sufficiency of the competing applications provision to achieve these goals will not be tested until the districts begin to significantly limit additional freshwater withdrawals.

Some think that the competing applications provision of Chapter 373, by itself, may not be sufficient for a number of reasons. Without additional guidance, significant legal and administrative costs to water management districts, renewing permittees and applicants may occur as the affected parties present their case to the governing board, mediate conflicts, and reach agreements. Renewing permittees who lose their permitted water quantities might not be compensated for their investment in equipment and land improvements associated with the water use activity. Perhaps, most importantly, the competing applications provision, by itself, may not encourage the movement of water to new uses as the economy changes over time resulting in temporal water use inefficiencies and constrained economic development.

Where feasible, the competing applications provision could be augmented through the use of market-like approaches that assist in moving scarce water from lower-valued uses to higher-valued uses while promoting water conservation and alternative source development. The intent of market-like approaches is to provide suggestions regarding possible reallocation of water from one user to another. These suggestions will be based on the maximum possible private net benefits of water use. The governing board then has the right to approve or deny each proposed water transfer based upon other public interest considerations.

The idea of using market-like approaches to reallocate scarce water supplies was incorporated into proposed water use permitting revisions for the Southern Water Use Caution Area (SWUCA) in the Southwest Florida Water Management District (SWFWMD). The revisions to Chapter 40D-2, F.A.C, "Water Use Permitting," also known as the SWUCA Rule, were passed by the SWFWMD Governing Board in November 1994.

The SWUCA Rule provided a forum by which water use permittees could voluntarily transfer all or a portion of their permitted and historically used water from the Floridan aquifer to individuals seeking access to the freshwater source. The provision was called "voluntary reallocation." Under the SWUCA Rule, the commodity being reallocated was not the right to own the water but the right to have a water use permit from the State of Florida, which can be amended or withdrawn given the provisions of Florida Statutes and the Florida Administrative Code. As the proposed rule was written, if the transferring permittee was compensated by the receiving permittee, the amount of the compensation would be a private matter between the two parties. The rule was silent on the subject of if and how much someone might be compensated for reallocation. Transfers of permitted withdrawal quantities to specific highly stressed areas would be prohibited and permitted withdrawal quantities in the source permit and the new permit would be modified to reflect certain conservation standards. Because SWFWMD had established a water use metering program affecting all water use permittees, the issue of water metering was not considered to be an undue burden for either SWFWMD or the permittees.

The SWUCA Rule was subsequently challenged by various parties through the Florida Administrative Procedures Act. The hearing officer found that the voluntary reallocation provision of the Rule "exceeds the scope of the District's delegated authority under existing Chapter 373."

The hearing officer's identification of which aspects were outside of the district's legislative authority can be inferred based on the following statements included in the Final Order: "The District's proposed reallocation provisions do not establish any prioritization of use for water quantities transferred nor do they provide for disclosure or impose any other requirements regarding the agreement between the transferor and the transferee. The establishment of such a program, without specific legislative authorization, exceeds the scope of the District's delegated authority under existing Chapter 373...there is no current statutory basis for allowing or authorizing the sale of permit rights," (Case No. 94-5742RP:517).

Thus, a "voluntary reallocation program" may be within the district's legislative authority if the rule revision specifically stated that a reallocation is only a permit to use the water and not a right to own the water and would be permitted by the district only if the proposed use passes the three-part test as specified in Chapter 373, F.S. Under this three-part test, the proposed use (1) is reasonable-beneficial, (2) will not interfere with any presently existing legal use of water; and (3) is consistent with the public interest.

In the SWUCA, historically used and permitted quantities have been beyond the district's estimate of safe yield from the Floridan aquifer. Therefore, water transfers via either competing applications or voluntary reallocation would not pass the three-part test and, therefore, could not occur without specific legislative authority or until permitted quantities are reduced below safe yield estimates. The SWUCA Rule, including the voluntary reallocation provision, had an overall method for reducing permitted quantities to safe yield estimates over a ten year period. Thus, perhaps without specific legislative authority, water transfers could possibly occur once permitted quantities were reduced below the safe yield estimate. Subsequent statutory provisions (373.0421(2) FS) allow for a phased "recovery strategy" when aquifer levels are below adopted minimum levels. These provisions may allow transfers to occur before quantities are reduced below their "safe yield" estimates as long as the transfers are included in the overall quantity reduction and recovery strategy.

Proponents of voluntary reallocation in the SWUCA see two main benefits. First, it would provide an efficient process of moving permitted freshwater quantities from one user to the another when it is mutually beneficial for both parties to do so, in a manner that is equitable. As a result, it would allow permitted water quantities to efficiently and equitably move from one user to another as the economy changes over time.

Second, a water "price" could evolve from the individual voluntary reallocation transactions. If the value of the freshwater is relatively high, is reflected in the water price and the price is well-known to the public, then the water price would provide an incentive for permittees to conserve water so that they can transfer the saved water to other water users in exchange for monetary compensation.

As a result, permittees use their permitted water allocation more efficiently while allowing other permittees and new applicants access to freshwater for beneficial use. Because the buyer is purchasing the permitted water withdrawal, he/she is better off obtaining the least amount of water necessary for profitable use. Therefore, water conservation and alternative water sources would be considered and used if they cost less than the water price.

Markets, when well-designed, may be able to process technical and economic information regarding the relative marginal value of water in different uses under different conditions and encourage existing and potential water users to consider water conservation and alternative source development. Such approaches would relieve governing boards of a significant and controversial burden of deciding which competing uses should use the limited freshwater sources from an efficiency standpoint. Thus, the governing board could concentrate on which competing uses best serve other components of public interest.

This type of market approach can be applied to a confined aquifer, a surface water source, a water storage facility, or an unconfined aquifer. Market-like approaches are tools for making water transfer decisions that consider the efficient use of freshwater resources. These approaches may not work in all situations and should be evaluated on a case-by-case basis. For example, the appropriate geographic boundaries of the water source within which voluntary reallocation could take place would have to be based upon the impact of the water transfers on the health of the associated water and water-related resources. This, in turn, would depend on the hydrologic characteristics of the water source and the proximity and hydrology of other affected water-related resources. In some cases, the boundaries of the water source would be too small for voluntary reallocation to be practical.

Some have criticized the use of market-like approaches to reallocate water by citing how certain water marketing arrangements in the western United States have not lived up to expectations and have resulted in significant negative third party impacts. A 1992 report by the National Research Council identifies three primary reasons why this has happened.

1. The prior appropriation doctrine used in the West is a major impediment to the consideration of public interest in the reallocation of water resources. This doctrine creates vested property rights that cannot be taken without just compensation. Thus, any water market in use under these circumstances will not consider public interest in the reallocation of water.
2. Existing laws, policies and procedures concerning water market transactions and other transfers in the West often fail to ensure either that third parties are protected from negative effects or that they share the benefits of reallocation.
3. In California, the lack of clear rules and procedures pervades the water transfer process which results in relatively high transactions costs and relatively few water transfers.

Florida water law does not have these impediments. Florida's three-part test and its water use permitting system protect the public interest and allow for the consideration of third party impacts prior to governing board approval of the transfer. Furthermore, water-related environmental resources are protected under Florida water law. The Florida Administrative Code can clearly describe the rules and procedures that would be used to evaluate potential water transfers. In fact, Florida may be one of the few states in which market approaches to allocating water may work the best. The Florida legislature from the viewpoint of some economists does not have to attach private property rights to water use in order to create market incentives to efficiently and equitably reallocate water from restricted water sources and to encourage water use efficiency. All water quantities would be attached to a water use permit with expiration dates consistent with current regulations.

When additional water quantities from a freshwater source are restricted, potential water users and those wishing to increase their permitted water quantity may have an economic incentive to pump more water than is permitted. Thus, monitoring and enforcement above historic levels, including individual metering of water pumpage and increased fines for non-compliance, might be necessary. Voluntary reallocation increases the benefit of effective monitoring and enforcement but does not increase the level of effort needed to prevent illegal pumping of water. Therefore, no additional monitoring and enforcement efforts would be required under voluntary reallocation.

When the voluntary reallocation system is well designed, reallocation should provide for equitable access to water use permits. Equity refers to the concept of fairness. To be truly fair the incentive system should favor no particular group of persons, income groups, geographic areas or water users over others.

The aspects of voluntary reallocation that promote the equitable allocation of water from a restricted water source are:

1. All potential water users would have the same level of access to the voluntary reallocation process especially if (1) the water management district becomes an information clearinghouse for the listing of potential buyers and sellers and the posting of water prices and quantities associated with successful voluntary reallocations and (2) the district implements measures to minimize unnecessary transaction costs.
2. Voluntary reallocation would allow for compensation to the permittee who is giving up his/her permitted water quantity. The compensation comes from the person who would benefit from the water use—the buyer.
3. Voluntary reallocation would not preclude the use of other methods to acquire water. Permittees whose permits are approaching their expiration date and who do not want to voluntarily transfer their water, would still have to renew their permit. Thus, expanding permittees and new water users still have access to freshwater through the competing applications process as described in Chapter 373, Florida Statutes. Applicants should be exempt from the voluntary reallocation process in cases of overwhelming public interest and where an applicant has already investigated alternative water sources, conservation, and voluntary reallocation and they were found to be unfeasible.
4. If the concern is that potable water prices might increase to levels where persons on fixed or low incomes cannot afford to pay, there are ratemaking mechanisms that can mitigate such potential problems.

In the long run, the water price plus the transaction cost will never be higher than the cost of additional conservation and alternative water source development. Furthermore, the public interest test becomes stronger under voluntary reallocation because the trading of permitted quantities is conducted in public view. In the absence of a voluntary reallocation system, private trades might still occur but public access to these trades would be restricted.

In the 1984 Florida Water Resources Atlas, economists Lynne, Moerlins, and Milliman discuss the potential role of water markets in Florida:

> From an economic perspective it appears that some mix of the public and private approaches could provide for economically efficient and equitable results. The private, market-oriented system tends to be very efficient; however, the public sector may be better equipped to identify the true social costs and thus the social and economic efficiency of certain activities and to evaluate appropriately benefits and costs in the public interest. Determining the appropriate mix of public and private involvement is an important economic policy issue that deserves further research and debate in Florida. (1984: 245)

The provision of a voluntary reallocation system in district rulemaking may be a good mix of public and private approaches to allocating freshwater from restricted sources. It has been argued that the commodity being reallocated is not the right to own the water but the right to have a water use permit from the State of Florida which can be amended or withdrawn given the provisions of Florida Statutes and the Florida Administrative Code. The water management districts consider social cost when establishing minimum flows and levels and approving individual water transfers. The private sector considers economic efficiency in the reallocation of safe yield among beneficial uses. These types of voluntary reallocation systems, however, should be designed and implemented on a case-by-case basis.

REFERENCES

Beecher, J.A., P.C. Mann, and J.D. Stanford. 1993. "Meeting Water Utility Revenue Requirements: Financing and Ratemaking Alternatives." National Regulatory Research Institute NRRI 93-13.

Babin, F., C. Willis, and P. Allen. 1982. "Estimation of Substitution Possibilities Between Water and Other Production Inputs." *American Journal of Agricultural Economics* 64(1):148-151.

Boman, B., and E. Ontermaa. 1994. "Citrus Microsprinkler Clogging: Costs, Causes, and Cures." *Proceedings of the Florida State Horticultural Society* 107:39-47.

Brajer, V., and W.E. Martin. 1989. "Allocating a 'Scarce' Resource, Water in the West." *American Journal of Economics and Sociology* 48(3):259-271.

Brown and Caldwell in association with J.J. Boland. 1990. *Empirical Water Demand Study*. Prepared for the South Florida Water Management District.

Brown and Caldwell in association with J.B. Whitcomb. 1993. *Water Price Elasticity Study*. Prepared for the Southwest Florida Water Management District.

Burchell, R.W. 1992. "Impact Assessment of the New Jersey Interim State Development and Redevelopment Plan Report II: Research Findings." Prepared for the New Jersey State Office of Planning by the Center for Urban Policy Research at Rutgers University.

Carson, J.R. 1979. "The Price Elasticity of Demand for Water." Master's thesis. University of California. Los Angeles.

Danielson, L.E. 1979. "An Analysis of Residential Demand for Water Using Micro Times-Series Data." *Water Resources Research* 15:763-767.

Gibbs, K.C. 1978. "Price Variable in Residential Water Demand Models." Water Resources Research 14(1):15-18.

Griffith, D.M., and Associates, Ltd. 1995. *Comparitive Rate Survey for the State of Florida*. Sponsored by the Florida League of Cities.

Harrison, D.S., A.G. Smajstrla, and F.S. Zazueta. 1983. "Sprinkler, Trickle, and Other Irrigation Systems: Cost Estimates for Citrus and Orchard Crops." Florida Cooperative Extension Service Bulletin 197. Gainesville.

Hazen and Sawyer. 1998. "Statement of Estimated Regulatory Costs for Revisions to Florida Administrative Code Regarding Minimum Flows and Levels in the Northern Tampa Bay Area." Prepared for SWFWMD.

Hazen and Sawyer in association with Resource Economics Consultants and HSW Engineering. 1994. "Economic Impact Statement for Revisions to Chapter 40D-2, FAC, Water Use Permitting, and Chapter 40D, FAC, Water Levels and Rates of Flow, Including Rules Specific to the Southern Water Use Caution Area." Prepared for SWFWMD.

Heady, E.O. et al. 1973. "National and Interregional Models for Water Demand, Land Use, and Agricultural Policies." *Water Resources Research* 9:777-791.

Herrington, P. R. 1987. "Pricing of Water Services." OECD Publications, Organization for Economic Cooperation and Development, Paris, 1987.

Howe, C.W., and F.P. Linaweaver, Jr. 1967. "The Impact of Price on Residential Water Demand and its Relation to System Design and Price Structure." *Water Resources Research* 3:13-32.

Kulshreshtha, K.N., and D.D. Tewari. 1991. "Value of Water in Irrigated Crop Production Using Derived Demand Functions: A Case Study of South Saskatchewan River Irrigation District." *Water Resources Bulletin* 27:227-236.

Law Environmental, Inc. in Association with Havens and Emerson, Inc. 1994. "Water Resource Development Plan (Draft)." Prepared for the West Coast Regional Water Supply Authority. Clearwater.

Law Engineering and Environmental Services, Inc. 1997. *Water Supply Needs and Sources Assessment*. St. Johns River Water Management District.

Lewis, K., R. Carriker, and R. Marella. 1981. *Analysis of Residential Demand of Water in the St. Johns River Water Management District*. St. Johns River Water Management District, Palatka.

Lynne, G.D. 1977. "Water Price Responsiveness and Administrative Regulation - The Florida Example." *Southern Journal of Agricultural Economics* 9:137-143.

Lynne, G.D., William G.L., and C. Kiker. 1978. "Water Price Responsiveness of Commercial Establishments." *Water Resources Bulletin* 14:719-729.

Lynne, G.D., J.D. Moerlins, and J.W. Milliman. 1984. "Water Economics and Finance." In *Water Resources Atlas of Florida*. Tallahassee, Florida: Institute of Science and Public Affairs, Florida State University.

Marella, R.L. 1992. *Factors That Affect Public-Supply Water Use in Florida*. U.S. Geological Survey Water Resources Investigations Report 91-4123. Tallahassee.

Mercer, L.J., and W.D. Morgan. 1986. "The Efficiency of Water Pricing: A Rate of Return Analysis for Municipal Water Departments." Water Resources Bulletin 22(2):289-295.

Metzler, M., and M. Peterson. 1994. "Florida Utility Rate Structures." *Florida Water Resources Journal* 46(6):25-27.

Moore, M.R., N.R. Gollehon, and M.B. Carey. 1994. "Multicrop Production Decisions in Western Irrigated Agriculture: The Role of Water Price." *American Journal of Agricultural Economics* (November):859-874.

National Research Council. 1992. *Water Transfers in the West: Efficiency, Equity, and the Environment*. Washington, D.C.: National Academy Press.

PB Water. 1998. "Seawater Desalination Water Supply Project of the Master Water Plan." Prepared for WCRWSA.

Pitts, D.J., and A.G. Smajstrla. 1989. "Irrigation Systems for Crop Production in Florida: Descriptions and Costs." Florida Cooperative Extension Service Circular 821. Gainesville.

Pitts, D.J., A.G. Smajstrla, D.Z. Haman, and G.A. Clark. 1990. "Irrigation Costs for Tomato Production in Florida." Florida Cooperative Extension Service Agricultural Engineering Fact Sheet AE-74. Gainesville.

Prevatt, J.W., G.A. Clark, and C.D. Stanley. 1992. "A Comparative Cost Analysis of Vegetable Irrigation Systems." *Horticulture Technology* 2(1):91-94.

Russell, D.F., and C.P.N. Woodcock. 1992. "What Will Water Rates be Like in the 1990s?" *Journal of the American Water Works Association* 84:68-72.

Southwest Florida Water Management District. 1992. "Water Supply Needs and Sources 1990 - 2020."

Tate, D.M., S. Renzetti, and H.A. Shaw. 1992. *Economic Instruments for Water Management: The Case for Industrial Water Pricing*. Prepared for Environment Canada. Social Science Series No. 26.

U.S. Environmental Protection Agency. 1997. "Drinking Water Infrastructure Needs: First Report to Congress." EPA 812R-97-001.

Whitcomb, J. Telefax to Jay Yingling. May 14, 1998.

Wichelns, D. 1991. "Motivating Reductions in Drain Water with Block Rate Prices for Irrigation Water." *Water Resources Bulletin* 27(4):585-592.

Williams, M., and B. Suh. 1986. "The Demand for Urban Water by Customer Class." *Applied Economics* 18:1275-1289.

Ziegler, J., and S. Bell. 1984. "Estimating the Price for Intake Water by Self-Supplied Firms." *Water Resources Research* 20(1):4-8.

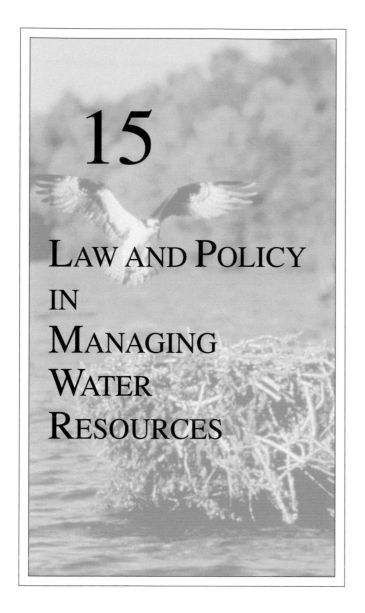

15

LAW AND POLICY IN MANAGING WATER RESOURCES

the early stages of common law development in England, and in the humid eastern states, water was commonly used in place for such purposes as navigation, fishing, bathing, and watering livestock. People had little technical capacity or need to remove large quantities of water from natural streams and lakes for use elsewhere. Before industrialization and the development of sanitary sewage systems, wastes were not concentrated for disposal into waters. The legal principles developed by the common law courts reflected these economic and social conditions.

Public rights in certain waters have been protected since ancient times. According to the Institutes of Justinian, a Roman codification of customary law,

> By the law of nature these things are common to all mankind—the air, running water, the sea, and consequently the shores of the sea.

The English common law recognized ownership, but vested it in the sovereign rather than in private individuals. Unlike other lands owned by the sovereign, however, these lands were to be held in trust for the use and benefit of the public, thus restricting the power of the sovereign to use or dispose of them when injurious to the public interest. As developed in the United States, this public trust was applied to all tidal waters and to all navigable waters. The Florida Constitution incorporates the doctrine thus:

> Sovereignty lands. The title to lands under navigable waters within the boundaries of the state, which have not been alienated, including beaches below mean high water lines, is held by the state, by virtue of its sovereignty, in trust for all the people. Sale of such lands may be authorized by law, but only when in the public interest. Private uses of portions of such lands may be authorized by law, but only when not contrary to the public interest (Article X, Section 11).

The public trust doctrine is an evolving concept. It has been applied to restrict the power of the legislature and the executive to alienate submerged lands, to limit the rights of private landowners to develop or adversely affect submerged lands, and to protect public rights to use submerged lands and their overlying waters.

Another ancient legal concept relates to the ownership of water. The fluidity of water makes ownership of it in the classic sense difficult to enforce. Water constantly moves from one parcel of land to another. The water in one portion of an aquifer, lake, or river cannot be isolated from the remainder of the water body and conserved, consumed, or used by a landowner without affecting all others who may use that body of water. When it is impossible for one owner of something to use his property without diminishing the property of other owners, market systems do not work. Water resources are therefore treated as a public resource, owned by no individual, but shared and controlled by all. Only when water has been reduced to individual possession and exclusive control does the common law recognize ownership of any quantity of water.

The common law did recognize certain private rights in water. In the case of a defined watercourse or water body—a pond, lake, river or stream—the owners of land touching the water had rights to use the water. In the case of land touching flowing water, i.e., riparian lands, these rights were called ri-

302

Florida's water resources have been shaped by our policy choices and the laws and institutions created to implement them. Until the 1970s, those waters were impounded, drained, filled, diverted, extracted, and contaminated on a massive scale, with devastating consequences for the natural environment and the sustainability of our society. Today, they are increasingly being protected, conserved, rationed, and restored. This chapter will discuss the development of the legal and institutional framework for water management and the policy issues facing Floridians in the Third Millennium.

Common Law Background

Conflicts over the use of water are not new. The common law, developed by judges presented with specific disputes over centuries of adjudication, resolved specific disputes among landowners and other individuals over the use of water. The kinds of disputes that came before judges under the common law reflected the uses made of water by the litigants. During

Richard Hamann

parian rights. Littoral rights were those appurtenant to land touching a lake or the sea. In practice these terms are subsumed in the word riparian.

Riparians share rights to a body of water with the public and with each other. If a body of water is navigable or tidal, riparians share a right with the public to navigate, fish, and swim. If a water body is privately owned, riparian landowners may still have shared rights to use the entire water body.

Riparians, however, control the use of their land to gain access to the water. They have a qualified right to build wharves, docks, or other improvements to facilitate their access to the water, and they have a right to view the water. Riparians also have a right to withdraw water and use it for a variety of purposes, from drinking it to cooling power plants.

Where these rights have come in conflict, the courts have developed rules for adjudicating such disputes. The earliest rule, the natural flow doctrine, gave maximum protection to those who used water in place. Under this rule, all riparians were allowed to use water but were prohibited from impairing the quality or quantity of water available for other users. In response to the economic and social pressures of the Industrial Revolution, the courts modified this doctrine to one of reasonable use. Under the reasonable use doctrine all riparians have a right to make reasonable use of the water. Riparians thus cannot unreasonably interfere with reasonable use by others. The determination of reasonableness, in turn, required a balancing of social, economic, and environmental interests. In a society seeking to industrialize, the development of water supplies is often viewed as "reasonable" as opposed to the "unreasonable" demands of those who seek to use the water in place or for lesser-valued purposes.

More recently, judges have been willing to give greater weight to other social concerns. The American Law Institute, an organization of eminent legal scholars, has identified nine factors considered by the courts in determining reasonableness. These are:

> the purpose of the respective users; the suitability of the uses to the water course or lake; the economic value of the uses; the social value of the uses; the extent and amount of the harm caused; the practicality of avoiding the harm caused; the practicality of adjusting the quantity of the water used by each proprietor; the protection of existing values of land, investments and enterprises; and the burden of requiring the users causing the harm to bear the loss (Maloney, Capehart, and Hoofman 1979: 256).

The use of water bodies for disposal of wastes required similar accommodations. The effects on downstream users can be substantial. Imagine, for example, the plight of a riparian landowner downstream from a growing livestock slaughtering facility or refinery. Such conflicts have been traditionally resolved through nuisance law, applying similar principles of reasonableness: one landowner cannot unreasonably interfere with the reasonable use of another's land.

Until recently, the technology for using groundwater, and for assessing the effects of such development, was not well understood. Consequently, judges were reluctant to apply any rules to govern its use. In the words of one court,

> The secret, changeable and unknowable character of underground water in its operations is so diverse and uncertain that we cannot well subject it to the regulations of the law, nor build upon it a system of rules, as is done in the case of surface streams (*Chatfield* v. *Wilson*, 28 Vt. 49, 54 [1856]).

Many early courts thus refused to find any liability for damage caused by pumping of groundwater, except in the case of proven underground streams. More modern doctrine recognizes advances in the science of hydrogeology and treats groundwater the same as surface water, subject to a rule of reasonable use.

Another common area for conflict over water relates to the drainage of unwanted surface waters. A landowner may increase the quantity and velocity of water flowing from a parcel by constructing channels and impervious surfaces, thus adversely affecting downstream properties through accelerated erosion or flooding. The diversion of water away from property is also sometimes a problem. A downstream proprietor may construct dams, dikes, or other protective structures, flooding upstream land.

If those waters exist in a defined watercourse or surface water body, then the rules of reasonable use would apply. Often, however, water that has not yet been collected into any channels, i.e., diffuse surface water, is involved. For such waters, the common law has developed several alternative rules. A "common enemy" doctrine allows each landowner to battle surface waters at will, with no liability for damage to neighboring lands. The "civil law" rule requires landowners to accept the natural quantity and rate of drainage, and prohibits upstream landowners from increasing the burden. The rule applied in Florida and most other states allows landowners to make reasonable alterations in the rate or quantity of surface water discharge.

There is a major difference in the law regarding consumptive use of water between the eastern and western states. As discussed above, the eastern states limit water use rights to the owners of riparian land, each of whom has a right to make reasonable use of the available supply. Conflicts are decided by reference to a set of social, economic, and environmental factors defining reasonableness.

The law of the West was developed from the customs of goldmining, which required the diversion of water for mining operations. To resolve the inevitable disputes, the miners recognized rights by priority of appropriation. Whoever first appropriated water by diverting it had superior rights to junior appropriators. In times of shortage, senior appropriators were entitled to their full allocation, while junior appropriators could be cut off completely. Only by diverting water could one claim rights to use it; instream uses and the environment could only use water that was being transported in a watercourse to downstream users. These rights were perpetual and often marketable. A later modification limited one's appropriative rights to that quantity used for beneficial purposes, to limit speculators from acquiring rights by diverting and wasting water. This doctrine of prior appropriation now controls most water use in the West.

The advantages of prior appropriation are in the certainty it gives to water users. Those with sufficient seniority can rely on receiving their full allocation into perpetuity. Junior appropriators, however, suffer when supplies are low, unless water can be transferred to them through markets. The environmental impacts are more problematic. Because instream users were not allowed to appropriate water under traditional prior appropriation systems and many streams are over-allocated, fish and wildlife, recreation, and aesthetic uses are suffering in many western states.

The doctrine of riparian rights is much more protective of water resources. Those who use the water in place— for fishing, swimming, boating or aesthetics— are entitled to that use, at least in theory, as much as one who withdraws water for irrigation or industrial use. The transport of water outside of a basin is generally discouraged. And because all riparians have a right to use the resource, new uses are more easily developed. The primary disadvantage is the uncertainly of it all. If a new user can come along at any time, limited only by a standard of reasonableness, then the expectations of existing users can be upset. Furthermore, the only way to resolve competing claims is through litigation. Even then the results may have to be changed in response to new users, technologies or information.

The deficiencies of the common law have led many states, both western and eastern, to develop administrative agencies for managing water resources. Under prior appropriation, there is a need to quantify uses, evaluate their beneficial use, determine respective priorities, record transfers, and enforce allocations, which the common law is ill-equipped to do. Under any system, there is a need to monitor resource use, research operation of the hydrologic system, reserve water for environmental, recreational, and other instream uses, develop new water supplies, and promote water conservation. Many of the disadvantages of riparianism can be offset through the implementation of permitting systems, under which water usage can be controlled while limited rights are created in use of the resource.

Institutional Development

When Florida was admitted to the Union in 1845, there was low population and a vast, swampy frontier. Most of the land was owned by the federal government. The rivers and coastal waters of the state were a primary mode of travel and source of sustenance. Beyond that utility, settlers viewed water, not as a precious resource, but as an obstacle to farming, development, and travel. Drainage, the construction of railroads and the improvement of navigation were the primary objectives of public policy.

Under the Swamp and Overflow Lands Act of 1850 Florida ultimately acquired about 21 million acres, for the purpose of transfer to private ownership to facilitate development and raise revenue for the fledgling state. To administer these lands and their privatization, the state created a board of improvement, composed of the governor and cabinet. During the late 1800s, the board granted vast tracts to railroad developers, canal builders, and drainage companies, eventually putting itself into receivership. To get itself out of debt, the board entered into a deal granting one million acres of South Florida to Hamilton Disston, a Philadelphia industrialist, for $4 million and half of another 9 million acres in exchange for improving navigation of the Kissimmee chain of lakes and draining the Everglades. Hamilton Disston, however, was unable to complete the project when his dredges hit the hard coral rock south of Lake Okeechobee. The Everglades Drainage District, was created in the early 1900s to complete the work. The Everglades Drainage District, also directed by the governor and cabinet, was authorized to levy taxes on lands within the district and to use those funds to construct and operate the drainage system. By the late 1920s, the system of major canals leading from Lake Okeechobee was complete.

To facilitate the construction and operation of secondary drainage works, the Florida legislature authorized the creation of special drainage districts, empowered to levy taxes on all the lands within their boundaries and governed by boards elected by the landowners on an acre/vote basis.

The state's submerged lands were also being developed. In 1857, the legislature had actually attempted to give all of the state's submerged lands to adjacent riparian landowners, but was prevented by the Florida Supreme Court through application of the public trust doctrine (*State* v. *Black River Phosphate Co.*). Through subsequent legislation, however, submerged lands were granted for dredging, filling, reclamation and other improvements, most notably the construction of Miami Beach from the bottom of Biscayne Bay. The validity of such legislation was barely questioned:

> The wisdom of a statute like the one under review was never more urgent than it is in this State. There are literally thousands of acres and thousands of miles of coast line affected by it . . . . Many of the lands affected by it are bogs and quagmires, fit for nothing but to breed snakes and mosquitos in their native state but acquired by private enterprise, they have been drained or filled and turned into valuable holdings.

> Deep waters have been made next to cities and attractive residential districts have replaced eye sores and unsanitary breeding places of every conceivable species of pathogenic bacteria. The potentialities of such sales nowhere approach the possibilities that they do in this State. . . *(Caples* v. *Taliaferro,* 144 Fla. 1, 7, 197 So. 861, 863 [1940]).

Miami Beach construction 1925

As the population swelled south of Lake Okeechobee, however, it soon faced environmental constraints. In 1926 and 1928 hurricanes swept the area, killing thousands of people. The drainage system proved inadequate to protect against hurricane flooding. The institutional response was to bring to bear the expertise of the U.S. Army Corps of Engineers, whose civilian responsibilities had, until then, been largely limited to improving and protecting the navigable capacity of the nation's waterways. The state of Florida first created a local agency, the Okeechobee Flood Control District, to improve the flood

Hoover Dike and drainage canal 1958

control system. In 1930, Congress authorized the corps to construct the Hoover Dike, a mammoth structure extending along the southern end of Lake Okeechobee to control hurricane-driven waters. In 1936, Congress expanded the national responsibilities of the corps to include flood protection, leading to the construction of dams and thousands of miles of levees, channels, and dikes across the country.

During the Great Depression, South Florida suffered a significant drought, compounded by the system of canals draining water to tide. Saltwater intrusion contaminated many coastal wellfields. Agricultural lands south of Lake Okeechobee suffered serious loss of organic soils through subsidence and oxidation. Uncontrolled fires blanketed the area with a dense pall of smoke.

Not until after World War II was there further development of water management institutions. The impetus was severe regional flooding in 1947 caused by widespread heavy rains. The corps of engineers was again authorized to develop a project addressing the problems, albeit on a much more massive and comprehensive scale. Congress authorized the Central and Southern Florida Flood Control Project in 1948. It included a complex system of levees, dikes, pools, canals, channels, spillways, pumping stations, and other water management structures in the upper St. Johns River basin, the lower west coast of Florida, and the entire Kissimmee River, Lake

Tampa Bay area flooding 1959

Okeechobee and Everglades basin. To serve as local sponsor for the project, the Florida legislature created the Central and Southern Florida Flood Control District, which was authorized to levy ad valorem taxes, acquire the necessary land, and build and operate structures. It was also authorized to regulate the discharge of water into the system and the withdrawal of water from it. The flood control district was governed by an appointed board. Flooding of the Tampa Bay area in 1959 and 1960 led to the creation of a similar set of institutions for Southwest Florida: the Four River Basins Project of the U.S. Army Corps of Engineers and its local sponsor, the Southwest Florida Water Management District.

Ironically, during the same period that it was creating the Central and Southern Florida Flood Control Project, Congress also authorized one of its greatest conflicting interests, the Everglades National Park, which was dedicated by President Truman in 1947. Conflicts over managing one of the central features of the project, the water conservation areas, began as soon as the discharge structures were closed on the Tamiami Trail. As water rose behind the levees and inundated water Conservation Area 3, it would adversely affect the area's herd of whitetail deer. Meanwhile, the Everglades National Park would be deprived of vital freshwater until, for flood protection reasons, it would be released in a torrent, unnaturally flooding alligator nests and wading bird feeding areas.

Competition for water in the Tampa Bay region has also influenced the development of water management. The city of St. Petersburg, located on a peninsula and thus vulnerable to saltwater intrusion into its wellfields, has had to look to other jurisdictions for water supplies since the early 1930s. As the area grew, and the water supply system was extended into Hillsborough and Pasco counties, the conflicts became more contentious.

In 1955, the Florida legislature established a study commission to evaluate Florida's water management problems and make recommendations for legislation. The resulting 1957 Florida Water Resources Act (Fla. Laws 1957, Ch 57-380) provided for state-level regulation by the Board of Conservation, which was authorized to permit the capture, storage, and use of water in excess of minimum flows and levels. Transport of water could be authorized so long as the diversion did not interfere with existing reasonable uses. In addition, the board could create and delegate authority to "water development and conservation districts." The first such district was established in Hillsborough County because of concern about water withdrawals by Pinellas County, but it proved ineffective. Its authority was ultimately delegated to the newly created Southwest Florida Water Management District in 1963, although wrangling over the specifics of regulation continued into the early 1970s. In 1974, the Tampa Bay water wars were suppressed, at least for a time, by the creation of the West Coast Regional Water Supply Authority, made up of all the major local governments in the area.

The next major climatic event affecting water policy was the drought of 1970-71. By that time the water control structures along the Tamiami Trail had been completed and closed, depriving Everglades National Park, located just downstream in the "River of Grass," from any water flows. As wildfires burned the Everglades and the nation saw photos of dying alligators, the residents of Florida's populous lower east coast knew that their water supply was threatened. The Governor's Task Force convened to address the environmental problems of South Florida, recommended major legislative changes, including

305

wetlands protection, state, regional, and local land use regulation and comprehensive water management. As the 1972 Florida legislature considered these recommendations, it discovered *A Model Water Code* drafted at the University of Florida College of Law by Dean Frank E. Maloney and his colleagues. This code became the basis for the Florida Water Resources Act of 1972. Other landmark legislation enacted during that session provided for the regulation of Developments of Regional Impact and Areas of Critical State Concern and initiated a state program for purchasing lands for conservation and recreation.

The Legal Framework for Water Management

The Water Resources Act of 1972, codified as Chapter 373 of the Florida Statutes, continues to provide the legal framework for water management. Although there have been numerous amendments, the basic structure and provisions of the act remain intact. Chapter 373 delegates comprehensive authority to manage water to five regional water management districts, covering the entire state, and the Florida Department of Environmental Protection (DEP). Two of those districts already existed in 1972, the Southwest Florida Water Management District and the South Florida Water Management District (created from the Central and Southern Florida Flood Control District). The three new water management districts, Northwest Florida, Suwannee River, and St. Johns River water management districts, were created to manage water in the northern and central parts of the state. One of the most important features of the districts is that their boundaries are drawn along surface hydrologic basin boundaries, cutting across political subdivisions such as counties or cities. Having the responsibility for entire watersheds greatly enhances the ability of a district to address ecosystem-level problems. The watershed of the Everglades, for example, is entirely in the South Florida Water Management District.

Each water management district is headed by a governing board, comprised of unpaid citizens appointed by the governor and confirmed by the senate. The governing board hires an executive director and is responsible for approving the district's budget, plans, acquisitions, rules, and orders. The districts have the authority to levy ad valorem taxes under an amendment to the Florida Constitution approved by the voters in 1976. The legislature sets a cap on the level of taxes and provides additional funds through appropriations. The activities of the districts are supervised and reviewed by a state level agency, the Florida Department of Environmental Protection (DEP). Much of the regulatory authority of the districts has actually been delegated by DEP. In addition, many district decisions are subject to review by the governor and cabinet.

The authority of the districts is broad and comprehensive. The water management districts can build and operate water management structures such as canals, dikes and pumping stations. They also have the authority to purchase and manage land for water management purposes.

The districts have extensive regulatory authority. The use of district lands and works can be regulated. The development of land for public or private uses is also subject to regulation under the Environmental Regulatory Permitting process. Virtually any construction or other activity that alters the flow of water across the surface of the land may be regulated by the districts to ensure that water quality is not degraded, downstream areas are not flooded, and aquifers and wetlands that

wildlife are dependent on are not adversely affected. If any development activity is proposed for a wetland, it must also meet a public interest test based on review of the impacts to fish and wildlife habitat, recreation and other wetland functions. Such impacts may be offset or compensated for by the preservation, restoration or enhancement of other wetlands. Mitigation banks have been established to facilitate this process and ensure the resulting mitigation areas have high ecological value. The districts also have a role in regulating the use of state-owned submerged lands and in coastal construction regulation.

Another major area for regulation by the districts is in the regulation of activities that affect the quantity of water available for use by humans or the environment. The districts have authority to regulate artificial recharge facilities and consumptive use of water. Consumptive use permitting is one of the most important responsibilities of the districts. Virtually any use of water that involves withdrawing or diverting it from its source can be regulated by a water management district under this authority. Local governments are prohibited from regulating consumptive use.

Consumptive use permits are granted for fixed periods of time. The maximum possible duration for most permits is twenty years. In practice, the districts have been reluctant to grant such lengthy permits because of the need to evaluate the availability of water and of more efficient techniques for using it. Permits can be revoked only under very limited circumstances. Thus, permittees are guaranteed a right to use water for the duration of their permit, subject only to water use restrictions imposed because of drought or emergency conditions. Permits may be freely transferred to the purchasers of the land or other facilities where the water is being used. Upon the expiration of a permit, the user must apply for renewal. New conditions may be imposed at that time to protect the environment or require more efficient use of available supplies. A competing user may be granted the right to use the water where there is some superior public interest to be served, although that has never occurred.

Three criteria must be met for obtaining a consumptive use permit. The applicant must establish that the use: (1) will not interfere with a presently existing legal use of water; (2) is a "reasonable beneficial" use; and (3) is consistent with the public interest. The requirement that a new use cannot interfere with an existing use ensures that the water allocated to one user under that law cannot be taken for use by another. It thus establishes legal certainty that water rights will be protected.

The reasonable beneficial use standard is the most innovative part of the criteria. The statute defines a reasonable beneficial use as "the use of water in such quantity as is necessary for economic and efficient utilization for a purpose and in a manner which is both reasonable and consistent with the public interest." The standard thus mandates water use efficiency and requires the districts to consider the same kinds of factors that were considered under the common law in making determinations of reasonableness. In addition, the public interest must be a factor in determining whether to issue a permit.

Environmental considerations play an important role in the determination of whether to issue a consumptive use permit. A wellfield permit, for example, that would result in dewatering wetlands could be denied for failure to meet the reasonableness or public interest standards. The districts are also required to establish minimum flows and levels as a limit for acceptable environmental impacts. Where those minimum flows and levels have been violated by existing conditions, the districts are required to develop recovery plans. They are also required, however, to consider the effects of hydrologic changes, and the feasibility of attaining minimum flows and levels, in establishing them.

Consumptive use permits allocate the water that is available during "normal" times. Florida, however, is subject to wide variation in climatic conditions, including extended droughts. To prepare for such events, each district is required to adopt a water shortage plan. Under the plan, permits may be classified by source, method of withdrawal, and use. When there is insufficient water available to meet all legal demands, or use must be curtailed to prevent serious harm to the water resources of the area from saltwater intrusion or other effects, then the water shortage plan may be put into effect. Restrictions under the plan may be imposed on all users or only on certain classes of users depending on the specific conditions of the water shortage. If implementation of the water shortage plan in not adequate to protect the public and the environment, then an emergency can be declared and orders issued to individual users to limit water use.

One area in which the Water Resources Act differs substantially from the common law is in the treatment of water transport. Under the common law, the right to use water was limited to those who owned riparian land or land overlying a groundwater source. Since 1957, Florida statutes have allowed the transport of water to more distant locations. The current law allows the districts to permit the holders of consumptive use permits to transport water "beyond overlying land, across county boundaries, or outside the watershed from which it is taken" where consistent with the public interest. The 1998 legislature directed the districts to consider a variety of factors in making that determination, mostly related to the availability and environmental impacts of alternatives. For transfers outside of a water management district, the district is required to consider the needs of both the receiving and producing areas.

The Water Resources Act provides for a variety of water management planning activities by the districts and the Florida Department of Environmental Protection (DEP). The DEP is directed to adopt a Florida Water Plan, consisting of its existing program and a "water resource implementation rule." Each water management district is required to develop a District Water Management Plan, regional water supply plans, groundwater basin resource availability inventories and Surface Water Improvement Management (SWIM) plans. This planning process should provide the basis for land use planning, restoration activities, water supply development, the establishment of minimum flows and levels, and consumptive use permitting.

In considering the legal and institutional framework for water management in Florida, several other governmental entities and programs must be discussed. Local governments have the broadest responsibility for protecting water resources, managing flood hazards and providing water supplies. Local government comprehensive plans are the vehicle for integrating these concerns with community development and other considerations. The Florida Department of Community Affairs and Florida's eleven regional planning councils have important roles in the planning process.

Local governments in several areas of the state have also joined together through interlocal agreements to provide water on a regional basis, most notably in the Tampa Bay area. The West Coast Regional Water Supply Authority controls an extensive network of wellfields, pipelines, and pumping stations to supply water to its member local governments, including Pinellas, Pasco, and Hillsborough counties. By working together in such cooperative arrangements, local governments can reduce regional conflict over water supply.

The protection and restoration of water quality is a vital part of water management. Water quality standards are established by the Florida Department of Environmental Protection (DEP), with the guidance and oversight of the U.S. Environmental Protection Agency (EPA). Both DEP and EPA regulate the discharge of pollutants by such major sources as industry, agriculture, mining, construction, and waste treatment. They are both involved with the cleanup of sites that have been contaminated by hazardous wastes, toxic substances, and petroleum. Other agencies with a role in protecting water quality are the Department of Health, which regulates septic tanks and other on-site sewage treatment and disposal systems, and the Florida Department of Agriculture and Consumer Services, which has jurisdiction over the application of pesticides.

Water managers and users increasingly face the need to consider impacts to the endangered and threatened species that inhabit or depend on Florida's waters as well as to other fish and wildlife resources. The Florida Game and Fresh Water Fish Commission, the Marine Fisheries Commission, the U.S. Fish and Wildlife Service and the National Marine Fisheries Service all play important roles in conducting research on fish and wildlife and bringing that information to the attention of water managers.

The federal government is actively involved in water management and has significant investments in such vital resources as the Everglades National Park, the national forests of Florida, and the national wildlife refuges. The federal government also holds several reservations in trust for the Miccosukee and Seminole tribes. The U.S. Army Corps of Engineers is engaged in a massive restudy of the Central and Southern Florida Project that will soon culminate in recommendations for a multibillion dollar reconstruction project to improve water supply, water quality and natural systems protection in South Florida. EPA along with he corps of engineers has wetlands permitting responsibilities throughout the state and has supported a great deal of research on the causes of water quality degradation.

Emerging and Recurring Issues

Florida's water management system has been the envy of many other states for over 25 years. Because the water management districts encompass entire watersheds, they are able to address environmental problems with less jurisdictional conflict than is usually possible. By having a stable source of ad valorem tax revenue, the districts are able to develop scientific expertise and information over years of data collection and analysis. With an independent source of revenue and appointed boards, the programs of the districts have been less subject to political whim than those of many other agencies. And finally, the scope of authority delegated to the districts has been sufficiently broad and flexible that they have been able to address problems that were only dimly recognized in 1972.

The districts have enjoyed strong political support. That is at least partly because their decisions have been supportive of agricultural, commercial, and residential development. They have provided drainage and flood protection, and they have denied very few consumptive use permits. Water seemed to be abundant.

That perception is now changing, and it will create enormous challenges for water managers and interested citizens over the next twenty-five years. Water is more scarce and valuable a commodity than ever, and the conflicts over how to use and manage this precious resource are certain to grow. One reason is that scientists have a much better understanding of how important the quality, quantity, timing, and distribution of water is to the natural ecosystems of Florida. Relatively minor changes in water levels can have significant effects on wetlands and the fish and wildlife dependent on them. In many parts of Florida, natural systems have been damaged by overdrainage, groundwater pumping, and surface water withdrawals. Restoration, or even the protection of what is left, will require leaving more water in the system. The demand for water, however, is certain to rise as the population and economic activity increase. Where will the water demanded by millions of new residents come from? Can we repair such damaged ecosystems as the Everglades and still meet those demands? In addressing such questions, a number of issues are likely to arise.

One set of issues revolves around the allocation of water for the natural environment through the establishment of minimum flows and levels, reservations of water, or the development of plans for restoring natural ecosystems. The first problem is in determining how much water is needed for the environment. Florida's wetlands, floodplains, and estuaries are all adapted to some degree of low flow conditions, as well as to floods. It thus becomes very difficult for scientists to determine the impacts that will result from withdrawing (or restoring) specific quantities of water. As water supplies become limited, however, the pressure to make such exact determinations becomes greater. Who should bear the risk if the current models of scientific understanding are wrong, the environment or the people who have invested in some activity with the expectation of a water supply?

Such determinations are complicated by the fact that there is seldom some threshold for environmental harm, i.e., a point at which harmless withdrawals become seriously damaging. Low levels of degradation may result from lesser withdrawals. Determining what level of harm is acceptable or significant, or determining what level of restoration is desirable and feasible, will be one of Florida's most important water policy debates in the coming years.

The determination of how to allocate available supplies to meet increasing human demands also raises a host of issues. Increased water efficiency is the most attractive option, but at some point the limits of cost and acceptability will be reached. The reallocation of water from existing users is at least theoretically possible. Upon expiration of a permit, water managers can transfer the supply to competing users who better serve the public interest. The economic and social dislocation that would occur, for example, from depriving agricultural users to serve expanding urban areas, makes this highly unattractive.

Existing users have been pressing in recent years to expand their protection. When permits are renewed, users are often forced to implement more efficient methods for using water or to use alternative sources that are more expensive or less desirable. Longer term permits protect users from having to make such changes. Another option that has been advocated for increasing the level of certainty for existing users is to give them either a guaranteed right to renew their permits or to give them a greater preference against competing users.

One way of obtaining more efficient use of water and providing for the transfer of water rights to new uses would be to provide compensation to displaced users. Some economists argue that water markets should be established, allowing the holder of water rights to sell them for new uses. They believe that a properly designed market would allocate water among competing users better than an administrative agency. Some of the arguments raised against such proposals relate to the practicality of establishing markets for something that cannot be easily transferred to different users without considering place-specific adverse effects. Others focus on the nature of water as a public resource and question whether it is fair to allow private users to gain monetary benefits from selling it. There is also concern whether markets place a value on all of the appropriate factors. The experience of the western states, where water rights are more freely traded, is instructive. In many places aquatic environments cannot be restored without purchasing expensive water rights from the private sector. In other areas, rural communities are being destroyed as the water rights necessary to support agriculture are transferred to more wealthy urban sectors.

Many of the foregoing problems can be avoided by developing new, alternative water supplies. Technologies are available for reusing highly treated wastewater, desalinating seawater or plentiful brackish groundwater, and capturing drainage waters or floodwaters for storage underground or in new surface impoundments. Implementing such solutions can be much more expensive, however, than utilizing currently available sources of "cheap" water. One common scenario developing in Florida is that a rapidly growing local government on the coast with limited freshwater supplies is forced to use more expensive alternatives, such as desalinization, while agricultural users and inland communities continue using inexpensive groundwater. Should all users be required to pay the cost of new facilities or just those who immediately need them? Should less expensive sources be reserved for certain users, such as agriculture, that may not be able to pay higher costs? Increasingly, such inequities are being resolved by asking the water management districts and state government to finance the construction of water supply facilities. Is it appropriate to place the burden of paying for new water supply sources on those who pay ad valorem or sales taxes, rather than the rate payers who will use the water produced? What about those who pay nothing for water, for example, self-supplied residential or agricultural users? Should a fee be assessed on those users to pay for alternative water supplies and the protection of existing water supplies?

Another option for meeting increasing demand or reducing environmental impacts (also expensive) is to allow the transport of water from more distant sources. One of the objectives of water resource legislation since 1957 has been to allow such transfers. They are always contentious, however, and disfavored by current policy. The "water wars" of the Tampa Bay region have occurred because Pinellas County, with insufficient local water sources, has gone as far as Pasco County for adequate supplies. Residents of the Suwannee River basin and all points south fear they may be next.

There are two fundamental arguments against transfers. One is the concern for adverse environmental impacts resulting from the withdrawals. Although not inevitable, they have frequently resulted in the past. Another concern, where water is limited, is that the future growth and development of the area where water originates may be stymied for lack of available water supplies, while another prospers at its expense.

Conflicts over the transfer of water are just one example of situations that require coordination among governmental entities. In many cases, the water resources of an area can be exploited more efficiently, with less harm to the environment, by developing a regional water supply system. By interconnecting wellfields, surface water sources, treatment plants and distribution facilities, supplies can be enhanced and made more reliable. Where a multiplicity of local governments and private water suppliers exist, however, jurisdictional conflict, reflected in disputes over cost-sharing and other issues, can inhibit the rational design and operation of a water supply system.

The need for regional and interjurisdictional coordination mechanisms is also evident when looking at how to protect and restore complex ecosystems. No single governmental entity has sufficient authority to protect and restore the Everglades, the Indian River Lagoon, Tampa Bay, or any river in Florida. Any successful effort requires the cooperation and participation of many local, regional, state, tribal, and federal agencies. For the many interstate rivers in north Florida, notably the Apalachicola, cooperation with Georgia and Alabama is essential. Given Florida's vulnerability to such global processes as the transport of mercury, climate change and sea level rise, successful management of Florida's environment will require international cooperation. Achieving effective coordination at appropriate scales, while providing for local participation in decisionmaking and management, will be a challenge.

One of the largest unresolved issues in Florida is how to make appropriate linkages between water management and land use decisions. Although any intensive use of land requires a water supply and thus places additional demands on available sources of water, land use planners are currently not required to consider the availability of water and the impacts of water supply development when making land use decisions. Inadequate consideration is given to the potential impacts of land use activity on water resources, through drainage, flood control, contamination, nutrient enrichment, boating traffic, and other effects. Some of the most difficult water management issues, such as how to reduce the impacts of stormwater runoff, manage flood hazards or preserve riparian habitat, must be addressed through land use regulation or nonregulatory controls on land use and development. Given the resistance of many private landowners to regulation and the primacy of local government control in this area, implementing effective policies for protecting Florida's land and water resources will require a substantial public commitment.

REFERENCES

Canter, B.D.E., and S.I. Holtz. 1996. "Water Law in Transition: Debates that Could Shape Florida's Future." *Florida Bar Journal* 70:77-88.

Christaldi, R.A. 1997. "Florida's Water Future: A Legislative Proposal for the Distribution of Water Resources in Florida." *Florida Bar Journal* 71:88-92.

Crosby, D.L. 1996. "Water, Water, Everywhere, But Not Enough to Drink?: A Look at Water Supply and Florida's Growth Management Plan." *Journal of Land Use and Environmental Law* 12: 153-170.

Earl, W., and T. Ankerson. 1987. "Slicing the Water Supply Pie: Competing Application Under Florida's Water Resources Act." *Florida Bar Journal* 61:87-90.

Gsteiger, Y., and J.P. Loftin. 1997. "For Sale: Florida's Water Supply?" *Florida Water* (Fall/Winter): 14-19.

Hamann, R.G. 1993. "Consumptive Water Use Permitting." *Environmental and Land Use Law*. The Florida Bar.

Hamann, R.G., and T. Ankersen. 1993. "Water, Wetlands and Wildlife: The Coming Crisis in Consumptive Use." *Florida Bar Journal* 67:41-46.

Harper, C., and E. Ross. 1990. "The Reasonable-Beneficial Test: Maximizing the Water Supply Pie Before Relinquishing the Last piece." *Florida Bar Journal* 64:68-71.

Kemp, D. 1982. "Interbasin Transfers of Water in Florida: Common Law and water Resources Act." *Florida Bar Journal* 56:9-21.

Maloney, F.E., S.J. Plager, F.N. Baldwin, Jr. 1968. Water Law and Administration: The Florida Experience. Gainesville: University of Florida Press.

Maloney, F.E., R.C. Ausness, and J. S. Morris. 1972. A Model Water Code. Water Resources Research Center Publication 8. Gainesville: University of Florida Press.

Maloney, F.E., L.C. Capehand, and R.S. Hoofman. 1979. "Florida's Reasonable Beneficial Water Use Standard: Have East and West Met?" University of Florida Law Review 31(2):253-283.

Maloney, F.E., S.J. Plager, R.C. Ausness, B.D.E. Canter. 1980. Florida Water Law. Water Resources Research Center, University of Florida, Gainesville.

Mann, S.B. 1997. "More than a Drop in the Bucket: Florida Water Resources Act II." *Florida Bar Journal* 71:30-37.

Niego, S. 1983. "Water Management in South Florida: Setting the Record Straight." *Florida Bar Journal* 57: 337-342.

Neigo, S. 1982. Wastewater Re-Use in Florida: An Idea Whose Time has Come." *Florida Bar Journal* 56: 626.

Nietzke, E. 1981. "Salt Water Intrusion: Florida's Legal Response." *Florida Bar Journal* 55: 759-764.

Parker, M. P., and S.B. Mann. 1996. "Water Management Reform: Mission Impossible?" *Florida Bar Journal* 70: 20-32.

Rea, R. 1983. "Drought in Florida: Nature's Response to 'Comprehensive' Planning." *Florida Bar Journal* 57: 266-269.

INDEX

Page numbers in bold italic indicate illustrations.

312